Holby City Episode Reviews

by Sue Haasler

Holby City Episode Reviews

Copyright © 2017 Sue Haasler

The moral right of Sue Haasler to be identified as the author of this work has been asserted in accordance with the Copyright, Designs and Patents Act of 1988.

These articles first appeared on the blog www.pauseliveaction.com

The characters and incidents mentioned are the property of the BBC TV series Holby City

SERIES 11 & 12

The first Holby episode I reviewed on the blog Pauseliveaction was Series 11, ep. 33, a dramatic episode that featured the death of long-running character Maddie Young. I didn't review every Holby episode to begin with, so there are only eight reviews from Series 11. Series 12 was when I got into reviewing Holby more regularly.

SERIES 11

The death of Maddy
(Series 11, ep. 33 'What Will Survive of Us' by Dana Fainaru 2.6.09)

Remember the old oil-and-bitches drama known as Dallas? Remember the entire series that turned out to be just a dream (Bobby wasn't dead, he'd just been in the shower for several weeks while Pammy slept)?

We had an episode of Holby like that last week. Maddy (the cute doctor who used to be competent but has recently been incompetent – Holby can be a bit variable like that) had been stabbed in the back and lay dying on the floor of a washroom. But hang on – she wasn't dying! Lovely Nurse Maria found her in time! The glorious (and totally competent) Linden Cullen stitched up her wounds, and three weeks later she was fine.

Phew. I've always thought Linden and Maddy would be a good couple, but she only ever had eyes for one man (apart from a drunken night when she had eyes for Sam Strachan) – Dan Clifford. And here he came, not on a white charger but a black Bentley (so much quieter), with a foxy outfit purchased from the Connie Beauchamp Boutique for Sexy Surgeons for her to wear at her interview for the Fellowship job.

Ric didn't want her to get the job. She wasn't ready, he asserted, but Maddy proved her worth, was offered the job, and Dan declared his love for her. And declared he was ready to move back to Holby to be with her.

Hurrah! A happy ending! But wait – this is Holby. And Maddy had been dealing with a patient (played by Paul Connor from *Corrie*) who may or may not have killed his wife and set fire to his house. She had the feeling she'd met him before, and this feeling of deja vu only got worse as she tracked him down to the basement* after he took an overdose. She was mentally confusing him with her own father, that's what was happening. Because she wasn't in the basement with Paul Connor from *Corrie* at all, she was actually still on the washroom floor, bleeding to death. Maria found her, but it was too late, and Maddy is no more.

*The basement. Isn't it strange that when someone goes AWOL on Casualty they usually find them on the roof, and if they go AWOL from Holby (same hospital) they turn up in the basement? Yet A&E is on the ground floor and Darwin and Keller are on the upper floors. These people just make life harder for themselves.

Joseph gets married

(Series 11, ep. 34 'Proceed With Caution' by Tony McHale 9.6.09)

The Holby City wedding of Joseph Byrne (the loveliest man in the universe) and Faye Morton (Patsy Kensit) was trailed by the BBC as being terribly dramatic. The bride was in red! Joseph had a text from Jac! Linden was looking tortured (so no change there, then)! As it turned out, as Joseph would probably say "It all went off quite smoothly, thanks."

There was a slight hiccup when Faye's dad turned up and they had a bit of a row. Ever so slightly embarrassing when Elliott, who'd been Faye's "surrogate father" for the occasion handed over speeching duties to the real father and didn't get quite the reaction he expected.

There was a bit of excitement when Joseph's ex threatened to put a spanner in the works, and a bigger bit when Linden confessed his love to Faye and they had a brief kiss (witnessed – or was it? – by Joseph's sister). Faye said later it was a mistake and it wouldn't be happening again.

Meanwhile, Jac was being horrible to some new cast members/medical students, as only she can, and waiting in vain for Joseph to call.

So, rather than being a huge cataclysm of plot lines coming together (like Tony and Carla's wedding in Coronation Street last year), this one just carried on simmering the story along. Linden still loves Faye, Jac still loves Joseph. Will they both forget about it and move on, or are there more twists to this tale?

Connie's new position

(Series 11, ep. 35 'The Honeymoon's Over' by Martha Hillier 15.6.09)

Connie Beauchamp has always had her eye on Ric Griffin's seat. The one marked "Director of Surgery." And now it's finally hers, that administrative Jane woman having become fed up of Ric's heavy-handed techniques with junior doctors (she ought to have seen how Jac behaved towards them last week; Ric is a pussycat in comparison). Will Ric go quietly? If he knows what's good for him he will, otherwise he'll be on the receiving end of several of those trademark Beauchamp killer stares.

The newlyweds were back at work, but neither of them looked blissfully happy. Faye was feeling edgy because she'd snogged Linden at the wedding. Joseph was feeling edgy because he knew Faye was edgy about something. He thought she was having second thoughts about him adopting Archie, which was convenient for Faye. Meanwhile Linden is being tortured by guilt and lust, which gives him every opportunity for visiting the hospital chapel and looking anguished.

In other news, Elliott's son-in-law, the man with the dopey miserable face, was even dopier and miserabler when he got the news that he's going to go blind. Martha was ready (if not exactly willing) to be his care assistant for the rest of their lives, but he rather kindly let her off the hook.

And Donna fancies the new junior doctor. Good old Donna, we can always rely on her.

Maria takes it lying down

(Series 11, ep. 47 'Long Day's Night' by Sebastian Baczkiewicz 8.9.09)

Phoebe Thomas, playing lovely ginger Nurse Maria, spent the entire last episode of Holby City horizontal. No, it hadn't been a heavy night at "the bar" (the one they all go to, although it's never full and no-one from Casualty ever goes even though they officially work in the same building). "The bar" hasn't been such a draw for Maria and Donna since Maddy died.

Poor Maria had been involved in a hit and run accident, and as a result she spent half of the episode lying on a bed with a plastic tube in her mouth surrounded by actors crying about what a great mate she was and how Ric Griffin mustn't let her die. The other half she spent lying on an operating table, her midsection covered in fake gore and what looked like a plastic squid, surrounded by Ric Griffin and Michael Spence competing over who wasn't going to let her die.

Meanwhile Dr Olly Valentine tried to protect Daisha from the knowledge that she was looking after the woman who ran Maria over. Obviously Daisha found out, and she was cross with him, but not so cross that she didn't agree to finish the programme by joining him at "the bar." Chrissie is going to be ropeable when she finds out.

And Joseph was all stressed out about Faye and Linden, and got quite cross with Linden at one point, which was rather magnificent to watch.

Connie's dream job

(*Series 11, ep. 49 'Spin' by Al Smith 22.9.09*)

Connie Beauchamp made no secret of the fact that she wanted to be Director of Surgery at Holby. A while ago I thought she'd cracked it, but that's the thing with Holby – if you take your eye off the political machinations for a minute, you can easily get confused.

So Michael Spence (who gets his trousers from the 1970s) is currently Director of Surgery. Connie pouted about this for about five seconds, and then carried on with her ambitious schemings as if nothing had happened. And this week, following some deft manipulation of the aforementioned Michael Spence, Connie was crowned – wait for it – Director of Robotics. Has there ever been a more apt job title in the history of the world? It conjures up visions of Connie at the head of an army of steely-eyed surgical androids (no, I don't mean Jac). "I always get what I want," she told Spence, in that voice she has that's like a hypodermic syringe dipped in honey.

Elsewhere on Holby lovely ginger nurse Maria is recuperating but still can't feel her legs. Donna forced her to cheer up and go and sit by the bedside of a girl with cancer. Chrissie told her dad that she is pregnant with the child of Dr Valentine, who wasn't yet born when Chrissie took her driving test. Her dad, who is very wise because he used to be Jesus (in the TV series Jesus of Nazareth, back in the olden days), told her to tell Young Dr Valentine, but she didn't get the chance because it was his boy scouts night.

And Joseph was having a few days off to get his head together. Coincidentally, Linden was also off sick. I wonder if they were resolving their issues online via World of Warcraft?

Joseph fails to punch Linden... again

(Series 11, ep. 50 'The Cost of Loving' by Cameron McAllister 29.9.09)

You have to admire Joseph Byrne's restraint (apart from when it comes to having drunk one night stands with Jac). A less Zen sort of man would have punched Linden's lights out several times over for canoodling with Faye on the day she became Mrs Byrne. Instead, in tonight's episode Faye's disabled son Archie had a medical crisis, which only served to make Joseph more devoted to her. We left them keeping vigil by the boy's bedside, a sleeping Faye encircled by Joseph's protective arm. Oh lucky Patsy Kensit.

Elsewhere, Maria was given a grim choice between a life in a wheelchair or an operation that could either make her walk again or kill her. She opted for the surgery. Next week her life will be in Ric Griffin's hands once again. Let's hope he's not too distracted by the news (via Dr Penny Valentine) that it was Jac who went to the press about the abysmal failure of his zero tolerance policy. Expect all kinds of sh** to hit hospital fans next week.

Another bad week for Maria

(Series 11, ep. 51 'The Uncertainty Principle' by Claire Bennett 6.10.09)

This week Maria had the surgery that could either kill or cure her. Surprisingly, Holby does not have the top spinal surgeon in the country, so they flew him in. He was one of those arrogant types, and the anaesthetist took an instant dislike to him. But hey, if he's the right man to get Maria walking again, we can put up with him.

Sadly, he was "doing a Nick Jordan" by trying to work when he wasn't medically fit – in this case because of epilepsy. Poor Maria's innards ended up looking like a steak and kidney pie, but thanks to Ric Griffin she survived. Whether she'll walk again, or even poo via the natural route, we shall have to wait and see.

Meanwhile, Chrissie had to tell young Dr Valentine that she was expecting his baby when she came over all funny and had to take to a side room. Sadly she had a miscarriage, and Young Dr Valentine proved that (I'm being kind here) he isn't quite ready for the demands of fatherhood, as he congratulated himself and Daisha on having lucky escapes from the world of nappy rash and nurseries. Daisha (whose child Little Joseph is being brought up by her sister in the Philippines) wasn't best pleased.

His sister, Dr Miss Valentine, was doing better this week as she convinced a worried patient to go ahead with a heart transplant, and did a load of admin for Connie, all in the same shift. Connie and Elliott are very pleased with her – the flip side of that particular coin of course being that Jac now hates her.

Maria walks, Connie shows off

(Series 11, ep. 52 'The Spirit Dancing' by Chris Murray 13.10.09)

Yet another tough week for Maria, as she struggled to make her legs work in a useful manner. She wasn't helped by the fact that she was assisted by two physiotherapists who were forbidden from uttering a word. This is what you get when you hire cheap extras at non-speaking rates. Her mate in the next bed who had cancer sadly died, but not before Maria had worked her magic and got her reunited with her mother. In return, the friend inspired Maria to make a proper effort to get her legs going again – and she succeeded, accompanied by Snow Patrol. By next week she'll probably be frowning sympathetically at patients and charging round with cardboard containers full of sick as usual.

Meanwhile Connie has a new sparring partner in the form of hospital CEO Leslie Ash, who seems to be in cahoots with Michael Spence somehow. Michael spent the episode at the bedside of Annalise, who was giving birth to another Junior Spence, and he carelessly forgot to sign off Connie's robotics equipment before he went, and Leslie Ash wasn't being very co-operative, so Connie did a bit of open heart surgery on a ward just to show off.

Elsewhere, Chrissie has started to think about having a baby without having a man around, and she's signed herself and her dad up for a spot of internet dating. Not with each other, I hasten to add. That would be wrong.

SERIES 12

Suspense!

(Series 12, ep. 1 'The Hands That Rock the Cradle Part 1' by Tony McHale 20.10.09)

Last night's first part of a two-part Holby started at the end, as episodes of Holby and Casualty are frequently apt to do. We had Joseph and Faye looking shattered and upset, Connie and Ric being defensive, and hospital CEO Leslie Ash determined to get to the bottom of things. Bottom of what? Cue flashback to twelve hours earlier.

Archie had inhaled a whistle. How could that happen, I hear you ask, as indeed I heard most of the cast members ask at one time or another. We never found out, but there it was, stuck in his windpipe and tooting softly with every breath. Connie made easy work of removing it, but while doing so discovered that there was some other medical problem going on, which as far as I could make out was that Archie's windpipe is collapsing. This requires lots of medical intervention, and Faye couldn't help thinking that the wee lad had suffered enough.

So had Faye done something to "ease his suffering," perhaps? Well, probably not because by the end it looked like there was about to be a mistake by one of the non-regular cast members, who had swapped medication intended for Archie with medication intended for the woman who stabbed Maddy.

Yes, the woman who stabbed Maddy was admitted to Holby, pregnant and suffering from the after-effects of being beaten up by her boyfriend (possibly the bloke hanging around pretending to be a charity worker – he ain't fooling me). Everyone tried to keep Maria away from her, because poor Maria has enough to cope with etc.

So we have a nicely set up scenario where possibly both Archie and the stabber are going to die/be very poorly indeed, with a range of suspects including Faye, Joseph, Maria, anyone who ever liked Maddy (i.e. everybody), the charity worker/boyfriend and so on. Tune in tonight to find out not who dunnit, but who works out who dunnit.

Meanwhile, Leslie Ash and Michael Spence have implemented a glossy brochure in the hospital which can mean only one thing – cuts. A new matron has been appointed, much to the irritation of Mark "Jesus" Williams, who doesn't like her even before he's discovered that the first cost-saving she's identified is him.

Suspended!

(*Series 12, ep, 2 'The Hands That Rock the Cradle Part 2' by Tony McHale 21.10.09*)

In the second of this week's Holby two-parter, Faye's disabled son Archie died. Patsy Kensit did a heart-wrenching job of showing Faye's grief, her entire body convulsed in sobs. But Joseph stole the grief show, as his normal stately composure broke down to allow one tear to glide artistically down his beautifully-sculptured cheek.

A post-mortem will no doubt reveal that Archie's death was caused by being administered drugs intended for the woman who stabbed Maddy. However, currently CEO Leslie Ash has suspended Faye, because she changed a bag of saline without proper authorisation, and Ric and Connie have been requested to "take leave" because they tried to cover this up.

Elsewhere, Connie proved that she'd be quite terrifying at the head of a mecha-army as she finally got to demonstrate her new robot. She couldn't do a proper demo, because Michael Spence had crashed the robot while playing with it earlier. Typical boy.

Maria came face-to-face with Maddy's killer, and cunning Mark Williams attempted to convince the aforementioned killer to confess to the police.

And Donna tried to set Young Doctor Oliver Valentine and Daisha up on a date, but Daisha was having none of it.

Elliot, step away from the pies!

(Series 12, ep. 4 'The Professionals' by Martha Hillier 3.11.09)

This week saw our favourite hospital a bit short-handed, staff-wise, given that huge swathes of the staff are still suspended/on enforced leave. Cardio-thoracics was particularly under-staffed, and Elliot Hope was particularly overworked as a result. Despite the valiant support of Dr Penny Valentine, something had to give, and what gave was Elliot, who collapsed. It turns out he has angina, but he's somewhat in denial about his lifestyle. "I don't drink, I don't smoke," he mused to Dr Penny. She waited patiently while he reached his own conclusion: it's the old sedentary lifestyle and over-reliance on doughnuts. Dr Penny (how cute would a May/September romance between those two be?) has promised to help him count his calories.

This all meant that Joseph had to step in and do a spot of surgery, even though his mind was really elsewhere. It was Archie's funeral, and Faye is still under suspicion. Joseph, looking impossibly handsome in a dark suit, took it upon himself to shout at people in an effort to clear her name.

An emotional one for Linden

(Series 12, ep. 5 'Home Truths' by Dana Fainaru 10.11.09)

What do you do when you have a difficult, emotional problem that you need to sort out? Maybe you talk to your best mates, or ring your mum, pray to your deity of choice or consult the tarot or I Ching?

What they do, invariably, on Holby City or Casualty is to go to work, and wait for a random stranger to utter some words of wisdom that, by happy coincidence cuts straight to the heart of the problem and resolves everything nicely. I call this "speaking your brains."

Last night Linden's long-lost daughter Holly turned up. Linden hadn't seen Holly for nine years, not since her mother died. She'd been living with her grandparents, which Linden had thought at the time would be best, but obviously and understandably Holly didn't agree and wanted to live with her dad and get to know him.

Well, we already know Linden a bit, and we know he's an odd character, guarded and a bit angsty. Not what you'd call adaptable. Anyway, he didn't think he could cope with a teenager in his life – until five minutes from the end, when a patient uttered the magic words about selflessness and thinking of others, and Linden had his Damascus moment, ran into the car park (accompanied by Paul Weller singing 'Wings of Speed' – it was a tearjerker, I tell you) and stopped the taxi from taking Holly away. Sniff.

Elsewhere, the Dr Mrs Griffin they were hoping for last week (Lola) has turned out to be everyone's nightmare Dr Mrs Griffin, Thandie. Elliot is understandably wary of the woman who practically killed half her patients last time due to incompetence and accused him of racism, but she seems to have improved a bit and helped Dr Penny Valentine do a tricky procedure. Elliot had advised Dr Penny to be mentored by Joseph rather than Thandie. "Why settle for silver when you can have gold?" he said. My thoughts on Joseph exactly.

Joseph wants answers

(Series 12, ep. 6 'To Have and To Hold' by David Lawrence 17.11.09)

The world's most beautiful heart surgeon, Joseph Byrne, continued his quest this week to find out who or what had killed Faye's son, Archie. He called in a few favours and obtained the toxicology report. What does it say? We don't know yet, because he only had chance to read it right at the end. Before that he was being distracted by having to do surgery, and having to deal with Thandie Griffin, who is still as devious as ever.

Consultant Nurse Mark "Jesus" Williams continued to take a shine to Matron, until he discovered that she'd recommended him for redundancy. She was wrong, she explained, and managed to convince Leslie Ash of the fact as well. Jesus has now forgiven Matron, but his daughter Chrissie is not the type to let bygones be bygones so easily.

It was a mixed week for Young Dr Oliver Valentine. Queen of the Night Jac Naylor gave him a massive amount of admin to do – like Chrissie, Jac doesn't forgive easily, and she hasn't forgotten that Young Dr Oliver went over her head to Michael Spence last week. Has Young Dr Oliver redeemed himself by taking the blame for Jac missing a diagnosis this week? Will she soften towards him at all? I'm not holding my breath.

Linden wasn't working this week but had brought his daughter Holly in as she's going to be working as a nursing assistant. They found themselves sharing a lift with three brides, accompanied by 'Sex on Fire' by the Kings of Leon. It would take far too long to explain why.

The most attractive staff in the NHS

(Series 12, ep. 7 'Break Away' by David Lawrence 24.11.09)

Connie, Ric and Faye are still away on "gardening leave" while the cause of Archie's death remains unexplained. Joseph (the world's most beautiful heart surgeon) thinks he has explained the death – he's got his hands on the toxicology report, and some unusual substances had been given to Archie before the point where Faye changed his saline drip – hence, the death had nothing to do with Faye doing that. The problem is that Joseph has nowhere to go with this information, because he obtained it somewhat illegally. Leslie Ash won't touch it with a bargepole – she's the kind of chief exec who plays things by the book, unlike Jane Grayson who was a feisty sort who would do whatever it took.

I just hope Joseph has a breakthrough next week. I can live quite happily without seeing Faye on a weekly basis, but Holby is just not the same without Connie. Jac Naylor does her best, and is extremely good at bitchy put-downs, but Connie is in a league of her own. She's like a sexy, elegant, kitten-heeled, non-swearing version of Malcolm Tucker. If you can picture such a thing.

This week's storyline revolved mainly around the stunningly beautiful Dr Penny Valentine (Holby really does have the most attractive staff in the entire NHS, apart from the anaesthetists, who are all weird-looking since Art Malik left). Dr Penny had been told to improve her people skills, and she did this by getting just a tiny bit over-fond of a hunky fireman who has only weeks to live unless he gets a heart transplant. One feels it can only end in tears and a particularly mournful song over the closing credits.

Linden's daughter Holly had her first day as a care assistant, and the radiant Donna Jackson was appointed to look after her. The radiant Donna wasted no time in trying to dig up some info about Linden, who has never divulged much about his personal life. Holly was at first as reticent as her dad, but Donna cracked her and discovered that Linden's wife had died in a car crash. But our Donna has matured in recent months, and when she got the chance to pass this juicy gossip on, she claimed that she didn't know anything because Holly was a very private person. I love Donna. She got the best line of the night – after saving a patient with quick thinking and prompt action, she modestly shrugged off Holly's admiration saying, "I went on a course. Free sandwiches."

Young Dr Oliver Valentine's tricky patient of the week was a boy who'd been stabbed by a gang of boys – using his own knife, which he was carrying because his father had told him he must defend himself. This father was severely in need of a trip to Jeremy Kyle for a word with Graham about anger management, and I'm a bit worried we'll be seeing him again, possibly "tooled-up" next time. We haven't had a hostage-type-situation on Holby for, ooh, a couple of months now – I'd say one is long overdue.

Joseph Byrne's beautiful mind

(Series 12, ep. 8 'And That's What Really Hurts' by Justin Young 1.12.09)

Joseph Byrne (the world's most beautiful heart surgeon) is wearing himself to a frazzle trying to get to the bottom of who killed Archie. We know this because he's started scribbling clues on sheets of glass, in a manner very reminiscent of the character Russell Crowe played in *A Beautiful Mind.*

Joseph has a beautiful mind too, as well as a beautiful face, even though derangement has meant he's temporarily stopped shaving. But he has cracked what killed Archie – it was potassium. And by the end of the episode he'd cracked who'd wrongly administered the potassium – it was Lauren, the nurse who is now conveniently away on holiday. All Joseph has to do is get someone to believe him, or support him, and no-one will, because he came about the evidence in a dodgy manner and it would never stand up in court. What we really need is for Lauren to get back from her holidays and 'fess up. Then Faye would be exonerated, and Connie and Ric could come back (hurrah!). And Joseph could have a shave and get back to saving lives and being wound up by Jac.

On the subject of Jac, she actually smiled this week! The smile was in the general direction of Young Dr Oliver Valentine, but it was more a smile of pleasure that she'd inflicted a very awkward patient on him than anything else. But still, the Ice Queen does seem to be thawing slightly towards Young Dr Oliver. He is quite a catch, too. Yes, he can be a bit of a dick, but he's young and male so we'll cut him some slack. He can also be rather lovely, as in this episode when he supplied said awkward patient with some chicken soup, because she'd told him her granny used to make her it when she was ill and he thought it would soften the blow of having to give her some bad news vis-à-vis her reproductive organs. He also paid for Daisha to go to the Philippines at Christmas to visit her son. Awww.

The Radiant Donna Jackson slipped on some sick early in the episode which was a great chance to swing the lead and spend most of the time having a little rest in a cubicle. Matron made her wear a support collar in case she had whiplash, and Donna blamed this for her poor performance in a test about hygiene on the wards (an initiative cooked up by Leslie Ash apparently for the express purpose of humiliating Chrissie, for reasons I couldn't quite work out). Maria came first in the hygiene test, meaning she is now ward hygiene monitor and gets a little pay rise. The Radiant Donna was not best pleased.

The twilight of the robots

(Series 12, ep. 9 'Now We Are Lonely' by Andrew Holden 8.12.09)

The world's most beautiful heart surgeon, Joseph Byrne, has still not had a shave, and his OCD is getting the better of him as well (the old obsessive hand-washing when not actually about to perform surgery). You sense he won't relax (as far as Joseph ever does "relax") until he's got to the bottom of who was responsible for Archie's death. The irony is that he has got to the bottom of it – it was Nurse Lauren Minster mixing up the drug labels. But having come so close to getting Lauren to crack and admit it, Joseph has now been persuaded to back off in case she makes a career-ruining complaint against him for harassment.

As well as all this detective stuff, he managed to fit in an impressive bit of surgery this week, performing an open heart operation on a woman while she was still awake. This woman had balls of steel – not only was she awake, but she could see what was going on in her opened-up chest reflected in one of the lights.

While all this was going on, The Stunningly Beautiful Dr Penny Valentine was doing a little stint on AAU, just in time to see her favourite patient, the firefighter awaiting the heart transplant, being admitted. Dr Penny is more than a bit in love with this man and she got into big bother with Matron for procuring a sandwich for him. Sandwiches aren't allowed on AAU, for some reason.

There was some nonsense involving a patient with a robotic camera which he managed to steer remotely into an operating theatre without anyone noticing. Given that this thing was about the size of the box I take our cat to the vet in, I found this a little implausible. Snake-hipped Dr Michael Spence had robots very much on his mind, though. A few weeks ago, Connie Beauchamp became Director of Robotics, but since then she's been on gardening leave, and the robot has remained idle and covered in a dust sheet. It seems that in the NHS the phrase "use it or lose it" applies, and the hunt was on for a robot-qualified person to come and do a spot of kidney surgery. Sadly the man chosen wasn't quite up to speed on the thoroughly modern model that Holby has, so it looks as though the robot will be making its way to rival hospital St James'. Connie will be absolutely livid when she gets back (if she gets back. Connie is coming back, isn't she? Please tell me she is). And a livid Connie could reduce Malcolm Tucker (from *The Thick Of It*) to a small heap sobbing for his mummy and his blanky.

Don't go breaking my heart

(Series 12, ep. 10 'Too Close for Comfort' by Sonali Bhattacharyya 15.12.09)

For several weeks now The Stunningly Beautiful Dr Penny Valentine has been getting increasingly fond of Scott James (Joshua Bowman), her hunky firefighter patient who is waiting for a heart transplant.

Last week she got into trouble for bringing him sandwiches, this week she got told off for bringing him a television to watch football on. Seeing a goal scored got him a bit too excited, and this is not what you want when your heart is only being kept going with the help of an electronic box.

Worse still, when Dr Penny was being pestered by a sleaze-bag patient (who also happened to be an old colleague of Elliot's), Scott James leapt in to defend her, scattering heart monitor leads in his wake. How thrilling! It gave Scott a funny turn, but how could Penny resist when he asked her to join him for a snuggly Boxing Day appointment with a DVD? As long as it was something fairly sedate and not too action-packed, as we have to remember his heart could give out at any moment.

Sadly, when you're a junior doctor there'll always be a senior doctor to rain on your parade, and this time it was Elliot, who reminded the beautiful Pen that professional boundaries ought really to be maintained. She had to tell Scott that he'd be tackling the Quality Street on his own come the 26th.

Better Boxing Day luck for Matron and Mark "Jesus" Williams, who have arranged a post shift mince pie assignation for that day. It was a fraught episode for Matron, whose son was brought in to AAU with alcohol poisoning with a side order of ruptured appendix. Then her estranged husband (Max Farnham/Steven Pinder from Brookside) turned up, and let's just say things between them are somewhat tense.

Not a great shift for Maria either, who was left in charge of the ward while Daisha was on a course. Naturally The Radiant Donna used this as an excuse to pop up to paeds to spread Christmas cheer among the kiddies, and Maria spent far too long sorting out a homeless woman whose pride had stopped her asking for help. That's the thing with Maria – her heart is as shimmeringly lovely as her hair.

I'm getting increasingly upset at the non-appearance of Connie Beauchamp. We haven't seen her or Ric for weeks now – are they possibly appearing in panto somewhere? There was no sighting of Joseph or Jac this week either (or Leslie Ash). I just hope they're all lying down in a darkened room, limbering up for those oh-so-dramatic festive episodes.

The ghosts of Linden's past

(Series 12, ep. 11. 'Stand by Me' by Tony McHale 22.12.09)

Holby City has never been a programme to shy away from the supernatural, considering it's full of doctors and nurses and scientific people like that. In recent memory we've had a whole episode that was in Maddie's head as she lay dying, and Donna talking with her father after he'd passed away to a place that hopefully smells less of disinfectant.

Last night, as Linden and Holly decorated their home for Christmas, Linden was being haunted by his late wife Olivia, who appeared in awkward places in a red coat, like a taller version of the scary midget in Don't Look Now. She also had a sideline in writing TELL HER THE TRUTH in condensation on various bits of glass. Obviously this stressed Linden out a fair bit, and Holly putting Stand By Me on his jukebox (who'd have guessed Linden would have a jukebox?) was the last straw. He yelled, Holly cried, and she ran away.

Linden was summoned to Holby at the request of a very ill patient, his Catholic priest. This man offered sage words of advice along the lines of TELL HER THE TRUTH (Linden was feeling a theme developing by this point), and asked Linden to borrow a pen, which he then put in his pocket. The pen, we felt, would have some Significance later.

By way of flashbacks, we discovered the truth of what happened the night Linden's wife died in a car accident. Linden had tried to save her by doing a roadside tracheostomy. This hadn't gone well, so Linden always blamed himself for Olivia's death. Holly had been present at the time, and Linden couldn't ever face talking about it so had given Holly into the care of her grandparents. Father and daughter had all this out by the side of a road, and I did think that Holly had thrown her backpack into quite a dangerous place on a bend. As she went to retrieve it, a car coming round the bend crashed into her. And guess what? Linden was forced to perform an emergency tracheostomy, using the very same pen that the priest had given him. This time it was successful, Holly was saved, everyone agreed Linden hadn't been in any way responsible for Olivia's death. Linden wanted to thank his friend the priest – but it turned out he'd died before Linden had the pen conversation with him.

It all ended rather emotionally, with Linden listening to Stand By Me on the jukebox that Olivia had given him, and dancing with the ghost of his wife. PLA Jr was in tears, so I feel a bit Scrooge for calling the episode more than a tad contrived (two roadside tracheostomies in one family? A heavy snowfall when the trees are all still covered in green leaves? The likelihood of the pen in your pocket being a Bic when you need one?), and just a bit slow and irritating.

It was left to The Radiant Donna Jackson to bring some light into the proceedings with her karaoke rendition of Stand By Me, at a fundraising do for her late father's charity (we'll pass swiftly over Mark "Jesus" Williams and his rendition of Slade's Merry Xmas Everybody). There was still no sign of Connie or Ric, but we're promised that next week Thandie is going to be putting pressure, as only Thandie can, on Lauren Minster, to reveal exactly what happened the day Archie died. Let's hope she's successful, so Connie can be de-suspended and come back in time to make Christmas crackers out of Michael Spence's knackers for losing her robots.

(Oh, and PS – Chrissie is pregnant again. Young Dr Oliver Valentine is not the father).

Oh, Dr Valentine!

(Series 12, ep. 12 'Resolutions' by Chris Murray 29.12.09)

"Just relax," Elliot advised Joseph. Has Elliot never met the world's most beautiful heart surgeon before? Relaxing is not in Joseph's nature at the best of times, and when your wife has just been charged with the murder of her son is not the best of times. Joseph wears anguish quite magnificently though, and I was rather loving his stubbly-faced, dark-overcoatedness.

I've also started to rather love Thandie, who carries on in the long line of strong, feisty Holby women. Thandie had spotted that Nurse Lauren Minster was getting antsy whenever Joseph or Faye were mentioned, and she decided to do a little digging. When Lauren let drop some remark along the lines of "I made a mistake," Thandie knew she was onto something, and went at her like a terrier with a rag, until Lauren finally confessed that she'd made a mistake with the drip bags and that was why Faye's son Archie had wrongly been given potassium. So, finally, Faye is in the clear, and just perhaps Joseph might be able to relax a teeny tiny bit. And have a shave.

Meanwhile, Young Dr Oliver Valentine was making eyes at Jac Naylor (or "Termi-Naylor" as Dr Penny Valentine aptly calls her) over an aortic aneurism. He had to admire Jac's icy-cool-in-a-crisis demeanour. "He's in VF!" shouts Young Dr Oliver. "How dull," sighs Jac, charging up the defibrillator. Young Dr Oliver tried to work out what motivated Jac to go into medicine. Was it being in control? That was it, wasn't it? She loved to be in control? The lad was fair dripping sexual tension by this point.

Operation successfully over, Jac let herself be vulnerable for a moment, showed him how her hand was shaking, and said she became a doctor because she can fix other people (but, by implication, not herself). Dr Oliver could contain himself no longer and pounced. His sister Dr Penny turned up to find out why he hadn't turned up at the New Year party, in time to catch a glimpse of her brother and Miss Naylor well and truly at it in the locker room. Luckily she had Donna's camera with her, so expect some fun and games when that photo gets shared around.

Faye has blood on her hands. Sleeve, at least

(Series 12, ep. 13 'Talk To Me' by Graham Mitchell 5.1.10)

I don't like to be the one to cast the first stone, but the facts are these. Faye Byrne, a lady with previous form for pushing husbands down staircases (thought we'd forgotten that, Mrs Byrne?) had a bit of a tussle with Lauren Minster next to a reservoir. Lauren Minster being the woman responsible for the death of Faye's son.

Next thing we know is that Lauren Minster is brought into AAU half-drowned, and Faye has got blood on her sleeve. You don't have to be Poirot, do you? But nothing's ever entirely straightforward on Holby, so we'll wait and see what really happened, probably via the medium of monochrome flashbacks accompanied by moody music in a couple of weeks.

Meanwhile, everyone received the shock news that Connie Beauchamp has resigned! Please let it not be true! Holby without Connie is an infinitely less pleasing place. I'm hoping Michael Spence will be able to lure her back.

After last week's lust in the locker-room with Young Dr Oliver Valentine, Jac was back to doing flashy bits of surgery this week. You never know with Jac whether she really is doing what she thinks is best for her patients, or whether she's just showing off. Ric knows what he thinks, and he doesn't like it. He had a word with Leslie Ash – either Jac was demoted back to registrar, or he'd follow Connie and resign. So Jac's precious consultancy has been whipped away from her, and I think it might be safest to avoid her for a while – you wouldn't like her when she's angry.

Cast aside, like a Holby storyline

(Series 12, ep. 14 'A Glorious Reunion' by Graham Mitchell 12.1.10)

The Holby City scriptwriters are a puzzling lot. They don't operate by the traditional rules of soapdom at all. Take this week, for instance, when two plot-lines which would have kept *EastEnders* happy for months and built up to a ratings-boosting climax were almost casually tossed aside.

Last week, Faye was tussling with Lauren Minster at a reservoir (which they kept calling a "river" this week, but it's a reservoir, and I should know because I walked around it on Saturday). Lauren was brought into the hospital with hypothermia, half-drowned and with various internal injuries which needed Holby's finest surgeons to sort out. And Faye was very much in the frame for this. Except, by the end of the episode, Faye wasn't in the frame any longer. Lauren woke up, told the police that Faye hadn't pushed her and it had been a suicide attempt because she couldn't live with herself after Archie's death, and that was that.

A couple of weeks ago, Jac and Young Dr Oliver Valentine had a lustful encounter in a locker room, which was photographed by Beautiful Dr Penny Valentine. This week, Donna (whose camera it was) emailed the photo to everyone in the hospital. How dramatic! Or – how comic! Actually, neither. Everyone more-or-less shrugged and ignored it, and the potentially embarrassing moment when Daisha, who Dr Oliver fancies, almost saw the picture was quickly averted by Jac.

So the main dramatic action of the week was the loss of Matron Judith. Ric wanted to propose a vote of no confidence in Leslie Ash for her handling of the Lauren Minster situation. Leslie Ash wasn't about to give in gracefully, but decided a head would have to roll to take the heat away from her, so Matron Judith was informed that her contract would not be renewed. Matron Judith has taken the news quite well. She fancied living in Manchester instead of Holby anyway, and she's still planning to see Jesus Williams at weekends, so it's all ok. Plus, she'd started wearing her hair down, which I didn't feel was a very professional look for a matron, so she really had to go.

Connie Beauchamp was mentioned a few times. She's officially gone from the hospital, but Amanda Mealing's name still comes up first on the credits at the beginning, and a little bird has told me that she's been filming recently, so I don't think we need to mourn her loss just yet.

Linden and Faye circling ever closer

(Series 12, ep. 15 'Stop All the Clocks' by Rebecca Wojciechowski 19.1.10)

At any given time Holby will feature only a certain number of departments. Back in the glory days of Mubbs (oh, how I miss Mubbs) and Owen, we never had our noses out of obstetrics. Before that there were lots of child-centred stories when paediatrics was one of the featured departments. Currently we concentrate our attention on Darwin (cardio-thoracics), Keller (general surgery) and AAU (acute admissions – kind of a Casualty overflow), with the odd foray into the twilight zone that is Holby Care and the beeping world of HDU.

Last night's episode involved machinations to get people into different departments. Linden is still hankering after Faye (your guess is as good as mine), so manoeuvred to pluck her from Darwin to AAU for the day, thus spiriting her away from under the nose of her husband, AKA The World's Most Beautiful Heart Surgeon, Joseph. Linden's daughter Holly was getting a tad suspicious about the way her father looked like he'd been struck breathless every time the fragrant Mrs Byrne heaved into view, so Linden put in a call – surely Darwin were a bit short-staffed (of course they are – you've nicked Faye) and needed Holly's help?

Linden and Faye are circling ever closer (this plot has been simmering away for what feels like years. They don't believe in hurrying on Holby), while things between Faye and Joseph are decidedly cool.

Not as cool as the relationship between Ric Griffin and the current Mrs Griffin, Thandie. She did a Jac Naylor by being flexible with the facts so she could assist in an operation with Ric and Elliot (it was one of those "you fix up the heart, and I'll dig around in his tummy bits" double operations that they enjoy on Holby). Ric was livid when he found out what she'd done, and he wants a divorce. Who remembers when Ric used to be fairly chilled out and not averse to the occasional relaxing herbal cigarette?

Meanwhile… when Nurse Nicky Van Barr, a man so pale and thin he makes Robert Pattinson look like Arnold Schwarzenegger, tottered into view, I said to my other half, "That man needs a storyline of his own." Previously we've only seen him being more or less background in the scenes when Archie died. Lo and behold, ask and the Holby writers will deliver. Not only is he hankering after Lovely Ginger Nurse Maria (bless! If they ever procreated their offspring would be so white of skin they wouldn't be able to venture outdoors without blankets over their heads. Like Michael Jackson's kids) – but he's also a carer for his mum, who has MS. Expect to see Mum Van Barr occupying a bed in AAU any time soon. Or, given that this is Holby, any time this decade.

Donna's big decision

(Series 12, ep. 16 'Promises' by Joe Ainsworth 27.1.10)

A while back, The Radiant Donna discovered she had a small female relative called Mia, who was something to do with her dad. Anyway, in last night's episode, the small relative and her granny pitched up at the hospital, quite literally as they used the tree at the front as a brake. Sadly, granny died after a heart attack, which left darling Mia (and my word, this child is adorable) all alone.

Apart from Donna. But could the ditzy party girl face up to the responsibility of suddenly being the sole carer of a five year old? In a plot-line which echoed the same dilemma that had faced Dr Zoe Hanna on Casualty not too long ago, and a final scene that had been faced by Linden and Holly even more recently, at the last minute Donna decided she couldn't let Mia be taken into care, and rushed down from the Window of Regret (the one on the stairwell overlooking the main entrance) to scoop Mia up from the nice social services lady.

It'll be interesting to see how that little relationship goes. Meanwhile, a relationship which is not going at all well is that of Faye and Joseph. Faye has taken to slumping in the hospital chapel for extended periods of time, clutching the little prayer card that Linden gave her. Is she seeking comfort in the Lord, or hoping for a bespectacled Scotsman to heal her pain?

Either way, it's all very upsetting for The World's Most Beautiful Heart Surgeon, Joseph Byrne, and it's affecting his work. He had to be bailed out by Jac, and that didn't sit very well with her at all. In fact, she's told Michael Spence that she will be going all out to try to get Joseph's consultancy job from him.

There was a new cast member, a locum doctor on AAU, George Kerwin (played by Joseph May). He's Canadian and he hardly ever blinks, and he's wasted no time in asking Maria out for a drink. What is it about Lovely Ginger Nurse Maria that men find so irresistible? Only the previous day, Pale Thin Nurse Nicky Van Barr was sighing about her. I assume he'll get even more pale and thin now.

Now some exciting news – apparently we're soon going to be treated to one of those rare episodes where Holby and Casualty collide (I love those), when Charlie-from-Casualty has a heart attack and has to be operated on by Elliot-from-Holby. Elliot Hope, the life of the world's most baffled-looking nurse will be in your hands.

A thorn in Ric's side

(*Series 12, ep. 17 '...And the Devil Makes Three' by Tom Bidwell 2.2.10*)

Marry in haste, repent at leisure, as the saying goes. Not a saying that Ric Griffin has ever paid any heed to, if his marriage and divorce record is anything to go by ("almost as many wives as Henry VIII," as someone pointed out in this episode).

When Ric sprang Thandie Abebe Griffin upon an unsuspecting Holby, she looked every inch the trophy wife. Beautiful, intelligent, sophisticated. And she turned out to be a right liability, a lethal combination of over-confidence and inexperience, with a whole heap of attitude on top. Everyone sighed with relief when she left.

A few weeks ago she returned, and she's a little different this time. The willingness to stretch the truth for her own ends is still there, but this time her heart seems to be in the right place, and she has occasionally gone out on a limb for a colleague – she was the one who finally got to the bottom of how Archie died, for example. And it seems that she is still in love with her husband. Such a shame that he can't stand the sight of her, so that this week, when she announced she would be going for the registrar job on Darwin, Ric did everything he could to block it. Sadly, as per usual Ric finds himself without allies, as Mrs Griffin has impressed everyone from board members to Michael Spence with her CT skills and empathy with patients.

Another youngish doctor whose empathy with patients is legendary is The Stunningly Beautiful Dr Penny Valentine. She almost got in hot water this week with weird anaesthetist Dr Green, but I sense that her caseload was not uppermost in her mind. She was late for work, she seems to have suddenly taken up smoking, and her brother has noticed she's acting a bit oddly. My guess is that this all has something to do with hunky firefighter and heart transplant candidate Scott James.

Meanwhile, Holly got on the wrong side of Faye and then back on the right side again.

Valentines and hearts

(Series 12, ep. 18 'Too Cold To Crash and Burn' by Al Smith 9.2.10)

Hunky Failing-Heart Firefighter Scott James had his heart transplant today. Via the medium of fuzzy-focus flashbacks, we learned that, as we suspected, Beautiful Dr Penny Valentine and Scott had definitely overstepped the boundaries of the doctor/patient relationship. In fact, they were in love, and it was really sweet because they're both adorable and it was Christmas and he gave her a little heart-shaped necklace. And there she was, in the operating theatre, with his heart literally in her hands. You have to thrill at the tragic poetry of it all.

When it looked like things were going wrong, she ran out of the room. She thought he was dead, but he wasn't, and as she sat by his bedside, Elliot hope told her he was very disappointed by her unprofessional conduct. Penny's career now hangs in the balance.

Her brother, Young Dr Oliver Valentine, wasn't having a good week either. Remember a while back when he had a bit of a fling with Jac in the locker room, and it looked like he'd got away with it? Well – he hadn't. Maria, who was having a dodgy week because she thought she was being messed around by The Unblinking Canadian Paediatrician, spilled the beans and showed Daisha the photo of Young Dr Valentine at it with Termi-Naylor. Dr Oliver found himself on the receiving end of a pretty hefty slap.

Jac has a bit of a soft spot for Dr Oliver, but not as soft as the spot she has for her career. Michael Spence used both these facts and her upcoming interview for the consultant job to mess royally with her head this week. He also ate a great deal of cake.

And hurrah and huzzah, Connie Beauchamp is back next week!

Charlie's best Hope

(Series 12, ep. 19 'Downstairs, Upstairs' by Mark Catley 15.2.10)

"You broke his heart!" Shona accused the useless Louis when he finally showed up at the hospital to see his dad. Holby has never been a programme to shy away from a medical metaphor, but in this case it was more literally true – stressing about his waste-of-skin son can't have helped Charlie's medical condition.

Elliot Hope, however, could and did help Charlie, but it was a bit touch and go in theatre. Elliot was not having a good day, what with being over-tired, his angina playing up, and having the life of the most revered man in Holby in his hands. Indeed, without Nick Jordan's timely intervention, it could all have gone horribly pear-shaped.

Meanwhile, Thandie was under threat of being deported if she and Ric didn't satisfy the Home Office that their marriage was real and not an immigration scam sham. Ric was in no mood to play happy families with the fifth Mrs Griffin, so when the immigration people turned up it soon turned into a proper bicker-fest, with both of them dredging up long-held grudges and niggles. And it was those very grudges and niggles which – ironically – actually persuaded the immigration people that they were a for-real couple. Apparently people who only marry for convenience try too hard to pretend they're in love. And, wouldn't you know it, no sooner were the snooping officials out of the door than Ric and Thandie were kissing. Bless! He'll probably be hating her again by lunch time.

Maria thinks she's found true love with the Unblinking Canadian Paediatrician, but we saw last week that he has a roving eye for the ladies. Tonight we discovered that his roving (unblinking) eye extends to the laddies as well, when he copped a feel of Pale Thin Nurse Nicky Van Barr. What we really need now is for Pale Thin Nurse Nicky to grow a pair and let Maria know what's going on, but since he's practically the living embodiment of the word "wimp," this may take some time.

Stunningly Beautiful Dr Penny Valentine has been ordered to repeat her Darwin rotation because of her misdemeanor with Scott James. But, now she's dumped Scott on Elliot's instructions, all will be well. But wait – she hasn't exactly dumped Scott. In fact, she hasn't even mentioned the d-word to him. Oh, Dr Penny, it'll end in tears one way or the other.

The return of the divine Connie Beauchamp

(Series 12, ep. 20 'Together Alone' by Dan Sefton 17.2.10)

Obviously, we've all missed Connie while she's been away. But I didn't realise how much I'd missed Connie until she was back on the screen in all her fabulousness. Quite simply, there's no-one like Connie Beauchamp – sexy as hell, cool as iced cucumber, supremely confident, bitchy, single-minded, but with just enough of a hint of vulnerability to keep you on her side. She's charisma in heels.

Michael Spence went to visit her at her new workplace, a hospital whose windows boast such brilliant views of London that you could shoot all the linking scenes of The Apprentice from there without ever going outside. And it has talking elevators as well! And I bet they don't break down while nurses are in labour inside them. In fact, I'm not sure this hospital even had nurses – there weren't all that many patients, and certainly none of the ghastly sticky stuff and vomiting onto shoes that you get on an hourly basis at Holby City.

The operating theatre involved colour-co-ordinated walls and scrubs and Vivaldi in the background ("Patient's choice," Connie was informed), and Connie's office was the size of the average Tesco's. Plus, there was some totty in the form of Irish Dr Greg, who turns out to be Connie's latest squeeze.

So what would tempt her back to Holby? Elliot pitched up later (he'd had a bad day, bless him) and begged her to come back. He'd straighten it with Leslie Ash, he promised. Connie said she'd at least want Leslie Ash's head on a plate, but as this didn't seem likely she'd stay put, with the roguish Irishman and the talking elevators. But you can see her heart isn't really in the world of private medicine and its rules and hierarchies. Connie likes her own hierarchy, which involves Connie at the top, and the rest of the world gazing adoringly up at her.

While all this was going on in London, back in the fictional city of Holby Scott James asked Beautiful Dr Penny Valentine (who was looking less beautiful this week due to stress, tiredness and fags) to move to Spain with him. Dr Oliver Valentine warned Scott that he shouldn't destroy Penny's career in such a cavalier fashion, so Scott pretended he'd changed his mind. Penny was having none of this and told him she'd very gladly thrown in her horrible medical career and move to Spain. But Scott said he wouldn't let her do that, so they must part. It didn't seem to occur to him that he could give up Spain and stay in Holby for the sake of Dr Penny's career. The fool.

Connie's replacement at Holby was a Mr Geddes – five feet tall ("Is he really that small or is he just far away?" Dr Oliver Valentine wanted to know) and with a habit of high-fiving his co-workers at the end of operations. This is not the kind of behaviour Joseph Byrne expects of a surgeon, and he ended up decking the aforementioned Mr Geddes. He won't get into trouble for this, because I'm willing to bet that if Leslie Ash asks for witnesses, no-one at all will have seen anything.

Things get personal for Thandie

(Series 12, ep. 21 'Amare' by Sebastian Baczkiewicz 22.2.10)

I've enjoyed Thandie Abebe-Griffin this time around. She's a really interesting character – a bit sly, a bit cheeky, a bit loyal, a bit disloyal. You never know quite where you are with her. She has a beautiful calm, graceful demeanor but you always sense there's all sorts going on beneath the surface, some of which you're probably best off not knowing.

But just as she was turning into one of my favourite characters, she's gone. The episode started well for Thandie and Ric.Last week's visit from the immigration people had put a new spark in their marriage and they were making eyes at each other above their surgical masks (as is the Holby way), and Ric was asking Michael to find her a permanent job.

Then Thandie's brother, Moses, turned up. Dying from various AIDS-related illnesses and in intolerable pain, he asked Thandie to give him more morphine and end his life. Knowing the consequences, she went ahead and did as he asked, but then told Ric what had happened and said she was returning to Uganda. I'll miss her.

Meanwhile, Pale Thin Nurse Nicky Van Barr had finally had enough of George, the Unblinking Canadian Paediatrician, and his innuendos, and the way he was treating Maria by flirting with anything with a pulse (apart from Chrissie, who has been around the block more than once and knows a player when she sees one). "Is anything wrong?" Maria wanted to know, sensing a bit of an atmosphere between her boyfriend and her pale, thin colleague. "Ask your bisexual boyfriend!" Nicky snapped. So Maria did – well, she asked him if he was bisexual, and he cheerfully admitted that he probably was, and that he was a bit tired of Maria and her couply behaviour.

Pale Thin Nurse Nicky seized his chance and asked her out for a drink, but she wasn't in the mood, what with just having been dumped and all. Best leave it, ooh, at least a week, Nicky. Till she's had a pep talk from Donna (who was still away this week, presumably plot-wise getting to grips with having a small child to look after).

Joseph bought Faye a first edition of *Our Man in Havana*, and she looked at it in complete bewilderment. Isn't that finally enough to make him realise she is not the woman for him? He was thinking of taking her on holiday to Cuba, he said. Faye didn't think it was a good idea. Joseph, you are banging your head against a brick wall with that one.

Duty before love

(Series 12, ep. 22 'The Butterfly Effect Part 1' by Justin Young 2.3.10)

With the folks in A&E overwhelmed by something or other, it was up to the rest of Holby City Hospital, and specifically AAU, to deal with the casualties from a bus crash and a hostage situation.

Cue Linden, Jac and Elliot doing extraordinary things under extraordinary stress, the stress largely due to the failings of their fellow staff members. Michael Spence and Leslie Ash made a total pigs ear out of ensuring that operating theatres, ICU and the wards were emptied of non-urgent cases. New consultant Mr Geddes made a fuss in theatre so Elliot had to shout at him and order him out, then he decided his shift was over and he'd pop off home. Young Dr Oliver Valentine was as much use as a bus ticket on a train.

Faye had earlier had an argument with The World's Most Beautiful Heart Surgeon, and Joseph had gone off in a huff in the car, with Daisha bagging a lift with the grumpy-yet-gorgeous surgeon. Faye was upset, and what with the pressures of the shift and everything, ended up snogging Linden under a fire escape, as you do. But wait! This was no casual snog – she was in love with him, she reckoned. It was enough to make Linden almost smile. Almost.

But then, when Faye finally tore herself away from Mr Cullen and got back to looking after patients, she discovered Joseph's blood-stained tie on the floor. News of two more casualties from the hostage scene came in – and everyone braced themselves for one of them to be Joseph. Faye had to rush to the chapel for a quick pray, and a quick bargain with God that if only Joseph was safe, she'd stick with her wedding vows and not skip off into the sunset with Linden.

The first casualty arrived, with a makeshift chest drain poking out of him. Who do we know who could improvise a chest drain on the spot? Joseph! And here he was, alive and well and dealing with the second patient, who was critically ill – and was also the lovely Daisha.

Will she survive? Will Linden let Faye walk back into the arms of Joseph yet again? Will Joseph want her back? How long will it be before Mr Geddes gets the sack and Connie Beauchamp is lured back to Holby? Tune in next week, when all, some or possibly none of these things will be revealed. It is Holby, after all.

Holby City: I can handle it. Trust me

(Series 12, ep. 23 'The Butterfly Effect Part 2' by Justin Young 9.3.10)

This week's episode carried on where last week's left off, with Joseph bringing a badly wounded Daisha into the hospital after a siege in town.

Then the action went back six hours, so basically covered the same time-span as last week's, but gave a different angle on the action, filling in pieces of the jigsaw which changed our perception of events.

This was particularly illuminating as regards Michael Spence. Last week it looked like he'd been incompetent in not dealing with the emergency properly, but this week we saw he'd actually been properly shafted by Leslie Ash, who made all the mistakes and let him take the blame. She'd agreed to clear the operating theatres and cancel elective surgery – and hadn't. So the fact that Daisha was left "like an animal" without the proper facilities of HDU that she needed was laid squarely at her door.

When the cry went up for a cardio-thoracic surgeon (the incompetent Geddes having left and Joseph being otherwise occupied), it was time for a hero to save the day. And they don't get more heroic than Connie Beauchamp. PLA Jr and I spontaneously applauded when Connie appeared, all scrubbed-up and ready to rock, and if the hospital staff hadn't had their hands full of blood and guts at the time, I'm sure they'd have joined us.

So how did Joseph and Daisha end up in the middle of a siege? Remember Joseph and Faye had had an argument, and Joseph drove off, with Daisha insisting on him giving her a lift. Joseph wanted alcohol, and when he found the off-license closed, he marched into the Indian restaurant next door for three bottles of red wine. And a popadom (they wouldn't sell him the wine without any food).

Unfortunately for Joseph, the young lad who'd decided to rob the off-license that morning had also found it shut, and also decided to try the Indian restaurant next door. "What sort of person holds up an Indian restaurant?" Joseph wanted to know. It turned out that it was a desperate, scared sort of person, just a young boy. Daisha got shot as the boy tried to leave the restaurant and was confronted by armed police. For some reason she didn't mention this, and sat in the car with Joseph giving him a pep talk about his hopes and dreams, till she passed out and Joseph spotted that she had a nasty-looking gunshot wound hidden under her coat.

So, will Daisha pull through? Will Connie and Michael manage to oust the incompetent Leslie Ash? Will Faye be able to keep her hands off Linden and make a go of things with Joseph? Or will Joseph finally realise that she is nothing but a misery drain?

The flipside of Joseph Byrne

(Series 12, ep. 24 'Faith No More' by Andrew Holden 15.3.10)

Apart from being The World's Most Beautiful Heart Surgeon, Joseph Byrne is a fascinating character. He's controlled to the point of being repressed, very literal, very correct. He's compassionate and caring, but doesn't exactly exude warmth.

There have always been signs that, for Joseph, self-control is a protective mechanism because he can't deal with extreme emotion. Sometimes outside circumstances get too chaotic, as when he was involved, against his instincts and judgement, in helping Elliot to break the rules to care for Gina. Joseph reacted to that by having a breakdown and suffering from obsessive compulsive disorder, something he occasionally struggles with when life gets too stressful.

Luke Roberts plays Joseph beautifully. From the way he angles his head to the little quickly-vanishing smile, there's always a feeling that Joseph's real personality is zipped inside him.

Last night, he unzipped spectacularly, when he finally realised that his wife Faye is in love with Linden Cullen. Joseph has always had a good right hook (as Mr Geddes discovered a few weeks ago), but this time he lost all control and it was like a volcano erupting. Linden is quite a big man himself but Joseph threw him around like he was a lightweight. And I have to say (though of course Hitting People Is Wrong) – he was absolutely magnificent.

Elsewhere on Holby, Connie still hasn't got Leslie Ash's head on a plate, but Leslie Ash seems to be making more enemies every week.

Chrissie had to reassess the doofus who is the father of her child, as she watched him being rather sensitive and lovely with a patient's relative.

And Daisha is determined to leave Holby and return to the Philippines to be with her little boy.

Holby City: A substitute for another guy

(Series 12, ep. 25 'Tipping Point' by Abi Bown 22.3.10)

Joseph and Linden were both bearing the scars of Joseph's attack on his bespectacled rival. Joseph, the world's most beautiful heart surgeon, had cut and bruised knuckles, but did this impede his surgical performance? No, he was still able to snap on the surgical gloves and wield the 2.0 Vicryl like the pro he is. But for sheer balls, the prize has to go to Linden for his self-suturing of his facial wounds. Nice bit of needlework, Mr Cullen.

While a physical beating didn't put Linden off the charms of the lovely Faye, Joseph managed to deliver a more telling blow. He told Linden that "Faye had you lined up, Linden. All through South Africa, our wedding, Archie's death. She's had you on the reserves bench." This hurt because it had the ring of truth, and when Faye told Linden that she'd loved him all along – but also loved Joseph ("I was confused!") – he started having serious doubts. And not before time.

If there's anyone more disliked in the hospital than Faye at the moment, it's CEO Leslie Ash. She might be able to get away with sacking Matron Judith, but when she started on Lovely Ginger Nurse Maria she incurred the wrath of both Pale Thin Nurse Nicky Van Barr and Mark "Jesus" Williams. Last week, Leslie Ash commanded Maria – who has recently recovered from a nasty spinal injury – to shift a load of boxes. It was just like one of those ads on daytime TV for no-win-no-fee lawyers, when Maria felt her back twinge. This week she almost dropped a patient and had to hit the prescription painkillers, she was in so much pain. Jesus, who also doubles as union rep, is now threatening to sue Leslie Ash.

This is a plan which will no doubt get the approval of Connie Beauchamp, who is no fan of Leslie Ash and indeed wants her out of the hospital. Her attention was distracted this week by Dr Penny Valentine, who made a bit of a gory mistake in theatre. "What is she still doing here?" Connie demanded of Elliot. He, of course, made her repeat her surgical rotation because of her relationship with Scott James, but Connie doesn't know this. Penny redeemed herself with Connie later via a deft bit of diagnosis.

Daisha left for the Philippines. As she was leaving the hospital she bumped into Joseph. I did wonder whether he might go with her, maybe just for a holiday to sort his head out a little bit. There was a little frisson between them in the car after the shooting incident, and there's always been a bond between them since Joseph delivered Daisha's baby, and she named the little boy after him. "You could always come to Manila," she suggested, and he was sorely tempted. Luckily for us, he said no.

Choose your Valentine

(Series 12, ep. 26 'Enemies Closer' by Paul Mari 30.3.10)

Imagine Dangerous Liaisons remade with Connie Beauchamp in the Glenn Close role. Not such a stretch, is it? It's a tad harder to think of Elliot Hope as John Malkovitch though. I was reminded of this film while watching last night's Holby.

Over a surgical procedure, Elliot and Connie debated which was the better of the two Dr Valentines, Penny or Oliver. Elliot, of course, champions Penny. Despite her faux pas with Scott James, Elliot likes her warm heart, her try-hard attitude and her lovely red hair (he didn't mention that, but how could you not love Penny's hair?). Connie, meanwhile, prefers Oliver, who is pushy, ambitious, cocky and attractive. Just Connie's kind of guy, once she's knocked him into shape.

So Connie proposed a little bet. She bet that Penny wouldn't be able to handle a day's responsibility without letting Oliver take over and make all the decisions for her. Elliot quoted Che Guevara at her, something about plodders being winners eventually. Connie quoted back. "You only get one shot," she said. "Make sure it's between the eyes." And the author of this quote? "Connie Beauchamp." You've got to love her.

Much of the episode, therefore, consisted of Oliver and Penny being sent on various errands, and it looked as though Connie was right. Penny defers to her brother if there's a big decision to be made, and he blagged his way into scrubbing into an operation that Penny had been promised, and took the credit for some research that she'd done about which heart valve should be used. The cad!

He got his come-uppance, though. All episode long he was hankering after a new nurse who wore red Doc Marten boots with her uniform (unconventional!), but she dumped him later in the bar because of his behaviour to Penny, leaving him with a bruised ego and a hefty champagne bill.

Now, a bit of a shock revelation.

We were all convinced Jac Naylor is an android, yes? Well, it turns out that she's actually at least 50% human, as last night we met her mother. Needless to say, it wasn't a terribly huggy reunion. In fact, Jac introduced the mystery patient who'd arrived in the hospital with kidney failure as the woman who "used to be my mother." Mummy had apparently run off to live in a commune in India when Jac was only 12 years old. Is this the reason why Jac is so cold and scary? Or is her coldness and scariness the reason her mother ran off?

In another shock, Mark "Jesus" Williams resigned from the hospital, after Leslie Ash got the upper hand over him re Maria's compensation claim. Is this the last we've seen of Jesus, or will he be back to visit Chrissie when she gives birth to her sprog?

Speaking of which, I'm very much warming to new doctor Sacha Levy (Bob Barrett), the father of Chrissie's child. Which is just as well, as his name is now appearing on the opening credits, so I guess he's here to stay for a while.

What lies beneath

(Series 12, ep. 27 'For the Greater Good' by Nick Warburton 6.4.10)

Oh my lord, Joseph Byrne is a seething mass of emotion under a beautifully tailored suit. Faye's betrayal of him has stripped away his controlled facade, and he's frankly a man on the brink. He's stopped shaving again, always a sure sign that Joseph isn't quite himself, and he's started screaming at junior staff members.

He also indulged in a bit of sexual seething this week. A patient's sister was smouldering at him throughout the episode, and frankly there was more sexual tension between them than he ever had with Faye. By the end of the episode they were getting frisky in his car in the hospital car park – most un-Joseph-like behaviour. Or is it? Is this shouting, fighting, shagging Joseph actually the real one? And can his personality cope with its own contradictions? I have to confess I'm a bit worried for the lad.

Meanwhile, don't you just love it when a plan comes together? Connie, Michael and Ric formed a triangular alliance to oust the horrible Vanessa at a board meeting. Michael was all for a softly-softly approach, whereas Connie – obviously – wasn't. It all looked like it had been scuppered when Ric arrived late and told the board he'd just been dealing with an incident that was proof of Vanessa's deft handling of tricky situations. Connie looked ready to destroy Ric with her laser beam eyes, but it turned out that the incident Ric was referring to was one more situation that Vanessa had mishandled and misread. Ric had a long list of others.

So Vanessa is out (or is she? I've learned never to take anything for granted on Holby), which means that Mark "Jesus" Williams, who had resigned, is now staying. Marvellous news, because where would we be without Jesus?

Holby City: Absolute Paradis

(Series 12, ep. 28 'Bette Davis Eyes' by Dan Sefton 12.4.10)

There haven't been any regular Obs/Gynae specialists on Holby since the departure of the very much missed (by me) Mubbs and Owen. Can we start a petition now to have Paradis Bloom (Ella Kenion) join the cast full time? She was absolutely brilliant as the feisty, eccentric private obstetrician Sacha Levy drafted in look after Chrissie when she developed pre-eclampsia and the baby had to be delivered by caesarean.

I'm delighted to say that mother and baby (boy) are doing well, and granddad Mark "Jesus" Williams is delighted. Sacha was lovely as well – apart from insisting on Paradis he kept in the background, respecting Chrissie's wish that he didn't get involved. Right at the end, though, Chrissie told him it was ok to tell everybody, which was just as well because he was bursting with pride, and Michael Spence was bursting with curiosity.

While all this was going on, Jac's mother got the news that only a perfectly tissue-matched kidney could save her. Guess who probably has one? Of course – Jac. She secretly tested herself, and has agreed that she'll have more tests to see if she's compatible. This doesn't mean that she's forgiven her mother for dumping her hen she was 12. Some broken fences aren't fixed by something as simple as donating an organ.

Faye needed to think of something profound to put on Archie's headstone. She went to Joseph to ask his advice, and he told her, huffily, to go to Linden.

It was the 500th episode! Hurrah!

Mother knows best

(Series 12, ep.29 'X-Y Factor' by Nick Fisher 19.4.10)

Holby City concentrated this week on mothers, in what was a cracking and, at times, very amusing episode.

Chrissie is, of course, a new mother, having given birth last week. Last week the father of the baby, Sacha, got down on one knee and proposed – that Chrissie meet his mother. This week we met Mama Levy, and let's just say she's a force of nature. Fulfilling most Jewish mother stereotypes in one fell swoop, she descended on Chrissie with smothering, chubby-armed hugs, Tupperware boxes full of home-made snacks, and an opinion on just about everything baby-related. She couldn't wait for Chrissie and Sacha to get married so Chrissie could be absorbed properly into the family, "absorbed" being very much the operative word.

I think we know Chrissie well enough by now to know what her response would be. She took the first opportunity to grab the baby, complete with his pea suit (Sacha's daughters had dressed him in a little suit that looked like peas in a pod, and it was the cutest thing I've ever seen, though Chrissie preferred her Egyptian cotton) and head for a good bitch with Maria and Donna (hurrah! Donna is back!).

Meanwhile Mrs Levy had called security. You can't have new mothers wandering around with their babies willy-nilly, you know. It all ended happily, with Chrissie informing the Levy clan that no wedding would ever – ever – take place, but that the baby would always be part of their family. And his name is Daniel Levy-Williams, which has a rather nice ring to it I think.

Meanwhile, Jac Naylor was preparing to donate a kidney to the mother who abandoned her when she was 12. She kept having nightmares about birthday cakes, and the day of the transplant also happened to be her birthday. The Radiant Donna tipped Jac's mother off about this, and later on presented Jac with a cake on her mother's behalf. Donna is just so precious sometimes. Anyway, the operation went well (there was a bit of a CT-style hiccup but we caught a glimpse of Joseph rushing in to sort it out), and Jac held her mum's hand afterwards. Of course it remains to be seen whether this will signal any permanent or detectable change in Jac's "Termi-Naylor" personality. I do hope not.

Back to the Radiant Donna for a second. From next week we must learn to call her Sister Jackson rather than Nurse Jackson, as Mark has promoted her. Motherhood (she's the guardian of a little girl called Mia) seems to have matured her, and if I was ill I'd want her to be my nurse (now that Abs is no longer in Casualty).

Following the departure of Leslie Ash, there's going to be a bit of restructuring. Connie worked her seductive magic on the chairman of the board. She's always had her eye on being Director of Surgery, and she hinted that, should she achieve such a position, she'd be very, very, Connie-style grateful to the chairman. Just as soon as she got back from a CT conference in Texas. Leaving him in a small, smouldering heap of anticipation, she shimmied away, murmuring, "As they say in Texas – yee har!"

Family-related shocks for Jac and Faye

(Series 12, ep. 30 'What Goes Around' by Al Smith 25.4.10)

I've said the words "poor Jac" once before. It was when she was trapped in a contaminated operating theatre with Joseph and she told him how she felt about him. Obviously feeling as I do myself about The World's Most Beautiful Heart Surgeon, I could relate. And also, Rosie Marcel plays Ice Queen Jac so well that when she crumbles, you have to crumble right along with her.

There were signs last week that the Ice Queen was melting towards the mother who abandoned her when she was 12. Having donated one of her kidneys to save her mother's life, this week saw them living together, and Jac getting almost touchy-feely – she was even buying flowers, and talking of buying a bigger flat so they could have a room each.

All wasn't well medically, though, what with Jac's wound getting infected and her mother apparently not tolerating her medication well. Michael Spence was worried. Not as worried as Jac was when her mother went AWOL, and she set off by car through the countryside to track her down at the home of her late grandfather. But when Jac passed out in a lay-by, she had to summon help from Michael Spence. Meanwhile she did a bit of ninja-level self-surgery to try and clean out her wound. I just hope no-one was eating while this scene was on.

When Jac and Michael got to her late grandfather's house, they discovered that rumours of his death had been greatly exaggerated. There he was, hale and hearty, and there was mum Paula, getting ready for a flight back to India. Jac, unsurprisingly, was distraught. Apparently her mother didn't care at all about her, and had only come back to England because she needed a kidney.

Even worse was to come. Paula had another daughter, a 17 year old sister Jac never knew she had, who lived with Paula and had a proper mother-daughter relationship with her. It's not surprising that Jac adopted this brittle, self-contained, selfish persona is it?

Back at the hospital, having had her nasty infected wound sorted out, Jac was visited by her sister (though not by Paula or her grandfather), but she refused to see her. The only person she can rely on is herself.

Meanwhile, Faye discovered that she's pregnant, and Joseph is the father. She tried to tell him, but Joseph has completely shut down towards Faye and can only react by being sarcastic and defensive (it's no wonder Jac and Joseph were attracted to each other), so she didn't tell him. Nor did she manage to say anything to Linden. It'll not stay a secret for long…

How would Jesus run the hospital?
(Series 12, ep. 31 'Apply Some Pressure' by Sally Abbott 3.5.10)

After the high drama of the last few episodes, this one was a bit low-key. It centred on a porters' strike, which meant big queues for CT scans and Young Dr Oliver Valentine pressed into service pushing people around on trolleys.

Cometh the hour, cometh the man, as they say. The man, in this case, being Mark "Jesus" Williams. His deft handling of the aggrieved porters impressed Chairman of the Board Cunningham so much that, at the end of the episode, he was encouraging "Jesus" to apply for Leslie Ash's old job as CEO. I can just imagine his job interview. "So, Mr Williams, how would you describe your management style?" He'd fix the interview panel with his trademark lugubrious stare, sigh a bit, and say, "Sorrowful yet irritated. But I'm good with a catheter."

Connie got back from Texas (yee-har!) to discover that, once again, she is not Director of Surgery. This role is being shared by Michael and Ric, who were both a bit scared to tell her. Michael said that her skills were really needed on the shop floor – Connie is at her best when elbows-deep in heart valves and aortic aneurysms rather than all the boring paperwork stuff, he suggested. Connie's facial expression (somewhere to the north of Norway, climate-wise) would suggest she has other views.

She was somewhat distracted by the appearance of an old friend of hers who needed surgery. This friend was from the days when Mrs Beauchamp was plained old "Con" from Peckham, and she doesn't like being reminded of her 'umble roots, so she was ready to bin the friend off to a London hospital. This was until Joseph, with whom Connie is writing a research paper, spotted that the friend is a perfect case for their research.

It was Donna's first day as a ward sister, and what with the porters' strike and everything, it's safe to say she didn't enjoy herself.

Just don't mention the time I had an affair with a patient

(Series 12, ep. 32 'Take No Prisoners' by Chris Murray 10.5.10)

It was the best of times and it was the worst of times for Young Dr Oliver Valentine in last night's Holby (rescheduled from Tuesday). To start off with, he got some good news. He's not an F1 any longer, he's an F2. Hurrah! That means he's on the same level as Lennie, May and Yuki on Casualty, which is a bit weird because Dr Oliver always seemed like a far more competent doctor than any of them.

Anyways, so he's an F2, and his sister Beautiful Dr Penny Valentine isn't. Penny, however, is used to being in the shadow of her gloriously brilliant brother, so she swallowed her disappointment and got on with the day's work. She even offered him some helpful hints and advice, which of course he dutifully ignored. He is the F2, and the brother, after all. And no surprises really when it turned out that Pen was right, and by ignoring her advice Olly almost killed Connie's old school friend and star patient. Oops.

While he was defending his actions to Elliot and Connie later, Dr Oliver, who has always been a bit of a slippery character, had a little hissy fit about how Penny is always given the benefit of the doubt – even when she's been sleeping with patients (or rather, one patient – Scott James). Oh my stars, you don't drop that kind of news in front of Connie Beauchamp and expect to live, but she turned her wrath on Penny, who was immediately dumped into the netherworld that is AAU (or sick-on-the-shoes-central as it could also be known). Since Penny's heart is really in heart surgery, this is a bitter blow. To be fair to Dr Olly, I didn't think he'd have the balls to admit to Penny that it was he who told Connie. I thought he'd let Elliot take the blame. But he owned up, and his sister is not a happy kitten.

The Radiant Donna's not happy, either. Being a mother is taking its toll on her, sleep-deprivation-wise, and she wasn't coping well with the new duties of being a ward sister. Lovely Nurse Maria, however, takes to responsibility like Connie takes to Jimmy Choos. Thank goodness her bad back seems to have been forgotten about. At the end of the episode both Maria and Donna had applied for the permanent ward sister job. There'll be tears.

Mark "Jesus" Williams had to deal with a few tears from a boy (Paul fromWaterloo Road) who had a promising future as a professional footballer. This was likely to be severely curtailed by the surgery he needed, which would involve removing a big chunk of his lung. Elliot told Jesus about a fabulous piece of laser gadgetry that would enable him to sort out the boy's problem while keeping the lung intact. If only they had one, they could sort out this particular boy, and also attract patients and fame from far and wide as only the third hospital in the UK to have such a device. The problem was, this laser thing was hideously expensive. There's nothing Jesus enjoys more than a challenge, so he leapt into action in a board meeting and argued the case for the kit. Not very well, though, as they refused. Jesus has another card up his sleeve, though. The Chairman of the Board wants him to apply for the CEO job. Jesus wasn't keen at first, but from such a position of influence, think of all the great and wonderful deeds he could perform.

Hell or high water

(Series 12, ep. 33 'Time and Tide Part 1' by Graham Mitchell 18.5.10)

Oh my lord. It was all kicking off in Holby last night. Picture the scene: the fictional town of Holby is experiencing non-stop heavy rain. Roads are flooding, rivers are breaking their banks, and the waters are seeping ever closer to the hospital.

Mark "Jesus" Williams is trying to hold back the floodwaters with sandbags, but this is even beyond Jesus, and he warns Linden that they might have to evacuate the operating theatres.

Busy as bees in various operating theatres are Linden (sorting out a road accident victim), Ric and Sacha (some palliative surgery for a woman with cancer) and Joseph and Connie (the brand new experimental surgery on Connie's old mate from her "Con from Peckham" days). And the power has gone off! The lights all go out, the machines that normally beep stop beeping, machines that aren't supposed to beep start beeping, everyone looks tense as hell, then the back-up generator kicks in… for now.

Back up generators are usually located in the basement, and the basement is going to be the first place to flood, despite the valiant efforts of Jesus and his sandbags (it would also help if he shut the door, but then we wouldn't be able to see him framed in the door phoning people while sandbagging goes on at his feet). Meanwhile Donna and Maria are trapped in a lift.

It can't get any worse, surely? Well, throw in a couple of missing kids, one of whom is Donna's Mia, and a paedophile on the loose, and yes it can get worse.

Luckily we only have till tonight to wait for the breathless denouement.

What a friend we have in Mark "Jesus" Williams

(Series 12, ep. 34 'Time and Tide Part 2' by Graham Mitchell 19.5.10)

The second part of the previous day's flood-tastic two-parter, and immediately we're pitched straight into the action. Donna and Maria are still stuck in a lift, Mark "Jesus" Williams is trying to hold back the floodwaters, two kids are still missing and there's a paedophile roaming around somewhere, and in the operating theatre Connie's sockets are on the blink and so, by the look of it, is her patient.

Tense. As. Hell. But when all hell is breaking loose, what you need is a man so calm and serene and wise that he could have once played the Son of God in a famous TV series. Holby is fortunate to have that man in the suit-wearing, gum-chewing form of Consultant Nurse Mark "Jesus" Williams. While the Acting CEO flapped around in her oversized high-visibility jacket, Jesus calmly took control.

Pretty soon Donna and Maria were freed from their elevator, though Donna's happiness was short-lived when she was informed that little Mia was missing. When the paedophile turned up, Jesus again took charge and gave him a gentle grilling ("You're the only one who's looked me in the eyes since I got here," the nasty man told him) and discovered that he didn't have anything to do with the children disappearing. He'd merely been off looking for some tools to try and fix the hospital's generator. And, even better, he knew a man who could get exactly the cables that were needed to plug Wyvern wing into the next door wing's mains and get the power back on. So where were the kiddies? Not entirely sure on that one, but they turned up safe and well anyhow, and that's all we care about.

Maria spent the episode reassessing her life's goals. She had been planning to go and work for VSO in Tanzania, but had taken the ward sister job instead. But when she saw (a) how brilliant Donna was at suturing and (b) how brilliant Donna was with Mia, she decided that Donna deserved the job more, and told Jesus she was withdrawing her application and catching the next flight to Dodoma (it's the capital of Tanzania. I googled).

Yesterday we left Connie busily grafting bits onto the heart of her old schoolfriend, being snappy with the anaesthetist, and exchanging meaningful glances with Joseph (I'm definitely sensing something brewing between these two). The operation successfully concluded, all that remained was to get the old schoolfriend safely installed in intensive care. But there was a snag – all the HDU's, ITU's, AAU and other places ending in U were closed due to lack of power. There was one still open in another wing, but it would involve carrying the unconscious schoolfriend up and down several flights of stairs and along Holby's maze-like darkened corridors.

Off they went, and at some stage old schoolfriend's breathing tube became blocked. She was "down" for several minutes, and a head CT (they had power to do CT's, by some lucky chance) showed she would possibly have brain damage. Not good news for Connie, who rather badgered the woman into having the surgery in the first place.

So Connie is down but not out. Maria is out, but not down. And it looks like Jesus is in – the Acting CEO told him she wouldn't oppose his CEO application, and the job is virtually his.

This is not a drill. Oh, hang on – it is

(Series 12, ep. 35 'Brutally Frank' by Joe Ainsworth 24.5.10)

I'm sure I remember someone in Holby having to drill into someone's skull with a hand drill, in Africa probably. Joseph, was it? Or Abra? It was impressive, anyway. I've always been impressed by that kind of on-the-fly improvisational TV surgery since Dr Clive Gibbons did a tracheotomy on Lucy Robinson on *Neighbours* with a Bic biro and a fruit knife.

It's not something you'd actually want to try yourself though (unless you're very, very disturbed), and it wasn't something Mark "Jesus" Williams felt like doing in Holby last night. He was locked in a tool cupboard with a porter who was suffering from a subdural haematoma. Linden was outside the door shouting out helpful advice. "He's going to die, unless you relieve the pressure!" "No!" Jesus yelled back, feeling under pressure himself. Luckily he was wearing scrubs for once rather than his suit – being his last day as a nurse before he took up the CEO job, he'd wanted to get his hands dirty. Not quite as dirty as covering them in bits of skull, though. "Drill slowly!" Linden instructed. "How slowly?" Jesus said. One sensed that he was just putting off the actual moment. He was right to do so, as a key was found, and the porter was rushed off to a more sanitary location to have his head drilled professionally.

Things went a bit pear-shaped for Connie and Joseph this week. Connie's old school friend Elaine is never going to be the same again following the oxygen deprivation she suffered due to the power cut following the experimental surgery Connie and Joseph did on her. Connie was naturally devastated, but also very keen to make sure that Elaine's husband Kev didn't find out that the procedure had never been done before on a live, living, actual patient. It's one thing disabling your old school friends; it's quite another possibly being sued for malpractice.

Kev, up till that point quite satisfied that Connie wanted only the best for his wife, stepped out for a soothing latte, and was standing at the coffee bar with Joseph when up popped Jac Naylor, very amused because Joseph's research project has gone tits-up. "Guinea pig numero uno is in a coma isn't she?" she grinned. And Kev realised she was talking about Elaine.

Kev was naturally upset, and nothing Connie or Joseph could say would calm him down. Later on, Connie discovered that her car had been smashed up. Was this Kev's work – or could it have been the grieving relative whose car she beat into a parking space earlier? I have to admit, I'm worried for her.

A bad day at the office for Connie

(Series 12, ep. 37 'Cross My Heart' by Dana Fainaru 7.6.10)

The trouble with these ice-cool, in-control types is that when they fall, they fall hard – and usually alone.

Someone was out to get Connie this week. She was getting nasty notes, and someone smashed up the photo of her daughter which sits on her desk. Was it former old school friend Kevin, whose wife had just died? Connie thought so, and told him she'd call the police if he didn't stop harassing her.

Then she was attacked in her office (quite savagely – Amanda Mealing twittered today that "I had serious bruises around my neck") – but it wasn't Kevin. In fact, Kevin was the one who rescued her. The attacker was the man from a couple of weeks ago, whose mother died. Remember Connie pinched his parking place, and he took so long to get to his mother's bedside that she'd already died by the time he'd arrived? Grief has apparently turned him into a surgeon-clobbering fiend.

This was a slightly clunky twist which I'd guessed was coming two weeks ago, but almost more troubling than physical assault, as far as Mrs Beauchamp is concerned, is that patients are losing faith in her. While Joseph and Irish Dr Greg were running around some housing estate trying to retrieve a heart, Connie was back at the hospital waiting for the tardy organ and defending her reputation. This is not customary Connie territory – her reputation (more of a legend, in fact) and skills are normally beyond question.

It's also usually a fact of the Connie Beauchamp persona that she really doesn't need other people for support or affirmation, but in her hour of need she reached out to Irish Dr Greg. However, earlier in the episode when she was still her former self she was a bit cool with him, and he chose to repay her by being cool in return and going out for a drink with Joseph instead.

Joseph needed a swift half after work because of all the running around chasing missing hearts, but also because Faye told him she is with child. She is also with Linden, but the child is Joseph's. It would be nice for Joseph to have a friend like Irish Dr Greg, who neatly balances Joseph's OCD tendencies by being maverick and laid-back and letting his heart rule his head.

I didn't blog about Holby last week because I was away, but I saw the episode (eventually) and loved the bickering/flirting between Sacha and Jac. I wonder if that's going to go anywhere?

Faye Byrne, the robo-nurse that men can't resist

(Series 12, ep. 38 'Thursday's Child' by Sebastian Baczkiewicz 15.6.10)

Faye Byrne has two facial expressions - disappointed sadness and sad disappointment - but despite this, men can't resist her.

This week, she discovered that the child she's carrying is a boy, which means he has a 50% chance of having the same profound disabilities as her late son, Archie. Clearly an awful situation and one for which we really ought to have the profoundest sympathy for Faye. But that's next to impossible when she spends an entire episode wringing her hands and being horrible to the wonderful Joseph, at one point telling him more or less to butt out of her business, conveniently ignoring the fact that the child is his as well. "She's cold," said my other half. Yes, she is.

Meanwhile, the Doctors Valentine literally almost lost a patient, because they were engaged in a brother/sister spat because of Oliver telling Connie about Penny's relationship with Scott James. While Penny pretended that the patient had died to upset Oliver, and Oliver pretended to tell the patient's wife he'd died to upset Penny, the patient himself had gotten bored waiting in a wheelchair in a corridor and had gone walkabout. Luckily he collapsed within easy reach of a nurse who uttered the Holby/Casualty official cry of "Can we have some help here?" and all was well. Apart, that is, from a dressing down from Connie and Mark "Jesus" Williams, and a humiliating stint in gorilla costumes as part of Jesus' bid to raise funds for laser surgery equipment.

On the other side of Holby, Michael Spence was attending relationship counselling with his anaesthetist wife, Annalise. We knew when we first glimpsed the counsellor sticking an inhaler thing up his nose that he wasn't going to last the session without crumpling into a collapsed heap, and thus it turned out. Luckily he had a consultant surgeon and an anaesthetist on hand, and to be fair to them they did remember to roll him into the recovery position before they carried on bickering.

Once they had him safely installed in the hospital, it looked for a minute like a reconciliation was on the cards. At least, Michael thought so, but he was left disappointed in the hospital coffee bar with nothing but a wilting bunch of flowers and two junior doctors dressed as gorillas for company.

Alright, who's got the laser?

(Series 12, ep. 40 'Swimming with Sharks' by David Lawrence 6.7.10)

I didn't blog about last week's Holby, but if I had I would have called the post "Where there's Hope, there's life." Because Elliot Hope spent the episode charming some lady from a medical organisation into promising the hospital one of these fab lasers that he needs to sort out Footballer Ben's lung, at a bargain price. It seemed he'd done a brilliant thing for Footballer Ben and all the other patients who'd benefit from a state-of-the-art laser, plus bagged himself a nice new girlfriend. Result!

Sadly this week, as Connie and Elliot lurked behind the hospital's front door waiting for a box containing a laser to pop through the letterbox (well, almost), it became increasingly clear that Something was Wrong.

Several desperate phone calls later, Elliot discovered that con artists come in many forms, including nicely-dressed, nicely-spoken, terribly nice-seeming ladies who work for medical institutions. She'd only gone and scarpered with Elliot's cheque, and no laser was forthcoming.

While Footballer Ben projectile-vomited blood all over the ward, Elliot continued (against all the evidence) to promise that the laser would arrive in time. Connie is sceptical. I'm sceptical. But there's something woolly and wonderful about Elliot's faith in human nature, and you just have to hope that, by some magic method, the laser will appear after all.

Meanwhile, Mark "Jesus" Williams was getting a bit over-enthusiastic in his new role as CEO. When Sacha Levy made a clumsy "blonde" joke and an irritable woman complained, Jesus swung into action. When he heard that Sacha had been giving Jac Naylor "unwelcome" hugs, rather than commending him for bravery, he started investigating him for sexual harassment. Of course it was all something and nothing, and the entire situation was beautifully defused by The Radiant Donna.

If only the tension between Dr Penny Valentine and Goth Sister Freda was so easy to sort out. Those two do not like each other, though Goth Sister Freda has taken a shine to Penny's brother, Dr Oliver Valentine. They even arranged to meet up for a drink, but Penny scuppered that by telling each of them that the other one couldn't make it. She took Oliver off to the cinema, leaving Goth Sister Freda at the bar with only the weird anaesthetist and vodka for company. Even that displeased her. Knocking back a glassful, she winced. "Vodka," she pronounced. "But not vodka."

Doctors love playing God

(Series 12, ep. 41 'Secrets You Keep' by Abi Bown 13.7.10)

I'm never any good with a new bit of machinery. Apart from the possible exception of my iPod, no piece of electronic equipment I've ever owned has worked properly, exactly as it should, straight out of the box. There's always a certain amount of tinkering to be done.

Now, either Elliot Hope is a bigger genius than we knew, or the Lung Laser 2000 (or whatever the new piece of kit is called) is completely user-friendly, because no sooner was it out of the cling wrap than he was using it to perform a bit of simultaneous "resection, coagulation and tissue sealing" on young Footballer Ben. There were the inevitable hiccups, of course. It wouldn't be proper Holby surgery unless there was a moment when the machines started to bleep and someone yelled "Pressures are dropping!" and/or "We've got a bleed!" But, all things considered, and with the help of the glorious Connie, things went off fairly smoothly and Footballer Ben was soon on a trolley on his way back to his whiny mother and a WAG-filled future.

This was such ground-breaking surgery that the rep from the Lung Laser 2000 company showed up to watch it in action, and it was from him that Mark "Jesus" Williams learned that the machine had only been ordered the previous day. Eventually he discovered that Elliot had been swindled out of the charity funds raised for the original machine, and had sold his house to pay for the second. This leaves Jesus with a bit of an administrative headache, and leaves Elliot living in his car with his dog.

Even when Faye Byrne isn't there, men are still fighting over her, such is her evil sexual power. Joseph and Linden continue to lock horns, though these days it's about the right to be a father to Faye's foetus. Joseph is the biological father, but Linden is kind of the sitting tenant of Faye these days, so he's claiming the moral right to bring the child up. He's a bit petty, though, that Linden. His dislike of Joseph runs so deep that, even when he had a patient literally dying on his operating table (sats were dropping!) and needed Joseph's expertise, he wouldn't let anyone get him. Luckily "anyone" doesn't include Goth Nurse Frieda, who obeys only her own rules.

It's not easy being Ric Griffin

(Series 12, ep. 45 'Man with No Name' by Martha Hillier 10.8.10)

Ric Griffin had a super master plan that was something to do with doing a chain of kidney transplants. It all involved delicate timing, a flow chart and a surgeon with ninja level skills (that would be Ric). If it went perfectly it would be massive kudos to Ric and one in the eye for Michael Spence, who was Ric's rival for some funding. If one person dropped out (or got pregnant, as was the case), the whole thing fell apart.

Meanwhile, Michael's ex-wife, the lollipop-headed Annalise, has set her sights on the aforementioned Ric. They've started having coffee mornings in her car, and Annalise is very much in the driving seat, literally and metaphorically. Of course Ric has a very long history of being "linked" with scarily strong women (Lola, Thandie – yikes, even Connie), so when Annalise (whose profession is putting people to sleep, so she is quite frightening) fixed him with her beady eyes and told him she wanted to take their relationship further he was powerless to resist. Michael will be ropeable.

Ric's harbouring a secret about his health, though, but we still don't know what it is (or do we? I admit I wasn't paying full attention last week as there were other things going on). Let's just hope he's not pregnant.

Down in AAU, Freda was convinced one of her patients was a serial killer or a rapist. She'd had some experience in this area, she told Dr Penny Valentine, who assumed that Freda had survived some unspeakable abuse in her past. Turned out she'd just been reading a book on the subject. Anyway, he wasn't a serial killer, so that was ok. He did need reviving at one point, which Freda managed by some manoeuvre that only doctors are supposed to do. She has a habit of doing stuff like that, which makes me wonder if she's actually better qualified than everybody thinks.

On Darwin, Connie had Dr Greg and Young Dr Oliver Valentine jumping through hoops as only Connie can.

Pain for Ric, and the drugs aren't working for Michael

(Series 12, ep. 46 'Skipping a Beat' by Rebecca Wojciechowski 17.8.10)

Ric Griffin has cancer. We know this because he keeps ignoring phone calls from the oncology department about his treatment, and every so often he clutches his stomach, doubles up and goes "Nnngh!" So far he's managed to pass this off as indigestion, but it can't be too long before his colleagues, who are all doctors and nurses lest we forget, start to draw conclusions.

Anyhoo, in between going "Nnngh!" Ric has also managed to fit in a spot of hanky-panky with Annalise, the estranged and lollipop-headed wife of Michael Spence. Only by the end of the latest episode Ric had dumped her (which made her cry like a 14 year old – that Ric must be Hot Stuff), presumably for the noble reason of not wanting to put her through looking after him when the nnngh!-ing gets too much. Or because she's very annoying.

Meanwhile, Annalise's estranged and tight-trouser-wearing husband Michael is spiralling into coke hell. He needs to have a quick word with Mark "Jesus" Williams, who spiralled into coke hell himself not that long ago and so is bound to have some sage advice. Like "Why not wear trousers more suitable for the 21st century?"

Goth Sister Freda this week recreated a memorable scene from Carry On Doctor/Nurse/Whatever (I'm not actually a fan of the Carry On movies, what with being over 11 and that) by leaving a nasty racist patient with a sunflower sticking out of his back passage rather than the rectal thermometer he was expecting. I just hope they rinsed it before they put it back in the vase.

And Young Dr Oliver Valentine continued to try and guess, along with the audience, whether Irish Dr Greg is nice or nasty. I have no idea, myself, but reckon Connie is wise to keep him at arm's length for now.

Dead man walking

(Series 12, ep. 47 'Transgressions' by Tahsin Guner 24.8.10)

It was Beautiful Dr Penny Valentine's first day as an F2! Hurrah! Elliot gave her some balloons to celebrate. He's lovely, is Elliot. Then Penny proceeded to fill the day with the kind of ninja-level doctoring that makes you wince and gasp at the same time – a bit of cardiocentesis here, a little chest drain there. And, following a pep talk by the aforementioned Elliot, even Frieda was being nice(ish) to her.

Meanwhile, the rivalry between Michael Spence and Ric Griffin gathered momentum. Ric discovered traces of cocaine on Michael's desk and stormed off to find him. Michael was in the middle of an operation – not ideal when you're off your box on Class A drugs. Ric tried to be subtle. "I found something on your desk." Michael wasn't into subtlety, what with being coked-up, cocky and cuckolded. "You found something in my house," he counter-accused. He meant lollipop-headed Annalese, having discovered that she'd had a fling with Ric.

Ric could have had Michael struck off for his druggy behaviour, but Ric is, by his own admission, a "dead man walking," as his cancer has spread to his liver. He didn't want to take Michael's career down, because Holby needs good doctors in tight trousers.

Doctors don't come any better, or more handsome, than The World's Most Beautiful Heart Surgeon, Joseph Byrne. I was speculating how very good he would look with a touch of guyliner, and thinking that he'd make a darn good vampire. But I digress. When Faye was rushed off to Obs & Gynae after she came over all woozly, Joseph rushed after her, concerned for the future Baby Byrne. Faye has been keeping him at the length of a couple of arms recently, but he was so adorable and concerned – and Linden was so Not There – that she was actually pleasant to him for a change and even let him feel her bump (good of her, since earlier he'd had to watch from the margins as half the hospital copped a feel of Faye's bump). And she's agreed to take the test to find out if Baby Byrne will have the same disability as the late Archie.

I can't believe this is happening to you

(Series 12, ep. 50 'Get Busy Living' by Joe Ainsworth 7.9.10)

Ric was recuperating from last week's life-saving surgery. "Why isn't he in a private room?" the assembled PLA family wanted to know. The answer was that he needed some inspiration to fight his cancer. Annalese perched on his bed and sighed a lot, and promised to be by his side till death them did part (this was meant to be up-cheering). The Radiant Donna gave Ric some of her most radiant smiles and cried a bit as well. Michael Spence was rather marvellous and, for Annalese's sake, organised a top-of-the-range treatment plan.

None of this changed Ric's opinion that he would just let nature take its course and go without treatment. What's needed in these situations is an Adjacent Inspirational Patient (much like the girl with cancer who gave Maria the oomph she needed to overcome her back injury). In this case it was supplied by a James Bond-reading man in the opposite bed. He ended up dying, but not before his remarkably perky attitude had made Ric reassess his options. This could never have happened if Ric had been in a private room.

The shock revelation this week was that Goth Nurse Frieda has previously trained as a doctor. We'd already guessed that, what with her ninja-level medical skills and that, but it came as a shock to Beautiful Dr Penny Valentine. I love Frieda – she takes no crap whatsoever from anyone, speaks her mind and does it with a beautiful accent. As well as saving patients' lives under the nose of Dr Penny, she found time to despatch an incompetent locum. "You have two choices: stay, and I will make your life absolute misery, every second you are on ward. Or man-flu. This terrible affliction will keep you off for two weeks," she offered, in her best deadpan style. The useless and terrified locum croaked that he would opt for the man-flu option. "Good," said Frieda. "Get well soon."

It was a good week and a bad week for Joseph Byrne, The World's Most Beautiful Heart Surgeon. He and Faye found out that their baby is not going to have the disability that affected Faye's late son Archie. It was such fabulous news that Faye even tried to smile, as much as her frozen face will allow. It was all looking promising for a future where Faye and Joseph would sensibly co-parent their offspring and Joseph would get plenty of access to his little lad. Then his mother, Lady Byrne (Jane Asher) stuck her aristocratic nose in, and put the foetus's name (Baby Byrne) down on the waiting list for Joseph's former prep school. This went down like a lead balloon with Faye, who has now decided to start ignoring Joseph again. It's going to take Jeremy Kyle to sort this one out.

You can't not be touched by it

(Series 12, ep.52 'Test Results' by Rob Williams 21.9.10)

Do you remember when Linden used to be all religious? The main symptoms were skulking in the hospital chapel for far longer than was necessary, and being able to resist Faye Byrne.

He's been away on a religious retreat and got his Christian mojo back, and once again the main effect is that he can resist Faye. Not good news for Faye, what with having dumped Joseph for him and that. Please excuse me if I laugh and say it serves her right.

Meanwhile, there was a new F1 on AAU. She'd had a bad experience in an ED in Manchester (I expect there's quite a few can say that, and not many of them actually doctors). There was something about her that suggested impermanence, so I wasn't surprised when she ended up getting acid thrown in her face by a patient who was trying to impress his way into a gang. Linden got all upset because he felt he should have been protecting her. There's something very wearying about the way Linden makes everything about him.

Some would say that Jac Naylor is, like Faye, a cold-hearted witch. But I am not one of them. I love Jac – underneath her beautifully constructed wall of cold, spiky cynicism, there's a vulnerable woman, and Rosie Marcel plays her with such skill that even when she's being a total bitch, you kind of have to love her.

Following her ill-judged remarks about the sainted Ric Griffin the other week, the nursing staff and Sacha were giving her the silent treatment. Actually, what they were doing amounted to workplace bullying, but as it was against Jac no-one seemed much bothered. Eventually Jac managed to get back on their good side by demonstrating she wasn't afraid to muck in and drain a stinky abscess when necessary.

You wouldn't get Connie Beauchamp draining a stinky abscess, but you would get her going the extra mile to help an elderly patient while still finding the time to deliver a presentation to the board that secured her the job of Joint Director of Surgery. Michael Spence is just thrilled.

An eventful night

(*Series 12, ep.53 'Long Night's Journey into Day' by Dana Fainaru 28.9.10*)

Connie Beauchamp (looking gloriously glam) went off for a night out, leaving Darwin in the capable hands of Irish Dr Greg. This didn't please Joseph, and you can see his point. He's been at Holby for ages, has been a consultant for a while and (lest we forget) is The World's Most Beautiful Heart Surgeon. It's got to smart when a whippersnapper who's been around five minutes gets put in charge of you.

It was similarly painful for Michael Spence when Annalese told him she was moving Ric Griffin into Spence Towers to look after him following chemo. So what you end up with is a night shift staffed by cross people.

At least things were looking up on AAU. For a start, Linden and Jac were off duty, which always makes for a more relaxing time. An agency nurse, Nait, was summoned to assist Sacha and Frieda, and as soon as we saw his guy-liner we knew he'd get on well with Frieda.

In fact he was an old friend of hers – they had private jokes, secret handshakes and he even made her smile. It was a lovely thing to behold. Sadly Nait had a slightly unorthodox way of dealing with difficult patients, and when Frieda discovered he'd given drugs to an old lady she had to sack him.

Things weren't going much better for Michael Spence, who was dealing with the sons of two old friends, who'd been injured falling from the roof of their posh school (Joseph's old school, as he kept telling everyone, but no-one was interested except me). One of them had knackered his liver due to years of heavy drinking, and the other one ended up brain dead due to his injuries. Michael decided to bypass all the proper transplant protocols and whip the liver out of one brother to give to the other one. He was stopped in the nick of time by Connie before he could commit career suicide – and kill his patient, because it turned out the liver wasn't a match for the brother anyway.

All of this confirms that Connie should never go off and leave the boys to run the hospital, not even for one night. They only get themselves in bother. Heaven knows what's going to happen when she leaves (which is tragically soon).

Heaven knows I'm miserable now

(Series 12, ep.54 'Revelations' by Graham Mitchell 5.10.10)

We're used to the Holby device whereby patients are used to "speak the brains" of one of the main characters. Recently an inspirational patient persuaded Ric Griffin to have treatment for his cancer, for example.

Linden Cullen is not such an easy nut to crack, however. This week, a patient who had tried to kill himself to be with his dead son (whose death was partly his fault) correctly spotted Linden's core problem – he was still wracked with guilt over the death of his wife Olivia, and this was stopping him from embracing love and happiness in the arms of Faye. The patient's advice was that you can either be alive, in which case leave the dead where they are, or you can go and join them.

So Linden toddled off to find Faye, who was languishing overnight in Obs & Gynae after getting a few twinges. Had he come to declare true love and pledge his full and cheerful ongoing participation in the life of Faye and Baby Byrne? No, he had not. He'd come to gaze sorrowfully at her before skulking off again. Miserable git.

A lot more fun was being had by Donna, who persuaded Sacha that Jac fancied him. Could it be possible? She was being unusually friendly, even helping him out in surgery – heck, even smiling occasionally. Sacha asked to see Jac at the end of the shift, and they had one of those amusing conversations where Jac insisted there was no "us," that she liked Sacha and he was a "lovely guy," but that there would never be any more between them. But I don't think I'm alone in hoping there will be something between them one day (staff Christmas party?), because they'd be the oddest, most fun couple.

A lot more fun than Linden and Faye by a merry mile.

The last of Linden

(Series 12, ep.55 'Misfit Love' by Andrew Holden 12.10.10)

The episode started at the end, as Holby often does, with Joseph and Dr Penny Valentine looking on in shock as paramedics covered up a body in the hospital garden. Then the action went back to seven hours previously. Who was the dead person? It would have been a mystery if the Sky EPG hadn't already helpfully informed me it was Linden (grrr!).

So Linden Cullen met his end by being cracked over the head with a vodka bottle, wielded by a heroin addict. It was all Faye's fault – she'd been stroppy and unsympathetic with the junkie (who also had a heart problem) and had him thrown out of the hospital. Belatedly, Linden had realised that you can't trust a word that Faye says. Joseph has been telling him this for months.

Maybe we can also blame Linden's habit of ducking into the hospital chapel – that's where he was when he was supposed to be on the ward giving the junkie some methadone. Whenever Linden has a problem he always rushes to the hospital chapel.

He started his Holby career by being rather splendidly enigmatic and tortured. He was a man who held a secret anguish: he was closed-off, unapproachable, staunchly moral and somewhat repressed. As such he was fabulously attractive, in a Thorn Birds kind of way. There's nothing a girl likes more than a challenge, and several people, including the late-lamented Maddy, tried to crack his holy facade.

No woman got close until he fell for the icy charms of Faye Byrne. Loving Faye came with a double dollop of guilt for Linden – not only was he still in love with his late wife Olivia, but Faye was married to Joseph. The Olivia problem was sorted out when her ghost gave him permission to stop feeling guilty about her death and move on with his life. The Joseph problem was a little messier, and Linden got thumped a few times for his pains. Was Faye worth it? You'd have to say no.

So Linden has gone (read Duncan Pow's farewell to Holby here), but Holby life goes on. The immediate future isn't looking too good for Michael Spence, who failed to take his kids to Alton Towers and ended up decking Ric Griffin in front of half the hospital and his own children. Not big, not clever, and he's now been suspended for that, and for falsifying the figures for Holby Care. Connie is now sole and glorious Director of Surgery – until next week, at least.

And what will the future bring for Goth Nurse Frieda? Dr Penny is very keen for Frieda to get the necessary papers to become a doctor in the UK (she's already a doctor in her home country of the Ukraine). Frieda was happily agreeing, but that was because she was in a good mood with Dr Pen because she had a date arranged with Pen's brother Young Dr Oliver. Unfortunately it wasn't exactly a "date" that Young Dr Oliver had in mind, more a couple of after-work mojitos. Frieda did not react very well. She's quite scary when she's angry.

SERIES 13

I don't like delegating. It's another word for defeat

(Series 13, ep. 1 'Shifts' by Justin Young 19.10.10)

Art closely mirrored life on last night's shiny new HD Holby. As the country faces hideous budget cuts, we saw the staff of Holby (the regular cast members, at least) huddled in a stairwell hearing new Joint Director of Surgery Henrik Hanssen telling them that it was "time for change" – costs would have to be slashed, staff may have to be "let go."

Hang on – rewind a bit – didn't Connie become Director of Surgery on her lonesome last week, after Michael Spence carelessly punched Ric Griffin? Yes, she did, and it's fair to say that the arrival of Henrik Hanssen (Guy Henry) has not gone down well with her. He is a fabulous addition to the cast, though – an arrogant surgeon in the mould of Anton Meyer and Nick Jordan, he oozes around the hospital ever so elegantly dropping bombs of unease and discord wherever he goes.

He had particularly bad news for Michael Spence, who had a lovely vision of himself saving the hospital by taking on lots of lovely lucrative cosmetic surgery. Hanssen has instead appointed him as the head of no-one's favourite ward, AAU.

The quote in the title comes from the glorious Connie Beauchamp, so we can be confident that Henrik Hanssen is not going to have things entirely his own way. Connie was, however, having a bit of a crisis about her young daughter Grace. She was left in tears when Elliot told her that, all too soon, Grace will be 18 and Connie will wonder where the precious childhood time went. The way is clearly being paved for Amanda Mealing's exit (sniff).

The other big story arc is, of course, the Joseph/Faye story. In the aftermath of Linden's death, Jac warned Joseph that Faye would try to reel him back in. She reminded him about Faye's dodgy past, particularly with respect to leaving a trail of dead husbands (under mysterious circumstances) in her wake.

This made Joseph suspicious, and he sought out Beautiful Dr Penny Valentine, who told him that Faye and Linden had argued loudly not long before his death, and when Penny arrived on the scene of his murder the only person she saw with him was Faye. Is Joseph now thinking that Faye killed Linden? Earlier on, she'd said something quite strange. Worrying about her baby she said that she couldn't cope if anything happened to the baby, because it was "all I have left" of Linden. But it's Joseph's baby, isn't it? He was certainly led to believe so, and has had a blood test done on the quiet just to make sure. Oh, Faye Byrne. The chickens are coming home to roost.

The sacrifice of Pale Thin Nurse Nicky Van Barr

(Series 13, ep. 2 'The Short Straw' by David Lawrence 26.10.10)

Oh, Pale Thin Nurse Nicky Van Barr, your Holby CV doesn't make for great reading.

We first glimpsed you as one of the two nurses looking after Faye Byrne's son, Archie, when he died. Luckily this wasn't your fault but that of your colleague Lauren Minster.

Then you pitched up in Keller for a while, where you had a little crush on Lovely Ginger Nurse Maria. Sadly, Maria was besotted with an unblinking Canadian paediatrician, who had wandering hands and the hands wandered in your direction.

We hadn't seen you for a while, so were thrilled when you appeared last week, less pale and less thin, as our commenter Barry pointed out. Sadly, it appears you've been fattened up merely to be sacrificed, as last night you were made redundant.

Henrik Hanssen (still suave but more nasty than marvellous this week) was determined that salary money must be saved, and his preferred person to be cut was Ric Griffin. He's only new to Holby, though, and he doesn't realise quite how much everyone (apart from Michael Spence) is besotted with Ric Griffin. Connie therefore took it upon herself to make a cut, and determined to save Ric. So several unnamed nurses have to go, and the figurehead of these is pale, thin and now very depressed-looking. It's a shame, really, as he's apparently the only male nurse in the hospital apart from Jay Faldren and Charlie.

Meanwhile, Michael Spence was doing his level best to pretend he wasn't really in charge of AAU, and left Penny in charge while he lurked lucratively in Holby Care. Of course everything went pear-shaped on AAU, and Henrik Hanssen was not impressed with Michael. Not a good time to be pissing off the man at the top.

Faye vague and expressionless. No-one surprised

(Series 13, ep. 3 'Tough, Love' by Martha Hillier 2.11.10)

The loss of Linden Cullen has hit Faye Byrne hard. She spent the episode wandering around the hospital clutching a little yellow box full of his bits and bobs (I mean his stethoscope and ID card, not his other bits and bobs which she's been wearing as earrings since she met him).

Joseph is a lovely man, but he's (a) had enough of Faye and her nonsense, particularly as she's telling everyone Linden was the father of the baby, which is not true, and (b) been to public school, so he told her in no uncertain terms to sort herself out. "If this is you holding it together then… let's just say it's not going well," he said. Luckily a spare psychiatrist was wandering around Keller, so she was pressed into service to try and help.

Ric Griffin's another one who needed sorting out. Frankly he's not at the top of his game, doctor-wise, and that's not what you want. His daughter Jess (Verona Joseph – looking absolutely beautiful) came back to tell him that he's about to be a grandfather, but he was so preoccupied with the impending hospital cuts and trying to pretend his cancer has gone away that he didn't even notice that she was a somewhat different shape from the last time we saw her.

Jess and Ric have always had a volatile relationship, and it took several arguments, Jess attempting to drive away (but failing due to a lack of petrol) and intervention by The Radiant Donna to get them to kiss and make up and get Ric to step down from his job until he's better.

There was some high-level flirting going on between Chrissie and Irish Dr Greg, which was upsetting Sacha, who is in love with the mother of his baby.

And Jac was, as usual, absolutely magnificent. The sight of her with streaming eyes after trying Chrissie's eye cream was hilarious, and I love the way she winds Sacha up. "Raindrops falling, Mr Distel?"

The see-sawing world of the Valentine siblings

(Series 13, ep. 5 'My No.1 Fan' by Rebecca Wojciechowski 16.11.10)

I've noticed that the gorgeous Valentine siblings (Young Dr Oliver Valentine and The Beautiful Dr Penny Valentine) are not capable of both having a good day on the same day. When it's Dr Oliver's turn to shine, Penny's usually busy being caught out shagging her patients. When Pen's having a good day, Ollie is spending his time almost killing people.

Last night Penny – eventually – had a good shift, when Michael Spence finally got round to writing the report on her AAU rotation, and it was somewhat glowing. Well, she deserves it – she's been running that place single-handed since Linden got distracted then killed. In recent weeks she hasn't even had Goth Nurse Frieda to hold her hand.

Meanwhile, Oliver was having a bit of a 'mare. He was looking after a young boy with a very bad heart problem, who was also an illegal immigrant. The boy's only hope of survival was to have a heart transplant, but since he wasn't in the country legally he would be on the B list for transplant – ie no hope at all. So his mother came up with a desperate plan – she would abandon him while immigration officer Angela Harris from *Corrie* was out having a fag and Dr Oliver "made a cup of coffee." He'd then be placed in the care of our glorious state and would have more of a chance to get the heart he needed.

You can see Dr Oliver's dilemma, and you could also see why he agreed to the plan and pootled off to the staff kitchen as instructed. Sadly what he'd failed to do was show Elliot a scan which revealed that it was too late for even a transplant to work, and the boy had only hours to live. Hours now spent without his mother. Poor Dr Oliver could only hold the boy's hand and try and be comforting, which meant staring at him with moist, soulful eyes.

And Henrik Hanssen constructed a self-assembly bookshelf. Well, he is Swedish.

I smell fear, and it doesn't belong in my theatre

(Series 13, ep. 6 'Betrayal' by Lauren Klee 23.11.10)

Henrik "The Swedish Scalpel" Hanssen apparently isn't satisfied by the sacrifice of Pale Thin Nurse Nicky Van Barr from the staff team. Nicky's salary of £Pittance hasn't produced the savings he was hoping for (who could've guessed?) and his attention this week focussed on a bigger fish. Elliot Hope.

"Elliot Hope?" I hear you cry incredulously. Kindly, twinkling Elliot Hope, who sometimes keeps a dog under his desk and sometimes sleeps in his car? Lovely Elliot, who's always sweet to Joseph and Dr Penny Valentine and any other upset redhead in the vicinity? Elliot who is, above all, pretty fab at his job most of the time.

Connie's task this week was to prove to Hanssen that Elliot was absolutely indispensable, which was difficult because although Elliot was pretty good in surgery, he needed a nice sit down afterwards, and his kindly twinklingness led to a patient being misled about her daughter's death.

Meanwhile, Jac was out to prove herself to Hanssen, which she did via the medium of ninja-level surgery in direct contravention of Hanssen's instruction to treat the patient more conservatively. Jac doesn't do conservative, though, and it's sometimes her undoing. It was also the undoing of the poor patient. Jac got the best quote of the night, though (apart from the one in the title, which was Hanssen). Someone mentioned shoe shopping. "I'm not really a shoe kind of person," she said. "The kitchen department's more my thing. It's the knives."

If there's anyone more scary than Jac or Connie in Holby, it's possibly Goth Nurse Frieda, who was prised off nightshift to do a day in AAU. And there we got a rather beautiful culture clash, as everyone's favourite tight-trousered American surgeon, Michael Spence, met "Angry Barbie." He was so impressed by her skills that he's offered her a permanent job on "Team Spence." This pleases me very much.

Jac's the better woman, and Sacha's the better man

(Series 13, ep. 7 'Future Shock' by Graham Mitchell 30.11.10)

Remember the episode way back when Joseph (The World's Most Beautiful Heart Surgeon) and Jac (Robo-Doc) were trapped together in a contaminated operating theatre and they thought Joseph was going to die, and Jac spilled out all her feelings for him?

Last night's episode had something of that intensity. The set-up was this: Faye had gone into labour but was refusing to leave the psychiatric unit, even though the baby was breech and in distress and she needed the facilities of a fully functioning maternity ward. This wasn't Faye being cussed, although Joseph kind of thought it was (you can see his point – Faye does have form on the cussedness front, and he was terrified for the safety of his unborn child). Faye was terrified herself – in her mind, Linden and Archie were with her in the psychiatric unit, and by leaving the room she'd be leaving them behind.

When Faye had some non-birth-related pains, Joseph summoned help from Jac. And, surprisingly, Jac understood Faye's fears. Jac knows what it's like to love someone so intensely your mind can't let them go; it was clear that everything she'd told Joseph in that operating theatre was still true for her. She tried to deny it to Joseph later, of course – she has her TermiNaylor reputation to maintain after all – but the chemistry between them was practically oozing out of the screen.

Meanwhile, Chrissie was on a promise from Irish Dr Greg. She'd even had a bikini wax (way too much info, really). But when Irish Dr Greg went all headstrong over a patient's treatment and risked his career by letting himself be dragged into an MP's publicity drive, he was saved by some deft work by Sacha. The MP, an attractive lady in an unpleasant blouse, responded to this by asking Sacha out for a drink. And was that a glint of jealousy we spied in the eyes of Chrissie, or were her eyes still smarting from her earlier depilation? Either way, Sacha turned the offer down, and Chrissie dumped Dr Greg, and they both headed home to put baby Daniel to bed together. Bless.

And Donna discovered that temporary nurse Kieran isn't the plonker she mistook him for.

Elliot doesn't meet modern NHS standards

(Series 13, ep. 8 'Losing Game' by Shazia Rashid 7.12.10)

Could someone please explain to me exactly when Elliot Hope turned from being a brilliant and capable surgeon who also had a nice way with people, to being a bumbling twerp who gets so involved with patients that he constantly messes up?

Or is it that the world has moved on, while Elliot's skills remain undimmed? Maybe, like Charlie Fairhead in Casualty, Elliot is just too nice and too caring for the modern world. At least, that's what Henrik Hanssen thinks, and what Hanssen thinks soon becomes reality in Holby these days. Goodbye Ric Griffin, farewell Pale Thin Nurse Nicky Van Barr. And now, it seems that despite Connie's efforts to showcase Elliot's talents as a heart surgeon, she's had to administer the Judas kiss after all.

Meanwhile, Joseph (who was The World's Most Beautiful Heart Surgeon before and is now officially The World's Most Beautiful New Father) decided not to divorce Faye, so he could look after her and Baby Byrne ("Has anyone signed a card for Byrne Baby Byrne?" Dr Oliver Valentine wanted to know. He is so witty). Baby Byrne is now called Harry, after Joseph's late brother. But no sooner had Joseph come up with this foolhardy plan (the one about not divorcing Faye, not the one about calling the baby Harry, which was actually Faye's idea) than Faye informed him she'd be taking herself back to the psychiatric unit just as soon as her stitches have healed up (again – but that's another story). So it looks like the divorce is back on again, and Joseph celebrated with a hot passionate team meeting in the staff room with Jac.

Jac needed something to take her mind off things, as the drama teacher from Waterloo Road whom she almost killed a few weeks ago by performing surgery when he was still full of Warfarin, has now decided to sue the hospital. Jac and Chrissie are both in the firing line, but Jac already covered her tracks by changing the patient's notes. Sacha, however, can't believe that Chrissie could have made a mistake – even though Chrissie admitted she'd been running on caffeine pills at the time due to sleepless nights with baby Daniel.

Knowing when to keep your mouth shut

(Series 13, ep. 9 'The Lying Kind' by Nicola Wilson 14.12.10)

Everything is falling to pieces for Connie Beauchamp. At one point in this episode she found herself on a stairwell being berated by Irish Dr Greg for betraying Elliot Hope, Elliot coming up the stairs to add to the berations in his sad, mournful way, and her father appearing at the top of the stairs clutching a bleeding wound as he'd gone walkabout not long after an operation.

When a person has a façade that's as controlled and controlling as Connie's, the natural assumption when she seems to have sold a colleague's career down the river and seems to be impervious to her ill father's increasing confusion is to think – what a bitch. The tragedy is that we're aware of how hard she battled to save Elliot's career, and we're allowed to see the pain in her face that she hides from her colleagues as she struggles with her father's illness (there were some truly upsetting scenes), but she doesn't let these feelings show to others.

Meanwhile, Young Dr Oliver Valentine (or "Boy Valentine," as Michael Spence calls him) was being incompetent again, messing up in surgery, messing up with patients' relatives and messing up suturing someone's face. He took the credit for a nice bit of facial needlework carried out by his sister Beautiful Dr Penny ("Girl Valentine"), so Michael Spence gave him another one to do. He proved to be as good at stitching as I am, and I was banned from the needlework room at school for breaking several sewing machines – by accident, I hasten to add. Goth Nurse Frieda had to help him out. "Where did you learn to do this?" Michael asked her admiringly, after he'd finished being growly because she shouldn't really have been doing it at all. "Not rocket science," she shrugged. Goth Nurse Frieda's stock with Michael is rising, but the same can't be said about Boy Valentine, who has a lot to learn.

And the weirdest/cutest thing happened. The Radiant Donna had brought a singing snowman toy onto the ward, but after a practical joke by Sacha she dumped it in a bin. Henrik Hanssen took a bit of a fancy to it, and at the end we saw him driving off from the hospital with the snowman sitting in the passenger seat of his car – with the seatbelt on. That man really is a heap of contradictions, and I'm looking forward to finding out more about him.

Is this a date?

(Series 13, ep. 10 'The Most Wonderful Time of the Year' by Tony McHale 21.12.10)

Young Dr Oliver Valentine has been a bit rubbish recently, and I find this strange. I referred back to a blog post I did about an episode in May, to confirm my suspicion that he hasn't always been rubbish, and found this: "He's not an F1 any longer, he's an F2. Hurrah! That means he's on the same level as Lennie, May and Yuki on *Casualty*, which is a bit weird because Dr Oliver always seemed like a far more competent doctor than any of them."

There. I knew he used to be good, but now he barely seems able to take someone's pulse without them screaming in pain and Michael Spence yelling at him. So what went wrong for the former blue-eyed boy? Well, his eyes are still blue, but if you can point at anything going wrong for him it can only be that sister Penny's star is in the ascendant, and it's knocked his confidence. Either that or it's just the scriptwriters being inconsistent just for the sake of it (which wouldn't be the first time on Holby).

Aside from the Valentine action this week, which saw Penny going for an after-work debrief (or was it a date? Frieda -hilariously – thought so, and the champagne would seem to suggest something) with Michael Spence, there was a heck of a lot going on in this episode.

I have to admit I'm worried for Joseph. He's gone all twinkly and smiley about Jac, and that is a lovely and precious thing to behold, but Faye still has her claws firmly embedded in him. She refused to go back to the psychiatric unit with baby Harry, and Joseph felt obliged to offer to spend Christmas with them. However, Faye was less than pleased when she discovered that Joseph's mum, Jane Asher (and possibly his very scary sister) were also part of this gathering. At the end of the episode Faye was making a mysterious phone call – and I'm a bit nervous about what it'll mean for Joseph.

Chrissie was getting on beautifully with Sacha after he locked them both in the basement (don't ask), but she went off him again when she found that he'd told Jac she was living off caffeine pills at the time a mistake was made with a patient's records. Jac used this information against Chrissie at a disciplinary hearing.

And Connie's father is destined for a care home over Christmas as Connie apparently doesn't want to cope with him – and no-one is very impressed.

Farewell Connie Beauchamp, toughest of all cookies

(Series 13, ep. 11 'Snow Queens' by Martha Hillier 28.12.10)

This episode covered, literally, miles. It started and ended at St Pancras Station, where Jac was collecting some organs for transplantation and heading back to Holby with them on the back of her motorbike. Or she was showing an ambulance how to get to Holby by leading them on her motorbike. Either way, it was all a bit odd, but they were special organs, what with being a very rare back-to-front heart and lungs combo and all.

Faye Byrne was Christmassing with the scary female members of the Byrne family, Joseph's mother Jane Asher and sister Cruella, plus Cruella's children. This was in a lovely Regency townhouse somewhere in the vicinity of Primrose Hill, London. But when Faye decided she'd had enough Byrne-type meddling in her affairs, she popped in a taxi and moments later was back in Holby again. This is Holby which used to actually be Bristol. The taxi driver must have been thrilled with that fare.

Faye's plan was to take baby Harry and a load of money from her and Joseph's joint account, and escape to France, but she's not very good with the Eurostar booking system, printers or online banking. This enabled Jac to apprehend her, once again at St Pancras, and off they went back to Holby again, to "tell Joseph."

Anyway, all's well that ends well on that front, as Faye agreed to let Joseph look after Harry (you'd only have to see him holding a baby and you'd ovulate just to oblige him) and she went off to Paris to work in a hospital there. Remind me to never get ill in Paris.

Meanwhile, Connie Beauchamp was getting increasingly stressed and upset by her father's illness and the way people have turned against her because she's perceived as turning traitor against her colleagues. Something had to give, and she told Hanssen she was leaving. Immediately.

I have to admit there was a tear in my eye as she said goodbye to Elliot Hope, because they were both in tears and I imagine not all of it was acting. I was glad that the writers gave Connie an upbeat ending once all the tears were done with. Back at St Pancras, over glasses of champagne she passed the baton of being Holby's top surgeon and super-bitch over to Jac Naylor, along with some wardrobe advice. Jac needs to ditch the autumnal colours and pay more attention to accessories, and then perhaps, one day, she'll be a worthy successor to the legend that will always be Connie Beauchamp.

And on that note, slinging an expensive-looking wrap over her shoulders, she headed to a train to a lucrative appointment in Brussels. A classy departure for the toughest cookie (as Hanssen put it) ever to grace the Holby corridors.

Not the big bad wolf

(Series 13, ep. 12 'Running the Gauntlet' by Chris Murray 4.1.11)

There's a new registrar on AAU (played by Jimmy Akingbola). He goes by the name of Malick – though his first name is, apparently, Antoine, like Lulu and Madonna he generally just goes by that one name, Malick.

Like Madonna, and to a much lesser extent Lulu, he's also a bit controversial. Is he a maniac or a genius, as Michael Spence pondered to himself? He has a certain way with patients which is part cajoling, part bullying, part charm, yet generally successful; but he does have form for thumping consultants he disagrees with.

Anyway, on balance Michael has decided that Malick can stay on Team Spence. This is odd, because Hanssen is still looking at ways he can reduce the staff salary budget, and surely AAU is pretty much well-staffed already? Mark "Jesus" Williams seems to have Goth Nurse Frieda in his sights as the next person to collect her P45, and, frankly, if she goes, I go too. But we already know that Goth Nurse Frieda has a few more strings to her bow so I'm sure we haven't seen the last of her fabulous Ukrainian surliness.

Donna and Kieran were all lovey-dovey, which of course couldn't last. It turns out he's in the army, and is being sent to Afghanistan as a medic next week. Donna, having seen what Afghanistan did to Gary Windass on *Corrie*, can't cope with having a boyfriend in a war zone, so they pretended they didn't love each other and that was the end of that. Which made me a bit cross, really.

And Chrissie didn't get sacked or anything following her disciplinary hearing (thanks to Jesus pulling a few strings). She just has to work under supervision for a while.

Farewell Joseph Byrne, the world's most beautiful heart surgeon

(Series 13, ep. 13 'China In Your Hands' by Martha Hillier 11.1.11)

Yet another "end of an era" for Holby, and a personal tragedy for me, as Joseph Byrne, The World's Most Beautiful Heart Surgeon (Luke Roberts), decided to become Joseph Byrne, The World's Most Beautiful GP, and move to Cumbria with baby Harry.

As if to underline what we'll be missing, the episode was packed full of Joseph goodness. He performed ninja-level surgery (the fabled and risky "elephant graft" procedure); he smiled several times; and he took his shirt off quite a lot. To top it all, there was a scene of him with his shirt off, holding the baby, and smiling all at the same time. Fabulous.

He started the episode by asking Hanssen (who was on top form throughout this episode – sarcastic, witty, odd, almost telepathic occasionally) if he could work part time. Hanssen instead offered him Connie's job.

Sadly there was a patient around who was just ready to speak Joseph's brains and remind him that what a boy really needs is a fully present parent. Elliot had heard of a nice GP job in Penrith which would be absolutely perfect for a young family: all that nice country air etc etc. Joseph could just picture what a lovely life he and Harry and Jac would have.

Jac? Well, can you really imagine Jac living a *Doc Martin* kind of life? Especially when she's just invested in a pair of "Connie Beauchamp shoes." Obviously she was going to say no, but you could see how much they love each other and how much it cost her to let him go. "I'd give up my life, my career, my identity, for a man who'll always put me second," she said, and asked him to stay. But of course he'll always put her second, because baby Harry comes first. So Joseph drove away (after first giving the door handle of his car a little polish – his OCD does come back at odd times) and Jac was left at the Window of Regret (the one overlooking the car park), in tears.

Meanwhile, Goth Nurse Frieda was made redundant, and also had a very difficult shift thanks to new registrar Malick, who'd decided she was lazy and incompetent. He'll have to eat his words, though, as Frieda has now decided to apply for an F1 position – meaning that I'm going to have to start calling her Goth Dr Frieda from now on (yay!). As one era ends, another begins.

Irish Dr Greg, you're in this blog

(Series 13, ep. 14 'My Hero' by Rob Williams 18.1.11)

Ooh, Matron! I felt like I was watching Carry On Doctor/Nurse/Whatever at the start of this episode. Nurse with tops of black stockings and ample cleavage peeping out of uniform? Check. Randy doctor making his way to an assignation with the aforementioned in a side room? Check. His boss catching them at it? Check.

Irish Dr Greg it was, caught almost in flagrante with Irish Ginger Nurse Mary-Claire, by Lovely Bumbling Elliot Hope. As a punishment, Elliot assigned Dr Greg to work with a particularly tricky patient. He was a blogger, and you know how difficult they can be. Worse still, he was a blogger on medical issues, which meant that everyone who treated him was kind of on test. "The only thing that could make me interested in a blog is if I'm in it," Irish Dr Greg told him, but regretted it a few minutes later when he was outed in cyberspace as being a bigheaded womaniser. I'm sure that if this blogger person had tried that stunt with Connie Beauchamp she'd have had a few choice words for him which would include "defamation" "sue" and "solicitor."

It turned out that the self-styled "human guinea pig" was scared of having a general anaesthetic (he said he needed to be awake during surgery so he could blog properly about it afterwards. This is going far beyond the call of journalistic duty, IMO). So Dr Greg agreed to do a tricky heart procedure on him with only an epidural. Sadly it all went pear-shaped and last we heard of the human guinea pig, the "harvest team" were waiting to get their hands on his corneas. But not before Dr Greg had convinced the patient that he was almost as good as Joseph Byrne (as if! Though I have noticed, now that I'm not dazzled by Joseph's beauty, that Irish Dr Greg does have a gorgeous nose) and convinced Elliot that he wasn't entirely a lost cause.

Meanwhile, Donna had to deal with an annoying Scottish nurse who'd rearranged her ward and convinced the staff, all the way up to Mark "Jesus" Williams, that he was the best thing since Florence Nightingale.

Donna didn't take well to his undermining ways, and occasionally she had a point, but what was really going on was that she was still upset about Kieran going to Afghanistan. On the subject of whom, Odd Little Nurse Elizabeth Tait has a photo of him, and was behaving oddly with a mug with his name on it. Keep an eye on that one – she looks timid, but I reckon she could very easily go Kelly Yorke on us.

Chrissie told Sacha – yet again – that there will never, ever, ever be a chance for them as a couple.

And accident of the week has to be the woman who fell out of her loft and impaled herself on a tiny bridegroom – wedding cake variety, not an actual human, which would have been an altogether different type of accident. Ooh, Matron!

You used to be Mark Williams

(Series 13, ep. 15 'Don't Go Changing' by Nick Fisher 25.1.11)

If Holby City was directed by M. Night Shyamalan, you wouldn't be surprised to find that the twist at the end was that Henrik Hanssen was actually a ghost. Supernaturally tall, he oozes around the hospital dispensing charm and iron-fist-in-velvet-glove evil in equal measure. He is universally feared and has absolute power, but seems to exist without personal context apart from some odd glimpses we've seen of a more playful, childlike nature – driving a toy snowman home after carefully fastening its seatbelt, for example.

His chief function so far has been to take a metaphorical scalpel to the staff team, though he manages to get other people to do the dirty work.

Mark "Jesus" Williams, as CEO of the hospital, was given the task this week of getting rid of either Ric Griffin or Elliot Hope – or preferably both. If this had been successful, Ric would have had grounds to claim for constructive dismissal, as he found he'd been moved from his office and was required to carry out his paperwork in the staff room. This didn't please anyone, least of all Chrissie. "I can't microwave pasta bake while Ric sits there writing his case notes," she complained to her dad. Well, exactly.

Everyone had a problem with Mark's suits. Before he started wearing suits he "used to be Mark Williams – friend," said Elliot. Ric preferred love-bombing to attacking. "Even if you do get sucked into management games, you've got the best interests of the hospital at heart," he said, little realising that Mark was planning Ric's leaving whip-round even as the words were leaving his lips.

Well, it was all too much, even for a man who has previously played the Son of God. Someone had to go, so in the fluid staffing configurations of Holby City Hospital, why not lose a CEO rather than two top-flight yet unhealthy surgeons?

And this left Hanssen looking quietly satisfied with his day's work. You feel that he has a grand plan in all this, and everyone else is just a pawn on his personal chessboard. We left him comfortably installing himself in the Director of Surgery office.

Meanwhile, Donna was visited by Kieran on the eve of his deployment to Afghanistan, trying to persuade her that they had a future together as long as he doesn't get killed (which he promises he won't). Donna turned down an offer of marriage, a decision which made more sense than the last time she turned him down, because she explained that her priority was adopted daughter Mia, and not wanting her to love a man who might not come back. Given all that Mia has been through in her little life, this is probably a wise decision, though she could still have kept her options open for when he gets back. But, then again, he didn't look half as good in army clothes as he did in scrubs (who does?).

The angry young black man routine

(Series 13, ep. 17 'Anger Management' by Patrick Homes 8.2.11)

Even by the weird staffing patterns of Holby City, there was a bit of a doctor/nurse imbalance going on in AAU yesterday. Four doctors of differing grades (Malick, Dr Penny Valentine, Dr Oliver Valentine and Goth Dr Frieda) and hardly any nurses. None with speaking parts, anyway (Chrissie was floating around, but is she on AAU or Keller these days? I lose track).

Being surrounded by all these junior doctors was sending Malick's showy-offy, competitive streak into overdrive. He's of the "treat them mean and keep them slightly intimidated" school of mentoring, which works to a certain extent with the Valentine siblings. Penny is slightly smitten with his smooth way with a scalpel, and Oliver is just scared. Of course it takes more than a surgeon with attitude to intimidate Goth Dr Frieda. When Malick told her to make him a coffee, she made sure it was a bad one. "He said I had to make coffee. He didn't say I had to make it well," she said. Atta girl. She also burst any romantic dreams Dr Penny might have had about Malick. He's gay, she told the Valentines. "I have gaydar," she pronounced, and of course she does – I have no doubt she has almost supernatural insights about many, many things. But as well as gaydar, she knows people who used to work with Malick.

So we know Malick is gay in the homosexual sense, but he certainly isn't gay in the old-fashioned sense of being blithe and carefree ("Humour," he observed. "I enjoy it but, like morphine, in small doses.") He has anger-management issues, and when he had to treat a racist patient he found it hard to be professional. At these times an older, wiser head is what you need, and in this case it belonged to Ric Griffin, who advised Malick to ditch "the angry young black man routine." Ric's been there, done that, and these days it's Michael Spence who makes him angry, rather than old ladies who don't want to be treated by black surgeons.

Meanwhile, Irish Dr Greg decided Sacha needed a bit of romance to cheer him up, and asked Mary-Claire to set him up with someone. But Sacha and Mary-Claire turned the tables and pretended they'd got together, and Irish Dr Greg was rather upset to find that he cares more for Mary-Claire than he thought.

The Ice Queen v the Yummy Mummy

(Series 13, ep. 18 'Blue Valentine' by Justin Young 15.2.11)

Cardio-thoracic registrars, huh? Like buses. You wait for ages, then two of them come along at once.

The first new registrar on the Darwin payroll was the ice maiden herself, the splendid Jac Naylor. She'd have preferred to be a consultant, of course, but in the game of chess which is Henrik Hanssen's staffing strategy, CT Registrar is what she currently is.

She wasn't alone for long, though, as she was joined in quick time by Laila Rouass, as Sahira Shah the Registrah. Sahira is just back from maternity leave, and in fact is still breastfeeding – much to Jac's disgust when she came upon her in the ladies' with the old breast pump. Jac does not feel this is what Madonna meant when she sang 'Express Yourself.' "Do you have a phobia of lactating women?" Sahira asked her, and this little exchange very much set the tone for their subsequent day together. Jac feels that you need bigger balls than any man to be a top surgeon, so scrummy mummies are a bit beneath her contempt. If only she knew how hard you have to work to be a mother of young children (Sahira has two) and work at the same time. Sahira is not about to be walked all over by Jac – particularly as she seems quite close to Hanssen.

Just a theory here – we know Hanssen likes children. Is it possible that he's the daddy? Could we be about to lift the lid on the previously mysterious area of Hanssen's home life?

And Jac's not as tough as she pretends – she's using Joseph's pager. It still has his name on it. Bless! She's missing him!

Meanwhile, Ric Griffin heard that he'd been accepted as one of the lucky few to receive a life-prolonging (fictional) cancer drug called Rafmonolox. When he found himself treating a young woman who was dying of the same type of cancer, he was in an ethical dilemma. This woman was the single parent of a 13 year old daughter (Shannon Flynn from Waterloo Road), and having the drug would mean there was a chance of her living till the daughter was 18, otherwise she had only weeks left. So Ric pretended there'd been a mistake, and said she could have the drug – which was his drug really.

The Radiant Donna was furious with him, and he also had ethical debates with Hanssen about how a very rare and costly drug can be fairly given to one person and not another. In the end it was a moot point, as the woman's condition deteriorated quickly and the drug was no longer of use to her. So it looks like we get the benefit of Ric Griffin for a few more years.

There was another new doctor in the form of Dan (Adam Astill), an unblinking orthopod with no lips and a penchant for inane sporting analogies.

Who's the Queen Bee?

(Series 13, ep. 19 'Open Your Heart' by Nick Fisher 22.2.11)

"If she's not shagging the Swede then I'm Kylie Minogue," Jac observed re her new colleague and rival Sahira Shah the Registrah. "You should be so lucky," quipped Irish Dr Greg, but exactly what is the relationship between Sahira and Henrik Hanssen? Is it really just that they've worked together in just about every hospital in the western world? My money is still on them being married – he did mention a husband, and muttered about her taking time off to have kids, but I reckon that's just to throw us off the scent. I've been wrong before, though…

Sahira's personal life may be intriguing Jac, but her professional life is driving her absolutely nuts. Connie promised the Queen Bitch role to Jac when she left, and she's ideally suited for the role. When offered a cupcake which Sahira pretended to have baked, Jac refused because "I don't do carbs or fat and I definitely don't do sweet."

When Elliot got stung on the face by a bee in his office, this was the cue for a bee lady to arrive and deliver a string of bee metaphors to further illuminate the spat between Jac and Sahira. "The only threat to [the queen bee's] power is another queen," apparently. Jac is "all sting and no nectar." You bet she is.

The bee sting had further ramifications in that Elliot couldn't do an operation that he'd been scheduled to carry out, so Irish Dr Greg and Sahira had to do it. Sahira decided the best approach was to operate on a still-beating heart, a prospect which turned Irish Dr Greg to a quivering wreck. Frankly he wasn't much use and was only slightly ornamental. Hanssen had asked Sahira to report back on Greg's performance in the operating theatre, and frankly he didn't exactly cover himself in glory, but Sahira is no-one's spy and refused to do what Hanssen asked. "You make everyone nervous with your bacon-slicer stare," she told him.

In an episode full of good lines, the best one was delivered by the very wonderful Goth Dr Frieda. Chrissie is now filling her father's old role of "nurse consultant," which for some reason means she has to be trained up in all sorts of procedures that either (a) she's been doing forever anyway or (b) she won't need to do because when Jesus was nurse consultant it just involved him wearing suits and looking sorrowful. Frieda summed up the role nicely: "The hermaphrodite of the medicine. Not one thing or the other."

While all this was going on, there was bad news from Afghanistan, where Donna's Kieran had been involved in an explosion. Was he dead? Was he injured? Was he even there? Did Donna care? Odd Little Nurse Elizabeth Tait cared – the poor wee thing has a crush on Kieran, apparently, but it seems she's not going to go bunny boiler on us (shame, that), but did her best to get Donna to face up to her feelings for her soldier boy. Donna spent the whole episode dithering and soul-searching, till PLA Jr was ready to give her a slap. Finally she made her mind up. "I must go to the man I love!" she told Chrissie (the hermaphrodite of the medicine, and also the one who has to cover for nurses running off to be by the bedside of injured soldiers).

Smells like team spirit

(Series 13, ep. 20 'No Credit, No Blame' by Mark Cairns 1.3.11)

Jac Naylor spent most of this episode looking close to tears. To Jac, life is a contest, and she's only happy if she's winning. She could handle the competition from Sahira Shah the Registrah if it was only about professional excellence, but what she can't cope with is that Sahira and Hanssen have a "special relationship" that means she often gets invited to do the tricky procedures that Jac enjoys, such as the odd crossover thoracoabdominal aortic aneurysm. And there's her fabulous parachute stitching and cupcakes (shop bought), lest we forget. Elliot advised Jac that she should drop her usual snipey attitude and become more of a team player.

Fat chance. In these circumstances, Jac always has a tendency to want to show off, and she managed it this week via the medium of the terribly tricky VATS procedure to get some shrapnel out of a patient's heart. It's like a heart surgery video game but "the risk of killing the patient is astronomical," according to Elliot, so not a thing to be taken lightly. In fact, not a thing to be taken at all, in the sense that Jac was supposed to let Elliot do it, but she went ahead, with Irish Dr Greg as wing-man, and despite the usual mid-op panic ("Pressures are dropping! We're losing him!"), all was well. Apart from the telling-off she received from Elliot, who had his teaching hours reduced by Hanssen as he doesn't seem to be able to keep control of his staff. "And I would have let you lead anyway," he told Jac, with one of his more-in-sorrow-than-anger faces which, I imagine, could reduce you to a whimpering wreck unless you were made of purest steel. Even Jac Naylor looked rattled.

Donna pitched up at the bedside of badly injured boyfriend Kieran. What we knew, and she didn't, was that he'd called her name as soon as he came round from his injuries. He loves her! But when he had to have his leg amputated he gave her the get out of jail free card by saying he didn't love her and had never really wanted to marry her anyway. The silly moo was on her way out of the door, but his mum stopped her and told her that he did love her really. So Donna went back, and told him she'd stay, and everyone cried a bit. Ok, yes, I admit it, even me. I do like Donna.

I don't know if I still like Young Dr Oliver Valentine after this week, though. There are two phrases no doctor ever wants to hear: "You left a swab in?" and "You've got to tell Malick." Yikes. When a patient returned a few weeks after surgery with an infection caused by Ollie not tidying up after himself in theatre, swab-wise, he persuaded Penny to take the blame for him, on account of he was on a final warning anyway and she wasn't. Then he compounded his crime by getting into Michael Spence's computerised records – luckily Spence had a very guessable password – and removing all trace of his presence on the op in question. Sadly, Ollie wasn't the only one who could guess a very guessable password, and before he'd had a go, Malick had already seen his name on the list. It wasn't hard for Malick to work out what had happened. And Penny has had quite enough of Ollie and his feeble nonsense. "You're toxic," she told him, and he reacted like they always do – by slapping his locker door. Hard.

No regrets for Donna

(Series 13, ep. 21, 'What You Mean By Home' by Nick Warburton 8.3.11)

I was very pleased that The Radiant Donna got such a lovely Holby exit. She's been one of my favourite characters for years – I've loved her mixture of fun and seriousness, her relationships with unsuitable men (and women) and her friendships with the other nurses. I loved her as a party girl and then when she settled down to become a mum to Mia, her frustration at not being taken seriously when she wanted to be a scrub nurse, her kindness, her stroppiness. Donna is, above all else, a real person you can relate to. And she has the most beautiful smile.

She leaves destined for Liverpool and a life with Kieran and Mia (with visits from Kieran's son). So the episode was full of goodbyes, most touchingly with Ric Griffin, with whom Donna has almost a father/daughter relationship. Symbolically, she handed that job back to his real daughter, Jess, who handily appeared in time to join everyone in telling Donna she was doing the right thing.

Also symbolically, Donna handed back to Michael Spence the necklace he bought her after their little fling. She said he was bound to need it again – and doubtless he remembered that he'd also given the same one to ex-wife Annalese. This little exchange took place at the Window of Regret, Donna claiming to have only just realised that she enjoyed standing there. Everyone enjoys standing at the Window of Regret – it's Holby's number one emotional destination. But no regrets for Donna, as her final touching goodbye was with funny little Nurse Elizabeth Tait. I still don't know if Elizabeth is in love with Kieran or Donna, or both, bless her, but it was a very sweet moment.

Meanwhile, the usual power struggles continued. Hanssen informed Jac and Sahira that there was a consultancy job on Darwin up for grabs and they should both go for it. I'm still trying to work out what the relationship between Sahira and Hanssen is. They exchange meaningful looks all the time, but my idea that they're married is clinging on by only the finest of threads since Sahira told Jac that her husband had come to take sick little son Indy home. And Hanssen showed no particular interest in Indy, though he did give a little smile to Donna's Mia earlier in he episode. So maybe our commenters Carla and Paul were right the other week when they said that Sahira was "the one that got away" from Hanssen. Or maybe Hanssen has a supernatural ability to separate home life and work life (it takes a lot to make me part with a theory – I could still be right…).

Frieda was engaged with power struggles of her own – with patients who won't believe she's a doctor rather than a nurse; with Chrissie who wishes Frieda was a nurse rather than a doctor; and with Malick, who doesn't really believe anyone's a doctor except him.

Just to make the day perfect, I kill an old lady

(Series 13, ep. 22 'Too Much Monkey Business' by Tony McHale 15.3.11)

Young Dr Oliver Valentine, aka Boy Valentine, looked so promising when he first appeared in Holby. He was confident, keen, clever and had a winning way with the ladies (Chrissie, Daisha and even – and you've got to be confident for this – Jac Naylor). Permanently in his shadow was sister Penny (aka Girl Valentine, aka Pitstop). Apart from her luscious hair, Penny struggled to stand out. Elliot Hope, who sees more deeply into people's souls than most, championed Penny, but to most people it was Boy Valentine who was the top sibling.

Recently, however, Oliver has been increasingly rubbish. He makes mistakes, he blunders, he lies and he hides behind Penny to cover up what he's done. And now, we know why. Following yet another error-strewn shift on AAU, during which he thought his carelessness had cost the life of a patient (it hadn't, as it turned out), Oliver ended up in the basement clutching a pack of sleeping pills. It took Penny a while to find him – I could have told her he'd be in the basement, because they always are. And he made a shocking confession: back in the early days of the Valentine siblings' medical career, Ollie had swapped their exam papers around. Penny had passed her exam, and he hadn't, but he made it look like she was the one who had failed. Apart from being a blight on poor Pen's confidence ever since, the fact that Oliver had never passed the original exam (no matter how many exams he might have passed since) means that he is practising medicine illegally.

It's all too much for Penny, who has gone on a little holiday, and wants Oliver to have told Michael Spence all about his crime before she gets back – or she'll tell him herself.

Meanwhile, my theory that Sahira and Hanssen are married has been bolstered somewhat by the fact that the writers are being so very cagey about mentioning her home life, and by the odd little looks that Hanssen gives whenever her children are mentioned. Irish Dr Greg thinks he's in with a chance with her, but if I was him I wouldn't be bothering with taking my best suit to the dry cleaners just yet.

The tedious Dan Hamilton, bone expert, has his eye on the lovely Chrissie Williams and spent the episode getting information from Sacha about her. Poor Sacha, he's the loveliest man but Chrissie is, as we know from her previous sexual history, far more likely to go for a boring man with a firm jawline than a complete angel in human form whose look can best be described as "cuddly."

We'll deal with the hand first and then we'll handle Hanssen

(Series 13, ep. 23 'Clash of the Titans' by Graham Mitchell. 22.3.11)

This episode's official title was 'Clash of the Titans.' Hmmm. Personally I would have given that accolade to the Nick Jordan/Henrik Hanssen face-off on *Casualty* a while back. Ric Griffin never quite strikes me as a "titan." Maybe it's because I recall his penchant for gambling and jazz cigarettes. You can't imagine Hanssen chilling out with a jazz cigarette.

However, what can't be denied is Ric's commitment to Holby City Hospital, so when he discovered that Hanssen was outsourcing all upper GI cases (Ric's field of expertise) to another hospital, Ric was not best pleased, despite the fact that his cancer hasn't been helped by treatment and he's started clutching his stomach and going "Nnngh!" again when no-one's looking. So Ric called a revolutionary meeting in the stairwell ("I will mobilise the staff and go over your head," he told Hanssen. You'll have to go quite high to get over Hanssen's head). He asked his colleagues to raise their hands if they thought Hanssen's scheme was outrageous. No hand went up, and Hanssen, who was standing watching, permitted himself a wry smile. Then Goth Dr Frieda raised her hand, and pretty soon everyone else followed. Maybe Ric is a titan after all, by reputation anyway.

With Hanssen, you've got to have the balance of a surfer because he's sure as hell going to pull that rug out from under you in a way you won't expect. Just when Ric had him pencilled in as public enemy number one, Hanssen made him an offer. The only chance Ric has of living longer than a few months is to have surgery so risky that there's only a five percent survival rate. "Only with me it's ten percent," Hanssen informed him. Well, that's one way to get a person on your side.

Elsewhere, someone was busy sawing their hand off. Seriously. A CT patient with mental health problems decided his hand was evil, so he wandered into an unlocked operating theatre, selected himself one of those electric saw things they use to get through sternums, and made quite a neat job of amputating the offending limb. Elliot blamed Jac, who was supposed to be looking after him but was apparently too busy trying to dress like Connie Beauchamp in her bid to get the CT consultancy job from Sahira. This time, however, Jac wasn't to blame as she'd called the patient's psychiatrist earlier and said he was at risk. This psychiatrist was the sort of older lady that Elliot has been taken in by in the past, and when she patted his hand and told him Jac had never phoned her, he believed her rather than Jac. Of course the truth came out in the end and Elliot apologised, and he and Jac had a great laugh about it. Only not that last bit.

This week's fictional drug: Vascamine. Don't ask for it in Boots because you won't get it.

Today we will save this man's life

(Series 13, ep. 24 'Second Coming' by Joe Ainsworth 29.3.11)

Considering that this was an episode where beloved-old-cast-member-who's-been-in-Holby-since-forever Ric Griffin looked death square in the face, it was one of the funniest episodes of Holby I've ever seen. Writer Joe Ainsworth got the balance between the high drama, tension and sadness of Ric's situation and some quite barking mad stuff going on elsewhere absolutely perfect. And he threw in a birth for good measure.

The episode started with a case conference, with Henrik Hanssen attempting to convince the surgical team about a very high risk procedure. There was one member of the team notably absent – Ric Griffin – and that's because they were talking about him. Hanssen was convinced he could save Ric's life with an extended right hemihepatectomy. Easy for him to say, I know, but not easy to do, given that statistics suggested a 90% chance of Ric dying on the operating table.

Elliot wasn't happy. "This is madness," he said. "No," replied Hanssen, unflapped as usual. "It's medicine." Hanssen was convinced he could do it, but it had to be done quickly. "If we don't operate immediately, even I will be forced to admit defeat," he said. Then Ric arrived, not best pleased at being the owner of the tumour under discussion. Waving away Hanssen's confidence and the "let me at that scalpel" gleam in Jac's eyes, Ric insisted he wasn't going to agree to the surgery and would dwindle away in his own time, ta very much.

We've seen before that Ric's stubborn mind can be changed by outside forces, and in this case the outside force was his pregnant daughter Jess. Her husband has left her, so she faced bringing up baby all alone and unsupported. This was motivation enough to get Ric to sign the consent form. He knew the risks, though, and started making a video for the grandson he might never see.

So Hanssen assembled a surgical team, and he needed a CT surgeon. Elliot was having none of it. Sahira was busy doing an operation with Irish Dr Greg and decided this was a good time to assert herself with Hanssen, so she refused to down tools and join him on Keller. Jac had her hands full as well, with a post-operative patient (pericarditis following a Croatian boob job) who'd gone into arrest. So Jac wouldn't be available, because surely she wouldn't abandon her patient in favour of some high profile surgery where she might help to save a senior surgeon's life and deeply impress the man who had the power to grant her a consultancy?

After barely the minimum resuscitation time, Jac decided her patient was a lost cause and left Funny Little Nurse Tait to sort the body out and break the news to the deceased's husband, while she dashed off to get scrubbed up.

A short while later, Goth Dr Frieda and Boy Valentine were practising their surgical skills on some corpses in the morgue. Not entirely conventional behaviour, but the mortuary staff turned a blind eye, and of course Goth Dr Frieda is perfectly at home with cadavers. A new one was wheeled in, and pretty soon Frieda spotted something odd – it was moving. Apparently Jac's pericarditis patient was not quite as dead as Jac had assumed.

Back in the operating theatre, Jess had discovered (after seeing Ric's video for his grandson, which he'd given to Elliot for safekeeping) exactly how risky the surgery was. She begged Elliot to try and stop it, but when it became clear that it was too late, she asked Elliot to go into the theatre and take care of her dad. So Jac was bumped out of the operation in favour of a more senior pair of hands. Obviously this made her cross, and her mood was not improved when she spotted her pericarditis patient apparently alive and well(ish). "Here's the one you killed earlier," Frieda said. The formerly dead patient wasn't one to hold grudges, though, and had quite enjoyed her near-death experience. She saw a bright light, she told Funny Little Nurse Tait, and heard a voice calling her. "It sounded like Barry White."

Meanwhile Jess had gone into labour, and it was one of those very quick TV labours. "The baby's coming now," Chrissie pronounced confidently, though Jess was still wearing leggings at that point so I'm not sure how she could tell. Baby Jake Griffin was delivered safe and well by Jac.

While his grandson was taking his first breaths, Ric was almost taking his last, as things had inevitably gone pear-shaped in theatre. Blood everywhere and lots of the bad beeping sound. Thank goodness, then, that Elliot Hope was there, because where there's Hope there's life, and he sorted out the problem and Hanssen managed to remove a tumour the size of a man's foot from Ric's abdomen. No wonder he kept saying "Nnngh!" So Ric will be fine, and baby Jake will be fine, once he gets over the shock of the first human face he ever saw being Jac Naylor's.

With all this going on there was still room for a bit of plot concerning Young Dr Oliver Valentine. Penny sent him a postcard telling him to "tell the truth." So he started writing a letter of resignation to Michael Spence. But after a day of corpse surgery and reanimation in the morgue with Frieda, he did a neat bit of diagnosis on a woman who ate lightbulbs. "The proper doctor just saved your life," Frieda told her (this woman had met Frieda before when she was a nurse, and still thought of her as one). Boy Valentine likes being a "proper doctor," and he deleted his resignation letter. Penny's not going to be pleased when she gets back.

The episode ended with Ric's video for his grandson. Life was short, he told him, so you you have to grab it with both hands and hang on tight, "Because, otherwise…"

All work and no play makes Jac the perfect choice

(Series 13, ep. 25 'Coming Second' by Joe Ainsworth 5.4.11)

It was the big day, when Sahira Shah the Registrah and Jac Naylor the Medibot 2000 would slug it out in the interview room for the title of CT Consultant. A particularly big day when you think that the boots you're filling are the kitten heels of the incomparable Connie Beauchamp.

Sadly neither Jac nor Sahira has Connie's flair with accessories. Sahira showed up for work having decided that red denoted confidence. Bright red dress, bright red lipstick. "I can see you've got your tactics worked out," Jac (in scrubs as usual) observed. "Couple of inches off the skirt?" Ouch. And double ouch that the wrong shade of lipstick will make you look ill and washed-out rather than confident.

Power dressing can't hide the fact that Sahira is more your touchy-feely type of doctor, as opposed to Jac who has only ever been really touchy-feely when around Joseph Byrne. So when Sahira found herself looking after a terminally ill patient who, to compound the poignancy factor had an adorable deaf son (Lewis Tompkins – sign him up for Waterloo Road immediately), she put patients before interview and missed her appointment. This, and trying to sugar-coat the fact that the man's cancer was inoperable, didn't go down well with Jac, who tells it like it is. "You want them all to fall in love with you," she told Sahira. "That's why you're not consultant material."

In the absence of Sahira from the interview room, Hanssen had no option but to give the job to Jac. My feeling is he wanted to do that anyway – he has a point to prove with Sahira, though we're not entirely clear what that point is yet.

Meanwhile, on AAU we were treated to another dose of Manic Malick, as his anger issues were stirred up by a man who'd been abusing his wife. Even before he had the evidence to prove what was going on, Malick decided the nasty man needed to suffer, and rather than giving him morphine for his pain he gave him saline instead. Hippocrates would shudder. Even Young Dr Oliver Valentine shuddered, and he's not always been the most ethical of chaps himself.

The man-magnet who is Chrissie Williams was fending off three men this week. One was the doggedly devoted Sacha, whom she doesn't have to fend off as he's so under-confident and lovely that he stays away and encourages everyone else instead. Another was tedious bone doctor Dan Hamilton (she can't marry him! She'd be Christine Hamilton), and the third was, somewhat bizarrely, children's TV legend Derek Griffiths off of Play School. He played a patient who kept pretending to have a relapse so he could spend longer in the radiant Chrissie's presence.

Before I go, could someone clear something up for me, please? At one point Chrissie said, "I'm just a lowly nurse." What happened to her being a consultant nurse and getting to wear a suit, avoid bedpans and swagger about like her dad Jesus?

And then there was one Valentine

(Series 13, ep. 26 'Boy Valentine, Girl Valentine' by Dana Fainaru 12.4.11)

Stunningly Beautiful Dr Penny Valentine is no more! Crushed beneath a crashed train while rescuing a patient, her fabulous skin and gorgeous hair will be seen on Holby no more.

It sounds like one of those Holby/Casualty crossover episodes, all action sequences and falling masonry, doesn't it? But it was all the more shocking because the action didn't leave the hospital, so there wasn't really any hint that such a huge tragedy would occur. In fact the first sign that all wasn't well was when Michael Spence and Goth Dr Frieda, who'd gone to the scene of the accident with Penny, arrived back alone, while Oliver was leaving a message on his sister's voicemail, trying to make amends with her and telling her that "life's too short." Oh, the dramatic irony of that little phrase.

There was loads going on this episode – power tussles between Dan and Sacha, and Sahira and Jac. But the episode belonged to Young Dr Oliver Valentine (brilliant work from James Anderson), under threat from his sister that if he hadn't told Hanssen that he wasn't actually medically qualified by the close of play, she would do it.

Boy Valentine has been a bit rubbish recently, medically speaking. Lots of mistakes, errors of judgement, lack of confidence. Then on what was due to be his last day as a doctor, there's a massive train crash, Holby is the designated receiving hospital for the casualties, AAU is on the front line, and Oliver is up to his knees and out of his depth treating a woman with a shard of glass sticking out of her abdomen and delusions that her daughter, who died five years ago, is still alive. He almost messed things up, "helpfully" allowing the woman to delay surgery because she didn't want to use up supplies of blood that her daughter might need (in the confusion, Oliver thought her daughter was being operated on elsewhere by Sacha and Dan). But, when pressures and sats and all those droppable things started dropping, Oliver was the only person who was available to perform life-saving surgery. Coached by the rather magnificent Malick, who yelled instructions at him down the phone while carrying out another bit of surgery in another theatre and then sprinted like a greyhound to AAU, Oliver proved that, when push comes to shove, he's got the balls and the skills.

A good day for Boy Valentine, then, and his first reaction was to share the news of his triumph with his sister, by ringing her. "I've had a bit of a day," he said, and then remembered she'd spent her shift at the scene of a terrible train crash. "I can only imagine what kind of day you've had." Then he got the news from Michael Spence – Penny was dead.

In the morgue to identify the body, Oliver confessed to Malick about cheating in his exams and swapping his paper for Penny's. Malick is only a few letters apart from the word "maverick" himself, and mere technicalities don't bother him. He'd seen Oliver's best work that day and didn't want him to waste his talents. "As far as I'm concerned, we never had that conversation," he said.

I'm glad Oliver will be staying, but I'm sad Penny had to go, and I'm sad that she had to be crushed under a train rather than joining Scott James in Spain for a happy life. But Spain would never have suited her colouring, and the tragic nature of her demise will no doubt inspire Oliver to be a better man, to be worthy of her.

And what a day to be starting a new job as CT consultant. Jac Naylor received a gift – a pair of kick-ass shoes from the glorious Connie Beauchamp, with the message "Fill them." And filling Connie's shoes is exactly what Jac proceeded to do, mainly by picking fights with Sahira. Jac doesn't really do "colleagues," she does "rivals," and Sahira, because of her close relationship with Hanssen, is the biggest rival of the lot.

However, by the end of the episode Jac had to concede that Sahira was sometimes right in her more conservative approaches (a lesson also learned by Dan, as he and Sacha disagreed over whether to amputate a teenage girl's leg). "Maybe you'd better look at your idiosyncratic management style," Hanssen advised her, before dropping the bomb that Darwin may be about to close. Oh, and Jac also received a punch in the eye from an annoyed relative. Like I said, what a day to be starting a new job.

If something's painful, keep your distance

(Series 13 ep. 27 'Rebound' by Martha Hillier 19.4.11)

Penny Valentine only died last week, so obviously her former colleagues will be suffering. It's conventional wisdom that what they need is a bit of counselling. "I trust you cascaded the note from HR about counselling?" Hanssen asked Jac. She sucked her cheeks in every so slightly (Jac is not one for management-speak), and replied that putting £50 behind the bar would surely be more therapeutic. She knows she's on thin ice with Hanssen, though, so when he argued she gave in. "Okay, I cascaded, I cascaded!"

She didn't cascade, though – whatever that means – with the result that Funny Little Nurse Tait ended up sobbing in a toilet cubicle. She takes things to heart, does FLNT, and wasn't coping with her grief. Jac was right generally, though, as everyone else ended up at the bar at the end of the shift, raising their glasses in honour of Penny's life. Young Dr Oliver Valentine wasn't present as he's presumably on bereavement leave.

Despite recent traumatic events, the usual power struggles continued unabated. After apparently burying the hatchet last week, Jac and Sahira are back at the sniping again. Indeed everyone's having a go at Sahira for being too touchy-feely and getting emotionally involved with her patients. Hanssen told her that, if something was painful, she should keep her distance. Good advice given that she ended up having urine thrown at her by an irate patient.

An early-episode basketball game between Sacha, Michael, Malick and Dan set the tone for the testosterone-fuelled shenanigans to come. A suave old friend of Michael's, Sunil Bhatti (Silas Carson), turned up with a mystery patient with nasty facial injuries. Bhatti was a maxillofacial surgeon with a nice string of private practices ("The Colonel Sanders of plastics," Michael called him). Michael was keen to get one of these for Holby, and asked Hanssen for some money to get the bits and bobs needed to perform some delicate plastic surgery on the mystery patient. "You give me the kit, I give you a Bhatti Clinic," he promised. Hanssen's fingers gripped the purse strings more tightly. "You give me a Bhatti Clinic, I give you the kit," he said. So it was up to Michael to impress with his ninja skills in theatre, which of course he did because tight trousers are no impediment to surgical skill.

The situation almost went tits-up, though, because it turned out that the mystery patient was a witness to some crime, and nasty people were trying to track her down and kill her – hence the mystery (and the police protection). Goth Dr Frieda almost ruined everything by ringing the patient's mother, which alerted the bad guys, but the day was saved when the patient was smuggled out while Frieda acted as a decoy. All a bit silly and unconvincing, but it looks like Michael will get his plastics unit.

I really don't like Boring Bone Doctor Dan, but I'm absolutely warming to Malick, so I knew whose side I was on when these two went head-to-head. They were disagreeing over the treatment of a very obese patient, and the arguments harked back to the days of Ric Griffin's famously rubbish zero-tolerance scheme. Dan didn't fancy operating on the leg of such an overweight person. Malick disagreed, and was proved right when the leg went very nasty indeed. Malick and Dan are quite a funny double-act (not least when Dan discovered that Malick's gay – who knew that the most macho man in the hospital could be gay?).

Hearts trump scalpels

(Series 13, ep. 28 'Crossing the Line' by Daniella James 26.4.11)

More basketball this week – Holby is turning into *ER*, isn't it? Except on *ER* they shout for "CBC and Chem 7!" while Holby prefer the old FBCs, U's and E's and LFTs. And they get fewer gunshot wounds. And they're much worse at basketball. Particularly Sacha, who played Michael for theatre time. "Jews and balls don't mix," Sacha said as he admitted defeat.

Jac was most unimpressed by all this laddish behaviour. "Nothing like the smell of rancid testosterone in the morning," she told Michael as they shared an elevator. "If you keep hitting on me I'm gonna have to report you," he replied. Ah, that easy American charm. Totally lost on Jac. "Call in the fantasy police," she said. "Maybe… if you were the last man on earth."

Michael wasn't having the best of days. Lollipop-headed estranged wife Annalese was bothering him about the divorce settlement, and plans for his lovely plastic surgery unit were not receiving the warmest of support from Henrik Hanssen. Given a choice between theatre time for a woman who needed to have some facial scarring sorted out, and a person with a cardiac issue, Hanssen knew where priorities lay. "Hearts trump spades – and scalpels," he said. Or do they? It seems that Hanssen may back the plastics unit after all – but at the cost of Darwin. Yes, that's right – Holby's award-winning, world-famous cardiac ward, which has seen the thrilling skills of Anton Meyer, Nick Jordan, Connie Beauchamp, Elliot Hope and Joseph Byrne over the years, may have to close. It's frankly unthinkable.

Meanwhile, Young Dr Oliver Valentine was back, and in a daring reversal we saw him staring regretfully up at the Window of Regret, rather than regretfully down at the car park. Quite daunting to be returning to the hospital where you've messed up so many times, where you aren't actually qualified to be a doctor, and where your sister recently died. Goth Dr Frieda thought it was too soon for him to be back, but Malick felt that work was the best thing to soothe a troubled mind. With Frieda's and Malick's help, Olli was just about managing, but then he missed an ectopic pregnancy (oh – duh! One of the most common ailments seen in medical dramas). No-one died, but it was a close call, and he had one of his traditional episodes of self-doubt in a store room. Frieda went and sat with him, and she was absolutely adorable – she even smiled! – and gave him a little kiss on his cheek. Remember ages ago when she thought she had a date with him but he only wanted to discuss work? Has Frieda been hankering after the blue-eyed boy ever since? And will he succumb to her idiosyncratic Ukrainian charms?

Irish Dr Greg and Sahira Shah the Registrah were both scrapping over a 15 year old patient with an exciting heart condition that they all wanted to have a go at. Dr Greg used his Irish charm, his beautiful nose and a camera "borrowed" from Elliot Hope to ingratiate himself with the patient, Ellie, but she was a seasoned hand at the hospital lark despite her tender years, and refused the exciting surgery. Irish Dr Greg found himself quite emotionally involved with the case. "Welcome to my world," said Sahira.

And the best line of the night came from Sacha, who described a patient's varicose veins as looking "like two blue snakes scaling a flesh-toned tree."

Detach, Mr Douglas

(Series 13, ep. 29 'Tunnel Vision' by Andrew Holden 3.5.11)

Ric Griffin is resurrected! After being almost dead and spending most episodes clutching his abdomen and saying "Nnngh!" he was back last night looking positively chipper. Five years younger at least. That Hanssen really is a miracle worker.

It wasn't long before the cares of Holby were settling around his shoulders like a manky old fur coat, though. It is a stressful job, particularly when you discover you have new colleagues as boring as Dull Dan, and that you have to share operating theatre time with them. This meant trading off one person's appendectomy against another person's dislocated knee and so on, and it all got quite competitive. Indeed, Ric had a bet with Dan about who would finish his list first. Old habits die hard, after all, and so, almost, do patients when this sort of thing gets in the way of the world-class surgery for which Holby is renowned. It all ended up with Ric having to bail out Dan when a bit of knee relocation went horribly wrong. Then Sacha had to bail Ric out.

Speaking of Sacha, he really is a beacon of normality in the super-competitive world of Holby, isn't he? He just gets on with things quietly and competently, is there with a man-hug whenever it's needed, and even bows gracefully out of the contest for the hand of the lovely Chrissie because if you sawed him in half you'd find he has "considerate" written right through him.

Maybe Irish Dr Greg will become a little more like Sacha after his experiences this week. Teenage patient Ellie, first seen last week, was still insisting she didn't want the heart surgery that would hopefully keep her going until she could have a transplant. She had a bad feeling about it, and she strongly felt she wanted to let nature take its course. She had Irish Dr Greg convinced to support her, particularly after her heart temporarily stopped and she reported a reassuring near-death experience which may have involved her late mum. Greg had had a near-death experience of his own once (he didn't elaborate, but we'll probably be treated to a flashback episode all about it at some stage), so he could relate.

Everyone got cross with Greg, particularly Ellie's father who was desperate for her to have the surgery, and his fellow doctors who all felt that the operation was the preferred clinical option and superstition shouldn't stand in the way of science. Hanssen took him off the case and advised him to emotionally take a step back: "Detach, Mr Douglas." And of course poor Ellie died during surgery, with Greg looking helplessly through the glass as Jac and Sahira tried to save her.

Meanwhile, on AAU, everybody's favourite Ukrainian goth medic, Dr Frieda Petrenko, took her makeup off. Not by choice, it must be stressed. It turned out that a patient was severely allergic to it. So out came the Pears soap, off came the slap, and Frieda emerged in all her fresh-faced glory. Is this going to be a tedious tale of a duckling turning into a swan, a "Without your heavy goth slap you're… you're beautiful!" yawn? Well of course not. This is Frieda we're talking about. The patient who was allergic to her makeup was a transvestite man who hadn't really told people about his dressing up habits. He was worried that his daughter would be shocked and horrified. He and Frieda bonded and had a good old chat about how what was underneath was certainly important, but what was on the outside was pretty important to, and you should be proud of whatever face you wanted to show the world. He put his wig and his bra back on and his daughter didn't look flapped at all, and as soon as he was safely off the ward Frieda reinstated her white face and eyeliner. "I'm still pretty," she said. "Underneath."

Never refer to Ric as "The Griffin"

(Series 13, ep. 30 'My Bad' by Tahsin Guner 10.5.11)

Ah, these young doctors. Just how do you keep them in check? They're so emotional, for one thing. There's Malick with his anger-management issues and over-inflated ego. There's Irish Dr Greg hitting the bottle after not sticking up for Ellie last week. There's Young Dr Oliver Valentine blinking winningly at everyone and hoping Malick won't tell anybody he isn't actually qualified.

The episode started with a woman going into labour right in the middle of the hospital entrance, just in front of the coffee bar. Enough to put anyone off their frothy coffee and breakfast muffin you'd think, but in fact the scene drew quite an appreciative crowd. The Malick was on hand to turn his cap the wrong way round in a businesslike style and get on with the delivery, almost as if they weren't in a hospital with a fully-functioning (though these days somewhat mythical) Obs & Gynae ward, porters with trolleys and wheelchairs and all the rest of it. He likes a bit of an audience, does The Malick, because he's not exactly the modest type. Shame he didn't think about the modesty of his patient.

Ric Griffin was a bit cross about it all, but Malick looks up to Ric. This makes Ric cross, too. "You're so far up my backside it's gotta be dark in there," he snapped, as Malick pronounced himself thrilled to be working on Keller alongside The Griffin. "I will not, nor ever will be, referred to to as 'The Griffin,'" Ric added. That told him.

But you can't keep a good ego down for long, and pretty soon the woman who'd given birth in reception was asking for The Malick's first name, so she could name the baby after him. Of course you can't name a baby "The," so he had to tell her his other first name, which is Antoine. This woman was a heroin addict who was wanted by the police for car-related crimes, and Malick pretended to the police that he'd discharged her, because she was claiming to want to start a new life, turn over a new leaf, bring up baby without recourse to drugs or Jeremy Kyle. Sadly her drugs habit caught up with her, as did the police, and she ended up in surgery with a nasty bleed that Malick felt could only be stopped with a hysterectomy. A drastic step, and Boy Valentine didn't agree, but these days all Malick has to do is fix Boy Valentine with his special scary "I know your little secret" stare, and BV just blinks back a tear and gives in.

It wasn't a much better shift for Irish Dr Greg, who started off by smashing a car window during a drunken game of something-or-other with Dull Dan in the car park. And it happened to be Hanssen's car. Not a good move. This earned Greg a warning and a breathalyser test before he was allowed anywhere near a complicated surgical procedure. Then he got another warning for panicking a patient (this was a man with a short-term memory of about 10 seconds, who kept asking "Is it serious?" Eventually Dr Greg said, "Yes! It is serious!" Because it was serious. But they weren't supposed to tell him it was serious). Hanssen wasn't impressed by Greg's behaviour, but is he also a teeny bit jealous of the way Sahira Shah the Registrah keeps covering for the attractive (and, temporarily at least, naked) Irishman? "Fraternising with drunken Irishmen is not a good career move," he told her. But when Greg failed to ensure there were decent supplies of a rare blood type on hand before they started the rare and tricky heart op, Sahira covered for him.

Meanwhile, Chrissie Williams was finding that her boyfriend Dull Dan was a little… well, dull, his idea of romance being to ring her up in the middle of the night and make a suggestion so rude it couldn't be uttered but could only be written down (and read by various people). Chrissie has been there and almost certainly done that with a merry succession of willing chaps over the years, and what she wants these days is a bit of romance. So Dull Dan commandeered the on-call room for a romantic surprise. And, fair play to him, I was expecting the usual table laid for dinner, candles, wine etc. What he did was much sweeter – he'd set the room up to be a cosy sleep sanctuary, because he correctly identified that what Chrissie really needed was a couple of hours kip, what with having a small baby and being disturbed in the wee hours by calls from pissed, lecherous doctors. Maybe there's hope for Dull Dan after all. Or maybe that's only because the radiant human being we know as Sacha Levy was having a day off, and so Dan's little star was therefore twinkling more brightly.

What's the big secret, Elizabeth?

(Series 13, ep. 31 'Step On Up' by Gillian Richmond 17.5.11)

Is it Bob Barrett as an actor, or Sacha Levy as a character, or a combination of both? Scenes with Sacha have an energy and a humour to them that's becoming more apparent the longer he's in the show. It's possibly that he's such an unusual character in the realm of Holby – genuinely nice, with no hidden agenda, no axe to grind, no skeletons in his cupboard – that other characters are able to respond to him in a way they can't with everyone else. He makes them drop their guard, because he has no guard of his own.

This week he was faced with the challenge of heading up AAU, the Ward of Doom. Full of emergency cases, where quick-thinking and prioritising are essential and it's not unusual to perform a bit of ninja-level surgery on the spot, AAU didn't seem a great fit for Sacha when Hanssen proposed it. Ok, Hanssen didn't so much propose it as decree it (and what a marvellous scene that was), and you don't say no to Hanssen.

You can never sustain trying to be something you're not, so Sacha's attempt to be all authoritarian ("It's Mr Levy from now on, Mary-Claire") was doomed to fail. When he messed up in the operating theatre because he didn't want to ask Dull Dan for help, he decided that AAU was not the life for him, and handed in his resignation to Hanssen. There's more than one way to skin a monkey, though (as Elliot told Jac later, apropos of something totally different), and Hanssen had heard about how Sacha had made a life-changing diagnosis for the same patient. "I like your approach," he told Sacha. So do I. I like his approach very much, and I was very glad to see that resignation letter torn up and flung in the bin ("And please call me Sacha, Mary-Claire").

Meanwhile, what was Elizabeth's big secret? Why did we see her at the beginning running tearfully down the Fire Escape of Despair (it's nowhere near the Window of Regret and has more of an outdoor vibe, but it's equally emotional)? Well, her granny (Mona Hammond – Blossom from EastEnders) turned up as a patient, and it's fair to say she was not exuding twinkly grand-maternal feelings. She was very cross with Elizabeth, who had left the family in the lurch by leaving home at 16 to pursue her selfish dreams of being a nurse. Granny and Elizabeth did make friends eventually, but sadly granny died on the operating table. When Ric finally caught up with Elizabeth on the Fire Escape of Despair, she told him her mother used to hit her, and her granny would give her sweets to try and make her feel better. At the end, she carried out her granny's wish, and rang her mother.

There was plenty to enjoy in this episode for fans of Jac Naylor, including some brilliant lines ("Saint Jac – patron saint of the minimally invasive bypass. I like") and several shots of her in her motorbike leathers. There were a lot of outdoor scenes in this episode – Hanssen in particular seemed to spend the majority of his time walking to and fro the car park. Jac's opponent this week was Bhatti the plastic surgeon, who had commandeered a bed on Darwin and some Darwin theatre slots for his own patients. Jac was outraged, as well she might be, that cardiac surgeries were being bumped in favour of tummy tucks. Elliot was no help, as he was apparently easily seduced by Bhatti's gift of donuts. Jac doesn't do carbs, and she doesn't do bribes, and she doesn't really do co-operation.

It would be nice to have the patients on your side at least, but her heart patient fell for Bhatti's tummy patient, and he gave up his theatre slot for her. This seemed all a bit odd to me – surely in the cash-strapped NHS theatre time would be allocated by clinical need? Or is that just me being old-fashioned again? Anyway, Jac had a right old go at Bhatti, and was very cross that Elliot didn't back her up, even when Hanssen materialised behind her. "There's more than one way to skin a monkey," Elliot told her, hinting that he's playing a long and cunning game. Connie Beauchamp would have slapped him hard with an icy stare, but maybe Jac, like Sacha, is learning that sometimes a different approach can work. She even ate a chocolate.

Manager of the year

(Series 13, ep. 32 'A Greater Good' by Rob Williams 24.5.11)

Authority was not sitting comfortably on Sacha's shoulders this week. He's just too nice, and his efforts to appear managerial came across, to Chrissie at least, as "cute." Well, he is cute, but when the machines start going beep, the floor's awash in bodily fluids and tough decisions need to be made, "cute" is not really what you want.

If the patients were the biggest problem he'd be ok, but it's always the staff who are hardest to control in Holby. Chrissie's used to getting her own way with Sacha, what with him being besotted with her and being the father to her child and all, and him being her boss didn't make any difference. This is the kind of thing that drives Goth Dr Frieda nuts, however, and she decided to give Chrissie a piece of her mind. And what a lovely sight it was. Frieda's still annoyed that Chrissie previously got to keep her job mainly because her father, Jesus, was the CEO of the hospital at the time. "You manipulated him," said Frieda, "And now you manipulate another weak man!" Weak man? Sacha must have been having thoughts along the lines of "with friends like Frieda, who needs enemies?' But the fact remained that he can't work with Chrissie, so she's been ousted to Keller – currently the domain of Dull Dan and his little fixator (it's for fixing pelvises. Pelvi? Whatever).

Dull Dan apparently can't get through a week without locking horns with another male staff member in a rutting stag sort of way. It's getting grindingly inevitable, and it's also getting grindingly inevitable that he comes off worse. This week he was up against the human challenge that is The Malick, but Malick was also charged, by Ric Griffin, with looking after Funny Little Nurse Tait, who is grieving for her granny and is therefore still funny (and little, but I'm not really expecting any change there). Malick and Dan were so busy squabbling over a patient that they didn't notice that FLNT had taken herself off to the Window of Regret for a quiet sob. This is not Ric Griffin's idea of people management, and he wasn't pleased.

Michael Spence and Plastic Bhatti got very excited at the prospect of showing off to a man from the health authority (Jamie Glover), a man so stern he made Henrik Hanssen look like Graham Norton. Their star patient was a young woman, Rose (Lauren Crace), who was having a mastectomy and then a breast reconstruction because she was at high genetic risk of breast cancer. But half way through the procedure, Jac demanded use of the theatre for a patient who was about to die without immediate surgery. This showed up what a daft idea the plastics/cardiac timeshare scheme is, and it also gave Michael time to discover that Bhatti got his breast implants (not his own personal ones, I mean ones to use on his patients) from a company owned by Mrs Bhatti. Corruption! But the fact remains that Plastic Bhatti is a very good surgeon, a point he was able to prove later when he and Michael did a very showy-offy double operation, with Rose in one theatre having her reconstruction and a helicopter pilot with a mashed-about face having his face done by Bhatti next door, and Michael Spence flitting between like a surgical bee.

He loves the buzz (see what I did there?) of a bit of ninja-level surgery, does Michael, so for now he's prepared to put up with his colleague being a tad dodgy. They shook hands on their continuing partnership – they even had matching watches.

Men. What are they like?

(Series 13, ep. 33 'Damage Control' by Tahsin Guner 31.5.11)

Apologies for the lateness of this post, but I've been on me holidays, where I discovered I tan about as well as Frieda Petrenko wearing a burkha. Money well spent, I'm sure you'll agree. So it was home to a Sky+ box literally groaning with accumulated televisual goodness. Hurrah! So much drama, so little time, what with John Stape and Becky Macdonald going even madder than usual on *Corrie*, and Jim on *The Apprentice* zapping everyone with his invisible mind-beams.

And, in Holby City, the character we've previously enjoyed dubbing Dull Dan locking lips with The Malick. Say what? Who'd have guessed that the burly, rugby-playing, Chrissie-fondling, blokey bone surgeon could turn out to have an eye for the laddies? Well, if you watch the episode back with the benefit of hindsight (which I sort of did, as I already knew the kiss was going to happen), the clues were all there, but it took him feeling extremely cross and getting all violent and strangly to make his sexual feelings come out, which I don't think bodes particularly well for Chrissie even if he does decide he errs more on the hetero side of life. My advice: run a mile. My second piece of advice: as a doctor, the man needs to be stopped. Every single week he makes bad decisions and mistakes, and he appears to be too arrogant to learn from them.

Away from all the testosterone being sprayed around Keller, a tragic love story was playing itself out on Darwin. Henrik Hanssen is quite clearly completely besotted with Sahira Shah the Registrah. I've finally dropped my cherished theory that they're married, and I now think that he's just in love with her and she's not in love with him, and he's jealous of Irish Dr Greg because of his easy Irish charm and the way he doesn't actually frighten Sahira. The patient they were looking after was a boy who was having a relationship with his teacher. Hanssen told the teacher he'd be reporting it to her school because it was "an abuse of power." Was he really talking about his relationship with Sahira? The mystery deepens.

Guy Henry has the most splendid and subtle range of facial expressions. Usually when actors are left, at the end of the scene, to do a facial expression to indicate how they're feeling, you get something broad-brush like "regretful," "elated" or "smug." With Hanssen you get "Regretful with perhaps a tinge of optimism but only under the right circumstances," with a side order of "Where did I leave my car keys?" It's quite beautiful to watch.

And Goth Dr Frieda's father died. Did she wail and cry? Not while we were looking. She finished her shift, because her dad had shown he loved her by working hard to put her through medical school, so she showed she loved him by being the doctor he'd wanted her to be. And she was nice to a little girl who'd been bullied. Bless.

Two new nurses, and about time too

(Series 13 ep. 34 'Rescue Me' by Kim Revill 7.6.11)

Chrissie, Mary-Claire, Elizabeth and the nurses who always hover in the background but never speak have been keeping Holby going, nurse-wise, since The Radiant Donna left for Liverpool. With Maria a distant memory, and Pale Thin Nurse Nicky Van Barr having been "let go," it was about time that some new nurses appeared. This week saw the arrival of not one but two: Eddi McKee (Sarah-Jane Potts) and Chantelle Lane (Lauren Drummond). I think it's safe to assume that these two are not going to turn out to be bezzy mates like Donna and Maria. Chantelle is all fluffy and ditzy and a wee bit useless, though to be fair to her she can "get a cannula in anything," a talent which instantly won her the approval of Young Dr Oliver Valentine.

She did not get the approval of Eddi, who arrived somewhat unconventionally when she accompanied a man with a penile injury. We weren't told exactly what he and Eddi had been up to in the back of a taxi when the injury occurred, but if you've read *The World According to Garp* you may think he had a lucky escape. Anyway, as an entrance to the show it beats the usual "almost having a car crash in the car park" route. Sacha assumed Eddi was a prostitute, but he was ever so glad when it turned out that not only was she a nurse, but she was a really efficient nurse. He offered her a job on the spot (without checking that she actually had any qualifications, that she was who she said she was and not an axe-wielding murderer and other minor administrative details). Eddi and Chantelle both have the makings of excellent characters. Chantelle is all soft and smiley – her first meeting with Hanssen was hilarious – and Eddi is spiky, brusque and independent.

Talking of women who are spiky, brusque and independent, the very apogee of those qualities, the divinity that is Jac Naylor, was a woman on a mission this week, the mission being to oust Plastic Bhatti and his little friend Michael Spence off her CT ward for good. Trying to reason with Hanssen wasn't getting anywhere, apart from an educational little foray into Swedish culture. Had she heard of "surströmming," he wondered. This was a dish of fish "fermented to the point of putrefaction." And, like sharing an operating theatre with the plastics people, it was "an acquired taste – but one I suggest you acquire sooner rather than later." I don't think they serve it at the coffee bar on the ground floor, though. Jac thought she'd found the ammunition she needed when she unpacked one of Spence & Bhatti's parcels of breast implants to discover they'd come from Mrs Plastic Bhatti's plastic booby factory. Corruption! Treachery! And surely enough of a weapon to take to Hanssen and get the gruesome twosome ejected from Darwin, if not the entire hospital. "I heart today!" a triumphant Jac told Michael, as she confronted him in the lift. But he was holding a trump card, or rather a trump file, which outlined management plans to move cardiothoracics to the dreaded St James's. But there just might be room at Holby for one CT consultant, he told her, and if Jac keeps quiet about the bogus boobs then that person could be her. Though would a one-woman CT department be enough of an empire for Jac? Surely what she wants in life is what Darwin was always supposed to be, a state-of-the-art facility renowned throughout Holby and, heck, even the whole of the UK.

Meanwhile, we gained further insights into why Funny Little Nurse Tait always looks worried, when her mother turned up. Not a mentally well woman, Ma Tait. A bit of a handful, in fact, and she is now a burden that Elizabeth feels she has to bear. Her perma-frown is soon going to be so deep that no amount of botox will shift it.

Show me some magic, Miss Naylor

(Series 13, ep. 35 'All About Me' by Nick Fisher 14.6.11)

"This place is run by cretins," sighs Jac Naylor. Well-spotted, that woman. It is indeed a bizarrely-run establishment that would bin off cardiothoracics (it's a dying specialism, apparently – who knew?) in favour of plastics. Never mind the unusual employment practices which mean that people who come in accompanying a patient one week can be practically running a ward the next week.

Oh well. If I wanted realism I'd watch *24 Hours in A&E* (which I do, in fact, watch, and it's rather good if at times a bit too gory for comfort). What I want to see, and what I did see, on Holby is Jac asking Hanssen, "Are the rumours true?" and Hanssen replying, "You'll have to be more specific. The one about me being undead is fallacious, for example." Fabulous.

The rumours – namely the ones about CT being binned off to the mythical St James' – *were* true, but Michael Spence is still waving his offer of Jac being the only CT queen in Wyvern Wing. How this happens to be his gift to bequeath, I have no idea, but he had a contract all nicely written up and ready for Jac to sign.

Meanwhile, Sahira Shah the Registrah had been busy slicing into someone's chest in a moving ambulance literally as it bounced over speed bumps. I couldn't help thinking she might have asked the driver to park up for the second it took to do the slicing, but that's me for you. By the time Sahira arrived at the hospital she was flushed with success, excitement and adrenalin and she'd had an idea. I wasn't entirely clear about her idea – it seemed to involve mobile CT units roaming Holby and lurking in Tesco's car park waiting for people to have heart attacks. Within minutes she was visualising entire convoys of surgical caravans, with her at the wheel, scalpel in one hand, Yorkie bar in the other (which I realise would make driving dangerous).

She needed a consultant to come on board with the idea, if not literally to come on board her cardio-van. Elliot was out, as he struggles with technology, so that left Jac. Two exciting job offers in one day! This left Jac ample scope for scheming and manipulation, which of course she loves. She signed Spence's little paper, but don't think that's the end of her scheming. Oh no.

Elsewhere, Malick was happily taunting Not-Gay Dan. "You're not the first straight guy who ever fell off the straight tracks by kissing a beautiful black man," he said modestly, exposing his buff physique just to remind Dan of the marvels of The Malick. They had to work together looking after a gay male patient, and Dan resorted to unpleasant homophobia and unrealistically snogging Chrissie every five minutes to prove that he wasn't even a tiny bit gay. It only made Malick taunt him more. "Dr Dan here is all bone," he told the patient, and we knew he didn't just mean his orthopaedic skills.

Nurse Eddi and Nurse Chantelle, despite or because of being chalk and cheese, were quite a sweet double act this week. Chantelle wants to be like Eddi: skilled, confident, with a proper contract, hungover. Maybe not the last bit. But she (Chantelle) continues to be charming and exasperating at the same time, the highlight of her work this week being putting a call from Sacha's mother through to the operating theatre where he was in the middle of a procedure – so Mama Levy could sing happy birthday to him.

Are you ready to start again, Dr Valentine?

(Series 13, ep. 36 'In Between Days' by Justin Young 21.6.11)

The episode dealt mainly with Young Dr Oliver Valentine's inner turmoil and journey through grief and self-pity to acceptance and a fresh start. It did this via the medium of flashbacks, which often took in little bits of action that we'd already seen in previous weeks. At times the effect was quite hallucinatory – was that really Nurse Eddi McKee that Ollie bumped into as he tried to start a fight outside a nightclub? (And that almost-fight explained the black eye he had a couple of weeks ago – here was I thinking I'd missed something).

Ollie pitched up at Penny's former flat to clear away her stuff, but ended up hanging around sharing reminiscences and a one-night-stand with Penny's former flatmate Lucy. It was obvious that Lucy and Ollie were really looking for Penny in each other, which I suppose makes sleeping together a bit weird, but we'll leave that to one side.

I did wonder why Penny had lived in a shared flat with second-hand (yet oh-so-shabby-chic) furniture, while Oliver had a swanky flat all to himself, but the reason for this became clear when his father, Simon, turned up. It seems that Penny was something of a disappointment to Simon – always wanting to fix things and make everyone better, the crazy fool, and, even worse, dragging her far more promising brother into the dead-end world of medicine. "Stop wasting everyone's time trying to be like your sister. You've got far more potential than she ever had," Simon told his son, handing him a cheque for £10,000 so he could have a little break and sort his head out. Apparently daddy loves Oliver and pays his rent.

Boy Valentine is a better man than all this, though, and he got his chance to prove it when a taxi driver he'd been treating was involved in a car crash. This was the same taxi driver, Mr Sharma, who popped up previously, the one who didn't seem to have anything wrong with him. Chantelle had diagnosed a broken heart, and it seems she wasn't far wrong. Oliver ended up pulling Mr Sharma out of the wreckage of the crash much as Penny had done at the train crash, and performing a venous cannula puncture in a moving ambulance to save his life. Ninja skills indeed.

He's a lad with a conscience, though, and he decided it was time to come clean to Hanssen about his lack of qualifications. Perching himself in Penny's favourite sulking spot in the basement, and sparking up one of the fags she'd handily left behind, he wrote a resignation letter. But Hanssen, like The Malick before him, wasn't about to let his only and best Valentine go that easily, not after that neat scalpel work in the ambulance and a glowing reference from Mr Sharma.

So Oliver stays, which is marvellous because we rather like him in this house. I like that thing he does with his eyes where he makes them even bigger because he's trying not to cry, and PLA Jr thinks that if you were standing on top of a cliff and he was at the bottom and said "I'll catch you," you could trust that he would.

While all this was going on, we were also finding out what had happened to Funny Little Nurse Tait since her mother showed up. This all culminated in Ric Griffin and the local pastor having a showdown about whether FLNT had a duty to sacrifice her own health and happiness (I'm presuming she does "happiness") for a mother who'd abused her. That showdown was the first time this story really caught light – it took Ric Griffin to inject some passion and drama into it, because all the emotion we've seen from FLNT herself is a kind of downtrodden acceptance. Whether she'll accept Ric Griffin's help from now on remains to be seen, as he and the pastor and a psychiatrist went hammering on FLNT's mum's door and terrified the poor woman into setting fire to the house. Ric should really stick to general surgery.

Is it the end of Darwin as we know it?

(Series 13, ep. 37 'The Bottom Line' by Stuart Morris 28.6.11)

Henrik Hanssen is only really comfortable when he's top banana. That's why he's so tall, so he can gaze down on everybody with his unnervingly calm stare. Sir Fraser Anderson is a higher banana status-wise, but can't compete with the Hanssen height. "Henrik! You get taller every time I see you!" he greeted the Swedish Scalpel. "What do you do – hang yourself up by your toes?"

The other thing that can flap the unflappable Scandinavian is Sahira Shah the Registrah, and she hit him with the shock news that, if there was no future for CT at Holby she'd be upping sticks to Newcastle (where, presumably, they're still old-fashioned enough to be having heart problems). So there was double pressure on Hanssen and he decided to go the traditional Holby route and do some high-risk, flashy surgery to prove to Sir Fraser that a multi-disciplinary Darwin was do-able.

He assembled a crack team of almost every surgeon in the hospital to help piece together a Polish man who'd been comprehensively mashed in an accident. Hanssen decided to go ahead with this despite a trace of amphetamine in the patient's blood. Unfortunately, it turned out the patient's mate had been slipping him speed on a regular basis, and his system was so entirely perky that he woke up half way through the operation. That's not what you want when you've got Elliot Hope and Henrik Hanssen poking about in your innermost self, and Plastic Bhatti and Michael Spence hovering impatiently waiting to fix up your externals.

Sir Fraser was not impressed: "You waste my time with this razzle-dazzle!" he said, as if he was talking to John Barrowman rather than the world's tallest surgeon. At the end Hanssen gathered assorted cast members and extras in the stairwell to deliver a bit of bad news. The main bulk of cardio-thoracics would be moving to the dreaded St James's, with only elective patients being treated on Darwin. Jac and Sahira looked stunned. Plastic Bhatti and Michael Spence looked insufferably smug.

Away from the cutting and thrusting on Darwin, Chrissie and Malick were getting friendly. Not in the way that Chrissie and Dan are friendly, and certainly not in the way that Dan and Malick previously got friendly. Malick was just giving Chrissie advice about her exams and mentoring her a bit, but it was enough to make Dull Dan get all insecure and jealous. When Dan is feeling insecure he likes to go into the closet – quite literally, as he likes to pretend there's not a gay bone in his body by messing Chrissie's hair up in a supply cupboard.

Meanwhile, Sacha was given the task of shooting Bambi. Not literally, but it was just as heartbreaking a task. He had to tell Chantelle that her services as an agency nurse would no longer be required. Poor Sacha hadn't seen the opening credits, or he'd have seen Lauren Drummond's face popping up and looking for all the world like a regular cast member. He made several attempts to break the bad news, but she thwarted him by being all smiley, adorable and lovely with the patients. What's a guy to do? Conjure her up a job out of nowhere, that's what. No sooner had he broken her heart by telling her that today was her last day, than he was telling her a permanent position had come up. Oh, the joys of the flexible Holby staffing arrangements!

I simply can't let you go

(Series 13, ep. 38 'Out on a Limb' by Lauren Klee 5.7.11)

Ooh, these buttoned-up, ice cool, intellectual types. Under a beautifully-ironed shirt, a suit and a sensible tie there's all sorts of passion absolutely seething away, and there's no moment more sexually charged than the one in which a bit of seethe is allowed to escape.

So we have Henrik Hanssen: Swedish, solid, sensible – like IKEA furniture but more scary. A man who would not be moved, apart from the fact that he is deeply in love with Sahira Shah the Registrah. She's his physical and emotional opposite, the sun to his moon, the yang to his yin etc etc.

Miss Shah does not want the CT service on Darwin to go down the pan. We're all with her on that one, and so are Jac, Elliot and Irish Dr Greg. Sahira, however, is the only one that Hanssen listens to. "What has she got that we haven't?" muses Jac, as the three of them eavesdrop on Hanssen and Shah slugging it out in his office. "Breasts?" hazards Greg, quickly adding, "Not that yours aren't spectacular." I loved the way Jac quickly readjusted her top just in case she was showing any unprofessional cleavage. She wasn't.

Such is the grip that Sahira has on Hanssen's soul that she almost literally gets away with murder. Gets away with keeping critically ill patients who shouldn't be there in the first place in the basement, and not noticing when they've been stabbed, anyway. Not a whiff of disciplinary proceedings followed this mad episode. Indeed it only made Sahira rave on even more about being passionate (we get it, love, you don't have to tell us every five minutes), and threaten to take her passion elsewhere (Newcastle, in fact) if her talents weren't going to be appreciated in Holby.

And it worked. Hanssen followed her into the corridor, and in a voice loaded with emotion told her, "Even though I know it's not what's best for this hospital, or for me, I… I simply can't let you go!"

So it looks like Hanssen will now pull out all the stops to save Darwin from the evil clutches of Sir Fraser. Never mind that Jac and Elliot do ninja-level work week in and week out, and Connie had built up a reputation of excellence for the department – it's obvious that the driving force in Holby is passion, of the romantic as well as the medical sort.

Which brings us neatly to Dull Dan, who should really stay away from that locker room, because every time he goes in there he's faced with a topless Malick, who taunts him rather marvelously. Dan is still pretending that he doesn't fancy Malick, and he's mainly doing this by trying to avoid working with him. Once again this backfired spectacularly and caused his patient extra pain and suffering, but once again Dan has escaped without any consequences. He's the poorest doctor to stalk the corridors of Holby since the tiny Mr Geddes.

Was it just me, or is sexual chemistry also brewing between Jac Naylor and Young Dr Oliver Valentine? I know they've got previous, but this week she had him jumping through performance-related hoops (he asked for her to be his mentor, so she had him practising suturing inside plastic cups), and he seems to like it. And she seems to like him liking it.

Another cute partnership, but certainly not a sexual one, was Eddi and Sacha. Eddi was bored of hearing Sacha droning on about Chrissie (I can so relate) and told him to man up. So he did! He actually told Chrissie he wouldn't switch the weekends that he sees Daniel just for her convenience. You can see why cynical, jaded types like Eddi and Jac like Sacha. You can be as sarcastic and snippy as you like with him, and you get sunshine in return. He's a joy-spreader, that's what he is, and even when he's putting his foot down, it seems to only make people love him more. Chrissie looked like she'd gained a new level of respect for him, anyway, but sadly still not enough to prise her from the arms of Dull Dan. Not yet, anyway.

Malick's got form, but Dan's got the guilty conscience

(Series 13, ep. 39 'Hand in Glove' by Sasha Hails & Nick Fisher 12.7.11)

We picked up where we left off last week, with Malick having just punched Dull Dan. And bravo to the makeup department for making Dan's nose look particularly gory and horrible. Gushing blood like the proverbial stuck pig, Dan staggered down several corridors leaving a messy trail behind him. He wasn't bothered about hygiene or the poor person who'd have to clean up after him. He was mainly bothered about what Chrissie would say when she saw him all busted up, and how he would explain it, without mentioning the "I kissed a boy and I liked it" bit. What Malick didn't want was to be sacked from yet another job for punching yet another consultant.

Dan's first attempt at an explanation went along the lines of, "I got in the middle of a fight between a father and a son." Chrissie is no fool, and she knew that wasn't true, otherwise it would have been the talk of the hospital coffee bar and Dan would be filling out incident report forms in triplicate. She also spotted that Dan was acting very weirdly around Malick – though he's been doing that for about a month now without her noticing anything. "It was Malick, wasn't it?" she said, and Dan fell to his knees sobbing, "It's always been Malick! He has something you can't give me, Chrissie!" Actually no, he didn't say that. What he said was that he'd tried to hit Malick first, and missed.

For reasons best known to herself, Chrissie marched off to Hanssen with this information, and he in return produced possibly the finest loom of his entire career so far when he materialised in a corridor to summon Dan to a meeting in his office at four o'clock. Never have the words "four" and "o'clock" sounded so ominous. So four o'clock was Dan's High Noon, and he took Malick along too, so they could both pretend they knew nothing and hadn't done anything and were both somewhere else when Dan fell and hit his face on a… thing. Hanssen's even less of a fool than Chrissie, but what can you do when people close rank?

Chrissie was still dissatisfied with Dan's explanations, so he said he'd been winding Malick up with some homophobic comments. This was plausible, because he's said a few unsavoury things in the past. Chrissie accepted it and let him off with A Look of Grave Disappointment, and they left the hospital arm-in-arm, leaving Malick pondering them from the Window of Regret.

Meanwhile, Michael Spence and Plastic Bhatti argued over who should be the Face of Plasticity in their shiny new brochure. Plastic Bhatti thinks it should be him, because people are willing to pay a premium for a bit of Bhatti magic, and he's terribly photogenic (he thinks). Michael had to do some reconstructive surgery on a girl who also had a heart problem. Miss Naylor being unavailable (boo!), Sahira Shah the Registrah was bleeped over, and she advised a postponement of the surgery, on the sensible grounds that the patient might die. When it all went tits-up (quite literally), Plastic Bhatti kind of saved the day with a spot of advice, but it was really Sahira and her proper medical skills that were impressing Michael. I'm thinking just give him a few weeks and we'll be able to woo him away from plastics, no problem.

Sacha appeared to be moving on emotionally this week. He removed Chrissie from a photo of her and Daniel that was in his locker, so it looks like he's given up all hope there. Then he went all flirtatious with an elderly patient's daughter. Well, flirtatious Sacha-style, which is only one step up the socially awkward yet sweet ladder from Elliot Hope. It was all going wonderfully, until he had to talk to the woman about her father's medical problem. As a side-effect of his medication, he (the old man, not Sacha) had a permanent and painful erection. She was far too grown-up to stick her fingers in her ears and shout "Blah blah blah!" but you could tell she wanted to, rather than hearing that her old man was having trouble with his old man. That, and the arrival of her husband, spelled the end of Sacha's ambitions in the romance department. Eddi did warn him.

It's emergency medicine – deal with it

(Series 13, ep. 40 'Going It Alone' by Rebecca Wojciechowski 19.7.11)

It pains me to admit it, it really does, but my overriding feeling watching last night's Holby was… irritation. Even the glorious Sacha was annoying, though he wasn't the worst offender.

The Worst Offender prize goes to Sahira Shah the Registrah. I've said it before and I'll say it again – we get the "passionate" thing. We do not need to see her cry, sweat and scream her way through a shift just to prove how much she cares. If that's what a caring doctor behaves like, I'd much rather have the cool Jac Naylor – a little less emoting and a little more action, as Elvis Presley didn't say.

The start of the episode had a weird atmosphere, like it was all going to turn out to be a dream or something. The camera angles were odd, the colours looked washed-out and there was a strange cast of non-speaking extras. These were Sahira's new team members in her £50,000 Cardiac Trauma Unit. "Why could she not just ask Hanssen for a pony?" muttered Jac between clenched teeth, and that nicely summed the whole, unfair situation up. The CTU had a lovely new telephone that was supposed to ring to let Sahira know a patient was on the way, but when a woman was wheeled in with a lump of metal sticking out of her chest and bleeding profusely, Sahira flapped. The phone hadn't rung! She didn't have any notes! Oh, woe! "It's emergency medicine," said Jac. "Deal with it."

Eventually – very eventually, and after a lot of histrionics – Sahira knuckled down, and even managed to save the patient when Jac had completely written her off. Was I alone in wishing the patient would die just to prove Jac right and Sahira wrong? She didn't die, Jac was wrong, Sahira was right, and we were supposed to admire her tenacity, skills and that bloody passion. Jac, being a better woman than me, did admire those things. I just felt cross and irritated.

Elsewhere, Chrissie was all sulky with Malick for punching Dull Dan, and Malick was sulky with Hanssen for not letting him do operations. So Hanssen said he would let him in on a particularly juicy operation. You know that when a junior doctor is offered this kind of opportunity, something will happen to stop them getting to the theatre on time, and thus it turned out. Malick badly mishandled a mentally ill patient, who managed to get his hands on one of the many sharp objects that they're fond of leaving around the hospital. So while he was meant to be helping Hanssen, Malick was busy stitching up bread-knife-inflicted wounds on his patient.

To complete a trilogy of tedious tales, Sacha had to decide between two junior doctors who both wanted Dr Penny Valentine's job. One of them was brainy but with no people skills, and the other one was the daughter of Sir Fraser and had a pashmina. It was all a fine opportunity for Nurse Eddi McKee to practise her gurning skills and for Sacha to be sweet, accidentally offensive and inept. He chose the pashmina woman, though I was past caring by then.

The one with the puking extras

(Series 13, ep. 41 'Sirens' by Patrick Homes 26.7.11)

Yes, I know there's usually a puking extra or two on Holby, but there were loads of them in this episode. It was coming thick and fast. Or thin and fast. Fast, anyway. Sacha and Eddi were at a loss. "It's not like normal food poisoning," they kept sighing. What could it be? Who would work it out? Turned out it was lead poisoning, caused by wine dissolving the lead from some fakey antique cups. The person who worked it out was new girl Dr Lulu Hutchison. She may be teetering on high heels and getting non-speaking-extra nurses to bring her cups of coffee, yah, but she can put two and two together, diagnosis-wise. That'll teach Eddi to make snap assumptions about people. Just because one looks like a duck and quacks like a duck, doesn't mean one can't also be a doctor.

But can one be both a mother and a doctor? This was the question Sahira Shah the Registrah was wrestling with, as she failed to really give 100% to her shiny new Cardiac Trauma Unit or her Adorable Son Indy, who was having a birthday. Her team of non-speaking extras from last week were apparently having a day off, so this week the CTU was staffed by Sahira and Jac, with Dr Oliver Valentine hanging around fairly uselessly in the background (Jac had him practising juggling 50p coins across his knuckles. It was partly a dexterity exercise and partly an exercise in Putting Junior In His Place).

Sahira seems intent on setting the cause of feminism back decades, such is her inability to separate home and work. When putting an emergency chest drain into a small boy, she had to get Jac to cover his face because she couldn't cope with the fact that he was roughly of a similar gender and age as her son. Pull yourself to-freaking-gether, woman! At one point she got in such a state that she smashed up the toy ambulance she'd got Indy as a birthday present. When we saw it in pieces on Hanssen's floor, we just knew he'd spend the rest of the day fixing it for her. He really is besotted. Once again, Sahira went wobbly in the operating theatre and Jac had to tell her to snap out of it, and once again she snapped out of it and did some suturing that "maybe only three surgeons in the world could have done," (according to Jac), and once again we're supposed to admire her and not think it's all a bit rubbish because Jac is by far the superior surgeon anyway.

And where is Elliot? Has he been quietly shipped off to the mythical St James, or are they hiring at The Hadlington again? And has Frieda gone with him, wherever he is?

Funny Little Nurse Tait's mother was brought into the hospital with a nasty infection and an advance directive saying not to make huge attempts to save her should the machines start going bleep. FLNT wasn't happy with Ric, blaming him for the fire in which her mother was burned. But when the bleeping started, Ric wasn't happy to leave her mother unsaved, and he dashed off to get Funny Little Nurse Tait to give him the go-ahead to save her mother's life. It all prompted a bit of soul-searching on the part of FLNT. "I've been so angry," she told him, her face registering its usually "mildly crestfallen" expression. Ric saved Mama Tait, and we left FLNT sitting by her bed, gently holding her hand. And looking mildly crestfallen.

When is a dark secret not a dark secret?

(Series 13, ep. 42 'Old Habits' by Fiona Peek 2.8.11)

I was all excited about this episode, because we were promised that we would find out a "dark secret" about Irish Dr Greg, when an old friend turned up. Since the loss of The World's Most Beautiful Heart Surgeon, Joseph Byrne, to the wilds of Cumbria, I've been warming to Greg, with his beautiful nose and lovely accent. So the thought of a dark secret was most bracing.

So what was it, then? Has he maybe falsified his exam results so he's not a doctor at all? No, that's someone else I'm thinking of. Has he been snogging other male doctors in the locker room? Nope, that's definitely not him. It wasn't anything as exciting as that, and indeed seemed to amount to Greggy and his old mate used to play football together and probably got into a fight at some point. Frankly, I wasn't really concentrating once I realised Greg wasn't going to turn out to be the long lost love child of Anton Meyer.

He did go to pieces in the operating theatre, though, which was a neat turnaround as it was Sahira who had to be calm, controlled and not screaming, "Oh my GOD! I'm covered in BLOOD and STICKY BITS and that!" like she usually does. Well done, Sahira.

Meanwhile, on Keller… "Everyone's acting weird!" says Chrissie. And she's surprised why? The reason they were acting weird was that Dull Dan was hatching a not-so-secret plan to whisk her off somewhere fabulous for the weekend. Chrissie doesn't like men organising her life for her, so she got all stubborn and even let her stubbornness cloud her usually acute clinical judgement. So, in another neat turnaround, Dan was right about a patient this week. All was well that ended well, and Chrissie popped into a pair of mentally high heels – just as well she had an orthopaedic surgeon on hand – and off they went for their weekend of – well, I don't really want to dwell on it if you don't mind.

Michael Spence paid a flying visit to AAU, just to check in on what the little people were up to, and spotted the attractive form of Dr Lulu Hutchison. This triggered his "flirt" reflex, and pretty soon he had her practising suturing bananas. As you do. The phallic nature of this exercise was not lost on Sacha, who advised Mr 70's Trousers that Lulu was Sir Fraser's daughter, so he'd Best Not Go There.

"Unhelpable" – is that even a word?

(Series 13, ep. 43 'Walk the Line' by Dana Fainaru 9.8.11)

It's amazing how the presence of Goth Dr Frieda lightens proceedings, which may or may not be ironic depending on how you feel about Goths. Her bullshit detector set as usual to 11, it wasn't long before she was busily winding up Lulu, and she found a willing ally in Eddi, a woman who similarly had a low tolerance for spoiled brats. Winding up Lulu proved to be all too easy.

Having a more difficult time was Funny Little Nurse Tait, who was busy trying to pretend that her mother didn't have a psychiatric problem. This meant that we had to endure a great deal of FLNT looking mildly put-upon and getting a bit snappy with Chantelle (which is like stamping on a fairy, really). It's got to the stage now where, as soon as FLNT's troubled visage appears on the screen, I start staring out of the window or try to engage the cat in a blinking contest, anything to lift the monotony.

Irish Dr Greg was still being bothered by his old mate Andy. Greg didn't want to face up to whatever it was that was The Dark Secret, but eventually it turned out that the old football coach had been sexually abusing those in his charge, which had led Andy to a lifetime of turmoil and a prison sentence for downloading child porn. Greg may or may not have been a victim of the football coach himself – it was a bit vague but I think he had been, though had clearly dealt with it better than Andy. Unusually for Holby, when Andy wanted to end it all he headed for the hospital roof. It's usually the basement (it's Casualty where people end up on the roof).

Wherever Greg is, Sahira is not far behind, looking annoyingly caring. Wherever Sahira is, Hanssen is not far behind, being sarcastic about anyone male and attractive whom Sahira might be looking annoyingly caring about. Greg found this so irritating that he actually dared to shout at The Swedish Scalpel. Yikes.

I did wonder when she took her clothes off

(Series 13, ep. 44 'One of Those Days' by Emma Goodwin & Patrick Homes 16.8.11)

I really think the Holby scriptwriters should have gone with my idea (and – hello? I am available, and ready to respond to the call whenever it comes) – that Henrik Hanssen and Sahira Shah the Registrah were secretly married. That would have been a very interesting dynamic indeed. As it is, he's besotted with the world's weepiest CT surgeon and I'm going to start calling him Hankering Hanssen if he doesn't shape up quickly.

Possibly those lovely scriptwriters have got something up their sleeves which will turn this whole situation around – after all, we've never met Mr Shah, we know nothing of Hanssen's home life and very little about their shared past, so skeletons may well tumble out of cupboards. Just pray they do it soon, because it's a waste of a tall, arrogant man otherwise.

Though it did lead to the best lines of the episode. A patient (who was the ex-wife of that Cunningham bloke who swans in occasionally and annoys people, but more of him later) was majorly flirting with Holby's tallest Swedish surgeon. It took Sahira to point this out. "She was flirting with you, Henrik," she pouted. "You do know what flirting is, don't you?" Hanssen looked bashful. "I did wonder, when she took her clothes off," he said.

Nasty Mr Cunningham informed Hanssen at the end that Holby's CT department is going to close. Close! Altogether! The legacy of Anton Meyer, Nick Jordan, Connie Beauchamp, Joseph Byrne, Elliot Hope, Jac Naylor… Closing! Altogether! (You can tell I'm upset). Anyone with a dodgy heart in Holby will, in future, be directed to The Mythical St James's. I think we should get a petition up.

Meanwhile… it was Sacha's turn this week to get over-involved with a patient, when he mishandled a case. This gave Eddi the opportunity to pull some of her "disapproving" faces at him and tell him off for not being professional. There was no sign of Lulu or Frieda, so Eddi had time on her hands to do this, not being busy winding up Lulu and pulling her vast range of "amused" faces.

Malick had a busy shift as well. Ric was going to let him assist with a kidney transplant, but it was just Malick's luck that, after weeks of not being allowed near an operating theatre, he was also called upon to do a bowel resection for a nervous patient, in the same afternoon. There was a lot of running around, the bowel resection man's mother died in the relatives' room, the nervous man legged it but Malick spotted him through the Window of Regret and legged it after him and… well, it all boils down to Lessons Learned about compassion and caring about your patient for Malick. Via this type of trial the eager, volatile young apprentice will eventually become as wise and omniscient as the Sainted Ric.

We saw the merest glimpse of Irish Dr Greg, who is reacting to his recent upsets by going out with Young Dr Oliver Valentine and getting hammered, in the proud tradition of Donna, Maria and Maddy. And FLNT smiled! She turned that frown upside down and actually seemed slightly happier this week. It can't last.

Standing in awe of Sahira's balls

(Series 13, ep. 45 'All Good Things' by Tahsin Guner 23.8.11)

The vultures landed in Holby this week, in the form of a team from The Mythical St James's. They wanted to see what they might be getting, in terms of surgical skills, when Holby's CT department is shifted over to their Mythical Premises. I actually visualise it like Darkplace Hospital (of *Garth Marenghi's Darkplace* fame), with lightning flashes overhead and a standard-sized hell-mouth beneath.

Not the sort of place Elliot Hope would be happy, and this was confirmed when he heard that they were offering him only one day of operating time a week. "The sheer joy of surgery – that's what I'll miss most," Elliot reflected sadly, as it became clear that the master plan was actually to oust him altogether. It made me wonder why he didn't cast his CV a little wider in search of a position where his talents would be more appreciated – after all, when his domestic arrangements were last discussed, he was living in his car with his dog, so it's not like he's not mobile.

This (ie realism) isn't the point, though. The point is that CT is the heart of Holby, and this battle between Holby City and St James's is, quite literally, a battle for hearts and minds. Everyone knew who'd come out of it well – Sahira Shah the Registrah. After all, she was Hanssen's golden girl, and he'd set up the Cardiac Trauma Unit especially to help safeguard her future at Holby. "Unlike myself, who somehow managed to get by on surgical brilliance alone," muttered Jac, echoing what we've been saying for weeks.

Sahira didn't like everyone thinking it was only favouritism that got her to where she is now, so she decided the best thing was to be not where she is now, and resigned. "I, for one, stand in awe of your balls," commented Jac, adding, "I'm less impressed with your brains, though." Ouch! But accurate. And if Sahira thought her gesture would have Hanssen immediately on the phone to St James's telling them the whole deal was off – well, he didn't. He just pretended he'd filled her job, and then she unresigned. All a bit wet, really. As is Hanssen, these days, although it pains me to say it.

The episode's general theme was coming to terms with loss. Specifically, Frieda's recent loss of her father, which was mirrored by Ric temporarily losing Jess, who's gone to live in Jamaica, and of course the CT staff losing their department. A rather surreal ending saw most of these people and a couple of patients and relatives out at the front of the hospital watching a lovely display of shooting stars. Via the medium of these glittering heavenly bodies they were each, in their own way, able to say goodbye. It was a bit obvious and mawkish, but quite sweet, too.

For the love of Spence

(Series 13, ep. 46 'Big Lies, Little Lies' by Peter McKenna 30.8.11)

I've seen this episode twice now. I've only actually heard it once, though, which is why I couldn't blog about it till now. When I watched it last week I was surrounded by a massed gathering of Clan PLA, who chattered throughout (I know! How very dare they?). So I got that Irish Dr Greg was being flirty/defensive, Sahira slapped him, FLNT's mother fed her daughter some tablets that made her puke, and Lulu sutured a lot of grapes, and that's about it.

When you can't hear what's going on, you miss those all-important details like Eddi telling Lulu that Michael Spence's nickname among some of the nurses is "Panda," because "he eats, shoots and leaves" (snork). This is important, given that Lulu and Michael spent the previous night taking the concept of "mentoring" to a whole new level. Upon arriving at the hospital together, Michael warned Lulu that the first rule of office relationships is discretion. Lulu doesn't really do discreet.

Does Lulu really like Michael, or is he just a passport to a nice piece of bowel surgery? Who knows, but she's a manipulative sort who isn't above putting her patients at risk just to get his attention. When the machines started going bleep, she made sure Michael was needed by pressing the mute button for a minute or two, just so things got nice and critical. But will this come back to bite her? We did get a close up of a flashing REC logo. Was the machine logging her unethical behaviour? Let's hope so, and hope it leads to her being booted out, because she's rather tedious. And anyone who is horrible to Goth Dr Frieda has to be taken out.

Meanwhile, Irish Dr Greg tried to pretend he wasn't affected by his recently-revealed childhood traumas, but Sahira Shah knew better, and pursued him with a furrowed brow and a worried expression. He paid a mandatory visit to Occupational Health (not the staff counsellor that people on Casualty get sent to), who was less effective than he could have been by virtue of being a non-speaking extra.

And Chantelle tried to get Funny Little Nurse Tait and Mrs Tait to be Good Mates by organising a picnic in the Linden Cullen Memorial Shrubbery. You can't expect a sandwich and a custard slice to heal that kind of rift, though, and later on Chantelle discovered FLNT doubled up and chucking up. Mrs Tait had tried to poison her with her medication. She's not daft, that Mrs Tait.

This is the first and last time I clean up after you

(Series 13, ep. 47 'Who Needs Enemies' by Justin Young 6.9.11)

Well, that was easier than we thought. Only yesterday, I was hoping that Lulu's evil ways with a mute button would be her undoing. And today – poof! She's gone. Vanished from Holby City and on a train bound for That London. Which leads me to speculate – how come Holby is the only fictional city in the Holbyverse? People leave there and go to Penrith or Brussels or London. Real places, not fictional places like Floppington on Sea, or whatever. Weird, that.

But I digress. It was Lulu's bunny boiler ways that ended her Holby reign of tedium, rather than being a useless/dangerous doctor (after all, Dull Dan is a useless/dangerous doctor, and he's still there). Basically, she got super-clingy with Michael and tried to ingratiate herself with his daughter, the fabulously feisty Jasmine, who was supposed to be shadowing her dad for the day as a school project.

When it became clear that Jasmine could see straight through Lulu, her thin veneer of niceness dropped away and she got all threatening. "Boarding schools aren't at all like Hogwarts!" she hissed at the unimpressed schoolgirl, shortly before giving her a slap. That was enough to get her dumped by Michael, but Lulu is not a woman used to being rejected, and she went all "Daddy, I want a squirrel!" on him and threatened to tell Sir Fraser exactly what Michael had been up to, vis a vis dodgy breast implant surgery.

It was all sorted out by Hanssen, on shimmering form (always filmed from below so we can enjoy the feeling of him looming over us), who arranged for Lulu to be "promoted" to a post in London. This wasn't because Hanssen particularly likes Michael – he so doesn't – but because the hospital's future viability would seem to stand or fall on the success of the Plastics department. "This is the first and last time I clean up after you," Hanssen informed him. Lulu went off to say good riddance to her bezzie mates on AAU, and, like me, they were only too pleased to bid her farewell.

Not only did we get to wave goodbye to Lulu, but the episode marked something of a turnaround for Funny Little Nurse Tait. She actually smiled! She and The World's Sunniest Nurse, Chantelle, bonded over a pervy patient. Indeed, Chantelle went so far as to write his name up above his bed as "Pepe Le Perv." Dull Dan, being dull, didn't realise it was a joke, and asked "Mr Le Perv" if that was the correct way to pronounce his name.

Elsewhere, Young Dr Oliver Valentine asserted himself with Jac by not letting her give a patient good news when she'd sent him to give bad news (if that makes sense). Jac always waits till Oliver's back is turned before she gives her little grin of approval – it wouldn't do to let your underling know you rather like it when he mans up.

And there was a new male nurse hanging around. Is my gaydar faulty for suspecting there was a frisson between him and Dull Dan? Frieda would know.

Compartment syndrome

(Series 13, ep. 48 'Night Cover' by David Young 13.9.11)

In last night's Holby City, Dull Dan was desperately dealing with compartment syndrome. This is a medical condition that, if left untreated, can be very nasty indeed. Dan was so busy flirting with Gay Nurse Stephen (the splendidly-named Lex Shrapnel) that he only managed to operate on part of a patient's arm, which required Henrik Hanssen to tear himself away from his sushi to sort out the ensuing emergency (there was more to it than that, but that's the general gist). Hanssen looked so blissed-out eating that sushi, as well. "I always thought you were reliable," he admonished Dan. "Boring, but reliable."

Compartment syndrome is also a nice description of Dull Dan's life at the moment. He has his square-jawed, sporty heterosexual compartment. And he also has his square-jawed, sporty homosexual compartment (or closet). He tries to keep the gay side of things under control by using poor, beleaguered Chrissie as a voodoo talisman. When he snogged Malick, he had to run off and drag Chrissie into a cupboard to reassert his straight credentials (that may or may not be a euphemism). When Gay Nurse Stephen got a little too close, Dan responded by jogging off and booking a honeymoon hideaway for himself and Chrissie. Yes, that's right. Honeymoon. It can't end well. Compartment syndrome doesn't just go away on its own.

While Hanssen was bailing out Dan, the most breathtakingly magnificent moment of the evening was the appearance of Jac, gliding along the corridor in a drop dead gorgeous evening dress. She'd been called back to sort out someone who was in a bit of a mess thanks to some rubbish work with a pacing wire by Young Dr Oliver Valentine, who was helping Irish Dr Greg cover for Sahira, who was asleep. "You called me out in the middle of the night because Nigella needs a nap?" Jac said to Greg. Never mind all that, what I wanted to know was where had Jac been and who with? Oh, Joseph Byrne, I just hope Penrith was worth it.

And Eddi got emotionally attached to Josh the paraplegic former snowboarder.

We do not admit to errors

(Series 13, ep. 49 'Broken' by Patrick Homes 20.9.11)

Deep, deep joy and jubilation. The little Plastics empire of Bhatti and Spence is coming apart, implant by leaking implant. Mrs Bhatti's Cut-Price Boobs do, indeed, appear to have been a bogus batch. Almost everyone who's had one seems to be turning up with complications and leakages. Not nice for the patients, obviously, but great news for those of us who want Darwin purged of all this Plastickery and reinstated as the domain of Holby's crack team of CT surgeons. And Sahira.

While Michael Spence can be an oily, smarmy little creep, he's our oily, smarmy little creep and we quite like him. Not everyone can pull off that 70's look and get away with it. And beneath the tight trousers and oiliness, he's actually a decent person with a sound moral core. The same cannot be said for his mate Plastic Bhatti, who would sell his own granny if there was a profit to be made. While Michael spent this episode getting increasingly concerned that his previous surgical work was causing more harm than good, Bhatti spent it covering his tracks, off-setting the blame and being generally evasive.

Meanwhile, in the calmer waters of AAU, Senior Staff Nurse Eddi McKee was becoming too attached to her ex-snowboarder paraplegic patient Josh. Not in the Dr Penny Valentine/Scott James sense of "close," mind. At least, I don't think so. She did warn his girlfriend off, but she also warned his mother off as well. It was like he was her pet project, and it was all very un-Eddi-like. She's always the one wagging a finger at others and telling them exactly what she expects from them in terms of professionalism. Maybe that was the point – it was this week's Lesson to be Learned. Anyway, the wonderful Sacha had a word with her ("Eddi, you scared his girlfriend away. How is that good patient care?" he reasoned), and she promised to maintain a nursely distance from now on.

Chantelle turned her smile up to 11 in an attempt to get Funny Little Nurse Tait to take some time off and lighten up. It would've worked as well, if it hadn't have been for FLNT's mother being brought into the ward with kidney failure. Chantelle had a go at not mentioning this to FLNT, with the result that FLNT got all cross with her. The FLNT frown, which Chantelle had tried so hard to turn upside down, was back with a vengeance.

We're not supposed to create emergencies

(Series 13, ep. 50 'Everything to Play For' by Nick Fisher 27.9.11)

Darwin's operating theatres are no longer ringing to the cheery buzz of sternum saws and bitchy banter as hearts are repaired and pulses are restored. Instead, they've recently been echoing with the slap of leaky breast implants being flung into metal dishes.

This is what happens when you let plastic surgeons use your lovely, shiny CT facilities, and particularly when the surgeons are as plastic as Plastic Bhatti and his little sidekick Mikey. This is a bit unfair on Mikey (aka Michael Spence) of course. He loves the money and the flash watches and the glamour of plastic surgery, but he also likes helping people, weird old-fashioned thing that he is. In some ways, he's even a tad naive. He certainly didn't see Plastic Bhatti for the slimeball that he is, until he realised the depths to which he'll sink. With Sahira circling the corridors clutching a box of dodgy boobs ("Unauthorised for UK use," apparently), Michael expected the wrath of Hanssen to descend on the plastics department – but what he didn't expect was to be totally shafted by his mate Sunil (who refers to this as "crisis management") and left to take all the blame. This resulted in what we might term an "uneasy" meeting between Michael and Hanssen. You know a meeting is not going well when Hanssen has to use his Outdoor Voice.

Meanwhile, we had an entire episode of FLNT looking particularly morose, as she tried to make her dying mother tell her why she abused her as a child. "She hates me!" she wailed at Ric or Chantelle, one of whom was at her shoulder almost constantly during the episode (poor Ric's sole function for the last few weeks has been to materialise sympathetically behind FLNT at moments of crisis). Frankly FLNT would try the patience of a saint. Chantelle must be well above sainthood, as she remained smiling and supportive no matter how much gloom was thrown her way. I'm thoroughly relieved that FLNT has apparently decided to leave Holby. She will not be missed, by me anyway. And it's lucky that La-Charne Jollie has escaped from the role while she's still young and before those frown lines became so permanent that she'd need industrial quantities of Botox to get rid of them.

Last week, the formerly mega-professional Eddi went all unprofessional by getting too close to paraplegic snowboarder Josh. This week she was all unprofessional in the way she tried to be professional by ignoring him. The poor lad ended up in the physio room on his own, trying to improve his upper body strength and ending up rupturing his spleen (which I impressed PLA Jr by diagnosing the moment he hit the floor – you don't watch Holby for all these years without knowing a minor yet important character isn't just going to fall and bruise himself).

Oliver always wanted to be a consultant

(Series 13, ep. 51 'Oliver Twists' by Joe Ainsworth 4.10.11)

What a delightful episode. I would have enjoyed it just for the neat demonstration of how character can be revealed via the eating of fruit. Henrik Hanssen peels his apple with a small knife, wearing a look of patient contentment and anticipation. Sir Fraser just grabs an apple from a bowl, sinks his teeth into it, and when he's had enough looks round for a bin to throw it in. Hanssen's pain at this callous disregard of fruit was etched on his face.

Etched on the face of Young Dr Oliver Valentine was a bruise – is he ever without a bruise? – caused this time by running into a lamp post. He was being distracted while jogging by his former patient, recruitment consultant O'Gorman. While Oliver was nursing his bruised head, O'Gorman hunted it, and offered Ollie a job as a hot shot high flying recruitment consultant. He would be earning a salary so enormous it could only be comprehended by looking at the figure typed on an iPhone and not spoken out loud. Recruitment is presumably not the type of consultancy Oliver was aiming for when he applied for medical school. What a marvellous use of several years of training and a qualification your sister worked hard to earn you. But Ollie had had enough of being Jac's puppet and spending hours in the wet lab suturing pigs' lungs – even his on-the-fly carotid sinus massage did nothing to impress her – so he wrote his resignation letter to Hanssen and told everyone he was leaving.

We knew he wouldn't get out without being faced with a tricky case which showcased his surgical skills (Jac accidentally cut her finger so he had to do the operation) and his people skills (he was rather good at dealing with a patient with a learning disability and his somewhat sensitive partner), and so it was no surprise when he changed his mind at the end of the episode. It certainly didn't come as a surprise to Jac. She hadn't spent all that time forcing him to learn to juggle coins between his fingers for nothing. It would have been a terrible slight to her work as a mentor if her mentee had metaphorically thrown her pigs' lungs in her face and left. In fact, she knew it wouldn't happen. So she'd taken the step of removing his resignation letter before Hanssen got to read it.

Hanssen had other fish to fry anyway, what with having his apple-eating interrupted, and with charging Sahira Shah the Registrah with the job of delving into the fake boobs. Bhatti was making himself scarce this week, leaving Michael Spence to mop up the mess caused by the exploding implants. Two patients with defective frontages were summoned for a quiet word. One of them promised to keep quiet as long as Michael threw in a free "Brazilian butt lift" (who knew?), but then she called a press conference anyway. Bad news for the credibility of the plastics department (hurrah!).

And it was bad news for Tedious Josh the Paraplegic Snowboarder. Apparently his paraplegia is permanent as, presumably, is his tediousness. Eddi spent the episode looking tragic. I just wish someone would find young Josh a place in a spinal unit so he can get on with rebuilding his life and Eddi can get back to being sarcastic again.

The natural order is finally restored

(Series 13, ep. 52 'PS Elliot' by Joe Ainsworth 11.10.11)

In everyday life, 52 weeks is generally considered to be a year. In the world of Holby City, 52 weeks is a Series. And last night was episode 52 of this particular series – which is kind of New Year's Eve, Holby-style. A time for reflection, for resolutions, for one era to end and another to begin…

And for all this idiot nonsense about carving Darwin down the middle and calling one half Plastic Surgery and the other half Sahira's Cardiac Trauma Unit to end.

It went right to the wire, though. Elliot Hope had packed up his office, all his bits and bobs, plastic models of hearts, leftover bits of pie, photo of Gina from the desk. I felt rather sad as he left for what he thought was the last time – the office he'd once shared with the Divinity Connie Beauchamp looking all lost and abandoned. As did Elliot himself.

Elsewhere, Irish Dr Greg and Sahira Shah the Registrah were admitting that they did actually like each other and would miss each other when he was at The Mythical St James' (or the less mythical Spain) and she was forced to cry her way through operations without him. And Hanssen was doing a lot of firefighting over the exploding boobs business.

Michael Spence was left to take the fall for that one (mainly on the say-so of Sir Fraser, who wanted "The Yank" booted out at the earliest opportunity, mainly for the cavalier way he'd treated his daughter, the appalling Lulu). His last piece of ninja-level surgery was to save the eyesight of Mrs Plastic Bhatti. She and Plastic had been involved in a car accident, from which Plastic did not recover. Excuse me if I don't bother mourning his loss.

Anyhoo, the upshot of all this was the very best news – plastic surgery has been put on the back burner (not literally – it would melt) at Holby, and the future is in lovely, gooey, dramatic, sexy heart surgery. Elliot can stay, Jac can continue with her very special mentoring of Young Dr Oliver Valentine and Sahira can try not to cry at just how bloody marvellous everything is. Yay! I'm wearing a smile bigger than anything even Chantelle can come up with.

On the subject of whom, this week she was pressed into action as a party planner for Dull Dan and Chrissie's engagement party, and a lovely job she did of it if you like pink. The balloons were pink, the bubbly was pink – it was all like a metaphor for Chantelle herself. Not feeling at all pink was poor Sacha, who loves Chrissie like a faithful old hound. All I can say to comfort him is – stick around. She will need someone to pick up the pieces when Dull Dan works out that he is, in fact, gay. Or when Chrissie works out that he is, in fact, a twat.

And it was tears all round when Eddi had to say goodbye to Tedious Josh, who set off in his new lightweight wheelchair for Whatever The Future May Hold.

As Elliot so perfectly put it – "Doughnuts all round!"

SERIES 14

Dig us out of this hole

(Series 14, ep. 1 'Keep On Keeping On' by Gillian Richmond 18.10.11)

A new series, and not much has changed (it's only been a week, after all), apart from a few people have had haircuts. Among them is Eddi. Frieda, who so often says what the rest of us have been thinking, asks her if she got tired of the helmet head look. I do love Frieda. I do love Eddi, too, now that Tedious Josh has wheeled off into the sunset. This week Eddi was required to hold her ruler of professionalism against Chrissie to see if she measured up. Chrissie is striving to be a Nurse Practitioner, whatever one of those is (I think it involves wearing a suit, like Mark "Jesus" Williams used to do), and this means she has to pass a module in emergency medicine. Since everyone pretends A&E doesn't exist most of the time, this means AAU and Eddi.

But this was a sub-plot. The meat of the story (vegetarian options are available) concerned Henrik Hanssen's continuing attempts to salvage what's left of the hospital's reputation following the Bogus Boobs Debacle. Sir Fraser (I know I should hate him, but I rather like his icy cold eyes) installed a small team of experts to scrutinise all the hospital's doings. Luckily one of them was an ex nurse, and when he pitched in to help Hanssen in one of those inevitable "Can we have some help here!" moments in a basement corridor, he witnessed the skill and passion of Holby's finest Swedish medic. He couldn't help but be impressed.

Casualty fans may remember a while back when Adam Trueman's "god complex" was illustrated via the medium of a fly trapped behind a glass. Holby treated us to a similarly heavy-handed animal-based metaphor last night when a bird flew at Hanssen's window and apparently expired on the window sill. But wait! At the end we saw its wee wing flicker with life. This touching symbol must mean there's hope for the hospital after all! Just as well, since there are 51 more episodes left in the series. On the subject of the hospital, Hanssen kept calling it Holby General yesterday. Has it always been Holby General? I thought it was Holby City. Anyway, Hanssen is the man who is, singlehandedly, going to save Holby Whatever Hospital. And he's had a haircut, too.

Irish Dr Greg was all perky following his snog with Sahira Shah the Registrah last week, but she has now decided they are to be "just good friends." Cue one very disappointed Irish medic. He did get to leap in an ambulance with her and do some life saving stuff. Was I alone in finding it peculiar that the paramedic who was with the patient didn't utter a word. There was no, "Male, 18, gun shot wound to the chest, GCS was 13 at the scene, he's a Gemini and he has a dog called Paul," like paramedics usually do. This is what happens when you staff your ambulances with non-speaking extras.

And Funny Little Nurse Tait was back from bereavement leave (too soon, surely. Way, way too soon). She was involved in a lot of business about a nun who didn't want to be a nun any more, and this helped her reach a decision in her own life. She's going on holiday. That'll put a smile on her face! Or not.

Keeping the hospital alive, one chunk of bread at a time

(Series 14, ep. 2 'Culture Shock' by Rebecca Wojciechowski 25.10.11)

Last week a little bird injured itself by flying at Henrik Hanssen's window. We thought it was dead, but it wasn't, and it wasn't just a bird, either – it was a metaphor for the very health and survival of the hospital.

This week we found that Hanssen was keeping the metaphorical health and survival of the hospital in his desk drawer and giving it water from a small pipette. This is how much he cares about and nurtures the hospital. He even cut up pieces of bread into small cubes with scissors to feed to it (the bird, not the hospital). So what he didn't need was some jumped-up management type irritating him and the rest of the staff with evacuation drills.

This management type, Mr Swann, was a man so irritating that I found myself actually liking Sahira Shah the Registrah because she stood up to him. Hanssen stood up to him, too, with the best speech of the night. When Swann asked him if he was serious (about the hospital) he said, "I have a level of seriousness beyond your four years hands-on experience in health sector strategic planning…" (tiny pause for maximum sarcastic effect) "..and your diploma in hospitality management." Yowch! That told him. Only it didn't, because people like Swann have a massively inflated idea of their own importance. No wonder all the stress made Hanssen accidentally cut himself later on when trimming bread for his bird. A drop of blood fell on the bread – yes, Hanssen will actually give his own blood to keep that bird/hospital alive.

I am slightly alarmed about the bird in the drawer, though. Having once hand-reared a baby blackbird (I used to live with a lot of vet students), I do wonder whether bread is the best diet and whether Hanssen shouldn't be out in the Linden Cullen Memorial Shrubbery digging up worms. Also I worry that one day he'll open that drawer and the bird will fly out and go smack straight into the window again. That would be bad news for the bird, and dreadful news for the metaphor.

Elsewhere, the glorious Sacha had to resort to trying to pretend a patient wasn't really ill, so she could go to another hospital and get better treatment. Thanks to recent cuts, Holby isn't doing laparoscopic procedures anymore, apparently. This poor girl would have had to have the full surgical shebang and long recovery time, but if Sacha signed her off as fit and well, she'd be able to get sorted out elsewhere. The plan was almost scuppered by Chrissie, who thought Sacha was being inept/unethical. How very dare she think that of The Sweetest Man In The World? Anyway, as soon as she found out what was what she was back on side, because Chrissie is a Good Sort, despite her strange infatuation for Dull Dan.

Look out, New York! The city that never sleeps might just be about to be put to its sternest test. Funny Little Nurse Tait is on her way, and she's planning to stay for some time. She had a leaving party and everything. Presumably people were bribed to attend by Chantelle, because Elizabeth has been the epitome of antisocial miserableness since she set foot in the hospital. Ric Griffin said he'd miss her, but that's because in recent months he's only ever been in a scene if it involves peering over her shoulder. Maybe he'll get a storyline of his own now.

Gimme a break

(Series 14, ep. 3 'Shame' by Graham Mitchell 1.11.11)

First of all, it's good news for the metaphorical and actual bird who was last week living in Henrik Hanssen's desk drawer. It has now graduated to a cage of its own, and is cheeping happily, until Hanssen throws a towel over it to keep it quiet. This is much how he treats his staff. Obviously the diet of bread and Swedish blood have done it the world of good, but I'm still a little nervous that it may fly into the window as soon as it feels ready to fly. Either that or we'll have a poignant moment when we see it soaring across the rooftops of Borehamwood, accompanied by Eva Cassidy singing something heart-tugging.

Anyway, let's not worry about that just yet. There's Michael Spence to worry about first. Returning to Holby for a disciplinary hearing, he found his erstwhile colleagues were giving him the cold shoulder. At Holby, it's not the done thing to look too ambitious. People don't like it when Jac does it, and they don't like it when Michael Spence does it either. His willingness to shaft his colleagues to get his plastics empire up and running has, understandably, miffed the likes of Ric Griffin and Elliot Hope, who are doctors by vocation rather than being in it for the glory or the cash. Of course, it's perfectly possible to be motivated both by helping people and by being the best in your chosen field, and again this is where Jac and Michael are very similar, and what not everyone gets about them. But more of Jac later.

Michael was exonerated by the woman who'd been brought in to probe him, but when he was let loose on the wards again he didn't find his path strewn with muffins and skinny lattes by adoring colleagues (it was Chantelle's day off). When Ric had to deal with a bit of a tricky operation, Michael volunteered his services – he can clip & tie faster than anyone else, you know. Anyway, mid clip & tie he had one of those surgical crises moments where the machines go beep, pressures are dropping, and the surgeon is staring into space and looking confuzzled. I don't want to think that this sort of thing happens in real life, but if it does I hope Ric Griffin is standing at the other side of the table ready to grab those clamps, remove that knackered kidney and save the day.

Michael Spence was about to take all the glory for saving the patient, but in the end he's an honourable man and he didn't. What he did do was tell Hanssen he was resigning. We know from experience that Hanssen won't let anyone resign unless it was his idea first, so he insisted that Michael works his notice. Presumably this is to give him time to experience a mind-changing incident and stay. I hope.

Now to the deeply wonderful Jac Naylor, who was making Young Dr Oliver Valentine jump through hoops as usual. But we saw a softer side of the fragrant Ms Naylor when a paediatrician, who doubles as Jonah's dad on Waterloo Road, asked her to take a look at a wee baby with a heart problem. Jac was all, well, Jac to begin with, but as time went on she rather warmed to the baby's mother, who felt inadequate and was trying hard to do her best for the baby. Having come from a background of total parental abandonment, Jac could sympathise with someone who was actually trying to be a good mother. It's lovely to see Jac's warm and cuddly side. She's even letting Young Dr Oliver Valentine take part in her therapeutic hypothermia project! (Is this where she treats a patient to an icy stare and scares them into getting better? Possibly).

This week Dull Dan managed not to kill or maim anyone (he's getting the hang of this doctoring business), but he managed to really irritate Chrissie with his wedding planning. Chrissie, have a long, hard think about this. It's not the wedding planning that's annoying you, it's the wedding planner. He's all wrong.

And Goth Dr Frieda had a phone call, muttered in Ukrainian a bit and sped off to the Ukraine in some rather fabulous boots. She didn't tell Sacha why she had to take time off in such a hurry. "I didn't think it was my business to ask," he said. You have to love Sacha. (Hello? Chrissie? I said You Have To Love Sacha).

Now, finally, a while back I wondered why Hanssen kept referring to the hospital as "Holby General" when I've always thought it was called Holby City Hospital. This week, TV news reports about Boobgate were referring to it as Holby General, but the sign on the wall clearly says Holby City Hospital. Someone help me out, please – when did it become HG?

You can live without a dysfunctional mother but you can't live without a functioning heart

(Series 14, ep. 4 'Under the Skin' by Rob Williams 8.11.11)

After a seriously arty opening concerning Eddi and a Mysterious Stranger on the roof (more of whom later), the episode settled down to be a true feast for fans of Jac Naylor. And, seriously, what's not to like about Jac Naylor? The motorbike leathers. The feline eyes. The pithy way with a put-down (loved her calling the paediatrician a "nursemaid in a novelty watch"). The breathtakingly brilliant surgical skills. The way she's more than a sum of all these parts because she's vulnerable under the toughness, but you have to look so darn hard to know it.

In short, she's magnificent – a fact not lost on the aforementioned paediatrician, Sean Dolan, who spent the episode flirting like all crazy with her. Brave or foolish or both? Jac was too busy saving her patient's life to seriously notice. The patient in question was Freya, the baby from last week whose mother left her. Jac didn't feel she handled the mother all that well, but she knew she could sort out Freya's medical problems. "You can live without a dysfunctional mother," she said, speaking from experience, "But you can't live without a functioning heart." Everyone agreed that Jac was amazing in the operating theatre, refusing to give up and literally keeping Freya alive by pumping her teeny heart with one gloved hand.

With all this going on, there was hardly any time left to make Young Dr Oliver Valentine jump through hoops, so he was left to wander the corridors of orthopaedics in search of material for his and Jac's supposedly joint study. What he found was a future career path. Seduced by the easy-going world of Dull Dan and his amusing antics with a mallet (not a euphemism), Oliver decided Dan would henceforth be his mentor. Dull Dan could see the attraction. "With Jac as your mentor, orthopaedics probably seems like Center Parcs," he said. Which was exactly Jac's view when she heard what Ollie had decided – but it's safe to assume that Jac would rather extract her own eyeballs with an ice cream scoop than holiday at Center Parcs.

And now we must return to the roof, and its panoramic view over Borehamwood, the Hollywood of Hertfordshire. Eddi was up there recovering from a hangover, and just as well, too. You really need the self-styled Best Nurse In The Hospital on hand when someone is about to throw themselves off the roof. Only he wasn't. Dr Luc Hemingway – for it was he – was merely taking a bit of air before starting his shift. Dr Luc is claustrophobic, and needed a bit of open space before plunging into the murky depths of AAU. Where he again encountered Eddi. Predictably, there was sexual chemistry and predictably they clashed over a patient. Dr Luc has a rather marvellous way about him. He's like a bit of Linden Cullen with a dash of Dan Clifford and just a suspicion of Joseph Byrne. In other words – I like. I like very much. And I liked the way he saved a child's life but didn't feel the need to correct Eddi when she told everyone that she'd done it. Eddi was so busy being the Best Nurse In The Hospital that she didn't notice Luc is claustrophobic, even though he made every excuse not to go into elevators or cupboards. What's the betting he gets locked into one or both in an episode soon?

I simply can't let a good bird metaphor go

(Series 14, ep. 5 'Devil in the Detail' by Marc Pye & Martha Hillier 15.11.11)

If you went looking for the Human Resources department at Holby City Hospital, you'd probably find a couple of stoned people giggling and making model ambulances out of Lego. This is the only explanation for the rather surreal approach to staffing which finds nurses hired on the spot, resignations accepted or not depending on the Director of Surgery's whim, and doctors being allowed to carry on working even though they either aren't qualified (Oliver) or maim people on a regular basis (Dan). And it's the only explanation for theatre liaison manager Gillian Kavanagh (Moya Brady). We were led to believe that Ms Kavanagh had just returned from a period of extended leave caused by either (a) back pain or (b) depression caused in part by Michael Spence insulting her at a barbecue. Had she been theatre liaison manager before? What, exactly, was a theatre liaison manager? Gillian interpreted her role as basically annoying as many surgeons as possible in the shortest possible time.

This was all part of Hanssen's micro management of the hospital, and frankly it didn't work. When a deputation, headed up by Sahira Shah the Registrah, informed him that they'd done quite well without Ms Kavanagh last week and they can definitely do without her next week, he told his staff that the power was now in their hands. Alone again in his plush office, he lifted the cover off his birdcage. Was it now time to let the symbolic bird fly free across the rooftops of The Hollywood of Hertfordshire? He opened the window a tad, and then thought better of it. Either he's just grown awfully fond of his little feathered friend and doesn't want to wave it goodbye, or the scriptwriters were telling us that he hasn't quite loosened his grip on our favourite hospital just yet.

Meanwhile, down on AAU, who's that hunk with the broken wrist? Why, it's none other than the Actor with the Fabulous Name, Lex Shrapnel. AKA Gay Nurse Stephen, who when last seen was doing his level best to prise Dull Dan out of the closet. Any regular viewer could guess what happened next. Chrissie grinned a lot and remained totally oblivious to the fact that her fiance and GNS kept giving each other Meaningful Glances. Dull Dan allowed his judgement to be clouded (what, Dan? No! Surely not) and let GNS walk out of the hospital with a hideously unstable fracture (which he seemed to get bandaged up somewhere between the ward and the car park). Dull Dan then pursued GNS to his taxi, where Irish Dr Greg spotted GNS giving DD an affectionate peck on the cheek, which made him Wonder.

Michael Spence continued his rehabilitation to All Round Good Guy by personally paying for an operation for a man whose surgery had been bumped by Gillian Kavanagh. The fact that the man turned out to be a con man provided amusement for The Malick and Young Dr Oliver Valentine and provided my favourite line of the night (possibly even better than Hanssen's imaginary children, "Little Benny, Bjorn and Agnetha"). "He owes £30 grand. How do you rack up that sort of debt?" Malick wondered. Chantelle knew: "Catalogues," she said.

Like Hanssen and his bird/tight grip on the hospital, Jac was not ready to let Baby Freya go. She feels personally responsible for the wee nipper (did the baby actually say "Mama" at Jac? I think so) and pretended she needed a scan rather than let her go to foster parents. I'm thinking it can only end in tears, and if she really wanted a baby to play with I'm sure Joseph would welcome her to Penrith, where they could play happily with baby whatever-his-name-was.

Tricky trousers to fill

(Series 14, ep. 6 'No Shortcuts' by Stuart Morris 22.11.11)

By leaving CT for orthopaedics, Young Dr Oliver Valentine has managed to shake off those tedious tasks that Jac used to set him. You know, stuff like learning to juggle coins with his fingers and spending long hours suturing bits of pig in the wet lab. Orthopaedics is so much more exciting. You get to do 3D jigsaws. Ok, so it was a skeleton he was piecing together, but it's still a jigsaw.

He also got to do a bit of surgery on a mashed-up fingernail, and I have a complaint here. Please, Holby directors, don't give us close-ups of gory stuff without preparing us with a slightly further-back shot first. I hardly had time to cover my eyes.

I'm waffling about this kind of stuff because, to be honest, it was a bit of a "meh" episode, one of those that comes along every now and again that feels like a bit of filler and doesn't move the story along too much. We got to see a bit more of Dr Luc Hemingway in action. Still grumpy, still locking horns with The Best Nurse In The Hospital. Sahira spent a lot of time telling Greg to keep the hell away from her, but really she was protesting too much – she knows she can't withstand that Irish charm and that beautiful nose for very long. And Chantelle sooo fancies Young Dr Oliver Valentine, and they would be the cutest couple on the planet.

With Jac busy at some meeting or other and Hanssen also absent, there was a dearth of witty lines and it was left to The Malick to fly the flag for ruthless ambition. Upon hearing that Michael Spence had resigned, Malick decided he'd be the best man for Spence's job. As usually happens with these cocky, maverick types, things went tits-up in surgery (not literally – we've finished with all that boob business), and Malick was left to reflect that maybe he has a bit to learn before he's fit to inherit the tight trousers of Holby's favourite American. He'd never fit in them anyway. Far too tight.

The bird has flown and the cat is out of the bag

(Series 14, ep. 7 'See You on the Ice' by Dana Fainaru 29.11.11)

Way back in April I said that Chrissie couldn't possibly marry Dan Hamilton, because then she'd be Christine Hamilton (don't anyone spoil my fun by telling me Chrissie is a Christina). If that was the only reason not to marry Dan Hamilton, Chrissie would be laughing all the way to the registry office. But there's also the inconvenient truth that he's (a) dull and (b) a bit gay. These truths have only remained hidden for so long because Chrissie, bless her, is (c) a bit thick.

After Irish Dr Greg spotted Dull Dan and Gay Nurse Stephen enjoying an intimate moment in the car park (not Malick/locker room type of intimate – not in the car park!) Dan knew he was on borrowed time. What you absolutely don't want in such a precarious situation is for an old friend to turn up, and for her to turn out to be a blabbermouth alcoholic who enjoyed winding Chrissie up. "He hasn't looked you in the eye all day," she told The Future Mrs Hamilton. All year, more like. Dull Dan's eyes are always gently gazing somewhere in the distance, as though he's contemplating a set of rugby goalposts from the far end of the field. When Chrissie had an odd discussion with someone who was supposed to be Dan's best man at the wedding, she realised there was something fishy going on, and she wanted to thrash it out on the Staircase of Secrets. And Dull Dan finally admitted that he does indeed have a roving eye, and not only does it rove to the far end of the rugby field, it has also probably roved to the far ends of a few rugby players over the years. In other words, Chrissie may not be man enough for him.

Casualty's lovely nurse Tess Bateman once spent an entire episode impaled on a metal spike. What Casualty can do, Holby can trump. Two people impaled on the same metal spike (as each other, not as the one Tess Bateman was impaled on. That would be a ridiculous coincidence). It was a father and son human kebab tragedy, and it fell to Sahira Shah the Registrah to sort it out. She needed general surgeon-type help, and she needed the best. Ric Griffin! Er, no. She needed Henrik Hanssen, but it took a bit of persuading to get him to come out of his luxury office, where he has his fruit bowl and his little bird in its cage (quite tame) and his lovely view of the Hollywood of Hertfordshire. Then they couldn't agree about the way to proceed with the case. I think she ended up being right, but I do somewhat glaze over and my eyes unfocus in a Dull Dan style whenever Sahira is on the screen, so I can't be sure. What I can be sure about is that the bird metaphor has literally flown. Hanssen opened his window and let the wee greenfinch soar across the Borehamwood rooftops. It was a beautiful moment. Another thing I can be sure about is Guy Henry's marvellously subtle acting skills. The way he manages to convey that a man who buttons his raincoat right up to the top and carries himself so formally is just crazy in love with a woman he can't have – well, it's masterful.

Elsewhere, Michael Spence was looking a bit grizzled. Was he growing facial hair for Movember, or was it to illustrate his inner turmoil and lack of sleep? He looked pretty good, anyway. This week he was sorting out a previous patient, who was possibly suffering from a leakage in one of Bhatti's batch of bogus boobs. Only she wasn't, and Michael managed to sort out whatever it was she was suffering from, because he's actually a genius doctor. Even The Malick gazes at him in admiration, and you have to be doing well to impress the man with the biggest ego in the NHS.

Chrissie wants to believe Dan, but...

(Series 14, ep. 8 'The Hand that Bites' by Lauren Klee 6.12.11)

Following the previous week's revelations about Dan and his complicated sexuality, Chrissie was, unsurprisingly, having a few doubts about their future together. She thought it might help if she got The Malick to clarify one or two points, but he clarified a bit too much when she realised that Malick and Dan's locker room moment was about five minutes before Chrissie and Dan's store room moment, which was (romantic, this) Their First Time. Chrissie had thought Dan was all combusting with lust over her, but now realises that the fire was actually started by Malick. Frankly, it's not a flattering thought.

She had a wedding dress to try on (in the beautiful city of St Albans), and who better to take with her (since she doesn't have any female friends) than the wonderful Sacha and their mutual child Daniel. Sacha was absolutely glorious, trying on a veil, giving a lovely rendition of something from Fiddler on the Roof in quite an acceptable baritone and just generally being adorable. How can Chrissie not see that Dan, whether gay, straight, bi or whatever, will never be half the wonderful human being Sacha is?

Henrik Hanssen treated us to a bit of Swedish this week, and he wanted to treat Sahira Shah the Registrah to a bit more Swedish by taking her to Sweden to a medical conference. She was going to go as well, because apparently the Stockholm opera house takes her breath away, but then she realised it was her wedding anniversary. So she told Hanssen he'd have to go on his own. Jac did volunteer her services. "I have a glittering array of pre-dinner anecdotes in my arsenal," she said, and I can quite imagine she has. Hanssen, however, felt he would rather be accompanied by someone who didn't have the temperament of "a disgruntled barracuda." Jac thinks she and Hanssen are rather alike, what with being cool, logical types who don't go all shouty and emotional the whole time like certain registrahs. They'd work well together. Hanssen was less convinced. "It'd be like staring into the abyss," he said, with the tiniest shudder.

And Chantelle failed her driving test, which made her go all sensible and unsmiley for about five minutes, until Ric Griffin harnessed her sunshine to take care of a patient and she realised that being a joy spreader is her main specialism. And somehow she managed to get Ric Griffin to agree to give her driving lessons. Well, he didn't so much agree as fail to disagree, which was enough of a green light for Chantelle. "Should I kiss you?" she grinned at the grizzled general surgeon. "Not... necessarily," he told her.

The ex factor

(Series 14, ep. 9 'Personal Injury' by Tahsin Guner 13.12.11)

Of all the hospitals in all the towns in all the world, Malick's ex, Paul, walked into Holby. He did walk, as well, because he was a relative rather than a patient. He was the brother of a man who'd knackered his kidney in a car accident. No problem for The Malick, who would whip it out. After all, a person can live quite happily with one kidney.

The problem (yes, of course there was a problem – this is Holby) was that one of his two kidneys had rather been earmarked for future use by Paul, who was in the throes of kidney failure. Whip it out and Paul probably dies. Don't whip it out and the brother dies. It would be a dilemma for any surgeon, but when it concerns your first love… It turned out that Malick hadn't been entirely nice to Paul and had dumped him as soon as things started getting serious. They were young, and Malick had his glittering career as The Biggest Ego in the NHS ahead of him. You know how it is. These days, Malick is a tad older and a tad wiser, and he decided he could save both brothers by only removing a teeny weeny bit of kidney in a ninja-level, high risk procedure. When we last saw him he was hunkering down in the wet lab with a tray of kidneys and a packet of crisps. I assume the crisps were to keep him going nutritionally, and the kidneys were to practice on, rather than the other way round. Just before he dived into the offal and snacks, his face assumed A Look which suggested he has a lot emotionally invested in the future health of Paul. Awww, Antoine – just an old romantic at heart.

Another ego on a stick who's been getting rather emotional recently is our Jac, who has rather become besotted by baby Freya. Possibly because, like Young Dr Oliver Valentine, Freya has big blue eyes. And, unlike Young Dr Oliver Valentine, she doesn't answer back. Anyway, Freya's mother wanted her back, and social services and the paediatrician who flirts with Jac agreed. Jac didn't agree. She knows what it's like to be abandoned, then kind of reclaimed, then abandoned again by a feckless mother.

It all ended with Freya being reunited with her mother, but not before we'd been treated to the once-in-a-lifetime sight of Jac sitting on Santa's knee. Holding a baby. And smiling.

Meanwhile, Chrissie was running from one well-known gay staff member (Malick) to the next (Gay Nurse Stephen – Chrissie has finally started to notice how he and Dull Dan smoulder at each other) to try and get reassurance that Dan only has eyes for her. Sadly neither of them was in a mood to indulge her dithering. Frankly, if you're so unconvinced about your loved one practically on Wedding Eve, it should be a clue that a wedding is not the best idea. Where is Goth Dr Frieda when we need some truth-saying around the place? In her absence it was left to a patient to voice what we've all been thinking. "What you need is a real man," he advised Chrissie. This was just before she had to re-glue his wig on, the point being that we've all got something to hide.

There was also a comedy obstetrician, Dr Samuel Tyler, who was rather marvellous. He was played by Fraser Burrows and I liked him a lot. Ideally what I'd like would be more scenes set in Obs & Gynae, with a staff team of Dr Samuel Tyler, Paradis Bloom and the magnificent Mubbs. What with that and my Jac/Joseph Christmas special idea, I should really be on the editorial team at Holby. No, really, I should.

The right man for the job

(Series 14, ep. 10 'Half Empty' by Andrew Holden 20.12.11)

Oh, the irony. Chrissie took delivery of the cake topper for her wedding cake, and when unpacked it turned out to be a groom & groom gay version. How splendid that these things exist, but not splendid for Chrissie, already a bit troubled by the idea of Dan and Malick's locker-room-lip-locking. Not the best mood in which to sit down to write a wedding speech – apparently Mark "Jesus" Williams can't make the wedding (Christmas is such a busy time for "Jesus"), so Dan thought Chrissie should make a speech in his place.

Help was at hand, however, in the form of the ever-dependable and utterly wonderful Sacha, who used to be a bit of a wordsmith at school. And what did he come up with? "When you walk into a room the rest of the world stops and all I can see is you." He was talking about her! Oh, Chrissie, love (as "Jesus" would say, shaking his head sorrowfully), what are you doing even contemplating marrying a man who has no idea who he is or what he wants, when you've got possibly the loveliest man in the world crazy about you?

It wasn't Sacha, a cake topper, or even "Jesus," but actress Maureen Lipman who really set Chrissie thinking. Maureen played a photographer whose brain tumour surgery was probably going to leave her blind. She was such a positive, feisty type, and a lot of it was due to her rock-solid relationship with her husband. With this template of marital perfection in front of her, Chrissie finally saw the light and told Dan she can't marry him. We'll permit ourselves a small "Yay!" at this point.

Meanwhile, Malick was breaking all sorts of rules to get the kidney that his ex, Paul, desperately needed. He was even thinking about donating one of his own kidneys. Then Paul's brother died, so Paul could get one of his kidneys after all. So the brother died, Paul survived, Malick admitted Paul was "the one," and Ric Griffin and Michael Spence got all huffy and cross about ethical issues. And it was Michael's last day, as well. He packed his belongings into one of those regulation-sized boxes that are issued for taking personal effects from an office and left the building. Only we shouldn't mourn his passing too soon, as a glimpse at next week's cast listing reveals he's still around (another "Yay!").

I wonder if new F1 Kip Maxwell will still be around next week, or whether he was just parachuted in to make Jac realise she wasn't over baby Freya? Dr Kip Maxwell's issue was that he was a father of twins. Jac refused to make allowances for him needing to answer the phone when his wife called, which almost ended in upset when the wife ended up giving birth prematurely to another set of twins and he almost didn't know about it, because Jac had made him throw his phone into a laundry basket. All a bit silly, really, and one of those weeks when casual viewers who don't know and love Jac like we know and love her would be saying, "That woman is such a cow!"

Warms the cockles of your heart

(Series 14, ep. 11 'Wise Men' by Justin Young 27.12.11)

A glorious episode with a triple fairytale ending – Sacha finally getting the woman of his dreams (it was Chrissie), and Frieda and Michael Spence heading back to Holby, where they rightly belong.

Chrissie seemed determined to scupper the happily-ever-after, though. After a deft bit of jazzy piano playing in the bar from Sacha (who knew?), Chrissie's eyes went all twinkly and she realised she was in love with the cuddly father of her child. Sacha wasn't convinced and asked her to name one thing she loved about him. And she couldn't! Idiot, idiot woman. I could have named at least ten without thinking. So Chrissie headed off to the airport with Daniel, en route to Sydney. She was in luck as well – you can't usually get a flight to Sydney from Stansted, but they'd apparently laid one on specially for her. We just knew Sacha would end up hurtling to the airport to catch up with her, the chase to the airport being very much a staple of the Heartwarming Romance, but we never guessed he'd do it on the back of Jac's motorbike. "That was the most terrifying 40 minutes of my life," Sacha said. Then we had the proper romantic ending, with Sacha listening to a message on his phone from Chrissie, who'd had a little think and could now tell him what she loved about him (she forgot the bit about him being a squashy snuggle bear, but otherwise her list was similar to mine). What a shame she was on the ImagineAir flight to Sydney! Only she wasn't, of course. She was behind him, still looking all twinkly, and it was snowing and everything. Squeeee!

Meanwhile, Elliot Hope had been summoned to Kiev to give a lecture, only he hadn't really. He'd been summoned to save the life of Goth Dr Frieda's former mentor. It took him a while to find this out, during which he came across a young boy who badly needed the services of a top notch plastic surgeon. Who you gonna call? Michael Spence, that's who. Having been en route to Florida, he arrived in the Ukraine in his usual tight trousers and skinny jacket combo, without a hotel room to his name, and ended up having to borrow Elliot's PJ's and half his bed, like a medical Morecambe & Wise.

They needed an assistant who could speak English, which meant Frieda had to face the former mentor's wife, who blamed her for letting her daughter die several years previously. Of course it hadn't really been Frieda's fault, and of course she performed wonders in both operating theatres, helping to sort out the young boy and then hand cranking a retro heart bypass machine and saving the life of her mentor. I must say, Kiev looked lovely and made me rather want to visit, but I'd take out top of the range medical insurance first, as the state hospital was not depicted as being terribly pleasant and was somewhat lacking in facilities. Even the surgical masks and gowns were made of rougher fabric than we normally see on Holby.

Elliot, Michael and Frieda celebrated with a paper cup of vodka, and Elliot wondered whether Frieda might be persuaded to return to Holby. There'd be little point, she said, as Michael Spence was no longer there. But wait! Michael, like Chrissie, had been having a little think about The Future and Priorities and that, and decided he would go back and face the Swede and eat some humble pie. He reckoned there was still room for a "shiny suited cowboy" at Holby and thought there'd also be room for "a Ukrainian emo with an attitude problem," too. Luckily she agreed, so we start the new year with Sacha happy and Michael and Frieda back where they belong. As Hanssen so beautifully put it, "It warms the cockles of your heart."

Sexual tension x3

(Series 14, ep. 12 'When the Hangover Strikes' by Joe Ainsworth 3.1.12)

After last week's festive and romantic journeys to the Ukraine and Stansted, we were back in Holby this week, and the place was seething with sexual tension.

Young Dr Oliver Valentine realised, as Jac had told him he would, that relocating dislocated shoulders and listening to Dan blathering on all day did not make him happy. When he had a bone patient with a cardiac complication, he was only too keen to get back to Darwin and make Bambi eyes at Jac over an operating table. Oliver and Jac really do have the best eyes for gazing at each other above surgical masks, and they spark off each other beautifully. There's obviously an attraction. She enjoys putting him in his place and being superior, but she loves it even more when he kicks against it and stands up to her. He rather loves it that she's a bitch and she pushes him to be better. And at the end of the episode he told her he wanted to come back to Darwin permanently, so expect a good deal more of this sort of thing in coming weeks.

On AAU, The Best Nurse In The Hospital, Eddi McKee (can I start calling her BNITH, please? I feel an acronym gap in my life since FLNT went to NYC) had a hangover and squabbled with Dr Luc Hemingway about how best to treat an alcoholic patient. They have a love/hate relationship, those two do, but because they're both fairly new I don't feel like I understand what attracts them to each other as well as I understand Jac and Oliver. Anyway, she told him she can't work with him any longer and AAU isn't big enough for both of them, so she reckons she's going to move to another ward. I hope it's not Darwin. There's already too much hysteria and passion up there courtesy of Sahira Shah the Registrah.

Ah, Sahira. Still capable of turning The Swedish Scalpel into a smorgasbord of unrequited longing, and also exerting a powerful attraction over Irish Dr Greg. This week, what with it being new year and everything, Irish Dr Greg decided he wanted to give up smoking. Luckily one of his patients was a professional hypnotist, so Greg paid him to hypnotise him to give up his nasty habit (smoking, not Sahira). That naughty Registrah asked the hypnotist to get Greg to be super-nice to a pain-in-the-backside patient who may or may not have been a mystery shopper, and Greg played along for his own amusement because – and, oh, we did laugh – the hypnotism didn't work. If you asked me to explain the attraction between Greg and Sahira I would say that she likes him because he has a gorgeous nose and the old Irish charm, and he likes her because she's female.

The champagne's chilling in the mini fridge

(Series 14, ep. 13 'Hide Your Love Away' by Rebecca Wojciechowski 10.1.12)

It was The Big Day at Holby. The day when they finally found out whether they'd achieve Foundation Trust status. It was a big deal, because without it they wouldn't get funding for research and equipment and Holby would die a slow death. Hanssen was confident, though. He even had a bottle of champagne in the mini fridge in his office, as we could see from the fridge cam cunningly placed inside it.

The day didn't start too well when the person who turned up to do the assessment was the horrible one whom I previously described as being "so stern he made Henrik Hanssen look like Graham Norton." The day didn't start too well for Irish Dr Greg, either, as he had a hangover and was put in charge of Darwin for the day. It got even worse when Sahira Shah the Registrah went off to pick up her adorable little son Indy from nursery and then news came in of a nasty car crash and a child with a coat labelled Indy was brought into the hospital. Greg went from being frantic that there was no Registrah present when the CTU Traumafone rang, to being frantic that the woman of his dreams may just have ended up tangled in some wreckage on one of Holby's highways. Greg was worrying about Sahira, Hanssen was worrying about Sahira and Jac was annoyed that everyone was busy worrying rather than knuckling down and suturing arteries. All this worry was a bit previous, though, because Sahira and her adorable son Indy were fine. She'd simply been at the scene of the accident and had been helping out, and gave the injured child Indy's coat to wear. How we all chuckled and heaved sighs of relief. Greg ended up kissing her (again) then they had one of those "let's pretend that never happened" conversations (again), and Jac finally got them to knuckle down to some artery suturing.

There was a feeling of deja vu hanging round this episode. As well as Greg and Sahira kissing and then pretending they didn't care about each other (again), we had another of Chantelle's attempts to be less sunny and more efficient. Malick gave her an "effective directive" and told her to care a bit less. That was never going to work, even when faced with a patient with a particularly annoyingly whiny voice. When are Chantelle's colleagues going to realise that her sweet nature is her biggest asset? Her smile alone probably has healing qualities.

The same can't be said for Goth Dr Frieda, who was in a particularly grumpy mood because Dr Luc Hemingway had caused the self-styled Best Nurse in the Hospital to be transferred to another ward, and AAU is so much less amusing without Eddi and her comedy facial expressions. Dr Luc was not impressed with his first experience of the charms of Frieda. "Ukrainian. Six words for cabbage and not one for excuse me," he said. Lucky for him she didn't rush straight off to HR to file a complaint of racism. She and Dr Luc disgreed about the treatment of a boy with a squirrel up his nose (not a real squirrel – that would be difficult enough with a modestly sized red squirrel and pretty much impossible with the more common grey squirrel. This was a small toy one). Isn't that the kind of thing that they would have whipped out in moments in A&E? Sometimes I don't quite get the point of AAU.

Anyway, very much against the odds, the stern man was impressed and "Holby City now has 'foundation trust' in its title," as Elliot proudly announced. And we were back to the fridge cam in Hanssen's office, to see him withdrawing his bottle of champagne. Did he crack it open with the senior staff and enjoy a bit of back-slapping and banter about the day? No, he did what he usually does with his foodstuffs and enjoyed it alone, quietly at his desk. That man is no fool.

Completely professional in the face of romantic disaster
(Series 14, ep. 14 'She's Electric' by Martha Hillier 17.1.12)

Much of this episode centred on the efforts of Eddi McKee, the Best Nurse in the Hospital, to find a niche that was appropriate to her massive and varied talents. She loves the hurly burly and excitement of AAU, because it's not a good day's work till someone's been sick on your shoes, but she can't stand Dr Luc Hemingway. So she goes off to Keller, where you have time to do a quick sudoku between ward rounds. There's no pesky Hemingway there, with his know-it-all attitude (don't you just hate a know-it-all?). But of course the Best Nurse in the Hospital is entirely wasted in a ward where people are quietly recovering from bowel resections and it's not long before she's back in AAU, bravely leading the troops through a power cut. With all this to-ing and fro-ing, you wouldn't think she'd get any time to do any actual nursing, but she's the Best, so she does. And she's got time to get all cross with Dr Luc when he makes more of his irritating assumptions about a patient. He's even more irritating when he turns out to be right.

Meanwhile, Irish Dr Greg spent the episode staring mournfully at Sahira Shah the Registrah as she swished past him on her way to various urgent bedside moments. Dr Greg loves Sahira, but he doesn't think she loves him back, what with the husband and the adorable little son Indy and everything. She's even planning to leave Holby! (We'll help her pack!). So Greg does what anyone would do, and goes to Dull Dan for advice. DD says he should be, like him, "Completely professional in the face of romantic disaster." If Dan can keep calm and carry on while his erstwhile fiancee is on honeymoon with the man of her dreams who isn't him, Greg can surely cope with a little knock-back from a registrah. Only Greg can't. He's Irish, and they have passion and poetry running through them like the word Blackpool runs through rock. Just ask Bono. In a strangely shot scene outside Hanssen's office, where Greg looks close one second and far away the next, he declares his love for Sahira. He knows her so well, he says, that he knows she constantly hums CBeebies theme tunes. Well, if she does I've never heard her. But that's love for you.

Not a lot of Jac this week, as she had to knock Oli's research project into shape so she was wearing a virtual Do Not Disturb sign. But she did have time to utter what will be our motto of the week: "Punctuality is next to godliness. Which is just one rung below consultant." Got to love her.

The indecisive registrah

(Series 14, ep. 15 'Butterflies' by Paul Matthew Thompson 24.1.12)

In the little recap segment at the beginning of the episode, we were once again shown Greg and Sahira's kiss from a couple of weeks ago. Nope, it's no good. No matter how many times I watch it, it's still not conveying passion, or a tragic love that can never be. It's not a Jac/Joseph kind of kiss. Or a Connie/Jayne Grayson's husband kind of kiss. They looked like a pair of reasonably attractive crash test dummies had been superglued at the lips.

And if you don't buy the intended passion in that kiss, frankly the whole Sahira and Greg storyline is a bit of a damp squib. Tedious, then, that the episode revolved around them revolving around each other. They want to be together, but Sahira has "everything to lose," what with the adorable son Indy, the invisible husband Rafi and... whatever. They had to go to a fundraising do, which gave Sahira the chance to wear a posh frock and gave them the chance to get drunk together and then get to the door of Sahira's room and almost give in to temptation, until they were interrupted by a timely text from Hanssen. Presumably this means that they'll spend the next episode with Greg trotting after her bleating, "Sahira! Sahira!" and she'll spend the episode muttering at him that it's got to stop and he must keep his distance. Again.

Back at Holby, Goth Dr Frieda was worried that she hadn't completed the assessments she needs to graduate from being an F1 to an F2, so she was given a tricky patient to diagnose and Michael Spence (still wearing the grizzly beard look and frankly looking a bit foxy) promised to get the assessment to Hanssen before the deadline. Frieda's patient was a very bad stand up comedian, but you just knew all the best punchlines would be Frieda's. It's her deadpan delivery. Weirdly, though, Dr Luc Hemingway had to talk her through intubating her patient. Wasn't that the sort of thing she was doing with her eyes shut when we still thought she was a nurse?

It was also a testing time for Chantelle, who had her driving test. Ric Griffin has been following through on his promise to give her driving lessons, and it paid off. Is our Ric getting a tiny bit fond of the World's Sunniest Nurse? He was staring down from the Window of Regret as she came back from her test, but maybe he was just making sure she didn't crash into his car again.

This was the first visit to the famous Window in quite a few weeks. I've missed it. Will Greg use it as a vantage point from which to stare longingly at the form of the divine Sahira as she heads off for Nottingham next week? We can but hope.

Shake yourself by the hand

(Series 14, ep. 16 'Here and Now' by Matthew Bardsley 31.1.12)

The power of love, eh? A force so immense and marvellous that at least five people have had a hit single about it. It's a force that's reduced Irish Dr Greg from being a rogueish charmer with a twinkle in his eye to being a moping, dopey fool constantly sighing about his unattainable love. If the unattainable love was Jac Naylor, I'd understand it, but it's only Sahira Shah the Registrah, a woman who has done little to impress us apart from show off her brilliant parachute stitching, cry a lot and bring cupcakes in for the staff.

Greg's devastating sex appeal hasn't been enough to convince the Registrah that he is the man for her. His witty banter and ever-available shoulder to cry on haven't done it either. What's a lovesick boy to do? Run off to Hanssen and try to get him to convince her not to leave, that's what. As if that's going to make him look any less spineless than he does already.

It's not a bad plan, as plans go, because Hanssen not only harbours fond feelings for the world's most emotional CT surgeon himself, but he also has Influence. Such is the reach of his mighty power that Sahira's invisible husband, Rafi, has now been offered a job at Holby. Well, they haven't had a proper anaesthetist since Annalese and Weird Dr Green left. Though his invisibility may present a bit of a challenge in theatre. Now Rafi has no reason to go to Nottingham and Sahira can stay under the wretched gaze of Hanssen and Irish Dr Greg for a bit longer. That's the plan, anyway.

Meanwhile, everybody's favourite Ukrainian emo, Goth Dr Frieda, had her F1 results. Things didn't look good, as she was summoned to Hanssen's office. Had she failed? She thought so, but no – she'd passed with the highest score in the region. Top F1 in the whole of Holbyshire! Or Wyvern District or whatever it is. Hurrah! After hearing this good news, Frieda felt it was only polite to give Hanssen a little compliment in return. "Nice job… running the hospital," she told him. "Shake yourself by the hand."

Chrissie and Sacha were back from their holiday in Australia, and looking all tanned and lovey-dovey. Sacha's attempt to be nice to Dull Dan backfired a little when Dan assumed Chrissie had told Sacha about Dan's complicated sexuality. It all ended amicably when Dan supported Sacha when a patient accused him of causing her to get an infection during surgery. This patient was a horse breeder, and in possibly the most blatant example of speaking-your-brains I've ever heard on Holby, she told Dan about a stallion she had who was somewhat reluctant to do his stallionly duty. "You can't fight nature, can you?" she said. This caused Dan to assume his Thinking Face.

Brains duly spoken by a gangrenous foot

(Series 14, ep. 17 'The Best Man' by Martha Hillier 7.2.12)

Ooh, but I loved this episode. There was so much going on. So many amusing sets of sparring people, so many funny lines, I hardly even noticed Jac Naylor wasn't there.

To Dull Dan first of all (he's a bit less dull these days, but it's so hard to let a good nickname go). Last week we had his sexual orientation being illustrated via the metaphor of a reluctant stallion. Apparently that was not enough to make Dan properly think about whether he's a gay man trapped in a dull man's body, so this week's speak-your-brains came courtesy of a woman with a gangrenous foot. If she didn't deal with it, Dan told her, it would have to come off. "What you don't deal with will eat you away," somebody said (it might even have been Dan himself). In case that was too subtle, Malick weighed in with, "Ignore it till it goes toxic." Dan's Thinking Face was in position for a great deal of the episode, apart from when it was replaced by his Confuzzled Face. This was generally thanks to Mary-Claire (hurrah! Given a bit of screen time at last), who spent the episode winding him up. As did Malick. "Orthapaedics. Real man's work!"

Goth Dr Frieda is rather like Sacha, in the sense that she lights up any scene she's in. Not bad for a surly Ukrainian emo. She also brings out the best in the other people in the scene, mainly because her bullshit detector is so finely tuned and so ruthless that people can't get away with any pompous nonsense. When Frieda's around, Eddi's rather fun and forgets she's supposed to be The Best Nurse in the Hospital and all the pressures that involves. One of the very best partnerships is Frieda and Michael Spence. They play off each other beautifully, Michael seeming to get Frieda's humour and appreciate her no-crap integrity. So it was a bit upsetting to discover that this was Frieda's last day on AAU. New consultant Alex Broadhurst (Sasha Behar) thought Frieda should try to get a place on Darwin. While there are a few up there (yes, you, Sahira) who could do with Frieda's brand of telling-it-like-it-is, I really want her to stay on AAU. So does Michael. "I'm gonna miss you, Petrenko," he told her, adding, "I can't believe I just said that."

Michael had other worries, as Hanssen, with his usual penchant for treating people rather like chess pieces, decided the clinical lead position should be open to competition. The competition includes the aforementioned Alex Broadhurst, who is seriously competent and doesn't have a murky background of exploding boobs to blot her copybook.

In the absence of Sahira, Greg channelled his energies into being horrible to Dr Oliver Valentine. He kept getting little digs in about Oli being under Jac Naylor's thumb (hello? Oli is not the one who spends most of his time wandering the corridors bleating, "Sahira! Sahira!"), but Oli had the last laugh when his and Jac's research project on therapeutic hypothermia came in handy and saved his patient's life. Oliver was really sweet with this patient. Her baby had been stillborn and she carried the ashes everywhere in a little urn. While Irish Dr Greg could only manage a very wooden, "I'm sorry for your loss," when she told him, Oli took the time to listen and help her. He's very good at all that touchy-feely stuff.

Don't let us down, Dr Valentine

(Series 14, ep. 18 'Awarded' by Matthew Barry 14.2.12)

As befits Valentine's Day, much of the episode centred on the man we know fondly as Young Dr Valentine. He and Jac were up for an award for their therapeutic hypothermia project (or he thought they were) and, as happens occasionally with Young Dr V, hubris got the better of him and the glory of being a doctor up for an award overshadowed the everyday glory of being a doctor who makes people better. Not that he didn't look adorable in a dinner jacket, though. But he got quite snappy with Elliot in theatre and was even brusque with Chantelle. Being brusque with Chantelle is like stamping on a kitten at the best of times, and was made even worse because she has a bit of a thing for Ollie and his fabulous blue eyes. It was a love that could never be, Lleucu advised her, what with Ollie being a doctor and being all posh and that, and Chantelle being Northern and a nurse. "You've been watching Downton Abbey again," Chantelle said. Chantelle was believing in a classless Britain and a world where doctors and nurses could live in perfect harmony (hello! Chrissie and Sacha!), but then a patient made her feel she ought to be happy to be a 'umble nurse and not get ahead of herself. And she fell out with Lleucu, because she thought she was making a move on Ollie, when she was actually only trying to intercede on Chantelle's behalf. Good grief, has she not read any Jane Austen? Ermm, probably not... I was glad Chantelle and Lleucu sorted out their little misunderstanding, though, because it's always nice to have a bit of friendly camaraderie between the nurses.

Meanwhile, Dr Oliver Valentine was arriving at the awards ceremony just in time to see Jac (looking, in Ollie's well chosen word, "Wow") picking up an award. But it wasn't for the therapeutic hypothermia project. It was for "Mentor of the Year." Say what? I can only assume that award was voted for by Henrik Hanssen or some other sadist, because Jac's mentoring style is harsh, to say the least.

But do you know what? Gosh darn, it may be harsh but it's effective. Ollie may have picked up some of Jac's bad habits (like referring to minions as "You"), but he's turning into a heck of a doctor. He returned to the hospital to apologise to Elliot and was praised for his superb spotting of a super-rare heart cancer. "I shall continue to keep a very close eye on your future, Dr Valentine," said Hanssen. It sounds like a threat but it was actually high praise.

Elsewhere, Sacha had money worries. He and Chrissie wanted to buy a lovely new house in one of the better parts of Holby (in other words not the Farmead Estate) and Sacha had an insurance policy that would just nicely cover the deposit. Only it wouldn't, because he wasn't able to access the money for several more years. But how to tell Chrissie and bring her dreams of a lovely school for Daniel in a leafy suburb come crashing to the ground? Sacha decided not to until he had a Plan B in place – he's going to take up the slack on Michael Spence's Tuesday morning Botox surgery. Selling his soul to the devil of private cosmetic practice for the sake of being in a good catchment area – oh, Sacha.

Best line of the night: Michael Spence was asked to give a talk about medicine to some of the local youths. "Do I look like a babysitter?" he complained to Eddi. "No," she said, "You look like someone who sleeps with the babysitter."

An operating theatre full of my admirers

(Series 14, ep. 19 'What You Wish For' by Philip Ralph 21.2.12)

Finally, finally we got a glimpse of Sahira Shah the Registrah's invisible husband Rafi. What have we learned? (a) He's not invisible. (b) His surname is not Shah, it's Raza (or "Razzer," in Irish Dr Greg-speak) and (c) he mumbles. That's about all we've learned, really. "Have you met Rafi?" Sahira said to Jac, by way of introducing them. "I've heard almost nothing about you!" said Jac. Having met Rafi myself now (televisually speaking), I can see why he wouldn't be a major talking point.

Irish Dr Greg was not pleased with the appearance of Dr Razzer, but at least it stopped him wandering the corridors uttering his desperate cry of "Sahira! Sahira!" Instead he was reduced to Gazing Mournfully and rescheduling people's operations to try and avoid his beloved Registrah. Of course it all went tits-up in theatre, when an under-age patient turned out to have an allergy he hadn't thought of mentioning to the aforementioned Dr Razzer when he did his pre-op checks. Speaking of which, isn't it funny how, when we have a main character who's an anaesthetist (Zubin, Annalese) they're always hovering around the wards and ITU. But the rest of the time, anaesthetists are confined to sitting at the head end during operations and not saying much.

Sahira had to pitch in and help save the patient, and Hanssen paid a visit to loom at everyone through the glass, so we had an operating theatre full of Sahira's admirers. I'm not including the scrub nurse in this, but she can't be immune to the charms of the Registrah, surely?

At the end of the episode, Hanssen marked Greg's card about tampering with other people's relationships – which is rich, coming from the man who schemed to have the invisible Rafi installed in Holby just so he could keep Sahira close by.

Meanwhile, in parts of the hospital where they care less about Sahira, Frieda found herself being mentored by Dull Dan. Her somewhat maverick style and – let's face it – superior doctorly instincts got up Dan's nose, but not as much as her closeness to Malick. Our Dan was just an eensy bit jealous, but whether it's because he's still hankering after a bit of hot Malick action or whether he's just jealous of Antoine's relaxed mentoring style I'm not sure.

And in other news, Michael Spence is going to be sharing the clinical lead job with New Dr Alex. And Sacha has been forced to store lots of his precious bits and bobs in the hospital basement, because Chrissie can't be doing with his clutter (it doesn't bode well for the longevity of their relationship, frankly). There's an armchair down there and a skeleton and everything. It looks so darn cosy he ought to consider renting it out to Dr Luc Hemingway, at least for the colder months. It's got to be better than a mobile home in the hospital car park.

If something works, why not use it?

(Series 14, ep. 20 'Fight the Good Fight' by Justin Young & Paul Matthew Thompson 28.2.12)

Darwin were having a clear-out of some old machines – the ones that go beep, only they don't beep as loudly as today's more modern, shinier versions, so they had to go. You didn't have to be a long time student at the Holby University of Televisual Medicine to know this was all really just an analogy for dear old Elliot Hope and his charming old-fashioned ways, but just in case you missed it the daughter of a patient was on hand to spell it out in nice big letters. "If something works, why not use it?" she said, of the machinery and of Elliot. She and her father had travelled from Kiev, and we know that Kiev's state hospitals are not over-endowed with machinery of any type. The father, Petro, had a serious heart condition (of course), and he and his daughter had come to find Elliot on the recommendation of the doctor he met at Christmas.

Would Elliot go out on a limb and offer surgery to a person who wasn't, strictly speaking, entitled to it? Of course he would, even if it meant going against Hanssen's orders and making Jac go all disapprovingly tutty. She wouldn't tell Hanssen the surgery was going ahead, though. "I'm a bitch, not a snitch," she told Elliot. Mind you, Elliot did have a brief wobble in mid procedure, but he pulled himself together enough to come up with the idea of using glue on the old man's dodgy ticker. I think it possibly shows I've been watching Holby too long when I tell you I came up with the glue idea about two minutes before Elliot did. Just ask PLA Jr. So Elliot saved the patient, and decided to parcel up all the old machines and send them to Kiev, where they'll be put to good use.

Speaking of old stuff, Sacha invited Dr Luc Hemingway to join him in his basement, and there they sat playing video games and bonding like Joey and Chandler on Friends. Eddi was in charge of looking after the key, and everyone was happy. Only Sacha wasn't properly happy, because he loves Chrissie yet he couldn't tell her about his secret basement den and his moonlighting job on Holby Care. But then one of his Botox patients ended up in AAU with a nasty rash (it was caused by a virus and was nothing to do with Sacha's bogus Botox technique) and Chrissie found out about his money-making sideline. And thanks to Eddi she found out about the basement. Was she angry? Possibly with herself for being such a dragon that Sacha didn't feel he could be himself around her. She told him to lock the door. Sacha and I both thought she had romance on her mind and, frankly, that basement room is probably the only room in the hospital she hasn't had sex in already, so for the sake of completeness it was worth a go. But no, she wanted to play his computer game. Oh, how we laughed.

While all this was going on, Hanssen was attempting to schmooze the Vice Chancellor of Holby University in an attempt to secure £12 million of funding. While he was doing this, he put Malick in charge of his clinical duties. "I need you to be me for the day," he told his registrar. Malick was up for that. "Involves a lot of looming and scaring the life out of baby doctors," he said, accurately. He had some baby doctors to scare, as well. He referred to them as Malickites. He and Dull Dan disagreed over how to treat a patient (it's now compulsory for someone to disagree with Dull Dan about how to treat a patient on a weekly basis), and Hanssen backed Malick. The woman from the university backed Dan, as she knew of him and his rugger skills (that's rugger skills) previously. She admired his rugger skills so much, in fact, that she wanted him to become Clinical Skills Lead. If she'd seen him in action as much as we have, she'd know "clinical" and "skills" weren't usually to be found in the same sentence when Dan is around. Hanssen thought Malick should be CSL. And guess what? Thanks to Hanssen, they've both got the job. Having to share a job and possibly an office with The Malick is going to make Dan twice as twitchy as usual.

What a start to a career

(Series 14, ep. 21 'Fresh Blood' by Rob Kinsman 5.3.12)

This week's New Member of Staff was F1 Tara. I liked Tara – she fainted while helping Young Dr Oliver Valentine pull a shard of glass out of a woman's abdomen. I'd have fainted too – partly because I'm squeamish, and partly because there's hardly anything more thrilling than Young Dr Oliver Valentine when he's being all competent and that. Tara suffered, or benefitted, from a bit of good cop/bad cop mentoring. Jac was as delicious as usual. Tara: "Hi! I'm Tara Lo, the new F1!"Jac: "Ugh." Ollie was rather more encouraging, which was badly needed after Tara almost killed a patient (though the patient didn't die and it hadn't been Tara's fault anyway).

I'm getting good at this medical lark. Last week I was suggesting using glue to fix a heart problem even before Elliot came up with the idea, and this week I diagnosed an aortic aneurysm about five minutes before Eddi and Luc worked it out. The owner of the aneurysm was a friend of Luc's, who was kind of casually employed as a security guard for Luc's mobile home. I may be good at cardio-thoracics, but I'm not so hot on psychology, because it's taken me till this week to realise that Luc's mobile home-dwelling is part of his claustrophobia. In the middle of trying to save his friend's life, he even had to take his shoes off in theatre because he was feeling a bit restricted. Eddi is being drawn to his quirky charms like a moth to a flame – but she really needs to do something with her hair first.

And Chantelle and Lleucu (or "Flakes") had a little falling-out over money, when Chantelle spent her flat deposit money on a holiday to Ibiza with some mates who weren't Flakes. But, like their last little spat, they sorted it out in the end.

Work mode

(*Series 14, ep. 22 'The Ties That Bind' by Graham Mitchell 13.3.12*)

To start with a handy, pocket-sized summary: No Jac, no Ollie, no Frieda, too much Sahira and Greg and a bit of Luc, Eddi and Malick. That just about says it all about the episode, but let's just send it for a quick ultrasound to make sure we haven't missed anything.

We got to see more of the formerly invisible Rafi this week. Someone must have had a word, because he wasn't so mumbly this time. In fact he's rather sweet in his way. The sort of calm, reassuring type that you'd want in charge of keeping you asleep during surgery. He was not, however, feeling calm about the nanny Sahira had appointed to look after their children (My Adorable Son Indy and the other one who is never mentioned by name). Not only was the nanny a mere slip of a girl at 25, but she had a nicotine habit. Sahira didn't want to talk about the Adorables while she was at work. "Work mode, remember?" she reminded him in her usual pompous style. Work mode, in Sahira's case, involves a lot of crying, shrieking and reminding Irish Dr Greg that they are Just Friends. And a bit of parachute stitching when there's time. "I can't do this!" she emoted to Irish Dr Greg later. The pressure of having a quiet husband, a smoking nanny, dying patients and a fondness for Irish surgeons with lovely noses is proving too much for her to bear. Something's got to give, and I don't really care what it is as long as it happens quickly.

In the department we fondly know as AAU, a mysterious young man with cheekbones turned up with a mysterious woman who mysteriously knew which street Eddi had lived on in Leeds. Was she perhaps some savant who could pinpoint regional accents with devastating accuracy? No, she was simply the girlfriend of the man with the cheekbones, who happened to be Eddi's brother. Family members turning up always throws light on the main character, and we discovered a bit about Eddi's troubled relationship with her mother. And it's all bringing Luc and Eddi a bit closer.

Hanssen gave Malick the Clinical Skills Teacher job, and frankly was a bit over-enthusiastic with the mentoring. At one point Malick was performing surgery and Hanssen was cheering him on from the observation window like a proud parent. All most odd.

With a little help from Faith

(Series 14, ep. 23 'Eastern Promise' by Joe Ainsworth 20.3.12)

He's a funny old soul, Elliot Hope. His heart is very much in the right place, but his methods are sometimes a tad batty. Thus, we found him squirreling away disused items of CT machinery in the basement (that basement must have vast numbers of unused rooms – there's always a spare one when you need it), pending being shipped off to the Ukraine to save loads of Ukrainian lives. But one man's life saving machinery is another man's scrap metal, and Elliot discovered someone moving the stuff out for scrap. An altercation ensued, during which Elliot sustained what my dad would call "a thick ear" and the other bloke had a heart monitor dropped on his toe. Double ouch. Some of the other staff found this rather amusing. "You really are a museum piece, aren't you?" Slinky Dr Alex purred when she discovered his altruistic plans. Jac took to calling him "Sir Bob."

So he had to go legit and take it to the board, whereupon he was helped by a patient he'd known for a long time. Faith was one of those feisty types who Gets Things Done – you know the sort, school governor, magistrate, volunteering at a Citizens Advice Bureau. She also had an aneurysm and wasn't well at all. Whenever a lovely woman like this appears in Elliot's life, you know it's going to go wrong in some way – she'll either die (Gina), have to be dumped for not being Gina (Lady Byrne) or rip him off (the woman with the laser), so it didn't bode well for Faith. She had one last bit of old-school activism left in her, though, and occupied the skip holding the disputed machinery. After a bit of persuasion, Elliot joined her and chained himself to it, throwing away the key, on the condition that Faith let Young Dr Oliver Valentine escort her back to her bed. Unfortunately she collapsed, and there was a frantic search for the key to unchain Elliot (I never thought I'd see Henrik Hanssen rooting about in bin bags), while Jac struggled to save Faith's life. Poor Elliot's face as he arrived at the operating theatre too late. Sniff. But she didn't die in vain – Hanssen came good and pledged the stuff to the Ukraine.

Malick handed Frieda the task of mentoring Tara Lo. This didn't go down well, particularly when Tara started out-diagnosing the Top F2 in Holbyshire. I did enjoy Malick taking bets on how long "Sweet and Lo" could last before fainting in an operation (12 minutes).

No such fainting problems with Eddi McKee's brother Liam, who appears to have quite a high gore tolerance threshold. Indeed, by the end of the episode he was happily dissecting a rat. Eddi had got him a job on AAU, serving meals (that wasn't the rat, I'm getting to that bit) and giving out water and books to patients. I think this is the first time I recall patients ever actually eating in Holby (apart from the time Beautiful Dr Penny Valentine brought a sandwich in for Scott James), although they never actually got to eat anything this week, either, because various accidents and incidents befell Liam and the trolley bearing the food kept ending up on its side in some corridor or other. You sense Liam means well, even when he messes up and drives his sister to despair. That girl's standards are impossibly high, anyway. Dr Luc Hemingway also sensed Liam was A Good Lad Really, and has offered to be his mentor. This involves letting him watch ghastly surgery (Liam's face when he watched a very big tumour being removed from someone was priceless) and dissecting rats, as mentioned above.

You are not the only surgeon at Holby

(Series 14, ep. 24 'Got No Strings' by Nick Fisher 27.3.12)

Poor old Rafi. He spent years being the invisible househusband of Sahira Shah the Registrah. He gave up the chance of a job in Nottingham (where they have miles of cycle paths, and he just loves cycle paths) to stay at Holby, and now he is completely unable to persuade his wife to leave work on time so he can spend quality (and quantity) time with her. The kids hardly know who she is any more, and she's forgotten the name of the one who isn't My Adorable Son Indy altogether. What's an anaesthetist to do? Well, he could drug her and prop her up in an armchair at home so the family could all admire her, but that would be unethical and more than a little weird. So what he did this week was put his foot down and tell her she simply must leave work on time so they could go for a posh meal, with wine and everything, and put their heads together to try and remember the name of their second child.

She agreed to this plan and even put some of the red lipstick on that she wears when she's trying to do posh, the one that doesn't really suit her. But of course Sahira may be a wife and mother, but foremost she is a Deeply Caring and Committed Surgeon. Henrik Hanssen, who loves her in a spooky, unrequited way, knows this about her and threw the tempting morsel of a girl with a thyroid cancer called Raymond (that was the cancer's name, not the girl's. Don't ask) in her way. Sahira made a huge effort to resist this gambit, by roping in Young Dr Oliver Valentine to do the surgery instead of her. I felt completely sorry for Boy Valentine. He knew he was out of his depth and so did Sahira and it was a shocking way to treat a junior colleague and a patient. Boringly, it meant that yet again Sahira could swoop in at the last minute and leave everyone marvelling at her supernaturally brilliant surgical skills.

For Rafi, it meant once again watching his wife put her job before him. He'd had enough, and he knew who to blame. Rather bravely, he confronted Hanssen. The Swedish Scalpel proved he was not above a bit of playing dirty, though. If Rafi wondered why Miss Shah was so keen on staying at Holby, he might ask Mr Douglas, who was similarly keen. Oh, Henrik. With one smooth sentence you have deflected attention away from yourself and possibly exploded both the Raza/Shah and Douglas/Shah relationships apart. Bravo.

Meanwhile, Michael Spence continues to look more gorgeous by the week, still rocking the grizzled look and teaming it with a rather nice suit. And Alex was being really horrible to him, pulling rank and being really rude to him in front of colleagues and patients. I wanted to slap her. They spent most of the episode disagreeing about a patient. Sacha and Chrissie were rather amused and Sacha said he'd spotted a bit of a frisson between them. "Oh big deal, she's attracted to me," said Michael, with his trademark modesty. "Who said it was that way round?" Chrissie said. So Michael went off and amusingly talked to Alex about their mutual frisson and she said it was a completely unethical thing to be talking about – but if he felt like inviting her for a drink, she'd probably say yes.

And Chantelle and Lleucu fell out again and then made friends again. Ric Griffin was once again relegated to the role of being a father figure for junior staff. It's time that man had a storyline of his own that didn't involve dishing out avuncular advice to nurses.

The passenger seat

(*Series 14, ep. 25 'Throw In the Towel' by Sean Cook. 3.4.12*)

Henrik Hanssen's favourite game of People Chess continued this week, as he drove a further wedge into the Shah/Raza marriage by telling Sahira he was going to take her off CTU duties. She was horrified. She's put passion into that CTU – oh lord, don't we just know how much passion she's put into it? We've suffered along with her as she's filled entire chest cavities with her tears. And now she's being told she's in the passenger seat. Jac had a little gloat, Irish Dr Greg felt Sahira's pain and Hanssen smiled enigmatically and waited for her to find out he'd done what he did because Rafi had a word with him last week. Hanssen just knew that this wouldn't go down well with Sahira.

Meanwhile, Rafi was in Poirot mode (he is actually a bit of a David Suchet lookey-likey in a certain light) and was keeping an eye on Irish Dr Greg, following Hanssen's tip-off last week. He just winds them up, and away they go… It all ended up with patients dying, Sahira getting all angsty in theatre (as per usual) and Irish Dr Greg being punched by Rafi. A satisfactory day's work for the hyper-tall Swede, apart from the dead patients bit.

He was also successful in getting his choice of candidate appointed as Clinical Skills Lead. Actually, The Malick didn't need a lot of help on this one, as he produced an absolute corker of an interview. Dull Dan tried to scupper his efforts by letting the lady from the university know about Malick's previous form as far as punching consultants was concerned, but Malick turned it round with a bit of neat "what you see is what you get" interview technique and the post was his. Dull Dan showed a bit of contrition afterwards by going for a drink with Malick instead of with the university lady (who wanted to discuss his job prospects). If I'd have been Malick, I'd have wanted to smack him one, the spineless lump.

I also wanted to smack Alex Broadhurst (Mad Maya). Michael Spence was happily intent on carrying on last week's flirtation, little realising that she was busy compiling reports about him "resembling a hyperactive child" for Hanssen. Then he did find out, and she suddenly seemed marginally less attractive than she had moments earlier. Michael also continued in his quest to replace Joseph Byrne in my affections by looking even foxier than he did last week and by being super marvellous with a patient. Alex greeted all of this magnificence with a bit of a sneer every time she passed by. Anyway, by the end of the episode Michael had won her over with his doctorly skills, if not with his charm. Even as she was inserting herself into a taxi (she was leaving Holby), poor Michael was still asking her out for a drink. He's a trier, that man.

A Ukrainian, a Chinese and a clown walked into a hospital...

(Series 14, ep. 26 'Equilibrium' by Patrick Homes 10.4.12)

There's a special magnetism between Greg and Sahira. That can be the only explanation for why every time they look at each other their beepers go off. It was happening constantly during the episode, and of course each beep was perfectly placed to thwart a Deep Meaningful Conversation. Greg did manage to tell her he loved her, but she was unable to reply as she was already hurtling off down a corridor at the command of her beeper. You'd swear Henrik Hanssen was in a control room somewhere coordinating all this. Greg has given up pursuing her along corridors bleating, "Sahira! Sahira!" He's on crutches anyway, which has slowed him down a bit. Now he's reduced to slumping in corners looking mournful, particularly when she said she was going to move to Nottingham with Rafi and enjoy all those cycle paths and finding out what their second child is called.

All this was just tedious, but the bit that really, really irked me was when Sahira was binned off an operation in favour of Jac, because "there's no place for domestic entanglements in theatre." Indeed not, and hurrah, but why did we then have to suffer the sight of Jac being unable to stitch up a heart that was shredding up like a used Kleenex and Sahira waltzing in, all scrubbed up, to save the day with some of her legendary stitching? Beyond annoying.

Thinking about Holby characters over the years, I realised that most of them are slight caricatures or one-dimensional when they arrive. You get a peg on which you can hang them – Donna the party girl, ditzy Chantelle, angry Malick, smooth operator Michael Spence, enigmatic Hanssen. Bit by bit, more sides of them are revealed. This can go on for years, as with Jac, whose story has evolved the whole time she's been in the show. But with Sahira, I think the mistake the writers made was trying to offer a fully rounded, beloved character right from the off. We were expected to believe she was a brilliant surgeon, loving mother, object of adoration etc etc. It was too much for one character to bear all at once and it tilted the emphasis away from characters we genuinely did know and love and made her irritating. Jac's comment to her this week, "Take a rest, Wonder Woman. Eat a cupcake," summed it up nicely.

Meanwhile, Tara Lo was getting to grips with the concept of patients dying, thanks to the hospital clown (yes there is one, and no, it's not Greg). This was a man introduced by Chantelle as being just the sweetest man imaginable, so kind, so funny, so great with the kids. You just knew with an introduction like that he'd be collapsed on the floor within a minute. It turned out he had cancer, knew it, but was refusing treatment because it stopped him being able to amuse the kids.

And Luc let Liam down, so Liam trashed Luc's van. Eddi helped him to sort it out again and Luc came good for Liam in the end.

The passion of the lonely Swede

(Series 14, ep. 27 'Ribbons' by Martha Hillier 17.4.12)

Finally we waved goodbye to Sahira Shah the Registrah. She was looking anguished to the very last, emoting left, right and centre and getting inappropriately "passionate" (not in that way) about a patient. No clinical detachment, that's her problem. Someone who has no problem with clinical detachment is Henrik Hanssen. His problem is more of the attachment than detachment type, and the person he was attached to was the aforementioned Shah. Once he knew she was leaving, he got ever so slightly tetchy, in a buttoned-up sort of way, telling her she could "drive her self-esteem from the fawning attentions of our finest beta males." It's a beautiful description of Greg Douglas, but it gave Sahira the clue that Hanssen didn't just like her because of the quality of her parachute stitching. Duh. "Are you in love with me?" she asked him, and he responded by shooing her out of his office. Literally. "Shoo! Shoo!" he said.

We're used to patients speaking the brains of the staff on Holby, but Hanssen found he could only speak his own heart about Sahira via the medium of trying to console a patient whose son was dying. In one of the most desperately sad scenes ever, all the more so for its restraint and calm, Hanssen finally told us how he was feeling. "The time of separation has come," he told the father, as Sahira looked on. "The acute anguish will diminish, to be replaced by a dull ache which will not go. That much I know." Lovely work by Guy Henry and a lovely piece of writing.

Elsewhere, Luc wanted to take a blood sample from Eddi for some reason, and to distract her he kissed her. This service is not offered by my local hospital and I want to know why. And Malick let the power of being Clinical Skills Tsar go to his head and got all arrogant and, well, Sahira-ish about a patient.

Learning from experience

(Series 14, ep. 28 'Half a Person' by Matthew Broughton 24.4.12)

Malick had himself a weird, slightly stalkerish fan this week. It wasn't Dull Dan, it was one Spike, a rather annoying medical student who somehow had the idea that The Malick was the greatest doctor since doctors were invented. Previously this has been very much Malick's opinion of his own worth as well, so surely having an adoring fan would only make him worse? Well, it didn't, because Spike was just plain annoying. He also went the maverick route by suggesting surgery to a patient after Hanssen had already decreed that surgery was not a viable option for him. Malick agreed with Spike, and sharpened his scalpel. Naturally everything went tits-up and Malick was forced to admit that sometimes there's nothing that can be done. And his acolyte was forced to admit that heroes were fallible and this doctoring lark was more complex than he'd first realised. The highlight of this storyline was a world-class loom from Hanssen. Having been missing for most of the episode, he materialised in spectacular fashion behind Spike to shake a sorrowful head at the eager young Clinical Skills Tsar.

Irish Dr Greg threw himself into his work as a way to get over the loss of his favourite Registrah, and found himself with a patient who was a bit of a madam, throwing herself at any man who happened to wander by (when you have the likes of Young Dr Oliver Valentine wandering by, why the hell not?). And she was only 15. It slowly began to dawn on Greg that maybe she was being abused by her father, but she wasn't saying anything. This is a topic that's been lurking in Greg's background for a while, biding its time in the usual Holby way. You think they've forgotten about an issue and then it comes back in dramatic fashion. Greg realised he had to stop the girl's father taking her from the hospital, so since he's still on crutches he despatched Ollie to leg it down to the car park to bring her back. When is poor Ollie going to get a storyline of his own and not just spend episodes hanging around waiting for someone to ask him to run somewhere?

Anyway, he succeeded and brought the girl back and Greg resorted to popping her in a CT scanner so he could speak to her alone for a minute. And he admitted that bad things had happened to him when he was 14, so she admitted that bad things had happened to her since she was 9. It was an intense scene, beautifully played by Edward MacLiam and particularly Antonia Clarke as the girl – she conveyed so much with just the expression in her huge eyes that the script didn't have to be at all graphic – we knew exactly what she'd been through. It was also well directed, with the nasty dad looming in a CCTV screen behind Greg in a most sinister manner.

Ric Griffin got the all-clear from his cancer – hurrah! And he's also got the all-clear from the lollipop-headed Annalese. Their relationship has "run its course," apparently. So now Annalese has decided to move to Florida for 6 months with her kids. Who are also Michael Spence's kids. He wasn't happy, but he received wise counsel from Ric, who advised him to take it on the (still stubbly, I'm pleased to say) chin and keep on friendly terms with his former wife and Ric's former girlfriend.

And there was a lovely big moon over Holby. I live just down the road, and I never saw it.

Goodbye, Irish Dr Greg

(Series 14, ep. 29 'Coercion' by Martha Hillier 1.5.12)

Irish Dr Greg, eh? He's been in Holby for over two years, and unfortunately for a large chunk of that time he's been forced to run up and down corridors moaning, "Sahira! Sahira!" What a waste. It all started out so promisingly, as well. We first encountered him as Connie Beauchamp's bit of Hot Irish Totty when she temporarily relocated to a posh private hospital in London. Subsequently he enjoyed a flirtation with the magnificent Mary Claire and the predictably flirtatious Chrissie and even a bit of a bromance with Joseph Byrne. He was a bit cheeky, a bit funny and – it was occasionally hinted – he might have Hidden Depths.

The depths got seriously hidden during the Sahira saga, when he became not much more than a sighing, hankering love-lorn loon. Then Sahira goes, and for his exit storyline Edward MacLiam is finally – finally – given a storyline to get his teeth into. Picking up from last week's sexual abuse plot, Greg found himself in all kinds of trouble this week when the abused girl, Lucy, stabbed her father with a pair of scissors. Mary-Claire got the wrong end of the stick and thought Greg was being "inappropriate" with Lucy. Greg almost let the evil abusive father die in theatre. And it was left to Elliot (kindly) and Hanssen (cunning) to sort everything out. Meanwhile, Greg was spilling out his heart about his own past abuse to Lucy: "I've never had a life, not a proper one," he told her. "I've never been close to people." Not for want of trying, we might say, but the point was that he didn't want Lucy to carry the shame and secrets in her life that he'd carried in his. It was touching and, like last week, beautifully written and played. Lucy was persuaded to tell all and get help, but it was all a bit of a scandal, nonetheless, and it was better for Greg's career for him to relocate to somewhere that wasn't Holby. "A few phone calls from me and a reference overestimating your ability will probably help," Hanssen told him.

The saddest scene was when Greg had to say goodbye to Mary-Claire. Niamh McGrady is another good actor who isn't given all that much to do, but when she does she's fantastic. Her poor wee face when Greg kissed her on the cheek was so sad.

And Malick was bailed out of a tricky spot by cunning, scary and rather magnificent new consultant Serena Campbell.

A touch of the Beauchamps

(Series 14, ep. 30 'A Woman's Work' by Justin Young 8.5.12)

What do we think of Serena Campbell, then? It's clear what we're supposed to think of her. The hallowed names of Anton Meyer, Dan Clifford and, particularly, the goddess Connie Beauchamp were invoked enough times for us to realise that the new consultant on Darwin was being lined up as a legend in the making. Whether she'll actually live up to her billing remains to be seen, of course, but for now I have to say I rather like her. She's well named, being in possession of an assured serenity that infuriates everyone around her. Such fun.

It was an amusing episode, what with Serena and her 3D stack (it's some kind of camera thing that turns surgery into a video game. Malick loves it) locking horns with Ric Griffin and his traditional way of doing things (ie not with a 3D stack). And we also had the fun of Jac Naylor being horrible to an F1 (Tara Lo – or, as Jac calls her, "F1"). I know a lot of people say Jac goes too far in her horribleness, but I'm endlessly amused by it. "Why do you always have to be so unpleasant?" Elliot asked her at one point. "I like to be consistent," she replied. She certainly does.

You can't blame her getting exasperated with Tara Lo, who seems to find a new way to mess up on a weekly basis. Just your average junior doctor, then, but Jac has above average standards. Tara is a bit dim. Even I know that showing a patient gory photographs of exactly what his chest is going to look like after you've smashed through his sternum to get to the juicy bits beneath, is not the way to calm his nerves. "She wants to cut my soul out with an electric saw!" the fearful patient (Sanjeev Kohli from *Fags, Mags & Bags*, who was hilarious) fretted. It was up to Elliot to calm him down and get him to sign his consent forms. When Jac discovered Elliot and Tara happily operating away on her patient, she was not best pleased and had a right go at Ms Lo in the middle of theatre, calling her a "foetus in scrubs." Ok, maybe not Jac's finest hour, and not her best timing, either, as Hanssen happened to be watching. Note to Holby staff: Hanssen is always watching. Even if you can't see him.

Tara was terrified. Young Dr Oliver Valentine, a man who can deal with Jac better than most, advised Tara to "go to her happy place" to cope with the scary Ms Naylor. "The library?" said Tara. But she didn't even need the library when Jac dropped by to utter the most marvellously brief apology, after having her card marked by Hanssen.

With all this going on, Hanssen found time to drop by and tell everyone the Cardiac Trauma Unit is going to close. It was just a toy for Sahira Shah the Registrah to play with after all. Jac looked like she wanted to stab him to death with her cheekbones.

Elsewhere, there was much sexual chemistry between Dr Luc Hemingway and Eddi McKee, but they were pretending like mad there wasn't. She even flirted with a patient's brother to try to make Luc jealous, or pretend she doesn't fancy the scrubs off him or whatever, but we weren't fooled for a minute. And Luc was positively seething with jealousy. It was a fine sight.

Just make sure she doesn't kill anyone

(Series 14, ep. 31 'Wolf's Clothing' by Lauren Klee 15.5.12)

Regular readers will know I usually lift the title of the post from a bit of the dialogue in the show that strikes me as particularly apt. Near the beginning of last night's episode, I jotted down, "Just make sure she doesn't kill anyone," which Michael Spence said regarding the new junior doctor, Ella Barnes. Michael was talking to Sacha, who had faith in Ella even if no-one else did. He's like that, Sacha – he sees the best in everyone, he wants to do right by people, he's kind and he's just all-round lovely.

So what kind of a shock was it when the person Ella possibly ended up killing was Sacha himself? Not directly, but via a chain of events that ended with Sacha being accidentally stabbed by a scalpel wielded by an angry boy. Ella rewarded Sacha for all his kindness by freaking out and leaving him to bleed on the floor in AAU, where thankfully he was soon found by Chrissie. I did find it hard to believe that, in a hospital where at least three consultants are only a paper aeroplane's throw away from any given incident, Chrissie was practically all alone and had no better idea than to ring Michael (who was in theatre) for advice. What about the A&E department downstairs, stuffed full of experts in stabbings etc? But let's fling that aside – I'm just too worried about Sacha to nitpick right now. Particularly as the last words of the episode were these ominous utterings from Michael Spence: "I've done my best, but I gotta be honest – the next few hours are critical."

Was this all arranged by cunning scriptwriters just to deflect our grief about the loss of Goth Dr Frieda? It's true. One of the most original, quirky and marvellous characters to ever grace the wards of Holby has left for pastures new, following a dispute with Serena Campbell over the care of an old lady with Alzheimer's. Frieda got to make a stand for what she believes in and delivered a passionate speech to some money-types who'd come to watch Serena in theatre, but it was a low-key exit. I'm hoping this means the door is open for her to come back at some point.

Jac went on her People Skills course and ended up sleeping with a Scottish neurosurgeon. Is it true romance for our favourite snappy redhead? Not judging by the speed with which she was out of the door afterwards, no.

Elliot Hope was offered the post of Professor of Darwin's new Transplant Centre. First, he was required to master the concept of paperless working, which essentially meant iPads all round. There was a bit of a cock up (not his fault – Ella Barnes again) which almost resulted in someone dying, and Elliot lost faith in his ability to deal with new technology. He resorted to good old fashioned textbooks to discover that his patient suffered from a very rare illness. "It's CIPA," I told him, five minutes before he discovered it himself. This is because I googled it on the iPad I was using to make notes on. Technology 1, Textbooks 0. Elliot told Hanssen he couldn't possibly take up the new post, because he was a dinosaur who couldn't get to grips with the modern world. We've learned time and time again that you don't say no to Hanssen, though, so it was no surprise when the world's scariest Swede told Elliot he had every confidence and was sure he'd get the hang of it all, with a bit of training.

Hanssen Loom of the Week came quite early on in the episode, when Jac was briefing the staff about the paperless workplace. "When was this decided? Does Hanssen know?" Elliot asked her. "I should think so," said Jac. "Since he's standing behind you." People, when will you learn? Hanssen is always standing behind you.

You know I can tell when someone's hiding something

(Series 14, ep. 32 'Double Bubble' by Martha Hillier & Paul Campbell 22.5.12)

The most important thing is, Sacha's not dead. He survived being stabbed last week and he survived an hour of Chrissie fussing over him and trying to force-feed him quiche this week. Oh, and a nasty infection which Michael Spence sorted out for him. By the end of the episode he was looking considerably perkier and I dare say the quiche was beginning to look appetising. Sacha looks like a man who enjoys his food.

The new transplant team arrived this week. The "team" consists of the wonderfully forthright and heavily pregnant Mo Effanga and the less pregnant and less forthright nurse Jonny Maconie. This is the Jonny Maconie Jac thought was a neurosurgeon when she shagged him last week. Although you can most certainly accuse Jac of being a snob generally ("I'm only jealous of thin people!" she said to Mo), she's an equal opportunities shagger and when we last glimpsed her she was helping Jonny get the store cupboard into a shocking state of disarray with some passionate shenanigans. I fail to see the allure of Jonny, myself, and I can't help thinking after sampling the delights of Joseph Byrne and Young Dr Oliver Valentine, Jac has rather downgraded this time.

I'm loving Mo, though, and I can only hope she makes good on her promise to take just two weeks maternity leave (and only that much if she really,really needs it), because I don't want her disappearing for long. Like any good new Holby surgeon, she got stuck straight in with a Terribly Risky Procedure – whipping out the heart from a patient who was receiving a new heart and lungs and sticking it into another patient, after patching it up a bit first. We were treated to the sight of a chest cavity with no heart in it and everyone went "Wow." Even Tara Lo, who was watching through the window. This is Tara Lo who couldn't so much as look at a bloodshot eye without fainting a few short weeks ago. The girl has come a long way.

It was a week for newbies, because we were also introduced to nurse Simon Marshall, played by Paul Nicholls off of *EastEnders*. I'm wondering how long it'll be before I can look at him and not hear the phrase, "I'm worried about Joe!" in my head, but it's possible he'll have gone again before that happens. He seems to be mainly a plot device to finally get Dull Dan to leap from the cupboard marked Closet and declare he is what he is and what he is needs no excuses. Simon's not only gay, but he's cute (not as cute as when he was Joe) and he and Dan go waaaay back. And Simon reckons he can always tell when someone's hiding something. You can imagine Dan's reaction to that news. He'll be laughing heartily and trying to look all heterosexual next.

Could do better

(Series 14, ep. 33 'Kids' Stuff' by Joe Ainsworth 29.5.12)

It's not like your humble correspondent to be lost for Holby words, but I find myself in that position this week. To be honest, my attention wandered onto such topics as whether to try shampooing the cat (she's a tad elderly and has given up on grooming) and whether the Queen is looking forward to her jubilee or just wishes everyone would shut up about how old she is (she's a tad elderly, but unlike the cat has not yet given up on grooming).

These "meh" Holby episodes do happen along once in a while and I don't particularly worry about them (I'm sure there'll be another good one along in a week or so). What I do worry about is Jonny Maconie, who I see has been installed in the opening title sequence and must therefore be considered a permanent fixture (or as permanent as cast members get on Holby these days). There's something about him that makes me want to slap him with a nice, fat wad of patient files – if only Holby hadn't gone paperless. I suspect slapping him with an iPad wouldn't feel so satisfying.

Following last week's unseemly behaviour in the store room, both Jac and Jonny seemed keen for a repeat. Some poor cleaner or other had worked hard to get those bedpans neatly piled up, as well. It didn't happen, though, due to timing issues caused by patients (they are so inconvenient). I can only assume Jonny has some amazing woman-pleasing tricks up his sleeve (ok, they're maybe not actually up his sleeve), because I see no other reason for his appeal at all.

Malick got slightly run over at the start of the episode and this might have accounted for his subsequent mad behaviour when he brought a child with a back injury into Keller without any spinal precautions and without contemplating for long that A&E was really the best place to take him, what with them having an adorable paediatric trauma specialist and all (ah, the lovely Dr Tom Kent. Now there's a man worth Jac's attention). It was the usual case of surgeons (Malick and Serena) disagreeing over how to treat a patient, and Malick did a spot of ninja-level surgery after first doing some rather Sahira Shah-like emoting. What's happened to his Clinical Skills Tsar job? Where are the Malickites these days? They're probably wandering around the basement lost. They won't be seen again until Oliver Valentine has his next emotional crisis and has to go down there to sit in the Penny Valentine Memorial Pondering Position. His pondering will be cut short when a troupe of hollow-eyed, emaciated medical students staggers past, in search of their beloved mentor.

Meanwhile, on AAU, Sacha was back at work. His powers of recovery are quite fabulous. That's what quiche does for you. His daughter Rachel turned up with a sore tummy. Was it appendicitis? Was it psychological trauma because her dad had recently been stabbed? Or was it an attempt to avoid an exam? Not too sure, to be honest. I totally lost interest in that storyline, which seemed to involve Chrissie looming over the poor girl's bed giving her a death stare every five minutes.

A rainy day in old Holby town

(Series 14, ep. 34 'Last Day on Earth' by Tahsin Guner 5.6.12)

There was ever such a lot of hurtling about in this episode. They used to send Jac on her motorbike to fetch emergency organs, but now they've got Jonny and Mo to do it and Mo's so heavily pregnant she probably can't fit on a motorbike at the moment, so they go by car. On this occasion they were sent to collect a heart, but arrived to find the father of the current owner of the heart wasn't emotionally ready to let it (or his son) go. Against his better judgement and protocol, Jonny found himself taken into the confidence of this poor man and eventually the heart got the thumbs up, as it were. I found I liked Jonny more when he was being kind and sensitive and nurse-ish than I do when he's back at Holby being a leery old Jac-magnet.

While all this was going on, the intended recipient of the heart had gone AWOL, as patients on Holby tend to do all too frequently. Tara Lo had taken rather a personal interest in this patient, and she took it upon herself to go and get her back. Young Dr Oliver Valentine took it upon himself to go with her. So off they went in the biggest downpour Holby has seen since that time there was a flood and Mark "Jesus" Williams had to deploy sandbags and his best sorrowful expression to keep the floodwaters at bay.

Someone at Holby HQ had clearly been having a think. "What could be more photogenic than Ollie and Tara?" they pondered. "Gosh, I know, we'll get them wet." Bravo for coming up with that idea, because it really worked.

In Tara, Ollie has found someone who can sort of fill the void left by The Radiantly Beautiful Dr Penny Valentine. Like Penny, Tara is intelligent, caring, a bit reckless, a little bit naive and very beautiful. And unlike Penny, she isn't his sister, which comes in handy during those "Oops, I just fell face down on you while you were lying face up" -type moments.

Tara is obviously harbouring A Secret Past. We've had a lot of secret pasts in the past (I have this way with words), what with Irish Dr Greg, Jac, FLNT and Oliver himself. Dr Luc Hemingway's secret past is still a secret. So I've no idea what Tara's is going to turn out to be, but I don't think it's that she used to be a man. I think we can safely rule that out. I think we can also rule out that she's secretly married to Hanssen as well.

While all this heart stuff was going on, guest artiste James Dreyfus was playing a man who was convinced it was the end of the world. Chantelle was pragmatic. "We can't face the end of the world without a cup of tea in our hands," she reasoned. "It wouldn't be British." Quite right, too.

It wasn't tea that Serena's daughter had been drinking, and she turned up at Holby somewhat the worse for wear, towing a friend who was even more worse for wear, given that she'd taken ecstasy and also had an ectopic pregnancy. It's been ages since we had an ectopic pregnancy on Holby. There was a time when there was at least one a week. Anyway, all this gave Serena the chance to bond just a weeny bit with Ric, when he told her he'd had a problem child of his own in the form of the late lamented Leo.

There was no Hanssen at all this week, but now he's had a week off I'm expecting an absolute mega-loom next week to compensate.

He's a big boy. He can handle it

(Series 14, ep. 35 'Unsafe Haven Part 1' by Patrick Homes 12.6.12 and ep. 36 'Unsafe Haven Part 2' by Dana Fainaru 19.6.12)

Bit of a fail on the blogging front last week, which was a shame because it was a cracking episode. There was an equal dose of romance and coughing. Dan and Simon were making eyes at each other and so were Ollie and Tara (and what beautiful eyes they both have) and Luc and Eddi. The episode ended with Luc and Eddi kissing in his caravan. So far so squeee, but there was that coughing to worry about. It turned out it was Legionnaire's Disease, and it was coming from Somewhere in the Hospital.

This week, the situation turned out to be so drastic that they even had to get some cast members from *Casualty* involved. Big Mac and Dr Dylan Keogh were drafted in for no particular reason apart from they probably fancied a trip to Borehamwood to see The Hollywood of Hertfordshire at first hand, because they didn't actually do very much. I was hoping to see Dr Tom Kent, particularly when a little paediatric case turned up in AAU, but sadly it didn't happen. The little paediatric case was called Noah, and his presence caused all sorts of problems for Dr Luc Hemingway. This was because young Noah not only had Legionnaire's, but he also had emotional problems. Our Luc doesn't really do emotional, not even when he's woken up to find the Best Nurse in the Hospital adorning the bunk bed of his camper van. It really exasperated Eddi, to the point where she declared she would just have to apply for a transfer. Again. At which point Luc asked her to remind him what comes between sleeping together and IKEA. Apparently the answer is "a date," according to Eddi. It's lovely to know that good old-fashioned romance isn't dead, isn't it? Oh, and Luc even had time to sort out where the Legionnaire's disease was coming from and sort out little Noah's various issues along the way, thus proving that he's not only a top doctor, but he's also emotionally worthy of the love of The Best Nurse In The Hospital.

Luc wasn't the only one who woke up with an attractive nurse in his bed. Dull Dan and Smouldering Simon had apparently also taken their relationship to the next level (it's only a short step after this to IKEA and some of their famous meatballs). It was rather lovely to see Dull Dan out of the closet. He actually looked happy for the first time in forever – certainly a lot happier than when he was pretending to be smitten by Chrissie – and he didn't even seem all that Dull anymore.

It was a shame it couldn't last. All it took was for Daddy Hamilton to rock up with a neurological complaint and an annoying line in "nudge, wink" comments vis a vis Dan and various (female) nurses, and Dan's new-found gay pride was disintegrating before our eyes. I actually felt sorry for Dan, but possibly even more sorry for Simon, who got the brush off despite being adorable.

While all this was going on, Elliot was mentoring comedian Andi Osho. And there was no sign of Ollie or Tara at all.

Happily ever after

(*Series 14, ep. 37 'Long Way Down' by Stephen Brady 26.6.12*)

He's not confused. He's not experimenting. He's not bisexual. He's not even Dull. He's gay! And he's proud of it! Hurrah! It's been a long time coming, but finally Holby's most incompetent orthopaedic surgeon got the backbone to admit to his father, a small crowd of onlookers and, most importantly, himself, that he's finally out of that closet and he's not going back in. Poor old Smouldering Simon had to suffer first, though, as we discovered just what a homophobic old bigot Papa Hamilton was and just what kind of conditioning Dan has been struggling against for all these years. Simon almost lost his job over Papa Hamilton's behaviour, but managed to keep it because he's a fab nurse, as did Chantelle because she's a fab nurse too, and Ric reckons her smile really ought to be available on the NHS. Which it is, obviously. So Dan is out and proud, and Simon is proud that he's out, even if he did it with n'er a hint of a show tune. I do like Simon.

I do like Tara, too, which is why it was a bit of a shock to discover the poor girl has a brain tumour. It wasn't a shock to her, as she already knew but had been keeping it quiet so it didn't ruin her chances of a medical career. One wonders, then, why she was quite so keen to jump into a CT scanner. It was supposed to be to allay the fears of a patient who was supposed to be having a scan herself, but would the radiographer really just allow staff members to pop themselves in for high doses of radiation willy nilly? Call me cynical, but it looked like a fairly lame way to get Tara's brain tumour out in the open. Well, it got as far as the wide open spaces of Hanssen's luxurious office at least, and Sweet & Lo soon found herself being suspended pending medical reports. All I could think about was how gutted poor Oliver is going to be when he finds out. I'm going to do a sponsored something or other immediately and get her sent for the very best treatment money can buy, because Ollie can't take any more suffering in his young life. He'll start to get frown lines and that.

Two people who were practically born with frown lines are Dr Luc Hemingway and Best Nurse Eddi McKee. They were getting serious this week – Eddi even gave Luc the key to her house, so they didn't have to spend every night in the bunk bed in his camper van, with Chrissie peering through the window. Bad luck, though – Luc's contract was up. Yet, good luck – Hanssen offered him a permanent contract. Hurrah! Time to bust out some champagne and a few more show tunes!

And yet… when Eddi skipped merrily to the Camper Van of Dreams after work, it had vanished. Has Luc taken fright and fled? Maybe being in possession of the McKee key was too much for his gypsy soul to bear.

H.A.P.P.Y.

(Series 14, ep. 38 'Stepping Up to the Plate' by Julia Gilbert 3.7.12)

I worry about Chantelle's eyelashes. They look like they might fall off and end up in open wounds. They need their own little set of scrubs, really, for hygiene purposes. But if we lay that worry carefully to one side and pull a curtain round it, everything else about Chantelle is pure joy and radiance. She has a smile that would keep Keller lit up even if the back-up emergency generator failed. She has a ready supply of snacks. And she keeps the patients happy.

This became a problem this week, when in an effort to keep the patients' relatives happy she promised a man that his wife was going to be ok. Only then she wasn't ok and he was appropriately aggrieved and Ric and Serena (especially Serena) got all frowny and disapproving. But wait! The not-ok woman was pregnant and Chantelle took it upon herself to go into bat for the chance for the unborn child to be a born child. Then it looked like the child, who was born, wouldn't survive for long and the husband was aggrieved again and Ric and Serena were even more frowny. But then the child was ok and everyone smiled and Chantelle smiled even more and the sun came out and baby lambs frolicked through the corridors of Holby. Only not that last bit. Not outside of Chantelle's imagination, anyway.

She really is a joy-spreader. Not a term we can apply to Best Nurse Eddi McKee, who tends more towards the snappy sarcasm side of humour at the best of times. This was not the best of times for her, as Dr Luc Hemingway was AWOL and he'd taken his camper van, too, which gave his absence a worryingly permanent air. Poor Eddi was left to contemplate what might have been if she and Luc had only got to the IKEA stage of their relationship, and left to cope with Michael Spence being rather less understanding than he could have been, given that he was missing his son's birthday to cover AAU in Luc's absence. In the end Michael decided to go and visit his kids. But who will look after AAU? Could it be that we haven't seen the last of Luc? I hope so, because, as Michael said, "I kind of miss his bizarre charm."

Elliot, meanwhile – or Professor Hope, as we must now style him – was again trying to mentor comedian Andi Osho. It turns out he's a very good mentor (Hanssen said he would be, and Hanssen Knows Everything) and all of his students passed their exams – apart from comedian Andi Osho, who in theory was the very best of them, but lacked confidence, or something. Anyway, Elliot now plans to give her more intense mentoring. That isn't a euphemism, though her husband thinks it might be.

And finally, how marvellous that Jac and Mo kind of get on and are partners in bitching. They're perfect together, because Mo loves her snacks and being mates with Jac means never having to share your crisps. Jac, as we know, Doesn't Do Carbs.

Mr 100%

(Series 14, ep. 39 'Only You' by Graham Mitchell 10.7.12)

Didn't we learn last week that we mustn't make promises of good outcomes to our patients? We've also learned over the months we've known him that Dan Hamilton and "good outcomes" aren't often to be found in the same operating theatre. Hence it would seem reckless for the man we know as Dull Dan to promise 100% success to a man with a broken neck who needs ever such delicate surgery, when Dan is the man who's going to be wielding the scalpel.

It was surgery of such a delicate nature that Serena wanted nothing to do with it in case everything went pear-shaped and she could remain all smug. The pressure was intensified by being under the watchful, worried gaze of the patient's best mate and Serena herself. No pressure at all, then, but it was only about two seconds before an artery was nicked and there was blood everywhere. What does a man need under such trying circumstances? He needs the love of a good man, that's what. And Dan had Simon, a very good man indeed.

Sadly, Simon was a man who was heading north (or north east if we're still pretending Holby's actually Bristol, but I think they gave that up ages ago, about the time Jac starting nipping to and fro St Pancras in five minutes flat). Simon had been offered a job in Leeds and was planning to take it. Dan was understandably upset. He didn't want his Mr Right being a Right Long Way Off. There was only one thing to do – he would relocate to Leeds as well. "Throwing his career away for a hot nurse," said Serena with something like a twinkle in her eye. I had a twinkle in my eye and a lump in my throat as Dan and Simon headed off for the wuthering heights of Yorkshire, I must admit. Dan and I haven't always seen eye to eye and I'm not completely sorry for calling him Dull Dan and worrying that he might be a bit of a danger to Chrissie with his barely repressed violent self-loathing, but he's been a bit of a sweetheart since Simon arrived.

On the subject of Chrissie, she spent most of the episode tutting and meddling and treating Sacha like he's about seven years old. Dan definitely upgraded by swapping her for Simon. Can you imagine what kind of helicopter parent Chrissie must be to Young Daniel? She's a helicopter girlfriend to Sacha. Only she was feeling too old to be called a "girlfriend." They tried various other descriptions during the episode: partner, lover, significant other, blah blah. You just knew the one they'd end up with. Wife. Yup, blow the cobwebs off your fascinator, dear reader, there's a wedding on the way.

Meanwhile, Tara's future hung in the balance, according to Hanssen. While she was officially declared fit for work despite her brain tumour, Hanssen remained to be convinced. Tara managed to convince him by a cunning mixture of being all sparky and cute and taking the credit for a clever bit of diagnosing which had actually been Oliver's work. The aforementioned Ollie, who doesn't know that she has a brain tumour and just knows she's helluva cute, was happily going for a post-work coffee with her, until Hanssen happened to mentioned her marvellous diagnostic work. Ollie got all hissy and decided he would rather drink his coffee alone. Before he gets all self-righteous, he should remember all the times he took the credit for something Penny did.

My personal life has never affected my work

(Series 14, ep. 40 'Last Man Standing' by Rebecca Wojciechowski 17.7.12)

In the world of Holby, the phrase "My personal life has never affected my work" was uttered by Serena and we knew that was a fib, too, because she'd just mentioned that she was being sued by the parents of her daughter's friend (the ectopic pregnancy one from a few weeks ago) and she was being all ultra-efficient and barking, "Have him/her prepped for theatre," every five minutes, much to Ric's professional dismay. Serena has a tendency to think of patients as statistics to be crossed off her list, whereas Our Ric likes to stare at them soulfully for at least a few minutes before operating. He decided to take his concerns about Serena's working methods to Hanssen. Oh, Ric, no-one likes a snitch.

Ollie's personal life was also affecting his work, because he absolutely *hearts* Dr Tara Lo, but isn't admitting it to her – or himself – yet. This has made him go all grumpy and bossy around her. Heaven only knows how he'll react when he finds out about her brain tumour, but I'm betting it'll involve close-up shots of his lovely eyes brimming with tears, like something in a Japanese cartoon.

Being grumpy and bossy is Best Nurse Eddi McKee's default setting, but there was still no sign of Luc or his camper van this week, so she was even grumpier than usual. She did soften a bit when she had to deal with a patient (played by legend Ron Moody) who was even grumpier than she was. She's quite sweet when she wants to be. I'm still optimistic that Luc will be back. Even though his face has gone AWOL from the opening title sequence, they mention him all the time to make sure we don't forget him. As if.

Labour pains for Mo – and Jac

(Series 14, ep. 41 'From Here to Maternity' by Martha Hillier 24.7.12)

This week we found out why Mo wasn't planning to be taking much maternity leave. It's because she wasn't planning to keep the baby, on account of the baby not being biologically hers.

When she went into labour, she tried at first to ignore it and then dispatched Jonny Mac to track down one Sorcha – who turned out to be Jonny and Mo's former teacher, and the mother of the baby Mo was carrying as a surrogate. So cue Jonny rushing around old hospital buildings and Mo trying to ignore contractions (no easy task). When Jac noticed that Mo kept screwing her face up, grabbing at counter edges and going "Oof!" every few minutes, she tipped off Hanssen who, rather unfairly I thought, assumed Jac was just trying to get Mo out of the way so she could grab her patient, who somewhat tiresomely was supposed to be involved in the Olympics opening ceremony. As if Jac would be that calculating and ruthless. Oh, wait…

The upshot was that when things got critical for Mo there was no one around to help apart from Jac. This meant the birth scenes were absolutely blissful from an audience point of view. Jac doesn't fit easily into a nurturer role: "Please can we get some help? She's going Gollum on me!" but she went in to bat for Mo anyway, blagging a bed in an over full maternity ward by pretending to be matey with Hanssen (her phone call disturbing him in the middle of his sushi), commandeering a wheelchair ("Leave that!") and dealing with a bossy midwife. Watching Mo completely ignoring Jac's discomfort because her own was far, far greater was a beautiful thing and their scenes were full of brilliant lines, my favourite being Jac's "Excellent hand crushing, Maureen. Not like I'm a surgeon or anything."

Birth scenes can easily be either overly dramatic or overly sentimental or both, but because of the feisty characters of Mo and Jac this one was perfect. I don't know whether Chizzy Akudolu has ever given birth, but she acted it brilliantly and there was just enough doubt in her face after the baby was born and she was faced with giving him away to Sorcha. It brought up some of Jac's feelings about her past and her mother, and she was keen for Mo to hold the baby and bond. Babies, she claimed, knew when they were being rejected. The bossy midwife didn't make the process easier, but Mo still didn't give in to tears and hysterics. She just went quiet and contemplative, which for a character like Mo said more about how she was feeling than a lot of weeping and wringing of hands would have done.

Talking of weeping etc, Eddi was in a "frankly horrific mood" according to Sacha and anyone else watching her. Still having trouble getting over Dr Luc Hemingway. That man must have been hot stuff beneath the camper van covers. This week she deleted him from her phone contacts, the modern equivalent of going to Nevada for a quickie divorce.

Serena, meanwhile, was once again trying to take on too much and this time Hanssen had to mark her card when she failed to spot a potentially serious Condition. She was doing twice the work, to be fair, as Ric Griffin was having a check up. Please don't say his cancer has come back.

Adorable

(Series 14, ep. 42 'Breathless' by Kirstie Swain 31.7.12)

Just how damn cute were Ollie and Tara in last night's Holby? I swear they're the sweetest thing since Joseph Byrne's smile. There's a proper on-screen chemistry between them – the looks they were exchanging while Jac was approving of Tara's ninja-level diagnostic work ("Nice work, St Trinian's. Not so useless after all") were so funny. Beautiful work from Jing Lusi and James Anderson, who is excellent at delivering comic lines. I still fondly remember his line about Mr Geddes: "Is he really that small, or is he just far away?" Last night's classic was, "I haven't seen Naylor that excited since…" with his voice dwindling away in some embarrassment as he no doubt recollected a certain locker room encounter.

It's just a shame the passage of true love is not running smoothly for these two. Some work-related Thing always gets in the way when things are going well – last night it was Tara having to stay back so Jac would help her with a study project, when she'd promised to meet Oli for a drink. I couldn't help thinking if she'd phoned him and explained, or sent a more explanatory text rather than "Got 2 bail," (Ugh! Txt spk!) he'd have understood. But that's not how romance works in telly land. Aside from that, there's always the spectre of her brain tumour to worry about. She had a CT scan this week and Hanssen assured her there'd been no change, but I can't help but be concerned.

Meanwhile, Serena was annoying all and sundry with some mad scheme whereby AAU wasn't allowed to refer patients up to Keller. No idea how this was meant to achieve anything positive, but Hanssen was convinced. Another person who's convinced is Mr PLA, who has happily accepted Serena as The New Connie Beauchamp. I tried telling him that Connie had passed the ceremonial kick-ass shoes to Jac, but he likes Miss Campbell's style. This is more than we can say for Michael Spence and Ric Griffin, whose feathers have been well and truly ruffled since Serena appeared. Ric was upset to see that Serena's "Bish bash bosh" approach to getting patients fixed up fast and sent on their way was rubbing off on Malick. "When did you become so blasé about patient care?" he sorrowfully asked him. Ric showed the young 'uns how it was done by sorting out an elderly man whose problems weren't so much medical as social (he couldn't read and had relied on his late wife to look after him). Ric can be so soothing when he's in this mode, but it's not that long since his zero tolerance policy was every bit as annoying and controversial as anything Serena has managed to devise.

Devastating loss of the episode: Michael's beard has gone AWOL. I'm going to start a petition to get it to grow back.

Hanssen Highlight of the Week: The sight of the World's Tallest Surgeon singing to a baby in Swedish. Förtjusande!

Let's hear it for the skinny rude girl

(Series 14, ep. 43 'Crime and Misdemeanours' by Steph Lloyd-Jones 7.8.12)

Is there any finer thing in the whole world than Jac Naylor in full, glorious, bitchy flight? All the more delicious when she's up against a worthy adversary, as she was this week when she came across Amanda Barrie's washed-up actress Annabel Casey. You know, *Annabel Casey* – she was in that film with the bomb. Anyway, Annabel may not have had many parts since the film with the bomb, but she was under no illusions about her own importance in the world – we're talking hashtag-diva here. And she only wanted to be operated on by the Best. We know this is Jac, but in Annabel Casey's world, surgeons look properly learned, wise and, well, male – somewhat like Elliot Hope, in fact. "You look like you sell beauty products," she told Jac. You can imagine how well that went down with The TermiNaylor, and she gave as good as she got, with interest. "I am not having that skinny rude girl anywhere near me!" was Annabel Casey's reaction, which was a shame, as Jac had the skills necessary to save her life.

Every so often the Holby scriptwriters decide it's time Jac learned some lessons about humility and being a team player. Luckily for us, she forgets all about it by the following week. This time she had an additional reason to try to be a team player – basically wily old Elliot Hope had to sign off a research project she'd done, and he'd only manage to find the time to do that if Jac could find the time to help him save Annabel Casey's life. Which she duly did, but not until she'd amply displayed how, if there was an award for Most Expressive Eyes While Wearing a Surgical Mask, she would win every time. "Why can't you be this charming all the time?" Elliot asked her. Because she's Jac, and if she was charming all the time, we wouldn't love her so much.

On AAU a locum, Max Schneider, arrived. He was a stand in for the recently departed Dr Luc Hemingway. He proved to be the perfect replacement, in the sense that he not only had the doctorly skills (though he mysteriously went missing for an extended period mid-shift) but he also found Best Nurse Eddi McKee utterly irresistible. He was played by John Light, who I last saw in The Lion In Winter, and he has a certain lupine charm about him that I like. Our Eddi needs to watch herself, I reckon.

On Keller, Malick had to look after a man who was a murderer, only he turned out to have only been acting in self defence. Malick had been warned to "just stay professional and uninvolved," but this is Malick we're talking about and he got about as involved as he could, in the interests of his patient. It was the usual Holby thing of "maverick surgeon breaks the rules/does something slightly unethical/ignores advice in the interest of his/her patient," (operating without proper consent in this case), but Malick does this sort of stuff with a manic intensity that's rather fun to watch and it was nice to see him stick it to the old guard of Ric and Serena. "Was that a tantrum?" Serena muttered to Ric. "Actually," said Ric, "I think you'll find that's us told." And it was.

Liquid hormones

(Series 14, ep. 44 'You and Me' by Peter McKenna 14.8.12)

Oh, Mo. Hardly any time at all since she gave birth to someone else's baby, and she was back at work. Ignoring the fact that she had puerperal mastitis, was in pain and her hormones were in shreds, she battled in to work with her very best "I'm a tough cookie, me" head on to look after a cheese enthusiast who'd had a heart attack. Because the cheese enthusiast had blood that wasn't suitable to use a bypass machine with (must've been all the cheese), Mo had to operate on him while his heart was still beating.

This would be pressure enough for the average person, without also knowing that the baby they gave birth to and haven't seen since is now called William and is currently in the very same hospital. Mo went to pieces slightly in the operating theatre, and had a heart to heart with Jonny afterwards. "They're not tears," she told him, "They're liquid hormones." It really works that Jonny is around. Because he's known Mo a long time he sort of puts her into context, because he understands her like no-one else in the hospital does.

Inevitably, Mo went to visit the baby. Inevitably, it was heartbreaking, but like the birth scenes a few weeks ago it was subtle and not overdone. She held the baby and said hello and told him he was beautiful. Then the baby sneezed and it was a genius piece of acting from Chizzy Akudolu. She said, "Bless you!" while she was smiling and crying at the same time. It was tender and spontaneous and absolutely, heartbreakingly real.

Comic relief meanwhile was supplied by a little man who'd been brought in as Business Manager for Surgery. His remit was to identify potential savings. Wasn't that Hanssen's remit when he first arrived? I suppose that was before his looming career really took off – he's too busy popping up and startling people now to really knuckle down with a spreadsheet. Anyway, young George Binns didn't exactly get off on the right foot. "You must be Henrik Hanssen," he said. "I was expecting you to be shorter." To emphasise their difference in size, George Binns was always filmed from a height, so we had a Hanssen's eye view of him. "What's he going to be when he grows up?" wondered Ric.

In AAU, Chrissie had a patient who was a farmer about to lose her farm and her leg. It (the leg) had to come off, declared Max Schneider, in between fag breaks and looking at Eddi with wolfish lust. Chrissie didn't think so, because she's idealistic and that, so she insisted that Serena come and have a look at the limb in question. Serena wasn't keen at first, what with the non-referral policy and so on, but Chrissie had a rant at her. "Every time I hear you speak all I hear is policy, never patients!" she told her. "Oh, that's really good!" replied Serena, with her best razor blade dipped in honey voice. "I might steal that for a paper I'm writing." Nonetheless, she was impressed by Chrissie's passion and agreed to do the surgery. She also asked Chrissie to scrub in and afterwards asked her to apply for a job on Keller. Chrissie wasn't going to, but after one sarcastic comment too many from Eddi she changed her mind.

Previously it would all have ended with a musical montage, with George Binns staring at his calculator, Chrissie staring in a satisfied manner at the two young farmers with four good legs between them that she'd managed to organise during her shift, Mo looking wistfully at baby William and Eddi gazing out of the Window of Regret at the space where Luc's camper van used to be parked, before going off with Wolfie for some rebound hanky panky. But they don't do musical montages any more, according to producer Justin Young. I used to quite like those montages, not least because whoever picked the music had excellent taste and some of the songs used ('Scale it Back' by Little Dragon and 'Till Your Ship Comes In' by Alexander Wolfe) I now love to bits. But it's probably just as well there wasn't one this time. I can remember when they used 'Fields of Gold' by Eva Cassidy when Chrissie and Owen's baby died, and I don't think I could have coped with sad music and Mo. There'd have been liquid hormones all over the place.

Suck it up or get out

(Series 14, ep. 45 'The Devil Will Come' by Fiona Peek 21.8.12)

Much of the episode revolved around Michael Spence's attempts to convince Tiny George Binns that AAU was brilliant and efficient and that, but the non-referral scheme just doesn't work. All he succeeded in doing was convincing Tiny George Binns that AAU was brilliant etc and the non-referral scheme worked beautifully and needed keeping. Bummer, as Michael Spence might say. George Binns is very amusing. He reminds me of Macaulay Culkin in *Home Alone 2* – I keep expecting someone to suddenly clap heir hands to their cheeks in horror and yell, "We forgot George!"

As suspected last week, Best Nurse Eddi McKee has been trying to get over Dr Luc Hemingway by succumbing to the dubious charms of Dr Max "Wolfie" Schneider. I still find Wolfie visually appealing, but as a character he's got nothing else to recommend him and frankly Eddi is showing all the taste and discernment of Early Chrissie – ie none. Oh, Luc, come back soon, please.

Dr Tara Lo was living on caffeine tablets to try and keep up with Jac Naylor's demands. Jac wasn't even there, but she'd left Tara with a mountain of work and a fear of failure to add to her usual work ethic and desperate need to please. It's a powerful combination and something had to give. The thing was Tara, who ended up fainting and knocking a locker over. Oli was concerned, but Tara shrugged it off and then attempted to show just how perky and competent she was by attempting to take an arterial blood gas without the supervision of Oli or Elliot. Luckily, the patient didn't die, though he did bleed like a stuck pig for a while. Adorably, Oli was going to take the blame – how contrary to his usual mode of behaviour – but all was well that ended well when Tara redeemed herself by spotting her patient had been full of cocaine.

On Keller, Chantelle proved for the umpteenth time that despite being sunny and cheerful and a bit ditzy sometimes, she's a damn good nurse. Heartwarming etc, because I do love Chantelle, but I think we got that particular message a while back.

Michael Spence. Hell, yeah

(*Series 14, ep. 46 'Taxi for Spence' by Joe Ainsworth 28.8.12*)

Little pen-pushing, calculator-prodding George Binns has been in need of a bit of lesson-learning. You know, the kind of lesson where patients cease to be statistics and you find yourself with your face shoved up against the grim reality of death.

Trust Michael Spence to take that quite literally. If I'd had a tiny American flag to hand, I'd have waved it merrily at the end of this episode, when our favourite tight-trousered surgeon decided he'd had enough nonsense from Little George Binns for one lifetime and frogmarched him through the hospital to show him exactly what the non-referral policy had meant in terms of human suffering, as embodied by guest artiste David Troughton, a nice man who ended up dying despite Michael's best efforts to find him a bed. George had been getting rather above himself (not difficult, as he's only about five feet tall) during the episode. When Michael started to leave a pointless managerial seminar early, Little George had a bit of an edge to him when he said, "I wouldn't miss it... if I were you." It was only a matter of time before someone punched him. The thought did cross my mind, "Where's Joseph Byrne when you need him?" but I think that most weeks anyway. As it turned out, Michael rose to the occasion magnificently. I do love Michael when he's full of righteous indignation.

On Darwin, meanwhile, Jonny Mac was doing a little bit of matchmaking for Mo. Her former obstetrician (he's still an obstetrician, but she no longer has need of his services) thinks she's somewhere north of wonderful. Sadly for him, Mo thinks it's somewhere south of spooky to go on a date with a man who's already shone a torch up your private bits. They both have a point, to be fair. Jonny was mainly matchmaking because he felt guilty for not going to a family do with Mo, because he was spending the weekend at a hotel with Jac. For some reason he decided to lie about it rather than just tell Mo why he couldn't go with her. Not a clever idea.

The non-referral policy wasn't a clever idea either. Wasn't it Serena who thought of it in the first place? She's regretting it now, as she spent the episode in the horns of an ethical dilemma involving one liver and two eager transplant recipients and ended it hearing about the death of Michael's patient. Not a good day at the office.

Something else you didn't know about me

(Series 14, ep. 47 'I'm Sticking With You' by Dana Fainaru 4.9.12)

So the non referral policy is over and everything's right with the world, yes? Actually, no. The shadow of the death of Nice Mr Mooney hung over everyone in this episode. Little George Binns was keen to lay the blame at the door of Michael Spence, who has a history of being maverick and so on. Michael has responded to adversity the best way he knows how – by letting his beard grow again (hurrah!) and by being ever more maverick, sending referrals up to Keller like it's going out of style.

All these patients turning up at Keller's door made Chrissie even more tense and irritable than usual. You'd think living with Sacha would make her all mellow and cuddly and want to make jam and bake sponge cakes (or is that just my reaction to Sacha?), but she's been quite the bitch recently. She was particularly horrible to the angelic Chantelle this week. We know how Chantelle operates, though. She just pushes through with her niceness agenda – because she genuinely just is nice – and everyone ends up smiling in a twinkly way at her by the end of the episode. Even hard cases like Chrissie and Serena.

Talking of hard cases, Mo had one to deal with in the form of a girl who needed an operation but didn't want a blood transfusion because she was a Jehovah's Witness. There was a way to do the op without a blood transfusion, but Mo wasn't confident as she'd done one previously that had gone pear-shaped, so she arranged for a top specialist to come from That London to do it. Before the specialist could get round the M25 and get stuck in, the young patient took a turn for the worse and her father persuaded everybody that it was okay to ignore the bloodless part and just crack on with the op in the normal way. Jac thought that was the best way to proceed. But Mo is a contrary and cussed sort (which is why I like her) and she decided she was not going to ignore the girl's wishes and was going to do the bloodless procedure regardless. There was part of her that wanted to stick it to Jac Naylor as well, I'm sure. Lord help the sister who comes between Mo and Jonny Mac. Jonny and Oli scrubbed in to the op, even though they could potentially get into trouble. Adorably, when Mo had a bit of a confidence wobble mid-procedure (the inevitable moment when there's a bleed and someone says, "We've got a bleed!" although they didn't this time because they didn't want to freak Mo out any more than she was freaking out already) Jonny and Oli supported her with a bit of a singalong. It was very cute.

Bad moon rising

(Series 14, ep. 48 'Devil's Dance' by Martha Hillier 11.9.12)

There was a moment in an episode a couple of weeks ago, which was repeated in the recap at the start of this episode, when Eddi was feeling a bit deflated and Wolfie said he had "something that would make her feel better."

"Aha!" I remember thinking at the time. "He's on drugs! That's why he keeps going for extended fag breaks." Only then he and Eddi went off for some store room shenanigans, and I thought I'd got it wrong. But I hadn't, had I? This week saw him scrabbling round among used needles and bloody swabs (ugh) for some precious Camoxidan tablets that had almost got thrown away. He ended up high as a kite with a scalpel in his hand, trying to perform surgery while Eddi tried to convince him to step away from the table because he was clearly not quite right, and a surgical team of non-speaking extras looked concerned and/or amused. That Camoxidan looks like good stuff, but don't try getting it either from Boots or from that dodgy bloke at the pub, because it's completely fictional. But did nobody notice how bizarre Wolfie's behaviour was getting? He did everything apart from swish his cape, twirl his moustache and cackle manically to signal he was Turning To The Dark Side.

The problem is that Wolfie has dragged Eddi into colluding and covering on his behalf. Sacha had his suspicions, and he was worried for the moral and professional well-being of the former Best Nurse In The Hospital. He took the drastic step of ringing Luc and telling him to get back to Holby ASAP. Hurrah! Expect industrial quantities of face-pulling next week when the Best Nurse finds herself torn between two lovers.

Talking of lovers, Ollie and Tara seem to have become a couple in a nice, quiet, low-key way while we weren't looking. They had a date, anyway, and Tara actually stood up to Jac ("I want a diagnosis and a latte, please") and put Ollie first. It was quite a lovely moment.

Junior doctors, eh? They just don't know their place any more, as Malick found out when he had a new bunch of Malickites to mentor. Ric attempted to show him how it was done, but he didn't fare all that better. Chrissie – who actually smiled quite a lot this week – gave Malick some feedback about the feedback the students were giving about him. "They said you were sweet," she said, "But that could be a young person's word for terrible." Fair point, Chrissie. She had valuable advice about how to show them who was boss, though: "Unleash hell!"

"I don't do slack"

(*Series 14, ep. 49 'A Crack in the Ice' by Lauren Klee 18.9.12*)

It was Chrissie's 40th birthday (but don't make a fuss because she still wants to be showbiz 30-something), but that was the least exciting thing that was going on. Cake, crisps and a signed card might be thrilling enough for Chantelle ("You've just described hell," muttered Chrissie), but we were busy being treated to the return of Luc, a radiation scare, lust and romance all over the place, ninja level surgery and Mo and Jac naked (but only because the part demanded it).

It opened with a pair of awkward threesomes. Who should happen to walk in on Eddi and Wolfie having one of their hair-ruffling encounters but Dr Luc Hemingway, sporting a new super-short haircut (no hair ruffling for him). Not even a gentle roar of a camper van engine to warn Eddi that her former beau was back, either. And who should walk in on Jac and Jonny having a quick snog in the lift than Young Dr Oliver Valentine, who could accurately be described as a former squeeze of the lovely Miss Naylor himself. Awkward.

To Darwin first, then, and a few weeks ago it looked like Jac and Mo might actually become friends, to whatever extent Jac actually "does" friends (probably about as much as she "does" carbs). A couple of things have put paid to that, one of them being Jac's relationship with Mo's bezzy mate Jonny Mac, which has made Mo feel a bit threatened. The other thing is that they're both successful, career-driven women in a profession that's as much about competition as it is about co-operation. Both these aspects collided in fine style during this episode, which saw them both having to deal with a man who was actually radioactive. Hanssen forbade them from operating until they had the all clear from the man with the Geiger counter, but it was a life or death situation so they operated anyway, with Hanssen frowning at them through the glass and telling them to watch the clock. Jac, being in possession of only one kidney, was ordered to leave, but she signed a waiver form and returned anyway. When her time was up, Mo took over, with Jac assisting from beyond the glass. It was heroic stuff. Afterwards, they had to give up all their clothes, in case they were contaminated. Jac looked all sweet and vulnerable in just a sheet and she looked even more sweet and vulnerable when Mo told her that Jonny Mac really likes her. When Jonny came in to give her a post shift-from-hell hug, she tried to push him away. "Shut up, you one-kidneyed freak," he told her and hugged her anyway. Awww. I never thought I would warm to Jac having Jonny in her life (I still hold out hope that Joseph might get tired of Penrith and come a-calling), but he's actually really good for her. I suppose it's because he's used to dealing with Mo – tough women don't freak him out at all.

Eddi McKee used to be a tough woman, but it was obviously all a facade, because all it took was for her to be abandoned by Dr Luc Hemingway and then for Wolfie to appear and she's gone all sloppy and reckless. Sacha thought all it would take would be for Luc to appear back in her life and she'd be all sorted out, but it's not going to be that easy. "Wherever you've been, it certainly hasn't been on a people skills course," she snarled at poor Luc. Well pot/kettle to you, missy. She did, however, draw the line at having a couple of Wolfie's Camoxidan pills. Along with their other fictional qualities, they're a "kick ass hangover cure," apparently. Luc obviously didn't like Wolfie, but he ended up having to bail him out in theatre when things were very much going belly-up with a patient who technically shouldn't even have been in theatre at all. Was Wolfie grateful? Nope. He just carried on being his usual horrible self and taunting Luc about Eddi now being with him. Frankly, Luc should have decked him. But there may still be time to deck him, as Luc is going to stick around for a while. Hurrah!

Is this something else that might require a doughnut?

(Series 14, ep. 50 'Hold On Me' by Martin Jameson 25.9.12)

The main action this week was in AAU and Keller, with Darwin as this week's comedy relief. And I never thought I'd hear myself say that.

To the hurly burly of AAU first, and the hot news is that Luc's camper van was clamped. The other hot news was that Wolfie had the chance of a nice job in Brighton – now Luc's back, there's no job for Wolfie at Holby. This was just as well, because Luc was noticing some troubling things about Wolfie. For one thing, he's hardly ever seen without having Nurse McKee attached to his face, which has got to be awkward and inconvenient, not least for the patients. For another thing, he had trembly hands. Again, not something to inspire patient confidence, and also a tell-tale sign of Camoxidan addiction. Luc did what any self-respecting maverick doctor would do, and covertly took a sample of Wolfie's hair – or should we call it pelt – from his jacket while Wolfie wasn't wearing it, and had it tested. This is not technically legal, but who cares when it came up with the evidence that Wolfie has been full of Camoxidan for at least months. This explains the trembly hands and the fact that he can't put a pressure bandage on to save his life. Or, more accurately, to save someone else's life.

There was a big showdown, Wolfie stomped off to Brighton and Eddi failed to stomp with him – but she did try to cheer herself up after his departure by popping one of his dodgy pills herself. Are we now going to have to endure Eddi's descent into drugs hell? I had enough of that when it was Mark "Jesus" Williams who at one stage was forever nipping off to the gents for a mid-shift enlivener.

Meanwhile, almost everyone on Keller was tense, awaiting the results of the report into the death of Nice Mr Mooney. Chantelle wasn't tense, because she's way too sunny for that type of thing and she also had a box of mini doughnuts as a relaxation aid. I do admire Chantelle's thinking. Serena didn't admire it that much, but she did have a sneaky doughnut anyway. Serena's controversial initiative of the week was to fast track patients by popping tubes up or down them to have a look-see before she'd done any X-rays or boring stuff like that. It saves time, but doesn't work when you have patients who inconveniently have all their organs the wrong way round. Victory for Ric and his old-fashioned, methodical approach once again, but he assured Serena this didn't mean he would let her take the blame over Mr Mooney.

As it turned out, no-one is getting the blame for Mr Mooney, as the report came back as "no blame attached." There were more than strong clues that this is not the last we're going to hear of this story, though. Not judging by the mass of emails Hanssen received with the subject line, "Blood on your hands." We do need to be concerned about our favourite super-tall Swede.

Darwin was a bit quiet, because Jac was away at a conference and Ollie had gone with her to carry her bag. He'd also left his phone behind, and Jonny Mac saw an opportunity to wind Tara up by sending her racy texts from Ollie's phone. She neatly (and a tad predictably, it must be said) turned the tables on him by sending back texts that seemed to indicate that Jac was having an affair with a millionaire. It was quite sweet, because Jonny kept pretending to Mo that he wasn't bothered – "This is Naylor we're talking about" – but he so is.

The things people keep in their drawers

(Series 14, ep. 51 'Blood Money' by Nick Fisher 2.10.12)

Have you noticed how people on TV have really tidy desk drawers? Typically the top drawer of any given TV desk will contain a few sheets of paper and One Thing important to the character or plot. If the character is an alcoholic, the One Thing will be a bottle of whisky. If they're a bit dodgy, it'll be a gun. If they're worried they might be pregnant, it will be a pregnancy test in a large pink box. If they've recently removed a huge nail from their own abdomen, it'll be a suture kit. But more of that later.

This episode had been hotly anticipated. The trailers looked tense – Hanssen kidnapped in the back of a van in the hospital car park by the son of the late Nice Mr Mooney, crazed with grief and after retribution. There were bottles of inflammable liquids and a lighter. There was a nasty-looking nail gun. But in the end, that part of the story wasn't very tense at all, because for tense you need someone who's looking scared, and Hanssen was as cool as could be. Little George Binns was flying the flag for "tense" and "scared" elsewhere, though.

This is not to say the episode wasn't magnificent, because it was, just not in the way the trailers had led me to believe. It was magnificent because Hanssen was magnificent. He has balls of Swedish steel and practically embodies the phrase "grace under pressure." When he was accidentally shot in the abdomen by the aforementioned nasty nail gun, did he crash to the car park floor gasping, "We need some help here?" No, he did not. He calmly pulled it out with some pliers, pulled his jacket over the blood stain and hijacked a camera crew to film a public apology to Mr Mooney Jr. And then he calmly opened his desk drawer, took out a suture kit and repaired his own wound. Bravo.

Jac's desk drawer was the one with the pregnancy testing kit. There was relief all round when it proved to be negative. Or was there? I'm sure I saw a trace of regret cross the brow of Holby's snappiest surgeon. All I can say is, if she's feeling the tick of the biological clock she should get herself to Penrith. I've warmed to Jonny Mac, but Joseph is the only man for her.

Meanwhile, Sacha told Chrissie he thought they should get married quickly to save on tax. It would be prudent and expedient, he told her. "Prudent and expedient," sniffed Chrissie. "The words a girl longs to hear." I am with Chrissie on this one. So Sacha went in for the big gesture and got Chantelle to hang a huge banner proclaiming his love out of a high window. This was enough to put a smile back on Chrissie's face, but she's told him she doesn't want a big wedding. She wants low key. But next week, Sacha's female relatives get involved. Can the key stay low?

All you need is love. And Camoxidan

(Series 14, ep. 52 'When Sacha Met Chrissie' by Justin Young 9.10.12)

An entire episode dealing with Chrissie's inner turmoil as to whether to marry Sacha or not does not sound like the stuff televisual dreams are made of. I mean, for one thing – duh! He might be built more for comfort than speed, but Sacha is officially The Nicest Man in the World, so why wouldn't you want to marry him? Particularly when you've sampled more or less everyone else. But it was actually one of the best episodes of Holby I've ever seen.

It took place across the five days leading up to The Happy Occasion. On Monday, the betrothed pair were planning to keep the wedding quiet and Chrissie was looking about as excited as if she was going for a colonoscopy. Meanwhile, Michael Spence was worried about letting Eddi have the keys to the drugs cupboard, what with her involvement with Wolfie and his druggy behaviour, and told her she'd only be able to do this if she got them signed off by another doctor (ie Luc) first. The only way Eddi could cope with all this suspicion was with liberal doses of Camoxidan.

By Tuesday, Eddi was getting numb hands. This is what Camoxidan abuse does, as we saw from Wolfie. It was also making her stroppier than usual and making her shout at Billy Corkhill from Brookside, whose wife was in a coma. "Eddi is a great nurse, but she's a little feisty," Sacha apologised. Eddi's Camoxidan supply ran out. The quiet wedding was turning into a slightly larger affair when Sacha's daughters got wind of it and proceeded to cry and sulk because they hadn't been invited. "They forced it out of me," Sacha apologised again. Only to Chrissie this time, rather than Billy Corkhill.

On Wednesday, love was in the air, as Ollie and Tara arrived at the hospital holding hands. I can't help thinking of them as "the Valentines" already. Meanwhile, Chrissie was arriving at the hospital in a hot car with a bunch of Sacha's relatives. Chrissie was having major doubts. "Am I making a terrible mistake?" she fretted in the general direction of Malick. This is Malick who was party to her terrible mistake with Dan Hamilton, don't forget.

On Darwin, Jac had found a use for Tara, when a Chinese patient needed a translator. Only the patient spoke Cantonese and Tara only speaks Mandarin, so she had to ring her mum for a translation. Plus she was in an even bigger fluster than usual because Ollie had casually let slip that he loves her (all together now: Squeeeeeeee!!!).

Thursday, AKA Wedding Eve, AKA Last Day of Freedom, depending on your viewpoint. If Chrissie thought she was going to slip quietly into wedded bliss, Chantelle had other plans as she'd arranged a hen party, complete with pink fluffy L plates for Chrissie. I think she passed that particular test some time ago. Marvellously, Sacha's stag do took place in Luc's camper van, and even more marvellously the only guests were Michael Spence, Luc – and Jac Naylor. It was perfect that Jac was there, because she's far more at home with the stags than the hens and her friendship with Sacha is a precious and lovely thing. It's also lovely to see Jac really smiling and looking relaxed and happy. Not that she wasn't her usual sarcastic self, though. Sacha was telling them about the night he met Chrissie. "By the end of the night we had conceived Daniel," he sighed, and everyone looked slightly queasy. Sacha didn't notice, because he was radiantly happy. "I wish you could all have what I have," he said. Jac didn't miss a beat. "In fairness, most of the hospital's had what you have," she said. As Jac was leaving, she bumped into Chrissie, who may or may not have been on her way to tell Sacha she was having second thoughts. Any nonsense of that sort was swiftly banished by Jac, who reminded Chrissie in no uncertain terms that Sacha is officially The Nicest Man in the World and not to go breaking his heart – or else.

In other news on the Thursday, Eddi was busy switching Tara's Chinese patient's medication – giving the patient aspirin, so she could grab a couple of those precious Camoxidan tablets. Oh, Eddi.

And at last, The Big Day. Thanks to some last-minute work by Chrissie and the female Levis, the wedding took place in the restaurant where Sacha and Chrissie had their first date. Only a stone's throw from the hospital as well. It was a magical occasion, with the groom looking like he couldn't believe his luck, the bride looking happy (albeit in a not entirely convinced way), Jac looking sceptical and Eddi off her box on Camoxidan. Mo and Jonny Mac turned up – in fact most of the cast were there at some point, though I was a little disappointed that Mark "Jesus" Williams didn't show up, because it's always handy to have "Jesus" at a wedding party in case the wine runs out. Eddi made a bit of a show of herself and had to be taken back to the camper van by Luc to sleep it off, and Tara said something to Ollie in Chinese which was probably that she loves him, too. Because that's what people do at weddings. They get romantic, or sentimental, or hammered. Or they just do a spot of dad-dancing, like Jonny Mac.

SERIES 15

The come down

(Series 15, ep. 1 'The Third Way' by Martha Hillier, Dana Fainaru & Julia Gilbert 16.10.12)

The sad truth for the intoxicated is that you either have to take more of whatever got you high to keep you there, or you have to face the come down afterwards.

This is very much how I felt watching this week's Holby. Not that the series opener (I love how a new series starts a mere seven days after the old one ended) wasn't a perfectly serviceable piece of telly, because it was. In parts it was actually pretty good. It just couldn't compare to last week's near-perfection.

Last week's episode had one writer (Justin Young) and this week there were three people listed on the credits (Martha Hillier, Dana Fainaru and Julia Gilbert). There were also three story lines, and I wonder whether they were given one each. If they were, the person who got the Eddi and Luc storyline fared the best. For her own good, Eddi had been ring-fenced. Luc had driven her in the camper van to the grounds of an unspecified stately home he's allowed to camp in and planned to keep her there until all the nasty Camoxidan was out of her system.

Ooh, it's scary stuff, that Camoxidan. In the space of a couple of weeks Eddi has gone from being the Best Nurse in the Hospital to being a puking, twitching mess in the throes of withdrawal. She tried to steal Luc's camper van to get away, but only succeeded in getting it stuck in the mud. Just as well – I can just picture her barrelling along the fictional byroads of Wyvern like a Casualty episode waiting to happen. It's clear that her drug of (Wolfie's) choice has addled her brain – who wouldn't want to be stuck in a pleasant field near a pleasant river with Luc and all the amenities of his luxury wheeled dwelling? I'd certainly be prepared to give it a go. Luc was adorable – and possibly feeling more than a tad guilty for abandoning her and thus being the cause of her falling into Wolfie's arms and evil ways – and it's clear he's going to sit it out with her and stand by her through whatever she's going to go through.

I expect Oliver Valentine would be just like that with Tara, but she's not giving him a chance, because she still hasn't told him about her brain tumour. She was given a patient this week whose boyfriend was unaware of her heart condition (top of the transplant list standard of heart condition, too). This poor patient was obviously only there to speak Tara's brains, and it was clear from Oliver's reaction that he feels loved ones should be kept in the loop with this sort of thing. Tara's own feelings about her illness influenced how she treated the patient, with the result that Elliot went to Hanssen to say that maybe Tara wasn't suited to the hurly burly of Darwin. Hanssen told Elliot the reason for Tara's behaviour – so now Elliot knows and it can only be a matter of time before Oliver finds out too, probably by Tara keeling over and going, "Nnngh!" in a corridor somewhere.

Hanssen, meanwhile, was mostly occupied by fending off an annoying reporter. This was the least interesting of the three story lines, mainly because I couldn't be bothered to follow the ins and outs of whatever set of initiatives Hanssen was, or wasn't, meant to be supporting. What I did enjoy was the little frisson between him and PR lady Sinead Bainbridge. Ms Bainbridge is attractive and smart, and there was definitely a little bit of flirting going on.

They tried to make her go to rehab

(Series 15, ep. 2 'Chasing Demons' by Julia Gilbert 23.10.12)

Eddi, Luc and the "love bus" were back at Holby this week, Eddi deeming herself ready to face the temptations of the AAU drugs cupboard with Luc's support. If only Michael hadn't given her the keys again, all might have been well. About five minutes into the shift she was already stuffing Camoxidan down her face like it was about to be made prescription-only. Oh.

What had been kept secret from the Holby-watching world was that this was Sarah-Jane Potts' last episode and all this Camoxidan business has been her exit storyline. Suitably dramatic it was,too, with Eddi at last finding true love again with Luc, only to collapse on the floor of the basement (nothing good ever happens in that basement) after taking erratic doses of her favourite medication. Luc had to take drastic action. When Eddi woke up, she found herself surrounded by Luc, Michael Spence, Sacha and her brother Liam, all gazing at her more in sorrow than in anger. Seeing Liam was the jolt she needed. She didn't want to end up like their mum, so she decided getting away from Holby was the only way to do it. So farewell Eddi McKee, one-time Best Nurse in the Hospital and Face Puller Extraordinaire. Who will we be able to rely on now for those all-important end-of-scene reaction shots?

This means there's a vacancy for the Best Nurse job, and there's only one person who could fill it: Chantelle Lane – the woman with the sunniest smile and the biggest snack collection in the NHS. There was a hurdle to overcome first in the form of an interview for a permanent staff nurse job. There was hot competition from the lovely (but very bitchy this week) Mary-Claire, and the pressure of being interviewed by none other than the legend who is Charlie Fairhead from Casualty. Chantelle's interview was suitably ditzy. "What's your biggest weakness?" she was asked. "Chocolate, definitely," she replied. But you can't help but love her, and when she's not being all fluffy kittens she's actually a darn good nurse, as she proved when she sorted out a man who was harming himself to get hospital attention. Did she get the job? Of course she did.

Hanssen had a spare pot of money to give away, so who better to give it to than Elliot Hope, the man with the artificial heart? Not his own heart – that's real enough – but the Herzig 3, a miracle of modern engineering just waiting to be tested on a real person. Will the real person be Aisha, who refused a heart transplant last week? She had a bit of a reality check when a patient she'd just met collapsed and died while they were driving round the car park together (don't ask). It was all an excuse for people to say things like, "You don't know what it's like sitting up at 4 AM having chats with the Grim Reaper" in the general direction of Tara, who gets her introspective face on because she certainly does know what that's like. Just stay away from that basement, Tara. Remember – nothing good ever happens there.

Where's the Camoxidan when you need it?

(Series 15, ep. 3 'Follow My Leader' by Stephen Brady & Nick Fisher 30.10.12)

I watched this episode with a befuffled head, thanks to having a very nasty cold. I say this by way of apology for the fact that this is such a poor-quality blog post. Having spent most of the day slumped in a sneezing heap watching *Judge Judy* from beneath heavy eyelids, frankly my powers of concentration weren't what they should have been come 8PM. Maybe Camoxidan would have helped, but I'm willing to bet, now Eddi's gone, Camoxidan will never be mentioned on Holby again. People will go back to getting good old-fashioned paracetamol for pain.

Seeing Ianto Jones from *Torchwood* popping up on Keller didn't help my confuzzlement. He (Gareth David Lloyd) was playing new boy Rhys Hopkins. I'm not quite sure what his job title was – I thought he said he was a radiographer, but he seemed to be doing generally doctorly stuff (and possibly dealing with aliens in the basement). As I said, I wasn't at the peak of my powers, concentration-wise. That naughty Mary-Claire tried to get Chantelle into trouble with him by letting him think it was Chantelle who'd confused saline for anaesthetic. Our Chantelle doesn't make mistakes like that, and as well as proving herself to be jolly competent on her first day as a staff nurse, she was also invited out for an end-of-shift drink by Rhys.

There was another new person on AAU in the shape of junior doctor Lilah Birdwood (Natasha Leigh). I'm not sure about her yet – I don't think we quite saw enough of her to know which way her personality is going to go.

And Hanssen and Jac had to grapple with their priorities when a member of the board's daughter needed an operation but Elliot also had the opportunity to try out his Herzig 3 on Aisha (that's not a euphemism).

Small things done in a great way

(Series 15, ep. 4 'If Not For You' by Jamie Crichton 6.11.12)

Not wanting to run into board member Cunningham, Hanssen pressed the B button on the lift and found himself in the basement. The basement is generally the place Holby cast members go to collapse, be attacked or have a sulky smoke. Nothing good generally happens there, but on this occasion, Hanssen found himself chatting to a Polish porter, Karol, whose job was under threat. This porter was a wise old sort, although he was blissfully unaware that he was talking to Henrik Hanssen, somewhat implausibly, given that Hanssen's face had been all over local newspapers and TV news for weeks. It reminded me of the encounter between Kevin and the owner of the toy store in *Home Alone 2: Lost In New York* (I'm sorry, but that film is my cultural touchstone). Karol was a people-person and liked to make a difference to the people he worked with. He had the following advice: "If you can't do great things, do small things in a great way."

"Small things in a great way" beautifully sums up Guy Henry's portrayal of Hanssen. It's all about restraint and control, with emotions leaking through the carefully positioned mask. In this episode, he was caring for the son (played by Ben-Ryan Davies) of his first ever patient at Holby, but he was unable to save the son's life. When Karol called by his office later to give his sympathies, Hanssen explained why the boy was so significant to him, and it was an incredibly moving piece of acting. "My first day here," he said, "I saved his father... And I thought that I could save him." The "him" just got lost, as he was so close to the edge of tears.

It was a classic Hanssen moment, and it was almost the last, for now at least. He packed a box with the things from his desk, and left the hospital. Watched from the Window of Regret by Jac, he put the box into his car and glanced around one last time before driving away. When will he be back? Will he be back? And what was the phone call about that he received in Swedish earlier?

Jac was also watching Jonny Mac – it was that rare beast, the three-way Window of Regret. The reason there was a pane of regret between them was that Jac had just dumped him, because he'd started to get in the way of her career, and when it comes to romance v work, there's no contest for Jac. Jonny had also managed to annoy Mo, when he tried to steer a middle path between both of the women in his life and get them to work amiably together with the slightly misguided strategy of being really annoying.

Meanwhile, Sacha was walking through a storyline which he and Chantelle seem to do on alternate weeks – trying to be something they're not, until they eventually work out that what they are is just fine as it is. For short, we'll call it "People skills save the day."

Who's sitting at Hanssen's desk?

(Series 15, ep. 5 'To Absent Friends' by Philip Ralph 13.11.12)

"Who is running Holby City?" Ric wanted to know when he discovered Henrik Hanssen had taken a leave of absence (that's "leave of absence," worried Hanssenites – they mentioned him so often in this episode that I'm quite confident he'll be back. It's Luc Hemingway all over again). Ric was not perked up to discover that the answer to his question was (temporarily) Serena Campbell, a woman with whom he does not exactly see eye to eye.

She's confident, that Serena. Her job interview was more like a sales pitch to the board. "I have what I believe is a compelling solution," she briskly informed them. "Me." The thing with Serena is, although she does display flashes of warmth, she is really all about the balance sheet. As such, she did look scarily comfortable in Hanssen's chair.

Everyone wanted Ric to go for the CEO job, because Michael Spence and Elliot Hope weren't interested in it and everyone is scared of Serena. The four of them seemed to be the entire candidate pool. I don't have any particular knowledge of NHS administration, but I couldn't help thinking this wasn't the most realistic scenario I'd ever come across. What it did do, however, was set Ric up for the classic patient v future-of-the-hospital dilemma. He had a patient who was about to have a kidney transplant, and the kidney she was about to get might or might not give her cancer. Serena thought it would be dreadful publicity for the hospital if they gave a patient cancer, but Ric felt the kidney was the only option for the patient. It wasn't ideal that his interview for the CEO job meant he had to leave the operation early and leave the suturing up in the capable hands of The Malick. Naturally the machines started going beep while he was away, and by the time he got back to theatre there was blood everywhere. "You take the vein, I'll take the artery," said Ric.

All was well that ended well, but Ric didn't get the job. He didn't really want it, not after almost losing his patient had reminded him of his priorities. Serena didn't get the job, either. An external candidate has been appointed, apparently, and we will be meeting her next week.

On Darwin, Jonny Mac was worrying about Mo's moral fibre, as she had spent the night with Albie, who owns the bar. He's married, you see. Personally, I think Mo could do much better than Albie, who as well as being married seems a wee bit creepy. Mo was in no mood to take relationship advice from Jonny, though, and said if it all goes horribly wrong, she won't even need him to help pick up the pieces. Sulky madam, she is.

There was another sulky madam on AAU, a new HCA called Ramona. She started off well by referring to Michael Spence as "a jerk." I love Michael Spence, but I also enjoy seeing him being put in his place by feisty juniors. With Ramona's direct approach and foreign accent, I couldn't help but be reminded of the glorious Goth Dr Frieda. I hope we'll be seeing her again and she won't end up disappearing like Lleucu and the now-you-see-her-now-you-don't Mary-Claire.

Michael wasn't in the best of moods because his children were supposed to be visiting him, but now weren't going to be coming until Christmas. Attempts to contact Annalese to shout at her failed, so he had to shout at staff and patients instead. Ramona wasn't taking any of that nonsense, and gave as good as she got. "How are things going with Ramona?" Sacha asked Michael. "Awesome," was the reply. "We're like the Borgias on crack." You can see why I want to see more of Ramona. Anyway, they ended up bonding a bit in the basement (something good happened in the basement for the second week running!). After he accused her of stealing a silver bookmark with photos of his kids on it, she threw a glass of water over him, then found the bookmark in a bin bag and showed him photos of her kids. Heartwarming.

Excellent! Onwards!

(Series 15, ep. 6 'Hail Caesar' by Dana Fainaru 20.11.12)

Looming is not a technique that suits everybody. It's best left to the tall, dark and enigmatic. The new CEO of Holby City, Imelda Cousins (Tessa Peake-Jones) doesn't have the stature to pull off a loom, so her technique is apparently to be everywhere at once, like the administrative equivalent of a flea infestation. Imelda comes across as a bit dotty and eccentric (she says things like "Lordy!" and her exclamation of "Onwards!" has already become a catchphrase at PLA Towers), but she's actually acute and tough.

Naturally, this was difficult for the other staff members to cope with. Ric said the last person they needed in charge was a "jumped-up nurse manager," particularly when she had strong views about staff deployment. She wanted Lilah back on AAU, so Ric decided to keep her on Keller, just to show who was in charge, come what may. "Come what may" turned out to be a near-disaster in theatre, after Lilah gave the patient Heparin and he bled all over the place. It wasn't Lilah's best day at the office – she got punched by the patient's wife as well. Imelda neatly pulled the rug out from under Ric by putting Lilah under Malick's supervision.

I felt sorry for Lilah, but not as sorry as I felt for Jonny Mac. I admit I didn't like him when he first appeared. He seemed like a bit of an idiot and I didn't think he was any match for the glorious Jac. I have now done a complete reversal and I think he's lovely – he's kind, funny, sweet, tries too hard, messes up. He's human, in other words, but "human" isn't quite enough for Jac, whose standards in all things are impossibly high. She really does like him, but whenever he questions her clinical judgement that's it – he's out. And then she went off on a date with paediatrician Prof Gleeson – on Jonny's birthday as well! And Mo was nowhere to be seen, either. Probably off with that creepy man from the bar. Poor Jonny.

In the department that we know fondly as AAU, Imelda had made her presence felt by ejecting Luc from the post-Eddi comfort zone of his lab to do some actual doctoring. Luc's bedside manner is my guilty pleasure – he's got no time for niceness and is pragmatic to the point of ruthlessness. Sacha's phrase, "Majestically up himself" covers it nicely. I also like it when he takes the piss out of himself. "If I went in for the human contact stuff, I honestly could hug you," he told the aforementioned Sacha (the world's most huggable man, admittedly). He's even going to let Sacha help with his research project. This has pleased Sacha, because Chrissie has told him he needs to push himself forward more. Poor man.

Cupcakes, kisses and kleptomania

(Series 15, ep. 7 'After the Party' by Emer Kenny 27.11.12)

It's always good to start an episode with Jac arriving at work on her motorbike and wearing her leathers. Jonny Mac thought so, too. Particularly as the fact that she'd arrived on the bike suggested she hadn't spent the night with the oily paediatrician of last week's episode. Later she confided to him that the paediatrician had ordered for her in the restaurant they went to. Ouch – schoolboy error, there. Jonny Mac looked amused – and relieved. He loves her to bits and, though I never imagined myself saying this, I'm rooting for the lad. If Jac would only let him, he'd be really good for her. He respects her, but he's not scared of her. Most importantly, he makes her laugh. She needs a bit of fun in her life to balance out her natural intensity.

She had good reason to be intense this week. Under orders from Imelda to get through her list efficiently and not take on any more cases, she took on another case, and it was a tricky one – Nina, a 15 year old girl with a heart problem, who was pregnant after being raped. Imelda ("She's like someone who collects cats and pretends they're real people," said Oliver, who's always reliable for an amusing quote) ordered Nina to be transferred to the Mythical St James, but Jac, Jonny and Oli cracked on and operated anyhow. Jac got emotionally involved with this case, possibly partly due to the humanising effect of Jonny on her life but also because it involved a child (two children, including the baby), and Jac's finer feelings are often stirred by children. She was magnificent, anyway, giving support to Nina and giving her dad a pep talk when he needed it.

Serena was hoping that Imelda's arrival would mean she would soon be able to escape from the Hanssen-imposed exile of AAU. Amusingly, it seemed that she and Imelda had already met. Serena couldn't remember it, but after a bit of a think remembered a former colleague she'd had a lot of fun with when they'd both basically harassed an overweight colleague until she had to leave. Embarrassingly, it turned out she was almost right – "Imelda was the biscuit thief," Serena explained to Michael after Imelda had pointed out her mistake. "And I terrorised her."

It's just as well Serena was warming to life on AAU, because Imelda won't be inclined to move her any time soon. She had to deal with a kleptomaniac patient who turned out to have an adrenal tumour. "It certainly beats vomiting tramps," Serena said. AAU was actually quite interesting this week. Ramona was back, and it looks like she and Michael Spence are an item. This could be fun.

On Keller, Lilah had baked cupcakes. Malick was not impressed and neither was I, given that the last cupcake-distributor at Holby was Sahira Shah the Registrah. Lilah bakes when she's stressed, apparently, and the reason she was stressed was because she had an assessment and she wasn't feeling confident. Ric Griffin was much more impressed than Malick by her cupcakes, and by Lilah generally. He's taken her under his wing, and when she failed her assessment he told her she could try again and accompanied her to the lab, where he more or less talked her through it. If this all seemed a bit too hands-on as far as mentoring went, it got worse when they ended up kissing. Uh-oh. That can't end well.

You want to cut a piece of my heart out?

(Series 15, ep. 8 'How Lo Can You Go' by Joe Ainsworth 4.12.12)

What a lifetime of suffering poor Aisha Bose had. Leukaemia, heart disease, failed surgery, failed relationship and, worst of all, her whole life being a metaphor and illumination for the problems of Dr Tara Lo. Aisha was brought back to Darwin with an infection, and it wasn't looking good. The only option was a spot of heart-rearranging surgery that would buy her some time, but Elliot was forced to admit they were now talking about months rather than years.

She was obviously upset and angry, and vented her anger on Dr Tara Lo, who was conveniently never more than a metre from her bedside, frowning at her in an upset way. Tara's attempts at empathy only got Aisha more and more cross, until she realised that Tara was ill herself. This explained why Tara had been so interested to find out how Aisha's boyfriend had reacted to her illness (badly) – because she's been grappling with the problem of whether, or when, to tell Oliver. "Tell him," was Aisha's advice. Despite a heart-to-heart in the Linden Cullen Memorial Shrubbery, Tara's default setting is to push people away. It wasn't until after Aisha had died on the operating table (poignantly, her last words were to tell Ollie to look after Tara) and Elliot had sent the emotional Tara to spend the rest of the shift in the wet lab, that Ollie finally managed to crack her. "What's going on in that head of yours?" he demanded, which prompted an ironic smile and the flinging of some brain scan pictures at him. Unlike most men, Ollie is now in the privileged position of having seen exactly what's going on in his girlfriend's head, but it wasn't good news.

There was more bad news for Michael, when Annalese informed him that their mutual children would be spending Christmas skiing in Aspen rather than Holby. Good call, as I've heard the skiing in Holby isn't much cop. Where one door closes, another opens, and he soon found himself invited to spend Christmas with the glorious Ramona, who got to speak Spanish during this episode, which only served to make her seem even more glorious. Serena meddled a bit – she's not keen on Michael, who is exactly the kind of seat-of-his-pants, only-on-nodding-terms-with-the-rules type of doctor that makes her go all beady-eyed and spiky.

Talking of spiky – that Lilah is a funny one. When she failed to spot that a patient had a hernia (mainly because the patient was a bit cagey about letting a strange woman fiddle with his nether regions), Ric had to mark her assessment as a fail. He wrestled with his conscience about it, what with Lilah being basically a good doctor and with the added complication of their kiss. He even sought advice from wise old Elliot (without mentioning the kiss bit, naturally), who agreed that failing her was the right thing to do. Lilah disagreed and said Ric was punishing her for not going "above and beyond." She complained to Chantelle, who mentioned it to Imelda, who sympathised. "I had to fend off the attentions of many a rampaging consultant," she told Lilah. Imelda has been looking for a stick with which to beat Ric since she arrived, and she may just have found it.

Ric's animal magnetism gets him into trouble

(Series 15, ep. 9 'Fault Lines' by Nick Fisher 11.12.12)

Is it just me, or does Ric Griffin get suspended on a regular basis? When the episode ended with him clutching the obligatory box of personal office items and gazing mournfully up at the hallowed structure that is Holby City Hospital, I had a distinct feeling of deja vu.

The reason for his current predicament was that Lilah had told Imelda about the kiss she shared with Ric in the wet lab, choosing not to emphasise the "shared" bit, but make it sound like he practically pounced on her. I'm still finding it hard to work out what's supposed to be going on in Lilah's mind. Is she (a) just a bit of an idiot (b) a troublemaker or (c) a cut-throat careerist? At the moment I'm tending towards a blend of all three. Imelda, full of sympathy for an abused junior (and thrilled to have something to pin on Ric) told Lilah to go home. "To Australia?" she bleated (lending force to theory (a) there). Imelda didn't mean Australia, she meant Lilah's Holby home, but Australia doesn't sound like such a bad plan to me.

Something that was a terrible plan was for Mo to get involved with Albie Who Owns The Bar, what with him being married and a bit creepy-looking and everything. Though, to give him credit where it's due, he does own the bar. This week he brought his wife (formerly known as Julie from *EastEnders* – the one who called Billy Mitchell 'Skidmark') in for treatment to the hospital, and because it was a lung condition and Mo has suddenly become the resident lung expert, only Mo would do. This whole scenario was 50 shades of unethical, which Jonny Mac persistently tried to point out. His suggestion that he summon Ms Naylor as a more ethically acceptable substitute fell on deaf ears (not surprising in Mo's case, as she and Jac have been involved in a territorial dispute for weeks now). EastEnders Julie ended up dead, an outcome which I hope doesn't come back to bite Mo.

There's all sorts of weird vehicles parked in that hospital car park. As well as Luc's camper van (of which more later), there was quite a swanky boat parked there this week, the property of a man who used to be Joe Carter in *Coronation Street*. Chrissie's head is easily turned by a show-off with a boat, even if he does have a key lodged in his intestine (don't ask). His tales of Christmases on Caribbean beaches were making her go all twinkly-eyed and breathless, and when he offered to take her (as a crew member – she'd come in ever so handy for splicing the mainbrace and whatnot), she'd have been tempted if only she didn't have to work, and didn't have Sacha, and little Daniel etc. Meanwhile, Sacha's plans for Christmas were coming on apace, and were mainly centred around eating. Chrissie is no Nigella as far as food is concerned. "Whoever thought of making a sauce out of bread?" she winced. It seemed her luck had changed somewhat when she discovered she had several days off at Christmas. "We could do something exciting!" she said to Sacha. His eyes took on a dreamy look. "Like a four-bird roast!" he said, also outlining his plan for a chocolate fountain "so big you could chocolate-coat a small dog." Chrissie was mentally calling the Calorie Police, and was not cheered further by the news that Imelda had evicted Luc's camper van from the hospital grounds and Sacha had offered him a parking spot outside their house – plus invited him to spend Christmas. But Joe Turner from *Corrie* told Chrissie how lucky she was to have such a lovely man as Sacha, so she cheered up a bit. Funny how it always takes someone else to tell her she's lucky to have Sacha.

How do you solve a problem like Imelda?

(Series 15, ep. 10 'Through the Darkness' by Martha Hillier & Dana Fainaru 18.12.12)

How did Imelda Cousins get the CEO job? What, exactly, is her job description? Because all that she actually does is to pop up in each of our key wards on a rotating basis, taking a dislike to the alpha males of the department (Ric, Michael) apparently solely on the grounds that they're alpha males, issuing random edicts and annoying people. She seems to be constantly pursuing an agenda based on people being horrible to her when she was a nurse. And she has a worrying tendency to appear in operating theatres to distract the surgeons at times when you'd think concentration would be essential.

This week she at least left Keller pretty much alone (Ric's already suspended, so there's not so much to interest her there), concentrating her meddling efforts on Darwin and AAU. In the department which is the spiritual home of the vomit-covered shoe, Ramona was doing some fine work helping Michael Spence with an emergency escharotomy, but she perhaps over-reached herself when the same patient needed intubating. Her cry of "We need some help here!" for once failed to summon any consultants at all, and she decided to have a go herself. Michael managed to defend her that time, but he wasn't able to defend her after she caused a patient to fall out of bed trying to escape the full onslaught of her compassion. Poor Ramona – she's read and fully absorbed the Holby Handbook which states that staff should go out of their way to try and sort out the social problems of all patients and their relatives, and she was only trying to help, but I couldn't help sympathising with the patient's need to get away from so much caring concern.

So Imelda suspended Ramona, and Michael was left in the doghouse with his prospect of a happy family Christmas up the spout. Serena decided it was time to take action. Who did she call? Hanssen. Looking tall and magnificent against a luscious wintery Stockholm backdrop, like a fine Swedish stag. Or something. But will he come back and save Holby from a fate worse than Leslie Ash?

Meanwhile, Imelda was making her presence felt on Darwin by trying to cancel the Herzig trial. Ollie was struggling to come to terms with Tara's brain tumour and eventually agreed to follow her lead and just "accept it."

On Keller, Chantelle was hoping Ianto Jones from *Torchwood* would take her to the Christmas party, but while she was busy trying to suture a chef with a needle phobia, that sneaky Mary-Claire was trying to wow him with her Irish charms. Ianto was having none of that and informed Chantelle that she's officially his girlfriend. Awwww.

Luc's heart of darkness

(Series 15, ep. 11 'And We Banish Shade' by Martha Hillier 28.12.12 and ep. 12 'Blood Ties' by Christian O'Reilly 2.1.13)

Since I was too busy being Christmassy to write about last week's episode, here are a few random thoughts about it. Serena was in full Connie mode (looking sooo A/W 2012 in a furry hat), manipulating away with the result that Imelda was somehow lured off to do Ric's job with Big Pharma in Las Vegas. All a little lame, plot-wise, though Serena was rather magnificent. I couldn't help thinking Las Vegas wasn't ever going to be the cleverest idea for recovering gambling addict Ric, anyway.

There was also some wonderful stuff between Jac and Jonny. I've thoroughly abandoned the idea that Joseph is the only man for her. He may have been the only man for Jac's younger self, when she was all about the career, but now she's older and more or less where she wants to be work-wise, she needs someone like Jonny to bring out the more playful side of her. Yes, she does have one. It was so sweet when she admitted she'd never decorated a Christmas tree before. I'm constantly impressed that the writers and the wonderful Rosie Marcel keep finding new sides to Jac and evolving her character and it looks like there's quite a bit of evolving to come in the next few weeks.

On to this week, then, and despite featuring a new year party with a Hawaiian theme, it was all rather intense. Luc had been working round the clock since Boxing Day on a new drug that would stop people bleeding to death. Sacha had been sweating blood bringing him blood to experiment on, but when the supply ran dry Luc started using his own. The lack of blood and lack of sleep was making him look like Eddi when she was withdrawing from the Camoxidan – all bug-eyed and shivery. Then a patient turned up with a tattoo that Luc recognised. It turned out that this patient and Luc had both (separately) been involved in the war in Sierra Leone and had seen terrible and gruesome sights. So Luc is not just weird and quirky – he's post-traumatically weird and quirky. He used his new drug on his patient when he was at risk of bleeding to death and it worked, but since it hadn't been tested and licensed etc, Michael Spence was not happy and marched off to read the riot act to Luc. He and Sacha found Luc in the wet lab in his undercrackers having a full-scale breakdown.

Gosh. We needed a bit of light relief, but it wasn't really to be found on Darwin, where Ollie was still struggling to come to terms with Tara's brain tumour and she was still pushing him away at every opportunity. Ollie was casually chatting to a patient when he suddenly realised he'd spoken his own brains by telling him you just know when you've found The One. He duly trotted off to propose, but she didn't make it easy for him and I was left not entirely sure whether they're now engaged or not.

I'll tell you who doesn't look in danger of getting engaged any time soon – Chantelle and Ianto Jones off of *Torchwood*. No sooner was her back turned at the party than he was off snogging that minx Mary-Claire. Chantelle attempted to pick up a consolation nerd (who will be Significant later on), but he wandered off, leaving her dancing round her handbag with Lilah.

Lilah had finally shown a more pleasant side to herself by helping to organise the party when Chantelle's original venue fell through (guess where it was finally held? Albie's! The very bar where every party has been held since Hippocrates was a lad). Lilah hadn't been best pleased to find that Ric was in Holby instead of Las Vegas. Luckily, after being a bit snappy and undermining Lilah's diagnostic skills, Ric eventually conceded that she's a fairly good doctor and she eventually conceded that he's not a predatory molester, and they agreed to let bygones be bygones. As an added bonus, Ric passed her on her next assessment, which means she can move on to the next stage of her career in the neurology ward. Since neurology is a place we don't normally visit, it's basically goodbye to Lilah.

Line of the episode: Ollie telling consultant oncologist Nathan Hargreaves (who we might see again because he was getting cosy with Malick at the party), "I'd shake your hand, but I'm holding a rather heavy tumour."

The past lives of two haunted men

(Series 15, ep. 13 'Hanssen/Hemingway' by Justin Young 8.1.13)

Everyone involved with Holby seemed really excited about this episode – even cast members who weren't in it. Cast members who *were* in it were duly despatched to daytime TV sofas to give out a few teaser details, but not give anything away. Video clips were posted on the internet. Expectation was running high. So did it live up to the hype?

Oh yes, and then some. We were promised "cinematic," and that's what we got, with beautiful panoramic views of Stockholm (the Swedish tourist board would have loved it) and gorgeous interiors – the austere elegance of Hanssen's flat ("I love what you've done with it," Jac said, surveying the almost total lack of furniture), the incredible library where Jac did her research.

That was the backdrop, but the two story lines and the actors who played them out were what made the episode so outstanding. Script-wise (brilliant, brilliant writing from Justin Young), Hanssen's back story must have been planned all along, because it answered so many questions about him. His fractured relationship with his father because of his involvement in using medical research data obtained by the Nazis, his mother who had committed suicide, his failed relationship and the son he had never met, all made sense of why he holds himself aloof even when he's passionately in love, his need to stay in control, even his slightly dodgy Swedish pronunciation was explained (English boarding school, Danish mother). Guy Henry was, quite simply, incredible. In a scene where he came face to face with his dying father for the first time, he didn't seem to move at all, yet somehow all his emotions were apparent on his face. It was masterful acting.

Back at Holby, Luc Hemingway was also coming face to face with the demons he'd tried to bury with work. In his case, it was the death of the woman he'd loved that haunted him. She had a blood clotting disorder – hence his frenzied hours in the wet lab trying to find a cure – and she'd died on the operating table in Sierra Leone when Luc had been too drunk to do anything to help her. Joseph Millson gave a raw and emotional performance.

In the end, both men found some sort of peace. Hanssen was reconciled with his father just before he died, and handed on his inheritance to his son's mother. He stood outside alone and a few snowflakes began to fall, harking back to his memories of waiting with his mother for the first snowflake of the winter to fall.

For Luc, his Holby career is, for the moment, over. With his behaviour getting ever more erratic and Michael and Sacha just about hanging on to the secret of what happened in the operating theatre last week, he had to go. Against the odds, he left heading for a happy ending, setting off in his camper van to join Eddi in Kerala. All together, Leddi fans – squeeeeeeeeee.

A heart stitched too tightly

(Series 15, ep. 14 'Push the Button Part 1' by Kirstie Swain 15.1.13)

Only last week I was full o' praise for the Holby scriptwriters. This week, they've upset me, the arch manipulators. No sooner had I grown to love the (initially unimpressive) Jonny Mac and think he's the right man for Jac, than she starts being horrible to him and takes another man home with her. Though she did have her reasons.

Jonny and Jac started the episode happily enough, having one of their famous store-room "staff meetings." Afterwards, they were actually twinkling at each other. Seriously – Jac was twinkly. Even paediatrician Sean noticed and told Jac she was glowing. "Only fat or pregnant people glow," she grumbled. Got to keep up that tough facade. Then she received a particularly tacky wedding invitation – from none other than The World's Most Beautiful GP, Joseph Byrne, and his fiancée who "looks like the kind of woman who would theme her wedding… unicorn," according to Jac.

After that, Jac was not in the best of moods – indeed we were treated to the full Termi-Naylor, and poor old Jonny Mac got the worst of it. Her patient didn't fare much better, as Jac was perhaps a little tense during surgery and stitched a heart up a bit more snugly than was good for her. This all ended up with Jac getting drunk and flirting a bit with Sean, before suggesting they polish off a bottle of whisky back at her place. Oh, Jac.

To cheer us up, we must tiptoe along the corridor of power to the CEO's office, where we can push the door back gently and find – Henrik Hanssen. Yes, he's back, and has asserted his right to still be CEO and Director of Surgery, much to the annoyance of Cunningham of the Board, who wanted Serena to stay in the post. She's much more corporate. To try to dampen down the Hanssen Effect, Cunningham decided to appoint an Executive Director to act as an intermediary between Hanssen and the Board. It was, as usual, a toss-up between Serena and Ric Griffin, and Hanssen ended up with the casting vote. He went – against expectations – for Serena, in a move that we might term "keeping his enemies closer."

Meanwhile, Our Chrissie had found a breast lump, but didn't plan to tell Sacha because he would make a fuss. It turns out that everything's probably okay anyway, but Michael Spence told her she really ought to confide in Sacha. You can tell a Holby staff member something, but they won't usually believe it until a patient speaks their brains for them. In this case it was a patient who knew she had Huntingdon's but hadn't told her husband: "If I said it out loud I'd have it."

The best line of the episode award goes to Michael Spence. Sacha told Chrissie that he was planning a treat that involved the word "dog" but didn't involve any animals. "He's arranged for a night of dogging," Michael suggested. "He doesn't even know what that means," said Chrissie, looking perhaps slightly disappointed.

You don't know what you've got till it's gone

(Series 15, ep. 15 'Push the Button Part 2' by Julia Gilbert 22.1.13)

Oh, Jac. Obviously you were devastated by the news of Joseph's impending marriage to a woman who puts sparkly bits in the envelopes with her wedding invitations. We all were. But we didn't all go off and spend the night with the first available paediatrician.

It's not as if Jac looked like she enjoyed this particular liaison with Sean, either, if her grim face in the taxi beforehand and the taxi afterhand was anything to go by. So why did she do it? Was she scared that Jonny Mac was becoming too important to her and she'd better explode the relationship before he got the power to hurt her as much as Joseph had? Or was she just being an eejit?

Consequences arrived fairly swiftly when it turned out that Sean's wife was practically bezzie mates with Caitlin (the patient whose heart Jac stitched too tightly last week), and that Sean had told his wife he spent the night keeping caring vigil at Caitlin's bedside. It all ended with Mrs Dolan giving Jac a hefty punch in the face as she pondered at the Window of Regret.

Dear old Jonny Mac was oblivious to all this. He's so utterly nice – he was really sweet and understanding about Joseph, when a lot of men would have been insecure, and he told Jac he was proud of her when she did brilliant work in theatre. "He's like a heart-shaped Creme Egg," observed PLA Jr. Yes, he is. He's the sweetest, squidgiest thing you could think of if you weren't thinking of Sacha.

Sadly, Jac has possibly realised this too late. Talking to Caitlin about her brother Liam she said, "You've got someone who cares. They don't come along all that often for people like us." But then she insisted on telling Jonny the truth about her night with Sean. Maybe she seriously thought he'd be ok with it, or maybe she really was pushing the Destruct button. That's the way he interpreted it, anyway. All he wanted was a quiet life, a wife, kids, roses round the door etc. In the Car Park of Broken Dreams, Jac insisted she could give him all that, but he didn't think she could. He walked off, and she walked to Hanssen, to take up the offer of a job in Japan.

While all this was going on, three new people had started work at Holby. Arthur Algernon Digby came third in his year at The Mythical St James's, so he's hot stuff. He's also the consolation nerd that Chantelle picked up at the new year party after she caught Ianto Jones snogging Mary-Claire. Arthur is your typical, good at the theory, not so hot at the practice type of medical student – his catchphrase seemed to be "I have had experience with…" before pitching in and messing up. But he'll learn.

On AAU, new F1 Gemma Wilde came second in her year (hah, Dr Digby!). She also came with a bit of a history, in that she had a previous career as the internet's "Dr Honey." Mildly racy pictures of her turned up in the locker room. Apart from that, she's a bit like Lilah in that she's keen, stubborn and pretty good.

So who came first in the year? Could it be the mysterious porter who was hanging round Keller being sweet and useful but constantly being mistaken for a troublemaker and/or criminal? Of course not. He was Malick's son!

Two strangers, nothing more

(Series 15, ep. 16 'The Waiting Game' by Matthew Barry 29.1.13)

Malick took to fatherhood slightly better than I expected, given that he only discovered he was father to a medium-sized porter last week. This episode found him offering the lad advice and money, two things that parents dish out all the time. Jake rejected both. When Malick discovered Jake had been sleeping overnight in Ric's office, he ended up doing a spot of emergency tidying up as well, again a thing that parents all too frequently find themselves doing.

Just in case all this is giving too much of a glowing impression of Malick's parenting skills, it must also be added that he started the episode by pinning his (presumably) first-born up against a wall in a threatening style, and ended it by recommending that Ric sack him and driving away with the bloke he met at the New Year party. "I'm a registrar, you're a porter," Malick said (this was when Jake was still a porter, before Ric decided to sack him). "Two strangers – nothing more." Hmm… a little way to go before they reach the father/son bonding fishing trip stage, then.

Jake is a good lad, as well. He messed up by telling a patient's relative that all would be well, when it wouldn't, but even top stars like Oliver Valentine have been guilty of that. He also got the blame for a bit of a messy incident in a lift, but I blame Arthur for distracting Chantelle due to his poor social skills, which meant the lift doors closed and Jake found himself in a stuck lift with a very poorly patient and her slightly hysterical boyfriend. Unfortunately for him, for once the lift didn't contain Hanssen (who spends most of his days riding up and down in the lifts and striding across the car park in search of prey), who would have been very handy.

Before we leave Keller, I just have to mention the Guts Cam, which gave us the view a spleen must have when it's being operated on by Malick and Ric. Artistic! Even more exciting than the Bath Cam, but more of that in a moment.

The Darwin plot was focusing on Elliot Hope's mentoring skills, with particular regard to one Hamish Richards, a medical student who was a bit over-fond of what we may describe as "partying." Like Jake, Hamish was a good lad at heart and Elliot was impressed by his kindness and his instinct to help. Sadly, this got him into bother when his patient choked on a large piece of confectionery and Hamish broke one of his (ie the patient's) ribs trying to resuscitate him.

What Hamish, Jake and the boyfriend of Malick's patient all needed was a good party. Oliver Valentine, with a shocking naivety about social networking, had posted details of a wine and cheese soirée at Tara's place on Facebook, so everyone turned up there. Hamish got wasted and ended up slumped in the bath vomiting quietly. Ollie had to break the door down, which was amusing, as was the Bath Cam which gave us a rubber duck's eye view of Ollie and Tara (looking incredibly pretty) as they entered the room.

Compared to all this, it was a quiet shift in AAU. Michael Spence tried to wind New Gemma up, but she's obviously not the sort to give up, cry and run away at the first sign of low-level bullying.

Living with a ticking time bomb

(Series 15, ep. 17 'Spence's Choice Part 1' by Tahsin Guner 5.2.13)

The official title of the episode naturally directs my attention towards AAU first. Spence's choice was whether to report a suspected case of child abuse to Social Services. The child had been hurt in a car accident, but X-rays showed some old injuries and the boy's step-father had a previous record of violence. You can see where Michael was coming from in jumping to conclusions, and Chrissie was right behind him, muttering sentences beginning with, "What parent in their right mind could…" at every opportunity. Gemma and Sacha, however, advised a more cautious approach. Week after week in Holby we see that a cautious approach is usually the right one, but Michael's not a naturally cautious man, and his judgement was a tad clouded by ongoing parenting tussles with estranged wife Annalese.

It all ended up with Michael almost getting punched, incurring the displeasure of Ric Griffin and causing the mother to try and take the child away from the hospital. She was spotted from the Window of Regret by Michael and Chrissie. The mother (Lucy Speed) said the family had all been ok until Michael started his meddling.

The theme of people being better off living in blissful ignorance ran through all three storylines this week. On Keller, Digby was having his assessment and his patient was a rather tricky case, what with him being from another planet and that. Different anatomy and physiology altogether from us humans. Digby's first impulse was to bin him off to the psych ward, but the radiant Chantelle had dealt with trickier patients than that in her time. Chantelle really is a brilliant nurse, and showed Digby that a bit of patience, understanding and empathy can get you a long way. Digby doesn't naturally possess any of these qualities, so he lucked out when he got placed on a ward with Chantelle – though he threw it back in her face later with a mean, "You're just a nurse so you wouldn't understand" comment.

It turned out that the patient was basically suffering from grief and loneliness following the loss of his parents and was self-medicating with a drug that was giving him delusions. He was possibly also self-medicating with the delusions, too, because he wasn't all that happy to discover he was only human after all.

If Tara didn't have the CT scans to prove it, we might suspect she wasn't human. She spends her entire life studying and getting cross with Ollie for organising social events to please her. As Mo advised her (it was nice to see the Mo/Jonny double act, albeit briefly), "Life's short. It's not about how many aortic valves you've repaired, it's about the things you did that made you feel like a kid."

In an attempt to show Tara a good time, Leonard Cohen-related activities having failed to excite her, Ollie gave her responsibility for Darwin for the day. Her over-zealous ordering of tests led to a patient being diagnosed with MS – but he wished he hadn't been told. "I'm supposed to live with a ticking time-bomb," he complained, and obviously was speaking Tara's brain (tumour) as well.

This very same patient required some emergency surgery, and when Elliot had to step out of theatre to take a phone call he left Ollie in charge. Ollie let Tara take over, and pretty soon there was blood everywhere. The upshot of all this was the patient lived, but Elliot let slip to Ollie that he knew about Tara's tumour.

Ollie is now moving in with Tara. What fun they'll have. Actually, there should maybe be a question mark after that sentence, because apart from both being pretty and being pretty good doctors (when they aren't over-reaching themselves), they seem to have nothing in common apart from a mutual admiration for the work of Two Door Cinema Club (PLA Jr is with them on that one) and don't seem to make each other happy at all.

Let's put our family concerns to one side, shall we?

(Series 15, ep. 18 'Spence's Choice Part 2' by Martin Jameson 12.2.13)

They're such a professional bunch at Holby City hospital. This week we had Michael letting his parenting feud with Annalese cloud his judgement (it was a continuing cloud from last week), Serena breaking the rules to put her mother first and then putting her mother second to her job, and Oliver Valentine in an almighty sulk with Professor Elliot Hope. Thank goodness there's Chantelle.

To AAU first, where Michael discovered that there are consequences to labelling people as child abusers, particularly when those people have the sort of neighbours who automatically think that means paedophiles, and that automatically gives them the right to set fire to someone's home. The mother of last week's abuse suspect, Mandy, was brought in with burns and various other injuries. And she did not want Michael Spence anywhere near her, because he'd had her son taken into care and he kept kicking off and going all shouty. Actually, Michael is quite marvellous when he kicks off, and so is Sacha when he has to be quietly authoritative, so I enjoyed the scenes where Sacha tried to calm Michael down very much indeed.

It all turned out that Mandy had brittle bones – a possibility Michael had thought of, but the genetic test would take months. But when Mandy needed surgery, Gemma spotted that there were tell-tale signs of the condition. This probably explained the child's injuries, and Michael did his best to persuade the social worker (Caroline Paterson) to reunite mother and child ASAP. If only Michael could be reunited with his own children so easily, but apparently Annalese's new boyfriend, Brad the Banker ("Sounds like a cartoon for children in *The Economist*" Sacha said last week) is moving in with them. Michael's not happy.

Oliver Valentine wasn't happy, either. In fact, he was in a major strop with Prof Hope for not telling him about Tara's brain tumour. He was so sulky he even turned down an exciting opportunity to do something or other with an alveolar adenoma. Imagine. Oliver wasn't the only irritating junior Elliot had to deal with, though. That Hamish from a few weeks ago surfaced again to make a complaint of bullying against snuggly, loveable Elliot, a man who is no more likely to be a bully than Jac Naylor is to join a knitting group. It was Hamish's evil employment lawyer of a mother behind it all, but the case rested on Oliver Valentine supporting Hamish's story. Even Oliver Valentine, whose moral compass has in the past been somewhat twitchy, couldn't bring down the career of his beloved mentor, and he told Hamish to drop the case, otherwise he'd tell Hanssen that Hamish had been drunk on the ward. So Ollie and Elliot are friends again, and the alveolar adenoma is back on the table, as it were.

Hot news just in from Keller: "Contrary to myth, Serena was actually born, not plucked from the thigh of the Royal College of Surgeons." And we can take that on good authority, as it came from her mother. Who also calls her "Rena." She was in the hospital because of some nasty business with her bowel (drawing a discreet veil over things here). Surgery was needed, but as a non-urgent (though in a lot of pain and distress) case, the waiting list was about a month. Serena easily sorted this by discharging one of Malick's patients, and got herself scrubbed up to sort out her mum's defective tubing herself. This is the sort of thing which is Just Not On, of course, and Ric swiftly appeared to tell her to stop. Holby therefore not being an option, Serena decided she'd pay for private treatment. A taxi was summoned to take her mum to Posh Private Hospital. Hanssen was a tad concerned. As deputy director of surgery (or whatever she is), Serena opting for private medicine for her nearest and dearest "might not appear to be a public vote of confidence," he said.

So Serena legged it to the car park to persuade her mother that a month of suffering really wasn't all that much to endure for the sake of her daughter's career. Bad, bad woman. "We all have to put our family concerns to one side if we're going to do this job properly," she told Michael Spence. Good luck with that.

Patient X

(Series 15, ep. 19 'Ask Me No Questions' by Jamie Crichton 19.2.13)

Good old Dr Oliver Valentine. He's only gone and found someone in Baltimore who can possibly sort out Dr Tara Lo's brain tumour. Hurrah! Problem is, the Baltimore expert has only had good results on tumours that have behaved themselves and not got any bigger for a long time – and apparently Tara's has started getting bigger. Ollie doesn't know this, because she doesn't tell him very much. He hasn't noticed, either, that she's gone a bit absent-minded (he's used to Elliot Hope) and when she passed out in the washroom and bashed her head on a basin, he was content to accept her explanation that a slippery floor was to blame. Meanwhile, Tara has included herself in her own study of 'The Psychology of Mortality in the Young' (it's going to be a gripping read when it's finished) as Patient X.

As if that wasn't enough excitement for one evening, we had Dr Gemma Wilde in deadly danger. Remember Dean, who'd been in the war in Sierra Leone and who forced Dr Luc Hemingway to start getting to grips with his past? He was back. His estranged wife was a patient and because Dean is more than a bit disturbed, he wasn't allowed to see her. It all culminated in Dean, Mrs Dean and Gemma locked in a room together and Gemma having to intubate the wife with the aid of Sacha on speaker-phone. Gemma did well with the intubation bit, but she was more than a bit daft to get locked in the room in the first place. She was right by the door and had ample opportunity to either leave or yell for security when it looked like Dean was getting a bit agitated. I can't imagine Charlie from *Casualty* making such a basic error. She's young, though, is Dr Gemma, and hasn't seen quite as many crazy people as Charlie has. Another piece of her background arrived at the end of the episode in the form of her son, Finn (Finn Wilde – excellent name).

On Keller, Malick (who's passed his consultant exams with an obscenely high score, apparently) was dealing with a stroppy American patient who was very dismissive of the care offered at Holby until Malick discovered that her American surgeon had left a small plastic beaker inside her during previous surgery. Hurrah for the NHS! Malick was more bothered about keeping his relationship with oncologist Nathan Hargreave a secret. This is not because Malick has decided to do a Dull Dan and get back in the closet, and not because Nathan Hargreave is an embarrassment to be seen with – he is so not. It's more about Malick getting to grips with the idea that he's in a steady relationship and might even be a bit in love. We saw in the episode when Malick's first love, Paul, turned up that Antoine is actually a bit of an old softie. He just hides it well.

The best line of the episode was from Mo. She and Sacha are on the Holby Fit Club Diet (aren't we all?) and neither of them is finding it easy. In fact Sacha is cheating and Mo is stressed. "If you say 'hungry' once again," she warned Dr Tara Lo, "I'll deep fat fry you, one limb at a time."

Forget that today ever happened

(Series 15, ep. 20 'Unravelled' by Frank Rickarby 26.2.13)

Why would any Holby City staff member allow a friend or family member to be treated at that hospital? They should know by now that it can't end well, and should insist that all loved ones either go private or go to The Mythical St James' (or The Mythical St Peter's, which was mentioned several times in this episode). Anywhere but Holby, which is far too dramatic if all you want is a nice, straightforward op and a speedy recovery. You're far more likely than the average patient to end up dead, permanently disabled or to have one of your visitors diagnosed with a nasty condition.

Serena's mum Adrienne was back for her operation, and everyone was feeling unreasonably confident, what with her being in the first class hands of Ric Griffin and Chantelle, and Serena keeping everyone on their toes. What could possibly go wrong? An oversight, that's what. Chantelle was about to do a post-op check on Adrienne and she put her initials and the time on the chart, but she had to dash away when there was an emergency at an adjacent bed. Then when Digby checked the chart, he assumed the obs had been done. This meant Adrienne wasn't really checked for two hours, during which time she had a stroke.

The scenes when Serena discovered what had happened to her mum were really upsetting, because Adrienne had been such a lovely, sparkly character. Serena reacted as I think any of us would react – angry and wanting to blame someone. Because she's Serena, and scary at the best of times, her anger was a fearsome thing to behold and it was particularly directed at poor Chantelle. So now Chantelle, who always wants the very best for patients, colleagues and woodland creatures, is facing a formal complaint.

In the dim recesses of Holby, in the ward of doom known as AAU, Gemma was trying to pretend she hadn't spent part of last week locked in a small room with a deranged man and a dying woman. A visit to the hospital counsellor wasn't very productive, although I did like his wallpaper. What use is a counsellor, anyway? What was really needed was for Gemma to work with a patient who could speak her brains. Ignoring the small point that the counsellor hadn't signed her off as fit for work, Gemma plunged into the day's case load, working with a man who was in denial about his wife's death. "You're just avoiding the truth," said Gemma, in a neat turnaround speaking her own brains while giving out advice.

It all went pear-shaped when Gemma had a panic attack after seeing Deranged Dean on television. Her patient helped her out and then tried to kiss her. Michael Spence (he is getting better looking every week, I swear he is) was, to put it mildly, not happy at all that Gemma was apparently canoodling with patients. He was even less happy to find she'd been working when she wasn't supposed to be, but he's going to cover that bit up.

Once again it was left to Darwin to provide the humour and light relief, and they were greatly assisted in this by the presence of the glorious Sacha, who was looking after a boy with a ruptured testicle (ouch) and breathing problems. While Jonny Mac was busy chatting up the patient's mother (who turned out to be a not entirely stable personality), Sacha and Mo were bonding over their mutual dislike of Holby Fit Club and Mo's sadness that it was the birthday of the woman she'd had the baby for and it was bringing up some difficult feelings for her. Mo and Sacha both just make me smile and I can't think of anything better than the two of them getting together. Except no one is happy for long on Holby…

Act as if...

(Series 15, ep. 21 'Recovery Position' by Nick Fisher 5.3.13)

Oh, but this was a good one. Excellently written, full of emotion, drama and quotable lines, and featuring three compelling storylines.

Malick started the episode in a good mood, looking forward to sampling Nathan's fried squid rings stuffed with pine nuts. Rather him than me, but still… He was also in the mood for some quality mentoring. "Act as if," he instructed Digby (who is really growing on me – he's very loveable and funny). "As if what?" said Digby. "As if you're me." Obviously.

When a patient was brought in with severe abdominal pains she'd been ignoring for a year, Malick didn't recognise her at first until he saw her little devil tattoo. "Is it some religious thing?" Digby asked Chantelle, as the very sight of it had provoked an extreme reaction in Malick and made him tell Digby to get lost. The tattoo was actually a reminder of Malick's younger, more carefree but less gay days, when between him and Anna they'd managed to produce Jake. You can see why Malick wouldn't want Digby knowing about that, but mentoring is mentoring and Digby had procedures to learn, which led to the poor lad having to do an ultrasound on Anna while trying to ignore the fact that his mentor and his patient were having a blazing argument about their mutual son at the same time.

Anna was a wonderful character. Played by Charlotte Randle, she teetered on the border between being incredibly irritating and being really sweet. When Malick discovered she had cancer and Nathan confirmed it was untreatable and she only had weeks to live, her main concern was for Malick to establish a relationship with his son. As we know, he was instrumental in getting Jake sacked a while back, so it's not going to be easy, particularly for the man who's previously been the biggest ego in the NHS. He's having to look at himself in a different way and it doesn't come naturally to him. As Malick told Anna, "I became a doctor – but I'm not sure what sort of man I became." Having both Nathan and Jake in his life is going to push Malick's character into different places and it'll be really interesting to see how he evolves.

Speaking of tough, driven, egotistical people who are reluctant to let their guard down and be emotional brings us neatly to the wonderful Jac Naylor, who was back from Japan. Hanssen said he was looking forward to her showing us what she'd learned in Japan, and I was getting very excited at the idea that she might start speaking Japanese in theatre. While that would have been spectacular, it probably wouldn't have been all that useful in Holby. What was far more useful was her new skill of being able to make an oesophagus out of a stomach lining via five tiny little incisions. Sort of like the way people put a ship in a bottle, only squidgier.

Her patient was a Young Farmer who'd ruined his own oesophagus drinking paint stripper, and this ground-breaking procedure was going to need the best CT team Holby could muster. Which meant Jonny Mac. He'd previously been in a bit of a flap at the sight of Jac, who'd arrived back at work a day early before he could perfect his poker face. "I need Jonny to be on his A-game," Jac told Mo. "When is he ever not?" Mo said sweetly. "He was hand-reared by me, remember?"

Things didn't go to plan, as the silly Young Farmer had caused further damage by eating curry, so Jac had to make do with a boring old standard thoracotomy. But never mind all that. When she slipped on some orange juice and cut her head, Jonny Mac was on hand with the stitches. And it was the loveliest scene ever, as Jac admitted she'd spent every night in her tiny Japanese bed thinking about what a cow she'd been to him. He was the most irritating man she'd ever met, she told him, and that's why she loved him. Well, cue a massed chorus of "Squeeeee!!!!" throughout the Holby-viewing land.

The third storyline was the aftermath of Serena's mother's stroke. Ric called Serena while she was in theatre with some bad news. "Can you speak?" he asked. "I'm holding a boy's ruptured spleen in my hands, but otherwise I'm all ears." The news was that her mother had been bumped down the waiting list for the stroke ward. This was the last straw for Serena, who has now had enough of Hanssen's advice that going private is not a great move publicity-wise. She wants the best for her mother and she wants answers about what happened.

The woman that never blinks

(Series 15, ep. 22 'Not Aaron' by Dana Fainaru 12.3.13)

The theme of parents and children ran through all three stories in last night's Holby City, both for the patients and the staff.

In Darwin Jac found an ideal patient to practise her exciting Japanese surgery on. It quickly became obvious that the patient was actually a bit less than ideal, as she had a phobia of hospitals after being in an accident in which her son died. Then it was discovered that she was pregnant, but it wasn't until she was in theatre and the cry of "We've got a bleed!" went up, that Jac realised she'd taken some medication to make her miscarry, as she thought having a new baby was betraying her dead son.

All complex enough, but made even worse because Jac was suffering from severe pains herself and had to leave the operating theatre. She tried to pass it off as period pains, but Jonny Mac wasn't buying that. "Come on," he said, "You're the woman that never blinks." He's actually wrong about that, as Jac has the most sarcastic blink I've ever seen. He was worried that the problem might be her remaining kidney, but Jac gave herself a quick ultrasound scan and ran the results (anonymously) past Serena, who said it was probably something gynaecological. Oh, typical. No sooner do we get Jac and Jonny happily back together – she even allowed him to be seen arriving at the hospital with her – and there's a spanner in the works. Not literally, as that would have shown up on the ultrasound.

On Keller, things weren't looking good for Anna and it was urgent for Malick to find Jake. Jake was understandably upset and angry when he found out his mother was dying, and most of his anger was directed at Malick, who seemed to be doing very little to help. Under pressure from Jake, Malick tried to perform surgery on Anna but was stopped by Ric Griffin. Ric's main role used to be hovering behind junior staff members (FLNT, Chantelle) in a kindly and reassuring way. His current role is to heave into view just as a colleague is about to inappropriately operate on a family member and tell them to stop. "You've lost your clinical judgement and you're about to lose your patient on the table!" he said, in what must have been the highlight of his week's script.

Meanwhile, in the House of Fun known as AAU, Dr Gemma had to bring her son to work and hide him in a side room. This happens at least once to every parent in Holby, and it's guaranteed that the child will go missing at some point. Wee Finn Wilde didn't go missing for very long. Basically he was just bored with his babysitter, Digby (or "Sniffles," as Gemma calls him), who tried to wow him with an exciting computer game about the Napoleonic Wars. "It's quite a pivotal period in history," he explained. If Roy Cropper from *Coronation Street* had had a previous existence as a junior doctor, he would not be that dissimilar to Digby.

In between running about after Finn, Gemma had to look after a young girl who turned out to have chlamydia. It was just as well she had an embarrassing illness, because otherwise Gemma was facing a formal complaint from the girl's father for being distracted and running off a lot. It looked like the game might be up anyway, when she found Michael Spence chatting to Finn. But he's a dad himself, and he's been at Holby long enough to know the thing about every parent having to take their child to work at least once, so he was in a forgiving mood.

I save lives while you hold my coat

(Series 15, ep. 23 'Holby's Got Torment' by Joe Ainsworth 19.3.13)

There was some shockingly unprofessional behaviour in tonight's episode and the staff need to get a grip. It was probably because Ric Griffin wasn't on hand to let everyone know what was ethically what. It's true that several staff members were grappling with serious personal issues, but still. Is this what we expect from the staff of Holby's finest hospital? (Actually, yes…).

To the fragrant Miss Naylor first, who was given the news that it's highly unlikely she'll ever be able to have children (note the word "unlikely," however). The casual observer may think she's the least maternal person on the planet and wouldn't be bothered at all by this turn of events, but we've known Jac for years and we know that she does, in fact, have a deeply-buried gentle side which is not immune to the charms of ickle babies. Or chirpy Scottish nurses. So it was bad news.

But onward and upward, particularly when you've got Susan Boyle (not that one) needing a spot of oesophageal surgery. Could it be third time lucky for Jac's famous Japanese ship-in-a-bottle procedure? There were a few hurdles to overcome, the first being Ms Boyle's son, who was a bit concerned about the surgery. "There's really nothing to be scared of," Jac assured him. "Except death," he said. Good point. Jac sent Jonny in to have a go at persuading him. "This is your area – bonding. All that touchy-feely crap."

That was harsh. After a honeymoon period of, ooh, ten minutes, Jac is back to giving Jonny a hard time.

It's easier for her to do that than to tell him what's really going on in her life. She knows he wants kids, but she doesn't have the confidence that he also wants her and that he might (probably would) be understanding and supportive. So she pushes him away and gets horrible. She got particularly horrible after the operation. She wasn't feeling well and Mo knew this, so when Jac felt a bit iffy she wasn't about to hand the scalpel to Mo. She gave it to Tara instead, who wasn't feeling all that well herself and messed up.

Jac rescued the situation and the procedure was a success, but the whole things was an omnishambles of unprofessionality. Jac shouldn't have been operating when she was feeling ill. Tara shouldn't be at work at all, as her brain tumour has obviously gone lively again. Jac shouldn't really have been so horrible to Tara when she messed up, and Jonny certainly shouldn't have given Jac a dressing-down about it in the middle of theatre.

Jac was furious and wasted no time in telling Jonny what she thought of him. "I save lives while you hold my coat!" she told him. His response involved something about any product of her womb possibly being the Antichrist, which was obviously more stinging than he realised under the circumstances and earned him a slap.

So things aren't looking rosy for Jac and Jonny, but at least she's got her funding for the Japanese procedure. And Susan Boyle's son thinks she's lovely.

After Anna's funeral, Malick didn't think Jake needed or wanted him in his life, mainly because Jake told him he didn't need or want him in his life. Malick is fairly new to parenting and still thinks that what kids say can be taken at face value, so off he went to arrange a dirty weekend with

Nathan. Then Jake and one of his mates turned up separately at the hospital, having been in a fight. Sacha didn't know Jake was Malick's son and called the police, which meant Malick had to get involved again and had a little bonding moment with his son in a bus shelter at the end of the episode.

Earlier, Malick and Nathan had been shockingly unprofessional in telling a man who they thought had cancer that he had just months to live. What happened to all the standard put-offs like, "We need to run a few more tests," and, "Let's just wait for the results of the biopsy. We'll know more then"? Luckily the man took the news quite well – both the news of his impending death and the news that it had been indefinitely postponed because he didn't have cancer at all.

Someone else who doesn't have cancer is Chrissie. She got the all-clear from her biopsy and Sacha saw her giving Michael Spence a celebratory and relieved hug. Any excuse, frankly. Sacha was naturally miffed that she hadn't confided in him that she had a lump, but he wasn't as miffed as Chrissie was when she found out that Sacha had been going to Rodolfo's with Mo instead of Fit Club. Sacha and Chrissie were married in Rodolfo's, so I don't think we can begrudge her thinking of it as "their" place. She needed to re-mark her territory and get the scent of Mo off it, so she booked a table and put extra mascara on (her eyelashes, not the table). "Let's make it a regular Tuesday thing!" she suggested. "But it's Holby night!" PLA Jr pointed out wisely. Sacha, meanwhile, was looking wistful. Was the carbonara not up to scratch, or was he perhaps thinking that Mo was more amusing company than his lovely wife?

And in other news, Digby was trying to impress Chantelle with gifts of chocolate (free samples from the coffee bar). Chocolate is usually the way to Chantelle's heart, but she was in an uncharacteristically unsunny mood.

What happened in the prayer room?

(Series 15, ep. 24 'Journey's End' by Patrick Homes 26.3.13)

Even to the casual observer, something is very wrong with Dr Tara Lo. When faced with Ollie in his PJ's asking "Why you aren't coming back to bed?" what right-minded person would opt to stay with the textbooks instead?

That aside, she's been exhibiting a few more symptoms recently. Little lapses of concentration, gaps in her memory, falling-over and so on. Then there was a recent MRI scan that showed her tumour had grown. She's on strict instructions to report that sort of thing immediately to Hanssen, but she's stubborn, driven, in denial etc, so she's been ignoring it, with almost fatal consequences for her patients as we saw last week.

Something had to give, and what gave was Tara's knees as she went crashing to the floor in the prayer room. It wasn't a bout of religious fervour, it was some kind of tumour-related seizure. Luckily she was with a rather calm trainee monk, who didn't bother shouting "Can we have some help in here?" but sat with her till she came round. Unluckily, the monk was a friend of Tara's patient, who was in line for the experimental Herzig 3 artificial heart, and the monk didn't think his friend should risk having the procedure. Persuade him not to have it, the monk said, and I won't tell anyone about your fits. You could tell from this that he wasn't exactly gold-standard monk material.

It was all a great excuse for some monkly brains-speaking about illness, death, the afterlife and so on ("I don't fear the destination, but only a fool wouldn't be worried about the journey"). But Ollie got wind that all was not well with Tara, got his hands on the missing MRI results and did the right thing – he went to Hanssen. And whatever journey Tara is on, Ollie has promised he'll be with her "every step of the way." Apart from the last step, presumably, if the worst comes to the worst.

On Keller, Digby continues to develop into a completely wonderful character. He's kind and clever and funny, but he finds people and their unpredictable ways difficult. It was Chantelle's birthday, but she was fed up about the investigation about Serena's mother hanging over her and she said she didn't want any fuss and wanted her birthday kept secret. Digby said he wasn't all that good with secrets, then he was handed another one to keep when he discovered that Jake (who is back working on Keller) doesn't know his dad is gay. It was all most bamboozling for Digby and provided some great comedy moments when he tried to protect Malick from the "embarrassment" of having to look at a patient's groin area. Jimmy Akingbola and Rob Ostlere are really good together in these comedy scenes.

There was a huge amount of brains-speaking going on with this patient, who was a reality TV star of some sort. "All I need to do is be myself," he told Digby. "I just have to work really hard at it." This didn't really help Digby. "Being myself doesn't really work for me," he said. He was totally confused when the other staff members set up a little surprise for Chantelle's birthday. He thought she'd be furious, but she was thrilled. That's women for you. In fact, that's people for you. Never do what you expect. Digby didn't expect Chantelle to kiss him on the cheek, and he certainly didn't expect her to agree to go out for a drink with him. But, bless him, it was probably more in line with his expectations when she decided to go out with former boyfriend Rhys instead.

On AAU, now that Chrissie has reclaimed Rodolfo's, Sacha has had to resort to going to Fit Club again.

Six hours earlier

(*Series 15, ep. 25 'The End of the Beginning' by Matthew Broughton 2.4.13*)

This episode started at the end and then flash-backed (back-flashed?) six hours earlier in a style that used to feature quite regularly in Holby. It even ended with a musical montage as staff members reacted to an email from Tara Lo, telling them about her brain tumour. Hanssen's reaction was to make sure the pencils on his desk were parallel, a brilliant little touch showing his need for order and control in times of stress.

The meat of the episode was about Tara facing the prospect of either death or surgery that may leave her drastically altered (or dead) – and either way the probable end to her career. It was intense and dramatic, with Tara demonstrating to the long-suffering Ollie how bad she was feeling by smashing up the windows of her car. "This is what the end of my career looks like!" she yelled as she took a metal pole to her windscreen. I couldn't help thinking that smashing up Serena's car might have ended her career even quicker, but that's me for you. While it's easy to sympathise with Tara's situation, she doesn't make it easy to sympathise with her as a person. She's so spiky, defensive and insular that it's Ollie I feel sorry for. "I'm concerned you're in a kind of denial," Tara's neurologist said to her. Tara's reply? "Well, I'm not!"

All this anguish was beautifully balanced by the Keller storyline, which showed Digby trying his best to win the F1 Prize against the mighty opposition of Dr Gemma Wilde. Every week I love Digby more. He needed to practise delivering bad news to patients (people skills aren't his speciality) and Chantelle offered to help by posing as a patient. It was a lovely scene as Rob Ostlere apparently tried not to laugh at Chantelle's funny reactions. Digby is actually a genius doctor and he managed to diagnose a real illness in someone who was only supposed to be pretending to be a patient, and helped Malick to sort him out in surgery. This meant Ric Griffin had to be called in to pose as a patient for the rest of Digby's test, and there was another funny scene as Digby managed to quote him chapter and verse of the rules about patients not harassing staff.

No surprise, then, that Digby won the F1 prize (hurrah!) – and he also went for a drink with Chantelle. Something of a red-letter day in the world of young Arthur Digby. Chantelle also had something to celebrate, as Serena decided to drop her complaint against her following the intervention of a patient who was also a journalist.

I do. I absolutely do. Yes, I do

(Series 15, ep. 26 'Promises, Promises' by Nick Fisher & Dana Fainaru 9.4.13)

The Linden Cullen Memorial Shrubbery has never looked lovelier. Twinkly fairy lights, hearts and flowers festooned the shrubs and turned it into a little grotto of sparkly festivity. The bride looked radiant – she had flowers in her hair and was wearing a cute little furry cape (essential as the episode was apparently filmed in December). The groom looked dashing and handsome, if a tad nervous, and the fairy lights were reflected in his lovely blue eyes. Blessikins.

Who'd have guessed at the start of the episode that the hour would end in the wedding of Dr Tara Lo and Dr Oliver Valentine? They weren't even engaged at the beginning. The proposal wasn't the most romantic of events, either. Tara needed a next of kin who wouldn't refuse her request to donate her organs if/when she died, as her parents were opposed to That Sort of Thing. Oliver was not opposed, and, as he confessed to Jac later, loves Tara to bits, so he agreed. On the eve of her horrible and scary surgery, they decided to get married. "Keep the champagne to a minimum and make sure she gets an early night," was the ominous message from Tara's neurologist.

Oliver wasn't entirely sure he could cope with the whole marriage/impending surgery/possible widowerhood thing, though. As often happens in times of pre-wedding crisis, Jac was on hand to offer sympathetic advice. "Ditch the self-pity – you're not the one with their brains being sucked out tomorrow." She has such a way with words.

So Ollie and Tara became the Lo-Valentines, in front of an assembled throng of their mates from Darwin. And don't think I didn't spot Jac shooting little glances at Jonny Mac whenever the word "love" was mentioned. The only thing that was missing was rice, for throwing purposes. Elliot arrived equipped with dried couscous instead. An unconventional confetti for an unconventional wedding.

While this was all going on, Malick was being impressed by (and trying to impress) a flashy surgeon from Newcastle. He was so impressed that he was even thinking of applying for a job there. "He's demonstrated a desire for self-improvement," Ric said, sarcastically. The flashy surgeon hinted that the job would be Malick's if he wanted it, but these days Malick has other responsibilities. His other responsibility, also known as Jake, was busy in the basement getting drunk with the daughter of his dad's patient. This is because he's still grieving for his mum, obviously, and needs the steady guidance of the biggest ego in the NHS. Malick realised this, and possibly also realised the difficulty of fitting in in Newcastle when you pronounce it Noocastle, so he decided not to go for the job. "The salary was crap," he told Jake. "The Malick doesn't come cheap."

We knew that Gemma's Dr Honey past would come back to haunt her eventually, and it did this week in the form of the son of one of her patients, who had previously been Gemma's stalker. His presence ruffled her a lot and she had to tell Sacha and Michael what was going on. Michael threw stalker-boy out, but he went and complained to Hanssen. There was a wonderful Hanssen scene where he was sitting looking at all the Dr Honey pictures on his computer while Gemma sat at the other side of the desk trying to maintain her professional poise. She explained that she'd been providing an essential public health service, in assisting teenage boys with their problems. There were many comments Hanssen could have made about this, but he is a refined man and he stayed silent.

You're a good girl, T-Lo

(Series 15, ep. 27 'Great Expectations' by Martha Hillier 16.4.13)

Apparently Jing Lusi knew right from when she auditioned for the role of Tara Lo what the outcome for the character would be. This being the case, you have to applaud her and the writers for not taking the easy route of making Tara completely lovable, sympathetic and sweet (Chantelle, basically) so we'd be devastated by her departure.

Instead, Tara has often been spiky, self-absorbed, stubborn and annoying. Although undeniably beautiful and although the situation she was in evoked sympathy, it was hard to warm to her as a person (unless you were Ollie). And still we were devastated by her departure.

The masterstroke in this episode was that we were given two different perspectives on Tara's operation. There was the operation itself, which looked absolutely horrifying – equipment like a sterile and sanitised torture chamber and the stomach-churning notion of being awake while someone else is poking about in your brain. Tara was being kept happy and comfortable by drugs – she even initiated a singalong – so the situation was possibly even more traumatic for Oliver and for Tara's mother, who had to stand by and watch.

The other perspective was of Tara and Ollie's colleagues and friends throughout the hospital, waiting for news. Writer Martha Hillier deployed Hanssen beautifully, having him turn up before the operation with – almost surreally – some home-made baklava for Tara. "I'm perfecting the recipe," he said. "This is to ensure a swift recovery." That such a stern-seeming man could do something as warm and homely as baking for her said more about his personality and his feelings for Tara than any amount of speechifying. Elliot and Hanssen discussed baklava while they waited for news. Jac and Jonny didn't exactly wait together, but they were never far apart.

There were non-Tara-related scenes, too. Malick's son Jake found out (thanks to Serena and Digby dropping clangers) that Malick is gay. Gemma was about to leave but was called back into work during an emergency. I couldn't tell if these scenes were a welcome distraction or not. I was impatient to get back to what was happening with Tara, but at the same time the scenes in the operating theatre were so intense that it was quite nice to get away for a few moments, especially when the moments involved Digby.

Some of the most emotional scenes were the ones in which Ollie and Tara's mum argued over who should be in the operating theatre with her. You could see both viewpoints, but Tara's father supported Tara when she said Ollie was her future. She needed to hang on to the idea of a future and there was even a little scene where she scribbled future dates in her diary – Ollie's birthday, Christmas shopping. In the end, the surgeon needed to test Tara's Chinese language as well as her English, so the mother was called into the theatre. Asked to write something in Chinese for her to read, Tara's mum wrote something down. Tara said she didn't know what it was, and then just as she slipped into unconsciousness, she said, "Love. It says love."

James Anderson has beautiful eyelashes, and they almost seemed to acquire an acting presence of their own as, in close-up, Ollie realised before anyone else that Tara had gone. He insisted that they checked her pupils, and got the dreaded response, "Fixed and dilated."

The most moving part of the episode was the reaction of the other staff members to the news. Hanssen received a call and Elliot understood what had happened from a glance. Jonny told Jac, and her eyes filled with tears. Chantelle told Digby and Malick that something awful had happened. When Hanssen gave the news to Gemma, Michael and Sacha, his voice choked on the word "dead."

In the final scene, Mo went to check on Tara, her body still being kept alive so her organs could be transplanted as she'd requested. There's such a tenderness about Mo sometimes. "You're a good girl, T-Lo," she said. "We're going to look after you."

Not a dry eye in the house.

The lads aren't coping well

(Series 15, ep. 28 'Second Life' by Paul Matthew Thompson 23.4.13)

Following last week's harrowing events it was business as usual at Holby, once you stepped over the Tara Lo Makeshift Shrine on the front steps.

How was Young Dr Oliver Valentine coping with his grief? You'd have to say, not well at all. That's what Jac said, anyhow. "How's the patient?" Hanssen asked her (about a patient). "Stable," she said. "Which is more than can be said for Valentine." Well, indeed. He was insisting on working, which was handy because then he could act out his anguish on his patients – or, more particularly, their relatives. The issue was a young man who'd inherited a life-limiting condition from his mother, but the parents hadn't told him about it because they didn't want to ruin his life with worry. Unfortunately this chimed badly with Ollie, who charged around like a bull in a china shop making sure truths were told. This was because he blamed Elliot for not telling him about Tara's condition sooner. He thought if he'd known about it, he could have persuaded her to have the surgery earlier and the outcome might have been less fatal.

Obviously it's not fair to blame lovely, kindly Elliot Hope, but equally obviously Ollie needed someone to blame and shout at, and Elliot is wise enough to mop it up. Equally obviously, we can't have Ollie cracking up and ranting all over Darwin. Heart patients need peace and quiet more than most. So Hanssen has given him a choice – either stay at home, or visit the hospital counsellor, who's been twiddling his thumbs since he sorted out Luc Hemingway and Gemma and has had nothing to do but gaze across the rooftops of Borehamwood and put his paper tissue collection in order of absorbency ready for the next bout of sobbing.

He might have come in handy this week, actually. At one point there was a deluded patient perched in an open office window high above the car park (even higher than the Window of Regret), believing he could fly. That's the sort of situation where an experienced counsellor could really help, but in this case all it needed was for Michael Spence to dash in, grab him and haul him back to safety.

The patient belonged (in the "he's my patient" sense) to Digby. Like Dr Valentine, Digby wasn't coping well this week. The poor lad was buckling under the pressure of being the best F1 in the hospital. "I only won that prize because Gemma had a hangover and Tara was dying," he fretted. While that is an accurate summary of the state of his main rivals last week, he underestimates himself, though it is true there's room for improvement as far as his practical skills are concerned. His comfort zone is books, computers and theory (yup, he's a geek), but when the yucky stuff starts flying he panics. Luckily, the Sunniest Nurse in the World, Chantelle, has his back, and she has a ready supply of paper bags to breathe into. They make a lovely team, and they'd make a very sweet couple, too, if Chantelle didn't keep getting phone calls from the odious Rhys just when Digby has plucked up the courage to ask her out for a curry.

For some reason, Michael Spence was on Keller this week (and am I very odd for finding the way he said, "Okay, he's peripherally shut down!" rather thrilling?), which bumped Ric down to the Hall of Doom known as AAU, despite Serena saying it was "a young man's game." He got the traditional AAU welcome – someone was sick on his shoes – and he found those flighty young things Mary-Claire and Gemma to be somewhat difficult to deal with. He's lucky it was Chrissie's day off. Maybe Ric is showing the signs of wear and tear. Not only is it getting difficult to control the young 'uns, but he can no longer properly interpret a scan picture without his specs. This almost led to a man going into an MRI scan (a huge magnet, basically) with a gut-full of pointy metal in him from an old shrapnel wound. "Lucky I was here," Gemma said, with a cocky smile. While this was technically true, I felt she deserved at least a withering glance from Ric for being a smug junior, but he issued her with an indulgent smile instead. See what I mean? He's losing his grip.

Worse was to come for him, anyway. Serena announced that Hanssen is "going back to the floor," which effectively means that Serena will henceforth be "effectively in charge." Ouch. There was good news for Mary-Claire, though. Serena wants her to take on a permanent job rather than just be agency staff. The bad news is she wont be allowed to read magazines while she's meant to be working any more.

Wise old heads

(Series 15, ep. 29 'Time Has Told Me' by Ian Kershaw 30.4.13)

Is Serena trying to get rid of Ric Griffin? Is that why she's banished one of Holbyshire's leading general surgeons to the reservoir of surplus emergency cases that is known as AAU, which everyone keeps insisting is a "young man's game"? She needs to be careful he doesn't have her for constructive dismissal if that's her plan. She claims his emergency medicine skills are "outdated." This would be because he's a consultant general surgeon. Honestly, it makes no sense, it really doesn't.

His comfort zone is very much the operating theatre, so he spent much of the episode there trying to hide from AAU (where someone yells "Mr Griffin!" literally every three seconds) by performing a laparotomy at the same time as an emergency procedure on a patient. It made clinical sense, and it also bought him a bit of quiet time away from the hurly burly of bedpans and puke. He also found time for a little bit of brain surgery, which obviously was excellent fun for him, but didn't go down well with Serena. "It's not an AAU procedure," she said. Well, no, but Ric follows in the proud tradition of Linden Cullen and Michael Spence in doing stuff on AAU that's ever so slightly a bit too risky for AAU, and therefore he's a better fit for the Ward of Doom than Serena perhaps anticipated.

Speaking of Michael Spence, his current gig is on Keller, where the collision of two of the biggest egos in the NHS (his and The Malick's) provided excellent entertainment. Malick wanted to impress cute new F1 Dominic Copeland (David Ames) and invited him to observe a procedure "that I, The Malick, will perform in Mr Griffin's absence." He was usurped by the higher power of Michael Spence, tucking into sushi (brought by Digby) and channelling his inner Mr Miyagi ("I'm the clinical lead. Wax on, wax off") in his mentoring style.

As an aside, is cute new F1 Dominic Copeland turning Malick's head away from the lovely Nathan? It looks like it. Maybe our Antoine isn't quite ready to settle down and meet his other half's mother just yet.

Dr Oliver Valentine continued to express his grief over Tara via the medium of looking moody and being horrible to Prof Elliot Hope. His grief is so profound that it's beyond the scope of the usual hospital counsellor to deal with it, and Ollie was pencilled in for a meeting with psychiatric doctor Sharon Kozinsky (Madeleine Potter). He didn't bother to turn up, but she appeared on Darwin anyway, because his heart patient needed a bit of psychiatric input as he was convinced the heart that had been transplanted in him was evil and had to be removed. Ollie failed to mention this bit of information to Dr K, with the inevitable result that the patient attempted the procedure himself with a lump of broken glass. Ouch. Dr K reported the whole thing to Hanssen, and both Ollie and Elliot are in hot water with The Boss (Hanssen, not Bruce Springsteen, who couldn't give a hoot, frankly).

Did Oliver thank Elliot for attempting to stand up for him and protect him? Nuh-uh. Walked straight past him at the end of the shift. I know the lad has to mourn and so on, but I do hope he sorts himself out soon and gets back to being a little bit flirty/scared with Jac, doing the big-eyes thing as opposed to the blank-eyes thing and producing amusing one-liners.

The episode ended on a philosophical note, with old-timers Ric and Elliot sitting outside, pondering the skies above Borehamwood, the Hollywood of Hertfordshire. Elliot remembered the days before there was so much light pollution, when you could look at the stars (and the fireworks from the *Big Brother* house on eviction night) rather than just see aeroplane lights. But, he mused, "there are still stars up there." Yes there are. And there's still room in a hospital full of smart juniors for a pair of wise, experienced seniors. As long as Serena's around to help them keep their skills updated.

A need-to-know situation

(*Series 15, ep. 30 'Only Human' by Rebecca Wojciechowski 7.5.13*)

For anyone who missed the throwaway comment the other week about Jac and Jonny sleeping together after the tragic loss of Tara, it was included in the recap at the beginning of this one, followed by Jac getting the news about her endometriosis. Keep these things in mind, because we'll be needing them by the end of proceedings.

But first to Keller, where Malick was given the task of looking after the girlfriend of a serial killer. Only he wasn't to think of her as the girlfriend of a serial killer. She was just supposed to be "a body on the table." He didn't bother to warn his staff about who they'd be dealing with and just told them not to react when they recognised her from television. They were probably expecting Lorraine Kelly or Gail from Coronation Street, which meant it was all a bit of a shock to find they were caring for Amanda, a woman who'd refused to give evidence against her boyfriend, a nasty man who'd killed lots of women. Chantelle found it impossible to even raise a smile, never mind get a cannula in straight. Luckily new F1 Dominic seemed pretty competent, when he wasn't busy casting adoring glances and compliments in the direction of Malick (dear Malick, he needs that, what with being so under-confident).

Malick himself found it difficult to maintain his professional judgement, and allowed a policeman who'd been on the case for 12 years and needed one last crack at it before he retired (don't they always) to question Amanda while she was just recovering from major surgery. Throw in the fact that the serial killer had just killed himself, and Amanda was in what we might call a vulnerable state. This led to her literally turning her insides inside-out (ugh).

Malick was carpeted for that one by Hanssen. "Ego is the distance between one's capabilities and one's actions," the Swedish sage informed him. Was this on Malick's mind when he grappled with himself later on about whether to resuscitate her or not? She also had cancer and had given instructions that she wasn't to be resuscitated if the situation arose from that. But he had thought she was suicidal and had called a psych consult, so the advance directive didn't apply. Or did it? It was a dilemma, but he went ahead and saved her life. And then got thumped by the mother of one of the serial killer's victims.

Guts hanging out, tales of evil deeds, Michael Spence looking cross… Keller was not a happy place to be this week. Don't even think of looking to AAU for light relief. Down there in the Hall of Doom, Sacha discovered that his daughter Rachel has leukaemia. Oh, scriptwriters. I know tragedy, conflict and upsets are the engines of drama, but not poor Sacha. I can't bear to see him unhappy. Isn't being married to Chrissie enough suffering for one man? Luckily, he has Ric Griffin on his side, a man who is practically the human embodiment of the phrase "pep talk" these days.

For laughs we need to go to Darwin, where the patient of the week was one of these hypochondriacs who turns out to have something real wrong with them in the end. But for most of the time, she was dramatically flinging herself out of a wheelchair she didn't need and being snarky to Jac. "Where's a better doctor?" she said. "One who isn't going to inflict their disappointment with life on to me?" She knew a bit about Jac's disappointments, as she'd read the letter from Jac's gynaecologist.

Mo – with a foxy new hairdo ('Better than being bald," was Jac's assessment) – had noticed something about the notoriously pie-averse Jac, which was confirmed when Jac received a call from the gynaecologist. "Your bum's changed," said Mo. "I knew you were pregnant!" Fans of the double-headed entity known as "Janny" may have squeeeed with excitement at that point, but let's not forget her one-night-stand with Sean. Whoever the father is, I just love the idea of Jac being pregnant. She's already one of the most multi-dimensional characters on TV, but adding in pregnancy and motherhood to a woman who's so famously controlled and controlling is going to be fascinating to watch. She's already let her vulnerable side show with baby Freya, and with Jonny Mac, but when you're pregnant you become public property, in an odd way. Jac's not going to take to that at all well, and you can bet Mo will be on hand for unwanted advice. I can't wait.

Serial killers, vampires and ghosts

(Series 15, ep. 31 'The More Deceived' by Joe Ainsworth 14.5.13)

There was some spooky old stuff going on in Holby this week, with a serial killer's accomplice still languishing on Keller, a vampire attacking Dr Gemma Wilde on AAU, Dr Oliver Valentine being haunted by the spectre of his dead wife ("How do you live with a ghost?") and Jac Naylor snacking on chocolate and anchovies. I mean, anchovies I can understand. But chocolate? Jac Naylor?

I'm going to start at the bottom (is AAU on a lower floor? I always imagine it is), because I need to show off. As PLA Jr will confirm, within two minutes of the goth patient trying to bite Dr Gemma Wilde because she thought she was a vampire, and then creasing up with abdominal pains, I'd diagnosed porphyria. It took handsome (oh gosh, yes he is) new doctor Harry Tressler (Jules Knight) most of the rest of the episode to reach the same conclusion, but at least he was doing better than Gemma and Ric Griffin, who'd had a dig about in the poor girl's insides before concluding they had no idea what was up with her. How did I become such a diagnostic whizz? I might have graduated from the Holby School of Televisual Medicine, but I did my early training at *St Elsewhere*, which once featured a similar storyline.

Back to Dr Harry Tressler, who's the new CT1. He's good-looking, charming and flirtatious – he's already got Gemma and Mary-Claire interested in him, and predictably the first round went to MC ("Hammer time!" – I do love Mary-Claire). While he's in his element with the ladies, Harry seems less at ease with black people, mistaking Ric Griffin for a porter (but… but… the gravitas of the man! He wears seniority like an invisible crown on his grizzled head!). When Ric put him right, Harry made a clumsy attempt to relate: "You lead from the front – man of the people stylee." Ouch.

For these amusing scenes alone you have to love an episode written by Joe Ainsworth, but he's also not afraid to get into the really serious stuff, and it was all very serious indeed on Keller. Amanda Layton, the serial killer's girlfriend Malick was looking after last week, was still there and still refusing to tell anyone where the bodies were buried. At the end of last week's episode the mother of one of the victims turned up and thumped Malick. This week she was demanding answers. Dr Dominic Copeland, who proved last week he's quite a good doctor, demonstrated this week that he's a rubbish googler (to be fair he wasn't using Google, but 'Whippet Search,' which may have been his problem) by concluding that this girl, Simone Harris, hadn't been one of the victims at all because her name hadn't been mentioned during the trial (though it had come up in other accounts). Anyhoo, Malick believed Mrs Harris and set things up so Mrs Harris would get the chance to confront Amanda Layton without a prison warder present (on the subject of whom, Judith Jacob was very funny in the scenes where she was flirting with Dominic – and totally barking up the wrong tree, as we'll see later).

The scene where the two women came face to face was very tense and emotional. Amanda ended up with a cut on her head, Mrs Harris ended up with an answer (but was it the right answer?) and Malick ended up looking totally traumatised. He was even more traumatised when he insisted on not resuscitating Amanda later (following her advance directive but ignoring his earlier opinion that she'd been suicidal and therefore not capable of making a proper decision) and she died.

When you've had the day from hell at work, it's really nice to be able to talk it through with your partner. Unfortunately Malick had annoyed his partner, Nathan, at the start of the episode and Nathan was in no mood to hold his hand and make soothing noises. The next best thing is an admiring junior doctor, and the episode ended with one of those passionate locker room moments which are a speciality of Malick's.

Before we leave Keller, can I just say that Jimmy Akingbola has been incredible in these two episodes? I do enjoy Malick, but his ego-driven, high-intensity character isn't especially warm or likeable, even during the episodes when he was bonding with his son. I felt like this was the first time I'd ever properly seen under the surface of him.

Darwin was a bit low-key this week. Jonny Mac still doesn't know that Jac is pregnant (no idea how Mo is keeping a lid on that one). As well as eating anchovies and chocolate (yum), pregnancy might be mellowing Jac, as she was really sweet to her patient.

Oliver Valentine has started his therapy sessions with Dr Sharon Kozinsky, but has been living in the on-call room because he can't cope with the Essence of Tara still lingering in their mutual flat. What I want to know is, will it be Oliver or lovely old Elliot Hope who has a romance with the fragrant Dr Kozinsky? Both are possible at the moment. Or maybe neither.

A tiny Naylor. There's a thought

(Series 15, ep. 32 'Divided We Fall' by Justin Young 21.5.13)

Oliver Valentine thinks the only people Jac Naylor can relate to are people who are anaesthetised and on her operating table. This is not actually true. The people Jac Naylor can relate to, or who can relate to her, are straightforward, honest people. People with, aptly enough, open hearts.

The living embodiment of this quality is Sacha Levy, which partly explains why scenes involving him and Jac are always so lovely. They're also rare, because they don't work on the same ward, so it was marvellous this week when an elderly patient (from a very sweet storyline) asked Sacha to be present in his wife's operation, thus putting Sacha and Jac in the same operating theatre.

Sacha was worried about his daughter, whose leukaemia isn't responding to treatment. Jac's response to this news was some of her top-grade emotionally expressive eye work, given that she was wearing a surgical mask at the time. Later, Sacha asked Jac to shave his hair, so he could show a united front with Rachel who was worried about being "puffy and bald." This was a completely perfect scene, as Sacha wasn't the only one with child-based worries. Jac was wondering whether she had the qualities to ever be a mother. Sacha said of course she did, and the expression on Jac's face was wonderful (like Guy Henry, Rosie Marcel's acting is ninja level). "A tiny Naylor. There's a thought," said Sacha, sweetly.

There was a thought, indeed. To add more food to the thought, writer Justin Young had thrown in a cute child for Jonny Mac to look after while all this was going on. A red-haired child, too – she could almost have been a tiny Naylor herself. Jonny's paternal qualities weren't lost on Jac, or Mo, who later told the child a story about the "skinny ginger witch and the annoying Scottish prince." Who could she mean?

Eventually Jonny Mac found out that Jac was pregnant, but Jac said she probably wasn't pregnant any more, because she'd been bleeding. He got her to do a test. Right at the end of the episode, he walked into an operating theatre where Jac was about to start surgery. "Are we going to do this thing?" he said. Did he mean the operation? I suppose if you were the anaesthetist or a nurse you'd have thought so, but we knew he meant having a baby. And her reply? "Looks like it." Hurrah!

Elsewhere, Digby, sweet old-fashioned thing that he is, had made a mix tape for Chantelle featuring some of his favourite tunes, the first letter of the titles of which just happened to spell CHANTELLE. And Channers, with her facility for wordsearch puzzles, worked it out in no time. Sadly, her reaction didn't look overwhelmingly positive, but her options are narrowing since we discovered that Rhys is "doing half the nurses in Paeds." That's the kind of behaviour that can have illiterate vigilantes daubing your house with red paint in the wee small hours.

If only Digby had the confidence of Harry Tressler. The ladies love Harry, and indeed I'm teetering on the verge of having to call him The World's Most Beautiful CT1. Dr Honey spent the whole episode making sarcastic comments about what he might or might not have been getting up to with that minx Mary-Claire. Not that she's jealous or anything.

Honesty is the best policy

(Series 15, ep. 33 'Back From the Dead' by Jon Sen 28.5.13)

I'm extremely sorry for the lateness of this post. I've been moving house – traumatic in itself – but no sooner had we started to unpack the boxes than the hideous truth dawned. We have broadband speeds of dial-up levels and the TV aerial is not working (I have no mobile phone coverage either). Though I'm still living in London and am only half a mile from my previous address, it feels like I'm living in the past.

So this episode of Holby has been watched on iPlayer in bite-sized chunks at off-peak times and I hope you'll forgive me if the quality isn't quite what you'd hope for.

To cheer myself up (did I mention I've also done my back in lifting heavy boxes and am sitting here wishing Camoxidan wasn't fictional?), let's start with Jac Naylor, Jonny Mac and the baby who shall henceforth be known as Jaccy Maccy Jr. There was the loveliest scene since the scene where he was stitching up a cut on her forehead (he did a great job on that, btw – no scar visible at all), when he gave her a wee ultrasound and they saw the baby for the first time. Jac gave one of her trademark looks – one of those that only lasts for seconds but says so much. Just in case the moment threatened to get too emotional, Jonny printed out a picture and she suggested he stick it on the his fridge at home, knowing how much he loved a cliche. The banter between Jac and Jonny was brilliant throughout the episode. I particularly loved it when they almost had a bonding moment on the Walkway of Wisdom and he put his arm around her shoulders as they walked away from the camera. How heartwarming, I thought, that she lets him be so familiar. "Don't touch me!" she snarled.

Chrissie was feeling a bit like that re Sacha, only in their case it was "Don't touch Daniel!" The fruit of her womb turns out to be a bone marrow match for Sacha's daughter, which would be lovely if only Sacha hadn't tried to have him tested without telling her. Understandably, she wasn't keen on wee Daniel having painful and possibly risky procedures, even if it meant a chance for Rachel to recover from her leukaemia. I did actually sympathise with Chrissie, who really only wanted to be consulted and feel part of the decision making, rather than being presented with a decision after it had been made.

Malick was suffering from the ramifications of his decision to let Amanda Layton die, and having a fling with Doting Dominic afterwards. Basically, Malick has been suspended and that might be the least of his troubles, as Doting Dominic may be about to go a little bit bunny boilerish after seeing Malick heading off home with Nathan.

Digby saves the day, if not the episode

(Series 15, ep. 34 'Home' by Nick Fisher 4.6.13)

Due to house moving etc, I'm still forced to watch Holby City on iPlayer with very poor bandwidth. Maybe it summarises my feelings about this episode when I tell you I didn't especially mind the regular pauses for "buffering."

What was wrong with it? No Darwin, hardly any doctoring, and two, rather tedious, storylines. I hate being critical, honestly I do, but once in a while a dud episode happens along and this was it.

The Coroners Court scenes were dull and even the presence of the sublime Guy Henry failed to lift them. It was only at the end when it really came to life. Dominic put his bunny-boiling scheme into action by claiming that Malick had given Amanda Layton a drug to suppress her respiratory system. Digby saved the day with a wodge of research to show the aforementioned drug would have a completely different effect (wouldn't Hanssen have known this?). It looked like Dominic's career as a doctor was in ruins and he'd have to fall back to being a hair model, but Malick stepped up to the witness-box and came clean about his "error of judgement" in ripping the jeans off his junior colleague. Understandably, Nathan was none too happy and left the courtroom, but it was the first time Malick has really shown much of a backbone.

Meanwhile, police had failed to turn up the body of Simone Harris, which Amanda Layton had told Malick had been "taken home." At the point where she said that, was there a single viewer watching who didn't think, "Hang on – that's a bit vague. Why not ask her whose home she means?" Malick was apparently satisfied with the obscure answer, basically so a bit of sleuthing could finally track down the remains of Simone Harris – conveniently including a necklace that said "Simone," just in case we were in any doubt. There was no suspense or drama about this at all, because it was all so contrived. Or has the "buffering" annoyed me more than I thought and everybody else was on the edge of their seats?

Back at Holby, there was even more nonsense featuring Dr Honey and her annoying child, Finn. This involved Dr Honey and Dr Posh chasing around the hospital after Finn, accompanied by a patient who couldn't be left alone for a second because she had a rifle (she was a deer hunter who'd been gored) and it wasn't allowed to be out of her sight until a policeman with suitable gun training arrived. Nobody noticed she was quietly bleeding everywhere because they were too focused on Finn. It was all just an excuse for Dr Honey and Dr Posh to kiss on the Walkway of Wisdom, which is being heavily used these days. Frankly Drs H and P make a lovely couple, because they both seem as dim as each other. The dumbest moment of the entire episode came when Drs P and H finally noticed the deer hunter woman was bleeding. Dr Honey fished around in the wound and came out with a sharp object. "What's that?" she gasped. At least Dr Posh was able to put two and two together and deduced that a woman who's been gored by a deer could well have a bit of antler sticking in her. Why, he'd even noticed there was a bit broken off when he saw the deer in a skip earlier! If there's a CT1 Prize, it should surely be his.

The problems of parenthood

(Series 15, ep. 35 'All Tomorrow's Parties' by Graham Mitchell 11.6.13)

Michael Spence is really at his finest when he gets emotionally involved with his patients (not in a sleazy sense, you understand; I'm talking purely professionally). When his heart is as engaged as his head, he gets all kick-ass like the time he thrust Little George Binns' head at a corpse.

This week he struggled with the difficulties of being an extremely long-distance parent, with daughter Jasmine about to land at Holby International Airport any minute and Michael still up to his elbows in gastric unpleasantness. The patient who tugged at his heart-strings (and mine, I have to admit) was Seb, a young man who was dying of cancer. Seb had the weirdest father ever – a beardy man who looked a tad like Brian Blessed and seemed to have the emotional range of Data from *Star Trek: The Next Generation*. Seb's mother had popped to Uganda on some unspecified business, neither of them apparently thinking that they should really be with their son. They were a stoic sort of family all round, with Seb fairly comfortable with the idea he didn't have long left – although he was afraid of pain. Michael decided he wanted to surgically buy Seb some more time to see his mother, and the only time the beardy dad showed he really cared was to kiss his son's forehead before he went into theatre.

The surgery was less successful than it could have been, and Seb had to get used to the idea of his death all over again. Michael felt guilty, but possibly not as guilty as he felt when Jasmine's plane landed early and Ric Griffin smugly did the chauffeuring honours. Jasmine is fantastic, and I loved how she swanned along the corridors with Digby struggling after her with a pile of luggage.

Michael isn't the only one with parenting problems, of course. Down in AAU, a depressing venue at the best of times, Sacha and Chrissie were still grappling with the concept of Daniel being a saviour sibling for Rachel. It turned out Daniel was a perfect bone marrow match and eventually Chrissie signed the consent forms.

What she didn't know was that tests had shown Daniel has a hole in his heart, which presumably means any kind of surgery would be more risky. And Sacha kept this information to himself (though Mo knows). Normally I would defend Sacha to the ends of the earth because he is The Nicest Man In The World, but he's wrong here. I know he's terrified that his daughter might die, but Chrissie should be aware of all the facts. She had my sympathy already, but when she talked in counselling about when her daughter Amanda died (still the episode that's had the highest tissue count for me), you really had to feel for her.

Someone else with a more recent experience of bereavement is Widowed Dr Oliver Valentine. Still sleeping badly (in the on-call room beside a picture of Tara), still snapping at his colleagues and going through the motions with his patients. Counselling hasn't helped, the kindness of Prof Hope hasn't helped. What's to be done? Wisely, writer Graham Mitchell decided to alleviate the anguish a bit this week by getting Dr Posh to work with Ollie on a tricky diagnosis. And I have to say that they made quite the duo. Dr Posh was a lot more fun with Dr Valentine than he was with Dr Honey last week, and having a bit of competition started to, if not quite bring Ollie's mojo back, at least remind him that he possesses such a thing as a mojo.

Pregnancy watch: Jac has become committed to the concept of eating for two, snarfing Jonny Mac's sandwich and cramming biscuits into her face like they're about to be banned by the government.

It's time to stop with the Tiny Tears act and man up

(Series 15, ep. 36 'Follow the Yellow Brick Road' by Johanne McAndrew & Elliot Hope 18.6.13)

Possibly it doesn't help that I watched the second half of this episode before I watched the first half, due to social circumstances, but even after I watched it again in the right order I still felt a little confused.

It seems I was completely wrong last week about Dr Posh and Ollie being a fun team. This week Dr Posh was being a bit of a dick and was apparently just there to be a thorn in Oliver's already aggrieved side. In fact, Dr Posh doesn't seem to have had the same personality for more than two weeks running. Is it any wonder I prefer Digby? You know where you are with Digby.

What I am sure about is that Ollie's scathing attack on Elliot at the end of the episode, even though we knew it was out of grief and he was turning on the person he feels closest to, was absolutely shocking. He wanted to make Elliot hurt as much as he was hurting, and bringing up the manner of Gina's death in such brutal terms was quite stomach-turning and far more shocking than him physically pushing Elliot.

Ollie really needs to follow Jac's advice and stop with the Tiny Tears act and man up. James Anderson has eyes which are perfectly designed to be brimming with tears ("Such pain hiding behind those beautiful blue eyes," as his patient pointed out), and his acting in this episode was brilliant, but he's also great at the comedy stuff, which he hasn't had the chance to do recently. Frankly I'm as worn out as Jac is by all the grief. Even Ollie's counsellor is thinking he's wallowing a bit.

Meanwhile, My Son Daniel had the operation to collect his bone marrow. I could feel Chrissie's pain as she insisted on being in theatre with him, then couldn't handle being there. As if she wasn't suffering enough, the machines started going beep. The friendly nurse with her said not to worry, it was just the hole in the heart thing and was quite routine. But of course Chrissie didn't know about the H in the H. At this point, the sympathy points she'd been picking up during the last couple of episodes dwindled away rather. Although I could understand her being angry with Sacha for not telling her about Daniel's condition, her behaviour in taking her son out of hospital when he was supposed to be on post-op observation just to get him away from Sacha was just stupid. Then what did she do but plonk him in Michael Spence's car – presumably without the legally required car seat, unless Michael has taken to ferrying three year-olds around in his car recently and had one handy – and leave him sleeping on Michael's sofa while she and Michael got rat-arsed and (luckily) didn't end up sleeping together. What kind of behaviour is all that when you're supposed to be the caring, nurturing mother?

This last bit was in the weird little red button segment, which was basically just a ten minute scene tacked on to the end of the episode. It didn't add very much to the gaiety of nations apart from banging another nail in the coffin of Chrissie's popularity and introducing us to Michael Spence's fabulous taste in interior design.

Much better were the scenes in the main episode between Michael, his daughter Jasmine and cancer patient Seb. There was another "Michael Spence – hell, yeah" moment when he rang Seb's father (conspicuous by his absence at the bedside). "This is a courtesy call. I'm wondering where the hell you are."

Pregnancy watch: There was a precious scene in which Elliot introduced Jac to the finer aspects of being a doughnut connoisseur. Her little face as he advertised the particular delights of a chocolate one, only to take a big bite out of it himself! All this carb consumption hasn't taken its toll on her physically yet. If there was any justice in the world she'd be the size of a gable end by now.

I was always a bit too good for you

(Series 15, ep. 37 'Break' by Nick Fisher 25.6.13)

Sacha and Chrissie. Did it all start out so promisingly? Not really. A one night stand that resulted in My Son Daniel. An intervening "romance" with Dull/Gay Dan. A wedding that probably wouldn't have happened if Jac hadn't issued a subtle threat. And months and months of patients and hospital visitors telling Chrissie that she's waaay too gorgeous and wonderful for dear old Sacha, and her blushing prettily and agreeing with them.

I wanted it to work out, because I want Sacha to be happy, but it was never going to last. Sacha never thought he was good enough, Chrissie always thought she was too good. I liked how, when the break came, it came as a result of a situation that was morally and emotionally complicated, rather than the more obvious route of Chrissie having an affair, or the less obvious route of Sacha having one. My sympathy for Chrissie has fluctuated over the last few weeks, with last week's behaviour in the red button episode being particularly unimpressive, but this week I did feel sorry for the way she was sidelined in the Levy Family Drama (Helen was good value, though).

Still, it didn't excuse Chrissie's rather nasty emphasis on the past tense when she was leaving Sacha in the Car Park of Grief. "What I loved – *loved*– about you was that I could trust you," she said. Ouch. So Sacha was left sobbing in the car park as Chrissie and My Son Daniel went to stay with Mark "Jesus" Williams (who else would you turn to in a crisis than "Jesus"?).

No Pregnancy Watch this week, as Jac wasn't around. Instead, for the night shift Darwin was being staffed by Jonny Mac, Mo (who seemed to be officially stationed in the coffee bar, as she wasn't actually on the ward much – maybe she was giving out healthy heart advice to people planning to order pies), Oliver Valentine and Dr Honey. Elliot was around, but was having a well-earned half with Dr Sharon, who told him to turn his pager off. Not content with deploying Dr Posh as an irritant to the already beleaguered Grieving Widower, Serena decided this week to torment him by having Dr Honey shadow him. It wasn't a terribly rewarding situation for either of them. The patient they were dealing with was somewhat high-maintenance and could have tried the patience of a saint. As it was, he was just trying the patience of a vicar, who also happened to be his partner. When he got stroppy with Ollie and refused a chest drain, Ollie got stroppy in return and stomped off, leaving Dr Honey to do a procedure she wasn't qualified for.

It's been far too long since we've seen Henrik Hanssen, but in his absence Serena seems to be taking on something of his persona. The way she asked Oliver, "Were you there, Dr Valentine? Supervising?" was pure Hanssen.

Meanwhile on Keller there was a sweet double-act of dying Seb and an old man called Mr Potter, who were both trying to encourage Digby to ask Chantelle out. Poor old Digby ended up letting Mr Potter's grandson think that Mr P was dead, when he was actually in theatre. Then he had to break the news that he had, in fact, died. Every week I love Digby more, and I did feel for the lad when Chantelle turned him down, although he could hardly carry on being the bumbling, hapless soul he is if he was stepping out with the prettiest girl on the ward. Just ask Sacha what a trial that can be.

Emotionally involved

(Series 15, ep. 38 'The Journey Home' by Julia Gilbert 2.7.13)

I think after this episode my love for Michael Spence, which has crept upon me with the stealth of Henrik Hanssen on a ninja activity day, is now complete.

Remember the days when people thought he was just in this doctoring lark for a fast buck, when he liked to inhabit the worlds of Holby Care and the more designer end of cosmetic surgery, shimmering from breast implant to buttock augmentation with as much graceful ease as his tight trousers would allow? These days his trousers are a slightly more forgiving cut, he's sporting that delicious grizzled facial hair look, and most of all, he cares deeply about his patients. In a storyline that reached an emotional climax this week, he became very involved in the case of Seb, a young man dying of cancer whose family had apparently abandoned him. Michael's own feelings of inadequacy as a parent came into play, particularly when his daughter Jasmine turned up on a visit from America and became friends with Seb herself.

As an emotional balance, Hanssen was back this week (hurrah!) counselling professionalism and detachment. Obviously Michael ignored him – "For an ice man like you maybe it's just another day at the office!" Michael told him, in yet another "hell, yeah" moment. The scene where Seb died was wonderfully acted by Hari Dhillon and Dylan Llewellyn (and beautifully written by Julia Gilbert), and I bet Michael Spence's weren't the only tears flowing.

On Darwin, Elliot Hope agreed to go to the opera with Psychiatrist Sharon, and then chickened out when Mo, Jonny and Jac told him it was officially a date. They then had to persuade him to re-invite himself. Mo offered to buy him new pants and Jac reminded him that he was the same age as Madonna and it was about time he had a life. I should think the same could be said for Sharon. That woman seems to be the entire Psych department at the moment. She gets summoned to sort out the problems of staff and patients alike, and even had Oliver Valentine ringing her up at home. She definitely deserves a night at the opera and a man with fresh pants.

Somehow mention of the word "pants" brings me to Dr Posh. Is it just me, or is he getting more annoying every week? He started off this episode by knocking Digby off his bike and ended it getting a dressing-down from Hanssen for helping a disabled man to smoke cannabis to help his pain. If Hanssen had had concrete proof that this had happened, Dr Posh would have been suspended, but as it was, he got away with a warning. And when Hanssen says "You have been warned," you know you have been.

I suppose we were meant to think Dr Posh was the sort of maverick like Michael Spence who would bend the rules for the benefit of his patient and good on him etc, but frankly he's just too smug and the way he plays off Dr Honey and Mary-Claire is very annoying. Not that I care about Dr Honey, and Mary-Claire can stick up for herself, but it's just that we're expected to buy into the notion that he's God's gift.

Talking of little gifts, it's time for Pregnancy Watch. Jac appears to be suffering badly with morning sickness, but is calling it "something I ate." She's gone off coffee, but her enthusiasm for carbs is wonderful to behold, particularly when she gets them via the medium of ticking off Elliot about his bad diet then snarfing his baguette. She's also showing her cheeky, fun side a bit more and is even acting like she's part of a team. Who knew hormones could be so powerful?

Then there were no Valentines

(*Series 15, ep. 39 'Mens Sana in Corpore Sano' by Patrick Homes. 9.7.13*)

It was the final episode for the man we've come to know fondly over the years as Young Dr Oliver Valentine. James Anderson has left for pastures new (including an episode of *Poirot*, apparently, which is excellent news – Mr PLA and I love to settle down in front of a good *Poirot* on a damp Sunday afternoon). I'll miss Ollie, but more for the character he used to be than the one he's been recently. As emotions go, sadness is not the most fun one to watch, and the poor lad has been immersed in sadness since the death of the lovely Tara.

James Anderson does misery beautifully, what with having those amazing blue eyes that brim with tears at the drop of a sad hat, and he also does anger really well – the scene recently where he nastily let rip at Prof Hope was shocking and upsetting to behold. Oliver's reaction to Tara's death, which was basically to put up a wall against the world, tell everybody everything was fine, and then shout a lot was realistic and consistent with his previous reaction to Penny's death, but from a viewer perspective it maybe went on a bit too long and got just a little bit boring. It overshadowed the things I've always loved about Oliver – his fun side, his way with a witty one-liner, his kindness, his relationships with the other staff members.

Thank goodness, then, that we had a little glimpse of this right before he left in two touching and perfectly crafted scenes, one with Jac and the other with Elliot.

Jac hadn't been around for most of the episode, and I was thinking there wouldn't be a Pregnancy Watch at all this week, but there she was, sitting in the dark in the staff room. "Is that – a muffin?" Oliver said, incredulously. Jac hugged the previously scorned cakey product. "My precious!" she said. This on its own was enough to give him a clue that something was up. "I'm pregnant," she told him, and the look on his face was a picture – laughing for a moment because surely it must be a joke, and then looking delighted. "If you hug me, I'll puke," she warned him, but he hugged her anyway and it was her turn to give one of her special Jac smiles. It was a lovely scene.

Ollie asked Jac to look after Prof Hope for him ("But who's going to look after *you*?" she replied. Don't you just love the new, improved, Nurturing Naylor?) and Ollie's final scene was with Elliot. It was full of forgiveness, understanding and genuine friendship. Oliver said he might return one day. "No, you won't," Elliot said sadly.

Before Ollie left, he (eventually) fessed up to stealing Tara's work for his CT2 test and for dropping Dr Honey in it over the dodgy chest drain business a couple of weeks ago. Added to this, of course, is the elephant in the room which is the fact that he wouldn't have been a doctor at all if he hadn't passed his sister's exam paper off as his own all those many moons ago.

This left Dr Posh to inherit the CT2 crown by default, but he said he didn't want it, because he likes to achieve his own achievements. Prior to that he'd said he would drop out of the race anyhow if only Ollie would tell the truth about Dr Honey and the chest drain. At that stage in her career, Jac Naylor would never have made such a rash promise. This leads me to suspect that Dr Posh doesn't have quite the right stuff for the hurly burly of Darwin, but possibly it makes him a nicer person than I thought.

It's nice that the patients have started using my nicknames for the staff, though. "Dr Harry Tressler," his patient said. "Posh, right?" Yes, he is. Or, more properly, Dr Posh.

Dr Honey is still besotted with Dr Posh. This manifests itself in a bit of bitching and a bit of Gazing Adoringly. In one scene, Posh managed to insert a colonoscopy tube into his patient without the patient even noticing it had gone in. Honey was hardly able to contain herself. "That was... beautiful!" she gasped.

On Keller, Malick was back and his confidence, which took a knock following the Amanda Layton business, was perked up by his latest patient, who was a blind photographer. At one point she went AWOL (they should really tag these patients or something, the number who go missing per month) and Malick found her in the Linden Cullen Memorial Shrubbery, which now has a little fountain and a fish pond. I'm going to call it the Tara Lo Memorial Water Feature, because even if it isn't, it should be.

The dangers that lurk in the car park
(Series 15, ep. 40 'Make or Break' by Rob Kinsman 16.7.13)

Lauren Drummond (Chantelle) was on daytime TV yesterday talking about tonight's episode. I didn't watch it, because I'm spoiler-averse, but I assumed she'd be talking about Digby's crush on Chantelle and whether Channers is ever going to see him as more than a friend.

As it turns out, the question we were left with at the shock end of the episode was – is she ever going to see him again, or is she going to expire quietly in the Car Park of Doom? Maybe I should have watched daytime TV to get a clue.

It all started quite well for Digby, as he received his results and discovered he's gone from being the third best F1 in the hospital (after Tara and Honey) to being the number one F2 (Honey is second, and Tara is out of contention. Hashtag RIP Tara). This has earned him new respect among some of his seniors. Serena even invited him out for a drink with the senior management team (her and Hanssen – what fun!). He deserved it, bless him – he'd put in a lot of effort. "I even read *Pancreatic Duct Obstructions: A New Perspective* from cover to cover," he told Serena. "Somebody had to," she replied, looking amused (I do like Serena when she's being amused).

When Michael Spence and Malick were required in theatre to do something complicated, Digby was left in charge of Keller. What could possibly go wrong? Well, more vomiting than an average morning in AAU, a neurotic patient who was scared of people and should really have been in his own room, a man with an anxious and slightly scary son (with magnificent eyebrows) who scared Chantelle a bit – with the result that Digby was soon resembling a geeky headless chicken and being all snappy with Chantelle.

All was well that ended well re the various patients, with the timely arrival of Michael Spence and Malick, but it wasn't a glorious first day for Digby and Chantelle was not impressed by his snappiness. She missed the old Digby, she told him.

So in an effort to apologise, he told Serena that he wasn't able to go for an after-work drink, and legged it across the car park to apologise to Chantelle and thank her for her brilliantly original gift of a congratulatory pen.

And out of nowhere – violent muggers! Chantelle was left horizontal with a bleedy face, calling to Digby for help, and he was left shaken and too scared to be stirred to do anything to help her. "Och, noooo," as Lorraine Kelly possibly murmured to Lauren Drummond on daytime TV. I should have watched.

Meanwhile, the Darwin plot was practically an hour-long Pregnancy Watch, as it was all about Jac's attempts to avoid going for a scan, because that would make it all official and there'd be nothing to stop Jonny Mac from blethering about his happiness to all and sundry.

She wanted to go private. "There's no way I'm going to let anyone in this hospital go near my womb," she informed the father of her child. "I did that once before, and look what happened." Aww, bless, she's such an old romantic. After much procrastination and prevarication and intervening bits of the day job, Jonny eventually got her to turn up 90 minutes late for an appointment at Holby's very own Obs & Gynae department, with the midwife-from-hell Jac had a run-in with when Mo was having her baby. "I don't appreciate your attitude," the midwife said to the never knowingly cooperative Jac. "Few people do," she replied. "I've learned to live with it."

The scan itself went according to plan. The baby seems to be healthy, Jac pretended not to care and Jonny grinned like he might explode and started jabbering. "The foetus can't hear you," sighed Jac. "I can. Shut up, Jonny."

It takes more real effort than that for Jac to rain on Jonny Mac's parade these days, and he couldn't wait to deliver the news, which he did to a room full of colleagues. Jac tried not to die of the embarrassment of having her personal space well and truly invaded. But at least now she won't have to hide her secret doughnut habit.

Meanwhile, Sacha was on pins waiting to find out whether Rachel's bone marrow transplant had been a success, or whether he'd subjected Your Son Daniel to surgery and annoyed Chrissie all the way to Australia for nothing. It was good news, and he shared a hug with Mo in the Linden Cullen Memorial Shrubbery (which gets more ornate every time we see it. It now features the Ollie and Tara Memorial Wedding Grotto).

Making yourself feel better

(Series 15, ep. 41 'A Night's Tale' by Dana Fainaru 23.7.13)

That Chantelle is made of sterner stuff than you'd think. She seems so pink and pretty that every time she laughs a new baby fairy is born, but she must be hard as nails really. How else do you explain going straight back to work after you've been mugged, with your false eyelashes glued firmly into place on your bruised and swollen eyelid? That's got to smart, but she bore it with her shoulders back, her head held high and a professional smile on her face.

The same could not be said for Digby. He was suffering from the aftermath of the attack. Not so much any physical injuries, although his glasses had to have first aid, but the realisation that he'd failed the woman he loves when she needed him most. He spent the rest of the episode trying to make himself feel better, as Chantelle pointed out to him, by being a bit too stroppy and ready to call the police on the potential mugger, who was the kid who was giving Chantelle trouble last week, Cameron.

In turn, Cameron accused Chantelle of trying to make herself feel better with her caring, sharing style. At the end of the episode, Chantelle and Digby sat on the curved bench of contemplation in an outdoor area I don't remember having seen before (they must have had Lottery funding to expand the Linden Cullen Memorial Shrubbery, as there seems to be more of it every week). She said she felt daft for being such a soft touch, and he said (I'm paraphrasing) that her soft touch was exactly what was lovely about her, and not to go changing because he loves her just the way she is. He was bold enough to put his arm around her shoulders as he said this, and was rewarded for his efforts with a kiss. It's been a long time coming (since New Year's Eve, when Chantelle first set eyes on her Consolation Nerd), and I hope now they can be happy for a while and neither of them will be diagnosed with a brain tumour or end up doing something they might regret with Mary-Claire after a drunk night at the bar.

Jac was away lecturing in Birmingham (I hope they have a branch of Dunkin Donuts there, or Birmingham is going to be in deep trouble). Jonny Mac was flying the flag for Pregnancy Watch, as he was bidding for a buggy on eBay. A practical choice, finance-wise on a nurse's wages, but I can't really picture Jac wanting to put Jaccy Maccy Junior in a second-hand conveyance.

Meanwhile, Mo was in charge of Darwin and it was nice to see her getting a storyline of her own again. This one involved a woman played by Waterloo Road's Eva Pope, who'd had the misfortune to have had two children with serious heart problems, one of them having died several years before. Mo was determined the second one wouldn't die, either, which obviously is an admirable attitude for a doctor to have. Her judgement may have been a bit influenced by the fact that it was the first birthday of William, the baby she gave birth to. At one point Eva Pope accused her of not knowing what it felt like to be a parent, but poor Mo does know.

And in AAU, Honey and Posh were circling around each other again, but it was Mary-Claire's birthday and she expected to be treated accordingly. So she took matters, and Dr Posh's credit card, into her own hands and booked a swanky restaurant and hotel. I do admire her style.

Sons and daughters

(*Series 15, ep. 42 'Never Let Me Go' by Julia Gilbert 30.7.13*)

Mo has placed herself firmly in the category of "maverick" this week (and what doctor worth his or her salt in Holby hasn't been in that category at one time or another?). Determined that her heart transplant patient Hattie wouldn't die, she told a teeny weeny fib when the heart donor's mother tried to withdraw consent, and said the procedure was too far gone and couldn't be stopped.

It was one of those cases where you could see everyone's point. Mo felt justified because if she hadn't done what she did, there'd have been two dead girls at the end of the episode instead of one. She also had it in her mind that Hattie's mother (beautifully played by Eva Pope) had already lost one child. On the other side was the grief of Nicole, the donor's mother (Lizzie Hopley, also heartbreaking – the scenes between her and Eva Pope were really touching), and poor Jonny Mac, caught in the middle and trying to do what was right and follow procedures.

Although Hattie survived and Nicole gave her blessing by leaving her daughter's heart shaped necklace for Hattie (I had a tear in my eye at that point), Jonny couldn't forgive Mo for putting emotions before protocol and potentially putting both their careers on the line and causing Nicole extra grief. Poor Mo looked devastated – she comes across as tough and feisty, but she needs his support and approval.

On Keller, Digby took some time off from gazing adoringly at Chantelle and being jealous that she was getting too close to a patient with amnesia, and did some first class diagnostic work. This impressed Hanssen so much that he invited Digby to scrub in on the ensuing surgery.

There are parallels, social-skills-wise, between Digby and Hanssen. Both of them are more at home with books than people, they like life to be quantifiable, they're occasionally brusque and awkward in their manner, but they can be endearing and charming. This was all highlighted by the arrival of Hanssen's ex partner, Maja, whom we last saw in the Stockholm episode. She was on a fact-finding mission, but she was also on a mission to see Hanssen and let him know he's about to become a grandfather (can you picture it? So sweet!).

Chantelle told Digby off for his attitude to his patient ("You haven't said one kind word…") and Maja told Hanssen off for his attitude to Digby ("You haven't given that boy any praise…"). Maja reflected to Chantelle that "some people need to learn those skills and some lose the ability to connect over time."

Indeed. But maybe connection is possible. At the end of the episode, Hanssen told Digby he was going to nominate him for a national junior doctor's award. Although he'd tucked the photo of his own son and daughter-in-law in his desk drawer, Hanssen seemed to be almost practising his paternal skills on Digby. All of this, naturally, conveyed by some of Guy Henry's trademark subtle acting. He hardly moves – it's like he has to just think an emotion and it'll somehow appear on his face without his face seeming to change its expression very much at all. And, I have to say, Rob Ostlere has a similar quality. Although Digby is all twitches and mannerisms compared to the very still and serene Hanssen, his great skill is conveying the person beneath the social awkwardness.

Meanwhile, on AAU Mary-Claire finally found out what Dr Posh really thinks of her when she overheard him in the operating theatre. She's "not the kind of girl you take home to your mother," apparently. I can only imagine what kind of ghastly nightmare of a mother Dr Posh has, and Mary-Claire is better off out of it. On the other hand, is Dr Honey the kind of girl you'd take home to mama, what with the dodgy website background, the child and the glottal stops?

There was a new face on AAU in the form of anaesthetist Edward Campbell. Now, who else do we know in the hospital with that surname? I've taken against Mr Campbell already, because he was very rude to Sacha, the Nicest Man In The Universe. In fact, he seems a bit of a dick generally. I can't wait to see what Serena makes of him.

Sometimes it's better not to know

(Series 15, ep. 43 'Digby Dog' by Martha Hillier 6.8.13)

You have to feel sorry for Prof Elliot Hope. He's known more human suffering than most men – the loss of his beloved Gina, living in his car for a while because he had to sell his house, being romantically pursued by Lady Byrne, almost being shipped off to The Mythical St James' during the Darwin-Goes-Plastic debacle.

Things have been looking up for him recently though, with the arrival in his life of Psych Sharon. This week we discover they're already at the arriving at work together, cheek pecking in public, dog walking phase. So sweet! Elliot even trusts Sharon with his beloved Samson!

And then she went and ran him over. Samson, not Elliot. It was only a little nudge, but enough to break his leg. I loved how Elliot's first reaction was to send for Jac Naylor – Elliot and Jac have operated on Samson before, so she knows her way around a dog. But they called a vet, and Elliot was given the bad news that Samson had bone cancer and the kindest thing was to put him to sleep. Sniff! As if poor Elliot hasn't had enough euthanasia in his life. And he doesn't know that it was Sharon who caused the accident.

Dr Sharon was very much in demand, with two whole patients and a dog to worry about. Just as well Oliver Valentine has left – she'd never have been able to fit him in as well. On Keller she was consulted about the memory loss patient from last week. Digby felt he was just stringing them along in order to lure the lovely Chantelle away. When they found out the true identity of Memory Man, Sharon's advice was Don't Tell Him Yet. So Digby told him. Well, it was clinically urgent to stop him flirting with Chantelle. It ended up with Memory Man running through the ward in his pants and getting in what's technically known as a "right state" and Hanssen having very stern words with his new mentee. I do love it when Hanssen has stern words.

Digby was entirely in the wrong and screwed up massively, but even worse for him was Chantelle telling him that their kiss didn't mean anything and she doesn't have a romantic thought in her head for him (and she does have thoughts in her head, you know – she gets really cross when people think it's just air).

On AAU, the new anaesthetist kept being referred to as "Edward…" because apparently nobody could remember his surname. Odd, that, when as a memory aid they could have remembered that it was awfully similar, indeed exactly the same, as that of Queen of the Hospital Serena Campbell. This was on account of them being previously married and that. Serena was on fine form, getting all shouty and irate at her ex (it's fair to say he rattles her – she ain't over him yet, I reckon) and sarcastic with her staff, while being kind and lovely to a frightened patient in theatre.

Pregnancy watch – Jac is apparently taking spinning classes in an effort to keep the weight gain under control, though I'm sure I heard Jonny Mac use the word "chubby" within her hearing (and she didn't destroy him with a Death Stare – how she's mellowed). In the bar for the wake for Elliot's dog (Sharon's idea) Jac was having to resist the peanuts.

Trouble for Chracha, Monny and Sedward

(Series 15, ep. 44 'Old Wounds' by Patrick Homes 13.8.13)

Sacha and Mo and Jonny were talking about these conjoined couple names that irritate me so much I generally refuse to use them. You know the ones – Brangelina etc. But it was quite funny when Mo mentioned ones that are commonly used by Holby fans – "Janny" for Jac and Jonny for example. It was like Mo had been reading the Digital Spy forums or Holby fan tweets, which would be weird as she's fictional (I know, it's a shock).

Anyway, one of the more apt names she came up with was for Chrissie and Sacha. I suppose it should technically be written "Chracha," but it's pronounced "Crasha," and it really fits their relationship, which has been a bit of a car crash all along.

Over Chrissie's long Holby career she's mutated from being the good time who was had by all, to a rather bitter, smug, superior woman who thought she was worth far more than being married to the Nicest Man in the World. It always seemed to be just a matter of time before she swanned off with a better-looking, more suave example of humanity (yes, you, Michael Spence), but the actual demise of her relationship with Sacha has been much more subtle. Driven away by Sacha's lack of trust in her and failing to properly talk to her about Daniel being a bone marrow donor for Rachel, Chrissie did turn to Michael Spence, but only as a friend. Even though Sacha believes that it was more than that (because he's never believed he was good enough for Chrissie), what has torn them apart has been the loss of trust and emotional intimacy (if it ever really existed). When Chrissie had her breast cancer scare, it wasn't Sacha she turned to and when she found another lump it was Michael Spence she went to again.

I do have sympathy for Chrissie. When Sacha said they should separate and then asked how her friend was doing (the "friend" being a cover for Chrissie's own medical tests), she said, "Frightened." And she really looked frightened and alone and vulnerable, knowing that she most likely does have cancer, and it was sad because Sacha would have been the most loyal, dependable, comforting friend she could have had.

Talking of best friends, on Darwin, Mo and Jonny were still dealing with the aftermath of the Poppy/Hattie heart transplant controversy. Hattie was trying her level best not to get better, because she felt guilty for surviving when her brother didn't. That was sorted out easily enough by Psych Sharon. What was harder to sort out was Poppy's mother Nicole, who was still haunted by the idea that maybe Mo had been telling a fib when she said it was too late to stop the transplant. Lizzie Hopley was fantastic as Nicole. She reminded me of Olivia Colman in series 1 of *Broadchurch* – so emotionally raw that she seemed drenched in tears. Mo and Nicole had a heart-to-heart (that wasn't meant as a pun btw) in the Linden Cullen Memorial Shrubbery, which was so full of non-speaking extras it was like Kings Cross on a bank holiday. I'm not going to get into the ethical issues of what Mo did (Jonny Mac covered that ground quite well), but there was no doubt her heart was in the right place (gah! another unintentional pun!) and I did feel sorry for her. "At this rate you'll take my place as the most hated doctor on the ward by… tea time," Jac told her, and it looked like it might be true. The problem is that Jac can cope with being hated and enjoys playing up to it, while Mo's toughness is more of a thin layer. It got sorted out eventually via Nicole meeting Hattie and then having a cry with Mo at the Window of Regret.

On Keller, Serena was being irritated by the continuing presence of her estranged husband, Edward. He may be an anaesthetist, but he's certainly woken up Serena's character, as she's most fun when she's annoyed and she's now constantly annoyed. This week he was writing a speech for a posh medical "do," which meant he was in her office and in her face for much of the episode. Serena had to find a plus one to take to the same dinner, so she plumped for Ric Griffin, with whom she's always had a flirt/hate relationship. Ric has just come back from America, where he's been modernising his thinking and has embraced a concept called Primary Defence. I've no idea what this involves, but if it's as roaring a success as his Zero Tolerance policy was, Serena is going to have her hands full. Particularly as Edward is a Primary Defence fan as well.

Pub quizzes. Not always a laugh

(Series 15, ep. 45 'All At Sea' by Laura Poliakoff 20.8.13)

As we approached our favourite hospital for yet another fun-filled episode, the first thing we saw was the Linden Cullen Memorial Shrubbery absolutely over-run with undesirable types (no, I don't mean Sahira Shah. She's not back). They really need to get to grips with that garden, otherwise no one is ever going to want a fairytale wedding there ever again.

Apparently the reason for so many bodies hanging around was that there'd been some sort of incident at the gig of ageing punk rocker and one-time support artiste to the Buzzcocks, Rex. It fell to Sacha to look after Rex, who had an abdominal aortic aneurysm, diseased kidneys and a fractured relationship with his marine biologist son to sort out. Rex also claimed to be able to feel the heat coming off Michael Spence's loins, which is frankly a skill I'd pay good money to have. It did nothing for Sacha, though, whose wife was supposedly the reason Michael's loins were in such a state of warmth.

Michael was actually just being a friend in need to Chrissie, who does have cancer and has to have surgery. She seemed to be partly confiding in Michael because of his winning bedside manner, but partly because he's proved to be good at getting procedures fast-tracked for her. To Sacha, though, it seemed like the inevitable had happened. His daughter Rachel said to him, "I always thought that if you and Chrissie broke up it would be because…" and Sacha finished the sentence for her: "She wanted an upgrade?" That's how Sacha sees their relationship and has always seen it. Sadly, that's also how Chrissie has seen it, too.

Sacha had organised a pub quiz to raise money for the Paediatric Oncology ward that had helped Rachel so much (when she wasn't in AAU so he could keep an eye on her), and when Michael and Chrissie sat having a heart-to-heart while Sacha was asking the questions, Sacha snapped and ended up punching Michael Spence (who admittedly didn't handle the situation with anything approaching tact) on the nose, ignoring my cries of "Not the face!" Luckily Jac was there to hold Sacha back before he did any further damage (or got damaged back). It made a change from being sarcastic about trivia. And Chrissie told him exactly what she and Michael had been talking about, so now everyone knows, including Rachel. Naturally Sacha is devastated, but he has Mo and Jac on his side, so I feel he'll be ok in the long run.

Prof Elliot Hope, meanwhile, was planning to take Psych Sharon for a weekend in Wales with a hot tub and a pool table, but she hit him with the news that she's off to do a PhD in Minneapolis (that's where she's studying, not what she's studying, which is actually mentally disordered offenders – you'd think she'd find enough of those hanging around AAU on an average Tuesday). So Elliot thought about cancelling Wales – ignoring Jonny Mac's kind offer of taking him instead – but then decided they should have fun while they lasted.

Elsewhere, I am very much enjoying how much Serena has been ruffled by the arrival of her ex, Edward. He's a smooth-talking sort and you can see what must have attracted them to each other in the first place. She's not entirely immune to his charms now, if her muttered quips about his "child bride" are anything to go by. Her mum Adrienne ended up in the hospital again this week, which gave another perspective on the situation ("Don't let him worm his way back in" was her advice) and gave Serena another chance to get all cross and guilty/shouty when it seemed that Adrienne wasn't coping well at home. The apple hasn't fallen far from the tree as far as feisty/independent genes are concerned, and Adrienne didn't want either of Serena's proposed solutions of a 24 hour live-in carer or a move to the box room chez Campbell. She prefers a retirement home, among people who are less guilty/shouty.

And Digby made an exciting diagnosis. "I'm one of the only doctors to have diagnosed a case of puffer fish poisoning!" he said. I diagnosed it two minutes before he did, in fact (I mentioned puffer fish poisoning in a book I wrote), but so far I haven't had any offers of mentoring from Hanssen.

I need you. No I don't

(Series 15, ep. 46 'Good Day For Bad News' by Johanne McAndrew & Elliot Hope 27.8.13)

If we hold this episode up against my patented PLA Relationship-o-meter™ we find Serena/Edward and Jac/Jonny going up, while Elliot/Sharon and Chrissie/Sacha (especially Chrissie/Sacha) plummet.

In a way, it makes me feel a bit cross that I was so happy about the fairytale Christmas episode where Chrissie failed to get on the ImagineAir flight to Sydney and Sacha hurtled all the way to Stansted on the back of Jac's motorbike, and it was snowing and everything was romantic and twinkly. Because ever since then, Chrissie and Sacha have not made each other happy. Apart from when he got stabbed and Chrissie fed him quiche in a desperate attempt to keep him alive, Sacha has been nothing but a disappointment to Chrissie and she's wasted no opportunity to agree with anybody who offered the opinion that she could do far better than him. And despite the thrill of knowing he's married to a woman so beautiful that it has to be remarked upon by everyone who meets her, Sacha has had only insecurity and a lack of proper emotional connection throughout the relationship.

This week Chrissie discovered that her cancer is not as bad as she was fearing, and the outlook is reasonably good. I can understand her not wanting to throw a party and scream "Hurrah!" from the rooftops, because obviously she's still terrified about her future and about Daniel etc. But where my patience runs a bit thin is the way she treats Sacha. Come home, she says. I need somebody there. But on the other hand – don't think things will be the same as before (i.e. it's not going to be the same as the first week we were married, before I realised I could have done a lot better and you started going to Fit Club with Mo because she was 100% more fun than me). On second thoughts – don't come home at all. "I can't do complicated," she sighed. Darling, you can't do anything else.

Meanwhile, up on Darwin, Jonny Mac was getting all assertive with Jac. "The whole biker chick look – you really think that's going to work for you when you're an egg on legs?" he said, risking a smack in the mouth. But he's decided that he's got to have some say in what happens to Jaccy Maccy Jr, so he told her the motorbike must be mothballed while she's pregnant. And, do you know what? She didn't kill him. She actually smiled. This is perfectly consistent with Jac's character. She's always liked people who stand up to her (Joseph, Oliver Valentine, even Tara and Sahira occasionally). I love how Rosie Marcel and the scriptwriters are handling Jac's pregnancy. She's a little bit warmer and smilier – but not too much. There was a lovely exchange with Psych Sharon, who'd been speaking to a patient. "He's egotistical, narcissistic, hedonistic, with no moral compass," said Sharon. "You make it sound like those are bad characteristics," said Jac.

This patient was a prisoner whose only friend seemed to be the prison warder who was chained to him. The chain proved to be a problem when the patient needed shocking and the key wasn't available, but there's always a silver lining and in this case getting a wee electric shock exposed the fact that the guard had a heart condition himself.

This relationship between guard and patient was mainly there to clarify a decision that Elliot had to make. Should he throw caution to the wind and go with Psych Sharon to the USA? "But what about the future of the Herzig?" I hear you ask, as indeed someone did ask during the episode. Jac was more than willing to step up and replace the Professor, but in the end he decided that work was dearer to his heart than Psych Sharon, and she went of to America on her own, after first confessing that she'd run Samson over a tiny bit. Well, she wouldn't be Psych Sharon if she didn't get some "closure."

Where one relationship door closes, another opens. It turns out that Edward Campbell's relationship with his child bride "Milly Molly Mandy" ("It's Mindy, actually") is over. But so was his short stay at the hospital. Except – a trial of the new pet project of Primary Defence (which seems to involve doing a little operation, leaving the patient with a gaping wound then going back to do a bigger operation later) was a great success, so Edward now finds himself with a six week contract to help Ric take the plan forward. Serena pretended to be displeased, but she loves him really. And I must say, after my initial disappointment that he wasn't being played by Aidan Gillen but the similarly named Aden Gillett, I'm pleased too.

The one with the unexploded device

(Series 15, ep. 47 'Point of Impact' by Lucia Haynes 3.9.13)

In light of the title of this post, I think we'd better put on our blast-proof clothing and go straight to AAU, where a patient was brought in with Something embedded in his chest. Dr Posh was assigned to talk to the patient's brother to try to get a clue about what it could be.

Prior to this, Dr Posh had annoyed Ric Griffin by being unexcited at the prospect of watching him perform an appendectomy. Posh was disappointed to learn that the procedure was going to be a ground-breaking, first-for-Holby, laser type of thing, but it was too late – Ric gave the gig to Dr Honey instead.

Posh discovered that the embedded Something was an unexploded rocket of some kind, and the army were duly called. Soon AAU was resembling outtakes from *The Hurt Locker*, with Dr Honey and Edward Campbell getting kitted out in helmets and body armour to go in and change the blood bags and keep the patient monitored. I loved how Serena looked just a tiny tad worried that her ex was in peril.

They decided the device couldn't be moved and they couldn't do anything else for the patient, who would therefore die. Dr Posh took it upon himself to take the brother in to say goodbye, and while they were there (without body armour) the machines started beeping etc and Posh ended up with his hand embedded in the patient's chest with everyone getting Very Cross Indeed because they now had no option but to operate and remove the device, otherwise Posh could explode at any second.

So poor old Ric had to come in and sort everything out. That man's hand doesn't shake even under the most intense pressure – if he gets bored with medicine he could always fall back on a career in bomb disposal. Posh was shaking like a leaf once his hand was free of the gloop – he actually did look like he was in shock (good acting, Mr Knight).

Ric was understandably a bit aggrieved that he'd had to risk life and limb thanks to his junior colleague, but Edward Campbell told him to cut the young 'un some slack because they need mavericks like Harry. "We were Harry once," he said, though I should think by the time Ric was Harry's age he'd already been married at least twice. You can't just go around disobeying your superiors and the army, though. "Serena wants my bits," said Posh, "Probably washed down with a fine Shiraz." Snork.

On Darwin, Prof Hope was in a very bad mood indeed. Jonny thought it was because of Psych Sharon going back to the US. "The dog's more of a loss than Sharon," Jac said accurately. Oh, if only there was a way that two adorable puppies could be brought onto the ward, with one of them suddenly requiring a loving home. It would be even cuter if they were named after members of Take That. Actually it *was* very cute, and Elliot looked very happy with little Gary, so well done Jonny and Jac.

Pregnancy watch: Jonny has started buying little baby garments (squeeee!), but Jac says she'll talk about baby stuff "when hell freezes over." Hell may be cooling faster than she'd like if the spoilers are to be believed (my advice: don't read the spoilers).

Digby let pressure get the better of him when he went down a diagnostic cul-de-sac and ended up with a very ill patient indeed. Then he had a panic attack. He spoke his own brains when he told his patient, "If your job makes you this ill, is it worth it?" and decided to tell Hanssen that all the stress was a bit much. Before he could say anything, Hanssen (wearing a shirt that was so white it was dazzling to the human eye) told him that he was the official, approved and only candidate for Doctor of the Year.

His approval rating with Chantelle is somewhat lower than it is with Hanssen, as he failed to join her in a mediation meeting with Cameron, who mugged them.

This stuff isn't meant to happen

(*Series 15, ep. 48 'The Kick Inside' by Joe Ainsworth 10.9.13*)

Jac Naylor was never going to be a stereotypical mother. Maternity leave? "You think some midget is going to halt my inexorable rise?" Nursery essentials? They're for "the slack-jawed, yummy-mummy, coffee morning crowd." And don't even think about referring to her as "preggers."

This is the thing with Jac, though – the things that are the most important to her are the things she gets most spiky and defensive about. And there's no doubt at all (even despite the "some midget" quips) that the baby she's carrying is the most important thing that's ever happened to her.

Because Jac is such a wonderful character and Rosie Marcel is such a wonderful actress, the scriptwriters don't ever give her an easy time. It was too much to hope that she'd have a normal pregnancy, give birth normally and go back to sarcastic normality. So it wasn't a total shock that her 20 week scan revealed that the baby had a congenital problem that means it only has a 50/50 chance of survival, but it was very, very sad.

The saddest scene was when Jac and Jonny attended a case conference about the baby and Jac spotted something on the scan: "It's a girl." Jonny took hold of her hand, and for a few seconds she let him. Just for a few seconds, though, because you get the sense that only the famous Naylor iron will is holding her together. As it was, she permitted herself a little cry in the ladies,' which is practically unheard of. This was intercut with a scene where Jonny had gone to talk to Mr Thompson the Obs & Gynae guy (still hankering after Mo, bless him), about the baby's chances of survival. "Let's hope she's as tough as her mum," he said, as we watched a tear roll down her mum's cheek.

Jonny wants Jac to do what's best for her, in his new man sort of way, but what she wants to do at the moment is blame him. "You gave me a 50/50 chance once of anything coming out of my womb being the Antichrist," she said. "It's one of the worst three things anyone's ever said to me." I wonder what the other two were?

The atmosphere on Keller was somewhat lighter, largely thanks to the arrival of new doctor Zosia (it's pronounced "Zosher") March, played by Camilla Arfwedson. When a Holby actress describes her character as "sexually voracious" and her very first scene includes Michael Spence, you think you can see which way the wind is going to blow. But no. The early object of her sexual voraciousness was none other than Arthur "I can't believe he's not a virgin" Digby. Was she attracted to him because they share an interest in antique pens? Possibly.

Zosia has a stroppy and frankly scary bedside manner (not a million miles away from Dr Lily Chao on *Casualty*), but she's beautiful and she's also brilliant at maths. If she ever gets bored with medicine, she should consider a job putting the letters and numbers out on Countdown.

I did enjoy Digby's little yelp of fear when Zosia pounced on him, but the patient walking into the lab and finding them in a state of disarray behind a desk was a bit silly. Still, silly was probably what we needed at that point.

On AAU, Edward Campbell decided to take Mary-Claire under his wing. It was marvellous to see MC having her own storyline in an episode. After some good work in saving a patient, she asked

Ric if she could be involved in his Primary Defence team (still not sure what that is). After being initially unsure about her commitment, he agreed when she did more good work with the same patient, and she joined the team in theatre.

I replayed what happened at the end of the surgery twice, and I'm still not entirely sure what happened – it was edited rather strangely – but I think Edward picked up the wrong drug from a tray, almost killing his patient in the process, and then let Mary-Claire think it had been her fault. This made Mary-Claire tell Ric that she didn't think she was up to the job. "Too much like hard work, is it?" Ric said. But he told her she's on the Primary Defence team (how exciting! Does she get to wear a cape?) and she will not fail. I hope she doesn't fail, because I like her stroppiness and her eyebrows. If she does fail, it will possibly have something to do with Edward Campbell (I just typed "Edward Cullen," but he's not in Holby). There's a bit of a frisson between them.

Chances of survival

(Series 15, ep. 49 'Contra Mundum' by Patrick Wilde 17.9.13)

Second only to the "last-minute-dash-to-the-airport-to-stop-loved-one-leaving" scenario, the "father's-last-minute-dash-to-the-abortion-clinic" has to be one of the most over-used scenarios in drama. We had it in Holby City this week, but because it was Jac at the clinic and Jonny doing the dashing, I actually cared about it.

I cared because I really want Jac to have the baby. It feels like this is a huge moment in her life, where she could open up and find out how it feels to love someone unconditionally and have them love her back. The alternative is for her to become ever more closed-off. You never know with Jac, though. She could have gone through with a termination, basing everything on cold logic and statistics.

Jonny Mac is the total opposite of her in many ways – he's all emotion. In fact he almost explodes with emotion sometimes, such as when he was running around the clinic yelling at Jac's voicemail on his phone (why did no one come out and ask him to shush?). He's also an enlightened, sensitive man who wouldn't dream of telling a woman what she could and couldn't do with her own body, and this has held him back from telling Jac how he really feels.

So it was lucky for him that Jac decided she's going to keep the baby anyway. Maybe there was a tiny tad of cussedness about it, as the doctor in the clinic turned out to be someone Jac had known (and disliked) a long time ago. "We called you Jac Frost at medical school," she said. "You had a nickname, too," said Jac, and when asked what it was, she said, "I don't use language like that any more." Advantage Ms Naylor!

If only Jac would let Jonny see how she really feels. We saw it right at the end, when she walked away from the hospital listening to Jonny's messages on her phone. "If our little girl inherits just one tiny gram of her mother's fight and spirit and downright bloody mindedness, I know she'll have the greatest chance in life, because you're her mum." And Jac allowed herself a little smile.

Chrissie didn't have much to smile about (does she ever?), because it was her first session of cancer treatment. What you really want under these circumstances is for a beloved Scouse entertainer to befriend you and cheer you up, and luckily for Chrissie, Paul O'Grady happened to be in the coffee bar (now weirdly branded 'Pulses' – nice play on medical words and healthy eating there, but considering they seem to sell nothing but coffee and muffins, maybe not so apt). Their relationship didn't get off to a good start, as Tim correctly identified that Chrissie is rude, selfish and a bit up herself. When they met again in the cancer clinic, they bonded like nobody's business and pretty soon she was laughing merrily and ignoring Sacha. Business as usual, in other words.

On Keller, Malick was fuming over a gangrenous leg and getting all angry because he passed his consultant's exam ages ago, but he's still a registrar and has to wait for Michael Spence before he can get stuck into a spot of surgery. Hanssen asked him which of his colleagues he'd like to be sacked so there would be a vacancy. Jac would have given him an answer without hesitating, but Malick didn't so he was sent off to mentor Zosia March for the day.

She didn't attempt to pounce on him, despite hearing that he was "Holby's answer to Colin Farrell" (say what??). I think Zosia is a natural predator, in that she likes to pick off the vulnerable stragglers rather than the head of the pack. Plus, she's probably heard that pouncing on Malick would be futile unless she had stubble and/or a quiff (that's not a euphemism – it's a hairstyle).

She's good at diagnosing stuff, though – these brilliant-at-books, bad-at-bedside-manner types so often are – and she spotted that the patient they were dealing with probably had bulimia. Malick ignored her, but then took the credit later on in Hanssen's office. Hanssen, however, was not fooled for a minute. That consultant's job doesn't look like it'll be happening any time soon.

Parental guidance

(Series 15, ep. 50 'Fredrik' by Julia Gilbert 24.9.13)

Parenthood was at the front and centre of proceedings in all three departments this week, with Chrissie wondering how My Son Daniel would fare without her should the worst happen, Jac and Jonny going to an antenatal class and Hanssen pondering whether to meet the son he's never seen. To add to the overall theme, Jac got a baby to hold and Hanssen got a young boy to look after. Chrissie got Paul O'Grady.

To Keller first, and Malick was out to prove himself to be consultant material. Hanssen said Malick would work with him for the day. It gave Hanssen the excuse to ask Malick what it was like suddenly finding himself the parent of a grown up son and to repeatedly lecture him about remaining rational at all times when dealing with patients.

Fredrik (Hanssen Junior) was on his mind, though, and it did make him overreact when it came to the welfare of young Josh, who had cystic fibrosis and needed surgery to sort out his spleen. Josh also had an absentee parent, a mother who'd left him because she was mentally ill, but who turned up to upset the apple-cart by taking him out of the hospital so he could collapse in the car park. He also collapsed in the stair-well earlier. If only he'd have collapsed in the toilets as well he'd have scored a hat trick.

The car park collapse caused Hanssen to actually run, which was a magnificent sight, but not as magnificent as him getting all shouty with the boy's mother. Unfortunately he blew it slightly when he was about to operate. With the mother's words of "treat him with the same care you would your own son" ringing in his ears, he went a bit wobbly and had to hand over scalpel duties to Malick.

Malick did well, though, in the sense that the boy didn't die. Hanssen not only handed him the scalpel, he also left him completely to it, which was odd given that last week Malick wasn't allowed to do urgent surgery until there was a consultant present.

Even stranger, at the end of the episode Hanssen was so pleased with Malick's work and attitude that he took him for a little walk in the Linden Cullen Memorial Shrubbery and handed him a consultancy post. Only last week he was asking which of Malick's colleagues he ought to sack to create a vacancy, and this week he's already moving his knickknacks into the spare desk in Michael Spence's office. But, such are the fluid staffing configurations of Holby City.

Up the stairs to Darwin we go now, where Jonny was left holding somebody's baby and singing it a lovely lullaby of 'Won't You Take Me to Funky Town.' "Can you find somewhere to put that? There's a cardboard box in my office," Jac told him. Oh, typical Jac, thinking you can file a baby away like paperwork! But what a lovely look on her face when she was discovered later in her office, with the baby happily and comfortably asleep in the aforementioned cardboard box. She might just be parent material after all.

Jac felt the baby kick, which gave Jonny the opportunity to do the standard, hands-on-belly, face-full-of-wonder thing while Jac smiled happily at him – for about a nanosecond, before she told him to get off.

To further prove that they're absolutely normal parents-to-be, Jac and Jonny went to an antenatal class. Jac rather enjoyed it, what with being able to dispense unwanted advice about overeating for two, the horrors of an episiotomy (OMG, I just googled that for spelling – you do not want to see what pictures come up), the risks of multiple births… the other mothers were left pale and trembling. They were also left bitching about what a cow she was – which Jonny overheard, and he defended her absolutely brilliantly. Even though she'd given the impression that he was a gay sperm donor.

Paul O'Grady was back, to tell Chrissie to put her best foot forward and show everyone "what a little ray of sunshine you are." Well, he hasn't known her long.

So she took his advice and tried to get on with business as usual (being brisk with the patients and horrible to Sacha) despite going "Nnngh!!" every five minutes just like Ric did when he had cancer andMo did when she was in labour (though Mo was "Oof!" rather than "Nnngh!"). They'll never learn to take it easy, these medical types.

It was My Son Daniel's first day at nursery and Sacha forgot to give him his toy monkey, which the excuse for Chrissie to get all cross with him. But she wasn't just being horrible for the sake of it this time. As she confided to Paul O'Grady later, it was because she was worried about dying and leaving Daniel, and whether Sacha would be able to cope as well as she does. I know that sounds like typical Chrissie – nobody, least of all Sacha, will ever measure up to her high standards – but on this occasion I knew what she meant.

Paul O'Grady implied that his chemo had worked, which cheered Chrissie up a lot, but we saw his face and I didn't believe him for a second. He's back next week, but will it be as a patient this time? Or will he get to live his dream of standing naked under a waterfall in Venezuela with Chrissie (best not to dwell on that image)?

Look out! Look out! Look out!

(Series 15, ep. 51 'The Cost of Loving' by Kim Revill 1.10.13)

Talk about emotional roller-coaster! I don't mean Serena's birthday, though I dare say it'll be one that she won't forget – and she doesn't even know (or care) about beloved Tim dying in AAU or Mo and Sacha kissing in the Linden Cullen Memorial Shrubbery. She doesn't even know yet about the car crash right at the end, but obviously she's going to, as half her colleagues were involved and there'll quite probably be some life-saving surgery to get stuck into next week.

Phew. Let's rewind a bit. It was the day of the Young Doctor of the Year award ceremony, and Digby was practising his speech – or his "rambling love letter to the Swede," as Zosia put it. And this would be a good place to mention that I really, really like Zosia. I think there's going to turn out to be a lot to her, and given time she could be one of the great Holby characters.

I also really love Digby and find him laugh-aloud funny. My favourite line was when his patient had just informed him that she was planning to call her unborn baby Destiny. Digby was explaining why she was in pain. "The appendix is being pushed up by the... by Destiny," he said.

He also has a beautiful smile, which he deploys less frequently, and therefore to even greater effect, than Chantelle. She didn't have a lot to smile about in this episode. Having blundered by suggesting to Destiny's mother that antibiotics were a useful option to surgery, she found herself on the receiving end of Hanssen's anger and teetering on the edge of a disciplinary. She got into even hotter water when she took a message from Maja that Hanssen was now a grandfather. Hanssen did not want one of Holby's chattier nurses communicating the happy news to all her mates and half the patients. He'd have had no chance with Mary-Claire, who'd have had it up on a web page before you could say "It's a boy!" (Which it was).

Digby made a half-hearted attempt to intervene, but wasn't much use. So to cheer Chantelle up, he asked Zosia for her ticket to the awards dinner so Chantelle could go.

Digby drove Chantelle, and Hanssen drove Malick (could they not have all fitted in one car, or did I miss something?), and off they went. Digby decided it was time to tell Chantelle how he felt, but while doing so he took his eyes off the road, and Malick, on the phone to Chantelle from the car behind, could only yell uselessly as Digby's car aimed for the back of a truck. And – blackness. Cue end titles.

Oh. My. Lord. Since we already know that three of those four characters are leaving soon, I'm going to be on pins till next week.

That would have been enough drama for most episodes, but down in AAU Paul O'Grady turned up, as a patient this time. He wasn't in Venezuela after all (yes, we had guessed) and had only pretended he was to keep Chrissie's spirits up.

Tim has been a sympathetic character mainly because Paul O'Grady is so popular and always comes across as being a lovely man. His deathbed scene was genuinely moving and proved once again that, whatever fans think of Chrissie as a character (not a lot, thanks to her terrible treatment of the glorious Sacha), Tina Hobley is a wonderful actress.

What was Sacha doing while all this was going on? Well, he was mainly trying to do his best for Chrissie as usual, and getting knocked back, as usual. So he went for a little stroll in the LCMS with Mo. Sacha and Mo's friendship has been built up well over the months, since their "Holby Fit Club" meetings actually took place over pasta at Rodolfo's. So it was no surprise when a comforting hug turned into a proper kiss. They both felt awful about it afterwards, but they really shouldn't. They'd be the most adorable couple, and the only thing that stops me from wanting them to get together is knowing how horribly the Holby scriptwriters treat anyone who's in love (see poor Digby this week). They wouldn't just let Mo and Sacha be happy and get married and have gorgeous babies and go to work cheerfully every morning with a spring in their step.

Look at the hoops Jac and Jonny have had to jump through – though, admittedly, being in a relationship with Jac was never going to be easy. This week, Jonny had taken himself to a support group in That London for parents with children with the same condition as Jaccy Maccy Junior. Jac wasn't happy about that at all, but these days Jac does see Jonny's point of view a little more than she used to. Jonny has now taken the bold step of suggesting they move in together, so they can support the baby better. I can't imagine that will be easy, for either of them.

When Henrik stopped being Mr Hanssen

(Series 15, ep. 52 'Like a Prayer' by Nick Fisher 8.10.13)

Henrik Hanssen has been one of the greatest ever Holby characters. A mystery wrapped in an enigma encased by a formal suit, he was always intriguing and fascinating. The character was beautifully written, especially in the early days when odd little clues about his background were leaked out bit by bit, but it was Guy Henry's stunning acting skills that really brought him to life. Having to work with the constraint that Hanssen was a character who didn't really show emotion, his inner feelings had to be revealed by the most subtle acting, and by clever, telling details like the way he ate his sushi and arranged his pencils.

The exit episode for such a special character needed to be very good indeed, and last night's episode was wonderful (beautiful writing by Nick Fisher). There had to be quite a lot of suspension of disbelief – that Digby was allowed to operate on the woman he loves even though he'd been a puking, shivering mess not long before; that no neurosurgeon was available at all (I'm sure in an emergency one could have been summoned from The Mythical St James' or the Hadlington or somewhere if there really wasn't one at Holby); that Ric Griffin took no part in the surgery to re-attach Malick's hand even though he's always been the go-to guy when veins needed sorting out; and so on. But, really, I wouldn't have wanted to sacrifice any of the drama just to make things more realistic. Having Digby and Hanssen outside the operating theatre biting their nails while a Guest Artiste Surgeon did all the vital stuff wouldn't have been the same as having them perform heroic deeds themselves.

The most touching scenes were the ones between Hanssen and Chantelle, whose sweetness and vulnerability completely cracked his cool facade. He went from telling Serena that Malick "doesn't need warmth, Miss Campbell, he needs a cold clinical surgeon with nothing in his head but the job in hand – no pun intended" to promising Chantelle that he would save her and she would live to have babies of her own. As ever, Guy Henry conveyed that Hanssen was full to the brim with emotions just by the look in his eyes and a tremor in his voice.

Later, when Chantelle was recovering, they talked about how he was nasty to her last week. Chantelle suggested that he was actually quite nice when he stopped being Mr Hanssen. He said he was ashamed of the father he'd been and the grandfather he might fail to be – and he said it in that tear-swallowing way that he occasionally does that carries more strength of feeling than if he broke down and sobbed. "You'll be great if you stop being Henrik Hanssen and just be Granddad," she said, and he gave her such a lovely smile. "It's high time I stopped being Mr Hanssen," he said. "Please don't ever stop being Nurse Lane."

And then he packed up his office, passed on the Chair of Power to Serena Campbell, and caught a plane to Stockholm, where he finally met his son and his new grandson. And the sight of him holding this "most beautiful baby" would have melted any heart.

I haven't mentioned Digby much in this, but it was a huge episode for him too, as he admitted to Hanssen, Chantelle and himself that he was in love with Chantelle and had been since the first time he'd met her (he did quite an accurate impression of the way she speaks as well). Once again he proved he's not really what you'd call a cool head in a crisis, but he's a gentle, sweet soul.

Jac and Jonny had the unenviable task of providing a secondary plot. It was a sign of the huge drama going on elsewhere that even the glorious Jac failed to completely capture my attention, because I just wanted to know what was going on with Malick and Chantelle. Jonny's old friend Bonnie Wallace turned up as an agency nurse, which riled Jac a bit. My favourite Jac line was, "Will you stop flapping like a baggy kilt?"

But it was Hanssen's episode. The end of a series and the end of an era.

SERIES 16

More than half the man he used to be
(Series 16, ep. 1 'If I Needed Someone' by David Bowker 15.10.13)

You can imagine that Antoine Malick wouldn't make a great patient even if it was only for something fairly trivial like an ingrown toenail. He'd be tetchy and stroppy and wouldn't do as he was told.

Now factor in that he's almost lost his hand and will only ever regain 85% of the movement in it at best, and you have to feel sorry for him, and maybe just as sorry for the people looking after him.

This comprised a crack team of new Queen of the Hospital Serena, Michael Spence, Digby and occasionally Ric Griffin. The episode opened with a strange dreamlike sequence in which the four of them were ranged at one side of a long table drenched in a heavenly light discussing the fact that Malick is only half the man he used to be.

Ric thought Malick needed counselling. "We have a very good counsellor," he said, though who that might be now that Psych Sharon has gone is anybody's guess.

Michael thought it might be therapeutic to show Malick photos of his severed hand, but I reckon that was mainly because the prosthetics team were very proud of that hand and wanted us to see it again.

On Holby the staff are always careful to make sure that there'll be someone in an adjacent bed who can shed light on your situation. Malick found himself next to Eva, who'd officially been slashed while protecting one of the pupils at her school from a random knife-wielding attacker. Eva couldn't let go of being a teacher any more than Malick could let go of being a surgeon, but after a rocky start they managed to support each other. "You've no idea what you can achieve if you put your mind to it," Malick told Eva, as well as himself.

In the short term, what he can achieve might be carrying on as a clinical skills tutor – if he accepts the counselling as Ric advised.

Someone else who might need counselling soon – ironically, as he's just lost Psych Sharon – is Elliot Hope. The latest thorn in his side is Zosia (pronounced "Saucer," according to Jac). Elliot was excited at the prospect of having her on his team. "Her clinical excellence is matched only by her questing intellect," he enthused. "There's bound to be something wrong with her," Jac predicted.

Well, obviously – but I really hoped it didn't mean she'd be pouncing on Elliot Hope like she pounced on Digby. He's a Professor and we must accord him some dignity. But she didn't. It turns out she isn't too interested in cardiothoracics at all and is just biding time till she can pursue her real interest of psychiatric medicine. "Biding her time" consists of trying to analyse patients' relatives and Prof Hope himself ("Elliot, are you a rejected misfit?"). This seems to be a new interest which she didn't exhibit while she was on Keller, but that must be her questing intellect.

She might have Elliot terrified, but she'll have to work extremely hard to frighten Jac. When she asked Jac about her urge to make babies, she got a Naylor Special Stare. "And what urge do you think I'm feeling right now?"

In the yo-yoing world that is Chrissie and Sacha's relationship, Chrissie has yanked the string back in and Sacha is, as we speak, moving his toothbrush and rom com DVDs back into the marital home. What has prompted this? Well, after Chrissie had a horrible day involving Tim's funeral in the morning (she was the only one who wore black) and radiotherapy in the afternoon, she was looking a bit fragile, bless her. Nice work, makeup department. So Sacha surprised her with a trip to stand naked under a waterfall in Venezuela. Always one to look on the bright side, Chrissie said it was because he thought she was going to die. Sacha reasonably pointed out that he wouldn't have spent all that money if he'd thought she was going to die and he promised she wouldn't. Not yet, anyway.

Their patient for the day was a man who was terrified of spiders. His wife had punished him for a suspected affair by putting a spider in his car. I wonder what Chrissie will put in Sacha's car if she ever finds out about him kissing Mo?

Arthur, you're not clinical waste – you're brilliant

(Series 16, ep. 2 'Friends Like You' by Helen Jenkins 22.10.13)

Arthur Digby is my kind of guy. The kind of guy who'll bring you breakfast in bed and then demonstrate the workings of your brain via the medium of a croissant. And he has the most beautiful smile. Still feeling guilty and worried about Chantelle, he installed her in Keller so he could keep an eye on her and so she could be among her friends and other ill people. She also came in handy by deploying her legendary people skills on a lady who was not being the most cooperative patient, because she wanted to put off her surgery till the man of her dreams arrived for a night in a posh hotel. The woman's niece and Digby thought this man was literally something from the old lady's dreams, but Chantelle had faith that he'd turn up because she's a romantic.

Later, when Digby suggested she move in with him, she accepted partly because she's scared to be by herself at the moment, but there was more to it than that. When the old lady was talking about her dream man, Chantelle was overcome by emotion for a minute and had to have a little cry. She wants true love and romance and security. Whether Digby is the person to provide it remains to be seen, but for now she's about to fill his no doubt unhomely home with cushions and fluffy items. He couldn't be happier, bless him.

While Digby was supplying Chantelle with croissants, Chrissie was informing Sacha that if he has a cake for breakfast he's not allowed a muffin at lunchtime. I'd have had the cake and the muffin for breakfast, just to show her who's boss, but in the Sacha/Chrissie relationship, she's boss and always has been. And Sacha, apparently, is "Mr Semi." This conjures up all sorts of images, so I have to quickly add that it means his kiss with Mo in the Linden Cullen Memorial Shrubbery was "semi-passionate." Mo was surrounded by men who admire her, as Mr T called her for a consult and when she diagnosed gallstones, Sacha was summoned. Unfortunately the men who admire Mo are either in a relationship (Sacha) or keep making clumsy jokes about her lifestyle choices (Mr T. And Sacha). Mo is getting just a little bit tired of this.

Down to the hall of doom known as AAU now, where Posh and Honey were competing over who got to help Ric Griffin with a laparoscopic nephrectomy. An old chum (I feel sure "chum" is the right word here) of Posh's turned up with his liver in a right old mess thanks to alcohol, and we got a glimpse into Posh's past. Lots of drinking and privilege, basically. Meanwhile, Honey's mum was ill and her son Finn was having a day off school, so Posh helpfully arranged for him to be brought to the hospital, because it always works out brilliantly whenever anyone's child is hanging around the wards. Posh was hoping to impress Honey, but he didn't impress her much when ecstasy tablets disappeared from Posh's friend's bag and everyone assumed Finn had taken them because he started throwing up.

Ric Griffin was even less impressed when he deduced that Finn actually had Norovirus and Honey's child had now brought a severely contagious disease into a ward full of already ill people. So Honey has been suspended and Posh is in the doghouse. Will his touching gesture of a pizza delivery complete with gift card redeem him? Who knows? Who cares?

The plumbing and the back to work bird

(Series 16, ep. 3 'Flesh is Weak' by Catherine Johnson 29.10.13)

Henrik Hanssen's parting words to Chantelle were, "Don't ever stop being Nurse Lane." But can she get over the car crash to continue being the sunny, joy-spreading nurse she once was?

She was back to work for her first shift. Serena told her she was on admin only, but that was never going to last for longer than it takes to shout "We need some help here!" Digby gave her a cuddly "Back to work bird" to bring her luck, which was adorable of him. It was all going reasonably well until Chantelle caught sight of Malick's arm while the dressing was being changed and the hideous sight made her throw up. After that she was in a bit of a flap.

She tried to compensate by spreading extra joy to her patients, including a woman whose pregnancy test had come back positive. Chantelle wasted no time in giving the happy news to the patient's boyfriend. Sadly it wasn't a pregnancy but a tumour, and the patient died in a very messy way in the operating theatre. I couldn't help thinking the scene in the Keller theatre was a bit frantic, with Mr T and Digby panicking a bit more than you usually see on Holby, where a spurting artery usually elicits nothing than a raised eyebrow and a call for some suction and 4-0 Vicryl.

In Darwin theatre, for example, Prof Hope was performing his usual miraculous deeds with a scalpel, but did it impress Dr Zosia March? No it did not. Surgery is "just plumbing" according to Dr March, who is more interested in the contents of people's minds than the contents of their chest cavities. This made Jonny Maconie Very Cross Indeed and he gave her a telling off which went right over her head. Zosia is Teflon-coated when it comes to other people's opinions of her.

She made the classic mistake of speaking out of turn and giving a patient an option that wasn't really an option. This time it was telling a young man with a badly damaged heart that the newly-developed Herzig 4 (yes! We're on to 4 already. Makes you feel old, doesn't it?) artificial heart would be a solution to his imminent death problem. Normally when a doctor or nurse proposes something that the more experienced doctors know isn't going to work, it's because they have the patient's best interest at heart and want to offer some hope. In Zosia's case, she seemed more interested in being able to psychoanalyse someone with an artificial heart and almost scaring him to death with a defibrillator first. She really is an odd person and she could probably do with a bit of psychotherapy herself. The way she pursues whatever interests her regardless of the consequences and seems oblivious to what people think of her – well, she is a tad sociopathic.

Elliot was so angry with her behaviour that he gave her to Jac. If anyone can sort her out, it's Jac. "F1, you might be entirely weird, but you're mine now," said Jac, sending young Saucer out to buy two jars of pickles. So nice to see that Jac is still on the pickles.

Elsewhere on Darwin, Mo had entered the world of internet dating. "They're always two inches shorter than they say they are," Jac told her, adding, "Not that I'd know." Zosia had some formula for internet dating success based on percentage points, and Mo had a date with Mr 73%. This was unfortunate, because after losing his patient on Keller, Mr T popped up to ask Mo out for a drink. He looked ever so disappointed to find her all dressed up with somewhere to go.

On AAU there was an annoying patient in a Cat Woman suit who kept distracting Dr Posh. Mary-Claire was cross about this, because she was hoping to take Posh to her sister's wedding in Ireland.

By the end of the episode, she'd phoned her sister to say that she would be going to the wedding on her own and her family had to stop feeling sorry for her because she's single. Hopefully this will allow Mary-Claire to have a storyline which doesn't involve her poaching other people's boyfriends or getting sulky about some man or other. Particularly when the man is as lame as Dr Posh.

Jac and Sacha friend-zoned

(Series 16, ep. 4 'Last Dance' by Simon Booker 5.11.13)

Jonny and Bonnie. It just can't happen. It rhymes, for a start, and it's impossible to make into one of those portmanteau names – though I have come across "BJ" on Twitter, which is almost certainly meant to be rude. Because the main reason Jonny and Bonnie can't happen is that it's making The Glorious Jac unhappy, and anything that makes Jac unhappy makes me unhappy.

Bonnie (she's nice, darn her, and pretty too) is no longer an agency nurse. She's a full-time, fully paid-up staff member, although obviously that means less within the fluid staffing configurations of Holby City than it would almost anywhere else. She is also "stepping out" with Jonny Mac, a fact which got our Jac so rattled she made a too-deep incision during surgery. Obviously she's Jac, so she saved the patient anyway and treated her to a most beautiful piece of post-operative Naylor sarcasm. When the (annoying new-agey) patient complained that Jac had done an open procedure instead of a laparoscopic one as promised, Jac replied, "This morning you were suffering pericardial effusion as a result of your own actions and now, as a result of mine, you can go back to shopping and having lunch."

Jac is aware of how she appears to other people, though. "I've just been called grouchy," she said to Mo. "On a good day, maybe," Mo replied.

But to get back to the person I may have to start calling This Bonnie Creature. The very worst betrayal, as far as Jac was concerned, was that Jonny told Bonnie about the baby's health condition – and Bonnie mentioned it to the patient as a possible reason for Jac's grouchiness, which was unprofessional and insensitive at the very least. Jac looked like she'd been slapped, and I rather hope it's Bonnie who gets slapped before too long.

On Keller, Chantelle was preoccupied with choosing paint colours for the kitchen at the place she's living at with Digby. It's not a love nest, though: "We're just sharing," Digby said. "I'll inform *Newsnight*," said Serena, who also does sarcasm beautifully.

Serena's mind was on her interview for the CEO job, but that didn't stop her having a very firm opinion about patient JJ Kirby, who also happened to be Malick's former mentor (he's had many students but only one Malick, apparently). He needed surgery that would have been life-changing in the digestive sense (let's leave it there, I've not long had breakfast), and Malick thought there was a better way to do it because you can't allow top surgeons to go round with life-changing conditions. Like 85% functioning hands. You can see that brain-speak coming a mile off, can't you?

Things took a critical turn while Serena was in her interview, which gave Malick the chance to use Digby as an avatar to do the surgery his way. This proved that Digby is an excellent surgeon, Malick is a great teacher – but also that Serena was going to be very, very angry indeed.

We don't know if she's got the job yet, but she occupies the seat of power fabulously. I thought Malick was extremely cocky with her and personally I'd have had him on a disciplinary for insubordination (hang on – is it too late to apply for the CEO job?), but Serena let him off while still giving him to understand she wasn't happy. "I do hope that's not a smirk on your face, Mr Malick." Indeed not – it's a non-smirking hospital.

We left Malick at the end practising one-handed suturing, failing to take Jake to a fireworks display and confusing Ella Fitzgerald and Billie Holiday.

What was Ella Fitzgerald doing in the hospital? She was providing a soundtrack for Sacha and Chrissie's last dance. Chrissie was given good news about her cancer, so Sacha went down on one knee and proposed a renewal of their vows. In the sumptuous surroundings of the Faith Room (or the Linden Cullen Temple of Anguish – LC has so left his mark on that hospital) they met to wait for the chaplain, but realised that they're never going to work as a married couple. "We're good together, but good just isn't enough," Sacha said. "I can't think of anyone on this earth I'd rather have as a friend than you," said Chrissie. The biggest bombshell was that Chrissie hates Rodolfo's. She always has, apparently, and only pretended to like Holby's premier budget Italian restaurant. I feel certain that Mo genuinely does like Rodolfo's and, in a nutshell, this is why I like Mo more than I like Chrissie.

I wondered whether Chrissie's decision to ditch her husband, a man so cuddly he's practically a human Slanket, was partly triggered by a little incident in the Linden Cullen Memorial Shrubbery. She was having a heart-to-heart with Michael Spence and just as he got up to leave he put his hand on her leg. I should imagine that one touch was thrilling enough to bring memories of Chrissie's glory days when her allure was in full force flooding back. You can see how Sacha might be a hindrance.

I can only love you like that

(Series 16, ep. 5 'Arthur's Theme' by Dana Fainaru 12.11.13)

If you'd asked me whether the theme from the film *Arthur* played by a massed band of amateur kazoo players (with a certain red-haired Irish nurse on vocals) could be emotional, I'd have probably said no. I'd have been wrong.

It was Digby's birthday. Chantelle's gift to him was a stress ball and a surprise party. I was going to say why do people on TV always insist on organising surprise parties for introverts who are going to hate it, but the answer is obviously that it's the only way to engineer big moments like the emotional kazoo playing. All the regular background cast members had kazoos, and frankly they've never looked happier, so it was worth it just to see their excited little faces.

It wasn't the easiest of birthdays even pre-party, given that the guest patient of the day was Cameron, who'd mugged Chantelle and Digby in the car park. Digby thought all of Chantelle's problems (she's now on beta-blockers for anxiety) could be traced back to that incident rather than the car crash, and, as these things are apt to do, it clouded his judgement when treating Cameron. As did telling Chantelle he loved her and seeing her less than exuberant reaction. Cameron died, which had Digby puking in the nearest bin, but Serena said it wasn't his fault.

Not the best background for a birthday party, but worse was to come for Digby. Outside Albie's (where they first met on New Year's Eve), Chantelle told him, "I do love you. Only not like that." Digby's poignant little reply was, "I can only love you like that." Awww, bless him. So Chantelle decided it was best for both of them if she moved on – to Ibiza, New York or wherever. He let her keep the stress ball, and she got on the bus and went home to pack. And poor Digby went back to the party.

Mo wasn't in a party mood, either. In fact, she was all partied out. She arrived for work in the passenger seat of a badly driven flashy car, having spent the night with Joey from the internet. Mr T's little face when he witnessed that – bless him. It was only a matter of time before Joey turned up in Darwin on a trolley. He had a dodgy heart, not helped by an over-reliance on cocaine. This was embarrassing for Mo, who had to reassure Elliot Hope that she has nothing to do with drugs herself, but worse was to come when she found out that Joey was awaiting the results of a HIV test. Nothing makes you think harder about your lifestyle choices than being potentially faced with a life-altering, work-affecting illness.

On AAU, Chrissie looked a bit put out after Sacha handed her the divorce papers to sign. Possibly he hadn't cried enough or spent enough time crawling on the floor moaning, "But Chrissie! You are the most wonderful woman in the world and without you I am nothing!" Indeed, he looked almost relaxed about the whole thing. There was a very real risk that Chrissie's ego would never recover from this setback, but cometh the hour, cometh the man in tight trousers with beautiful eyelashes. "If you were my wife, I'd never let you get away from me," murmured Michael Spence, sounding only a little bit stalkery. So she had no option but to snog him, which displays excellent judgement on her part. But please tell me he's not going to be running away with her to Venezuela!

After the year she's had

(Series 16, ep. 6 'Merry-Go-Round' by Patrick Homes 19.11.13)

"After the year I've had…" Chrissie kept complaining throughout this episode, and I think we were meant to sympathise with her and think, "Yes, Chrissie love, you have had a horrible year and you deserve to run off into the sunset with the most attractive American medic in the hospital."

But instead of thinking about poor Chrissie's breast cancer problems, and My Son Daniel's traumatic bone marrow donation and Sacha's deception re same, all I could think about was how horrible she's been to Sacha. It was left to the ever-wonderful Jac to sum up the car crash that has been Sacha and Chrissie: "You sleep with him – you break his heart. You have his child – you break his heart. You literally beg him to marry you and you break his heart. And now you've even found a way to divorce him, yet still give him a little bit of hope so you can break his heart again." It was all true, and Chrissie wandered through the episode being as smug, self-righteous and manipulative as she has been recently.

I was glad that writer Patrick Homes used the device of having Chrissie sorting through a box of ID badges of former colleagues to remind us that Chrissie hasn't always been so annoying. Seeing Owen's face again reminded me of the episode when she lost her baby, which is etched permanently on my mind as the Holby episode that made me cry the most. So many faces from different eras of Holby highlighted what an important character Chrissie has been, and in that sense it was a beautiful send-off for her. And, thank goodness, she didn't take Michael Spence with her.

It would have been more useful if she'd taken Malick, because frankly his behaviour is getting a bit difficult. Digby thinks he's having a nervous breakdown. He ought to put Saucer on the case – she likes to psychoanalyse people and she'd probably tip Malick right over the edge. Malick spent most of the episode trying to live his surgical life via the medium of poor Digby, his chin practically balanced on the lad's shoulder while he was trying to operate. On the up-side, Digby did get to have a go on the Gastroscopy Simulator, which looked to be such fun I'm going to ask Santa for one for Christmas.

On Darwin, in case we were under any illusion that Mr T isn't the nicest person in the world (maybe jointly with Sacha), Mo confirmed it. "You really are the nicest person in the world," she said. Obviously he is – he loves Mo, and he can knit. He can even make pom poms! Mo is still resisting him, but when she's feeling mellow after a mince pie and a glass of sherry at the staff Christmas do – well, I'm sure she'll see the advantages of a man with charm, humour and an intimate knowledge of the workings of the female "downstairs" (I don't mean Chrissie, I mean gynaecologically-speaking).

A new man

(Series 16, ep. 7 'Sink or Swim' by Jon Sen 26.11.13)

It was Malick's farewell episode, and didn't we just know it? He was given maximum opportunity to do all the classic Malick things – rush around going "Grrr," shout at Digby, have an almighty strop, mess up a bit of surgery and try to worm out of it, and wrestle with his conscience about what kind of father he was to Jake. The only typical Malick thing that he didn't get to do was have a steamy encounter in the locker room, but there was hardly time for any of that nonsense because he was so busy elsewhere.

It was actually all rather magnificent (apart from the sloppy one-handed chest drain incident – what happened to the standard cry of "We need some help in here"? And surely there's a call button in the CT scanner room?). Since he damaged his hand, Malick has (understandably) been a tad immersed in self-pity, which has at times been fairly tedious to watch. By the end of this episode he'd recovered his mojo, but incorporated a few life lessons into it and become a humbler and wiser man. He's The Malick again, but he's Malick 2.0 – teacher, mentor, father. Ego restored and off to Sweden with his son and a James Brown soundtrack.

Before I start getting too sentimental, I shall leap on a trolley that's going in the direction of Darwin for a quick summary of events there. It was Elliot's medical silver jubilee, which means it's 25 years since he became a heart surgeon. Jonny and Bonnie (or JonBon, if you will) thought this was a hilarious opportunity to wind up Saucer and make her believe that they'd arranged a stripper as a gift for Elliot rather than a strimmer. Oh, what rib-tickling fun. Zosia was actually quite funny when she attempted to lecture Elliot on what harm his supposed fondness for strippers would have on his psyche, but Jon & Bon were just tedious. After working extremely hard to convince me, against my better Joseph Byrne-worshipping judgement, that he is a suitable partner for The Magnificent Jac, in this one episode Jonny has thrown all that away and made me think he's just a giggling tosser. There. I've said it.

Fun and games on the ward is all well and good, but there was a major incident going on at the same time, and the staff should really have been more focused. A ceiling had collapsed at one of Holby's fine array of leisure centres, so all wards were full of people in various stages of "Nnngh!" I never thought in all my days I'd have reason to use the phrase "human kebab tragedy" again (the first time was here), but here we had two unrelated people impaled upon the same pole. It fell to Serena Campbell to uncouple them, and it was exactly what she didn't need on the day she found out she hadn't got the CEO job. Nor did she need the person who did get the CEO job, Karl from *Corrie* ("I love yer, Stella!"), hanging around and questioning her judgement.

Frankly I haven't warmed to this new CEO, Guy Self. It's a silly name for a start (apologies to Will Self and any other Selfs [or Selves]), and I thought he was extremely uncooperative considering there was a major incident in progress. No amount of speechifying in the stairwell can make up for being a twonk when the mucky stuff is hitting the fan.

No wonder Serena was driven first to a failed attempt at smoking and then to a successful attempt to get her ex, Oily Edward, to cheer her up by accompanying her back to Campbell Towers. This was a good result for Edward, who'd spent the rest of the episode flirting with Mary-Claire and then asking her to cover for him – once again – when he messed up in theatre.

What do you reckon he's hiding up his bottom?

(Series 16, ep. 8 'Fait Accompli' by Johanne McAndrew & Elliot Hope 3.12.13)

This week we got to know more about Guy Self (or "Selfie" as he's never called, but he should be). He lost his wife, which knocked his surgical confidence for a bit, but now he's back. And he likes Miles Davis.

Do we know this because he confided in Sacha over a lemon and poppy-seed muffin at Pulses? No, we know it because a former colleague of his has arrived in the form of Colette Sheward. She appeared like a terrifying amalgam of Sahira Shah the Registrah and Best Nurse Eddie McKee – briskly efficient, stroppy and northern like the latter, and apparently indispensable to the CEO like the former. Irritating, in other words.

Colette had brought a patient with her. He was a former patient of Selfie's and only Selfie could cure him blah blah. Which he duly did, and Colette couldn't wait to get on the phone to the hospital the patient was supposed to be treated at and gloat a bit. Selfie then offered her a job. "I'm nothing without you," he bleated. But is he anything with her? We'll have to wait and see, because I remain to be convinced about either of them.

Meanwhile, Serena "Should have been CEO" Campbell was busy dealing with a man with something up his bottom. He wouldn't say what it was, because he was too focused on being sleazy to Serena and threatening to sue Sacha for cutting his designer jacket up. He then tried to get Serena sacked for assault after she gave him a rectal examination. To be fair, as an examination it did carry a whiff of "revenge attack" about it, but he deserved it. Selfie managed to get both Sacha and Serena off the hook after it was discovered that the item up the bum was a roll of cash the man had won in Las Vegas. He'd imported it rectally to avoid paying duties on it, so Selfie levied a little tax of his own in the form of a donation to paeds oncology. The maverick!

Elsewhere, Jac and Jonny were informed by Mr T that the best date to deliver their baby would be February 4th. This is weird, because if the baby was conceived on the night of Tara's death on 17th April, that puts the due date at the beginning of January. I can only assume it's a red herring to make us drop our guard in January so we aren't expecting a surprise birth.

Anyhoo, the two of them reacted in their customary ways. Jac closed in on herself and assumed her professional, business-as-usual head. And Jonny didn't. They were looking after a patient who was pregnant with what turned out to be a Downs baby, and Jonny didn't think Jac could cope, so he said he'd keep an eye on the patient while Jac got on with her paperwork.

Jonny's idea of keeping an eye on the patient was to get all emotive about her baby's future life chances. The parents didn't really need him by the bedside waving leaflets at them and hectoring them. It was lucky that Mr T was there with his special brand of quiet bedside manner. At this point I have to mention that I just noticed in this episode what a gorgeous voice Mr T has. He really is adorable.

Despite Jonny's efforts and the machines going beep and a drama turning into a crisis, the baby was delivered safely and Elliot sorted out the mother's heart problems. Jonny, who'd spent the episode being a whiny lump, had a mutual brain-speak with the baby's father along the lines of you have to stay strong for the mother. Then he toddled off to find Jac to apologise for being a muppet.

In one of those rare moments when she peeps over the barricade of her own defences, Jac thanked him for being a muppet. It's almost like he's emoting so she doesn't have to. If only he didn't have to inflict it on the patients.

Edward gets nasty

(Series 16, ep. 9 'Heart of Hope' by Mark Stevenson 10.12.13)

If Serena Campbell stopped amid issuing Christmas invitations to reflect for a moment, there must have been a good reason why she and Edward split up. I urge her now to remember that reason(s) and run away from him faster than you can say "laparoscopic cholecystectomy." Or even faster than that, actually, because the man is Bad News.

He's making a habit of messing up at crucial times in theatre – but, handily for him, he's always been able to get Mary-Claire to cover up/take the blame for him. The reason she's been willing to do this so far is that she's been sleeping with him. The reason she's no longer willing to do it is she discovered this week that he's back with Serena.

It's sad that Mary-Claire still values herself more in terms of whom she's sleeping with than in terms of her career and ethics. When she told her sister she'd be going to the wedding in Ireland on her own without a plus one, it did seem like she might have turned a corner in how she viewed herself. Never mind – the point was that she threatened to tell Serena what had been going on – and Edward got all nasty and arm-grippy.

Later on, he made another mistake in theatre – he really is the most incompetent staff member since Dull Dan – and this time he's determined to firmly pin the blame on Mary-Claire.

Luckily for her, she has a champion, in the form of Queen of Nurses Colette Sheward, who popped up at the last minute and is going to support her nurse. This made me instantly like Colette a whole lot more than I did last week.

Another thing I liked was the banter between Mary-Claire and Honey. Posh even got involved, and it was quite like the old days of Donna/Maria/Maddie. I wish Honey had been used more in this kind of role throughout her time in Holby, rather than being stuck with the Honey/Posh nomance.

Remember when Hanssen was fairly new to Holby and he would suddenly manifest in various wards like a tall, Swedish ghost and frighten people? Selfie tried a bit of that this week, but because he's not tall or Swedish the effect was less dramatic. For some reason, he decided to bother the good folk of Darwin, who were busy preparing for a heart transplant. The patient had Asperger's and didn't like people he didn't know touching him. He knew Elliot, so Elliot had to do it. This explains why those dedicated transplant experts Mo and Jonny were nowhere to be seen.

When the donor heart became unavailable, Selfie had a plan. Giving the patient the Herzig robo-heart would be excellent publicity for the hospital. Why, he even had a "mate in the States" who was all agog to hear about the Herzig. A live video link-up of the procedure would be set up immediately!

Jac had reservations (she also had the best line of the night: "Who buys flowers nowadays? They're more of a garnish than a present"), but Elliot couldn't resist Selfie's flattery and the lure of putting his precious Herzig on view to a wider audience.

Predictably, it all went pear-shaped. Jac was right, Elliot was wrong, and he was left contemplating a rather disgusting-looking pizza. This is not a metaphor for the mess the patient's chest was in – it was an actual pizza, designed by the patient specially for Elliot.

Keller was a bit strange this week. Zosia was there, though she's been on Darwin recently, and so was Sacha. He's inherited Malick's teaching mantle and had a herd of students following him around. In honour of the occasion he'd chose a shirt/tie combo that I can only describe as "busy."

Zosia wanted to move into Chantelle's old room in Digby's house, but he wasn't keen, doubtless fearing that his quiet existence of nerdy pursuits and heartbroken sniffling would be interrupted by having Zosia pouncing on him at tediously regular intervals.

It didn't matter anyway. What Saucer wants, Saucer gets and by the end of the episode she was moving herself in anyway and insisting that Digby got some decorating done.

There's something going on between Saucer and Selfie (I know what it is but I'm not spoilering) – she walks away whenever he appears, which seems like sensible behaviour to me.

Digby was hilarious – I love his attempts to empathise. His patient was a man who was found to have a wooden initial M piercing his colon. It was a pendant that had belonged to his late wife. Digby, maybe channelling Chantelle, adopted his best concerned voice. "Did you swallow the pendant so your wife's initial could be close to your heart?" The man said no – perhaps he'd accidentally dropped it into his minestrone. "We've all been there," sighed Sacha.

A-hole averse

(Series 16, ep. 10 'Father's Day' by Joe Ainsworth 17.12.13)

My gosh but Keller was a mixed experience this week. On one hand there was a patient's relative (who became an actual patient, as they so often do on Holby) played by Gary Cargill, a man with a speaking voice that makes me come over all unnecessary. It's the Scouse accent. But on the other hand, we had the loss (maybe temporary, but who knows?) of the snake-hipped wonder that is Michael Spence.

Cargill played a man whose son needed a liver transplant. Dr Honey messed up by sourcing a liver that was from a donor of the wrong blood group (but I'll return to Honey later). The patient's dad had a liver, obviously, and he was super-keen to part with a bit of it to help his son. Michael went ahead with the operation despite discovering the father also had angina. When he suffered a heart attack after the surgery and it looked like he wouldn't have long to live, he didn't mind too much because he'd saved his son's life. That's the kind of selfless, devoted father he was.

Michael Spence has been guilty of being a tad less than devoted and selfless where his own kids are concerned, but he may be able to spend more time with them now. He was Summoned by Selfie (actually, Selfie sends Serena to do his summoning, which I can't help thinking is a bit of a waste of Serena's manifold talents and doesn't do anything for Selfie's credibility – Hanssen would have staged an Über-Loom), who suspended him for three months for swerving all kinds of protocols in his liver transplant case. "I'm not risk-averse," said Selfie. "I'm A-hole averse." In which case, he must find himself very hard to live with.

Michael left Holby with a souvenir in the form of a busted nose, courtesy of Sacha, who got all cross about Michael's fling with beloved Chrissie. Hopefully that's got Chrissie out of Sacha's system now and he'll be ready to move on with storylines that involve less sighing.

Michael wasn't the only one who left. Dr Honey, upset by her liver mistake and worrying that she hardly gets to see her son Finn, decided to quit. Holby City is the only hospital in the NHS which apparently doesn't require its staff to work a notice period. Indeed some of them aren't even required to give "soap notice" by packing the traditional box with three lever-arch files and a houseplant and giving the hospital an over-the-shoulder glance as they unlock their car. It's all very casual.

The big excitement on Darwin was the revelation that Saucer is Selfie's daughter, but she has wisely decided she doesn't want to be known as "Zosia Self," because that would sound extraordinarily silly. There was a touching scene where Zosia told Elliot why she wrote down his (Elliot's) words of wisdom in a little book. It was because her late mother had a "beautiful way with words" but Zosia hadn't written any of them down at the time, and now found that her memories were fading. It was a really well-written bit of dialogue and Camilla Arfwedson acted it perfectly – it actually made me feel a bit tearful. So Saucer's relationship with her father is complicated – she maybe blames him a bit, but she also wants to have a relationship with him if only he wasn't too busy with Colette.

Elliot Hope, meanwhile, was wracked with guilt about the mess he made last week with/of Steven Parker and the fact that his patients seem to die more than most people's (it's because he takes on more high-risk patients). He went all paranoid thinking Selfie was trying to sack him and had sent

Zosia to spy on him. Jac gave him a pep talk and amusingly tricked him back into the operating theatre by pretending she felt sick.

It was fairly quiet on AAU, and events there focused mainly on Edward being a tit to Mary-Claire and Colette supporting her. I'm still not quite sure what to make of Colette. I like her no-nonsense, capable approach – she reminds me ofEve Montgomery in Casualty. I also like the way she sticks up for the nurses. I don't like her relationship with Selfie, because I don't like Selfie. I'm A-hole averse.

Festive spirit

(Series 16, ep. 11 'All I Want for Christmas is You' by Julia Gilbert 24.12.13)

There was Christmas spirit all over Holby yesterday, embodied in the form of a patient on Keller, who loved Christmas and knew the Christmas traditions of every country in the world. This would come in handy later. It was also embodied in the fine figure of Mr T, who was dressed like an elf. Frankly, this was a wonderful thing. I was temporarily distracted (I'm currently Christmasing at the parental home), so I didn't see what made him decide to do a striptease, but it was before the watershed so he was stopped before he got even to a half Monty. It all served to make Mo realise what a catch he could be. He's charming, sweet, can knit, is fully qualified in Lady Parts and he's always thought Mo was adorable. Surely, what with it being Christmas and that, the Holby writers would let Mo and Mr T get together under the mistletoe and go home to roast chestnuts on an open fire (which may or may not be a euphemism, depending on how things went)? But no. No sooner had Mo decided to ask him out, than she was pipped to the post by a patient's relative. Nooooo!!! But there's always new year. I'm an optimist and it Must Happen.

Meanwhile, Edward Campbell was getting into the Christmas spirit – literally, as the spirit in this case was vodka. Yes, it turns out that the reason Edward makes so many mistakes is because he's quietly plastered a great deal of the time. This worked out well for Mary-Claire, because once the news got out about Edward being drunk in charge of an anaesthetised patient, he was sharply out on his ear and Mary-Claire had an apology from poor Serena, who was forced to face the fact that Edward was a philandering drunk. Once again, the unseen Holby HR department has been shown to be woefully lacking, as apparently Edward was "let go" from his previous post due to his drinking and nobody thought to pursue this until he was caught red-handed and red-eyed with his fist clamped around a bottle.

We found out a bit more about Zosia and Selfie. It seems that Zosia's Polish mother died only recently and this is her first Christmas without her. Selfie had a present for her, something her mother had asked him to give her, but she refused to take it. For the first time I actually liked Selfie a bit in this episode. He understood that she needed some space and he gave the present to Digby to give her. Digby proved to be the perfect choice, as he prepared a Polish Christmas with all the Polish trimmings. It was so lucky he had that Christmas expert of a patient as a resource. Digby is absolutely adorable, and I'm completely warming to Saucer too.

It wouldn't be Christmas without some festive singing, and the carols this year benefited enormously from the presence of Dr Harry Posh – Jules Knight had a previous career as a singer and it was a good excuse for him to show us his stuff.

Needless to say, Jac Naylor was not to be found singing under the tree in the LCMS, but there was a nice little scene where Jonny Mac prised his face away from Bonnie's for long enough for him to remember that last year he discovered Jac had never decorated a Christmas tree, and to promise her that next Christmas she'll have a tree – and a family – of her own. We'll just have to keep our fingers crossed that he's right.

Some people come good

(Series 16, ep. 12 'Ring in the New' by Julia Gilbert 31.12.13)

Thank you, Julia Gilbert, for letting us celebrate the new year without anything too traumatic happening. There were no deaths, no serial killers, no beloved characters departing on buses or under trucks, Darwin didn't explode. It was what the staff of Holby would probably term a fairly quiet shift. That's not to say there was no drama and nothing happened, because there was and it did, but it mainly revolved around the emotional wellbeing (or otherwise) of various staff members.

I have to admit I'm beginning to accept Selfie in his triple role of CEO, neurosurgeon and Saucer's dad. It's a lot of work for one man to handle, and at first I thought the fact that he was loathsome Karl from *Corrie* would always get in the way, but John Michie is bedding in nicely now. This has mainly been due to Selfie's relationship with his daughter, which is satisfyingly complex and realistic thanks to Camilla Arfwedson's quirky portrayal of Zosia.

This week a patient with a brain tumour and a dodgy heart meant that Selfie was on Darwin a lot, where Zosia currently is (though it was her last day, apparently). Both Selfie and Elliot Hope are keen for Zosia to specialise in surgery, because, according to Prof Hope, she has potential he hasn't seen since Jac Naylor. If Sahira Shah the Registrah heard that she'd be spitting at how soon her near-legendary suturing had been forgotten.

As well as some brain surgery, some brains had to be spoken to illuminate the Saucer/Selfie situation. This was neatly done when it turned out the brain/heart patient had a girlfriend and a son who had opposing views about what was best for him. Through this we learned that Selfie had kept quiet about Zosia's mother's cancer returning, because he didn't want to worry her when she had exams looming. This meant she didn't get the chance to say goodbye and always felt that Selfie placed more importance on her career as a doctor than on her as a person.

Zosia is in a lot of ways quite childlike. She sulks, she speaks without thinking, she acts out, she has tantrums. I can understand that – she's a young woman who is very intellectually brilliant, but I can imagine that a lot of parental attention went missing because of her mother's illness and her father's job, so emotionally she isn't mature at all for her age. She kicked off in thoroughly unprofessional style at her father, because any time it looks like she has his attention, patients or Colette take priority. She was wrong to behave like that, but I also think Colette was wrong to come over all *Supernanny* and advise Selfie to basically leave her on the naughty step for a while.

So Zosia went to the bar, downed a few tequilas and then went home and pounced on Digby. "I need the warmth of another human being, and you're the closest," she told him. I'm not sure whether she meant he was physically the nearest person to hand, or whether he's the closest thing to a human among her circle of acquaintances. Or both.

While I'm warming to Selfie, I'm also warming to Dr Posh. Yes, I know it's a bit obvious of me to start liking him just because he was kind to a dog, but I also like that Mary-Claire made him work hard for forgiveness from her. Previously he's coasted by on being a pretty face, but that's not working for him any more because everyone is wise to the fact that he can be a bit of a slime ball. But, as the dog-owning patient told Mary-Claire, "There are some people who come good if you give them a chance."

I did wonder what any vets watching the episode will have made of the fact that a junior doctor and a nurse can between them manage to take a blood sample from a dog, send it to a lab where they detect pancreatitis but not the fact that the blood isn't from a human (would they spot that? Can any medically knowledgeable readers tell me?), identify the necessary drug and the correct dose without even resorting to Google and five minutes later the dog is right as rain. But let's ignore that, because a heartwarming doggy story was just the thing for New Year's Eve. And Dr Posh topped off his redemption by pretending the homeless dog-owning man won the raffle prize. Bless.

Serena was at work despite the recent embarrassment of her ex husband turning out to be a scheming and unpleasant rat. Everyone was sympathetic – a bit too sympathetic in most cases (yes you, Digby), though Selfie was the exception. He blamed her for not spotting the gap in Edward's CV when she was acting CEO. It seems I was wrong for blaming the HR department – they clearly don't have one.

Serena was holding it all together nicely till she had a rare meltdown in theatre. Luckily she has Ric Griffin on her side, so she will live to fight another day. Unfortunately it looks like her recovery is going to be somewhat hampered by the reappearance next week of Edward himself.

I can't imagine life without her now

(Series 16, ep. 13 'Self Control' by Rebecca Wojciechowski 7.1.14)

A few years ago, you wouldn't have put money on Jac Naylor being the maternal type. Indeed I remember remarking on the trauma likely to be faced by Ric's grandson Jake because the first face he saw was Jac's. Not because it isn't a beautiful face (it is), but because it has a default setting of Terrifying.

In this episode, in the final moments before Jac gave birth, we got to see what kind of mother she's going to be, and it's glorious. I'll be honest and say I was primed to cry from the outset in this episode, but I became tearful very early at the sight of Jac's face when she told Mo that the baby "likes lights." It was like a little window into a whole relationship that she's built up with the baby during the pregnancy. She talks to her, not in the "yummy mummy" way she despises, but in her own quirky way, telling her about the scientific reason for a red sky at night, educating her about the importance of numbers. I can imagine that Jaccy Maccy Junior's life (if she gets to have much of one – and I'll be devastated if she doesn't) will be full of as many chemistry sets as dolls, as many trips to science museums as funfairs. It'll be a no-bullshit upbringing, but one full of love and care. Jac might tell her child that a red sky is just caused by a refraction of the light, but they'll both be up early the next morning to see how lovely the dawn is.

This was such a well-crafted episode. I wasn't expecting secondary stories to be taking up much time and at first I thought the storyline involving Ric and Serena was going to be irritating and just make me want to be back in the labour ward with Jac, but as things went on I got more and more absorbed into the story of Ric and his former love, Kathy. Yes, it was a tad contrived – Kathy was the life and soul of the party until she told Ric she had cancer, and then poignantly died as he rowed them on the river – but it was so beautifully acted, with Cherie Lunghi and Hugh Quarshie very touching as the former lovers reunited too late. There was a lot of comedy in it too, with Ric's karaoke turn, Serena fabulously drunk and flirting with a man who's previously been an Unblinking Canadian Paediatrician at Holby (though he was a different, very amusing, character here) and Edward trotting up at regular intervals with a bunch of flowers to try and win her back.

The second time I cried was after Kathy had died. Ric made a phone call, and there was only going to be one person he'd call – Jess. Because the episode was all about parents and children – specifically daughters.

Back at Holby, Jac was trying to keep her daughter safe, by not letting her be born. It was the only way she could maintain any control over the situation. Wise old Elliot Hope sat with her in front of a print of The Lady of Shalott (I used to have that picture on the wall of my room at university) and explained how the story of it touched her own situation – that sometimes keeping safe is no substitute for the chance to really live. (The Lady of Shalott was also referenced in Ric's story, in Kathy's white dress and the early morning boat trip).

Where was Jonny Mac while all this was going on? He was right beside Jac as much as she would let him be, trying to be strong for her and feeling helpless, but the important thing was that he was there and she wanted him to be.

The baby was eventually delivered by caesarean, and was rushed off to NICU looking apparently lifeless. Jac shut down her emotions to prepare for the worst, then Jonny came bursting in to tell her the baby was breathing. She's "so tiny and so beautiful." And ginger, apparently. Jonny was lovely – he'd brought a "wee piggy" called Ralph for the baby and was going to put it in the incubator "as soon as it's been sterilised."

While Jonny was all optimism and happiness, Jac looked like she didn't dare hope and you could see that in her thoughts she was far away from what was happening in the room. In an episode full of brilliant performances, Rosie Marcel's was amazing. For a woman who's been called Termi-Naylor and is often accused of being cold and unfeeling, at times in this episode it was like Jac had no skin at all, she was so vulnerable and emotional.

Mr T broke the good news to Mo and Elliot, and Mo kissed him. Lovely Mr T got a bit flustered and completely sidetracked, bless him. After this story is over, can we please find a way to bring Mr T in as a regular cast member? I want to see his face on those opening credits.

I loved this episode so much. It was beautifully written, with lovely details like discovering that the midwife who's formerly been Jac's enemy has had some tragedy in her own life, and Serena necking a bottle of wine so she and Ric would have an excuse not to go back to Holby. Catherine Russell was marvellous in those comic scenes. She's her father's daughter, after all.

A whole day (almost) spent trying to make people better

(Series 16, ep. 14 'Intuition' by Lucia Haynes 14.1.14)

After last week, the question on everyone's lips was, "What will Jac and Jonny's baby be called?" It wasn't on everyone's lips for long, because it had already found its way into programme information for a few episodes hence, and from there people couldn't wait to plaster it all over Twitter and any other available outlet.

So when the paediatrician kept telling Jac and Jonny that they really ought to give the baby a name, I already knew it was going to be Emma. The only remaining suspense lay in who would come up with the name, how and why.

I said last week that as soon as the birth was over, Jac had shut herself down emotionally, prepared for the worst. This week she carried on with that, by going back to work straight away, not visiting the baby, and pretending life was normal. Jonny Mac couldn't understand it, because he was busy emoting all over the place, like he does.

What he still doesn't realise about Jac, even after all this time, is that the only public displays she's happy with are of her surgical skills. Otherwise, she is the most private person you could imagine. We only found out just before she gave birth what a bond she had with the baby, and this week we saw that she's providing breast milk for her, but sends it to NICU via a nurse who's sworn to secrecy. Obviously the NICU staff must know – I don't imagine they dish out random breast milk to the babies in their care – but as far as the rest of the world is concerned, Jac isn't bothered about seeing her baby.

It's a self-protective device, and what she needs to learn from Jonny Mac and what the paediatrician tried to tell her is that she has to take a risk and let herself bond with Emma, because the baby needs her.

So how did she come up with the name? No idea. Maybe she's a Jane Austen fan (yup, that sounds likely). Maybe she thinks it's practical because it's easy to spell, having grown up with "Jacqueline" as her own name. Maybe it was the first thing she thought of that wasn't Morven, Storm or Destiny – which was the direction Jonny Mac was heading in. Maybe we'll find out next week. Or maybe never.

What we did find out this week was that Mo has a sister. Her name is Adele, and she rocked up on AAU looking like the fairy off the Christmas tree. Fairly soon she was wearing scrubs, because she wasn't a patient (a fate usually reserved for friends and relatives of the staff) but an HCA. She arrived in the car park just in time to pick up a patient on the way, which got her into instant trouble with Colette, who didn't think a fairy should be treating patients.

Colette wasn't in the best of moods anyway, because it turns out she may not have got her job entirely legitimately. Well, about time. I've been questioning the free-and-easy employment practices on Holby for ages now, and had reached the conclusion that there couldn't possibly be an HR department, because appointments were made and resignations accepted apparently on the whim of whoever happened to be in the CEO chair at the time.

It turns out that there is an HR department after all, and her name is Sophia. She decided to keep a close eye on Colette to see if she was really up to the lofty job that Selfie had handed her. The conclusion was that Colette is going to have to re-apply for her own job through the proper channels – now that we've discovered there are some proper channels (I think it probably involves being interviewed by Charlie from *Casualty* the next time he's in Borehamwood).

I think we were supposed to react to this news with horror that "our" Colette has been treated so badly, but frankly I'd have sacked her on the spot. Not for her casual approach to staff discipline – giving a mild ticking off to some non-speaking extras who were caught snogging in a cupboard is fine and I'm sure Charlie from *Casualty* himself would have no problem with that. I can just about forgive the fact that she didn't believe Adele when she had a strong gut instinct that there was something dodgy about her patient's sister. After all, she's only just met Adele and she probably doesn't know Medical Soap Rule 2723(a) that you should always believe the hunches of junior staff members and 2723(b) that the juniorer they are, the righter they'll be. I can just about overlook the arrogant, stroppy way she ordered Dr Posh to run tests on the patient. He may be junior and he may be Posh, but he's a doctor and therefore surely deserving of respect at least in front of the patients? But the thing I'm rapidly finding I can't cope with about Colette is her vocal delivery. It works for dry sarcasm, but then it never shifts out of dry sarcasm mode, no matter what's going on in the rest of the scene. Frankly it's driving me nuts in a way I haven't been driven nuts since Faye Byrne left. Grrr!

And... relax. But maybe not in the way that Zosia March likes to relax, which is by having her wicked way with Digby. Dear old Digby doesn't mind being Zosia's plaything at all, but he's an old fashioned boy who's been brought up to follow a night of passion with a morning of coffee and croissants, and probably making sure the bed is properly made and the room is nicely aired too. He's a good old-fashioned lover boy, in other words. The problem is, as far as he's concerned, that Zosia is not interested in the trappings of cosy coupledom. She just likes having a little shag-buddy handy when she needs one.

To add to Digby's misery, she's also inflicted another flatmate on him – and it's That Dominic, the one who got Malick into trouble. He's now back at Holby and working on Keller with Digby and Zosia. Their patient was Ian Lavender off of *Dad's Army*, and it was obvious he was a famous person because he seemed to have four doctors all to himself, what with Sacha also being around. Dominic taught Zosia and Digby a few lessons about bedside manners, which Digby was able to put into practice when Ian Lavender went missing and was tracked down to the Linden Cullen Memorial Shrubbery (the basement was already occupied by Colette who'd gone down for a soothing e-cig). He hated hospitals, he told Digby, who told him he should be more positive about them because "people spend their whole day trying to make you better." When they're not bitching, sniping, undermining each other and snogging in cupboards, that is.

I wouldn't want to be anywhere else

(Series 16, ep. 15 'Life After Life' by Katie Douglas 21.1.14)

We already know that Jac Naylor is most comfortable when she's in control, and is most in control when she's working. There's that lovely professional distance thing, where you can refer to the person you're treating as "the patient" and it makes them seem that bit less emotional and vulnerable and more like an interesting problem to be solved.

It was therefore entirely in character that she should describe her baby daughter as "the patient" when talking to the paediatric surgeon who was about to operate on her. Jac had done the research, and was of the professional opinion that "the patient" was ready for the surgery.

Leaving Jonny Mac to cry over the crib, Jac went off to join Elliot Hope in looking after Robbie, a cystic fibrosis patient who would die without some bits of donor lung. In the process she received a hefty amount of speaking-your-brains from Robbie's girlfriend Laura, who insisted she wanted to watch while Jac transplanted bits of Robbie's parents into him (we never got to see these parents – Laura phoned them and the next thing they knew they were anaesthetised and having chunks of their lungs carried from one operating theatre to the next, poor souls). "You can't possibly want to stand there and watch him die," Jac said, cracking a bit and revealing that Emma's surgery was very much on her mind. Laura – who was a tad annoying – said that if you love someone, you're there for them. "If I have to watch him die… I wouldn't want to be anywhere else," she said.

Robbie went bleep in theatre, but Jac (with Elliot's calm help) got him sorted out and then she was out of her surgical cap and gown and hot-footing it to Paeds, where she had the novel experience of sitting in a corridor with Jonny Mac, like any other terrified relative, while Emma had her operation. The good news is that Emma is apparently doing well. Jac popped back to talk to Laura about Robbie. "He'll get through this and you'll be there," she said, speaking her own brains this time. Then she went back to sit with her daughter.

It's been a while since the phrase "Walk with me" was a regular feature on Holby, but Sacha used it this week when he had to get tough on Digby. The reason for this was that Digby was getting seriously irritated by Dominic, who as well as being the little worm who dumped Malick in hot water is also genuinely irritating in his own right. Sacha made them work together on a tricky case – once again on Keller one patient gets at least two and usually three doctors all to herself. Dominic knows exactly how to wind Digby up ("You sound like a tiny Bond villain in scrubs"), but took his competitiveness too far by binning test results and not sharing information. Digby had some support from Zosia, who glides around with a tiny ironic smile playing about her lips, and eventually he and Dominic between them managed to reach a tricky diagnosis that wasn't even Addison's disease.

A similar "we must work together for the sake of the patient" situation was going on in AAU, where Mo had been summoned for a CT issue and had to work alongside her sister. They're actually quite friendly and Adele's hair even matches Mo's coat, but the main issue was that Mo didn't really value her sister's job as an HCA. For the second week running, poor Adele had a gut instinct about a patient which proved to be correct but was ignored by her "superiors." In that respect she's like an under-qualified Frieda Petrenko, but I can't imagine for one minute that Goth Dr Frieda would have found Selfie attractive, as Adele apparently does.

Top quality doctor material

(Series 16, ep. 16 'Prince Among Men' by Nick Fisher 28.1.14)

New boy Rafaello Di Lucca is known as "Raf" to his friends and to people who can't be bothered typing out his full name. Raf it is, then. But he's not riff Raf – he's Top Quality Doctor Material, as he wasted no time in informing Ric Griffin and Selfie, who were interviewing him for the post of new registrar on AAU. Perhaps unsurprisingly, there was no sign of the HR woman from two weeks ago, so appointments are again being made on a nod and a whim and someone can be interviewed and then start work five minutes later.

Ric likes a maverick, and this Raf practically has 'Maverick' written on his forehead, just under the words 'Arrogant' and 'Up Himself.' Selfie wasn't as keen as Ric, but Raf came prepaid (something to do with the NHS already having paid for him), and what CEO can resist a bargain? Also, what CEO could resist the challenge, "Henrik Hanssen had a vision… I'm gambling on you having a vision, too."

Raf didn't employ any kind of dimmer switch to his brilliance once he hit the Ward of Doom, either. The first thing he did was rip into Dr Posh for his rubbish CPR technique. Presumably Dr Posh has been employing this same technique in front of various tutors, mentors, Sacha, Ric and so on for months, but none of them has spotted just how badly he does it. Did Raf take him quietly aside and spend some time demonstrating how it should be done? Nope. Humiliation was sufficient. Honestly, if Raf has been sent as a way of making me side with Dr Posh, he's succeeded.

He mentioned his wife quite a few times, and I'm absolutely terrified of meeting her. She can do "everything," apparently, including making croissanty-type treats and packing them into jolly Tupperware, and all of this while shielding her eyes from the dazzling brilliance of her husband. Please tell me she's not going to appear in a few weeks as an anaesthetist?

A maverick, brilliant new doctor has to have a suitable challenge, and in this case it was a boy whose lungs were pretty much useless as a consequence of eating wild fungi. Never, ever eat wild fungi without Bear Grylls or Ray Mears with you to advise, because this is the kind of thing that can happen. It was all far too messy for Raf and Mo to fix up, and required a special machine called an ECMO. Which Holby didn't have. Not to worry – with Raf's maverick brilliance and a few bits of tubing from the supply stores, it was no trouble at all to build one on the spot. Makes you wonder why they're so rare if they're so easy to knock together.

To the relative sanity of NICU now, where Baby Emma had done her first poop (which "speaks volumes" apparently) and was ready to be held by her parents. Jonny Mac was up for it, but Jac ("I'm not 'Mummy,' I'm 'Ms Naylor'") had a little squirt of hand sanitiser and then legged it. She still can't quite get her head around this whole motherhood thing and no amount of nagging or persuasion from Jonny or Mr Solis would persuade her. What did the trick was seeing That Bonnie Creature holding Emma, and then Bonnie seeking her out for a chat afterwards. "I hate it when I hear you say her name," Jac told her, looking like she was only resisting decking her because a surgeon has to be careful not to damage her hands.

Back at NICU, Jac demanded to hold Emma. Mr Solis protested a bit that it wasn't the best time for the baby, but I think he was just making sure she really, really meant it. Then we finally had a very sweet scene with Jac holding Emma and agreeing with Jonny Mac that their daughter smells of toast.

In case we might fear that this would turn her all yummy mummy, there was a brief scene where she was called to deal with a mitral valve replacement and just for a second she seemed like she would rather look at pictures of Emma on her computer instead – but it was just a second, and then she was grabbing her stethoscope and was off out the door.

On Keller there was a silly story about a woman who had a 2,000 year old mummy she needed scanning. As you do. Zosia volunteered to stay with her (and as usual the woman ended up being a patient herself), mainly because she wanted to avoid getting involved in an operation, because she thinks surgery is just plumbing. Selfie had a (somewhat threatening) word with Sacha and told him to get Zosia in theatre, which he duly did and it ended up with blood everywhere. Sacha is trying to be tough and has told the joined-at-the-hip threesome of Zosia, Digby and Dominic that they're having a test in the wet lab tomorrow and if one fails – they all fail. There's nothing like a bit of peer pressure.

A multi-slap episode

(Series 16, ep. 17 'Things We Lost in the Fire' by Natalie Mitchell & Julia Gilbert 4.2.14)

I spent the majority of the time during this episode wanting to slap one or other of the characters. Looking on the positive side, I suppose this meant there were characters I cared enough about to make me want to slap people who were being horrible to them, but still... all this aggression can't be good for my blood pressure. Each story line had its own slapable person in it – some of them even had two – and the worst part of it was that one of them was Sacha, formerly the Nicest Human Being on the Planet.

As the slapability count was highest on Keller, let's get that one out of the way first. Following on from last week, Sacha was carrying out his threat of making Digby, Dominic and Zosia do tests in which a failure by one meant a failure by the group. This despite the fact that Digby is a year ahead of the other two and has only recently been crowned Doctor of the Year. Sacha, meanwhile, has morphed from being Mr Cuddles to being all stern and cross, and I don't like it at all. Power used to not sit comfortably on Sacha's shoulders – I remember once when he was put in charge of AAU and had a half-hearted attempt to get Mary-Claire to call him Mr Levy, which lasted for about twenty minutes. Maybe it's because he's been so horribly treated at the hands of Chrissie, but he seems like a different person now.

He did redeem himself a little bit when he discovered Digby had thrown away his Doctor of the Year certificate, and he tracked him down to the Linden Cullen Memorial Shrubbery (which looked particularly splendid) to have a quiet, and more sympathetic, word.

The reason Digby was sulking in the Shrubbery was that the other slapable Keller character, Dominic, had spent the episode winding him up. Sacha had the pair of them competing with each other to sort out a sick fireman. Dominic came up with the diagnosis – cyanide poisoning – although he only stole the idea from Zosia and spent the rest of the time flirting with the patient ("Jamie Foxx would play you in the movie"). It was Digby who made the bigger discovery that the fireman wasn't a fireman at all, but not before things had gone pear-shaped and the fireman was left with permanent changes to his digestive system. Digby was out of his depth, and without Chantelle standing by with a paper bag for him to breathe into he was soon in high-anxiety mode, but being undermined by Sacha forcing him to compete with that little worm Dominic can't have helped.

There was no relief to be found on Darwin, where That Bonnie Creature was trying to decide whether to call Jonny "Daddy Mac" or "Mac Daddy." Ooh, which is best? A clue: neither. To be fair to Jonny for just a second before I start properly slagging him off, Jac was being a bit of a nightmare, too. She's started looking for a nanny for Emma, which is fair enough because the last thing I want her to be is a stay-at-home-mom – because then she wouldn't be at Holby doing what she does best (ie ninja level surgery and sarcasm). But she's also put Emma's name down for the Elmswood Academy for Girls, which is a bit previous and sounds dreadful. It sounds like something Lady Byrne would have done – in fact, did try to do for wee Baby Byrne, as I recall.

This made Jonny go into eye-popping emoting mode, and he was aided and abetted by former patient Lexie and her Herzig heart and hotline to God. Jonny decided he wanted Emma to have a hotline to God too, and arranged for Lexie to christen her in the Linden Cullen Temple of Anguish. "The Jonny Mac I knew wouldn't take no for an answer," prompted the irritating robo-vicar, who only escapes a slap from me because Elliot is very excited that she's a walking, talking Herzig owner.

I'd have expected Jac to tell Jonny where to stuff his religious twinges – she strikes me as the kind of woman who has the concept of God filed neatly between Santa Claus and the Tooth Fairy – but she agreed to the christening. Just at a better venue than the LCMS, which makes sense because that place is probably a total infection risk.

On AAU, it was Selfie who was looking for a slap this week, first of all for telling Serena to take off her "ridiculous shoes." I would like to see him try that kind of crap with Connie Beauchamp or Dr Zoe Hanna, and I would dearly have liked to have seen Serena throw her coffee at him – she was handily holding a cup. But she did as he asked and presumably spent the rest of the episode in Crocs, which was a shame as she was looking extremely foxy and the plot called for her to do a great deal of flirting, which is not so easy in Crocs.

The person she was flirting with was the charming Mr Tressler. No, not DrTressler/Posh – this was MrTressler/Rich, father of the aforementioned Posh, who was having a hernia repair. Father and son weren't the best of friends – like Oliver Valentine, Posh's choice of career had been a big disappointment to his money-loving father. Tressler Senior had some spare cash kicking around, and in no time at all Serena had persuaded him to part with it in the direction of the hospital. Then Selfie showed up, diagnosed a neuro-thingy and Tressler Senior decided all the money from his newly-hatched Tressler Foundation should go to neurosurgery.

Serena was understandably miffed. "You said you'd give me my voice, but every time I try to use it you silence me," she complained. Selfie said he didn't give a damn about her ego. Vile, odious man. Serena decided a bit of power was better than no power at all, so she agreed to be in charge of the Tressler Foundation anyway.

Emma's christening and other rare events

(Series 16, ep. 18 'Eat Your Heart Out' by Nick Fisher 11.2.14)

Sometimes two extremely rare things come along at once. Rare things like the christening of your only daughter. Rare things like a ruptured congenital aneurysm of the left coronary sinus – "the rarest heart condition Holby has seen since Roman times," apparently. Anyone would be conflicted, but most people would prioritise the christening. Jac Naylor isn't most people, though, and she's far more comfortable in a nice sterile operating theatre than she is with the more complicated world of emotions and conventional public displays. She knows how to behave as a christening guest (it involves kick-ass £300 shoes, makeup and a new dress), but her knowledge doesn't extend as far as what to do when you're the one who produced the baby in question. How would she know that she was supposed to get a christening gown for Emma?

Jonny has known Jac for quite a while now, and he still doesn't get her. He never will, and in that respect he's far better off with That Bonnie Creature, who knows what's expected and is conventional and straightforward. Jac is better off with people who do understand her, like Sacha and Elliot – she exasperates them too sometimes, but they don't want to change who she is. Easy for them, I know, as they don't have to share parenting of a small baby with her.

I've said in the past that Jac respects people who stand up to her, and this is the approach that Jonny seems to be taking at the moment. This involves behaviour like storming into operating theatres shouting, "Get yourself out of here and to that chapel now!" I'm not sure the alpha male approach was particularly helpful in this instance, though. Actually, I'm understating that a bit – it was an outrageous way for him to talk to a senior surgeon while she was in the middle of surgery. It was an outrageous way for a man to talk to the mother of his child, come to think of it.

It was a shame Mo wasn't around (quarantine due to chickenpox, apparently) – she'd maybe have been able to rein Jonny in a bit and been supportive of Jac, who may not actually have post natal depression, but at the very least has the baby blues and the confusion that comes from finding yourself in a new job where the definitive textbook has yet to be written.

Dr Posh was pondering new jobs this week – specifically, what did he want to specialise in? Where was his passion? The arrival of Annie, an overweight patient who was pencilled in for a gastric band gave him a clue and he decided on the spot that bariatric surgery was where his future lay. He could see it all laid out before him – a golden future full of people with artificially reduced stomachs, embracing a gloriously pie-free life all because of him. It was all so dazzling that he ignored another patient whose leg ulcer turned out to be necrotising fasciitis. He also ignored the fact that his bariatric patient was interpreting his interest in her as more than just professional. There's every chance she's going to go bunny-boiler on him next week.

Occasionally a guest patient turns up on Holby who is so wonderful I want them to be in it every week. One such patient was Anthony Dransfield, a plain-speaking northerner with a throbbing rectum. "Not being funny, lad," he said to Dominic, "But are you a poofter?" Serena gave him a little lecture on political correctness and told him she'd have to have a look to find out why it had been two weeks since his last poo. He wasn't keen. "Have you ever had a beam shined up your jacksie?" He insisted that Zosia had to go on privacy watch while Serena snapped on the rubber gloves, which meant we had a very funny view of Zosia's face framed prettily by the cubicle curtain while Anthony yelled, "It feels like you've stuck a stingray up me hole!"

He needed to have an abscess sorted out, but he refused to have a woman do it in case the ladies laughed at his tackle while he was asleep. Come on lads, you've all been there. The only man available to do the job was CEO and top neurosurgeon Guy Self – I know, not the most plausible scenario in the world, but a delightful opportunity for Serena to get revenge on him for being such a twonk last week. Understandably he wasn't keen, but Anthony insisted. "You operate on brains but you can't do bums?"

Zosia and Serena were bonding quite well, and Zosia confided in Serena all about her mother's death and the way Selfie kept it from her because she was doing exams. The reaction was not quite what she expected – "You need to look at your own stuff," was Serena's advice.

Posh up, Jonny down

(*Series 16, ep. 19 'Aftertaste' by Kit Lambert 18.2.14*)

My opinions about Holby characters don't remain static. A case in point is Dr Posh. In fact, I might actually start referring to him as Harry now and again, that's how fond of him I'm getting.

His character has become much more interesting since he had Raf to antagonise him. Raf is a man who thinks your medical qualifications are worth nothing if you haven't at least got an NVQ Level 1 from the school of hard knocks. He dismisses Harry because he grew up with the advantages of having a rich dad, and in Raf's eyes this means he hasn't earned the right to very much respect. In some ways, he's right – Harry still expects opportunities to fall in his lap and still feels he can get what he wants with a dazzling smile and a bit of smooth talk, but he's increasingly finding that's not the case and there's some doubt and anger in him which is making him much more interesting. I found myself actually rooting for the lad, despite his terrible treatment of vulnerable bariatric patient Annie Hinkley.

I'm not rooting for Jonny Mac, however. Oh Jonny, what have the Holby writers done to you? Jonny used to be a sweet, genuine, no-hidden-agenda kind of guy. And now his whole focus is on this childish game of one-upmanship with Jac and at the centre of it, as Jeremy Kyle would say, is an innocent child. I thought both Jac and Jonny were out of order this week, though I felt there was no intentional malice in the way Jac behaved by hiring a nanny without consulting him. It was initially thoughtlessness, which turned to aggressive defence when challenged. Jac can be as spiky as a hedgehog when threatened and it's not nice and it does sometimes teeter on the edge of bullying (saying she'd hired a male nanny because Emma needs "a strong male role model in her life" was a low blow), but Jonny's response was dreadful. Basically he tried to frame her with Colette and portray her as a monster, so he could be given a promotion which five minutes earlier hadn't existed in the fluid staffing configurations of Holby. Now apparently he's going to use his new job as Acting Clinical Nurse Manager to make Jac's life difficult in ways which sound like they would contravene the Sex Discrimination Act.

Meanwhile, on Keller there was a bit of movement in the fractious relationship between Dr Zosia March and her father, Selfie. Sacha gave Zosia a bit of psych evaluating to do, with a patient who thought she could smell her dead husband. "Ewwww!" said Digby. Burnt toast and coffee rather than decomposing corpse, though, so not all that bad. Zosia got into trouble for not seeking a psych assessment for the patient and getting consent for a procedure while there were doubts about her mental health. This led to a showdown in Selfie's office which turned into a heart-to-heart about Zosia's mother. Zosia ended up in tears and Selfie gave her a hug. Later on she called him "Dad" in theatre and was impressed by his brain surgery skills. So that was all very heartwarming and lovely, but – ugh – brain surgery is disgusting to watch, even when it's only pretendy.

If only work didn't get in the way of my personal life
(Series 16, ep. 20 'Anything You can Do' by Dana Fainaru 25.2.14)

Thanks to the fluid staffing configurations of Holby, Jonny Mac is now King of All the Nurses on Darwin. That's him, Bonnie and a handful of mostly non-speaking extras (though the one with the blonde ponytail gets to say "Thank you" or "Yes" when it's her birthday). It's a hefty responsibility and with it comes a new set of scrubs in "hunter green." "Straight from the garden centre," according to Jac. Jonny thought she just couldn't handle the fact that he was now at the same level as her – and anything she can do, he can do better. Let's have a parachute stitching contest and we'll see if he's right about that.

The thing is, he can actually be helpful when he gets the chance. He had an excellent idea involving a diathermy loop in theatre, and when he and Jac work together on either work things or baby-related things, they're a very good team. The problem is, with Emma just about ready to leave hospital, they haven't quite negotiated how life is going to be. At least they admitted as much by the end of the episode.

I hate to admit it, but I felt a bit sorry for That Bonnie Creature. She can see that her hold on Jonny's affections is a bit precarious, but she still gives the occasional bit of good advice about him having to work as a team with Jac for Emma's sake. As a nurse, I'm less impressed with her. When two patients went AWOL, Bonnie's response was that she was a nurse and not a security guard. "We don't assume our patients are going to run out on us." Hello? Has she not noticed that hardly a week goes by when a bed isn't suddenly and mysteriously empty and nurses have to jog from toilet to car park to basement to Linden Cullen Memorial Shrubbery to retrieve their patient? In this case the patients only got as far as the grassy interface between the car park and the LCMS, which is a shame because it's been a while since we saw the Tara Lo Memorial Water Feature.

On AAU, Dr Posh was acting all posh again and booking himself a trip to Cuba with his mother's air miles. Raf, who is apparently intent on waging a one-man class war against his privileged colleague, pointed out that Posh had missed 17 basic skills from his log book. Posh said he'd done them all, but he hadn't written them down. Obviously this wasn't good enough, so he had to enlist Adele's help to get all 17 ticked off by the end of the day so he wouldn't miss his flight. In return, he promised to take Adele to dinner. The fact that he had no intention of doing so ("She'll take a rain check") possibly proves that I was a bit previous last week in deciding he was quite nice really. Raf called him a "Lazy, inconsiderate, over-indulged prat," which I think is a bit harsh, but only a bit. I'm wondering what Raf's deal is. Is he harbouring secret romantic yearnings for his junior colleague? Or has his past been blighted by Dickensian maltreatment of his poor-but-honest family by some rich baron or other? I'm sure we'll find out eventually.

On Keller there was some kidney transplanting to do. Despite Ric and Serena being perfectly handy at this sort of thing, someone called Catherine O'Malley was drafted in to do it and Zosia was drafted in to help her. This was basically so Selfie and Zosia could have another run-in, when it turned out that Catherine was (a) of the cut-them-up-and-ask-questions-later school of surgery and (b) was having a romantic "thing" with Selfie.

A kitten, a birthday and a loose cannon

(Series 16, ep. 21 'Instinct' by Patrick Homes 4.3.14)

Keller has acquired a new little wing which was temporarily dubbed the "Tressler Neurological Wing," as it was funded by Dr Posh's dad. I say "temporarily," because by the end of the episode the nice new sign was being removed and Tressler flounced off after calling Selfie a loose cannon.

What had happened to provoke this reaction? It seems it was Selfie's habit of letting patients with a very poor chance of survival clutter up beds. It's "not a good look" for a showcase neurological facility, apparently. So it's goodbye to Tressler Sr., but what will Selfie do with himself now his neurological wing is no more? He'll have to find something else to do, because gazing mournfully at "Zoshy" and frightening Sacha are not full-time occupations, and he never seems to do much administrating.

In the part of Keller which is just plain old Keller, Dominic was dealing with a patient, Mr Bing, who had a kitten under his blanket. That's not a euphemism, it's a baby cat. The kitten was the clue to why the man was acting very strangely, and I diagnosed toxoplasmosis half an hour before anybody else did (that's worth a free muffin and frothy coffee at Pulses, surely?). The main point of this story was the spotlight that it shone on the somewhat weird Dominic, who got quite nasty with Mr Bing at one point. We didn't see whether Dominic actually stabbed him with a needle or not, but I wouldn't be surprised if he had. Especially not in view of the charming anecdote he told Digby later about the pet hamsters he had when he was a boy. One pair of hamsters had six babies, but when he and his brother put a different female hamster in the cage, she bit the heads off all the babies. Digby was aghast, but Dominic thought it was quite sensible behaviour. "When threatened, react violently – end threat," he said.

Maybe these are words Ric Griffin could reflect on in the coming weeks. His daughter, The Beautiful Jess, turned up unexpectedly, with her son in tow. This is the same son who was delivered by Jac Naylor and Chrissie Williams while Jess was still wearing leggings, but he seems to be a perfectly healthy child despite that.

Which is more than I can say for Jess, who went "Nnngh!!" and was diagnosed with a hernia. When the X-ray revealed old, healed fractures and Jess told Ric she'd left her husband, he put two and two together and made a promise: "If he comes anywhere near you… (long dramatic pause accompanied by Intense Stare)… I'll kill him."

A similar fate might befall That Bonnie Creature when Jac finds out that Bonnie squashed her motorbike with her silly little car (which she was driving rather recklessly considering it's a hospital car park where there are generally at least three people collapsed on the ground at any given time). The rather wonderful Denise Black was playing a lung cancer patient who had a penchant for giving out advice via tarot card readings. She predicted disappointment for Bonnie, which came true because Jonny had forgotten (or didn't know about) her birthday and Jac thwarted her plans for a romantic getaway to the Lake District by letting Jonny have Emma for the weekend. I kind of lost track of who was supposed to be looking after Emma when and why, because I was too busy wondering why Jac was getting involved in scrapping over Jonny. I know he's the father of her child and blah blah, but it's really time she moved on.

The thin line between love and hate

(Series 16, ep. 22 'Exit Strategy Part 1' by Robert Goldsbrough 11.3.14)

Ricin had been discovered in the ED. Or was it a raisin? There was some linguistic confusion, but the upshot was that emergency patients had to be channelled towards other wards (rather than to the Mythical St James's) while Charlie implemented a quarantine-type situation. As RoboNurse5000 strode around with a clipboard acting like she was Deputy CEO rather than queen of nurses (she's presumably passed the HR woman's test as we haven't heard anything since), Selfie said he thought it was about time the ED had a consultant who could whip it into shape. We have seen the future, people, and her name is Connie Beauchamp.

But, with all the extra bodies arriving in AAU, it was all too easy for Jess's nasty husband David to turn up and persuade her that, even though she'd had her operation moments before and was still groggy from anaesthetic, it was time she legged it away from the hospital. So off they went in his car, hotly pursued by Ric (also in a car – he's not as fast as he used to be on foot). Seatbelts, emergency braking and freshly inserted surgical stitches don't mix, and pretty soon Jess had become as unzipped as PLA Jr's purse in Topshop. Ric caught up with them, there was a bit of an altercation and Jess ended up running David over. Ric and Jess dashed back to Holby so Serena could fix Jess up again. Soon afterwards, David was brought in with a ruptured spleen and a policeman who was worried about MRSA. "We run an incredibly clean ward," purred Mary-Claire, enjoying the fact that she had the best line of the night, "but I could find you a dirty little corner if you asked me nicely." Ric obviously doesn't want to see his daughter sent dahhhn for running over her abusive ex, so he owned up to doing it himself. Oh, Ric. Such noble self-sacrifice.

Let's haul ourselves up the stairs (or even take the lift) to the lofty heights of Darwin, where the "love triangle" of JonBonJac is grinding on. If a triangle can grind. This week's development saw Bonnie get all cross and anxious because Jonny seemed to be getting on too well with Jac. "How can I compete with her being the mother of your child and all that?" she wailed (I'm paraphrasing) in the Linden Cullen Memorial Shrubbery. Simple – by becoming Mrs Maconie. Jonny dropped to one knee to propose in Holby's second most romantic location (after Rodolfo's). I wonder if Jac will get to be a bridesmaid when she, Bonnie, takes him, Jonny, to be her lawful wedded etc. She would probably rather be force-fed confetti with a dirty fork.

On Keller there isn't a love triangle, but there is a thin line between love and hate-type situation still going on between Selfie and Selfette, or Dr March as she prefers to be known. I really think we should get a petition going to get Psych Sharon back from wherever in America it was that she went, because if anyone is in urgent need of counselling it's Zosia. Just a glimpse of her father is enough to make her go all tantrumy and start throwing her toys and her stethoscope out of her pram. She took her resentment of the way he handled her mother's death to another level this week, when she had a disagreement with him over a patient's care. Deciding that he was putting funding issues above the patient's interests, she incited the patient's militant granddaughter to shift him (the patient, not Selfie) to a different hospital (predictably they only got as far as the car park) and then to put in a formal complaint against Selfie.

The one with the nude portrait of Serena

(Series 16, ep. 23 'Exit Strategy Part 2' by Joe Ainsworth 18.3.14)

This is going to be a quickie, and late too, thanks to me being in the middle of packing to move house and having internet that works about as often as the HR woman on Holby.

This episode was part 2 of the one started last week and continued with the triple shocking storylines of Jess running her husband over and Ric taking the blame, Zosia making a formal complaint against her father, and Jonny's out-of-the-blue marriage proposal to Bonny.

Starting with the JonBonJac situation… Mo is going to be Jonny's best man, which is excellent news because you couldn't think of anyone better to make a speech and arrange a stag do (plus, Jonny doesn't have any other friends). On the downside, Discretion is not Mo's middle name, so it wasn't long before Jac found out. Was she ruffled or bothered at all? Well, yes she was. But apparently not as R and B as Jonny was – he did his best to make Jac beg him not to marry That Bonnie Creature and marry her instead, but she didn't, because she's Jac (and he isn't Joseph. I'll never give up on Joseph, you know). So the wedding of the year is still on, Rodolfo's is booked (or it should be) and Mo is after ideas for her speech. It's just a shame that Jonny doesn't seem to know a great deal about his bride-to-be.

It's a mistake to go into a marriage without fully knowing what you're getting into. Just ask Jess Kilburn nee Griffin, who found herself with her guts hanging out, her abusive husband on life support and her father possibly facing a manslaughter charge on her behalf. I bet she didn't see all that coming when she said "I do." Frankly, it would have been easier for all concerned if the abusive husband had just died, and when he started going "Nnngh!" and only Ric was in the room, Ric hesitated a good long while before calling the crash team. In the end he did what his conscience told him he must do, but he also knew that he had to get Jess away, so he asked Selfie for a few months sabbatical while he gets Jess settled in an undisclosed location with her son. Selfie had a look in the "Fluid Staffing Configurations of Holby Handbook" and said of course, off you pop, it won't be any problem to fill a consultant surgeon/head of AAU job with no notice at all.

On Keller, it was round two of March v Self, and to cut a long story short, Self won in the sense that a disciplinary panel concluded that he'd acted professionally and she'd acted like a petulant teenager. Really we didn't need a disciplinary panel to tell us that. Almost every episode involving Saucer at the moment seems to require her to decide a patient needs a psych evaluation, and then discover they actually have a neurological problem. It was the same again this week, but the patient was a vicar who had sexual urges towards the radiant Serena Campbell. I'm not sure whether that really requires a psych evaluation, because she's lovely, but the nude drawing he did of her on the wall of the Linden Cullen Temple of Anguish was a bit disturbing. It was done in a sketchy sort of style, apart from the eyes – they were unnervingly realistic. It looked like someone had cut peepholes in the wall and real eyes were looking through. It certainly livened up the usually drab LCTA, though.

Henpecked

(Series 16, ep. 24 'Green Ink' by Paul Matthew Thompson 25.3.14)

Due to moving house and living in a circumstance that looks like an episode of Extreme Hoarders before the tidying people come in, I only got time to sit down and watch Tuesday's Holby last night and my recollections about the episode might be a bit confuzzled due to having to watch it through a canyon between cardboard boxes accompanied by the faint smell of cat poo (our traumatised cat had decided the new sofa was the best place to go to the toilet and the smell is taking days to shift).

So… Predictably enough, Bonnie has turned into Bridezilla and her head is full of wedding cake (metaphorically-speaking) and she wants everyone to share her happiness (say that aloud in a kind of breathless squeak for the full Bonnie effect). This includes Jac, because they're going to be all mums together as far as Emma's concerned, aren't they (grrr…)? So Jac is invited to the wedding, but obviously wouldn't be seen dead at the hen night. Or would she?

Yes she would, you know, and it provided an opportunity for her to tell Bonnie what she really thinks of her. This wasn't as much fun as I'd have expected it to be, mainly because I just can't accept the idea that Jac would care so much about Jonny – who has his sweet side but is increasingly often a complete arse. Jac can do (and has done) so much better.

On AAU, Dr Posh had a hangover and having to poke at a pair of gangrenous hands didn't help. What did help was the hangover cure administered by consultant pharmacist Dr Amy Teo. And Dr Teo herself, who was exactly Dr Posh's type – female, with a pulse and not Adele (poor Adele). I don't think we've seen a pharmacist on Holby before, apart from the occasions when you see a non-speaking extra hand a bundle of Camoxidan through a hatch, so when Dr Teo suddenly found her skills to be essential to every scene on AAU, there was obviously going to be more to her than met the eye. Unfortunately she's not a serial killer – she's only the wife of Raf. The one who makes the croissanty treats and packs them in Tupperware (Amy, not Raf).

For a serial killer, or at least someone with a psychopathic tendency, we need look no further than Keller, where Dom is going all "Mwah ha ha!" on us and only Digby has noticed. I have to say I was worried for Diggers when he followed Dom down to the basement. Nothing good ever happens there (not since Sacha dismantled his den), and finding Dom in the wet lab clutching a scalpel and threatening to self-harm might turn out to be only the start of Digby's problems.

Three little words

(Series 16, ep. 25 'The Cruellest Month' by Martin Jameson 1.4.14)

Jonny and Bonnie's wedding day. What could possibly go wrong? Given that the groom's heart didn't seem to be entirely in it, there was scope for quite a lot to go wrong. A jilting at the altar seemed the most obvious choice, and when Jac contrived to have Jonny assist her on a tricky piece of surgery on the bride's brother, of all people, it looked like there was every chance he'd see the error of his ways and decide he wanted Jac.

There was a lot to love about this episode, but one thing bothered me a bit – even assuming that no one wanted to give Bonnie the news that her brother was undergoing heart surgery in case it spoiled the wedding, didn't she notice he wasn't there? Didn't anybody else? And wouldn't she have rather been at her brother's bedside?

Anyway… while the wedding party was assembled at the registry office, with Bonnie looking gorgeous (possibly only just outshone by Mo), back at Holby Jac was taking Decisive Action. The action which has worked on Jonny in the past involved pouncing on him and slamming him against a shelf full of bed pans, so she had a go at that and was a bit flustered when he pushed her away. Then we got an insight into their thinking (something which has puzzled me for the last several episodes, I must admit). "What am I to you, other than some kind of twisted security blanket?" he asked her. Her reply: "My whole life, I've never had anyone like you." In other words, even though she's known the love of the quite remarkable Joseph Byrne, there's something about Jonny that speaks to her soul. That thing, I think, is the emotional straightforwardness of him. That's the very thing that finally kept them apart, because in his world view, if you love somebody you can tell them, in words of one syllable. No matter how he tried to get her to say it, she couldn't say "I love you." And Bonnie, bless her, was having a hard time stopping herself from saying it (thinking it was bad luck on a wedding day), because she's one of these uncomplicated types, too.

So he chose Bonnie, and off he dashed by taxi to the wedding. If only he'd had a fiver in his wallet, he wouldn't have had to ask her for the cash. And if only she'd remembered her Green Cross Code, she wouldn't have walked into the road while delving into her little bag and not looking where she was going. If only the lorry driver had slowed down in anticipation of a distracted bride crossing the street… It was an absolute shocker and I had to rewind and watch it twice. Thanks to Tumblr, if you're that way inclined you can watched Bonnie getting run over on a two second repeat, which does lessen the shock a bit and actually becomes quite hilarious.

Jonny's anguish made it clear he really had loved Bonnie and she wasn't just a cheap Jac substitute, but my worry is that with Bonnie out of the way, the writers will drag the whole Jac/Mac saga on and on and on. It would be nice for Jac to have a story line that didn't involve romantic/parenting tussles with Jonny Mac.

Comic relief was supplied on AAU by the magnificent Serena. When Adele told a patient whose life was being ruined by snoring that she'd read in a magazine at the hairdressers that singing was a cure ('Roar' by Katy Perry was attempted), Serena did some research. She found that vocal exercises may indeed help, but they had to be quite specific. Her demonstration, which sounded like an operatic version of the start of 'Living On A Prayer' by Bon Jovi ("Unga-unga-unga-unga"), was hilarious. She has a very pleasing voice, and I think a trio with Sacha and Dr Posh needs to be arranged ASAP.

Keller is where we tend to go these days for a bit of something dark and twisted, but Dominic was more or less behaving himself this week. The twistedness happened to Zosia, who was having a hard day anyway because it was the anniversary of her mother's death. What you don't want when you're drowning your sorrows at Albie's is for a patient's socially awkward brother to attempt to spike your drink with something to help you "relax" and "go with the flow." She definitely didn't want to go with the particular flow he had in mind, so she swapped the drinks and later found him fitting in the car park. I can't remember whether she got suspended again or not, because I was still reeling from the double effects of Bonnie's death and Serena's singing.

Indispensable

(Series 16, ep. 26 'The Win' by Bede Blake 8.4.14)

It's all ready to kick off on AAU, with an epic love triangle of Hanssen /Shah /Douglas proportions (read that any way you see fit) about to ensue, as Dr Posh and Dr Smug (aka Raf) fight over Mrs Smug (aka Dr Amy Teo).

Now they have a Consultant Pharmacist on AAU, no pharmaceutical can be dispensed without Amy having to worry about contra-indications and whatnot. It's practically criminal that they've been dishing out Camoxidan left, right and centre for years without as much as running it past (and usually through) Best Nurse Eddi McKee first.

So Amy was on hand at the bedside of Posh's patient, a former glamour model (whose image had apparently enlivened many a lonely midnight hour while Dr Posh was at boarding school), giving out advice and prescriptions and looking a bit queasy. There's usually only one reason women in soaps look queasy, but she's not pregnant. We can still file it under "hormones," though, as she's going through IVF. That and being married to Dr Smug is all a bit of a strain, so how lucky Dr Posh was on hand with his blue ("blacker than black") dinner suit and his suave ways picked up at boarding school when he wasn't hunched over a photo of his glamour model patient.

Moving swiftly on to Keller, we find Dr Dominic Copeland apparently doing some decent doctoring, and making excellent work of sorting out the troubled medical and social history of a patient (a touching performance from Scott Chambers). I'm getting very fond of Dr Dom – he's got this cute, innocent face and he walks as if he was propelled by a brisk breeze. And he's quite probably a psychopath. The way he took every scrap of his patient's tragic story and pretended to Digby and Zosia that it had all happened to him was quite delicious.

Darwin was naturally engulfed in grief and mourning, what with it only being a week since Bonnie was mown down by a big truck on her wedding day. The Linden Cullen Temple of Anguish had been festooned in small brochures with her face on them, in preparation for a memorial service. Jonny Mac wasn't going. He didn't want to think about Bonnie being dead. Even Elliot Hope, who made a speech, didn't want to think about Bonnie being dead, although the best anecdote he could come up with about her being alive was something rather generic that could have been about anybody. But hey, that was Bonnie for you – just the gal next door.

Not like that horrid Jac Naylor woman, a person so toxic she destroys everything she comes into contact with, according to Jonny. Yes, I get it, he's just lashing out. But he announced that he's going to take his lashing out a step further and go for custody of Emma. My advice to Jac: take Emma and head for the hills. Or, more accurately, fells. Joseph will look after you until Jonny has had time to see the staff counsellor and calm down a bit.

Not so smug now

(Series 16, ep. 27 'Cold Heart, Warm Hands' by Nick Fisher 15.4.14)

When I said last week that the Smug/Smug/Posh love triangle was like the Hanssen/Shah/Douglas one, there was another parallel I wasn't thinking about at the time. Dr Smug, AKA Dr Rafaello Di Lucca (which is possibly Italian for "smug") is reminding me worryingly of Sahira Shah the Registrah. Remember when everyone used to stand round gasping at her parachute stitching? Remember when she had that exciting new initiative where she would sit in the back of a converted ambulance in Tesco's car park and wait till someone had a heart attack, and then operate on them as they hurtled back to Holby over speed bumps just because she could (something like that, anyway)? Remember how loathsome that all became?

Raf Smug is rather like that. People get tearful just at the thought of what he can do with his ECMO pump (he has a shop-bought one now and doesn't have to make do with the one he made out of Tupperware and tin foil). This week he and his little pump brought a frozen man back to life and a nation sobbed and cheered, while women swooned and felt inspired to go back to medical school so they could be that brilliant as well.

Luckily there were people who were a bit less impressed. One of them was Dr Posh, who looks at Dr Smug and sees the word RIVAL hovering over his head. Mo also failed to go all fangirl with him, because she has ninja level surgery skills (though I'm worried that the two of them are being lined up as future love interests. I do not want this to happen. The only man for Mo is Mr T [or Sacha, if he stopped being stroppy/serious and got back to being cuddly again]). Mrs Dr Amy Smug was also unimpressed, mainly because Dr Smug has a problem no amount of ECMO pumps can solve. Even though he can coax life out of almost dead people, there is no life in his sperm. A bout of mumps caught in Malaysia has all but ruined his hopes of being a father.

This upset Amy to such a degree that she was forced to go out to the Linden Cullen Memorial Shrubbery and punch some trees. That's no way to treat a relaxing green facility. Amy wants to go down the sperm donor route, but Dr Smug isn't prepared to bring up someone else's baby. Even if it has the lovely blue eyes and singing skills of Dr Posh? I fear that's where we may be headed, as he was lurking in the background of nearly every scene and seems determined to win the hand of the fair Amy. Will he be able to resist showing off the fabulous quality of his sperm?

If I dwell on this too long I may need to chunder into a cardboard bowler hat, as Dominic so nicely described the cardboard sick bowl he handed to his patient, Kevin. Then he proceeded to whip it away again so Kevin vommed down his hospital gown instead. This was because he recognised Kevin as someone who'd bullied him when he was at school, back in the days when he was called Darren. The kids called him "Gay-Dar" and this was part of the reason he changed his name to Dominic. And because it sounds posher than Darren.

Dominic is a brilliantly twisted individual. As the "big wheel of karma" had put Kevin in his care, he used every sadistic opportunity to get revenge on him and even enlisted Zosia to help. Maybe it wouldn't have been so bad if we had the idea that Kevin was really a bully... but he certainly didn't give that impression. In fact when he was telling Digby about how lovely Dom/Darren's mother was, he seemed rather sweet. Digby was confused, though. Wasn't Dominic's mother supposed to be dead, according to the tragic story Dominic told them last week? A quick Whippet Search was all it took to confirm that Carole Copeland was alive, well and Employee of the Month at her local supermarket.

Digby confronted Dominic with this information, and with a casual shrug Dominic admitted he'd lied about having a dead mum because Zosia had a real dead mum. Digby's face when he heard that was a picture – shocked and quite gleeful that perhaps now Zosia would believe what a psycho Dominic really is. She was definitely cross – but she ended up going to Albie's with Dom for a post-shift pint regardless. Poor Digby – what does a guy have to do?

Jac and Jonny were in no mood for a post-shift pint, though they had a patient who was so annoying he'd drive anyone to drink. Alan thought he had post-profusion syndrome, or "pump head syndrome" – mental impairment caused by being on heart bypass during previous surgery. Jonny and Elliot didn't think this was even a "thing," but Jac did. It turned out Alan was only using it as an excuse to try and get off some criminal charges. It was all an excuse for a bit of brains-speak about lawyers, as Jonny was still threatening to take Jac to court for custody of Emma. Elliot attempted to calm things down, and right at the end it seemed that Jonny was maybe ready to discuss things with Jac – but she'd misread the way things were going and had already instructed a "Rottweiler in kitten heels" of a solicitor. I can't wait to meet her.

Friend of Selfie? You're in

(Series 16, ep. 28 'Battle Lines' by Julia Gilbert 22.4.14)

I know I overuse the phrase "fluid staffing configurations," but they were once again at play in this episode, as Selfie's best mate Jesse Law was given a consultant anaesthetist job despite the fact that he had a dodgy CV and Serena didn't like him at all. He was the Sammy Davis Jr to Selfie's Dean Martin, and that was the main thing. "Get yourself up to HR," Selfie told him, hilariously trying to pretend they actually do have a HR department. Even Jesse, who'd only been in the hospital for five minutes, looked like he wasn't buying that one.

I wanted to like Jesse, because Don Gilet is very attractive and I loved him in EastEnders, but it may be difficult because his character is a bit of a prat, on first glimpse. Though he does call Selfie "Selfie." When Digby disagreed with Selfie and Lawsy about a patient's treatment (and Serena agreed with Digby, so obviously he was right), Jesse blindfolded Digby and frightened him on the Parapet of Persuasion (it's that elevated walkway we haven't seen for a while). This was some kind of macho initiation test thingy, and the upshot is that Digby now fancies being a neurosurgeon and being Frank Sinatra. RoboNurse2000 and Sacha agreed that this would be a short-lived phase and I can only hope they're right.

The big shock on Darwin was that Jac's mother turned up. This didn't happen till right at the end, though. For the rest of the time there was the far less shocking – indeed tedious – Jac v Jonny tug-of-love (you never hear that phrase any more, do you?) for baby Emma. Frankly, I don't care. Jonny is so spitefully loathsome that anything that gets him out of the way is fine by me. It would almost be the best outcome if he got sole custody, as long as he promised to be a stay-at-home dad and not bother the hospital ever, under any circumstance.

To get out of the way of her warring colleagues – and who could blame her? – Mo volunteered to spend the shift on AAU, where she had to cope with her sister Adele and a radio DJ patient. The DJ had the best line of the night – saying that he preferred to be treated by Serena rather than Mo he said, "It's nothing to do with your 'ethnicity.' I've been on tour with the Four Tops." He liked Mo's voice and said it had a "soft, velvety timbre" that would be good for radio. As luck would have it, he had a mate who was looking to fill a slot for an on-air medical agony aunt. Mo was quite tempted – and she's going to be very cross when she finds Adele got in ahead of her. Especially as Adele is about as qualified to be a medical agony aunt as I am.

Jac is tormented and Posh pounces

(Series 16, ep. 29 'Wild Child' by David Bowker 29.4.14)

I'm going to start with Darwin, because frankly I've had enough. I get that the essence of drama is conflict. I get that Rosie Marcel is a brilliant actress and Jac Naylor is a wonderful, complex, contradictory character the fans love. I understand that, for these reasons, Jac has to suffer. But please, enough already. Jac has gone through a pregnancy that had a high possibility of ending with the death of the baby. Her relationship with the baby's father has been volatile, to say the least, and for most of the pregnancy he was with another woman and the pair of them were hardly the essence of tact and sensitivity. The baby was born early, endured surgery when she was still tiny, but has survived. Jac had problems bonding with her but now seems to be fine.

Apparently Jac still hasn't suffered enough, so now we have Jonny Mac, becoming more odious by the week, threatening to take the baby away from her. And then last week her mother turned up.

"What's the scam this time? Have you come back for the other kidney?" Jac asked her. Paula said she'd come back to show Jac some photos of her alleged father, who is now dead, and to have a quick check-up because she's been having breathing problems. She turned out to have incurable lung cancer (which was initially missed because for some reason Elliot Hope was being bumbling and useless). Was this a chance for mother and daughter to bond before it was too late? Paula seemed willing to give it a go, but from experience Jac knows that Paula only bonds when she wants something. In case she was in any doubt, a patient's daughter was on hand to speak her brains. Against the current evidence, this woman's cuddly-seeming brain-damaged dad used to be abusive and violent. "You can't build a better future by denying the past," the daughter told Jac. So Jac gave Paula £20,000 to go away. Money which Paula promptly gave to Jonny to help him win the custody battle and take Emma away from Jac.

I honestly don't think I can watch any more scenes with Jonny in them. The sight of his gleeful triumph at the end of the episode made me want to do all sorts of violence to him, and the fact that he's acquired a sidekick who has the capacity to hurt Jac more than anyone else in the world has made him worse. Watching Jac basically being bullied (at the start of the episode it seemed that all the nurses were deliberately ignoring Jac to show solidarity with the pathetic Jonny) does not make me feel entertained. It makes me feel cross and irritated, but not entertained. Where's a rampaging patient with a scalpel when you need one? I just want Jonny gone so that Jac can concentrate on kick-ass surgery and riding her motorbike and being brilliant.

Parenting issues were also to the fore on AAU, where Mr and Mrs Dr Smug got the news that they'd been accepted by their private IVF hospital of choice – hurrah! – but the appointment was three months away – boo! This led to a lot of bickering in side rooms and corridors. Raf is allegedly the love of Amy's life, but I can't actually picture them ever having fun together. They look like they've spent every day since meeting each other being snappy and hostile and having joyless "trying for a baby" sex. Raf thought having a three month break from the trying for a baby thing was a good idea. They could concentrate on "finding themselves" again.

Wherever the Smugs are, Dr Posh is not far away, stirring the situation with his little silver spoon. "What are you looking so smug about?" Amy asked him at one point, perhaps confusing him with her husband. Posh pulled some strings and got their appointment brought forward, so the relentless grind of trying for a baby can recommence without the finding each other break that Raf wanted.

Raf was not happy about this, and Amy was not happy that he wasn't happy. He was looking all cute and fatherly as well, getting on brilliantly with a little girl who'd spent her early years chained to a radiator and was therefore understandably a tad apprehensive about strangers – apart from strangers who were required to dramatically demonstrate that they'd be a brilliant father.

The upshot of this was that Raf had to go away on a business trip, and Amy ended up in Albie's in the willing arms of Dr Posh. Is this going to result in a Posh-Smug pregnancy shock-type situation? I expect so.

Amy is a man-magnet, but she's a mere amateur compared to Zosia, whose date from the previous night turned up on Keller in a bit of an embarrassing situation. Not only had he done his back in during his encounter with Dr March, but he also had a perma-stiffy thanks to taking too much Viagra in order to keep up with her demands. Even Dominic, "the world's leading authority on men's bits," had never seen anything like it. He actually fainted while it was being fixed (which involved a large syringe). Between having his man-parts syringed and his back operated on, this unfortunate patient had the chance to observe the body language of Zosia and the man she refers to as "Uncle Jesse." They fancy each other, he reckoned. They had a laugh about that in the locker room afterwards as he tried not to notice that her bra was showing and she pretended she wasn't admiring his manly frame when he took his shirt off. She really is going to have to stop calling him "Uncle Jesse" very soon, or it's going to get all types of weird.

The only person who cares about you is you

(Series 16, ep. 30 'My Name is Joe' by Johanne McAndrew & Elliot Hope 6.5.14)

Jules Knight (Dr Harry Tressler-Posh) must get quite excited when he gets a new script. Which Dr Posh will he be this week? The up-his-own-bum self-important rich kid? Or the misunderstood wants-to-be-a good-doctor-and-forget-I'm-rich version? My personal favourite, the one who likes a bit of banter with Mary-Claire and has a sly sense of humour? The sleazy loverboy perving around after confused pharmacists and just about anyone with a pulse? Or just a tosser? At least he's never going to get bored by some tedious old linear character development.

This week we got the tosser version, when Dr Dominic "Possibly Psycho Yet Adorable" Copeland was assigned to AAU. Everyone bears a grudge against Dr Dom for the Malick business, but Dr Posh went out of his way to be snarky and unpleasant. I forgot to mention that in most of his guises he's competitive anyway, so he wasted no time in trying to get Dom into Serena's bad books. Flatter her by mentioning she's wearing Chanel perfume, he advised. Dom did. "It's Dior. Any gay man worth his salt would know that," Serena said.

She had a point, and maybe it was a lesson for Dominic to follow his own nose rather than what other people were telling him. Unfortunately when he tried to put this into practice literally, he ended up with said nose being broken by an angry patient who was trying to escape in a waiting taxi.

By the end of the episode, Serena had rather warmed to our Dom, and even got a bottle of wine out and kicked off her shoes. "Jimmy Choos?" said Dom, wisely using his observational skills and reading the label.

While Dominic was away, Zosia and Digby were left to play on Keller without him. For some reason Digby has taken up magic tricks and was trying to impress Selfie (I think it was all part of this Rat Pack bonding thing with Selfie and Uncle Jesse). Zosia, meanwhile, had a patient to look after who was an old Polish war hero. Or was he? There was a possibility he'd been in the SS (I confess this made me giggle – I know it shouldn't, but I kept thinking of the episode of *Friday Night Dinner* where the eccentric Jewish dad gives his son a book about the SS for his birthday. "Weapons of the SS… heroes of the SS… It *is* a bit SS-y").

Zosia is supposed to have this fascination for psychiatry that makes her want to delve into the minds of her patients, and being half Polish herself she was more interested in this patient than most, but she really has no clue how to handle people and invariably ends up upsetting them on a scale from mildly miffed to seriously traumatised. This particular encounter ended up in her failing to get a DNR properly signed and acted upon, so that Sacha ended up resuscitating the patient in theatre against his wishes. This made Sacha go particularly shouty and Zosia was once again sent home early. I don't think she's done a full shift for months.

On Darwin, Jonny Mac was bonding away with Paula, who is biologically if not socially and emotionally the mother of the glorious Jac Naylor. However, it seems that he was unaware of most of Jac's history and accepted Paula's version of events. When he found out that Jac had given Paula one of her kidneys, he thought it must mean they used to be close. Jac soon put him right. As she told a patient, "The only person who cares about you is you." That could be – and probably is – her life motto.

Jonny, however, is still willing to take Paula's money if it means getting Emma away from the evil influence of the terrible Jac. *Bangs head on desk* There may be a glimmer of hope next week though – the episode preview hints that there may be an "end to hostilities." Every digit I possess is crossed.

I thought you would understand

(Series 16, ep. 31 'No Apologies' by Anna McPartlin 13.5.14)

The conclusion to last week's story about Joe, the patient who may or may not have been a former SS guard, started fairly comically, with Zosia having forced Digby to stay up all night researching the man's background on th'internet. Zosia reported their findings to Sacha, who held the opinion that a patient's background should have no bearing on their medical care. "I thought you would understand," Zosia pouted. Because he's Jewish, she expected him to have the same knee-jerk reaction as her.

But because Sacha is Jewish, and because he's played by the wonderful Bob Barrett (who hasn't been given a lot to do post-Chrissie but was absolutely at the top of his game here), the story turned into something far more subtle and moving.

The scene between Sacha and Joe as the old man lay dying, having already confessed his past to his beloved granddaughter, was a masterful piece of writing (from newbie Anna McPartlin) and acting (from Bob Barrett, and Julian Glover as Joe). Resisting the cliche of a deathbed transformation, Joe held on to his belief that what he did had been the right thing – he wasn't simply "just following orders," he was actually proud of what he'd done.

Nobody would have blamed Sacha if he'd walked away, but he stayed and did what was physically necessary for his patient, while not letting him avoid how much Sacha – and the world – loathed what he'd done. As Sacha said, in the end he was the better man, even though it took every bit of humanity and every bit of his medical training to keep him by that bedside. It was an amazing scene. I was in tears.

Comic relief was provided by the lovely Effanga sisters. Mo accidentally overheard her sister on a radio show, giving advice as "Dr Mo." The advice was rubbish, until Mo rescued her with some swift text messages to ensure she wasn't telling patients with potential heart problems just to pop a Gaviscon and forget about it. Adele's career as a radio agony aunt was pretty short-lived.

Mo was still hiding in AAU, which was sensible of her because in Darwin a familiar story was once again playing itself out. Baby Emma was rushed into hospital but turned out to be fine. Jac and Jonny stood on the other side of the glass smiling at her and looking a bit tearful, and decided, as they usually do when they're at Emma's bedside, that they should really be more cooperative with each other for her sake. Jonny had finally realised what a nasty piece of work Jac's mother is, too. So all was going to be well. Until – there's always an "until" in this storyline – Jonny's phone rang and it was Paula wanting to know how to work the burglar alarm in his flat. The cad! He's only got the Kidney Thief living with him! So as swiftly as mediation was agreed, it's now off again.

Elliot fails to thrust

(Series 16, ep. 32 'Keeping Mum' by Joe Ainsworth 22.5.14)

What's wrong with Elliot? He's making mistakes and forgetting things and generally behaving like the bumbling old incompetent he briefly turned into when he was almost shipped off to The Mythical St James's. A quick blood test revealed it was only a bit of a virus, so phew – but at the end of the episode Elliot looked, frankly, worried. There's more to it than just a spot of man-flu, it seems.

He was under pressure, too, thanks to Selfie's insistence on selling the Herzig 5 to the world. Not in an online store sort of sense ("Dragons, I'm here today to ask for a million pounds in exchange for a 5% equity share in my new online artificial heart business"), but more in a "great PR for the hospital" type of way. Anyhoo, Elliot was pencilled in to pop a Herzig 5 into Mandy Jordache from *Brookside*(Sandra Maitland), who had a dicky heart and had started being relentlessly happy since she had a TIA. Anyone old enough to remember *Brookside* would know that relentlessly happy is quite an unnatural state for Mandy Jordache, so everyone was concerned.

Elliot promised her husband that he wouldn't go ahead with the surgery without consulting him first, given that Mandy was perhaps not in the most sensible frame of mind to give consent (Psych Sharon would have been there like a shot in former times, but the Psych department is currently being run by invisible non-speaking extras). Swayed by Selfie, Elliot went back on his word and also made a few more big mistakes during the episode. Luckily, Jac and Jonny had his back (apart from when he forgot to do a broncoscopy he'd promised to do for Jac).

This was the first episode in months in which Jac and Jonny shared a lot of scenes and didn't once mention Emma or get snippy with each other. It was quite like the old days, in fact. Some of their scenes were really funny – such as Jac's advice to Elliot: "Mr Self might require a little more… thrust, if you're going to be his poster boy," and Jonny telling the patient's husband that Elliot was the Lionel Messi of cardiac surgery. This set up the line, "I thought you said he was Messi." "He is."

We're going to need them to pull together if there's something properly wrong with dear Elliot. They might even have to lure Mo back to the department she specialises in. This would come as a relief to Adele, because this week Mo was getting a bit full of herself, what with being a proper doctor with her own stethoscope and a proper radio agony auntie with her own headphones and everything. She was quite looking down her nose at lovely Adele, who is occupying the position formerly held by Chantelle as The Sunniest Staff Member in the NHS.

Serena had to juggle the demands of Selfie (who wanted a report on his desk by the close of play, like he usually does), her mother (who wanted a cup of coffee and a chin wag) and her patient (who wanted more access to his son). When there's a child running around the corridors of Holby, tragedy can't be far behind, and it ended up with the father on the roof being talked down by Serena, Colette and the child's mother – until the son dashed up to give his dad a hug and they both toppled off. Luckily it wasn't the big roof, it was one a bit lower down, so the son was okay once Serena had sorted his spleen out, but sadly the father will never walk again. On the upside, it did mean he got to stay in the family home, so every cloud has a silver lining.

I really loved this episode. It was a departure from some of the more tired recent story lines (Custodygate and Smug/Posh/Smug) and had plenty of Jac, the Effanga sisters and Serena. Serena blew on her coffee! Everybody does that in real life but nobody ever does it on a soap, and for that alone I love her.

Life finds a way

(Series 16, ep. 33 'Crush' by Glen Laker 27.5.14)

Where was Ric Griffin in this episode? He was behind the camera, as Hugh Quarshie had his first bash at directing.

Content-wise, we were back to Smug/Smug/Posh (which took a not completely unexpected twist) and Custodygate (which didn't). More amusingly, Mo has gone all showbiz and Adele has gone all Darwin.

The most engrossing storyline was Serena's. Her mum Adrienne reappeared, this time as a visitor, come to see her friend Roger, who was a patient. It quickly became clear that Adrienne was suffering from the Curse of the Holby Visitor – nine times out of ten they end up having something worse than the patient has. In this case, Adrienne was showing signs of dementia, which Selfie verified with a quiz after Adrienne nearly killed Roger by giving him soluble aspirin, which he was allergic to. It was clear that Adrienne was going to need support, and Serena was soon on the hunt for a nice care home. It's not that she doesn't love her mother and care about her – it was etched on her face that she does – but both mother and daughter are feisty, independent types. Serena was left with no choice but to have Adrienne move in with her for now – an arrangement which is bound to take its toll.

On AAU, Dr Amy Smug was feeling queasy, which wasn't helped by being leered at by Dr Posh every five minutes. It turns out she's pregnant (I know. Shocker. *blank expression*). Who's the daddy? Could one of Dr Raf Smug's inadequate sperms have hit the target? Or is Baby Smug the result of Amy's one night stand with Dr Posh when she was bladdered? Either way, the news has made Dr Smug go even smugger, but obviously this may be temporary. Meanwhile, Dr Posh is unaware that he may have sired a Smugette, but is busy blackmailing Amy to get her to get Raf to be nicer to him. Amy is so fed up with this she's considering moving to Denmark.

The best thing about the Baby Smug storyline is that it involved the very welcome appearance of Mr T, who was on AAU for a quick consult, had time to advise Amy on the likelihood of rubbish sperm doing the trick ("Life finds a way") and then had a little flirt with Mo. He should really try harder at this "flirting with Mo" business, because she really likes him but he's not very good at reading the signs.

Mo is going all showbiz thanks to her side job as "Dr Mo." I'm not entirely convinced that a weekly medical slot on a local radio station would seem quite that glamorous for a woman who spends her day job doing heart surgery, but that's just me and my muddled priorities. Whatever, it gives Mo the chance to swan about in fabulous frocks. Unfortunately, it also makes her very bitchy towards poor Adele, who took refuge in Darwin under the wing of Jonny Maconie. This also brought her face to face with the force of nature that is Jac Naylor. Possibly because she has Mo as a sister, Adele is completely unintimidated by Jac as a doctor or as a person. It's always funny to see Jac's face when she comes across someone who hasn't read the "We're all terrified of Ms Naylor" script – it's a lovely mixture of rage, confusion, amusement and respect.

A proper cad

(Series 16, ep. 34 'Collateral' by Dana Fainaru 3.6.14)

There's been a massive development in the Smug/Smug/Posh triangle! I can exclusively reveal that the Triangle will henceforth be known as Smug/Queasy/Posh, since Dr Amy Smug spent most of the episode gipping into her own mouth and unable to look a muffin in the face. Lightweight. By this stage of her pregnancy Jac was on a heady combination of chocolate and anchovies.

There's a sinister side to the triangle, too, as Dr Harry Posh (currently unaware that Dr Amy is pregnant because, unlike Selfie, he hasn't had his hands on thousands of pregnant women in his career yet) is blackmailing Amy. Basically she has to smooth the path of his career-haltingly troublesome relationship with Dr Raf Smug, or else Posh will spill the beans about their night of drunken lust. The cad! "I'm a proper cad," he told Amy. The proper cad!

As previously mentioned, Selfie knows at a glance that a woman is pregnant – it's just one of his billions of skills – so he twigged that the Smugs are multiplying and took Amy to Pulses for a heart-to-heart, where he also worked out that Posh might be the father. Just why he thought Pulses was the venue for a woman with a muffin aversion is a puzzle, because muffins are the only food they sell.

The upshot of this is that Amy has now taken it upon herself to mentor Dr Posh, in an effort to try and get him promotable, at which point he'll hopefully leave. It's obviously a plan which is doomed to fail, and would indeed be a ticking time bomb, if I could manage to care about any of the three of them.

AAU was getting a bit crowded, so Mo was back on Darwin this week. This meant she had to work with her sister, whom Jonny has taken under his wing as new best drinking buddy and trainee phlebotomist. They were looking after a patient who was totally star struck at the thought that Mo was the Actual Real Dr Mo Off Of The Radio. It's not been nice seeing Mo be all sarcastic and horrible to her sister, but I have enjoyed her diva moments – Chizzy Akudolu seemed to be having great fun swanning about in fancy frocks and shades and enjoying her stardom. It looks like she'll be toning it down now, though, as she turned down a fashion shoot so she could go and visit Mama Effanga for her birthday and admitted to Adele that being "Dr Mo" had enabled her to feel as confident as Adele always seems. I hadn't actually noticed Mo lacking in confidence previously, but maybe she hides it well.

On Keller, meanwhile, Zosia started the day badly when she scored 22% in a patients' survey of her bedside manner. The day ended with her slamming Uncle Jesse lustfully against the lockers – if she has a moment she could possibly analyse her need to slam men against things.

Bring your daughter to work day

(Series 16, ep. 35 'Masquerade' by Lucia Haynes 10.6.14)

Don't tell me Holby isn't educational. Aside from learning all manner of instantly forgettable stuff about crustaceans, I also discovered, via Jac Naylor and the power of Google, that *Gigglebiz* is a real TV series for kids. I'm no longer up on that sort of thing, what with PLA Jr being nearly 17 and that, so I had to check.

We learned a lot about Emma and her preferences, as Jac had sacked the third nanny in a row (for putting Emma to bed too early so Jac never saw her) and was forced to bring her daughter into work. The crèche was full. The crèche is always full, and if Selfie wasn't so busy building his empire and obsessing about Zosia, he might usefully employ himself in sorting out better crèche facilities.

No staff member's child has ever spent a day at Holby without going missing, but Jac was fairly confident in leaving Emma with Elliot while she was in theatre. Unfortunately, as we've glimpsed previously, Elliot isn't quite his usual self and he wandered off and left Emma to her own devices for a bit, during which time she promptly vanished. My money was on her being with Paula, who was in the hospital with pneumonia. Emma did end up with Paula, but that was via Jonny Mac after he found his daughter being looked after by Adele.

I can't actually believe I'm dwelling so long on what I could have quickly summarised as "Custodygate: the latest chapter." Basically, the court date is looming (and can't come soon enough for me), Paula is dying (ditto) and Jonny Mac continues to be an annoying whine-bag.

But the important question still remains – what is the matter with Elliot?

In the bowels of the hospital known as AAU, don't say the word "bowels" or Dr Amy Smug might well chunder on your shoes. Dr Harry Posh proved that he's not really cut out to be a doctor by not twigging that his colleague and former bed-mate is pregnant, but that's probably because he lives in a bubble which reflects his own ego back at him so sparklingly that he can't see much of the real world outside it. When Amy wasn't hurling into the nearest staff sink (nice), she was forging ahead with her scheme to mentor Harry within an inch of his life in an effort to get him qualified and promoted to Anywhere But Here. Would this really be the job of a consultant pharmacist? Anyway, it all went pear-shaped and now Serena has her eye on the pair of them.

Also on AAU, Essie – the granddaughter of the Nazi war criminal, who is now a nurse – is getting mysterious phone calls. This will be important next week.

Love was in the air on Keller. Zosia and Uncle Jesse are now very much An Item (it's not as weird as I expected it to be), but don't tell Selfie because he wouldn't like it. Digby didn't like it, either, but he was distracted by a pretty marine biologist, who turned out to be every bit as nerdy as him. It was a match made in heaven, and provided ample opportunities for Digby to demonstrate that he has the most beautiful smile in the NHS.

Surgeon or mother?

(Series 16, ep. 36 'Little Star' by Julia Gilbert 18.6.14)

I suspect this was an episode that was supposed to be a roller-coaster of emotions, but at the end of it the feeling I was left with was one of depression.

The climax of Custodygate didn't take place in court, but more appropriately perhaps in the Linden Cullen Memorial Shrubbery. Shortly before taking her last breath, the totally toxic Paula Burrows made sure that Jac's confidence in herself as a mother was fatally undermined. Jac told Jonny she was going to Stockholm (following a phone call from Hanssen – how I would love those two to have their own spin-off series) and therefore she was giving him the baby full-time. At this point he desperately tried to back-track and unsay all the horrible things he's said to her in an effort to get her to reconsider and to come to some co-parenting arrangement. At the start of the episode Sacha had reassured Jac that she wasn't a "heartless automaton," but Jonny has made the mistake of thinking she was, and that he could say anything he liked to her and it wouldn't get through her bomb-proof shell. It turned out that everything had been getting through all along – and when you have people telling you that you have no heart and you're cold and selfish and incapable of love, eventually you'll believe it.

So despite Jonny's last minute dash to the airport, Jac has gone to Sweden and Jonny has been left with a baby strapped to his front. "Don't worry Emma, we'll get Mummy back," Jonny said, so I hope this isn't the end of the story. I know, I've been banging on for weeks about wanting Custodygate to be over – is there no satisfying me? But what I mean is that it's just not satisfactory to have Jac giving up her baby like that. She's been through so much in terms of character development, and having a baby has opened up aspects of her we never knew about before. I'm just hoping the wise and wonderful Henrik Hanssen will convince her not to give up on her daughter, the way he gave up on his son for so many years. I think that's a conversation they might have over a glass of Akvavit one evening.

Meanwhile, I was once again left to ponder the question – exactly where is Holby these days? Sacha drove Essie to the Gower Peninsula without her realising it (she wasn't drugged, either – just snoozing). This would be easier if we still believed Holby to be a thinly-disguised Bristol. Frankly Essie would have had to have been off her head on Camoxidan to have slept through the car ride from Borehamwood to west Wales.

It was absolutely stunning, scenery-wise, but the storyline of Essie hiding out from the press (one journalist) who wanted her to go to Poland to apologise for the Holocaust was a bit tedious. The presence of Sacha's mum (Frances Cuka) livened things up a bit, but between Essie nodding off in the car and Sacha nodding off under a comfy blanket under the stars it wasn't very dynamic. It didn't add anything to the very intense drama of the episodes about Essie's grandfather.

So I was left feeling a bit depressed, a bit irritated and a bit jealous (of whoever owns that cottage overlooking the sea). But at least Jac has finally got herself a new coat. It looks a bit like a dressing gown, but it's an improvement on that camel-coloured thing she's been wearing for years.

Nice hair, shame about the adultery

(Series 16, ep. 37 'Every Dog Has Its Day' by Nick Fisher 26.6.14)

You know when a love triangle is reaching critical mass. It's when every corner of the triangle gets a haircut the very same week, which was the case for the Smug/Posh/Barfs in this episode. It's like some sort of adultery telepathy. Dr Amy Smug-Barf was still covering for Posh's mistake the other week, because she needs to get him moved on to another department and can only do that if everybody thinks he's competent and he passes all his tests.

So far so Smug. And Posh. What it all needed was a hefty dollop of brains-speak and a Big Reveal (and then more brains-speak). That's exactly what we got, but in the capable scriptwriting hands of Nick Fisher it was quirky, funny and very dramatic.

AAU Patient of the Week was an ice cream man who'd been shot in the face by a crossbow bolt (still in situ when he rolled up in the car park and Posh attempted to buy a 99 from him). The patient seemed quite blasé about his injury. "You got shot in the face!" Posh repeatedly exclaimed. "It's not ideal, granted," was the reply.

Dominic has been fairly quiet for a few weeks, but the crossbow incident also gave us a delightful reminder of just what a beautifully twisted soul he is beneath his cute exterior. "If someone shot me in the face with a crossbow I wouldn't want them to get into trouble till I'd had a chance to shoot them. In the face. With a crossbow," he said.

Big praise also to the prosthetics department, who must have been proud of their work with the crossbow/face case. Thoroughly, yuckily convincing.

But back to the Triangle of Doom. Raf was suspicious of the way Amy's story about the disciplinary incident differed from Posh's. I can't help thinking it wasn't in the best interests of the patient to interrogate Posh about it while he was trying to remove the crossbow bolt from the man's face ("Gently… in an anticlockwise direction"). Despite this pressure, Posh did good work and some beautifully neat stitching, which was ruined moments later by the ice cream man's wife's fingernails, because he'd been seeing her hairdresser on the side (the crossbow bolt had been delivered by the hairdresser's husband).

By this time, Raf had managed to get Amy to confess about her night of lust ("Twice" – TMI) with Posh. It's fair to say Raf didn't take the news well – particularly the realisation that the baby might not be his. There was a lot of brain-speaking going on when he took the ice cream man off to have his face fixed again. "I'll do my best to repair it, but it's never going to be pretty."

Something else that's not going to be pretty, and indeed will quite possibly be heartbreaking, is finding out What's The Matter With Elliot. He's a worried man, and even the lure of a doughnut couldn't tempt him out of his lab, where he's busy tinkering with the Herzig Whatever Number He's Up To Now.

He popped out for Pot Noodles in the Linden Cullen Memorial Shrubbery and fancied he could hear a sea shanty. He wasn't hallucinating, though – he really could hear a sea shanty, as a posse of singing sailors had found a parking space in the ever-accommodating car park and one of them was preparing to check into Darwin. Mo and Adele thought the man had taken Viagra,because there was something he wasn't telling them and it was embarrassing him, but Elliot took him out to the LCMS for a man-to-man chat and it turned out it was Botox, because he didn't want to look wrinkly on telly. It was all a good excuse for a brains-speak about ignoring symptoms, and Elliot booked himself in for a MRI scan. The results worried him, but we still don't know What's The Matter With Elliot. At the end of the episode he was hearing piercing ringing noises, like the kind that always made Captain Kirk and the crew clap their hands over their ears and run side to side on *Star Trek*. I bet Digby knows what I mean.

Speaking of whom, Digby is on a roll as far as wooing the ladies is concerned. This week another attractive geeky gal crossed his path in the form of Marieka, who had a dog that was capable of sniffing out *C. difficile*. He'd been exposed to thousands of stool samples ("And I thought I had a rubbish job," said Colette, who wasn't keen on having a dog on one of her spotlessly clean wards – until the dog spotted some *C. diff*).

Colette was preoccupied anyway, because she'd noticed that the linen cupboard was sometimes locked, sometimes not – and when it was locked, Zosia and Uncle Jesse were nowhere to be seen. She decided to give Jesse a warning about what Selfie would do if/when he discovered what was going on. This was delivered in her best "Exterminate! Exterminate!" voice, but telling Jesse how Selfie would rip off his man-parts etc didn't sound as threatening as if she'd simply reminded him that Selfie was Killer Karl from *Corrie*.

Posh baby or Smug husband?

(Series 16, ep. 38 'All Before Them' by Kate Verghese 30.6.14)

Someone at Holby HQ had been raiding the Camoxidan cupboard for last night's episode (possibly it was left unguarded while Dr Amy Smug was busy barfing in her mouth somewhere else). It was one of those episodes with odd camera angles and general randomness, and a particularly hallucinatory scene where Elliot Hope wandered off into the basement in search of the source of a ghostly moaning sound. Was it in his own not very well head? Was it the ghost of Linden Cullen, doomed forever to walk the corridors in search of Faye? Was it a corpse who wasn't actually dead (it's happened before)? Or was it a live patient who believed he was a corpse? It was Leonard Bloom, a live patient who believed he was a corpse. "I am already dead," he announced to Elliot, adding disturbingly, "You are as dead as I am." As if Mr Bloom wasn't being metaphorical enough, he was also a watchmaker and he had a special watch that stopped the moment he "died" – and started again the moment Mo fixed him, because he wasn't really dead, he was just spooky and unwell.

Adele proved once again that's she more than just a HCA, and when she has a hunch you darn well should listen to her, and Elliot was left to get on with working on his presentation for the Herzig 5. Was it significant that he addressed his presentation to the late lamented Tara Lo? In an episode Loaded With Significance, you have to bet it was.

Reluctantly I'm now dragging myself to the lower floors of the hospital. The Smugs were still at odds over Dr Amy Smug's drunken decision to "sleep with" Dr Harry Posh and not take a morning after pill the morning after. The stress made Raf Smug have a panic attack, and he said if the baby wasn't his, Amy would have to choose – Posh baby or Smug husband. He insisted that Amy went immediately to see Mr T and get a paternity test.

I'm going to pause here for a fangirl moment re Mr T. He's so tall! So smiley! And his voice is so gorgeous!

That has distracted me so much that I can't actually be bothered to go into any more details about Smug/Posh/Barf except to say that Posh now knows that Amy is With (Possibly His) Child, she's decided to keep it never mind who the father is, and Raf has decided there's no way he can bring up a Posh child, so he left Amy on the roof gazing into the Borehamwood sunset and walked off, blinking his super-long eyelashes tearfully.

On Keller, Zosia is teetering on the brink of going total bunny boiler on Jesse. He decided to back off a bit as Colette's words ("Exterminate! Exterminate!") were still ringing in his ears. You're only allowed to back off from Zosia if she says you can, and she hadn't said anything of the sort. When an old friend of Jesse's turned up as mother-of-a-patient, Zosia turned into seething ball of jealous crossness. Jesse told her they needed to cool off their relationship – he's like a rock that people smash themselves against, apparently. Zosia looked like she wouldn't have minded smashing herself against him in the linen cupboard a bit more, but Jesse wasn't keen. So Zosia ended up getting very drunk indeed, and Digby rather magnificently told Jesse what he thought of him, before taking Zosia home to hold her hair back while she puked.

Fun with Mo and an open chest cavity

(Series 16, ep. 39 'Captive' by Lauren Klee 9.7.14)

Jonny Mac was making plans for him and Emma to move to Scotland this week. I'm not sure how that ties in with his promise to Emma to "get Mummy back," but it's irrelevant anyway as it doesn't look like he's going (sigh) – not now he's remembered how much fun he can have with Mo and an open chest cavity.

The Darwin story involved a pregnant 49 year old, which was excellent news because it provided an excuse for Mr T to be summoned. Surely it can only be a matter of time before we see his face in the opening titles? Give him his own ward, get Mubbs back and I think we'd have a dream team right there. But on the topic of "dream team" – did you notice Mr T pop his arm around Mo as they walked out of shot in his first scene? Bless!

To Keller now, where Jesse, a man people like to smash themselves against, spent the episode almost resisting Zosia's attempts to smash herself against him. Selfie had offered him a job which sounded like the best job any anaesthetist in the history of laughing gas has ever been offered, Selfie was that thrilled with it. Jesse turned this fantastic opportunity down, and when pressed as to why, he said it was so Zosia didn't keep smashing herself against him. So Selfie smashed his fist against Jesse's nose instead – what we might term a "Self-inflicted injury."

Jesse drove away (has he gone for good now then?) and Zosia was left staring sadly at his departing vehicle and angrily up at the Window of Regret, from which Selfie was staring down at her in a Greek tragedy type manner.

Keller high point: Digby giving Jesse advice between the shelves of a trolley.

AAU was a pool of Smug/Posh/Barf gloom. Dr Amy Smug spent most of the time lurking in her medicine cupboard, where she was ever so slightly menaced by an upset patient. Dr Raf Smug spent most of the episode teetering on the verge of tears (he's far more tearful than Dr Oliver Valentine ever was), and Posh looked apprehensive. Eventually Smug told Posh that Amy had had a paternity test and the father of the child was not Posh. Posh was so thrilled he tossed his car keys up in the air with a cheery gesture. Smug went to find Amy in her medicine cupboard to tell her what he'd done. The high point on AAU was Smug climbing into a toilet cubicle and kind of abseiling down the walls.

Stage fright

(Series 16, ep. 40 'The Spirit...' by Chris Lindsay 15.7.14)

It was the day of the grand unveiling of the Herzig 5. It hardly seems any time at all since we were gasping and marvelling at the Herzig 1, does it?

The problem was that Elliott, as we know, hasn't been well. He's been dropping things, falling over and getting tetchy. He's had an MRI. He's looked at the results in a troubled manner. It's something scary and big, and it's not what you want when there's a ground-breaking, life-saving piece of kit to showcase and Selfie is relying on you to sell it to the world.

It all culminated in Elliott going wobbly in the middle of doing the operation, just at the point where the machines were going beep. It was all going to go horribly wrong! Elliott's life's work would be in ruins! If only there was someone who could take over...

Then she arrived, like a Venus in scrubs – Jac Naylor, straight off the plane from Stockholm and into a Darwin theatre like she'd never been away. Jonny asked her why she came back. "Something isn't right," was her reply. Elliott hadn't been replying to her messages, Mo was sounding concerned – Jac had the idea Elliott might need her.

So she saved the patient's life, gave a brilliant presentation and the orders for the H5 were soon rolling in. She really is magnificent.

More important to her was Elliott's health: "Despite my cold and passive exterior I am moderately fond of you," she told him. In fact she showed just how fond she is of him when he was being wheeled off for an MRI scan and Jac wanted to go with him rather than give the Herzig presentation. My, how she's changed.

Rather worryingly as far as I'm concerned, it seems she's caught the eye of the odious Selfie. I do not want to see a romance developing between those two, but I fear that's where we're headed. He's impressed with her surgery and presentation skills (a turnaround from thinking she had "the people skills of the Ebola virus"), and she'll be impressed when he saves Elliott's life, as it turns out Elliott has a probably benign but needs-to-be-out tumour that Selfie is pretty confident he can remove.

While Elliott was having a traumatic time upstairs, down in AAU it was a bit of a day for Serena, too. She was about to be sued by a relative of that man who jumped off the roof, Selfie was on at her for something or other, she had a patient with puzzling symptoms – and to top it all off, she had to look after her mother by giving her a bed in AAU and expecting her not to go AWOL at any point. I think we have to leave the ethics of doing this in the bay marked "artistic license," because the point was Serena's conflict at wanting to do the best for her mum while also wishing it was a problem she didn't have to face (once again some beautiful work from Catherine Russell and Sandra Voe).

This is a story that can't have a happy ending, and at the end of the episode, while Serena had managed to sort out her legal difficulties and had gained Selfie's respect, things with her mother took on a worse turn when her mother hit out at her in the car park.

Darwin wasn't the only place for broken hearts this week, because Zosia was nursing one on Keller, and it was her own. Jesse was ignoring her calls, and Zosia was so upset she started smoking. Luckily she had Dominic on hand to go "Ugh!" and deter her from the evil weed. She also had Digby, everybody's consolation nerd, but he rejected her when she pounced on him because he's going out with Marine Maria and he's a very, very nice man.

Today, Professor Hope, you are a patient

(Series 16, ep. 41 'A Heart Man' by Rebecca Wojciechowski 22.7.14)

One thing I really loved about this episode was the way Elliot Hope was properly placed in context, with friends past and present and even a visit from his miserable son. There were numerous references to Charlie Off Of Casualty. Elliot had get well soon messages from Joseph (Joseph! Oh, please come and visit Elliot next week. Cumbria isn't that far) and Connie (who will be visiting next week – hurrah! She's wasted on *Casualty*). A box arrived from none other than Henrik Hanssen, and it contained baklava. Remember he brought baklava for Tara Lo when she was facing brain surgery, "to ensure a swift recovery." That didn't end well, but he did say at the time that he was "perfecting the recipe," and the message with this batch was that he has "perfected" it – so its healing powers must be awesome. And the wonderful Mr T wanted to get Elliot a kitten. I do like his thinking.

Elliot had solid support from Mo, Jonny, Sacha and especially Jac, who was at her absolute cuddliest. She was also distracted by a former Herzig patient who'd decided that Elliot had been negligent. Obviously he hadn't, and Jac sorted it all out, but by doing so she's caught the eye of someone called Patsy Brassvine (seriously), who has influential power re the future of the Herzig and thinks Jac would be a much better figurehead than its whiskery, eclair-scoffing inventor. Not for the first time in his career, people are plotting to dump Elliot.

Might Jac be persuaded into the "pro dumping" camp? She might have been nudged in that direction when Elliot's angry and petulant son told her that Elliot had been less than complimentary about her parenting skills, but I don't think so.

So what of the op? It all seemed to take place via Elliot's nose, which made me absolutely cringe and I had to look away, so I couldn't tell you any details apart from it was apparently successful (a bit of tumour has been left behind in case further drama is needed at some point) – so hurrah, and well done Selfie. Digby, who was assisting, didn't impress the CEO, though, and he's been dumped from neurosurgery. I really hope Digby's next job is in Obs & Gynae, because a Mr T/Digby double act would be a gorgeous thing to behold.

Talk of "double acts" brings me to that radiant twosome, Mr and Mrs Dr Smug. They actually smiled this week, because they saw their baby on a scan (which also made Dr Raf Smug cry – maybe he thought the foetus looked a bit Posh) and also it looked like they might be getting rid of Dr Posh. Despite being the most useless doctor ever to hang a stethoscope nonchalantly around his neck, if you believe Raf, it turns out that through either genuine skill or Amy's relentless mentoring, Dr Posh came 15th in the national exams. American institutions are therefore desperate for his services, so it looked like the Smugs might get rid of him.

The problem is that Raf is not convinced that the examiners have got it right and Posh really is all that, and the move to America was dependent on him writing a glowing reference. He had a tussle with his conscience, which was reminiscent of Linden Cullen during his more anguished moments, but minus the visits to the chapel, and told Serena that Posh wasn't ready for the bright lights of California.

Hurricane Zosia

(Series 16, ep. 42 'One Small Step' by Alex Child 29.7.14)

Following a short spell in neurosurgery – as a doctor, not even as a patient – the previously competent Digby has gone all under-confident and generally a bit useless now he's back on Keller. Possibly this is in no small part due to the fact that he lives with Zosia (a woman on the edge of a nervous breakdown) and Dominic (a part-time psychopath with an endless string of gentlemen callers). He doesn't just live with them and their histrionics, but he has to work with them, too. It's apparently official Keller policy that all junior doctors must work in groups of three at all times. This leads to the interesting patient of the week finding his/her view of the ward obscured by a solid wall of (appropriately) wine-coloured scrubs at any given time.

This week's interesting patient was a buff trainee astronaut, so Zosia and Dom went into flirt overdrive. When it transpired that the astronaut's mother was dying of cancer and she didn't want the astronaut to know, Zosia went into meltdown, because it reminded her so much of her own situation. It all culminated in her getting off her face on what the tabloids would call a "lethal booze and drugs cocktail" and collapsing. Luckily this happened in the hospital, and luckily Digby was on hand and was entirely sober and saved her life. It was very dramatic, not least when Digby had to go scuttling off to find the correct meds and was forced to make small talk with Selfie en route. "Treating a colleague with stolen meds is at least a GMC hearing, if not a spell in prison," Dominic told Digby, comfortingly.

When he wasn't making small talk with Digby, Selfie was offering Jac the double crown of Darwin and the Herzig project. She said she didn't want them – she wanted a spare pair of hands on Darwin while Elliot was laid up. It's just possible that Selfie could actually be a Machiavellian genius, because the hands he came up with were those of Connie Beauchamp – the one person in the world calculated to turn Jac's ambition dial up to 11. It was wonderful to see Connie back on Darwin. For some reason she just isn't Connie when she's onCasualty, but here it was like she'd never been away. I think I actually squirmed with delight during some of her dialogue with Jac – as a sparring partner only Serena could come close. With my feminist head on, I suppose it was a shame that their barbs were mainly about their children, and their romantic failings ("How is Sam?" "He's in New York. I hear Joseph found himself a nice little wife"), but it was highly amusing anyway and Connie gave Jac a pep talk about letting her feelings for Elliot get in the way of pursuing her career goals. And as a parting shot, some fashion advice: "Remember… autumn tones!"

On AAU, Serena summed up everyone's feelings about the arrival of Dr Raf Smug's brother as a patient: "There are two of you. What a treat!" Guiseppe Smug had been in a fight or something, but the main reason he was in hospital was so he could create lots of awkward situations by talking about Baby Smug while Amy, Raf and Dr Posh were all present. It made Dr Raf Smug even more tense than usual, but Serena gave him short shrift when he said he didn't want Harry operating on his brother. At least he's agreed to get the nursery ready for the arrival of Baby Smug, and Amy's eyes lit up in thrilled excitement when he presented her with a ticket to Glasgow to visit his mother. Either she's glad that he's finally accepting Baby Smug/Posh, or she's a big *Taggart* fan.

Carer or consultant?

(*Series 16, ep. 43 'Affair of the Mind' by Johanne McAndrew & Elliot Hope 5.8.14*)

This week we discovered that Serena's mother, Adrienne, has "a penchant for a silver fox." Luckily for her, a thrilling example of the genre had just arrived back in Holby in the form of Ric Griffin. Apparently he's got Jess all sorted out and safe somewhere, and now he's back.

His presence was good news and bad news for Serena, under fire from Selfie who thinks her role as a carer for her mother means she can't give her best, medically-speaking. She thought Selfie was only trying to edge her out because Ric was back, but on the other hand Ric is an enormously reassuring, calm presence. This is just what you need when your mother's dementia has reached the stage where she's smashed every mirror in the house and most of the mirrors in the AAU toilets. "At least 21 years of bad luck," calculated PLA Jr.

Speak-your-brains patient of the week was, kind of disturbingly, the copper who is currently investigating Lucy Beale's murder on *EastEnders*. She was an alcoholic (which is possibly why she's not made much headway finding out who killed Lucy) and also a psychologist, who had plenty of advice about dealing with dementia. Serena has, as a result, decided to be more proactive and get a grip on the situation. Selfie looked doubtful, but he always looks doubtful unless the subject under discussion is his own magnificence, so no change there then.

The whole storyline is lifted (and made even more sad) by the sensitive performances of Sandra Voe and Catherine Russell, and the scene where Adrienne was dancing with Ric was very touching. There was a female patient on Darwin with "problems down below." Never before has this phrase been much of a call to celebrate, but these days it means that the glorious Mr T will be summoned. His visit coincided with Mo being in a very grumpy mood. It wasn't just because in the absence of Jac and Elliot she'd been landed with an entire department to run. It was because it was two years ago that she gave birth. Mr T remembered, which of course he would because he's (a) lovely (b) an expert in matters "down below," including births and (c) crazy about Mo.

Digby is also apparently crazy about Marine Biologist Maria, so when she appeared in Keller with possible appendicitis, he wasn't keen on his all-kinds-of-crazy flat-mate Zosia being responsible for her care. Zosia was particularly distracted by a new F1, who found himself being pounced on in the linen cupboard in what must have been a memorable first day on the ward. Unfortunately for Zosia the main emotion he experienced was fear. She can be a bit full-on, as Digby knows only too well.

The best man (or woman) for the job

(Series 16, ep. 44 'Star Crossed Lovers' by Claire Bennett 12.8.14)

Honestly, the way staff are wandering willy-nilly between Holby City and *Casualty* these days, you might be forgiven for thinking it was the same hospital.

Following Connie Beauchamp's recent-ish manifestation on Casualty, this week it was the turn of staff nurse Adrian "Adrian" Fletcher (or "Fletch") to don the attractive dark blue scrubs of The Big Hospital Upstairs. He took to life on AAU very readily – he'd even heard of Albie's, though no one from Casualty has ever gone there. Ric Griffin wasn't that pleased to see him – Ric and Tess Bateman go back a long way, apparently, so obviously Ric wasn't that impressed by the married man who messed Our Tess around. Ric has apparently forgotten the old saying about "two to tango" and that Fletch only recently saved the life of the blessed Tess, but still… At least by the end of the episode Fletch had won the admiration of Ric via the medium of some nifty work with a Sengstaken tube. Even Dr Smug was impressed by that one.

Harder to impress was Colette, who only had to clap eyes on Fletch and she would go all snarly. It turned out that she'd once turned down the opportunity to become Mrs Adrian "Adrian" Fletcher, presumably before he got married to the one he was married to when he was being a married man dallying with Tess. Who knew?

Before I move swiftly on to more dallying on the wards, I just want to say that Fletch on Holby works just fine, in my opinion. Not sure the history with Colette was entirely necessary, but as a character he just seems to fit and it's like he's always been on Holby.

I can also say the same for Mr T (I feel I know him well enough to start calling him Derwood now, but Mr T suits him so well), a character who is rapidly turning into a legend. This week the legend was added to when Sacha suspected him of being a two-timing love rat, and we discovered that not only (a) is he nothing of the sort (he's actually single – information which made Mo's day), but (b) he has his own corset and likes dressing up as Frank N. Furter. If we don't see some of that at the staff Christmas party this year, I'll be sorely disappointed. It would totally eclipse last year's elf costume.

On Darwin, Elliot Hope was back at work. He's recovered well from his brain operation, but he may recover less well from being stabbed in the back. This latter injury is metaphorical rather than actual, as Jac Naylor has signed the contract which puts her at the head of Darwin and the Herzig project, and it's going to hurt.

Brand Naylor

(Series 16, ep. 45 'The Art of Losing' by Katie Douglas 19.8.14)

You only have to look at Elliot Hope and you want to give him a cuddle. He always seems a bit sad, a bit lost, a bit too nice for the world. Just in case this isn't obvious enough, he has an adorable sidekick of a dog called Gary (#RIP Samson) which he brings to work to cheer up the geriatric ward in his spare moments when he's not saving lives on Darwin. Or in lifts.

You couldn't hurt a lovely man like that unless you were Jac Naylor and Selfie had offered you the career leap you'd always wanted. Even so, Jac wasn't comfortable with sticking the knife between the shoulder blades of her former mentor. It even made her cry to tell him that she was now the face of the Herzig project, which had been his ever since he concocted the Herzig 1 out of twigs and pine cones in the wet lab. "It shouldn't have been you who took this from me," Elliot said, in a scene of Shakespearean tragedy proportions (Elliot was part King Lear, part Julius Caesar and Jac was part Cordelia and part Lady Macbeth). Technically it was the odious Selfie who took it from him ("Guy wants consistency... brand"), but of course Selfie was keeping such a low profile that he's probably face down under a filing cabinet in the basement.

The upshot is that, as usual, Nobody Likes Jac. And Gary chewed up her presentation pen (a gift from Selfie) – before she even got a chance to show it to Digby and Zosia. They love a good pen, those two.

Digby and Zosia were having a day off (hangovers, probably), leaving Dominic to do his cute/ cheeky thing on his own on Keller. The main story on Keller was that Sacha was trying to progress his relationship with Essie by getting her to meet his daughters. She wasn't keen. "When are you going to tell your Jewish children I'm related to a Nazi?" she asked him and it's a reasonable question, but I imagine all Sacha heard was the voice of Chrissie, who'd always been too good for him (in her own mind). Patient of the week was George fromGeorge and Mildred, whose toe had fallen off.

Meanwhile, guest artiste of the week on AAU was Helen Flanagan, formerly *Coronation Street*'s minx extraordinaire, Rosie Webster. She's still doing the pouting thing. Fletch had "found" her in Albie's and got her a job by "pulling a few strings" with the largely fictional HR department. Fluid staffing configurations etc. I'm not sure whether she was actually a qualified nurse, but I presume she must have been. She didn't go down well with Colette, what with the pouting and everything, and then a mobile phone went missing and latex gloves were used on a patient who was allergic to latex. Fingers (non-latex-covered) were pointed at Helen Flanagan and she had to be "let go" by Colette and Fletch. I did quite enjoy her turn as basically Rosie Webster in scrubs, and I'm still very much enjoying Fletch's work.

What a strange girl you are

(Series 16, ep. 46 'Going, Going…' by Joe Ainsworth 26.8.14)

Percutaneous fetal balloon valvuloplasty. It's easy to say (the "balloon" bit is easy to say, anyhoo), but very, very tricky to do. Indeed, it's so risky and rarely performed that Jac Naylor described it as "groundbreaking" to Selfie, and that was enough for him to give it the thumbs-up. Jonny Mac wouldn't have given it the thumbs-up if he'd been CEO, because he thought it was way too risky and was just about Jac showing off. He should know by now that Jac does, indeed, enjoy showing off her surgical skills – but only when she's reasonably confident of a good outcome for the patient.

The unborn patient in this case was the result of a one night stand, and Jonny had plenty of advice for the baby's father. In fact he came over quite misty-eyed when talking about Emma, and is still describing her as being strong because she takes after her mother. He hasn't given up hope of a friendly co-parenting set-up for Emma, but to Jac it's apparently off the table. "I can't do this, ever," she told him, twice. Is it because she's afeared that if she becomes a "proper" parent she'll go all Sahira Shah and have to make cupcakes and hide the faces of child patients in case they make her cry?

Normally when there's groundbreaking surgery going on, Selfie would have been on the phone to America and got lots of press and investor types earnestly peeking through the Darwin theatre viewing screen at the wonder of it all. Not this time, because he had a party to go to. The top line of his CEO application form did mention that he had "the ability to prioritise."

So it was left to something of a dream team of Jac, Mo and Mr T (Mr T!) to get the procedure successfully done. Mo "felt an inappropriate high five coming on" afterwards. Jac replied that normally she'd laugh in her face, but she permitted herself a small fist-bump of celebration.

Talking of "celebration," let's get to this party, which was actually a fund-raiser of some sort and was a splendid excuse for some regular cast members and a lot of non-speaking extras to don their glad-rags. The highlight of the evening was a charity auction, in which the star attraction was a sporty wee car. The winning bidder was Dr Raf Smug, who managed to get into a bidding war (or willy-waving contest) with Dr Posh and bid well over the odds for something that's going to be entirely impractical as soon as Baby Smug-Smug/Posh arrives.

When last seen, the car had a sitting tenant in the form of Serena, who was using it to hide from new board member Billy Tressler-Posh. Selfie's advice on how to handle Billy Posh ("Just smile and nod") brought the brilliant response, "I'm not a bloody geisha!" Serena and red wine really do make a delightful combination.

Something else I enjoyed about Serena this week was the solidarity between her and Colette, who helped her find a carer for her mother. It makes a nice change to have female colleagues on Holby being friendly and supportive rather than back-stabbing and bitching (though obviously this doesn't mean I want Jac Naylor to go changing any time soon).

Back to that car auction, and driving up the price along with Posh and Smug was Dr Zosia March, who was having a very strange week. She should really be kept well away from all cancer patients, because it always makes her think of her mother and she gets all unhinged. This week she took it upon herself to make a dying man (Roy Hudd) happy by reducing his medication so he wasn't sleepy (but was in pain), eat a steak in front of him so he could enjoy it by proxy (Pulses apparently don't mind if you bring your own food in from outside, which is handy to know if you want to eat anything other than a muffin), and then take him to the party. Her heart's in the right place, but sadly her judgement and self-control are shot to shreds. While the auction continued, Zosia's patient was barfing blood all over the place and Digby and Zosia had to rush him back to the hospital, where he died. And Digby, who is Zosia's self-appointed guardian angel, was left to peer at her with a worried frown on his face as she danced by herself in the dark in the Linden Cullen Memorial Shrubbery.

A car crash of a marriage

(Series 16, ep. 47 'The Looking Glass' by Kate Verghese 2.9.14)

Recovering from the dual indignities of Jac taking over his Herzig project and then presenting him with a new chair that exploded like a clown's car when sat upon, Elliot Hope was startled to find a man hiding behind Jac's coat and frothing at the mouth. I hasten to add that Jac wasn't in the coat, or indeed in the room, when this occurred.

This man turned out to be a prospective patient, Louis, who had an impressively caved-in chest. It caused him no end of social distress (it did look like it would be a handy receptacle for party nibbles, but that would have to be the right kind of party). Elliot knew a risky technique to fix up that kind of thing, but Jac told him he couldn't do it because it was a cosmetic procedure and the budget wouldn't stretch. Adele tried to object. "Sage input as always from Holby's Next Top Model," said Jac. She's always on top of contemporary references, which makes me think she really does do normal stuff like reading magazines and watching telly, rather than spending all her down-time in a specially constructed basement wet lab at Naylor Towers honing her suturing skills.

The upshot was that Elliot did the surgery, which looked absolutely brutal, and everyone went "Wow." Even Selfie.

Meanwhile Jonny Mac had sent Jac a video of Emma saying her first words, which sounded very much like "daddy." This is probably because "d" is easier to say than "m" (*waves little-used linguistics degree*), but that probably doesn't stop Jac from wanting to wrench Jonny's head off.

The person whose head I wanted to wrench off this week was the Keller patient, who was a deeply annoying woman who thought she was Alice in Wonderland (no love, Wonderland is actually AAU, not Keller). "Pills don't fit in my tiny mouth" – that sort of thing. It turned out to be abdominal migraine, the symptoms of which are hideous pain and, apparently, being very, very twee.

While Essie and Sacha were sorting all this out, Essie kept getting texts from an 049 number. "What is my mother-in-law doing texting Essie?" I couldn't help but wonder, but it wasn't her. It was a great-uncle that either Essie hadn't known she had or had forgotten about. She'd been invited to Munich, and despite being just about to move in with Sacha, she's going to go. Let's just hope that a few days of beer and Bratwurst will help her to put her Nazi grandfather into perspective and cheer her up a bit. Even Alice in Wonderland could see that she was only smiling on the outside and was still miserable inside, despite having the world's cuddliest man to cuddle.

Remember the wee car Dr Raf Smug purchased in an auction last week? He's only gone and crashed it into the Linden Cullen Memorial Shrubbery. The shock of this made Dr Amy Smug go "Nnngh!" so off she popped to see Mr T (Mr T!) for a quick scan to check that all was well. All was well, and not only that but the baby is a boy and Amy wants to call him Callum, despite "Callum Di Lucca" sounding like a herbal remedy. Or maybe that's quite apt for a pharmacist's child.

I actually rather warmed to the Smugs this week. They weren't even smug, because they were so upset. Not about the car, but about their relationship. "We're too damaged, Raf," Amy told him. She's going to stay with her brother for a while. Is this the end of the road for the Smugs?

Digby seizes the chance to shine

(Series 16, ep. 48 'Hoops' by Fiona Peek 9.9.14)

Ooh, Arthur Digby! A man of many fine qualities, including being the top F1 in the world (or thereabouts) and having the most beautiful smile in the NHS. He's not usually what you would call dynamic, though. Indeed, he was seen sporting a rucksack with wee horsies on it in this episode and I don't think you'd ever see Michael Spence with that kind of accessory.

But in this episode he had a moment which made me go, "Hell, yeah!" in a way I haven't done since the aforementioned Michael Spence went on sabbatical. It was when he told Zosia to go home and followed it up with, "It's not a request, Dr March." Thrilling! The lad is manning up at last.

What had Zosia done to elicit this kind of behaviour? It wasn't because she was late for work due to doing a visualisation with a random pensioner in the Linden Cullen Memorial Shrubbery. It was because she got heavily over-involved in a case, like she does, and decided what was needed was a muscle biopsy on a young girl, which was both unnecessary and a thing she wasn't trained to do. Double unethical.

Sacha had left Digby in charge, and when he disagreed with Zosia's proposed course of action she trotted of to tell Selfie and Sacha, who showed that he is probably not cut out to be in charge of juniors when he relieved Digby of his responsibilities and put Zosia in charge instead.

At the beginning of the episode Sacha had told Digby that he should "Seize the chance to shine," and he kind of did, in that he worked out a diagnosis and stopped Zosia from doing a career-threatening procedure. He found that shining comes at a price, though, as he felt like he betrayed Zosia to her father, and Dominic was on hand to agree with him via the medium of his best snarky face.

This week's Darwin patient was the lovely Michael Starke, formerly Sinbad in *Brookside* and assorted other roles. I always enjoy his appearances – as well as being a Scouser, he always comes across as a lovely warm, genuine man. Darwin is sooo the place to be warm and genuine, too, because it has Adele and she's always smiling and always has time for the patients. Indeed she's so good at her job that Jonny Mac wants her to do a nursing degree. The shift seemed to involve more downs than ups, and by the end she'd almost decided to go back to her old job as a holiday rep and had put some holiday trousers on to signal her intent. This is what you have to do on Holby if you want to leave – never mind giving notice or any of that bureaucratic nonsense. Just change into leisure clothing. Sinbad from *Brookside* helped her change her mind, though, which is good news because one Effanga is good, but two Effangas are better.

On AAU, Fletch started the shift listening to Temples, but things went rapidly downhill from there. It seems that he's a bit rubbish at doing staff rotas and organising cover and so on, which isn't surprising because Tess and Charlie did all that for him in his previous job. So when AAU found itself short-handed, Fletch donned the apron of hospitality and served the patients' meals himself. It's good to see him prioritising nutrition, but it's only about the third time I can remember when patients have ever been offered any meals on Holby.

A man that's hurting inside

(Series 16, ep. 49 'Forgive Me Father' by Nick Fisher 16.9.14)

I had a bit of a flashback watching last night's Holby City. As Dr Raf Smug shimmied into a confessional booth and began pouring out his tortured Scottish soul (he wants to kill Dr Harry Posh), I couldn't help but be reminded of the sainted Linden Cullen and his anguished moments in various hospital chapels. My advice to Raf: avoid the shrubbery. My advice to Harry: avoid Raf.

I don't think Raf would actually kill Harry, though obviously he has more reasons than just Harry being all posh and blue-eyed and sparkly and that. There's all that business about Harry's sperm (possibly) succeeding where Raf's sperm (possibly) failed. But still – was this any reason to behave the way Raf did, by concealing a life-or-death bit of patient information so that Harry would mess up royally in theatre under the stern gaze of Ric Griffin? The upshot was that Harry is now suspended (it must have made a change for Ric to be the suspender rather than the suspendee), and a patient almost died.

Raf took the Linden Cullen way out, which was to go snivelling to God to ask for help: "I'm a healer, so would you heal me please so I can continue healing others?" he pleaded with his invisible chum. Or with the priest, who was partly visible and owed Raf one because Raf had sorted out his ingrown toenail earlier. I think the phrase God is possibly fishing for at the minute is "Physician heal thyself."

"There's something about a man that's hurting inside," Prof Elliot Hope told Adele, who'd spotted that Jonny Maconie has recently become something of a lady-magnet on account of being bereaved and having an adorable child. Elliot could just as easily have been talking about Tortured Dr Raf, but he wasn't. Adele was naturally drawn to the powerful force of the tragic Jonny and they had a go at kissing, but decided it was just a bit weird and they're better off as mates.

They had their hands full anyway – not with each other, but with those two annoying young farmers who turn up on Darwin at regular intervals. "What things do I hate the most?" Jac asked Jonny. He offered up a varied, if incomplete, list: "Managers, drugs reps, puy lentils, British wine, whiners, Americans, the French, any pastry with a French name…" All true, but the thing Jac hates the most is "idiots," as exemplified by the young farmers. One of them had swallowed an electric dog training device, thus giving him even more of a static charge than Jonny Maconie and his romantic air of tragedy.

My favourite scene of the episode was Digby and Dominic, in "his and his" kimonos, being surprised in the middle of a little domestic moment by Selfie. David Ames and Rob Ostlere are so brilliant at these funny scenes and their facial expressions were precious. Why was Selfie walking unannounced into their flat? He was picking up some things for Zosia, who was staying with him. And she wouldn't be coming into work either because she was too fragile. Except that by the time they got to the hospital, Zosia was already there and hard at work on one of those hard to diagnose patients that Keller gets so many of. As usual, she eventually made the right diagnosis, but not before a lot of very worryingly manic behaviour – including getting the patient to start thinking about funeral plans.

She was being shadowed by Dr Amy Teo, looking rather lovely in a plain black dress rather than her usual florals, and far more interesting away from the Smug/Smug/Posh triangle. Amy had pointed out to Selfie that she wasn't a psychiatrist and hence wasn't qualified to asses Zosia's mental health, but he pointed out in return that if his daughter saw a psychiatrist it would go on her record, and these things didn't happen in his world. Amy wasn't comfortable with this Self-centred view, but Selfie pointed out that Zosia wasn't the first person to have an inappropriate and damaging fling with another member of staff. He didn't wink meaningfully, but Amy knew what he meant so she dutifully did as asked and observed Dr March in action. Her verdict? Zosia's not well.

The episode was dedicated to lovely Clare Cathcart, who played the wonderfully snarky AAU patient, Joy. Clare died on 4th September.

Crisis point for Serena

(Series 16, ep. 50 'Mummy Dearest' by Nick Fisher, Johanne McAndrew & Elliot Hope 23.9.14)

The storyline about Serena's mum has been bubbling along for quite a while. When we first met Adrienne we saw how intelligent, funny, independent and kind she was. We saw the relationship between her and Serena was loving, mutually respectful, but with the standard tensions that two women who are more alike than they care to admit will have when their circumstances change and the daughter starts to become the carer. The progress of Adrienne's dementia has therefore been upsetting to watch, and in last night's brilliantly crafted episode it reached a crisis.

Serena brought her mum to hospital, suspecting that she was suffering from TIA's. Raf (not at all Smug in this episode) thought A&E or Keller were more appropriate places for her, but Serena insisted she stayed on AAU where she could keep an eye on her. What would Raf do if Adrienne was his mother? she asked him. Raf agreed to keep her on AAU, but said he would be in charge of her care. Then Raf and Fletch noticed nasty bruises on Adrienne. She accused Serena of hitting her and stealing her rings. Fletch and Raf didn't want to believe it, but the signs were all there. It all climaxed in a devastatingly emotional scene in Pulses, where Adrienne attacked her daughter and it became clear that Serena had been putting up with violence and abuse, because she loves her mother dearly and doesn't know how else to cope. I have to admit I was in tears. It was one of those scenes where I completely forgot I was watching acting and I was just believing in the characters. Catherine Russell was wonderful.

At least now the truth is out and perhaps Serena will get some support, rather than people being suspicious and wary of her. Raf was very sweet and kind and offered a way forward.

I was going to say it wasn't all doom and gloom elsewhere in the hospital, but it actually was – though when it's Dominic being doomy and gloomy, there's always some comedy in there as well.

One of his former one night stands appeared at the hospital in a tiger onesie. He was a nurse from The Mythical St James', collecting money. He was quite cute as well, and sort of familiar, given that we've previously seen him on Holby as Pale Thin Nurse Nicky Van Barr. Only this time he was called Kyle and he was coughing up blood. This was handy for Dominic, who'd been ordered by Sacha to get some interesting diagnostic cases under his belt (it was Farmer's Lung, apparently). It was less handy in that it brought him face to face with relationship/commitment issues. "Are you not 'out' at work?" Kyle asked him. "Are you kidding?" said Dominic. "The coma patients know I'm gay." So it wasn't that. And it wasn't really that he didn't date nurses. "I'm a strictly one-time guy," Dominic said, but Sacha gave him a pep talk and he set off to talk to the by now discharged tiger, who was on his way down the stairs. But then he allowed himself to be headed off by Zosia (who was relatively calm this week) and ended up eating ice cream on his own.

On Darwin, there was a man whose heart was on the wrong side of his body, and he needed a transplant. Jac thought they should stick a Herzig 5 alongside, but Elliot disagreed. Elliot also remembered that Mo was supposed to be the transplant specialist of the team (this often seems to be forgotten) and said she should be involved in the case. When things went beep in theatre, Jac was forced to call Elliot for help. Elliot and Mo sorted things out between them and Jac walked out of theatre. This disagreement had the unfortunate effect of sending Jac off for a drink with Selfie. Heaven help us, Jac's taste in men is deteriorating more and more! Though he is a bit better looking than old Lord Byrne at least.

Genius at work

(Series 16, ep. 51 'Inside Out' by Anna McPartlin 30.9.14)

In an episode where I was equally interested in all three wards/stories (not something I can say every week), I'm going to start with Keller, and the glory that is Dr Dominic Copeland. I know not everyone agrees with me, but I love him to bits. He's sweet, adorable, bitchy and quite possibly just as messed up as Dr Zosia March, though he manifests this by pouting a lot and having the odd Psycho-Dom moment rather than self-harming with alcohol and drugs and emoting in the Linden Cullen Memorial Shrubbery.

"I know what you need," Sacha told him. "Sex… money… an entourage?" said Dominic (I do like his thinking), but Sacha's thinking was that Dominic needs love. Sacha needs love, too, but Essie is away in Germany reconnecting with her roots (and with someone on Facebook called Heiko, which freaked me out a bit because that's my husband's name and he's German and 42 as well. He's not a lawyer and he doesn't like The Hoff, though, so it's not him. Phew). Luckily for Dominic, the next patient through the door happened to be the brother of Kyle (formerly Pale Thin Nurse Nicky Van Barr), who "may be a vacuous northern nurse," according to Dominic, but he's a darn cute VNN. Dom decided to pounce for a kiss in the Linden Cullen Memorial Shrubbery (such a romantic setting), but his advances were temporarily repelled. Kyle is a sensible, persistent chap though, and later on he told Dominic he thought they should start afresh and get to know each other better. In a blink-and-you'll-miss-it moment, Dominic revealed that Psycho-Dom is still alive and well by mentioning that the One Who Broke His Heart (Malick) is dead, which as far as we know he isn't. Dominic just can't resist adding a bit of drama, can he?

There was a lot of drama taking place on AAU – or rather, in a boardroom somewhere, because it was the day of Dr Harry Posh's hearing about his apparent mistake t'other week that almost killed a patient. I found myself totally rooting for Harry, not just because he looks bloody good in a suit (I know, I'm so shallow), but because he was completely innocent and had been set up by Dr Raf Not-So-Smug-Now. As well as this, Harry revealed at several points what a good doctor he is/could be. Amy told Selfie what was what, but it took Raf going to pieces in theatre (again with shades of Linden Cullen as his homophobic religious patient kept mentioning that God sees everything) before he confessed to Serena. Harry is now reinstated and Selfie has sent Raf home. Obviously he'll be fired immediately, yes? Struck off and that? Um… no. Selfie is going to cover it all up for reasons best known to himself, one of them possibly being that the more people who owe you favours, the more powerful you are.

The shock news on Darwin was that Prof Elliot Hope has taken up painting, and everyone agrees he's not very good at it. Bless him, he's lining up hobbies for his retirement, which now seems to be closer than he once thought it was on account of the Herzig being wrestled out of his hands. Jac was trying so hard to be friendly with him, but he's not having it. Nor was he having much of Adele and her relentlessly chirpy attempts to reassure him that he's the finest heart surgeon in the whole of the known universe. He did benefit from an absolutely lovely patient, Mr Lu (the one Serena and Adele cured from snoring via the medium of Katy Perry), who needed the kind of ninja-level surgery that Elliot specialises in. And Adele cleaned out a spare room that nobody had really noticed before for Elliot to use as an office. It even has a window. Oh, the luxury.

The girl's wired

(Series 16, ep. 52 'True Colours' by Jon Sen 7.10.14)

These Holby wet labs are entirely unregulated. If you want to appropriate one for your own personal use and stick post it notes all over it and have a prog rock freak-out, then go ahead. That's what it's there for, and that's where Dr Digby found Zosia, full of manic energy and having worked out the secret to something or other that will surely see her as cover star of the Lancet sometime soon. If they have cover stars.

Her behaviour round patients (and colleagues) was as confrontational and bizarre as ever. She's been getting away with it, but not this time. The patient was Colette's old mate Sophie, and while Sophie was blonde, she was most certainly not Blonde. "Can't you see there's something wrong with her?" she said to Colette. "The girl's wired." Sophie had a brain problem, which is Selfie's area of expertise, but Sophie was wary of letting him operate on her. "You can't even see your own daughter's running wild and you want me to trust me with your life?" This is the kind of truth-saying that Holby could do with more of (I can just imagine what Dr Frieda Petrenko would have made of Zosia. And, indeed, Selfie). Sophie even identified that Colette is in love with the charm-free CEO, despite Colette having spent the last several weeks flirting with Fletch.

Was it her love of Selfie that made Colette substitute her own blood for Zosia's when a drugs test was needed? Digby and Dominic finally 'fessed up about the time Zosia overdosed, and in a tearful encounter on one of Holby's many mysterious outdoor walkways, Zosia admitted to Colette that she'd taken an enlivener the evening before. I can't help thinking Colette's actions were seriously misguided (or mis-Guy-ded) and it's all going to come back to bite her. Guy is still in denial about his daughter's health and despite Colette's efforts he literally shut her out of the charmed axis that is the Family Self.

Someone else who was getting doors shut in her face, though more metaphorically this time, was Jac Naylor in her attempts to hold out an olive branch to Prof Hope. He was all excited about a new invention. It's not another Herzig, it's something quite new, and he wants to keep Jac's "grubby little fingers" off it. I'm sure she was trying to help rather than steal it when she told Selfie about it, and he agreed to let Elliot present a proposal for funding to him. Elliot, however, has his New Bezzie Mate, the ever-present Adele. As soon as she was finished serving breakfasts, she was apparently free for the rest of the day to hover around the Prof, bolstering his ego, calling in favours from a range of expert mates and revealing pitching skills that would have Duncan Bannatyne reaching for his wallet if she was to ever go on Dragons' Den, and negotiation skills that would have Lord Sugar telling her she was hired. "I have a valve replacement at six. Perhaps you'd like to have a go at that, too," sighed Jac.

Two good things to report about AAU. The first was a very nice mention of Jeff, who perished so spectacularly a couple of days ago on *Casualty*. Harry gave his condolences to Fletch, who of course worked with Jeff for a long time. I do like it when we get glimpses that it's all the same hospital really. And I do miss Jeff.

The other lovely thing was the return of the magnificent Mary-Claire, who'd hardly set foot on the ward before she'd worked out the whole Smug/Posh/Barf triangle, including pointing out to Harry that statistically it was much more likely that the baby was his. This prompted him to run off and tell Dr Amy Teo that he wanted a DNA test to find out if the baby might be a little bit Posh.

SERIES 17

Godzilla v Bambi

(Series 17, ep. 1 'Not Waving but Drowning' by Julia Gilbert 14.10.14)

Only last week I was wishing that there was someone on Keller who would speak the plain truth. My wish came true in fine style this week with the arrival of the new Keller consultant, Fleur Fanshawe (Debbie Chazen) – a woman who apparently has no self-editor at all and doesn't give a hoot whom she offends.

"You're the eternal registrar with multiple wives," she greeted Sacha (multiple wives? Wait till she meets Ric Griffin), "And a penchant for a floral shirt." Dominic was rather smitten. "She's deliciously diva-esque," he sighed. He wasn't so keen when she started calling him Doris, but her description of Sacha as "Pudsey" was cruelly accurate. She's cruel only up to a point, though, and this is where Fleur Fanshawe's true brilliance lies. Some people need the sharp sting of a thorn in their side to bring out their A game, and Sacha is one of those people. When Fleur barged into his theatre and took over a procedure over which they'd disagreed ("It's like Godzilla versus Bambi," said Dominic), Sacha finally found the nuts to stand up for himself. "What I did expect was your professional respect," he said. And he got it, because Fleur isn't a monster. She doesn't care what people think of her, but she's not being horrible for the sake of it. She's blunt with patients for their own good (though the way she spoke to a patient this week was very similar to the way Zosia speaks to them, and when Zosia does it she gets into trouble) and blunt with colleagues if they need it. She's also very funny.

On AAU they were all excited about a visiting American dignitary from a hospital in Chicago. Was it a ground-breaking Holby/*ER* crossover? Sadly not quite, but the visiting dignitary was a bit spectacular. It was none other than everyone's favourite snake-hipped, smooth-talking medic, Michael Spence – clean-shaven these days, but still thrilling. Everybody was gobsmacked: "Shut the front door!" said Mary-Claire. He's in Holby on a mission to see if they're worthy of some Chicago funding, but he's also escaping the glare of publicity after having an affair with a senator's wife, the rogue. It seems that he already knows Fleur Fanshawe (nobody arrives in Holby without knowing somebody else), but at least he won't be having an affair with her because Fleur told Dominic he's not the only gay in the village. She meant her, not Michael – that would be a shock indeed, and besides, Michael has already spotted Zosia.

The main AAU story was still the fallout of the Smug/Posh/Barf triangle. Thanks to his personal life being in tatters and having to face the smiling visage of Dr Posh every day, Raf's concentration isn't what it should be and he missed a ruptured spleen and then went to pieces in surgery. Luckily Michael Spence was on hand to sort things out. Fletch, sticking up for Raf, told Harry to tell Michael what was going on re the triangle, though I couldn't really see that it was Harry's responsibility to do that. Anyway, Michael has told Selfie that Raf is a liability, and as Michael has his hands on the American purse strings, Selfie is going to have to do something.

On Darwin Jac was happily amusing herself with four back-to-back heart valve replacements, but then the ward started filling up with babies. Well, two babies anyway, and one of them was her Emma. The other was the newborn baby of a patient who didn't even know she was pregnant. Another opportunity to see the glorious Mr T, so hurrah for that, and also a chance to see that both

Mo and Jac, highly skilled professional women, still have a bit of a hormonal struggle when there's a birth taking place. Jac is having to be absolutely brutal with herself in her attempt to keep a distance from Emma. Jonny can't understand it and desperately wants her in Emma's life, but Jac still thinks she'd be as toxic for Emma as her own mother was for her, and is pretending to be cold and horrible. You're not fooling us, Ms Naylor – we've seen your face when you think nobody's looking.

They call him Dr Smug

(Series 17, ep. 2 'Bounce Back' by Nick Fisher 21.10.14)

What kind of doctor is Dr Raf Smug? "What kinda doctor are you?" asked Michael Spence. See – he wants to know as well. He's a magical doctor, according to Fletch, who wanted some of that "Di Lucca magic" for a plastics case. Normally Michael Spence would be your go-to guy for this kind of thing (plastics, not magic), but he was busy elsewhere, and no other plastic surgeon was to be found in the whole of Holbyshire, so it was time for Raf to gather up what was left of his self confidence after Smug/Posh/Barf-gate and snap on those latex-free gloves.

The patient was Crazy Eric, and he was all about risk. Life wasn't worth living, he explained, unless you were balanced on a tightrope somewhere very high, or bungee jumping or any of that other mad stuff that lands people in hospitals. But when he went blind, could Raf risk sorting out his eyes with an incredibly delicate and complex procedure that would normally only be attempted by a fully paid-up ophthalmologist? He wasn't sure, so Fletch had to give him another pep talk along the lines of "you just have to man up and ignore the fact that your wife has left you because she's probably pregnant by a man whose sperm is far friskier than yours and who has a dazzling smile to match." Fletch was qualified to give this advice "because my private life is full of cock-ups" (you can take that almost too literally). "Same here," chimed Michael (ditto).

When Raf described this eye operation it sounded truly disgusting, and the op itself was possibly the most revolting thing I've ever seen. Or not seen, because I couldn't actually look. Even the snipping noise was traumatic enough.

Procedure successfully completed and Crazy Eric well on the road to recovery, Raf went off to confide in Amy. "'Dr Smug' – that's what some people round here call me," he said. Yes they do, and I would love to take the credit for that. Amy grabbed the concept. "Go! Be Smug! Be Great! It's what you do best!" she said, in what was presumably intended to be a compliment. It's fair to say that Raf's mojo is restored, as he had enough of it left over to lobby for a new 3D printer for plastics purposes. "They don't call him Dr Smug for nothing," sighed Fletch adoringly. Again, this was intended as a compliment.

Meanwhile, Dr Dominic Copeland was planning a surprise holiday for Kyle – yes! cosy coupledom already. But then disaster – he spotted Kyle with another man. But then hurrah – the other man was just Kyle's cousin, and Kyle is so sweet he prepares nice breakfasts for Dominic and has given him his own drawer to keep his smalls in when he stays over. He even brought the empty drawer in to work. Possibly slightly over the top as gestures go, but Kyle is adorable, so all's well that ends well. Except Kyle still thinks that the reason Dominic is a bit wary of commitment is that he's recovering from the death of his One True Love. That's Malick. Who isn't dead. Dominic had a delightful patient, Myrtle, who'd been having an affair for 30 years. She spoke Dominic's brains, saying "A big fat lie in a relationship is always going to hurt." But he just couldn't bring himself to tell the truth, not with Kyle being so sympathetic and everything. He's like "a bucket of greased eels with the moral compass of a stoat," was Digby's assessment.

Question: What's the best fluid – blood or spinal? We were actually treated, if that's the word, to an argument along these lines between Jac Naylor (Team Blood) and Selfie (Team Spinal Fluid) who were busy doing one of those two-procedures-at-once operations and trying to score points off each other. They were being observed by Olive Fincher, the secretary of the Friends of Holby City, the most important and formidable fundraising body in the whole of Holbyshire. I don't remember hearing about them before, but maybe they work on a masonic kind of basis. Anyhoo, what Ms Fincher really came to see was "The Legend" Jac Naylor (and to get lobbied for that 3D printer by Dr Smug). This helped Selfie to fully appreciate The Legend's legendary qualities.

Heart and brain ops complete and all fluids mopped up, we then had to endure some dreadful flirting between The Legend and the CEO based on the motif of the sun shining from Jac's backside. Later on Colette turned up at the Office of High Authority to whisk Selfie off to a booth at the Blue Note (I'm guessing it's a late-night jazz club in Rodolfo's basement), but he already had plans. He was taking Jac to dinner. "This could be the start of something really big," he mumbled, and I felt even queasier than I did when Raf was operating on Crazy Eric's eyeball.

Sometimes people can surprise you

(Series 17, ep. 3 'The Science of Imaginary Solutions' by Robert Goldsbrough 28.10.14)

Mo might be "Doctor Mo," star of Radio Holby's crowd-pleasing medical phone-in, but that's not really where she wants to be career-wise. She wants to be Miss Effanga, Holby's well-respected hot-shot CT surgeon. In the zone, but not, as Jac pointed out, "the comfort zone."

So Mo did what CT surgeons seem to do when they have a point to prove – she decided to do a spot of risky, history-making, ninja-level surgery that makes everyone else go, "Surely you're not going to try that?"

Was she over-reaching herself and putting her patient at risk? At one point in theatre even Mo thought so. It was the point at which the machines go beep and people start wanting to page Jac. What Mo needed at that point was a pep talk. Possibly a pep talk from a devilishly handsome anaesthetist who just happened to have pitched up on Darwin that very day. It was only Jesse, back to be a thorn in the side of Selfie, but more importantly for this episode, to help Mo believe in herself, carry on with the procedure and save the patient's life (and buy him a surfboard afterwards). Career credentials restored, Mo resigned from her Doctor Mo job – from now on we must once again call her Miss Effanga.

How did Selfie and Zosia react to Jesse's return (given that it was Jac's idea and Selfie knew nothing about it)? Selfie unnerved his former bezzie mate by not yelling at him or punching him, while Zosia greeted Jesse with, "Please tell me you're here with a ruptured spleen." She looked somewhat rattled, but perhaps she's moved on as she was picked up right at the end by a flashy man in a flashy Audi. It was none other than our favourite visiting American VIP, Michael Spence. Oh dear. This sort of thing has been on the cards since he and Zosia exchanged Meaningful Looks about ten minutes after he showed up at Holby.

There was lots of fun on Keller with Fleur and Sacha. "She's not the boss of me," Sacha told Jac. "Yeah, but she is though," said Jac. I love Jac and Sacha scenes.

Fleur is tiny, but she can loom almost as well as Henrik Hanssen and several times popped up behind someone just as they were saying something indiscreet. In a team that includes Dominic, indiscretion is not uncommon.

Their patient was Barbra ("Just the two A's, like Streisand") and she was one of these diagnostic puzzles that they often get. Sacha was determined that he and his little trio of juniors ("Doris, Digweed and The Girl With The Face-ache Tattoo" according to Fleur) would get to the bottom of this without Fleur's interference, and eventually he did. Fleur, in a very rare move for a senior doctor at Holby, actually gave Sacha the credit for this. So a lovely new partnership could be flowering. "We're like Butch and Sundance!" said Sacha. "You're Sundance," said Fleur. Robert Goldsbrough's script was full of funny lines like that and everybody seemed to be enjoying themselves enormously. There was even some comedy business with beanbag chairs.

Enjoyment was not on the menu in AAU (for the staff at least), where Serena had to deal with another crisis when Adrienne went missing from home and turned up at the hospital in her nightie, suffering from pneumonia. She was found in a confused state by Raf, heartbreakingly saying that she was late picking Serena up from school.

Serena at least has some support now. Her daughter Elinor turned up (Amy McCallum, who plays her, looks amazingly like Catherine Russell) and after a heart to heart with her mum in the Linden Cullen Memorial Shrubbery she's planning to take time off from college to help look after granny. And Raf was so lovely I'm going to have to stop calling him Smug (typical – just when he started calling himself Smug as well). He offered to look after Adrienne so Serena could spend some time with her daughter.

Serena had been looking after a patient with a drink problem, who was reluctant to call his wife and let her know. Serena told him he should make the call. "Sometimes people can surprise you," she told him. And she was right: Mo, Jesse, Sacha, Raf, Elinor – there were people behaving in surprising ways all over the hospital.

It's just grey matter

(Series 17, ep. 4 'Chaos in Her Wings' by Kate Verghese 4.11.14)

Imagine you were given this choice: you could either go and work in a hospital in Chicago, where all the doctors look like George Clooney and Noah Wyle (or they used to). Or you can stay at Holby and spend your days being belittled in front of bigwigs and taken for granted by Selfie.

This was the choice offered to Top Nurse Colette Sheward, and the only surprise was that it took her almost 60 minutes to reach her decision.

I've never been a fan of Colette – the character was initially promising, but a combination of being tainted by association with Selfie and her deadpan delivery made her hard to warm to. It's only been in recent-ish episodes, in her interactions with Serena and Fletch, that a softer side to her personality has really come out. But in this episode, I really felt for her. She so much wanted to fix everything for Selfie – sorting out his patient with her top quality people skills and doing her best to help Zosia, only to have it all thrown back in her face by a man who's so arrogant and so wrapped up in himself that he has no idea that other people have feelings. Or maybe he does: "I spend all day manipulating people's feelings," he told Colette. "It's just grey matter." Says it all, really.

The saddest bit was when Colette appeared all glammed up for a night at the opera with him, and all Selfie could say was that she didn't need to bother going if she didn't want to. And there was Jac Naylor looking even more glam. Selfie had obviously had a better offer.

Via the medium of a patient who collected butterflies and had a paper replica of a rare one, Colette finally realised there was more to life than the paper replica version she was currently living, and decided to spread her wings (the butterfly metaphors just won't stop now) and fly to a new life.

Maybe Colette's departure will be a wake-up call for Selfie and he'll finally get some proper help for his daughter, who's struggling. Zosia had made a DVD for Colette, and it was basically her rambling incoherently to the camera about her "research." Camilla Arfwedson is playing Zosia's mental illness beautifully. Sometimes it's so understated that you could think there was nothing wrong, but there's always a brittleness about her. At other times, like in this episode, it's clear that she's very unwell and desperately needs help, but so far people seem more inclined, for various reasons, to cover it up and pretend nothing's happening.

Down in AAU, Antony Costa from popular beat combo Blue arrived fresh fromSaturday's episode of *Casualty* (not exactly "fresh," poor lamb, as he was quite badly burned) and in need of some highly specialised plastic surgery. Dr Raf Smug decided he'd do it himself, but Michael Spence wasn't best pleased, accusing him of "swanning around like a tourist with a scalpel."

The situation was further complicated for Dr Smug because he'd kissed Antony Costa's girlfriend in Albie's earlier. Really, if he was going to get back on the romance scene he should have gone a little further afield than the nearest bar.

Darwin was the romantic hotspot of the day, with Adele Effanga and Jesse Law doing the classic bickering/sexual tension thing. She thought he was trying to steal Elliot Hope's latest invention, but he was only trying to help, while he teased her constantly about her "days of the week" pants. At some point when I wasn't looking Adele has graduated from being an HCA to being in joint charge of Prof Hope's research project. "We'd love to have you on board," she told Jesse when it became clear that he not only had the Prof's best interests at heart but also had handy skills. Unfortunately Jac Naylor was too busy getting glammed up for the opera – where's a handy verbal take-down when you need one?

There was a also a brief appearance from Connie Beauchamp, who materialised in Selfie's office. To be honest I have no idea why she was there, but it's always nice to see her anyway.

The one with the mobility scooter

(Series 17, ep. 5 'We Must Remember This' by Elliot Hope, Johanne McAndrew & Joe Ainsworth 11.11.14)

The writers of this episode used the fact that it was being screened on Armistice Day to add another poignant angle to the story of Adrienne's dementia – and to give us the magnificent sight of Serena driving a mobility scooter.

Serena encountered Eric (Dudley Sutton) in the car park. He was an old soldier in full military regalia, selling poppies and riding the aforementioned mobility scooter. He also had an excellent line in persuading senior doctors to part with cash. Unfortunately we know that the car park is never the safest place to be, and Eric got mugged. He wasn't too badly hurt (he had a dislocated shoulder, but he popped that back in himself. The piece of broken samurai sword that had been embedded in it since the war was a bit trickier to deal with), but his injuries meant a short stay in AAU – where Adrienne had just returned, having been ousted from the ward she was in for plot reasons. She's (understandably) not keen on AAU. "This is the worst hotel you've ever taken me to, George," she complained to Raf, "and the staff are appallingly rude!"

We've seen Adrienne relating (or not) to her daughter, her granddaughter and hospital staff, but we haven't seen her relating to someone of her generation who was able to share reminiscences with her and understand how she was feeling. Eric was lovely with her and made her smile. His wife had had dementia, and he had some wise advice for Serena: "Your mum is still in there somewhere. You want to go looking for her before it's too late."

The most distressing part of her mother's illness for Serena has been that Adrienne often no longer recognises her, but in a scene where she was helping to tidy Adrienne's hair, her mother asked her when she was going to get her own hair sorted out: "You've had that boy's haircut for years." Serena's smile was heartbreakingly lovely – just for a moment she'd got her mum back. Once again, Catherine Russell and Sandra Voe were brilliant, as Adrienne faced the fact that she was ill and mother and daughter wept in each other's arms.

This is not the time for Serena to be going off to America for a lecture tour, but she has been asked to do just that. She asked Fleur if she would be interested in going instead. Michael Spence was also up for the gig, and they both wanted it. So when this week's Keller Patient With A Mystery Complaint arrived, Michael suggested that whoever figured out what was wrong would get the job. They should have gone straight to Digby, because he's usually the man for a rare diagnosis. Fleur did actually ask for Digby (or "Clark Kent") to assist her in theatre, but Dominic was up to his old tricks. Fancying a ticket to the US as Fleur's assistant, he told her that Digby was already at lunch. Then he told Digby to treat himself to a nice lunch. Then he volunteered to assist in the operation. Cunning.

There was a further, non-surgical, complication in the form of Fleur's ex, Sophia (Nina Toussaint-White), who is working as a nurse on Keller. Fleur got rather cross when Michael Spence said he fancied "taking a run at Sophia," and threw him out of theatre. But technically he worked out that the problem with the patient was dead bowel (ugh), so he used his out-of-theatre time well. Fleur got the lecture tour anyway, but by then Dominic had already started to back the wrong horse by running off to get Michael a latte with sprinkles and whipped cream.

Talking of backing the wrong horse, on Darwin Jesse Law was continuing to turn Effanga heads, but this week the head was Mo's. And everybody knows that she really needs to be with Mr T. Jesse is rather lovely, though. He's obviously easy on the eye, but he's also very kind and supportive. Mo needed that this week, because she was doing a double lung transplant and things went horribly beep in theatre. At times like that you need someone calm at the head end. Jesse suggested doing the procedure on bypass and Mo settled down and got on with it and saved her patient's life. She would have taken "Team Transplant" further, but was disappointed to see that Jesse already had a date. Luckily Jonny Mac had a two-for-one curry offer, so the night wasn't entirely wasted.

Time's up

(Series 17, ep. 6 'Severed' by Joe Ainsworth 18.11.14)

Adrienne's story line was never going to end happily. The actors and writers haven't flinched from showing the emotional devastation, the little highs but many more lows of dementia for both the sufferer and those around her, particularly her family.

Sandra Voe gave the character of Adrienne great intelligence, humour and grace, which made it even harder to watch the disease make her act in ways that weren't really "her" – physically attacking Serena being just an outward sign of her deterioration.

So when Adrienne looked her daughter in the face and asked her to "pull the plug" on a life that was increasingly slipping out of her control, we knew she meant it. Serena knew she meant it as well, but as a doctor and as a daughter she pushed it away. In the end, she didn't have to make the decision and Adrienne's death (following another stroke) was quiet, gentle and very, very sad.

A photograph in her mother's purse of Serena as a child was a final precious proof that Serena had been loved, and as she walked down the corridor to leave she looked so vulnerable and alone, and her tears started to flow. I always think this must be such a hard thing for an actor to do, but Catherine Russell's acting throughout this story has been absolutely perfect. And I have to add a little cheer for Raf, who's been gorgeously kind and supportive to Serena and her mother and whose shoulder was there to cry on when needed.

On Keller it was business as usual in the sense that everyone was being competitive, self-absorbed and working to their own agendas. Michael Spence wanted to lie low at Holby for a bit longer, because it was all going pear-shaped in the US with the senator's wife scandal. So he asked Selfie if he could stay: "There's no better knife man" than him, apparently. His knife skills were soon put to the test when the team were required to re-attach the two severed legs of a man who'd been in a road accident. The left leg was much worse than the right, which meant that Fleur and Michael were competing over who got to do it and Digby and Dominic competed over who got to assist. Both the juniors still have their eyes on accompanying Fleur on her American lecture tour and they wanted the chance to impress. Digby even took an opportunity to ask Michael what qualities Fleur was looking for. "You need skin like a rhino," Michael said. "And a horn to match!" said Digby, quickly adding, "Please don't say I said that." Bless him.

Everyone went to Albie's to celebrate the successful reuniting of man and legs, but Michael went off to find Selfie – to let him know he's going back to America after all. He hinted that he may return to Holby, but next time he won't be doing it just to hide from scandal. And hopefully next time he'll stay for longer and grow his beard back.

On Darwin Adele was struggling to fit her work, her studies, her role as Elliot Hope's research assistant and her new job as Secretary General of the United Nations into her life. The work almost suffered (excellent prioritising, Adele), but once again Jesse Law was there with Operation Encourage An Effanga (Any Effanga). When he made a move on her in Albie's she made it quite clear that she didn't need that kind of encouragement, ta very much. Not when she has to get home and file her astronaut application to NASA.

Getting back to normal

(Series 17, ep. 7 'Flesh and Blood' by Jamie Crichton 25.11.14)

"The best way of getting me back to normal is getting me back to normal," Dr Zosia March told her father. Hard to argue with her logic, apart from the fact that "normal," to Zosia, means being at work.

For the past week or two she's been at an expensive and exclusive-looking clinic and the verdict from the doctor in charge of her was that she may be bipolar. As usual, Selfie was in denial. Mental illness? Goodness. Nothing that assisting with a bit of seriously tricky brain surgery won't sort out!

Obviously that didn't work out well at all, and even Selfie was finally forced to admit that having a grown-up daughter who writes all over the table in Pulses in salt isn't quite right. He went back to see the psychiatrist and admitted that his views of mental illness were "unenlightened." You don't say. Even so, despite Sacha offering some father-to-father advice and Zosia's odd behaviour being the elephant in every room she sets foot in, Selfie is still determined to keep the issue just between the two of them.

It's when your life has been through upheaval that you really find out who your friends are, as Serena discovered this week. Apart from clutching a biodegradable urn containing her mother's ashes (and yes, it did look like a big takeaway coffee cup), she was trying to pretend that she was getting back to normal by getting back to normal. During Adrienne's illness a lovely bond started to develop between Serena and Dr Raf (not smug at all these days) and he was adorable again this week. There was a beautiful scene where he brought two bottles of Shiraz and he and and Serena got pleasantly drunk in her office, talked about her mother, talked about his wife being pregnant possibly with Harry's baby ("My gast is well and truly flabbered," was Serena's response to this) and then went to bury Adrienne's ashes in the Linden Cullen Memorial Shrubbery (will I have to start calling it the Cullen/McKinney Memorial Shrubbery now?). "I'm glad she's somewhere I can see her all the time," Serena said, adding, "You're going to have to help me stop the drunks peeing on her." Brilliant. To top it all, Raf had arranged a trip to Paris for her – it was a place she'd visited with Adrienne. You have to say, what a man. I take back every negative thought I ever had about him (unless he starts being smug again).

To Darwin now, and I have to wonder where Jac is getting all this money from? She gave a load of cash to her mother to try and get rid of her, she presumably gives Jonny Mac money to pay for Emma's upkeep, yet she still has enough lying around to secretly finance Elliot Hope's latest invention, which was so expensive that the normal Darwin budget wouldn't go near it. Do you think she's won the Lottery? Can you imagine Jac popping into her local newsagent's for her regular copies of Take A Break and Cardiothoracic Sarcasm and a scratch card? Anyway, she's become Elliot's secret benefactor because she's lovely really and she adores him and believes in him and feels guilty for appropriating his Herzig. So he can now buy as many batteries and rolls of Sellotape as he needs to finish his invention and save lives. Hurrah!

Healthy body, healthy mind

(Series 17, ep. 8 'I Am What I Am' by Chris Lindsay 2.12.14)

How would Zosia cope with a busy day on a ward where Fleur has "upped the tempo"? Selfie didn't worry his grey matter with that sort of thing. As long as she's taking her medication and looking like the hot-shot junior doctor she's supposed to be, that seems to be fine with him.

Her shift wasn't made any easier by the presence of Lisa (her former roomie from the clinic), and a patient without a penis (not rare, I know, but this one was a man) who presented a particularly tricky case and kept speaking Zosia's brains at regular intervals.

Lisa, an artistic type, was convinced that her prescription drugs changed her personality too much, so she refused to take them. She was a wee bit obsessed by Zosia and pretended to have a heart problem so she would be admitted to Holby, but obviously she ended up on Darwin because that's where people with heart problems are put. This brought her in contact with the fragrant Jesse, who decided she was faking illness and sent her on her way. When Lisa's sister arrived and explained about Lisa's mental illness and tendency to take cocaine to self-medicate, Adele told Jesse that if he'd only spent more time with Lisa he'd have spotted that something was wrong. This is because as well as being a HCA, studying for a nursing degree, co-producing the latest life saving heart invention, being Secretary General of the United Nations and just commencing her astronaut training, Adele is also a Top Psychologist.

Jesse seemed to get the blame (and blame himself) for Zosia's condition, but I'm going to borrow Adele's Top Psychologist badge for a minute to speculate that she's had her illness for a long time – the whole time we've known her at least – and Jesse was almost a symptom rather than a cause. He was a contributing factor at most.

Back to the man without a penis on Keller. Not only had he had his manly part hacked off by an angry girlfriend (there was a lovely scene where Dominic was reading about this aloud from the internet, while Digby was about to eat a banana. The way he removed the banana from his mouth and let it hang limply was poetry in motion), but he'd had a childhood injury that meant he couldn't safely be anaesthetised – hence there was no chance of having his bits reconstructed. "Do you have any idea what it's like to lose a part of yourself?" he asked Zosia, and of course she does because the hyper part of herself was currently being chemically subdued.

Zosia has the makings of a brilliant doctor, and she worked out a way for the patient to have surgery for his stomach problem, which meant the reconstructive surgery would also be a possibility for him in the future. And then she dumped her pills and, worryingly, went out on the lash.

Angus Farrell, the man from the health authority who was previously so stern that he made Henrik Hanssen look like Graham Norton, was hovering around AAU. That's hovering, not hoovering.

There were so many non-speaking extras in this episode that there was probably someone hoovering somewhere in the background, I just wasn't quick enough to spot them. Angus was there for a bed blocking review. He wanted to send patients home within 24 hours over Christmas, and Serena wasn't having any of it – a bit of a turnaround from her former "bish bash bosh" approach to moving patients on, but she's been on the staff of Shoe Sick Central for quite a while now and knows what's what. One thing she knows is that sick people have to eat (unless they're nil by mouth or have just been sick on your shoes) and Angus had decreed that eating was a luxury AAU couldn't afford, so she ordered healthy takeaways for everybody from Wyvern Organics. I bet they aren't cheap.

Later on everybody was at a pub quiz. Serena and Raf were enjoying another bottle of Shiraz when they were joined by Angus, who is a pub quiz whizz, apparently. And was there a bit of flirting going on between him and Ms Campbell? I think there was.

Finding Mr Right

(Series 17, ep. 9 'Estel' by Patrick Homes 9.12.14)

Not an episode to be watching if you're feeling at all sensitive about babies for any reason (or sensitive about tinsel, but that's another story). There were two births, neither of them straightforward – lots of screaming for the first and Mr T up to his elbows in afterbirth with the second – but at least the outcomes were good. The births were also the background for much soul-searching and quite a bit of brains-speak. And, obviously, a chance to bask in the loveliness that is Mr T (MR T!).

AAU was the centre of these neonatal goings-on. There was a newborn with a CDH (the same condition as Jac and Jonny's Emma) who needed Jac's surgical skills and Raf's special ECMO pump. It's a scary piece of kit for a tiny baby to be attached to, and her mother Helen (Nathalie Cox) didn't at first consent to the procedure. Later on, Helen talked to Raf about how a mother is supposed to protect her child from nasty things like that happening. She spoke to a backdrop of Jac trying not to be emotional while operating on a tiny child with the same problem as her daughter – and to Raf, who in this episode may or may not have become a parent himself.

After barfing dangerously close to Dr Harry Posh's shoes, Amy went to see Mr T, who diagnosed pre-eclampsia and whipped out Baby Smug-Or-Posh by caesarean. Harry and Raf both appeared for the procedure ("You wait all day for a birth partner then two turn up at once," quipped Mr T). Baby S-O-P was born safely, but there was the standard post-childbirth hiccup for Amy, who needed a bit more of Mr T's skill to sort her out.

Raf went to visit the baby and reported back to Amy. The wee one has his mother's eyes, hair and temperament, apparently, and he also has a lot of willpower. Raf wondered if he dared suggest that the willpower came from him. Poor Raf – he so much wants it to be his baby.

Before I relinquish all thoughts of Mr T for the week, when is Mo going to realise that he is actually her perfect man? He was her Secret Santa and gave her a John Coltrane CD (he's so obviously a keeper). She was Secret Santa to Jesse and gave him a DVD of her favourite film *Strictly Ballroom* (incidentally the first film I ever went to see with Mr H) – which he promptly passed on to a delighted Mr T. See how well matched they are? But silly Mo still thinks Jesse is more of a catch, just because he goes surfing and wears a jazzy hat (though not while surfing, presumably). I did enjoy watching her face as she pictured Jesse wearing a thong, though.

"It looks like an elf sicked up," said Dr Dominic Copeland. He wasn't talking about Jesse in a thong. He was talking about Zosia's way with Christmas decorations. "It's very shiny," said Digby. "It's very magnificent," said Zosia. It was all of the above, and a bit more, and was a twinkly manifestation of Zosia's too-sparkly mind.

Dominic had other things on his own mind, as he was still trying to impress Fleur and get the LA lecture tour gig. It didn't help at all that his patient of the week was Mr Bing (Shaun Prendergast) – the man he may or may not have stabbed with a needle last time he was in the hospital. On that occasion I diagnosed toxoplasmosis before any of the doctors did, and this time I beat them to a diagnosis of Lyme Disease. I really should get out more.

At some point Zosia let slip in front of Kyle that Dominic used to be Darren, so now Kyle is all cross with him. Just wait till he discovers that Malick's not dead. But at least Fleur was impressed with his diagnostic skills. Just as well she didn't find out about him taking blood from other patients. He really is a loose cannon, but I find him very enjoyable.

What I didn't find enjoyable was the sight of Jac kissing Selfie at the end of the episode. Luckily, for whatever reason, Selfie knocked her back. "I thought you were a lot of things," said Jac, "But boring wasn't one of them." I'll just leave that thought hanging, I think.

Baby, it's cold outside

(Series 17, ep. 10 'Star of Wonder' by Julia Gilbert 16.12.14)

There's something about Christmas that makes everything more emotional, isn't there? The decorations, the lights, the singing, the excessive alcohol.

Just about everyone in this episode got emotional at some point, and none more so than Zosia. Oh, but it was sad. Zosia got it into her head that Anita Dobson off of EastEnders was her mum, come back to her for Christmas. Anita played Betty Stern, and she wasn't stern, she was sweet. And anyway, Stern is German for star, and through a random selection of star-based stuff, Zosia decided Betty was her mother. And, like Zosia's mother, Betty had cancer. Zosia was on a mission to save her, even if that meant some rather frightening fundraising on the ward and at the staff Christmas party.

Digby and Dominic tried to be helpful, but Digby was run off his feet with doctorly duties (dull, but someone has to do it) and Dominic was busy being terrified at the prospect of Christmas with Kyle's alcohol-free family.

Things got even sadder when Zosia visited a post-operative Betty, who now didn't recognise her, and then tried to find her mother under the Christmas tree next to the Linden Cullen Memorial Shrubbery (looking spectacularly festive). It was like that scene in Home Alone 2: Lost In New York, when Kevin's mother finds him under the Christmas tree, but without the happy ending. "Mama's dead, isn't she?" Zosia said to her father, who had no option – finally – but to put her in the care of mental health services. Once again Camilla Arfwedson was brilliant – Zosia's pain seems so exposed that it's sometimes hard to watch. Even Selfie was very touching, and Zosia has a real friend in Digby who always does his best to help her.

Mo thought she was on to a good thing when Jesse said he wanted to duet with her at the Christmas party. That's got to mean more than just singing 'Baby It's Cold Outside,' right? It made her go all flirtatious in theatre, but luckily she's such a good surgeon and multi-tasker that she can sort out a heart valve while still making eyes at the anaesthetist. The patient was Margie, who was in the episode in which Mr T dressed as an elf. In this episode, Mr T dressed in his finest going-out waistcoat to accompany Mo to the party – at the request of Adele [Memo: add "matchmaker" to increasingly long list of Adele's Skills]. Margie had advised Mo to "follow her heart," and Jonny Mac also gave her the same advice – dump Mr T kindly, to clear the way for Jesse.

Mr T may dance like he's being tasered, but he's the sweetest, nicest man in the world. He told Mo she was far too good for the likes of him – and then went outside and failed to start his little car, he was that upset. Meanwhile, Mo had spotted Jesse and her sister kissing. Ouch.

There were tears on AAU, caused by baby Callum Teo, the new baby of Dr Amy Smug-Teo and... well, who? Amy decided it was time everyone found out. Serena sorted out the paternity test (and had a little eyes-filled-with-tears moment at the sight of wee Callum, who was extremely cute). In my best Jeremy Kyle voice (picture me perched on a step at the front of the stage) I can now reveal that the father of the child is... Dr Harry Posh. Yes, Callum is semi-Posh. Harry told Amy he wanted to support his son in every way possible, but she said she and Callum were moving to Singapore. This made Harry cry.

Dr Raf Previously-Smug didn't cry, but he said that's because he'd told himself that it couldn't be his baby anyway because of his rubbish sperm. He and Serena decided to swerve the Christmas party and go for a few consoling bottles of Shiraz instead. Probably a wise decision.

A Valentine for Christmas

(Series 17, ep. 11 'I Will Honour Christmas in My Heart' by Elliot Hope & Johanne McAndrew 23.12.14)

Ric Griffin's back! And his very first action was to rescue a tramp who was being beaten up by a bunch of Holby's disaffected youth. It wasn't not just any old tramp, though – it was only the blue-eyed charmer formerly known as Young Dr Oliver Valentine, looking somewhat the worse for his bereavement-induced career break.

"He's one of ours," said Ric as he wheeled him into AAU, because for now, Ollie is a patient rather than a doctor (though he still knows his U's and E's from his LFT's). Months of not looking after himself very well and a brush with a nasty virus in the Andes had knackered his heart, and his liver wasn't far behind. There's only one man who can sort out a mess like that – Elliot Hope and his untested-on-humans Assist Device, and that's what Oliver had flown all the way back and hitch-hiked from Heathrow for.

This raised all sorts of moral, ethical and, yes, financial questions, and Jac put her foot down. "You are thinking with your heart and not your head," she told Elliot, but that's Elliot for you. Jac wasn't being horrible for the sake of it – she knew what failure would mean to Elliot personally and professionally, and for Ollie it would mean he was dead. "I'm not going to let you kill Oliver and this project at the last hurdle," said Jac, thinking of all the future patients that could be saved if the Assist Device only had time for a bit more tweaking.

Of course the operation went ahead – Ollie signed something to absolve the hospital of any blame should the outcome be bad. Jac told Elliot she was right behind him, and suggested the Assist Device was given the name Kibo – which is Japanese for Hope. Neat.

Most people know by now that James Anderson is coming back to Holby permanently, so the chances were good that he'd get through the surgery successfully. Even so, the operation itself was rather suspenseful – would the new device work? Could Ollie's weakened body cope with it all? Jac and Sacha waited nervously outside. Even Harry Posh was worried.

But Kibo worked, and Ollie lived to open his lovely blue eyes and blink handsomely at Elliot and Jac. He even had the cheek to ask for his job back, bless him.

Later on, Jonny (who knows Jac financed the prototype of the Kibo) brought in a package for Jac. It was a motorbike helmet – a gift from Elliot. And she'd been eyeing up a motorbike in the car park with longing in her eyes at the beginning of the episode, too, so I think fans of Jac in leather won't have long to wait.

She was fixing up her own teddy bear for Jonny to give to Emma – but she still won't take the step of seeing her daughter herself. She thinks Emma is better off without her in her life, but really what better role model could a little girl have than a kick-ass motorbike-riding top surgeon of a mother – who is also, in her heart, a good friend and very kind.

After his heroic tramp-rescuing, Ric's shift settled down to nothing more than a bit of low-level bickering with Serena. "What's been going on, Serena?" he asked. "My mother died and there's been a spot of bother with the boys," she said, summing up months of AAU storylines in one elegant sentence.

Selfie and Digby had to do brain surgery on Entertainer Darren Day, and Digby was rather tense because Jesse had told him that Selfie once went to pieces in theatre due to his wife's illness. Would he hold himself together now that Zosia has been sectioned? He did, although he spent worrying amounts of time waffling on philosophically about jigsaws. Zosia had been refusing to see her father, but Digby managed to get them talking again by commanding them to do a jigsaw together. As a strategy this was rather successful and Selfie has now asked Digby to call him Guy (only his very close friends get to call him Selfie).

In other news, Dominic is LA-bound after impressing Fleur with his essay, and Sacha received a pressie from Essie.

My dead ex is getting married

(Series 17, ep. 12 'Should Auld Acquaintance Be Forgot' by Tony Higgins 30.12.14)

Isn't it awful when your deceased One True Love decides to get married and you find yourself stuck in a lift with his dangerously ill fiancé? Come on, we've all been there. But why was Dr Dominic Copeland there (as in, anywhere near a Holby lift), when we last saw him packing his sunnies and about to go to LA to carry Fleur's briefcase for her?

He came home early because he missed Kyle, he told Kyle. There were complaints made about him by conference delegates because they were homophobic, he told Ric and Serena. Basically, he messed up and got sent home in disgrace. This and a telling off from Ric weren't enough to make him any humbler – he was soon busy slagging off Kyle's Christmas present to him. "A beige jumper. Medium." [Gives Kyle A Look] "You think I'm a medium." [Looks at the label] "Viscose." He didn't care at all that Kyle obviously adores him, and is gentle and honest and kind. What sort of qualities are these if you can't even manage to purchase natural fibres?

It was time Dominic learned a proper life lesson, and it came courtesy of Nathan Hargreave, who is now engaged to Malick. Wedding invitations have gone out and Henrik Hanssen is going to be best man (how I would love to hear his speech). When Nathan got knocked off his bike in the super-dangerous Holby car park, it only became obvious how bad his head injury was when he lost consciousness in a broken-down lift with only Dominic for company. Ric Griffin managed to lower down a fairly hefty-looking drill, and Dominic had to crack on and drill the skull of his former love rival. When he lost confidence, a little phone call to Kyle soon set him right.

This was despite Kyle having recently just discovered that Malick, who Dominic told him was dead, is very much not dead (indeed we heard his voice when he rang to congratulate Dominic on a job well done when his fiance pulled through safely). "You're just one big lie aren't you, Darren?" Kyle told Dominic later. Dominic's response was to propose, but Kyle is too sensible and northern to be taken in by that kind of thing. "I think you really need some help," he said. So via a good cry in the arms of Digby, Dominic toddled off to theatre to ask Sacha and Ric if he could scrub in. "I have a professional career to carve out," he informed them, but it remains to be seen how long he can keep that up.

On Darwin Mo was looking after Lauren, who had a heart problem and was also pregnant, which necessitated a lot of visits from Mr T (MR T!!!). The pregnancy had started out as a surrogacy, but when it was discovered that the baby had spina bifida the other parents didn't want to know, and Lauren decided she would keep the baby and look after it no matter what. This of course brought up a lot of feelings for Mo about her own surrogate pregnancy, and Mr T was sensitive and sweet as only he can be, especially compared to That Jesse. This combined with Mr T's natural wonderfulness and the fact that he brews his own elderflower wine convinced Mo to ask him to her sister's wedding (not Adele; there's a third Effanga sister apparently). "I'm asking the right man for the right reason," she said, and Mr T looked thrilled, until she friend-zoned him a few minutes later. Good grief, it's two steps forward, one step back for that poor man and his romantic ambitions.

There wasn't all that much going on down in AAU. They're ever such a matey bunch down there at the moment, with the whole lot of them piling down to Albie's to see in the new year together. Following a short burst of high-level flirting, Mary-Claire and Harry wandered off together. Nobody really noticed – Serena had just ordered a round of shots.

The outsider of the family

(Series 17, ep. 13 'Brand New You' by Rebecca Wojciechowski 6.1.15)

There were two stories in this completely brilliant episode. One of them, involving Zosia, was a continuation of the story of her illness and the fractured relationship between her and her father. The other story, focusing on the wedding of Mo's youngest sister Celia, brought in a completely new element of Mo's background. That this didn't feel like an add-on was down to Rebecca Wojciechowski's script, which beautifully drew in things that we already know about Mo (the surrogacy, the way she tries to hide an occasional lack of confidence), supported by key people from Mo's life as we know it – Mr T, Jonny Mac and Adele.

It was clear even as she arrived at her mother's house in Mr T's little wedding-bedecked Smart car (he is so precious), that there were tensions between Mo and her mother. The reasons for this were uncovered gradually throughout the episode, culminating in an emotional scene back at the hospital in which Mo discovered that the person she'd always known as her mother was in fact her aunt, and her birth mother had been an unmarried alcoholic who had a nasty death with only the two year old Mo with her. Ma Effanga had done her best to provide for her but had always resented her and blamed her for everything that had gone wrong in her life.

What I loved about the reveal scene was the way Mo asked Jonny Mac to stay with her while she had the conversation with the old family friend. That seemed so realistic to me – to want your oldest, bestest friend with you at a time like that. I like to be reminded of how close Mo and Jonny are.

I also like how much Mr T loves Mo and how this has been consistent ever since we first saw them together. I definitely think Mo should take Aunty Rose's advice to "Enjoy Derwood before I do," and she almost did enjoy a kiss with him (I'm confidently assuming she'd have enjoyed it), before they were interrupted by Elliot and Jonny.

Chizzy Akudolu was once again brilliant in the big emotional scenes and it was an episode that really showed her range, from the funny scenes of wedding dancing with Mr T to the devastation of learning that her past wasn't what she thought it was.

Another brilliant actress is Camilla Arfwedson, and in the second story we found Zosia was in a depressed phase of her illness, and once again the aptly-named Selfie was finding it hard to cope. Lisa, Zosia's room mate from the clinic, needed brain surgery following a suicide attempt, and Zosia was named as her next of kin. So Zosia was once again at the hospital, and Selfie was once again struggling to cope with the idea of an ill daughter.

If only he could be more relaxed about it, like Sacha, Serena, Digby and Dominic, who have formed a wonderful little Zosia Support Team. Serena was particularly helpful, realising that Zosia needed to feel normal and giving her some admin to do so she could still feel a part of things. Serena told Selfie that she'd suffered from depression herself in the past ("Leonard Cohen would have crossed the street to avoid me"), and maybe this revelation and the fact that it hadn't been career-breaking is the most helpful thing Selfie has heard on the subject, as when his daughter speaks he never seems to hear what she says. Anyway, father and daughter had a nice little moment in Pulses at the end of the episode.

Not really any AAU action this week, with Serena apparently on Keller for the day. At the beginning of the episode she was also at the gym, underlining exactly why she really is a role model to us all. She'd made the effort and put on a bit of Lycra, but on hearing what was involved in a healthy new year regime, she was unimpressed. "No booze..." she said, heading for the door. "This isn't really my bag."

We have contact with Miami

(Series 17, ep. 14 'Wages of Sin' by Elliot Hope & Johanne McAndrew 13.1.15)

Just before Jac Naylor was lured away to America to teach the Americans how to use the Herzig, there was the problem of Emma to address. It was Little Miss Jaccy Maccy Junior's first birthday, which meant that Jonny Mac had arranged a party complete with jelly, balloons and a rendition of 'The Wheels on the Bus,' because he believes in doing things properly. Jac had got a present for her daughter which was tastefully wrapped, but frustratingly we never got to see what it was. The box looked a bit too small to be 'My First Wet Lab,' but maybe she gave her one of those for Christmas.

The Americans offered Jac a generous childcare package, including extra trans-Atlantic flights for Jonny Mac so he could visit – but would Jac be able to deprive him of daily contact with his offspring?

In a word, no. I have to admit I didn't much care either way, as I'm somewhat over Jaccy Maccy Junior as a plot device until she comes back in a few years as a wild child (see below). It was the right decision under the circumstances – Jac does need to repair bonds with her daughter at some stage, but depriving Jonny of daily contact with her at this point would have been very cruel indeed. Not as bad as snogging Selfie as a consolation prize, though.

There was much excitement on Darwin as the Americans wished to see a Herzig procedure for themselves, so a live video link-up was arranged. Mo was lined up to do the surgery, all the better to showcase Jac's teaching skills. "We have contact with Miami, if you'd like to proceed," Selfie told Mo, because he enjoys being pompous and show-offy.

Mo was a bit nervous about doing her first Herzig on the telly in front of Miami and that, but she held her nerve – even when it became clear that the patient wasn't suitable to have a Herzig after all. Selfie and US representative Patsy Brassvine got a bit cross about this, but Jac supported her colleague and eventually the Americans conceded that Mo had made a good call and was exactly the type of well-mentored surgeon they hoped Jac would soon be turning out for them.

On Keller we discovered the dangers of taking those fictional over-the-counter enliveners 'Keepy-Ups,' when Sacha's daughter Rachel appeared at the hospital with amphetamine in her blood and a septic tattoo on her arm. She's obviously going the Grace Beauchamp route and turning into a Wild Child, and she'll have to get a grip on that tendency if she really wants to be a vet.

And on AAU, Mary-Claire was doing her best to resist the charms of Dr Harry Tressler ("He's like a budgie with a mirror," she told their mutual patient, accurately. And like a budgie, he's been careless with his seed in the past so she should think on). Harry was also trying to resist Mary-Claire. They couldn't manage to resist for an entire hour, so a clothing-ruffling visit to the on-call room was required. This could be fun, as there is actual chemistry between the two of them, though I hope the story doesn't go back down the old path of "Mary-Claire isn't the sort of girl you can take home to meet Mummy."

The first day of the rest of Fletch's life

(Series 17, ep. 15 'Sucker Punch' by Martin Jameson 20.1.15)

Since his transfer from *Casualty*, Fletch has been floating decoratively around AAU being funny, relatable, supportive – but without having anything very much to do apart from a bit of banter. This was fixed in dramatic style this week, as he was given what we might call an "emotional rollercoaster" of an episode to get his very nice teeth into.

Bleary from working extra shifts, he wasn't best pleased to see his ex-wife Natalie turn up on AAU, bladdered. Despite being bladdered she wasn't there as a patient, but as a patient's friend. She didn't realise the danger she was in – we all know about the Curse of the Patient's Relative/Friend, and the even more powerful Curse of the Staff Member's Relative/Friend (see below). Both of those groups of people are highly likely to end up in a very bad way indeed, and being both a patient's friend and a staff member's (ex) relative, Natalie was doubly cursed. It was no surprise that what started as a hangover ended up in an operating theatre with Selfie poking about in her brain.

Not a surprise for us – but definitely a shock for Fletch, and Alex Walkinshaw stepped his acting up a gear as Fletch went from "that nice guy who's fitted in brilliantly since he arrived" to being newly bereaved, blaming himself and having the care of four children to worry about. The scene with him struggling to say the right things to his children was beautifully done – Macey Chipping, as Fletch's oldest daughter Evie, really worked well with Alex Walkinshaw to make it touchingly real.

Children, eh? A constant worry. Just ask Sacha, whose daughter Rachel was still on Keller thanks to an infected tattoo. When she started being sick for no apparent reason, Sacha ordered all her tests to be done again. All of the tests. And Digby was not looking forward to Sacha finding out the result of one of the tests. It turns out that darling Rachel is pregnant, and Sacha didn't take the news too well.

Jonny Mac didn't take the news that Jac and Selfie are an item too well, and I think the entire Holby-watching world is with him on that one. So Jonny was in no mood to cooperate with Selfie's latest big plan, the "elective throughput initiative," which basically means fitting in as many operations as humanly possible, pausing only to run a damp cloth around the theatres in the wee small hours. It occurs to me that Jac, Mo and Elliot aren't going to be able to cover that kind of schedule on their own, so I'm hoping they'll need more staff. My vote would be for Oliver Valentine and (I do feel the need to mention his name at least once a month) Joseph Byrne, just to keep things ticking over. But I digress.

Jonny's patient this week was a rather wonderful monk-type person who called himself Sau Dharma, possibly because his real name was Gordon. He was in heart failure, but what with being a monk and that, he didn't want any more treatment. Sau Dharma had a proper monk beard and a properly spiritual tendency to wander round the multi-faith room nude. Not even Linden Cullen managed that level of holiness. He also had time for a little bit of brains-speak in Jonny Mac's direction when he said he'd worked very hard to get to a state where he didn't care – because Jonny Mac so does care about Jac and Selfie, so much so that he fronted his CEO out on his mad initiative and even called him "Guy." And not in a friendly way, either.

Bigger, stronger, wiser, kind

(Series 17, ep. 16 'Good Girls Don't Lie' by Kit Lambert 27.1.15)

In adjacent Keller beds, for convenience, we had Sacha's daughter Rachel still recovering from an infected tattoo, and a woman who during the course of the episode became a convicted murderer (the court case was proceeding without her). They usually flank criminal types with prison staff or police, but this woman had some vague connection with Selfie, so there was no need.

Last week we learned that Rachel is pregnant, and the father was assumed to be her best friend, the rather lovely Lloyd. Unfortunately for Sacha and especially Rachel, it turns out that the father is her teacher, Kreepy Kerrigan. Was I the only one who felt a bit queasy when he told Rachel he loved her?

Sacha (new motto: "Bigger; stronger; wiser; kind." It's some parenting thing) employed a great deal of compassion when dealing with the convicted criminal, Leila. He thought her murderous behaviour might have a medical basis and wanted her to appeal. He – understandably – was far less tolerant about the actions of his daughter's teacher and was ready to smash his face in and/or call the police. Rachel showed how absolutely mature she is by stamping her foot, going sulky and saying more or less that she would scweam and scweam until she was sick. Kreepy Kerrigan showed his maturity by legging it at the first opportunity.

Poor Sacha. I only hope that Essie has got her flight from Munich booked, because he needs all the help he can get at the moment.

On Darwin, Mo had a charming patient called Raheem who was eagerly awaiting becoming a British citizen. Meanwhile, Mo was trying to pluck up the courage to tell Adele that she was her cousin rather than her sister. Adele took the news fairly well, and the two Effangas decided that not being officially sisters wouldn't stop them being sisters. Adele threw a little party for Raheem's citizenship, and was the only person in the known universe who knew an obscure verse of 'God Save the Queen,' which contains a line about everyone being one family. We can therefore add to the long list of 'Adele's Skills' being able to brains-speak via the medium of song.

Meanwhile, in Shoe-Sick-Central, Mary-Claire has only gone and fallen for the dashing Dr Tressler-Posh. Well, he is dashing. And posh. They're still pretending that they're just "friends with benefits," though (and that might be how he thinks of her). They thought their patient was posh, but she was a cleaner. They also thought she had rabies from a bat bite, but actually she had hot tub lung (who knew?). These mistakes are bound to happen when your mind is confuzzled with romance.

Don't give your heart to just anybody

(Series 17, ep. 17 'The Beat Goes On' by Joe Ainsworth 3.2.15)

The Darwin and AAU stories intertwined this week. Darwin contained a boy who was brain-dead and was therefore a potential organ donor. At the top of the list for a heart/lung transplant was another Holby person, so to keep the families separate as protocol demanded, the potential recipient had to stay on AAU.

That's the bare bones of it, if you also throw in the 'parents disagree about whether to donate the organs' angle. It's a story we've seen before (not surprisingly, as Darwin contains a specialist transplant team), but it was beautifully played out by everyone involved and in fact was a bit of a heartbreaker, if that's not an insensitive word to use under the circumstances. Melanie Gutteridge was particularly good as the mother of the brain-dead boy. There was also lovely work from Jonny Mac, Mo and Jesse, who handled the issues and the parents' grief with great professionalism and sensitivity.

On AAU, Mary-Claire was accused of being a bit less professional and sensitive when the transplant recipient and his wife worked out that the donor family were up on Darwin. "Back to form," Serena tutted at her (a bit rich considering it was Serena's idea for MC to go for a permanent job), and MC got no support at all from Harry, who seems to be interpreting 'friends with benefits' as being more about the benefits – for him. Mary-Claire had her hands full anyway, as she was in charge of the ward while Fletch had to look after his kids, and one of the people she was looking after was Pat the Tramp, a frequent visitor to Holby and someone she knew well. He was concerned about his missing dog, but he was also concerned about Mary-Claire, as he could see that Harry wasn't valuing her properly and he had a go at him about it.

Serena's "back to form" quip could be better directed at Harry, who was once again being superior, insensitive and a bit of a twonk. When Pat died, Harry totally ignored MC's feelings by saying it was just as well that Pat had no family and nobody to grieve for him. Mary-Claire had had enough. She told him Pat was a real person just like she is, and she's bloody good at her job. Yay, MC! Then she turned down his offer of a 'social engagement' with him and went out into the Linden Cullen Memorial Shrubbery. I was writing down 'where she finds Pat's dog' even before she found Pat's dog, because it was kind of inevitable, but it was lovely anyway because he was a lovely dog and Mary-Claire took him home with her. A reliable, faithful and cuddly friend is really what she deserves.

Which brings me on to Sacha, though maybe 'reliable' isn't the word for him, as he'd completely forgotten that it was Rachel's birthday. Standard teenage girl behaviour would have been to drop so many hints you wouldn't be able to forget, but Rachel has had other things on her mind recently. One of the things on her mind has been Kreepy Kerrigan, the father of her pregnancy. Sacha thinks they aren't in touch any more, but they are – and they're making plans. Oh-oh. Sacha's plans for Rachel's birthday consisted of sending Dominic out to buy party stuff. He came back with a brilliantly disturbing cake (it looked like a peculiar hybrid of 'Mary Had a Little Lamb' and 'Baa Baa Black Sheep' rendered in icing), which Rachel threw up on in a spectacular 'blowing out the candles/morning sickness' mishap.

Sacha tried to make up for this by giving Rachel a driving lesson. Is he going to regret this when she steals a car and heads for Gretna Green with Kreepy K? He can't say I haven't warned him.

Worried about the Kidds

(Series 17, ep. 18 'Love Divided By Three' by Matthew Broughton 10.2.15)

By inserting triplet brothers into this weeks cast and giving them the surname Kidd, writer Matthew Broughton more or less ensured I'd have to have some sort of Kidd-related title this week.

The Kidds – River, Hector and Marmaduke (I can just picture their parents) – had a rare blood group, which meant poor River ended up being a blood bank for the other two and for his late mother. Yup, he was a veritable River of blood. Mo didn't think that was very fair, especially not when it compromised his own health, and when his position in the family was vaguely reminiscent of her own as the Effanga who's always been a bit different. On the subject of which, Ma Effanga popped in for an Outpatient appointment and gave Mo a shoebox containing old family photos etc, to try to help her make sense of her place in the Effanga dynasty.

While River Kidd was relaxing on Darwin waiting to see which of his brothers was in most urgent need of his precious blood, Marmaduke Kidd was on AAU waiting for gall bladder surgery and Hector Kidd was on Keller with a tear in his kidney. This all resulted in a multi-ward case conference, in which Mo went in to bat for River before his brothers bled him dry, Harry argued the case for Marmaduke to have the elective surgery he needed because he had to get out of hospital and sort out the family finances, and Sacha trumped everybody because Hector had just become an emergency case. It was all quite thrilling.

With all that going on, it was hardly surprising that Sacha didn't notice Rachel sneaking out of the hospital, stealing Digby's bike and heading off down one of Holby's picturesque forest paths to rendezvous with Kreepy Kerrigan.

The only person who had a clue where she might have gone was Digby, who'd read coded messages from Kreepy on her phone (she asked him to, for some reason – did she really want him to stop her?). I absolutely loved the little disapproving shake of his head when he said "Text speak." By putting two and two together, Sacha was soon heading off down the same forest paths in his Merc, which was a lot faster than a bike ridden by a very ill teenager (she had a heart thing by now, it wasn't just the infected tattoo). He was able to spot her route because she'd left a handy trail of bloodstained tissues, and her found her collapsed and bleeding from her face.

Back at Holby Jac did her usual wonders in surgery and Rachel will be fine, but she lost the baby. There was no news about what happened to Kreepy Kerrigan or (more importantly) Digby's bike.

Down on AAU, it looks like Dr Harry Tressler-Posh has fallen in love – with the wonderful Mary-Claire. Since she withdrew the benefits from their friends-with-benefits arrangement, he's now seeing her in a more rosy-tinted light, perked up by jealousy that she's dating someone called Adam who wants to take her to Berlin for the weekend.

And on the subject of the males in Mary-Claire's life, the adorable Norman (the dog she acquired last week) followed her to work. He really is a keeper.

And thanks to everyone's efforts in all three wards, the Kidds were alright.

Excellent work, Nurse Carter

(Series 17, ep. 19 'Be Bold, Be Bold' by Catherine Johnson 17.2.15)

In this episode, Mary-Claire faced everyone's worst nightmare – trying not to laugh at a very poorly executed tattoo. But she's a professional, and the tattoo was on her patient, so she didn't laugh. James, the patient, thought she was laughing at one point, and fairly soon she was barricaded in a cupboard with him while he insisted that she removed the tattoo for him with only a sharp knife to help her. That's how much he really hated that tattoo (which had a look of Michael Jackson crossed with Davina McCall on Camoxidan about it).

Luckily for Mary-Claire he also had a collapsed lung, because it was a bit of a tense situation before that, with James having a crack at getting the tattoo off himself, and then holding Mary-Claire at knifepoint.

When you're in a cupboard with a distressed man with a knife and a collapsed lung, what you really want is to hear the calm, assured voice of authority, and luckily Ric Griffin was making one of his rare appearances at work and was able to talk her through an improvised chest drain. Meanwhile, Dr Harry Tressler was fretting because his favourite girl was in peril but he hadn't managed to kick the door down. I'm glad he didn't – Mary-Claire coped fine under pressure and impressed Ric, and she didn't really need a Jules Knight in shining armour to save her. She even turned down the offer of a post-trauma drink with him, preferring a night on the sofa on her own instead. This left Harry sighing longingly after her, before distracting himself with an anal abscess as big as his head.

On Keller, Sacha briefly went to pieces in theatre because of all the pressure of the Rachel/Kreepy Kerrigan situation. Luckily he had Digby on hand to calm him down and he was soon back on track saving the life of Llovely Lloyd's foster mother. Meanwhile, Llovely Lloyd was out in the car park vandalising Kreepy Kerrigan's Kar. To be fair, Sacha had punched Kreepy on the nose at the beginning of the episode, but it really took Lloyd's direct action to show Sacha that he had to be extremely firm. He made Kreepy tell Rachel that their "relationship" was over, and then the police arrived.

On Darwin, it was round two of Guy Self v Jonny Maconie. Jesse's money was on Guy. "He's K2," he said. More like R2D2 if you ask me, but still. A very annoying posh girl called Minty, whose father was on old friend of Selfie's, made a nuisance of herself on the ward by making selfies of Selfie and a video of staff disgruntlement and putting them up on Holby's answer to YouTube, "GreatVid." This is the sort of stuff that gets militant nurses sacked, but Selfie isn't going to sack Jonny – the threat of a sacking is much more powerful and has ensured that, for now, he's got Jonny Maconie on side in his quest to fill the operating theatres to capacity at all times.

I have to admit that I'm as worried as Jonny is by Selfie's plan. As the cry, "Let's get him/her straight to theatre" goes up at least twice an episode, what are they going to do if the theatres are all constantly full? Or will they keep a spare "straight to theatre theatre" handy, just in case? And what happens when Sacha, Jac and Serena all need to get somebody straight to theatre at the same time? I can't help thinking Selfie hasn't thought this through.

Measuring contests

(Series 17, ep. 20 'Domino Effect' by Katie Douglas 24.2.15)

Why is Selfie doing chest compressions on a Darwin patient? Why does Jonny want to keep going with the resuscitation attempt even though it's been 30 minutes already? Why do Elliot and Selfie think they should stop? Why does Jonny Mac start trashing stuff afterwards?

And… flashback to several hours earlier. Julie Kale is a patient without long to live (we know that already because we just saw her die) – and all that's standing between her and the Grim Reaper at this point is Elliot and his shiny new, only ever tested on Oliver Valentine, Kibo device. Julie's ready, her husband is ready (he has short-term memory issues following an accident – which will be important later), Elliot and the staff are ready – and Selfie is ready, because it's another chance to show off the world-beatingness of Holby.

Unfortunately with hospitals, those squidgy, inconvenient things known as patients keep cropping up to ruin the very best laid plans, and an accident at the docks meant every ward was swarming with at least one extra patient.

Julie and her Kibo had better wait until the next day, reasoned Elliot and Jonny. Selfie disagreed. "I'm striving for excellence," he muttered between clenched teeth at Darwin's top nurse, adding a little threat: "Not everyone will make the cut. You're looking tired – I do hope you're getting enough rest." (He wasn't, thanks to extra shifts and Emma not being well).

So it was off to theatre with Julie, the Kibo was installed, and all might have ended happily. But remember how the Kibo is 50% toilet roll middles and pipe cleaners and 50% batteries? Jonny showed Memory Loss husband how to change the battery, but was called away (on account of the ward being super extra busy) before he had time to properly log it on the chart. When things were getting a bit beepy later, Memory Loss husband fixed the problem – by changing the new battery back to the old battery. The battery died and Julie soon followed it, and now Jonny is going to be right in the frame when Questions are asked. And Jac is probably going to shout at him too when she finds out Emma is ill. I predict an unhappy week for Jonny next week.

When there's been an accident at the docks you expect more mayhem than usual on AAU, but there was still plenty of time for us to ponder Mary-Claire's romantic life. A rather thrilling helicopter medic called Tom, who had no qualms about taking someone's leg off at the scene without anaesthetic, turned out to be an old flame of Mary-Claire's. They had planned to move to Australia together once upon a time, but he'd bottled out. As luck would have it, he was once again just about to go to Australia and he offered Mary-Claire a job with him. She was tempted, not least because he was a bit of a hunk. Dr Harry Posh was jealous, and the two men got all competitive. "I hate to break up the measuring contest, guys," Mary-Claire said, in an effort to keep their minds on work.

Mary-Claire's mind is on work as well as romance, and Ric (we've seen him two weeks running!) told her she'd been doing her job rather well recently. What she really wanted was for Harry to beg her not to leave, and she gave him a chance to do it but he didn't take it. So she's told Tom she's interested in the job, but not in him – when he kissed her, it was just "fine," and she really wants more than fine.

There were men being competitive on Keller as well, to complete a full house. In this case it was Digby and Dominic. Digby asked Dominic to cover for him while he took his girlfriend Maria for breakfast, because he'd hardly seen her recently. Dominic was about as cooperative as Selfie (though obviously with much better hair). By the end of a shift where they eventually had to collaborate to solve a tricky problem (which either of them could probably have sorted with a quick call to a senior colleague or Doctor Google), Dominic agreed that Digby could go out for his breakfast. "We're not about to form a band or get matching tattoos," he added, just in case Digby was getting ideas above his station.

The three unluckiest men in Holby

(*Series 17, ep. 21 'Trust in Me' by Jon Sen 3.2.15*)

This was the episode when Dr Harry Tressler-Posh finally realised that he was in love with the radiant Mary-Claire Carter, and decided to tell her. It was either that or watch her swan off into the Australian sunset with Helicopter Tom. Mary-Claire assured Harry that Australia was only a work arrangement and she and H-Tom weren't an item. Anyway, "You're the one who told me I deserved the best," she reasoned. "Yes," he reasoned back. "I meant me." Bless him – modesty still intact even in the face of imminent heartbreak. Mind you, if he'd known how the day was going to turn out, he might have agreed to accept "imminent heartbreak" as a less painful alternative.

What happened instead was that a patient's boyfriend, getting cross at the amount of time it was taking for a Darwin doctor to pop down to AAU to have a look at his girlfriend, decided it was time for a Dramatic Gesture. Breaking with years of Holby tradition, he didn't immediately make his way to the basement. He didn't even bother with the roof. Instead he ended up on one of those window cleaning platform thingies and, because no Holby relative/friend is safe from the Curse, became ill himself. Harry overcame his fear of heights (briefly mentioned last week in response to H-Tom's offer of a chopper ride) and climbed out of a window to the rescue. What happened next was both inevitable (this is Holby, after all, and I'd seen the spring preview) and dramatic – I actually emitted an involuntary sound something like "Eeep!" when Harry fell.

Thanks to the surgical skills of Serena and the never-give-upness of Raf (no former love rival is going to die on his watch!), it looks like Harry is going to live – but will he ever be the same? His liver is mashed, his brain may have been starved of oxygen for too long, and there's been damage to his precious, pretty face. Surely Mary-Claire won't be able to go to Australia and leave him in that state?

On Darwin it was all about the repercussions of the death of Julie Kale last week. Ric Griffin, achieving something of a record by appearing in three episodes running, was Selfie's "objective ear" as the staff were grilled by the charm-free CEO in an attempt to find out what happened. Selfie was fairly satisfied that Jonny was at fault, despite Jac rather marvellously sticking up for him ("He is a brilliant nurse and a good man"), and when Jonny was discovered fishing the missing battery out of a bin, it seemed he'd been caught red-handed. He's now helping the police with their enquiries – a mere year(ish) after Bonnie's death, as well. If Harry Posh hadn't fallen off a window cleaning platform and smashed his face and his liver, you'd have to call Jonny Mac the Unluckiest Man in Holby.

Compared to all this, Digby could only rank as Third Unluckiest Man in Holby. Marine Maria apparently dumped him after their breakfast last week, proving that she must be a bit of an idiot, because he's lovely. What Digby really didn't want was the support/sympathy/smirks of his two housemates, but Dominic and Zosia had other ideas. Sacha was relieved about this, as it distracted Dominic from his attempts to revamp Sacha's wardrobe.

Jonny be good

(Series 17, ep. 22 'Blindside' by Anna McPartlin 10.3.15)

(This review guest-written by Emma Chaplin)

I'm counting down the days until Henrik Hanssen is back in the captain's chair on the bridge, or wherever the person in charge of this hospital keeps everything running smoothly. Selfie is a vain, inept twonk, and I don't like it when there are staffing shortages and confusion over shift patterns, however fictional. Jonny can be irksome at times, but it's preposterous that he should be on remand awaiting trail for murder. Great that it transpires at the end of the episode that Jac is paying for a high-class defence team for him (as well as supporting Elliott's Kibo development. She must have a hell of a salary), but I'm not sure why he couldn't get bail, neither do I understand why he has no memory of explaining how to change the battery of the 'Kibo' to the memory-deficient partner of the patient who died.

And talking of Kibo. I know we're supposed to suspend disbelief that the kindly (and adorable, of course) Professor, apparently powered-by-donut, Elliott Hope, is a brilliant inventor of lifesaving devices, but was it just me who found the plastic sandwich bag inflated by a straw didn't quite cut it as believable as a piece of medical genius?

Other plot lines this week – one benighted family are spread over three wards, each with different and distressing medical crises. Mother (heart problems – recipient of the balloon/straw sandwich bag device technique), plus autistic son and rugby-playing daughter.

The daughter is treated on Sacha's ward of anal warts and other gastro-intestinal problems, by the adorable, but sadly less than fragrant (and cruelly nicknamed by evil genius Dom 'vomit boy' this week) Digby. We see him dithering about his medical future, as he attempts to summon sympathy and a supportive bedside manner, by relating memories of bad games lessons, where his genius for strategy was never truly appreciated by his rugby teacher. Digby's on "a journey" (at which point I vomit) that will end in a GI speciality, you mark my words.

And then we have the Posh story. "Hero" Harry Tressler, apparently wearing an empty chocolate box wrapper to hide his poor, broken cheekbones after last week's window cleaning hoist heroism, has two women in conflict at his side. The lovely NHS-powered MC v Posh's Hermes-scarf-wearing mother, who clearly believes medicine is only clinically effective if you pay top whack for it, trying to whisk her son away to a private clinic. I was going to say fictional, then I remembered it all is. She seems to feel that the surgeon who tried to end her son's career (Raf) isn't necessarily best placed to save his life. MC, Fletch and the rest of us who watch Holby know better, obv, and they/we are proved right. Raf saves Posh's sight. Hurrah for the NHS! And it's sweet that MC and Harry end up with a tender moment, and not just because of his bruises.

Plot-wise, Jonny's cruel porridge means his adorable daughter Emma (and, my how she's growing up fast) gets a cuddle from Elliott and Mo, and to sit on the knee of her hitherto absent mummy Jac. And that was a smashing ending.

Now, where's Hanssen?

Picking up the mantle of Michael Spence

(Series 17, ep. 24 'Rock and a Hard Place' by Elliot Hope & Johanne McAndrew 24.3.15)

I haven't blogged for a couple of weeks, during which time Jonny Mac has been incarcerated, Jac has been reunited with Emma and Dr Harry Posh has been starring in his own version of The Phantom of the Opera while Dr Raf Smug works out how to use his new 3D printer. Or something.

"Make me pretty again," Harry said to Raf at the start of this episode, and Raf was all set to do just that, having studied the Tressler face more closely than even the most besotted fangirl clutching a signed copy of a Blake CD. Then Raf's brother, Thug Smug, turned up with the news that their mutual mother, Mama Smug, had passed away. As always with a McAndrew/Hope episode, the writing was spot on. Serena telling Raf about her trip to Paris when she found herself sobbing about Adrienne in front of a Chateaubriand and a nice Bordeaux was a lovely scene and it was nice that Serena could support Raf as he'd supported her.

Raf had to decide between dashing back to Glasgow to support his dad and staying at Holby for another day to sort Posh's face out, and despite a lot of emoting from Thug Smug (not happy to learn from Mary-Claire about the Posh/Smug/Barf triangle – now he knows how we felt all those weeks) he chose to operate on Harry. Just as I was thinking fondly that Michael Spence used to be the go-to guy for that type of thing, Ric Griffin spoke my brains by telling Raf, "You are picking up the mantle of Michael Spence." And what a mantle it is.

Meanwhile, Ma Effanga was admitted to Darwin with chest pains and Elliott thought she might bleed to death at any minute. This meant that Mo really had no choice but to talk to her about the mysterious man in the photograph (Clifford, Mo's father). She greatly benefited from a pep talk from the glorious Mr T (MR T!!!), but I can't imagine anyone who wouldn't benefit from five minutes of Mr T wisdom.

For reasons best known to himself, Digby told Serena he wanted to specialise in emergency medicine (hello? You do know that Connie Beauchamp is in charge of that gig don't you? If you think Serena's scary…), so she gave him a man who'd been injured in a caving accident to look after. Everyone assumed it was just the heartbreak of his recent break-up with Marine Maria that has made Digby go all useless ("Any idea what's hampering the erstwhile Dr Digby?" Serena wanted to know), and I hope they're right. When he's being outperformed by Dominic, something is very wrong. He got more interested in the causes of the accident, in a manner very reminiscent of the way Zosia often behaves, and that's not the Digby I know and love. He needs to sort himself out.

Selfie fails to impress anyone

(Series 17, ep. 25 'The Last Time I Saw You' by Julia Gilbert 31.3.15)

Shall it be Holby or The Mythical St James's for the Cardiothoracic Super-Centre? And doesn't that question have a familiar ring about it? It seems like a CT contest between Holby and its mythical rival is almost an annual event.

The decision-making power this time seems to rest in the hands of one Dept of Health bigwig, Neil Maclin (unseen), and his wife Francesca – seen, because she had a cough that Elliot needed to sort out. Luckily (for Selfie) she also needed some spinal surgery, which gave him a chance to show off his fabulous surgical skills. It also gave Francesca the chance to observe his personality at close quarters. "I don't like him either," she confided to Elliot at the end of the episode, and she offered to make sure the Super-Centre went to St James's just to spite him. Elliot convinced her that he'd rather like to have the Super-Centre all the same – so if Holby gets it, it will be despite, rather than because of, Selfie's efforts.

If only the charm-free CEO had realised that his own Self was the hospital's greatest liability, he mightn't have worried so much about Prisoner X, or Jonny Maconie as we've come to know him, littering a side room with his inconvenient presence. At the time of writing, Jonny Mac has been returned to the Wyvern County Jail, but thanks to Mo's efforts in helping Memory Loss Steve to recall changing the battery that Jonny had just changed (oh, I did feel sorry for Steve), we can be fairly optimistic about an early release. And will he, Jac and Emma skip off happily into the sunset together? It's looking increasingly likely.

It's looking less likely that Harry and Mary-Claire have a future together, though, as she's just decided to accept a job working with Michael Spence and Colette in Chicago (nooo! Don't leave, MC!). Don't they have any doctors or nurses in the US? They always seem to be casting their recruitment net in the direction of Holby.

Dr Harry Posh was making plans to go to Chicago too, but it was mainly because he hoped Michael Spence could give him his own beautiful face back rather than the rather lumpy job he's been left with as a result of Dr Raf Smug's efforts. Not that Dr Raf hasn't done a brilliant job, because he has – but Harry's expectations of facial reconstruction were unrealistically high. Everyone agreed he wasn't ready to relocate to Chicago, particularly as it's known as the Windy City and everyone knows that "if the wind changes direction your face will stay like that."

Meanwhile, Digby carried on pursuing his detective theories about last week's caving accident, while merrily ignoring some actual internal bleeding. Dominic bailed him out more than once, with the rather implausible result that he impressed Serena and she's given him a job on AAU. That could go horribly wrong – but on the other hand Digby isn't a million miles away from Dr Ethan Hardy off of Casualty, personality-wise, and Ethan does very well in a trauma setting. We'll have to wait and see – but I'm sad the Dig & Dom partnership has to be split.

Jonny learns to live a little

(Series 17, ep. 26 'Squeeze the Pips' by Nick Fisher 7.4.15)

When Jonny Mac left the Wyvern County Jail with a friend he'd met inside, it was inevitable the friend (Archie) would end up being a patient on Darwin before the hour was out. He only had time to steal some drugs from the pharmacy, get bladdered and utter some life guidance to Jonny, before he was whisked away to theatre to die on the operating table with a heart turned into a soggy sponge by a lifetime of poor lifestyle choices.

Jonny's made a few of those in his time, but starting a relationship with the stunningly out-of-his-league Jac Naylor wasn't one of them. Not only did they mutually create Wee Emma, but Jac also paid for the hot-shot lawyer who sprang Jonny from prison (with the loose change she had left over from funding the Kibo prototype). When he had a post-Archie meltdown, Jac was there to deliver some honesty. "You sound like a moaning, whining, crying little bitch," she told him sweetly, adding that he should cheer up because he had Wee Emma and if he wanted, he could have her too. Yes! She really said that.

We were then treated to possibly the finest Jonny Maconie moment ever, when he found Selfie and delivered a little straight talk in his direction ("You, Mr Self, do not get to squeeze my pips"). Then he left the hospital arm in arm with Jac, who'd even purchased a 'Welcome Home Daddy' balloon to celebrate the fact that she's possibly gone a little soft in the heed. Nevertheless, a suitably warm exit for Jonny, who's been by turns cuddly, human, exasperating, downright nasty and back to cuddly again. Also nice for Jac to have some happiness, and I like the way the writers have built up to this gradually. I can't help thinking that if Joseph Byrne became available, Jonny might seem a less attractive proposition, but that's possibly me projecting my own feelings on to Jac.

Also being welcomed home this week was Essie, which is marvellous news because there aren't any other nurses on Keller who speak (and she speaks sign language as well as English, as a bonus). Sacha was thrilled to see her for that reason, but also because he hearts her romantically. Unfortunately, he's not great at communicating with the women in his life, particularly when My Daughter Rachel has a health crisis of any description. It happened with Chrissie, and it's happened with Essie. While he wasn't communicating with her while she was in Germany and Rachel was ill/pregnant, she sought solace with someone called Dirk. This news made Sacha decide to push the self-destruct button on the relationship before it could really get going again, because he's sick of being a cuddly teddy and he doesn't even want to be a spaniel. We'll have to wait till next week to find out what he does want to be, though.

What Digby wants to be is a good doctor, but he found his first shift on AAU rather bamboozling (Digby in blue scrubs – winner). This is because on Keller he's been used to the luxury of every patient having at least three junior doctors and a consultant at the bedside at all times. On AAU all you've got is Raf pretending to be stern and Mary-Claire and Fletch being a bit giggly and undermining. That could all get very wearing, but Digby was still able to pull one of his brilliant diagnoses out of the bag and impress everybody. "You out-smugged Dr Smug," Fletch told him admiringly. I do like it when they get the staff names right.

Everything must go

(Series 17, ep. 27 'Go the Distance' by Alex Child & Andy Bayliss 14.4.15)

This episode left me with a warm, fuzzy feeling – which is surprising considering that large swathes of screen-time were occupied by Selfie blustering around the hospital corridors.

The writers did their best to reposition him as a man of integrity who really just wanted to do what he does best – drill people's skulls. The CEO life wasn't really for him, he realised. He wanted to be there at the soggy end with his fingers in a brain. To add to the sympathy factor, his late wife was invoked (it's hard doing something when the person who loved you doing it is no longer there, or words to that effect) and he seemed more than a tad affected by Jac's sudden disappearance (taking her deferred maternity leave, it turns out). The lack of Jac also worried Ric, who was at Selfie's shoulder at regular intervals looking concerned. "There's a super-centre roaring down the highway with no one at the wheel," Ric said, and I wasted too long in trying to picture what that would look like.

Selfie even apologised to Elliot for taking his Herzig away, though it was a fairly limp apology: "If I hadn't taken away the Herzig you wouldn't have discovered the Kibo," he reasoned, with a classic bully's defence, before promptly giving the Herzig back to Elliot because of that super-centre roaring down the highway. Because Selfie hasn't really changed. Even though he no longer wants to be CEO, he's not content with just being Mr Average Brain Surgeon (if such a thing exists). A quick phone call to the deep-pocketed Patsy Brassvine instantly secured funding for 'The Guy Self Centre for Neurosurgery and Neurology' (or Self Centre, for short). See? Just a normal Guy.

He announced all this to a bemused board of non-speaking extras and Ric, before putting Serena's name forward as his replacement and assuring them that he'd work his notice – because despite having just given himself a new department and a new job, given Elliot a new job, suggested Serena for one and ruined the chances of Raf getting his Max Fac funding, he does like to stick to protocol wherever possible.

Right at the end, we paid a brief visit to the scene of domestic bliss that is the Naylor/Maconie household, to see Jac, Jonny and Emma playing Connect 4 (not a sentence I ever thought I'd write) and playing host to Elliot and Mo. It was absolutely adorable, as they all basked in happiness and the knowledge that the Reign of Self is all but over.

Also over was the Holby career of the glorious Mary-Claire, who has been one of my all-time favourite characters, and it was a fittingly lovely send-off for her (and for Jules Knight, leaving to continue his musical career). Filling all the wards with many boxes of her old toys, she prepared to say her goodbyes and go off to Chicago with her lovely dog Norman. But what of her true love, Dr Harry Posh? Well, I have to report that he's made the best recovery from plastic surgery since Chrissie Williams and her vanishing scar, because he looks more or less back to normal. Having a bashed-in face made him reassess his priorities, though, and his priority now was revealed when an engagement ring fell out of his jacket pocket. It still took a bit of manoeuvring by Raf, Serena, Fletch and Digby (hilariously dressed as John Travolta in Grease) to get them together, though, and it could only be achieved by shutting them in the back of a fairy-light bedecked ambulance together. "Are you trying to bloody marry me, Harry?" said Mary-Claire. He is, too – and 'MC Posh' has quite a ring about it, I think.

Romance was also in the air on Keller, where Essie and Sacha eventually said they loved each other. Sacha had apparently spent the night in his car, which I think he should do more often because it made his hair look pleasantly fluffy.

Welcome to the Self Centre

(Series 17, ep. 28 'All About Evie' by Joe Ainsworth 21.4.15)

This was always going to be a transitional episode – last week's festival of happy-ever-afters tied up so many loose ends and saw so many departures that it feels like Holby is moving into another phase (which thrillingly will involve the return of Henrik Hanssen and Oliver Valentine).

There was already a new arrival in the form of neurosurgeon Annabelle Cooper (Nina Wadia). When she arrived to start her new job at the Self Centre for Brains And That, she was surprised to discover it closely resembled a general surgery ward, namely the ward we usually refer to as Keller. It was a work in progress, explained Selfie to a clearly disappointed Annabelle, who'd been led to expect a facility like the one on Critical. She seems like a can-do sort of person, though, and rolled her sleeves up and got stuck into a day pleasantly filled with taking Zosia under her wing mainly to annoy Selfie. I like her already.

Also on Keller, Sacha approached Dominic for interior design advice, because he doesn't want his cushions to disappoint Essie. Dominic is normally fairly happy to play up to a stereotype, but on this occasion he was a bit miffed. "You know, I too have a wotsit," he said. "Please don't talk about your wotsit," said Sacha. In the preview version I watched originally, Dominic and Sacha actually said "penis," but maybe you aren't allowed to say "penis" on iPlayer, even in a medical drama. Even though it made the line funnier.

There wasn't much comedy to be had on AAU, where the Holby Finger of Fearful Fate was pointing at Fletch and his struggles to cope as a single dad. A school bus crash gave Fletch the double worry of discovering that daughter Evie is being bullied because he forgot/couldn't afford to buy her some new shoes for school, and having to care for a malnourished young woman called Roza. He found Roza's problems easier to deal with, by sending a social worker friend round to check that her family were okay. "You shouldn't be too proud to ask for help," he told her. Then he promised Evie that they would manage and he would get her some new shoes. Once again Alex Walkinshaw and Macey Chipping were very sweet as father and daughter.

Fathers and daughters were also on the agenda for Adele, who decided that Mo has been dithering too long (ooh, all of a fortnight) about whether to find out more about her biological father, and started rooting through hospital records. It wasn't long before she had a name and full medical history, because apparently he's no stranger to Holby (and it can only be a matter of time before the Finger of Fearful Fate beckons him in again). Mo wasn't best pleased.

We need to talk about Guy

(Series 17, ep. 29 'Small Disappointments' by Patrick Homes 28.4.15)

The episode was officially titled 'Small Disappointments,' but the only small disappointment about it from the point of view of thousands of excited Hanssenites was that the man in the black raincoat took so long to appear. There was an early sighting of him eating a sandwich in the Linden Cullen Memorial Shrubbery, but it wasn't until the last minute when he was properly seen and actually heard.

Until then, we were presented with a couple of red herrings as to who would succeed Guy Self as Holby City CEO. It was fairly certain it wouldn't be Serena. The shoes gave it away. She was wearing the kind of shoes that on Holby symbolise A Powerful Woman. We may term them 'Connie Beauchamp shoes.' Three steps later and Serena was on her bum on the newly washed floor, because the shoes of office were not for her (though we know she's a Jimmy Choos rather than a Crocs kind of gal in general). A few minutes after that she was flat on her back on the floor with the scary man from the board, Angus, on top of her with a dislocated shoulder. This led to some funny scenes with Angus on morphine (Catherine Russell is so brilliant at comedy stuff – it's the way she has Serena maintaining her elegant poise whatever happens), which resulted in Angus and Serena arranging a date for Saturday, but reinforced how those shoes were just not her. Ric understood the shoes were metaphorical as well, and he agreed that they weren't the right fit.

It turned out that Selfie had other plans anyway. There's a woman we've never heard of before in orthopaedics called Olivia Sharpe, and she is apparently just the sort to wear a red shoe with an animal print and an impractical heel for work. Perfect CEO material as far as Selfie was concerned, plus she'd be nicely in his pocket.

Serena had had enough of Selfie and his B grade manipulating. It was time to call in someone who has manipulation down to a fine and elegant art form. As Selfie left the hospital for the evening, Serena pointed him out to a mysterious figure in the shadows. "He won't be happy when he finds out why you're here, or that I called you," she predicted. "Well, life's full of small disappointments, Ms Campbell," said Henrik Hanssen. And a nation cheered.

Mo had also been calling a man from her past – her father Clifford. Mo rang him on the pretext of wanting to do some kind of medical study. When he turned up in person she didn't explain who she was, but used the medical study story to get some information about him.

Mo wants a steady male influence in her life, but he's there already in the form of the glorious Mr T (MR T!!!). There was a fabulous Mr T moment when Mo had been complaining to him that she was all alone and unlucky in love. As she walked off he said, "You're not alone," in such a sweet way – but she didn't hear him. Later on, Clifford (who was by now aware of what his relationship with Mo was supposed to be) watched her doing her brilliant doctoring thing. He didn't know her, he said to Mr T. "Her name is Maureen Effanga and she saves people's lives. She's a hero," said Mr T, fairly glowing with pride. Good grief, you can keep *Poldark*. Mr T is my idea of what a proper romantic hero should be like.

On the ward formerly known as Keller but currently serving as the Self Centre until he can turn his cardboard model into reality, Dr Annabelle Cooper continued to lock horns with Selfie over her approach to patients. It seems that she has more invested in neurosurgery than just a glittering career, as we discovered that she has the same kind of brain tumour as this week's patient. How unlucky are Holby staff with brain tumours? Nick Jordan, Dr Tara Lo, Prof Elliot Hope and now Annabelle. Maybe there's something in the water. Whatever it is, I'm sure it's not anything Henrik Hanssen can't fix with his exceedingly good baklava.

Looming marvellous

(Series 17, ep. 30 'Homecoming' by Dana Fainaru 5.5.15)

The new CEO was going to be introduced at a specially convened meeting. Everyone sighed and looked a bit bored or cross as they trundled towards the board room. Many of them expected to see the mythical Olivia Sharpe installing her shoes under the table of corporate power (though Elliot had bumped into Olivia and she hadn't mentioned anything), or some tedious pen-pusher in a suit. Nobody noticed that Serena Campbell was wearing a Knowing Expression. Then the door opened to reveal... an empty table.

It just wouldn't have been dramatic enough to have had Henrik Hanssen being reinserted into the hospital at a boring meeting. Instead, a riot and a scaffolding collapse in Holby kicked off a full-scale emergency situation – and who was there to direct the troops with a brief, no-nonsense pep talk ("Let's to it!")? Obviously it was the once and current CEO of Holby City Hospital, Henrik Hanssen – who also had time to introduce his deputy CEO, Serena Campbell. That's a dream team right there.

It's wonderful to see that Hanssen still has the power to unnerve. He'd learned everybody's names before he even set eyes on them ("Don't ask me how, but he does that," said Dixie off of *Casualty*, who was there delivering casualties to the episode and interfacing with former colleague Fletch).

Hanssen also staged a couple of perfect looms, on one occasion hilariously spotting Dominic trying to hide from him. Most magnificently, he left Selfie under no illusion about who's boss by taking away his Self Centre and his delusions of grandeur. "My agenda is to restore the moral compass of this hospital," he informed Selfie. It's an agenda we can all sign up to, I think.

Also back where he belongs is Young Dr Oliver Valentine, who is less young now, biologically-speaking, and a lot less young in terms of life experience. He's gone all snappy and cross. Indeed I wrote in my notes, "He's a bit more Jac," and then Jesse (who was being less than helpful with the new/old boy) spoke my brains by asking Adele if she was quite sure that Jac hadn't just gone away for gender reassignment. This assessment would have made Jac extremely proud of her mentoring skills, I'm sure, but if Ollie carries on in this manner I'm going to start calling him O. Negative.

I'm not sure where the loss of the Self Centre will leave new neurosurgeon Annabelle Cooper, but we – and now Zosia – know that she has more personally riding on it than just career prospects. Zosia isn't happy knowing that Annabelle has a brain tumour, but of course she can relate to people hiding medical diagnoses for the sake of their career so she hasn't said anything to anyone yet. It can only be a matter of time before Hanssen finds out, though, because he Always Finds Out.

In other news, Fletch got Dixie to put a bet on for him because he's strapped for cash. The horse didn't win, but luckily Dixie hadn't put the bet on anyway (does Fletch have a history of a gambling problem that I missed when I wasn't watching *Casualty*? It seemed to be implied). Raf loaned him the money he needed anyway, because he's not very smug at all these days and his moral compass is nicely calibrated.

Danger – unauthorised spectators, infested dogs and trembling hands

(Series 17, ep. 31 'Lifelines' by Fiona Peek 12.5.15)

"Stick to your work and don't try to fix everything," Dr Oliver Valentine told Adele. He was being Managerial because Elliot had left him in charge (and he's also still somewhat O. Negative) and he wasn't taking any nonsense. And, frankly, I cheered him. I'm getting more than a bit tired of Saint Adele of the Trillion Skills, and there's been nobody to take her down a peg since Jac disappeared.

Most irritatingly even when Adele is wrong, she ends up being right. "I was just trying to hold on to somebody I love," she said, in her best surely-you-can't-argue-with-that voice, and Ollie didn't argue with that and assumed his Thinking Face. Was he thinking about Penny (his patient was a twin) or Tara, people he loved and couldn't hold on to? Or was he just wondering what was in the fridge for tea? Such is the magic of Adele that it could have been all, some, or none of these things.

The "somebody she loves" is of course Mo, and Adele was trying to hold on to her by means of summoning her biological father Clifford to the hospital to try to make amends. It looks like it worked, too, eventually, but not before Mo got very cross. Especially when Adele brought Clifford to watch Mo in action operating on a patient, surely contravening all sorts of regulations.

Once again there was an adorable dog running loose around AAU, but the perils of dog ownership were all too scarily illustrated when Raf found the dog owner's intestines were full of worms. Still, a deft bit of diagnosis never does any harm, particularly when you're trying to impress Hanssen. Hanssen actually was impressed by Raf's bid for funding for his Max Fac facility, despite the dog and despite Raf's presentation featuring a superb photo of Hanssen modelling Scandi knitwear. Hanssen has an uncanny ability to be able to tell the good guys from the bad Guy.

Talking of whom, Selfie was busy harrumphing round acting all aggrieved and nobody was much bothered apart from Zosia, who has finally decided daddy is a good Guy after all. The thing she's most bothered about is Annabelle Cooper being able to do her human trials of the brain treatment that might just save her own life. All of this has revived some of Zosia's obsessiveness, so what with that and Annabelle's trembling hands, Keller is not the safest place to be a patient at the moment.

Line of the week and Top Hanssen Moment: "I didn't have you down as a ballet buff," said Sacha to the world's suavest Swede, who replied, "Well, I've yet to share my life history with you, Mr Levy." Smooth.

Looks better in blue

(Series 17, ep. 32 'The Ides of March' by Peter Mattessi 19.5.15)

"I picked you because you're bloody brilliant," Dr Annabelle Cooper told Dr Zosia March. Zosia must be brilliant, too, because the thing Annabelle picked her for was to operate on her own brain (Annabelle's, not Zosia's, obvs). This made me mumble crossly to myself the way I do, wondering exactly when it was that Zosia got so brilliant at brain surgery, considering she's only been doing it for five minutes. Scriptwriter Peter Mattessi got round my objections in a cunning scene in which Zosia listed all of the relevant experience she's had. My word, she really is an expert. So that left only Selfie to convince. He wanted his daughter to "steer clear of the Annabelle thing – given your situation." Was he genuinely worried about Zosia's mental health, or his own ego? It's never easy to tell with Selfie.

Hanssen was tempted to give Zosia the benefit of the doubt (while initially supporting Selfie), but Selfie threw a golf analogy at him. "I don't play golf," replied Hanssen, in a new voice that I'd have to term The Whisper With The Dangerous Edge. Quite thrilling it was, but not for Selfie, who had a go at calling his boss "Henrik" but was firmly corrected and told it was "Mr Hanssen." How I treasure these moments.

Eventually it was decided that Zosia would operate on Annabelle, Selfie would supervise and Ric, Hanssen and assorted non-speaking extras would watch tensely through the glass. This proved useful when Zosia went a bit wobbly during the procedure. Everyone was set to grab the tools from her trembling hands, but Hanssen made them wait while Zosia calmed herself down with a little mantra. All ended well, and surely a glittering career in neurosurgery beckons for Dr March.

But no. She's already asked for a transfer to Darwin. "I just look better in blue," she told Dominic, but if getting away from the maroon/wine/berry coloured scrubs was the main consideration, Keller wouldn't have any staff left. Mainly she wants to get away from Selfie's orbit, and who can blame her?

She's going to Darwin in the nick of time because apparently Mo is about to join Michael Spence in Chicago for six weeks, so once again they'll be a woman down. What is it with all the staff leaving for Chicago (apart from Ric, who is off to Australia with Jess)? Are the production team lining up a Chicago special or something? And if so, will Noah Wyle and George Clooney be in it?

To keep up the Effanga count at Holby, Mo's dad Clifford is now a porter there. I know he isn't officially an Effanga, but I'm talking genetically. He seems very nice, anyway.

Someone who didn't seem very nice, but in a good way, was the daughter of Raf's patient on AAU. The mother had messed up her innards with alcohol, but the daughter, former medical student Lucy, was far more interesting to Raf. She had a nasty facial wound caused by some previous face-fixing surgery that went wrong, and she was fabulously snarly and sulky. This was helped no end by a beautiful Welsh accent. At one point Raf suggested Lucy might enjoy a little walk in the Linden Cullen Memorial Shrubbery. "There's a garden, and you want me to walk in it?" she said, in a voice that was only just slightly less scary than Hanssen's Whisper With The Dangerous Edge.

Luckily she's come to the right place, what with Raf being the expert who reconstructed the Posh Visage and that. Lucy's response to being shown photos of Posh was to smash Raf's phone (rude), and Serena was not best pleased with his handling of the situation. I'm expecting Lucy to be back next week, because there's obviously a lot more to this story.

Talking of interesting characters, this episode marked the end of Annabelle Cooper's brief employment at Holby, what with recovering from brain surgery and all, so it's farewell to Nina Wadia. It's a shame, because I hardly had time to stop thinking of her as Zainab and she was gone.

Blue eyes, old soul

(Series 17, ep. 33 'All Coming Back to Me' by Kate Verghese & Sally Tatchell 26.5.15)

Following last week's Whisper With The Dangerous Edge, this week Hanssen showcased his mastery of the Long Scary Pause. He gave Elliot a little talk along the lines of needing to have everyone working well because a team was only as strong as its weakest link. Elliot tried a bit of humour with "You are the weakest link. Goodbye." To which Hanssen replied, "I beg your pardon?" followed by that LSP. Not an Anne Robinson fan, then.

The weakest link on Elliot's sadly depleted team is currently Oliver Valentine, because he's still being O. Negative and his "gap yah" (as Jesse insisted on calling it) hasn't really helped him sort his post-Tara life out.

His gloomy mood didn't go unnoticed by his patient, Derek Winger. "Took an O-level in nihilism did we, Blue Eyes?" he asked him, and not in a flirtatious way either. Later on he referred to Ollie as a "teenybopper," and suggested he'd never known the heartache of losing the things you most love in life. Oh, if he only knew. Ollie was so distracted by the heartaches of life that he failed to notice Derek's heart was occupied by "vegetation." I was rather relieved to hear that "vegetation" in the heart means bacteria, and not ferns and moss and stuff, but apparently it was still a thing that should have been spotted and dealt with. "Buck up, Oliver – I expect more from you," Elliot chided him, but the situation was so bad it required a high level loom and some enigmatic advice from Hanssen. "You can give up, or you can take the same gamble as everyone else," he said. Go on, Ollie – choose life!

Down on AAU, Raf spent most of the hour trying to persuade last week's patient, Lucy, to consent to some of his fabulous face-fixing surgery. We discovered that her injuries were the result of domestic violence, when her mother-in-law turned up and Lucy eventually told Raf that her partner was in prison for what he'd done but was about to get out. Lucy was less scary this week as she gradually allowed herself to trust Raf. Raf is doing that classic Holby maverick thing of getting too involved, ignoring his superiors (Serena was very cross for most of the episode) but achieving good outcomes against the odds.

On Keller, Essie was whingeing because she didn't want to meet Sacha's children and she feared she couldn't relate to teenagers. Then she found herself relating brilliantly to a teenager on the ward who'd managed to get locked in some handcuffs, and on the strength of this agreed to go bowling with the Little Levys after all. Patients and their relatives, eh? Always handy for a life lesson. The best part of this story was Dominic's little shudder when Essie took home the handcuffs, presumably for fifty shades of fun with Sacha later.

Finally (so that isn't the last image I leave you with) some exciting news from Darwin. Adele has been taking mindfulness classes! I knew you'd be thrilled.

A few people get out of their depth

(Series 17, ep. 34 'Tug of Love' by Patrea Smallacombe 2.6.15)

Adele had a dizzy turn, which for an otherwise healthy female on Holby generally leads to a visit to the glorious Mr T (MR T!!!). Was Adele pregnant with a little Law? The home pregnancy test said yes, but the scan said no. What she had was actually a cyst that may or may not be malignant. Mr T has whipped it out and sent it to the lab, but we'll have to wait for the results.

What was Jesse doing while all this was going on? He was being offered a job on Selfie's neuro team and some kind of temporary gig in America (though in LA rather than Chicago, because Chicago now has its full official quota of ex-Holby people). Jesse had about five minutes to ponder this before Hanssen loomed up to tell him that Selfie's offer was career suicide. "Putting one's self first isn't always the best way forward," he said. Was the pun intentional? Obviously it was, because I can't imagine anything about Hanssen being unintentional.

When Jesse finally rocked up at Adele's bedside (he also had Sensitive Patient Issues to deal with, it wasn't all about himself and Self), he'd bought her a wetsuit. This wasn't a random gift – they were just about to go surfing before she had her dizzy spell. There was some weird brains-speak which compared wetsuits to – what? The human body? Love? Both? "If we treat it with care, it'll last," anyway.

On AAU there was a guest appearance from Jean Slater off of EastEnders (Gillian Wright) playing a former teacher of Fletch's daughter, Evie. Evie was also around, because it was her birthday and Fletch had promised to take her for lunch, which Raf paid for because he's not smug, he's bloody lovely. Father and daughter ended up on the roof (in a good way – it wasn't a suicide pact), where Evie reassured her dad that they'd be okay and Fletch gave her her late mum's engagement ring, which he'd been thinking of pawning earlier because they're strapped for cash. I say this every time, but I do like Fletch and Evie – I can totally believe in them as father and daughter and they're very sweet together.

To Keller now, where Serena seems to be currently based. This is good because she gets scenes with Dominic, but bad because Essie seems to be unnaturally interested in Serena's love life. This is non-existent anyway, because the relationship between Serena and Angus of the Board has fizzled out, due to his reluctance to address her Womanly Needs. While Serena's idea of a cosy weekend away involved breakfast in bed, Angus was thinking golf.

Drives and juices were uppermost in everyone's mind thanks to a patient who was a professional stripper and seemed to need to take his clothes off every time he heard 'Le Freak' by Chic. This was inconvenient for him as it was the ringtone on his phone and he got quite a few calls, though it certainly enlivened the shift for Serena, Essie and Dominic.

So much more than wee, poo, pus and sick

(Series 17, ep. 35 'When a Man Loves a Woman' by Nick Fisher 9.6.15)

Darwin guest patient of the week Talesha (Emi Wokoma) and Jesse had to work hard for the entire episode to try to persuade us that there was "something going on" between them behind Adele's back – snatched conversations, Jesse muttering "Am I doing the right thing?" at every opportunity and making desperate attempts to keep Adele and Talesha as far apart as possible. We know that Jesse would never be unfaithful, though, because there is no one – no one, I tell you – who is as special, incredible or wonderful as Adele. Everyone says so, even if they don't always appreciate her many talents. "All I ever deal with is wee, poo, pus and sick," she moaned to Elliot, who reassured her that he also relies on her for teabags, shortbread and ring binders. Way to make a girl feel special, Elliot. Then he gave her Talesha to look after (Nooo!!! They must never speak to each other!!!), which prompted Jesse to run about with a worried look for a bit and wonder again if he was doing the right thing. He even asked for advice from Mr T (MR T!!!), a man who is properly qualified on this subject because he specialises in Lady Parts and he can knit.

It turned out that Talesha was a singer and part of a girl group Jesse had hired to sing 'When A Man Loves A Woman' while he proposed to Adele, and Mr T acted as ring bearer. The singing was rather impressive (and if Talesha's that good now imagine how good she'll be when she doesn't have fluid on her lungs). Jesse seemed to be down on one knee for long enough to develop arthritis before the singing stopped and he could finally pop the question, during which time Adele was forced to stand still and maintain a surprised/delighted expression on her face. She still made him wait for an answer, though, and this necessitated a Proper Grown Up Conversation at the Window of Regret, after which Adele said yes, she would become Mrs Law. And to cap off a marvellous day, her test results from last week came back all clear. She's free to resume her astronaut training just as soon as she's finished calibrating the Large Hadron Collider. She's so special.

From one special woman to another, and what was Sacha thinking when he replaced Chrissie with Essie? Their names are too similar for one thing, and recently Essie has taken to wearing the same exasperated/put-upon/superior expression when she's around Sacha that adorned Chrissie's face for much of their relationship. She had a right go at him for bringing her a chocolate-dipped wafer instead of proper chocolate. I can see her point, but any confectionery in a crisis is my motto. Essie has "instincts," and she's not afraid to use them. Despite her instincts leading her to surely break all sorts of confidentiality rules by taking one patient to gaze upon some (unconscious) others and divulge their medical histories just to teach him a Valuable Life Lesson, she's won the approval of none other than Henrik Hanssen. "People who agree with me are manifold," he said (I agree with him). "People who feel obliged to agree with me in this hospital are in the majority." Essie left his office following that speech with the kind of look on her face that's usually accompanied by someone tossing their car keys a couple of inches up in the air and then catching them.

Which wasn't what Fletch was doing, because his car had been clamped and his car keys had been confiscated. This happened while he was looking after a really annoying patient who'd collapsed in the car park. This was a Stereotypical Activist type of person (he had his own megaphone) who called himself Spike despite really being called Quintin. He acted more like a Quintin most of the time, but at least he tried to help Fletch get his car back. The person who really helped Fletch get his car back was Clifford ("I've been in your shoes and I know how tight they feel," he told Fletch. Possibly Fletch takes a different size), who has also given him a bin bag full of duty-free ciggies to sell for profit. Is peddling death sticks really the solution to Fletch's debt crisis?

New girls on every ward

(Series 17, ep. 36 'The Children of Lovers' by Lucia Haynes 16.6.15)

There was a new female face on each ward in this episode. Darwin had Zosia March, newly redeployed from Keller. AAU had new nurse Cara Martinez, and Keller had a baby girl.

The baby got the best welcome, her first glimpse of the outside world being Mr T (MR T!!!) and Dominic, whose reaction at a forced glimpse of birthing lady parts was a delicate "Eurgh!" It hasn't put the lad off, though – he went back for a cuddle of the baby once the new arrival (middle name: Dominique – bless!) had had a bath and was looking more human. Is he getting broody? Possibly, but he's still queasy about lady parts, resisting Mr T's attempts to beckon him to a life in Obs & Gynae. Aside from Dominic, is Essie getting broody? Who knows? Presumably Sacha will be informed in due course.

On Darwin, Dr Oliver Valentine was being even more O. Negative than usual, thanks to it being Tara's "anniversary." It must have been her birthday, because she died in April so it wasn't that anniversary. Anyway, he brought her a flower which he was going to place in the Linden Cullen Memorial Shrubbery, where they got married on that lovely day of fairy lights and smiliness.

He hardly smiles at all these days, and his voice is different too. It's got a harsh edge to it that it didn't used to have. Maybe having to work with a soul even more tortured than he is would make him cheer up? But no. The very sight of Dr Zosia March made him go even grumpier. Their first operation together didn't go at all well, when Zosia made a slip with the sternum saw (we've all done it) and made a bit of a mess. She redeemed herself later, but by then she'd caused all sorts of aggravation by getting typically too involved with an ethically tricky patient situation.

Will it be a classic Mills and Boon case of Ollie and Zosia hating each other on sight (he has "no warmth or empathy" according to Zosia) only to fall in love a bit further down the line? Possibly. They're being given every opportunity anyway because Prof Hope wants them to carry on being a team.

A team rather like Jesse and Adele (who couldn't wait to remind Zosia that Jesse is her fiance, just in case Zosia had any Ideas). Jesse booked a surprise weekend to Paris, because he's never one to shy away from a romantic cliché. We discovered that Adele failed her nursing degree module (shocking under normal circumstances because of her being Saint Adele of the Many Skills, but we have to remember she's not been well) and preferred to stay at home and revise for resits.

Finally to AAU, where Lucy Mottica was back for her face improving surgery. I'm pleased to report she's back to being quite snarly again. Raf was all excited because Hanssen was due to be watching the op through the glass in the company of one of these teams of silent dignitaries with big pockets, so there was a lot resting on it. Then new nurse Cara Martinez almost rained on his parade by getting Lucy's psychiatrist involved. Was Lucy really ready for the surgery, given that she was only doing it to please the abusive boyfriend who'd caused the facial damage in the first place? To cut a long story short, yes she was, Raf impressed the Big Pockets in surgery, and Hanssen hinted that the funding may soon be his.

I'm reserving judgement on Cara for a few weeks – so far she seems like an amalgam of Mary-Claire (Irish, feisty), The Radiant Donna (cheeky, reads magazines) and Dr Honey. I mention Dr

Honey because Cara was about to join the others for a drink but then her phone started to ring and she got a bit flustered and left, and I wondered if she had a small child at home. We'll soon find out because if she does she'll have to bring him/her to work soon to re-enact the lost staff child scenario. Or maybe she has a nasty husband (like Nasty Warren off of *Casualty*) and that's why she got so upset on Lucy's behalf? Or maybe she simply has a secret Nazi grandfather.

Fletch is being dragged deeper into a life of crime by Mo's dad Clifford, who is the Del Boy Trotter of Holby. Last week it was cigarettes, and this week it was dodgy alcohol. When Hanssen caught them loading boxes of it into the lift, they had to pretend it was for a surprise party for Adele and Jesse. When Hanssen said he might drop in, they had to quickly arrange an actual party. Hanssen did drop in, and his face when he tasted the cheap imported booze was a delightful thing to behold. "Certainly clears the head," he said.

The good that comes from being in hospital

(Series 17, ep. 37 'Spiral Staircases' by Andy Bayliss 23.6.15)

It's heartening to see that Henrik Hanssen hasn't given up being enigmatic. This week he communicated some staffing advice to Elliot Hope via the medium of a children's book about a gorilla, and a strategically presented banana. This was far more subtle than saying, "Prof. Hope, I really think you ought to be paying more attention to Dr Zosia March," though being less subtle might have avoided Elliot having to spend so long pondering the meaning of the gift – time he could have spent paying more attention to Dr Zosia March.

Zosia had a deeply annoying patient and the patient's even more annoying sister to deal with. They were convinced they were both afflicted by a fictional parasitic worm disease, and this was preventing the woman agreeing to treatment for a real heart problem. Dr Oliver Valentine – who is nowMr Oliver Valentine, if you please – wanted to take the direct approach, which was basically to bang heads together, and I was with him on that one. Anyway, what was needed was a Psych consult from new Psych guy Seb "Call me Seb" Coulter, who is going to be popping up everywhere now, just like when we had Psych Sharon. He's an "arrogant narcissist" according to Zosia, and we must believe her because she's read all the Psych text books. He also has a flashy little car which he drives wearing driving gloves to keep the smell of ciggies off his hands. Doesn't that sound attractive? Zosia thinks so, anyway, and he's asked her out, so she may get to find out even more about him. She was a bit worried that getting into an emotional entanglement could set her health back, but Dig and Dom delightfully reassured her that this wasn't the case. She also got the fake parasite woman to admit that she'd been using the fake parasite illness as a bit of an emotional crutch (there was some kind of brains-speak going on there, but it was even more subtle than the gorilla book and the banana). Zosia is "the good that comes from being in hospital," apparently.

The same can't really be said for her father, who continues to be odious even though he isn't the CEO any more. He's a very good brain surgeon, but I really didn't need the down-the-throat view of his through-the-mouth brain surgery. Ugh. What Selfie needed for that surgery was a top class anaesthetist, and by various means he managed to get Jesse (the only anaesthetist in the hospital who actually speaks, so you know he's the best). Hanssen is glad of this because he's hoping Jesse can keep Selfie in check.

Hanssen is "seeing rogue elements everywhere," and I think he might need to turn his attention to AAU very soon, because Mo's hitherto fairly genial dad Clifford is turning out to be a bit of a villain. He got quite nasty with Fletch at one point. Fletch has only dipped his toe into a life of crime so far, but he wants out because he's basically a Good Bloke. But will Clifford let him?

Back to Darwin again, and fans of the double-headed entity known as "Janny" will have been thrilled to see Rosie Marcel's and Michael Thomson's names on the cast list. They appeared in Elliot's office via the medium of the interweb, as Elliot apparently makes a point of having cosy family chats with them when he should be paying attention to Zosia. They're looking very well, I must say – though domestic harmony seems to have made Jac far too relaxed and smiley. She needs to get back to work very soon before she forgets how to be horrible. That would never do.

Pinkie promise

(Series 17, ep. 38 'Losing Control of the Wheel' by Julia Gilbert 30.6.15)

There was so much to love about this episode that I hardly know where to start – we had Mr T (Mr T!!!) manning up, Dominic's mum flirting with Selfie, and the best new character debut for ages.

Dr Morven Shreve (Eleanor Fanyinka) is the new character. She's on AAU and she could easily have been another "more book learning than people skills" type. She arrived all nervous, but as soon as her scrubs were on she was spouting medical terms like she was born to it. But she does have her own quirky way with people, too. She knows when a patient needs a hand to hold, and when a mentor (Digby) is in need of a bit of support himself. She's clumsy, funny and entirely adorable.

AAU is brilliant at the moment. Raf wasn't even in this episode and there was still more than enough goodness to spare, what with Fletch and his school-shy daughter Evie, the glorious Serena (key advice this week: "Never ignore the build-up of limescale"), the aforementioned and always good value Digby, and new nurse Cara.

Darwin was also considerably enlivened by the return of Mo from her stay in Chicago. Absence seems to have made the heart grow even fonder for Mr T, and he planned a welcome home party for her. Mo's dad Clifford has taken against Mr T, because he's not alpha male enough. But when Tosh fromEastEnders (Rebecca Scroggs) required an emergency caesarean, it's hard not to go misty eyed at the man with the skills to get a baby born safely. Mo was suitably impressed.

Mr T had a go at asking Mr Oliver Valentine for romantic advice, and received a suitably bleak and bitter response. Indeed I'm coming to the conclusion that O. Negative is actually an android who's being remotely controlled by Jac Naylor from an underground bunker somewhere in the Wyvernshire countryside.

Despite this, Mr T is not going to give up on Mo easily, and he found the backbone to man up to Clifford in a rather wonderful scene. Clifford got the last word, though, when later on in Albie's Mr T was just about to kiss Mo and Clifford beckoned her over and ruined the moment. Poor Mr T.

Dominic's day started quite well, till he spotted something bright pink in Pulses. It was his mother, Carole (Julia Deakin), and she was rather marvellous, albeit in a totally embarrassing way for a man who's tried so hard to build his "Dominic" image and leave his 'Darren' years behind. Despite promising to stay quietly in the staff room, Carole was soon out and about on the wards, giving head massages to brain patients and cupcakes to people who were supposed to be nil by mouth. Best of all, she told Selfie he looked "more like James Bond than a real doctor." I'm hoping next week we'll find out what she makes of Hanssen.

He has a good heart

(Series 17, ep. 39 'Beneath a Mask' by Elliot Hope & Johanne McAndrew 7.7.15)

O. Negative has finally started to veer back into the positive (neutral, at least), and it's all thanks to a rather wonderful combination of Elliot, Hanssen, Mr T, Zosia and especially a lovely patient called Jade (Anna Krippa).

The day didn't start well for him. Does Zosia really not know about his dead Chinese wife? Was she being entirely thick asking him about his Chinese tattoos, or is she just distracted by Slimy Seb? Either way, she and Ollie were soon sparring away like a proper rom com couple. He hasn't had that much fun since Jac Naylor had him juggling coins.

The glorious Mr T (Mr T!!!) was required for a consult when patient of the week Jade said she had period-style cramps. He diagnosed fibroids, and then there was a stand-off between him and Ollie about which bit of Jade should be treated first to give her the best chance of (a) survival and (b) the ability to have children. Mr T pulled rank, which was a rather fabulous thing to behold, but it was Jade herself who convinced Ollie to take her childbearing future as seriously as her heart. She also got him, for the first time, to talk about Tara, with whom he liked to share a Twirl (it's chocolate) for elevenses. "It was the best part of the working day, seeing her smile," he said. Bless.

Elliot told Zosia about Tara and Penny, and in her heavy-handed way she told Ollie she was available if he ever wanted to talk. "Never have, never will," he snapped, his defences all back up – but then he went to find her in Albie's. And they were starting to get a bit close, too, till Slimy Seb turned up. Darn you, Slimy Seb!

Ollie left them to it and went back up to the ward to check on Jade and enjoy a little Twirl (it's chocolate) on his own. On seeing this, Hanssen permitted himself an enigmatic smile, because despite his scary Scandinavian exterior he likes his staff to be happy.

Line of the week was Hanssen's reply to Elliot (the whole scene between the two of them at the beginning was beautiful), who said that Oliver kept himself to himself these days. "You see this as some kind of issue, do you?" said Hanssen, flying the flag for introverts everywhere.

You couldn't accuse Dominic of being an introvert. He probably gets it from his mum, who has now got herself a job in Pulses. You know how gossip rages around Pulses. It wasn't long before Carole was fully up to speed on the Malick/Dominic situation. Dominic's patient was Mandy (Josie Walker), who seemed ever so nice but turned out to be someone who specialises in "curing" gayness. This brought out the tiger mother in Carole, who was furious on her son's behalf. Dominic, however, showed a lot of self-restraint and maturity in rising above it all. Sacha was almost as proud of him as Carole was.

Digby topped off a difficult day by getting home to find Carole and Dominic in matching onesies in front of the telly – but worse than that, Carole had tidied Digby's bedroom and put all his little soldier figures away. He'd just got them in proper battle formation as well. Ouch.

I'm not sure what's going on with Digby. He's having panic attacks and easily feels undermined in a way he didn't on Keller, even despite AAU being a rather nurturing environment these days. Is it because Morven hero-worships him and he can't live up to it? Not sure, but I'm worried about him.

Meanwhile, Fletch and the little Fletchlings have been evicted and eventually found themselves sleeping in the hospital basement (watch out for serial killers, scalpel-wielding maniacs and the remnants of Sacha's furniture). It's a desperate situation and it's led to desperate measures – Fletch has told Clifford (whose apparent niceness has actually been a type of grooming) that he will get involved in his planned crime.

Fletch's life of crime

(Series 17, ep. 40 'U-Turn' by Rebecca Wojciechowski 14.7.15)

I wouldn't have wanted to have been a patient on AAU last night. The most senior doctor and nurse available were both bundles of nerves and distractedness.

In Digby's case, I'm still not exactly sure what's the matter with him. He did say that Morven is "driving him mad," plus he was super-keen not to have to summon on-call back up, who happened to be Connie Beauchamp (Morven thinks with that name Connie must be like a little mouse nibbling cheese. She'll learn). During a day spent totally ignoring the machines when they went beep and staring into space with a look of terror, Digby mentioned a time when he was the cause of an accident which really hurt someone he loved. Is the car crash that he, Hanssen, Malick and Chantelle were involved in still haunting him? I need to know, because he's popping pills and he's just not himself.

Fletch is still himself, in the sense that he's a very good and competent nurse and a loving father, etc etc. He isn't a criminal, but he is desperate for cash, so he was going along with Clifford's scheme to rob a drugs delivery van. This was bad enough when Fletch thought the drugs were going to the needy and the van driver was the unpleasant Alan, but when he found out the drugs were going to the criminal underworld and the driver was the pleasant Vince (Ray MacAllan) – who even offered to help Fletch out with some money – Fletch just couldn't do it. He thinks that's the end of it now, but Clifford's already had a warning kicking from the crims and there's certainly more trouble heading Fletch's way.

Maybe he should think of promotion, which is exactly what was on Essie's mind this week, when she wasn't bitching about Chrissie (with her on that one) and being self-righteous about a patient. She went for an interview for the role of Transplant Coordinator, but she wasn't very well prepared because Sacha never passes on her post so she didn't know about the interview, and she'd only brought a pair of jeans that Chrissie's "My Son Daniel" had scribbled on. The best part of the interview was when she got a phone call. "I'm being harassed by a satsuma," she explained to Hanssen. "Sister Williams, I presume?" he replied.

The thing is, I'm convinced Essie is turning into a less orange version of Chrissie herself, in the sense that she has a rather superior, condescending, bossy manner with people in general and Sacha in particular. This annoys me even when she's supposed to be right, as she was in this episode. It doesn't annoy Hanssen, though, who finds her very convincing and gave her the job after she pitched herself to him again.

She's not a million miles away, personality-wise, from Adele Effanga and her million skills and "You know I'm right, babe" attitude. Maybe it's a double case of opposites attract, because Jesse, like Sacha, is rather laid back and calm. He was a bit less calm when Adele forged his signature on a petition because she was convinced her opinion was right and his was wrong. I think we were supposed to side with Adele, but if I was Jesse I'd be packing my surf board and heading for Anywhere But Holby about now.

A shock in the shrubbery

(Series 17, ep. 41 'Family Fortunes' by Joe Ainsworth 21.7.15)

Digby's been having a lot of bad shifts recently, and in this episode it culminated in him getting all shouty and unnecessary with a patient. He had to rush out into the balmy night air of the Linden Cullen Memorial Shrubbery to calm down.

What you don't want to see in these circs is an apparently lifeless hand protruding from said shrubbery, but that's what Digby saw. It didn't spur him on to anything resembling doctorly activity, though – he just stood like a panicking plank and left Morven to summon help.

Help for whom, though?

Cue flashback to several hours earlier, and an entire day of setting Mo up to be the victim of ghastly violence. Clifford was being threatened by the Mr Big of the pharmaceutical van robbing world. If Clifford didn't come up with cartons of Camoxidan on cue, his beautiful daughter would get hurt. Clifford managed to miss the drugs delivery, then Mo refused to lend him the £10,000 which would have kept him in the clear and her out of danger (she didn't know that bit). So after that, every time someone tapped Mo on the shoulder, or she was summoned to the car park to look at a cake topper or get balloons (it was Jesse and Adele's engagement party) it looked like she was in deadly danger.

In a twist, though, it wasn't Mo but Adele who ended up being bludgeoned in the bushes, by someone who couldn't tell one Effanga from the next. Despite the lack of early first aid from Digby, Adele was soon being treated to the finest service Holby can offer, with Henrik Hanssen and Serena Campbell operating on her to try and save her life. Did they succeed? We still don't know – Jesse and Mo are keeping vigil by the bedside as we speak.

PLA Jr hasn't watched Holby for a long while (exams and that), and hadn't seen Essie before. I explained who she was. "But she looks just like Chrissie," was her assessment. Acts like her, too. In this episode, Sacha noticed she was "a bit off." She was quite a lot off, in fact, and has been for a while. She was looking after Ros (Carol Starks), a terminally ill woman, who at one point was trying to line Essie up as a replacement wife for her husband and mother for her children. Ros must have really hated the husband and children. Essie said no to the scheme anyway, because she already had someone and – do you know what? – he just might be "the one." Everyone knows The One is Keanu Reeves, but nevertheless, Essie is rather fond of Sacha and to show her devotion has taken to copying his tendency to wear shirts that look like wallpaper. Sacha favours florals and Essie likes her geometrics, but the principle's the same. And she also wants a baby (I told you she'd inform Sacha in due course). Is this going to cause conflict, with Sacha thinking that My Son Daniel, Rachel etc are more than enough of a genetic legacy?

Hope, faith, camomile tea and doughnuts

(Series 17, ep. 42 'Return to Innocence' by Elliot Hope and Johanne McAndrew 28.7.15)

With Adele's life still hanging in the balance, everyone was rallying around Mo. Most notably the adorable Mr T (MR T!!!) was offering a listening ear, chocolate and a relaxing cup of camomile tea. Hanssen offered "hope and faith," and his continued medical services, and Elliot Hope placed his emergency stash of doughnuts at Mo's disposal. Even Oliver Valentine and Zosia were caring and concerned (indeed Ollie smiled a lot more than he has for months, and he's stopped being all growly and cross).

One notable exception to all this supportive behaviour was Clifford, Mo's dad. Lest we forget, it was very much his fault that Adele ended up in such a critical condition in the first place (though he tried to blame Fletch for not going through with the drug van job), so there was an element of guilty conscience, but it seems that Clifford is not the genial chap he likes to pretend to be.

By the end of the episode, Clifford had decided to leave Holby, to carry out some unspecified deeds as payback for the criminals who were now threatening Fletch's children. So maybe he's not entirely bad – just a bit bad and a lot stupid.

Meanwhile, Adele found herself in need of the services of Selfie to sort out a brain-related problem. The charm-free former CEO managed to use this as a chance to score points against Hanssen and Jesse, and he did his usual trick of prioritising brain over heart (I did wonder why Hanssen didn't pull rank at this point, as he was clearly uncomfortable with the idea of not having any heart specialists present when Selfie was operating). It all culminated in Mo having to dash in and sort things out. Adele isn't out of the woods yet, though.

In AAU, patient of the day was a friend of Serena's, Sian (Andrée Bernard). She was the sort of woman who defines herself by her sexual allure – she was sporting what we were led to believe was an absolutely stunning pair of surgically modified breasts (typing that sentence has weirdly made me reminisce fondly about Michael Spence) – and she absolutely terrified Digby. In recent weeks he's been very easily terrified, so it wasn't long before he was scuttling off to pop some of his pills. Morven almost caught him at it, but not quite. She gave him a talking-to about being more relaxed around patients. "A bit of humour goes a long way," she told him. In the end, he was able to relax enough to let some of his old Digby brilliance shine through, as he thought of a way they could ensure that Sian continued to wee via the normal route, realising how traumatising the alternative would be for a woman who was actually as insecure (and pill popping) as him.

It's not chocolate – it's a fresh start

(Series 17, ep. 43 'A Good Man' by Patrick Homes 4.8.15)

July must be a slow month in the Holby calendar as far as births are concerned, because for the second week running top Obs & Gynae consultant Mr T (MR T!!!) was busying himself being supportive by Adele's bedside, and laying on frothy coffee "and a selection of delicious cakes" to comfort the worried relatives. This didn't include Jesse, who spent most of the episode looking after the daughter of a former girlfriend who had to have her brain fixed before she could speak his and convince him that he was proper fiancé material.

With Adele not showing much sign of improvement, Mo got rather emotional by the bedside and told Adele to come back, because Mo needed her. There's nothing Adele likes more than being needed, so she woke up. Hurrah! She needs to get better ASAP, because that Nobel Prize won't win itself.

Fletch's conscience was bothering him, because he is A Good Man (as the episode was properly titled), so he 'fessed up to Mo. She said as soon as Adele woke up, she'd be going to the police. After Adele did wake up, Mo decided she couldn't deprive Fletch's kids of their dad (because she is A Good Woman), so she's given him a month to find a new hospital. There's a mythical one just down the road he might try…

Meanwhile, Fletch had promised his son some chocolate, and when he found a pound coin he tried to use it in the vending machine. When the chocolate failed to drop, he gave the machine a good kicking, which was witnessed by Dr Raf Not-Smug. In the second big emotional scene of the episode, Fletch told Raf how he got into debt, and Raf – sweetheart of a man that he is – said he would give/lend Fletch all the money he needs to get out of trouble, plus he offered to put Fletch and the Fletchlings up at Not-Smug Towers so they didn't have to stay in a dodgy B&B.

When fortune turns, it turns good and proper – and as Fletch was walking past the vending machine, the chocolate bar dropped out. He did a little happy-dance just as Hanssen loomed behind him. "I hope the chocolate bar you're wielding lives up to the expectations you're ascribing to it," said Hanssen. "It's not a chocolate bar," said Fletch. "It's a fresh start." It's a metaphor, that's what it is.

On Darwin, Elliot has decided to dub the Valentine/March combo "Team Oz," not because they're off to see the wizard, but because it's their initials. They do make a lovely team, too. They snipe like they're in a rom-com, they infuriate each other and they make each other smile. They're adorable. There's just one fly in the ointment – Slimy Seb, or "my boyfriend," as Zosia refers to him. Gah! Can't she see that the man has terrible dress sense and his red sporty car is just a little phallic symbol on wheels?

Don't panic!

(Series 17, ep. 44 'Speak True' by Katie Douglas 11.8.15)

It's always a dramatic episode when you have half the cast having to wear protective face masks and at least one of the wards on virtual lockdown. It was Darwin's turn for that sort of thing this week, as Brigitte (Sally Dexter), an old colleague of Elliot's, arrived with a couple of patients with drug resistant TB who needed the high quality care – and publicity – only Holby can provide.

This meant regular patients having to be sent home, but one of them was refusing to go quietly. He did get as far as Pulses before crashing to the ground amid the muffins. Luckily Mr T (MR T!!!) was heroically on hand to do CPR and save him.

Elliot decided this patient was the priority, and Dr Oliver Valentine was more than capable of whipping the lung out of the TB patient (a simpler procedure, apparently). This wasn't good enough for Brigitte. She tried to get Mo back to do the other op, but when Mo wasn't available Brigitte just went ahead and pretended she was. This left Elliot to attend to the TB patient.

Was Brigitte justified in her actions, given that she thought the publicity of having world class surgeon Elliot Hope operating on her patients was like gold dust as far as raising money to treat other people was concerned? Or was she putting patients at risk and behaving unethically? Elliot, Oli and Hanssen were of the latter opinion, and Hanssen told her in no uncertain terms that she wouldn't be welcome back at Holby. He can't have people arranging press conferences on the steps and that sort of thing without his say-so.

Meanwhile on Keller, Essie was still broody and was inviting Sacha to consider having his vasectomy reversed. This brought tears to his eyes for all sorts of reasons, but he's been well trained and he agreed that what Essie wanted, Essie could have. He was surprised by her reaction, which was what I would call a "double reverse Chrissie" – she managed to look irritated and disapproving while telling him that she wasn't one of those Chrissie-like women who would treat him like a doormat, and if they weren't both on board with the baby plan it wouldn't happen. No wonder Sacha looks confused most of the time.

On AAU, Serena decided it was time Morven moved out of the shadow of Dr Digby and handled a patient on her own. She did this spectacularly badly, because she still had to learn that new doctor lesson about not speaking your scary diagnoses out loud and terrifying your patient. Serena knows that beneath all her quirks (talking in rhyming slang this week) and insecurities, Morven has the makings of a brilliant doctor.

Catering news now, and I was thrilled to discover that Pulses has branched out from coffee and muffins and you can now enjoy a panini. The choices seem a little limited – ham and cheese or cheese and ham, apparently – but a change is as good as a rest, menu-wise.

Bring on the day

(Series 17, ep. 45 'Beautiful' by Julia Gilbert 18.8.15)

How adorable is Dr Dominic Copeland? You'd have to say "very adorable," unless you were Hanssen, who remains to be convinced.

This week, the medic formerly known as Darren was charged with looking after a group of girls, A level students who were thinking about a career in medicine. They were a bit of a handful, at one point practically storming the ward and causing Hanssen to have to use his Cross Voice to sort them out. I didn't think their behaviour was the most realistic thing I'd ever seen, but it gave Dominic plenty of opportunities to be snippy and sarcastic and put-upon, all of which he does gloriously well.

When the inevitable Curse of the Holby Visitor struck down one of the girls and she ended up as a patient, Dominic came good with a diagnosis. Hanssen said he'd pop by to watch Dominic operate on the girl, and when he got there he found everyone scrubbed up and ready to go – but where was Dominic?

He was on the roof, sorting out a girl who'd been bullying his patient. Very sweet of him, and in the long term probably just as much use to his patient as the surgery was, but not the sort of thing to score brownie points with the world's scariest Swede. At the end Hanssen staged perhaps his finest loom ever. Dominic was telling Essie that one day Hanssen would "bitterly regret all those times he misjudged me as a complete and utter waste of space." As he spoke, Hanssen glided around the corner behind him and uttered, "Bring on the day, say I."

Meanwhile, Lucy Mottica was back on AAU with an infected wound and a pair of souvenir cufflinks for Raf. Cara – given something to do at last – had a word with Raf, telling him gifts from patients could be "misinterpreted," and suggesting Lucy was getting a bit too fond of him. She was right. It turned out that Lucy had been messing with her wounds so she would have to go back to hospital and be looked after by Raf. He told her that he cared about her, but not in a romantic sense. Will she get the message? Or is Raf going to need a bodyguard?

Up on Darwin, Prof Elliot Hope has been offered a new job. Hanssen wants him to be Director of Research (Adele would have been first choice, but she's still convalescing). Elliot munched on a doughnut and mused that he could "now make his artificial lung dream a reality." Everyone told Elliot that this was the job he'd worked his whole life for, and hurrah and everything, but Elliot's response was to do a 360 degree gaze around the ward in a 'how can I give this all up, even to pursue my artificial lung dream?' manner.

A breath of fresh air

(Series 17, ep. 46 'Infallible' by Kate Verghese 25.8.15)

Why is Selfie still at Holby? And why are we still having to endure him working through the loss of his wife? I know that sounds heartless, but he's fictional so I don't feel too bad about it. He's had some brochures printed for his Self Centre of Neurosurgery. They have a picture of him on the cover (just to tempt any funders who may be enticed by craggy features) and they reminded me of Plastic Bhatti, another ego on a stick who liked pictures of himself in brochures. Look how he turned out.

Anyways, the Self Centre was temporarily shunted down to AAU this week, because Keller was apparently full, but it turned out to be handy when a face from Selfie's past appeared with a broken wrist. Milly (Amber Aga) had gone through chemotherapy with Selfie's late wife, so it was almost inevitable that she would have more than a broken wrist wrong with her. What she had was cancer in her brain, and Selfie persuaded her (against her wishes, really) to have surgery. This was only partially successful and Milly died, leaving her husband distraught and Selfie drowning his miserable sorrows in Albie's and picking fights with Jesse (who apparently used to be a surgeon. Did we know this or is it new?).

Hanssen was also on the move. His lovely office was being "fumigated," (possibly fleas brought in by the symbolic bird he reared during his first spell there). If only Adele had been around she'd have found him a spare room and had it fitted up as a plush new office suite in no time, but she's still convalescing, so Hanssen was forced to move in with Sacha for the day as it was the only spare desk space available in the entire hospital.

The point of this was that Sacha felt the eyes of Swedish scrutiny upon him all day long, but it was one of those occasions where Sacha's instincts paid off and he improved his patient's life. Hanssen was pleased. "Days like these are a breath of fresh air," he told Sacha, and thanked him for having him on Keller like a very polite and supernaturally tall child at the end of a play-date.

Sacha's patient (Lorraine Stanley) was a pregnant heroin addict (disappointingly there was no sign of Mr T, who is usually on hand at the very first sniff of an occupied uterus). After he'd fixed up her surgical problem and sorted her out with various support services, he told her she would be a great mother. She said he would be a great parent too. Despite reading in Rachel's diary that she thought he was a rubbish dad (and you could argue that the fact he'd read a private diary is further proof of that), he's decided to give parenting yet another go, and told Essie he wants them to have a baby. Dominic is going to literally heave when he finds out.

On Darwin, Oliver Valentine and Zosia March were flirting like nobody's business. It's a beautiful thing to behold, because it's put a spring back in Ollie's step and he's very much O. Positive these days. The only fly in the ointment is the bearded, badly dressed fly known as Psych Seb – the "pound shop Carl Jung," as Ollie called him. You know Ollie's feeling better when he says stuff like that.

I'm still wondering whether Psych Seb is going to turn Psycho Seb. It's not just the cardigans. There's an odd glint in his eye and he seems ever so possessive. Frankly, I'm worried.

Fight club

(*Series 17, ep. 47 'Man of Conscience' by Tony Higgins 1.9.15*)

Thought we'd seen the last of Clifford? No chance. Back he came to AAU, this time as a patient, with a black eye, some broken ribs and intestines full of little packages of drugs. Oh, Clifford. This is what happens when you mess with Nasty Men.

Speaking of whom, on the next bed we had the Nasty Man himself, the very one who threatened to harm Clifford's daughter and then got it a bit wrong and harmed her sister/cousin instead.

This gave Fletch, and then Mo, opportunities for Revenge. Fletch had an encounter with Nasty Man in the lift, in which Nasty threatened him and his lovely children. "Threatening the bloke that gives you the morphine isn't the best idea," said Fletch through clenched teeth, making it quite clear where the balance of power lies if you happen to be lying on a trolley with tubes stuck in you.

Later on Mo had her chance when she went to confront Nasty and spotted that he was bleeding profusely. Mo actually looked extremely kick-ass in this scene and looked well ready for a fight, but both she and Fletch are good people and medical professionals first and foremost.

Nasty Man ended up dying in theatre anyway, so that's him out of the way. And the legal system will be dealing with Clifford, but not before he had a father/daughter bonding moment with Mo.

Fletch, meanwhile, has taken a job at the mythical The Grange. Maybe this is the new brand name for The Hadlington. The main thing is it will get him some regular shifts and get him away from the disapproving gaze of Mo.

So there was drama on AAU, but for a proper fight we need to go to Darwin. Sexual tension simmered all episode long between Ollie and Zosia. At one point they found themselves in The Zone – the one where two people get their faces fairly close and then they go a bit still and their gaze flutters between eyes and lips and a kiss looks imminent. She actually pounced on him (only a little pounce because they were sitting down. It wasn't one of those lunges she used to do to Digby) but he jumped away like a scared wee beastie because he's not yet ready for That Sort of Thing.

There's the additional problem of Slimy Seb, who is still officially Zosia's boyfriend. This week he wanted to take her to New York to meet his father, or "Pops," as he's known. Throw all of this together and add in a disagreement about the way to best approach a patient who wants a gender reassignment but doesn't want her father to know, and you have an explosive situation. This culminated in the funniest fight, with Ollie and Seb grappling like schoolgirls. If I tell you the cry of "Not the hair!" went up, you can guess just how brutal the encounter was. It was Seb who was worried about his hair (snork) and he ended the encounter moaning, "That's an £80 shirt!" I think we know who claimed the victory there.

Unfortunately Seb is still the official boyfriend, and Zosia is going to New York with him to meet "Pops." The way Seb ostentatiously kissed Zosia at the end of the episode and waved Ollie away with a flutter of his fingers was totally creepy, and I think Ollie should spend the time while they're away in New York taking martial arts lessons, so he can give the £80 shirt a good kicking when it returns.

In other fight club news, Selfie and Jesse faced the wrath of Hanssen for last week's scrap in Albie's. Selfie whined that it wasn't a hospital issue because it had happened "off-site." "There's no such thing as 'off-site,' Mr Self," said Hanssen. For the rest of the episode Selfie and Jesse stayed on-site and bickered.

I'd catch a grenade for you

(*Series 17, ep. 48 'An Eye for an Eye' by Nick Fisher 8.9.15*)

When I say this episode was an absolute joy (as Nick Fisher episodes usually are), it wasn't just because Selfie had to hold a live grenade for most of it. There was also the delicious banter between Mr Oliver Valentine and Dr Zosia March ("Makes my toes curl just thinking about it"), and Dr Dominic Copeland trying to maintain his perkiness between the twin difficulties of getting evils from Hanssen and having to deal with the world's gloomiest (and funniest) man.

But first we'd best keep an eye on that live grenade. Ron (John Bowler), the husband of the recently deceased Milly, was wandering around the hospital carrying a Napoleonic era box (thank you, Digby) containing photos of his late wife. He wanted Selfie to see them, to see the woman Milly was and had been rather than a set of symptoms. Selfie proved to be a hard man to get to, what with being locked away in the ivory tower of the Self Centre. Adrian 'Fletch' Fletcher is an easier man to get to, because he wanders around previously unseen areas of the hospital exterior just for the purpose of finding upset people to be nice to. He's been trained on *Casualty*, where they do a lot of that sort of thing. He's kind and he's lovely (Dr Raf Not-Smug adores him and the Fletchlings and wants them to stay forever at Not-Smug Towers) and he oozes empathy. So he said he'd bob up to the Self Centre and get Selfie to come down and talk to Ron.

What he didn't know was that Ron's Napoleonic era box also contained a little gift for Selfie – a grenade (or Mills bomb, as we now know it must be termed. Holby is so educational). If Selfie had been apologetic, humble and half way human, I imagine the bomb would have stayed in the box, but he was his usual pompous, arrogant Self ("hand-holding isn't his forte" – who knew?). In no time at all he found himself holding a live grenade – and if he let go half the hospital would be blown to kingdom come in four to seven seconds (depending on exactly how old the grenade was).

The next half hour was thoroughly exciting as the hospital was evacuated and armed police roamed the eerily quiet halls. Fletch could have evacuated himself, too, as Ron had no wish to blow up such a nice man, but instead he did his best to keep things calm and stop Selfie doing anything stupid. When the bomb was dropped, it was Fletch who went running outside with it to try and fling it as far away as possible – and after the explosion it was Fletch who was left in a pool of blood.

Will he pull through, or will Dr Raf Not-Smug end up having to look after the orphaned Fletchlings full time?

When the bomb scare happened, Zosia, Elliot and Oliver were in the middle of surgery, so they had to try and evacuate a patient whose heart was visible to even the most casual observer. It was a tense and stressful situation, but Zosia had already admitted that there was nothing she liked better than cutting people up, and days with Oliver and Elliot in theatre were the best days of her week. Bless her. She said it was even better than sex, but considering her current partner is Slimy Seb, that's not such a surprising statement.

When the bomb went off, Ollie and Zosia went flying. He was flat on his back and looking lifeless, but oh so pretty. When he opened his eyes Zosia was so happy and relieved that she had no option but to give him a thorough kissing. Bless.

No such fun for Dr Dominic Copeland, who was busy looking after the world's most lugubrious man (played by Dai Bradley who was in *Kes* – and it's spooky how you can still see Billy Casper's eyes looking at you from an older face). Richie Hicks wasn't only a committed pessimist who could "produce more pus than they've ever seen," he needed a tricky vacuum dressing and was also in the middle of a malpractice claim against another doctor. Dominic thought he'd been set up by Hanssen, but he and Richie eventually developed quite a bond ("Dominic, the treatment is doomed!"). When Dominic found Richie smoking in the toilets when he was supposed to be being evacuated, he called him a drama queen. "I'm not lucky enough to even create a vacuum," muttered Richie.

Dominic dealt beautifully with all this, but he still didn't get Hanssen's approval. I really think this has gone on long enough and if Hanssen doesn't recognise soon that Dominic is (a) trying hard and (b) adorable, I shall be writing him a memo.

And in other news, Digby doesn't high five. Ever. It doesn't sit right with him.

Career suicide

(Series 17, ep. 49 'Shockwaves' by Dana Fainaru 15.9.15)

AAU was all about Digby this week, but obviously the first question we wanted answering was whether Fletch survived last week's explosion. It looked quite grim at the beginning, as the patient Raf etc were working on went beep, and despite everyone's desperate efforts, he died. But we never saw his face, until we'd already seen the face of Fletch, watching through the window and very much alive. The dead person was Ron, and Fletch had escaped with just a flesh wound. "You're a bloody hero," Raf told him.

Selfie was bloody, but he wasn't a hero. He slumped about in a shirt covered in Ron's blood for so long I was screaming at him to get himself to the scrubs cupboard and get something clean to wear. He did manage to mumble a thank you to Fletch, who said not to mention it because Selfie would have done the same for him. You could tell by Selfie's face that he wouldn't have done any such thing, but that he wasn't proud of himself for it.

Back to Digby, whose anxiety dial was turned up to 11, what with things exploding, people dying, and having to deal with two brothers who were annoying and tricky respectively. And his shoes got vomited on – twice.

So it wasn't long before he was unlocking the drugs trolley and helping himself to something calming. And he was seen by Morven. Trying to cover for him, Morven found herself in the middle of an impossible situation and Serena, thinking it was Morven who was stressed, sent her home. She left, but not before making a brilliant diagnosis on the tricky patient and telling Digby she didn't want to be around when he killed somebody.

Digby went to confess all to Serena and Hanssen – which is such a brave thing to do that he must have still been firmly medicated at that point. Hanssen just looked at him with his face set to 'inscrutable.'

What Digby really needed was a friend and champion, and he has that in the form of the totally wonderful (and getting more wonderful by the week) Dr Dominic Copeland. As we know, Hanssen doesn't have the same high opinion of Dominic that I have, but when Dominic went and pleaded on Digby's behalf ("He just needs someone to believe in him") Hanssen relented a little bit. Digby now has two weeks to get drug-free and Hanssen will review the situation.

The question I had re Darwin was why Oliver Valentine was still working, given that he'd been knocked unconscious (albeit briefly) in the explosion. He should have been resting and watching out for signs of concussion. Anyhoo, he was sent off to collect a donor heart so we didn't see him for much of the episode. This gave Zosia time to reflect on their kiss, and time to tell Slimy Seb (who was lurking around Darwin with muffins and unwanted psych interventions) about it. He didn't take it well, and as soon as Ollie got back Seb confronted him. I was squealing "Not his face! Not his precious surgeon's hands!" but Seb went for the psyche rather than a physical attack (saves wear and tear on the shirts). Whether this had anything to do with Ollie's later reluctance to commit to a relationship with Zosia I'm not sure, but it didn't do Seb any good. He told Zosia he loves her – but she said she doesn't love him back. Ouch. Time to get those rabbit hutches firmly locked.

There was a new nurse on Keller. Fran Reynolds is an old friend of Essie's from their student days and her main function in this episode was to make Sacha feel even more insecure than he does already by telling him that Essie used to go for "hard-bodied blokes." Poor Sacha.

And Serena went for a drink with the hunky police chief.

Taking the leap

(Series 17, ep. 50 'At First I was Afraid' by Julia Gilbert 22.9.15)

I'm not sure I can even start to do justice to last night's episode. The only word for it is "special." There were only two stories. One was based in the hospital, as Elliot contemplated taking up his post as Director of Research and ended up taking a completely different path, and the other largely took place at the seaside as Dominic tried to help Digby with his demons and in the process confronted some of his own. Goth Dr Frieda made an unexpected but entirely welcome reappearance, as did Jac Naylor (how can that woman even look beautiful in yellow scrubs?), and Digby kissed Dominic on the lips. It was brilliant.

There have been numerous attempts over the years to put Prof Elliot Hope out to pasture (at one point he was even teetering on the brink of being shunted to The Mythical St James's) but all have failed, because Darwin was just about unthinkable without that lovely teddy bear, carb-craving genius of a man. Sadly we now have to contemplate a future where the Darwin consultants' office isn't full of doughnut crumbs and dog hairs, because he's gone.

His old friend Brigitte returned again, and this time she had an even more serious patient with her – who happened to be Goth Dr Frieda, who'd acquired TB while working on a TB programme in Pakistan. She was doing it to get money for her family and to assuage her guilt after a friend died in an explosion. Despite being make-up free, weak as a kitten and coughing blood, Frieda was still recognisably her old snippy, sarcastic, wise and practical self. Spotting immediately that there was chemistry between Oliver and Zosia, she advised him to go for it: "With luck she won't die on you."

We also discovered that Elliot and Brigitte were once nearly married, but then he discovered that she'd had a termination without telling him. Soon after that he married Gina. Jac Naylor – handily arriving just in time to do some of her ninja-level surgery and save Frieda's life – saw how much Elliot still cared for Brigitte. "She's better than that redhead Yank who ran over your dog," she said, because she's not a million miles away from Goth Dr Frieda, personality-wise. Jac does let her hard-as-nails guard down with certain people, though, and Elliot is one of them. A bit later on there was a scene between them that was as lovely as the one just before she gave birth to Emma. Jac said that Elliot's face lit up when he talked about Brigitte, and she understood because it's how she felt about Joseph (squeee!). She said that when Joseph asked her to leave with him, she refused because she thought he would always put his child before her. Now she has Emma, she realises that Joseph had no choice but to put Harry first, but it didn't mean he wouldn't have had enough love for her. Basically she was saying that with hindsight she'd have made a different choice and followed her heart, and Elliot should do the same. And she told him she and Jonny didn't work out (I am desperately hoping this means that Joseph is on his way back. That would make me very happy indeed).

So Elliot decided to leave to work in Pakistan with Brigitte – and Frieda, when she's better (though I was also hoping Frieda would decide to stay at Holby). There was a tearful farewell with Jac, and then Elliot left the building, to be greeted by a line-up of his colleagues forming an arch with doughnut-decorated crutches, and Brigitte waiting in a taxi. It was a funny, touching, lovely send-off for a character who's been a stalwart of the show for many years, and an actor who is clearly going to be missed by his Holby family.

To the seaside now. To save Digby from turning into a total hermit because of his anxiety, Dominic took him to his parents caravan at the seaside. They were supposed to be away on holiday. The caravan was how you'd imagine having met Carol – kitsch and tasteless and full of bottles of gaudy-coloured liqueur and cuddly toys ("They're all staring at me," said Digby). Amusement arcade visits and a spot of paddling would have been amusing enough, but things took a deeper turn when Dominic's parents arrived home early and we met his father, Barry. Barry was a bully who dominated his wife and felt nothing but contempt for his son, who was just a disappointment to him. "He doesn't like bloke things," Barry told Digby while they were fishing, "He likes blokes" (Digby is hardly Bear Grylls himself, but they bonded over a shared interest in military history). It was clear that Dominic suffered badly from Barry's lack of affection and approval, and poor Carol was stuck in the middle trying to smooth things over and compensate for her husband's coldness by being too bright and cheerful.

Things came to a head at a karaoke bar. Digby and Carol both stuck up for Dominic in a stand-up argument with Barry, and Dominic said he wasn't scared of him any more. Then Digby and Dominic, hand in hand got up on the stage and sang 'I Will Survive,' during which Digby gave Dominic a big kiss on the lips. It was like an outtake from Pride – which I mean as a huge compliment. Barry choked on a peanut, and Digby finally got his medical mojo back and calmly took charge.

So Digby is on the road to recovery; Dominic is finally free of the need to please his father and – by extension – "The Scandi Man;" and Jac has inherited Darwin and Elliot's dog Gary. It's a new dawn.

Undercover heart

(Series 17, ep. 51 'Cover Story' by Joe Ainsworth 29.9.15 and ep. 52 'Ever After' by Elliot Hope & Johanne McAndrew 6.10.15)

First of all, I apologise for the lack of review last week. I watched the episode with family members I haven't seen in a while, so there was more talking than watching going on. It's just as well that last week's and this week's episodes pretty much form a unit, with the continuing stories of Cara and her husband, and Adele and Jesse's wedding, featuring across both.

I thought the Cara/Jed storyline was really interesting and well done. Cara hasn't had much to do since she arrived except be a bit cheeky and take wedding rings on and off a lot. We discovered why there was so much emphasis on the wedding rings when a 'friend' of a patient turned out to be none other than Cara's husband Jed, who is an undercover cop. This led to some hanky panky in a store cupboard (handily, one that locks on the inside), but it was clear that spending months not knowing where her husband was or what he was doing was taking its toll on Cara. Worse was to come, when she discovered he was the father of the patient's baby. It was all excellently set up for last night's episode, when Jed returned as a patient (the Curse strikes again), badly battered. Cara was torn between wanting to protect him, wanting to batter him herself and having to keep his cover story intact in case worse happened to him. Niamh Walsh was very convincing, giving Cara just the right mix of strength and vulnerability. I couldn't help thinking Cara could do better for herself, though. Yes, Dr Raf Not-Smug, I'm looking at you.

Meanwhile, Adele was back at work for the first time since she was attacked, and inevitably found her first shift difficult. Not as difficult as guest artiste the radiant Denise Welch, who spent most of the episode gasping for breath and having an on/off wait for a lung transplant. Adele spent the shift being a bit flaky and looking sideways every time Jesse was mentioned. From this we could conclude she was Having Doubts.

This week was the wedding itself, but before they could even rehearse, the wedding planner collapsed (the Curse striking yet again). For plot reasons it was decided that Adele would take her to hospital rather than Mo, because the chief bridesmaid (Mo) was deemed to be more necessary at the wedding venue than the bride.

This gave Adele the whole episode to run back and forth between Pulses and Darwin, sometimes at almost supernatural speed. "How did she get there so fast?" Mr PLA said at one point. "It's like a horror film. She's always behind you." The wedding planner turned out to have an unconventional marriage – she was a gay woman happily married to a gay man, an arrangement which has suited both of them beautifully until the man decided to leave. This made Adele look sideways again.

Jesse, meanwhile, was busy helping Selfie with some terrifyingly ninja-level surgery. Jesse had to put his foot down when it seemed that Selfie was putting his patient in danger with his willingness to take risks. This earned Jesse the approval of Hanssen and also of Selfie, who likes people who stand up for themselves. Selfie also likes nurse Fran Reynolds, and after a barf-inducing flirting scene they both went off together at the end of the shift.

Jesse and Adele got dressed for their wedding, but it wasn't long before Adele was muttering the dreaded words, "I can't do this," and dashing off. There was an emotional scene in the multi-faith room (formerly the Linden Cullen Chapel of Torment) and Adele said she couldn't possibly be with a man who thought it was acceptable to release doves and sea eagles at the same time at a wedding. It was clear that it would end in carnage. That wasn't really what she said, but it was part of him wanting to always be in charge and take control etc etc. Like the sea eagle, Adele is a free spirit who can't be confined by that sort of behaviour. Jesse looked stunned, bless him.

SERIES 18

New responsibilities for Mo
(Series 18, ep. 1 'The Sticky Mess of Being' by Kate Verghese 13.10.15)

Three years just flies by, doesn't it? It only seems like yesterday that Mo was almost fracturing Jac's hand while giving birth to baby William in one of my favourite episodes ever. When she handed the baby to his biological mother Sorcia and they emigrated to Canada, she probably thought she wouldn't see much of him apart from a progress report in a round-robin email at Christmas. The lure of Holby proved too much for Sorcia, though, so the family was only a few miles away from the hospital when the Curse of the Holby friend/relative struck and so did a passing vehicle. The result was that Sorcia's partner ended up in a very bad way indeed, and after an apparently healthy pause, so did Sorcia. Despite the best efforts of Mo and Sacha, she died. Meanwhile little William (Jackson Allison), now three years old, was wandering around the hospital being quietly adorable (apart from when he smacked Oliver Valentine in the face with a colouring book).

At the start of the episode we saw Mo telling Hanssen that she was up for the challenge of filling in for the recently departed Elliot Hope. It was therefore a tiny bit inevitable that she would end up having to take on the responsibility for looking after the little boy she gave birth to. She's always felt a strong bond with him, but even if she hadn't his little face when he said to her, "Please don't go," would have been impossible to resist. I just hope this doesn't mean we'll see less of her while she's at home getting acquainted with CBeebies.

For students of the tall enigma who is Henrik Hanssen, the way he looked at the little boy ("He couldn't be in better hands, Miss Effanga") – a mixture of kindness, sympathy and sadness possibly indicated that he's missing his grandson. Maybe we'll soon find out what made him leave Sweden again and return to Holby.

In other news: Cara and Raf bonded after she admitted to him that she and her husband have split up. Raf knows what it's like to be cheated on, bless him.

Jesse – apparently absolutely over being jilted last week – has decided he fancies being a surgeon again. He was working with Sacha for the day, which made Selfie go all sulky.

It was Oliver Valentine's birthday, and apart from being hit in the face with a colouring book, his main preoccupation was Zosia. There was a lovely scene in which he told William (happily colouring in and ignoring him) about his feelings for her. At the end of the shift she agreed to go for a birthday drink with him, so progress has been made.

Sacha is getting fed up with Fran slumping drunkenly on his sofa on a nightly basis. Frankly he's not the only one getting fed up with Fran. Some aspects of her I quite like – she seems like a real nurse and she has a relatable warmth and sense of fun about her. But I find all this "good time girl" business a bit tiresome, and it does Sacha no favours as a character to now have him being browbeaten by two irritating women instead of the usual one.

And get ready to deck the halls! Christmas must be coming, because they now have a bowl of satsumas on the counter at Pulses.

Well this is awkward

(Series 18, ep. 2 'Cover Up' by Joe Ainsworth 20.10.15)

I wonder what first attracted Beautiful Nurse Cara Martinez to DC Jed "Alias" Martinez? Did he woo her with elaborately sculpted balloon animals and love tokens crafted out of delicate sugar-work? Or was it just his ability to hold her gaze while clenching his teeth and making veins pop in his forehead?

Thank goodness he still has some of his skills intact, but only the nasty ones because The Job has knocked out any sweetness he may once have possessed. He's been too busy getting undercover-and-on-the-side girlfriends pregnant, because his intensive police training apparently didn't cover contraception.

Poor Cara was faced this week with the prospect of assisting in the birthing of her husband's undercover secret love child, when for plot reasons there were no beds at all in Maternity even though the baby was breech. Not even a side room or a stable could be found, probably because it was Mr T's day off and his department was in the hands of anonymous midwives.

So the little Jedling came into the world, and Cara had to stand silently by and stare mournfully for a lot of the episode while various configurations of happy families got to hold the baby. It was no surprise that the poor woman was stressed and accidentally let slip that the baby was six weeks early rather than two, thus letting Brady know he couldn't be the baby's father. He still didn't twig the daddy was his bro Jed, but Nicole knew he wouldn't take the news well and she had to escape.

Dr Raf Not-Smug finally noticed that Cara had become a little over-involved in this particular case, to the extent that I don't think she as much as glanced at another patient for the entire shift. Cara had to tell him what was going on, and he helped to get Nicole and the baby safely away. He may regret this, if next week's preview is to be believed.

On Keller, Henrik Hanssen was keeping a close eye on Selfie, and he was right to do so. Selfie – apparently human and not simply an EgoBot 5000 – was suffering the after-effects of having almost been blown up by a grenade a while back and he wasn't himSelf at all. Hanssen was observing through the glass as Selfie went a bit blank and useless in surgery, and ordered him out of the theatre. Selfie is now on a "sabbatical" until he sorts himSelf out.

Zosia and Ollie were mainly concerned about whether Mo was coping with having little William (he calls her Momo – cute!) to look after. It seems that she's coping very well, apart from having to adjust to a diet mainly consisting of sausages.

Meanwhile I want to start a campaign. "Zollie" must not happen. Yes, they are absolutely delightful together and there's a real chemistry and rapport between them. They would be a gorgeous couple and could potentially have the most beautiful children imaginable. But you know how it would play out. They'd no sooner get together properly and we'd all be going "ahhhh" and it would be lovely – and then things would go wrong, there'd be problems, there'd be heartbreak – and Ollie would end up O Negative and Zosia would end up being all sad and distracted again.

Oh, Holby City, you've destroyed my faith in True Love.

It'll be alright by quiz night

(Series 18, ep. 3 'Calling Time' by Nessah Muthy & Julia Gilbert 27.10.15)

Mo was only just getting used to parenthood and she's had it whisked away again. Not for the first time, she's had to give little William up just as she was beginning to bond with him.

She was helped in this heartbreaking task by the knowledge that he really was best off with his stepfather, and also by having the counsel of two wise women. One of them was her sister/cousin Adele, who seemed to be constantly at Mo's shoulder for the purpose of pointing out Uncomfortable Truths. The other was a patient, a rather marvellous lawyer type called Lizzie (Polly Hemingway), who approached death as fearlessly as she'd approached life. "Feisty girls like us don't give up," she told Mo.

So Mo brought little William and all his bits and pieces to visit his stepfather, and consoled herself by hosting a much anticipated but poorly attended quiz night at Albie's.

Talking of feisty women, Nurse Cara Martinez is fairly feisty herself, but you'd really need a Masters degree in feistiness to cope with what she's had to put up with recently. Just in case she might have been starting to relax, up popped Nasty Sean Brady, the husband of Nicole, the woman who's just given birth to Cara's husband Jed's son. He wanted to find out where Nicole is, so he was a bit menacing to Cara. Then Jed "Alias" Martinez turned up, to inject his own special brand of charm (Phil Mitchell with a quiff) to the proceedings. When Dr Raf Not-Smug accidentally referred to him as "Mr Martinez," Jed responded by giving him a good kicking – for potentially letting his undercover cover slip, for being too friendly with Cara, or simply for having lovely eyelashes. We may never know. What we do know is that Raf had to struggle bravely on with nasty bruising and possibly worse, because the AAU Patient of the Week needed him in surgery.

Afterwards, Raf and Cara had a little Moment in the locker room. She winced at his bruises while trying not to admire his manly physique, and told him from now on she's going to keep well away from him for his own good. He blinked his lovely eyelashes at her in a manner that suggests he doesn't want Cara far away from him, and he doesn't care if it's for his own good or not.

I'm worried that there's an anaesthetist void elsewhere in the hospital, because Jesse is now being a surgeon on Keller. I know there are other anaesthetists about, because we see them – but they don't speak, and I always think speaking is a useful skill for a doctor to have.

Jesse was approaching his new role with his usual cocky confidence, and it made Sacha go all introspective. Essie kept giving him pep talks, because he needs to be confident if he's ever going to be a consultant. She also helped by being a bit rude and undermining to Jesse, because she's the consummate professional. She needn't have worried anyway – Jesse was really trying to run before he can walk, surgically-speaking, and Sacha had to save the day with a diagnosis. Then Sacha and Jesse bonded by forming a team for Mo's quiz night, while Essie went home to make voodoo dolls of anyone else who may be considering applying for the consultant job.

How to restore your confidence

(Series 18, ep. 4 'What It Takes' by Michelle Lipton 3.11.15)

I think my favourite moment of Selfie's entire Holby career came in this episode. The sight of him sitting on a bench with Digby munching popping candy was rather delightful.

As Digby is Selfie's daughter's flatmate, it wasn't so outlandish that they'd both be sharing a little confidence-boosting brains-speak in the Linden Cullen Memorial Shrubbery. They both had something to prove in this episode: Selfie that he was over the shock of being almost blown up by a grenade, and Digby had to show his AAU colleagues that he could cope with his anxiety without resorting to the drugs trolley. Digby's new drug of choice is the aforementioned popping candy – a trick he learned from Zosia. Apparently the odd sensation it produces is enough to take your mind off any other odd sensations, or something. It's the food-stuff of the devil, that's all I know.

The episode was punctuated by Digby doing little confessional pieces to camera, which I assumed were actually taking place in the office of the staff counsellor. At the end it turned out he was in Hanssen's office. He finished telling him how he had no people skills and people just confuse him (luckily, for people skills he used to have Chantelle and now he has Morven). Hanssen merely gazed an enigmatic – yet kindly – gaze and said, "From what you know of me would you think I consider myself a people person? And yet here I sit. Consultant General Surgeon and CEO of this fine hospital." The message being that, as far as Hanssen is concerned, people skills Aren't All That.

Which brings us back to Selfie. Brain surgery is a high pressure job at the best of times, but he had the extra stress of having to operate on the son of Patsy Brassvine (Caroline Lee Johnson), the woman who holds the purse strings for all sorts of medical funding. Selfie didn't think he could cope and tried to find an alternative surgeon, but boosted by popping candy and with no replacement surgeon in sight, he was forced to scrub up. In theatre he had the standard panicking moment, but a bit of shouty advice from Jesse and then some calm advice from Hanssen put him back on track. The operation was a success and Patsy Brassvine was so pleased she's going to fund his Self Centre.

Selfie's immediate response was to start calling Hanssen "Henrik." It seems the Monstrous Ego is back.

Darwin was a little bit low-key in comparison to all this. Zosia ("Selfie Junior" as Mo was calling her) was keen to be involved in a bilateral lung transplant. Well, who wouldn't be? So Mo made her jump through hoops for the entire shift just to wind her up. Mo seems quite comfortable being in charge of Darwin, but she shouldn't relax too soon – it seems that Jac's return is imminent.

Lots of pain caused by small things

(Series 18, ep. 5 'Left Behind' by Rebecca Wojciechowski 10.11.15)

Mo Effanga is a wonderful character. She's strong, skilful, feisty, funny – and she can break your heart. So it did seem a bit odd a few weeks ago that she seemed to give wee William back to his father without too much of an effort and quickly console herself with quiz night. Where was the big emotional leave-taking?

They were saving it up for this week. Faced with the possibility that William might be going to live with his granny Viv (Sorcia's mother, with whom Sorcia had had a difficult relationship), Mo and the little boy got in her funny pink car and headed off. She didn't seem to have much of a plan – by then she was operating completely on instinct and emotion and wasn't thinking much at all. Mr T, who knows her better than most, tracked her down to the local bus station.

William likes buses and Mr T likes Mo, and I'm certain I wasn't the only viewer who was thinking what a lovely family they'd make. In fact I'm certain that was exactly what Mr T was thinking. He persuaded her to come back to Holby, and there was such a lovely scene in the little pink car when Mr T assured her that one day she'd have a family of her own and be happy. Oh, let it be with Mr T, Mo. He's perfect.

William's stepfather Brett finally decided he would look after William after all, but Viv proved to be a lot more sympathetic than Mo first thought and understood how Mo felt. And how did Mo feel? "How can he not be my son?" she said. "I feel him, right here."

From pain caused by the love of a small boy to pain caused by having a small cavalryman embedded in your upper arm. A small toy cavalryman, I hasten to add. This was the fate of Digby, who'd fallen over Dominic's gym bag and managed to get the aforementioned object embedded in him. "Looks like you fought a toy soldier and the toy soldier won," said Serena (who was on excellent form in this episode). "I'm at risk of blood poisoning," fretted Digby. "You don't know where Dom hides my cavalrymen." Best not to dwell on that.

Digby was a spectacularly (amusingly) bad patient, though he insisted his anxiety is under control. Morven did her best to help, but he was having none of it: "I think Junior Doctor of the Year 2012 knows what he's talking about," he said. Attempting to self-treat later on, he promptly fainted at the sight of his own blood (he went down like a felled tree) and needed half the AAU staff to revive him.

Serena, meanwhile, was having a bad day herself following the arrival of a wedding invitation. Her ex, Alcoholic Edward, was marrying his much younger girlfriend (or "foetus") and Serena wasn't happy. Not that she'd ever have him back, but he just has this way of unsettling her that she doesn't like. Digby reassured her that she was way too good for Edward, and obviously that's true.

Patsy Brassvine, the Keeper of the Big Medical Purse, now has more titles to her name. She's been appointed to the mysterious post of Innovations Consultant (she may want to start with Pulses – they've been overdue a menu revamp for years) and was also heading up the panel to appoint the new Keller consultant.

Sacha had his shoes polished and his suit cleaned ready for the interview. Hanssen dropped by to not wish him luck – why, that would be unethical. "Impartiality rules prevent me from wishing you good luck," he said, "but were you to assume that is what I'm wishing you, that would be your prerogative… entirely." How Guy Henry manages to deliver lines like that so smoothly is always a marvel.

It was unfortunate that Patsy was on the interview panel as well as being Innovations Consultant, because she meddled with one of Sacha's cases and tried to get him to Innovate when he strongly felt that the un-innovated method was the best. He turned out to be right, but Patsy's influence had made the patient insist on the Innovated approach. The outcome wasn't good for the patient, and it was a disaster for Sacha, as he let rip at Patsy after the interview: "If the price of a consultant's badge is sucking up to some flash idiot who's just bought their way on to the board then you can keep your damn job!"

Hanssen dropped by later to tell him he hadn't got the job, but as a man with the moral compass of the hospital on his agenda, Hanssen let Sacha know that his attitude was appreciated.

But we're so close to an arrest!

(Series 18, ep. 6 'Beneath the Cover' by Lindsay Williams 17.11.15)

The Mythical St James's is apparently real enough to have its own quiz team, according to Fletch. In fact I'm sure they have an A&E department as well (which occasionally gets used if Charlie is a bit over-stretched on *Casualty*). If only Nicole Brady had gone to St James's to haemorrhage, Nurse Cara Martinez might have had a quieter shift and we wouldn't have had to endure her husband, Jed "Alias" Martinez, bleating on at her again about how he's so close to making an arrest he can't possibly peep out from behind his undercovers.

Instead we had Bad Man Sean Brady stalking the AAU corridors holding the baby and eventually discovering the truth about who the real father is. Pausing only to put the baby down, he proceeded to give Jed the good kicking we've all felt he deserved for weeks, until Cara knocked Brady out with a swift whack with a crutch.

To the very end Jed was trying to persuade Cara to trust him, and she might have done if Nicole hadn't given her a swift summary of exactly what kind of things his undercover life had involved: sex, violence and a heavy reliance on hair products.

At least Cara has one man she can rely on. Adorable Dr Raf Not-Smug protected her by not telling anyone – not even Serena – exactly how Cara was involved in the situation. Bless him.

And bless Dr Dominic Copeland, too. Last week's patient, Lee, was back on Keller for the surgery to sort out his cancer. Dominic was a bit funny with Lee last week – all cross and snappy in a way that made me think I'd missed something. He was like that this week as well, but he had to be nice to Lee because he wanted to be involved in the surgery. Lee took advantage of this by sending Dominic to get him magazines.

They say there's a thin line between love and hate, and in Dominic's case there's a thin line between irritation and attraction. He started to rather like Lee, so that by surgery time he was promising him that everything would be fine, medically speaking. We know by now that doctors shouldn't promise positive outcomes when there are no guarantees, and when it was discovered in theatre that Lee's cancer may have spread, Dominic had one of those distracted moments. Later on he went to visit Lee – and they ended up holding hands. It was very sweet and I just wish I could promise Dominic a positive outcome, because he so deserves it. I'd have to say (because this is Holby) the prognosis is not good, though.

Mo, meanwhile, has given up looking for Mr Right. He definitely wasn't the man she'd gone to a salsa class with. He turned out to have a heart condition and seven kids ("He's a Sperminator," said Mo). Mo realised that what she really wants is a baby, as looking after William has made her hear the ticking of the biological clock very loudly. Zosia pointed out that she didn't need Mr Right to have a baby, so Mo is thinking of going the sperm bank route.

If only she knew a man who is kind, warm, funny, handsome, good with kids, can knit, knows his way professionally around lady parts and is crazy about her and likes the idea of having a family with her. If only she knew a man like that, just think how happy she could be.

Jac back. Everyone on their A game

(Series 18, ep. 7 'A Delicate Truth' by Katie Douglas 24.11.15)

Jac Naylor was back full-time at Holby from her maternity leave (hurrah!). Was this the reason that everyone was on their A game in this episode? Not just character-wise, but acting-wise and writing-wise, too. It was an absolute cracker.

The main effect of Jac's return on Oliver Valentine was a tad odd. He started the episode feeling all confident and looking forward to getting his hands on a very unusual tumour (it was called Howard). As soon as Jac appeared, his confidence drained away. She wasn't helpful: "Have you found a Yellow Pages to stand on in theatre, or do you still need to borrow one?"

I don't recall Ollie as being particularly scared of Jac before. Indeed what she respected about him was his tendency to stand up to her. Maybe it's a side effect of all the traumas he's had in his life and his re-emergence as Valentine 2.0. At these times, what's needed is a little brains-speak, and this was supplied by the patient with the tumour, Mr Duffy (Nick Raggett). He quite liked having his tumour because it had made him rather a star on his tumour forum and he wasn't quite sure if he could cope with a tumourless life. Ollie told him he needed to have some confidence. "Bet on yourself, because no one else will," he told him. "Is that what you're doing?" Mr Duffy replied, and Ollie realised he had to man up and get into theatre, without a Yellow Pages because he's quite tall enough on his own.

While all this was going on, Jac had returned to find that there was a nasty little bug on her ward, and one that couldn't be sorted out with hand sanitizer and bleach. It was Selfie, who's been given a corner of Darwin to play with. I have no idea why this has happened, given that he was recently squatting on Keller, and Patsy Brassvine has offered to fund an entire Self Centre. And why does Hanssen – normally the most sensible of men – keep giving away little portions of his innovative, award-winning CT ward? We'll just have to file it under "plot reasons" (so Jac and Selfie are thrown into conflict) and move swiftly on.

Jac was not best pleased to see Selfie. "You have four beds. Take one step towards a fifth and I'll gut you like a fish, and enjoy doing it," she told him. I'm very much hoping that the barbed exchanges between Selfie and Jac aren't pointing to a revival of their relationship, but the omens aren't good.

As far as Oliver was concerned, it was handy that Selfie was nearby because Mr Duffy needed a neuro person to be on hand when his op got more complicated than expected. Jac seemed to be a bit childish and unprofessional in her reaction to this, but Ollie had to ignore her and do what was right for his patient. Later on Jac told him it had all been deliberately designed as a learning experience for him, just like the good old days when she made him juggle coins between his fingers.

This was all fairly light-hearted compared to what was going on in AAU. Morven also had lessons to learn, and in her case the lesson was that not everybody could be (or should be) saved. Her patient was Beth Musgrove (Jenny Lee), who turned out to have such messed-up innards that there was nothing that could be done – at least nothing that would have left her with any acceptable quality of life. Beth's husband Hugh (Keith Barron), like Morven, wanted to do anything possible to keep Beth alive, and when Morven mentioned the possibility of a transplant, Hugh went straight to Hanssen. This was a beautifully played scene with two wonderful actors. Hanssen agreed with

Digby that a transplant wasn't a viable idea, and Beth asked Morven to help Hugh come to terms with the idea that she would die. The scenes between Morven and Beth and Hugh were beautifully written (by Katie Douglas) and played, and so sad.

Back up to Keller for some light relief, though I worry that it's only temporary. Dominic is in love with hunky plumber Lee (Jamie Nichols). And who wouldn't love a man with big brown eyes who surprises you with a picnic on the roof and a white vest as a gift, despite having a nasty infected wound? Thoughtful *and* brave. What I love about this story is that usually Dominic is all perky and cheeky, but when he has real feelings about something or someone he goes rather quiet, and almost shy. It's like his own feelings take him by surprise. At the end Lee got the good news that his cancer hasn't spread, and he and Dominic hugged. So it's happy ever after – for now.

Nothing in this hospital is normal

(Series 18, ep. 8 'In Which We Serve' by Ed Sellek 1.12.15)

After the flashy new title sequence (I like it), yet another episode to cherish. Particular highlights: Morven's hair, Digby's smile, Jac's brilliant one-liners and Dominic generally.

I'm going to start with AAU, which continued the story from last week featuring guest artiste Keith Barron as newly widowed Hugh Musgrove. Digby has been gradually working his way back from the low point that saw him helping himself to the contents of the drugs trolley to cope with his anxiety. His medical skills are fine, but it's always been people skills that have caused him the biggest problem.

Luckily he found some common ground with Hugh – Digby's interest in military history gave him a connection to the ex army man, who reminded him of his grandfather. When Morven recommended grief counselling for Hugh, Digby knew that he wasn't the sort of person to welcome that approach. By the end of an episode in which Hugh had gone walkabout, fallen down the stairs and needed emergency surgery, Digby had bonded with him and was being so kind and lovely.

It didn't go unnoticed by Morven, who later on in Albie's decided Digby was ready to put his glasses on again and become The Full Digby. This made him smile, which is excellent news because he really does have the most beautiful smile in the NHS and we haven't seen it for a long time. And Morven was looking rather fondly at him.

Digby's flatmate Dominic, meanwhile, spent his day trying to pluck up courage to ask Lee the Plumber (Jamie Nichols) out before he was discharged and disappeared into the wilds of Holby forever. In this endeavour he was aided by a nun (Liz Izen) who couldn't speak because she was about to have thyroid surgery. This was ideal for Dominic because she was the perfect sounding board – listening, not speaking, offering to-the-point written replies. Never mind that some of her replies were actually about her own fears about her surgery.

It seemed Dom had missed his chance when Lee left while he was busy, but he caught up with him on the Stairs of Romance, and while Dominic wavered and hesitated, Lee kissed him.

In other Keller news, Adele has now joined the team and she has her very own special uniform as worn by nobody else in the hospital because she's Unique.

Fran had moved up to Darwin for the day – possibly so she didn't spot Adele's new uniform and become insanely jealous. It was also so she could cross paths with Jac, which will become significant in a later episode if the previews are to be believed.

Jac was on top form, if you enjoy barracudas in heels. Which I do, obviously. Her finest line was to Selfie: "You know what my role is here," she told him. "To remove useless or…" [pause to cast withering glance at him] "…harmful tissue."

I also liked her response to Zosia, who was attempting to be chummy by asking about a staff member Jac had just sacked: "Does it look like we're in a hairdresser's?"

During this exchange, Zosia noticed that there was a question mark next to her name on Jac's handy staff wall-chart. Needing to prove herself, she took it upon herself to persuade a patient that he should have surgery that was a tad riskier than the course of treatment favoured by Jac (and you know it must be risky if even Jac thinks it's risky). Zosia's handling of this situation veered very close to being a disciplinary matter, if I'd been in charge, but when things inevitably went pear-shaped and Zosia's treatment option became an emergency necessity, she impressed Jac in theatre. And the question mark disappeared from beside her name.

Someone should admit her

(Series 18, ep. 9 'Skin and Blister' by Joe Ainsworth and Kate Verghese 8.12.15)

You know I'm not a violent person, but by the end of this episode I wanted to kick something. Anything, but preferably Nurse Fran Reynolds.

Alarm bells should have been ringing as soon as she announced to Jac that cardiothoracics is her "passion." That's a word that's used all over the place – we've probably all bought a sandwich from a company that declares itself to be "passionate" about sandwiches.

Passion goes down very well at Holby these days. Essie has already been praised for hers, and in this episode Jesse was praised for his (passion and compassion, but more of that later). Passion manifests itself in different ways, though. For Jac Naylor, passion for the job means working hard, being excellent, always improving. What it doesn't mean is all the touchy-feely stuff that Fran thinks it means.

It was fairly obvious to even the most casual viewer that Darwin patient o' the week, Seymour Orson (Daniel Hill) was on the autistic spectrum, but Jac didn't notice it at all and Fran only noticed it when he had a Rain Man moment and told her which day of the week her mother had died on many years ago. Until then, Jac had him written off as an awkward cuss and Fran had seized the opportunity to be annoyingly caring and dreadfully undermining to Jac. She led a vulnerable patient into saying that he wasn't happy with Ms Naylor's treatment of him, and she handed the case over to Ollie behind Jac's back.

This would have been enough to have had her on a disciplinary, but in the end it was Jac who had a complaint made against her for negligence – by Fran.

I'm not sure if we were meant to have any sympathy for Fran's position, but I certainly didn't. Jac was no more brusque than usual with Seymour, and indeed she correctly realised that the best way to reassure him was to give him facts and statistics about her success rate.

I'm going to turn my attention to another ward now, because my blood pressure can't cope with this. On Keller Jesse came face to face with the past when he found his patient was the sister of the patient who'd died during surgery last time he had a go at being a surgeon. Unsurprisingly, her mother was not thrilled to see him again. He tried to avoid getting involved in the case, but in the end was on hand in theatre (as an anaesthetist) and was able to give Hanssen a vital piece of information to ensure the operation was a success. So everyone was happy and Hanssen was pleased with Jesse's work and can now possibly imagine him settling into a surgeon's role.

AAU was a bit silly. Raf, Fletch and Digby were more or less joined at the hip so they could try and match-make between Cara and a patient. I'm not sure how ethical it all was, but Cara wasn't interested anyway, because it was too soon after the hideous revelations about Jed "Alias" Martinez (currently Banged Up). I think what we were supposed to take away from the storyline was that Raf kept looking a tad wistful, and was probably rather relieved that Cara wasn't seduced by a man who could still have a crack at some capoeira moves while on crutches and recovering from a back injury that had had them all terribly worried only twenty minutes earlier.

A perfectly deadly aneurysm

(Series 18, ep. 10 'Bad Blood, Fake Snow' by Nick Fisher 15.12.15)

Carli Norris must be a brilliant actor. Fran Reynolds started her Holby life as a fun-loving, funny, caring person (I think I described her as "relatable"), friend of Essie, amusing thorn in Sacha's side, always available for a bit of plain-speaking relationship advice whether it was asked for or not. And in the last couple of episodes I don't think there's been a character I've wanted to slap more – at least not since Sahira Shah left. To be so believable in both roles (as the same person) takes skill.

Character-wise, I suppose Fran's fondness for Selfie should have rung alarm bells, but otherwise there was nothing to suggest that the mere sight of Jac Naylor would have her turning to the dark side so thoroughly. There's obviously something behind it – there's history between the two of them, which Jac is unaware of and which looks like becoming clear in the next episode.

This week saw her escalate her apparent vendetta against Jac, with that old chestnut of mortality figures. We've seen before with Prof Elliot Hope, and Zoe Hanna on *Casualty*, that the best doctors always seem to have more patients dying on them. This gets folk ruffled until they realise it's because those doctors are the ones brave enough and skilful enough to take on the sickest patients. Fran showed these figures to the sister of a patient who was pencilled in to have a frozen elephant trunk inserted in her (it wasn't made of elephant). She also spent much of the episode chasing Henrik Hanssen around corridors. He really should have swatted her back to her ward (actually a different ward – it was clear she wasn't a very good fit for Darwin), but then he mightn't have been present when Jac rather brilliantly took things up a notch and goaded Fran into hitting her. Smacking a consultant is the surest way to have you escorted off the premises by two non-speaking extras. Fran's last hope was that Selfie would save her – or at least buy her a glass of wine and some artisan crisps at Albie's – but he wasted no time in clearing off, leaving her bleating, "Guy! Guy!"

Fran wasn't the only one having a bad day, and while I'm in slapping mode I could possibly slap whoever decided that Dominic wasn't entitled to just one more week of happiness with Lee. I know Dominic's "happiness" was keeping Digby awake at night, but still… Lee has only gone and emptied Dominic's bank account and cleared out almost everything in their flat, including Digby's grandfather's medals and Dominic's mum's running away money, which was stuffed in a teddy bear. Possibly it's been a character-building experience for Dominic, who finished his shift and then went back to check on a rather wonderful shoplifter patient he'd been looking after. I can't help thinking that being in love was a character-building experience for him as well, though. Bless him.

And God bless AAU, every one. The majority of them – Fletch and the Fletchlings, Raf, Cara, a random patient and probably the non-speaking extra who spends his time checking drip bags – are all going to be spending Christmas at Serena's. She's been whizzing around Waitrose buying up all their Christmas goodies, only to be let down by daughter Elinor who prefers to Christmas elsewhere. Gazing around her domain, Serena realised that most (all) of her staff have had a traumatic year, what with one thing and another, so everyone is going round to Campbell Towers on the Big Day to help her with a crate of Shiraz (or a soft drink for the Fletchlings) and Downton Abbey.

Cherish it

(Series 18, ep. 11 'Blue Christmas' by Julia Gilbert 22.12.15)

There was so much packed into this episode – a shocking revelation, atrociously bad carol singing, two Christmas kisses, a proposal, a new job, and Hanssen as Santa. It was absolutely glorious.

The best thing about it was that I realised how many wonderful characters there are in Holby at the moment. Every ward is full of lovely people. I especially love AAU, and would put up with any amount of sick on my shoes if I could be part of Serena's gang. It looks like they have such fun together (as actors as well as characters). I loved the scene where Serena was auditioning for inter-ward competitive Christmas carols. Morven was amusingly dreadful. Serena dismissed Raf's offer to solo: "Far too rugged and world-weary," she said, and he looked rather thrilled. Digby had the right choirboy look, but his voice was no better than Morven's. Serena sighed and said she was missing Dr Tressler's dulcet tones.

The storyline on AAU was all about Morven and Digby. I feel that Morven herself would use the phrase "keen as mustard," and she really is. She has all the skills to be a great doctor, but lacks the life experience of old hands like Fletch as far as difficult patients is concerned. This got her into trouble with a very unpleasant man this week, and Digby did his sometimes misguided best to help her out. The two of them make the most adorable couple, and their funny little kiss at the end was perfect for their characters.

Despite me having been ready to slap Fran for the last two episodes, she once again thoroughly turned things around this week. Carli Norris really has been brilliant in this role. She turned up at the hospital trying to bribe first Hanssen then Selfie with a bottle of alcohol before giving up and downing it herself. Ending up as a patient having taken some stolen prescription drugs still wasn't enough to get Jac to listen to her, so she hit Jac where it hurts, by taking Emma from the creche and taking her walkies – to the roof.

We finally discovered Fran and Jac's shared history. They'd both been at the same children's home, and while Fran was the target of abuse from one of the staff, Jac had avoided it by keeping her head down and her guard up. Fran blamed Jac for not doing something to help her. It was a shocking story, handled beautifully by all concerned, and added another totally plausible piece to the jigsaw of Jac Naylor.

To Keller now, and Sacha was wearing possibly his finest shirt ever. It was so bright and festive he really didn't need the turkey-shaped Christmas hat to complete the look. When you picture a general surgical consultant, do you picture a cuddly man in a Santa shirt and a turkey hat? This is what we need to start doing, as Sacha finally decided to go for it, went for it, and got it. This was in part thanks to an old acquaintance of his, Hugo (Daniel Flynn) who was one of these competitive, somewhat bullying types. Sacha initially crumbled under the pressure, but when Hugo was found to have inoperable cancer, Sacha's strengths as a doctor and a person came to the fore and he impressed the interview panel. He celebrated by proposing to Essie.

Romance was a bit in the air, what with Digby and Morven, and Sacha and Essie. So what about Oliver and Zosia, who've been circling around each other for some time? Well, he did sprint towards her and give her a proper kiss – but afterwards he sprinted away from her just as fast. She looked confused.

I've not really mentioned Henrik Hanssen yet, but he was very much in evidence throughout the episode – at one point turning up in a Santa costume after the Santa who'd been booked to dish out presents at the creche failed to turn up. The booked Santa obviously had much shorter arms and legs than the tallest CEO in the NHS, but somehow Hanssen even manages to wear an under-sized cheap Santa suit with panache. But what's going on in his family life? Why was he looking sadly at a Christmas card depicting his family (it was his family, wasn't it?). Why did the Christmas card only contain a question mark?

In the final scene, Jac was leaving the hospital with Emma and Gary the dog. She told Hanssen that Jonny would be spending Christmas with them, and invited Hanssen to join them (can you imagine what fun that would be?). He declined. "I think Christmas is for families," he said, adding rather sadly, "Cherish it while you can."

Ric didn't get the memo

(Series 18, ep. 12 'Beginnings' by Andy Bayliss 29.12.15)

After all the drama of the last few weeks, Holby City was ready for a relatively quiet episode. To ease us into a spot of post-Christmas relaxation, there was really no better man for the job than Ric Griffin. Following his stay in Australia ("Expensive") with daughter Jess ("Expensive"), Ric was all ready to add his own brand of calm authority to his old post in AAU. But he hadn't been reading his emails. AAU is very much the Queendom of the blessed Serena these days. Ric was actually pencilled in for Keller.

He wasn't best pleased, because his heart and soul is in AAU (though he practically had to be prised away from Keller once upon a time). Still, he's a professional, so no problem there. He could easily fit in as the boss of Keller. Oops – another email missed, as Sacha is currently fulfilling that role. Poor Ric was left not quite knowing what his place was, and I can't say I blame him.

At least he knew he was in a position of authority over Adele, because she's a very junior junior nurse who used to be a holiday rep. When she got too big for her boots, as she so often does, he put her in her place sharpish. He was right to do so as well, in my opinion – it just isn't on to scare patients into thinking they might have cancer when it hadn't occurred to them before and they probably don't, and to assume that your patient is being groomed for terrorism just because she has a Turkish boyfriend.

But once again, he hadn't got the memo. The one that says that Adele must be treated with kid gloves because (a) she got whacked in the Linden Cullen Memorial Shrubbery, and that's got to hurt, and (b) she's Special. Hanssen swiftly put Ric right about these things, and Ric apologised, and realised for himself just how special Adele is.

On Darwin, there was a lot of that double act of Mo and Mr T (or MoT), and it was brilliant. Chizzy Akudolu and Ben Hull really work so beautifully together, it makes the relationship between them seem totally real and effortless. As we know, Mr T loves the bones of Mo and has done for years. It's love without any agenda except for her to be happy, and it's a rare and beautiful thing. She, the silly sausage, can't quite see this, or doesn't quite feel the same way, though she loves him a lot in her own way. So when she decided she wanted a baby by a donor father, he was only too pleased to offer himself as a donor (he's worn loose boxer shorts every day since he was ten years old, so quality isn't an issue).

This was the cue for some lovely comedy sequences – Mr T primping himself in the mirror before he went to outline his plan to her; the look on Mo's face when she saw a small jar of opaque liquid with his name on it on the staff room table (it was egg nog, apparently); and a very badly coded discussion about it between them in theatre, which led to Zosia exasperatedly saying, "Just take his semen, will you?" I love this story line – there are so many possibilities as to how it'll develop, and any reason to see more of MoT is fine by me.

Remember that hunky policeman who was in charge of proceedings when Selfie was left holding a live grenade? He appeared this week and did a lot of lurking around AAU. Frankly I thought he was a bit of a nuisance and I'd have got a non-speaking security guard to see him off the premises. Instead, he and Serena have gone on a date, and a nation rejoiced because it gave Serena the chance to wear her famous fur hat.

Squeee level set at 11

(Series 18, ep. 13 'Young Hearts, Run Free' by Johanne McAndrew and Elliot Hope 5.1.16)

For plot reasons, Henrik Hanssen sent Dominic, Digby and Morven to one of these adventure camp places where you get to pretend to be in a video game and make do without comfy beds and nice facilities in exchange for having your character built. Notice that Hanssen didn't go himself, because his character is already built and he's got more sense.

Also for plot reasons, the person running this adventure was Morven's dad Austin (Clinton Blake), who turns out to be so famous he has his own Foundation. He's also rather scary/thrilling, depending on whether you're Digby or not.

This storyline was excellent fun, because we got to see Morven being all feisty and gung-ho, we got to see Dominic telling his relationship woes to a hen (marvellously named "Henriketta"), and we got to see Digby manning up and proving that he's worthy of Morven's affections and respect. And there was a happily-ever-after ending with Morven and Digby sharing a proper kiss, and Dominic getting himself a date with a posh boy.

As if that wasn't all heartwarming enough, back at the hospital Oliver Valentine was eventually persuaded to crack and admit he's in love with Zosia, and the pair of them also ended their shift with a proper kiss. He didn't even run away after this one.

He took a bit of persuading, though, because he'd spent Christmas mooning about in Mexico feeling all guilty for having feelings for another woman when he was really supposed to be enslaved to the memory of Dr Tara Lo. It was going to take drastic action to stir him, and this came in the form of a twin-pronged attack from Jac Naylor and that nun who pops up sometimes to give him good advice. Jac told Zosia about a fabulous research opportunity in Edinburgh that meant she'd have to leave immediately. This seemed entirely reasonable to Zosia, because the fluid staffing configurations of Holby mean that people can come and go at the drop of a hat and not even have to think about who's going to pay their share of the rent in Holby or anything practical like that. A word from Ollie would have made her stay, but he was busy being moody and upset. It took a tearful chat with the nun in the Linden Cullen Temple of Anguish to make him see sense. And when Jac walked in on Ollie and Zosia enjoying a Tender Moment, the penny finally dropped that the research job in Edinburgh had probably been made up by Jac just to give Ollie a bit of a motivational kicking. Jac always did employ unorthodox methods with him.

We were also treated to Mr T (MR T!!!) worrying that he would never be good enough for Mo, just to ensure that the sound of Holby fans going "Squeee!" could be heard up and down the land.

Honest, objective and ethical

(Series 18, ep. 14 'The Hope That Kills' by Patrick Homes 12.1.16)

I think we're supposed to dislike Selfie. Jac says he's after Darwin. Hanssen says he's after everything, and since Jac and Hanssen are the intellectual and moral centres of the hospital respectively, I take them seriously. In this episode he was even prepared to risk the life of a woman who'd been nothing but a friend to him, in order to pursue more glamorous and headline-making surgery, and that's not the behaviour of a nice man.

And yet, Holby likes its villains to be nuanced. Apart from out and out monsters like Jac's mother, most Holby baddies have a back story that grants them at least a tiny bit of sympathy. In Selfie's case, the tragedy of losing his wife has perhaps been augmented by the near death experience of having a live grenade in his hands. Something has been sending him to support groups alongside other tortured geniuses. Something upsets him so much he has to absorb himself in a daily sudoku to cope.

He's still a rampaging ego on a stick, though, and try as I might I can't have any sympathy for him. But if all this is ultimately leading to a massive showdown with Hanssen to once again restore the moral compass of the hospital, well that gets my vote. You can't have a hero without a villain.

Talking of heroes – Arthur Digby. What an extraordinarily lovely man he is. Morven asked him to keep their relationship on the down-low, and the silly pickle kept it so down-low that when Serena asked him if there'd be any problem giving Morven an "honest, objective, ethical" appraisal he said of course not, and toddled off. And of course it was a problem, but instead of ending up with them getting all cross at each other and ruining a beautiful thing before it had even properly begun, Digby decided to announce his feelings for Morven, loudly, spectacularly and poetically, in front of the whole ward. He was egged on by a man with a screw through his tongue (a piece of prosthetic work so disgusting it should have come with its own advisory notice and a helpline for the traumatised to call afterwards). Serena, who was on very amusing form during the episode, told Digby that he was a "brave boy" to declare his love, after she'd just told him she couldn't abide office romances (while being deliciously gossipy herself about Ollie and Zosia).

The other ongoing office romance is Sacha and Essie. Sacha was having a day off, but Essie was very much in evidence, coordinating transplants, acting on her usually rock solid instincts and getting things a bit wrong but only a bit, and finding out she's not pregnant. A busy shift indeed.

See you back on the ice

(Series 18, ep. 15 'Sins of Our Fathers' by Kit Lambert 19.1.16)

There was a moment in this episode when I thought things were turning against Henrik Hanssen in his battle with Selfie for control of the hospital. Selfie was trying his best to line up allies. He had Ric Griffin on Team Self for pragmatic rather than heartfelt reasons, but still, Ric is a very big deal. Selfie also offered Jac Naylor the post of Clinical Ambassador if she would support him and it briefly seemed like she might be swayed. She turned it down, which was obviously the right decision, but it cheated me out of the opportunity to use the phrase, "Ambassador, with these balloon stents you are really spoiling us."

Firmly on Team Hanssen were Serena, Digby, Oliver Valentine, and just about any sensible person in the whole wide world of Wyvernshire.

The biggest asset to Team Hanssen is, of course, Henrik Hanssen himself, and he was absolutely magnificent in this episode. He has his eye on the big picture of the future of the hospital, and ensured some funding went in the direction of carrying on some old research that Jac and Elliot had been doing. At the same time he's very aware of his staff and patients, remembering that it was a year since Fletch's wife died and sending him home to be with the Fletchlings, offering Sacha some wise advice (and giving himself a bit of deep brains-speak in the process), and taking personal interest in the case of a homeless man he found outside the hospital.

We still don't know what's been going on in Sweden – why he came back to Holby, why he was thinking of returning to Sweden. This is a good thing, because an air of mystery only adds to his general marvellousness.

Elsewhere, Digby realised that he isn't cut out for the hurly-burly of AAU and decided to move back to Keller. This is also wonderful news because he'll get to work with Dominic again.

Essie was worrying about how well a woman with a Nazi grandfather was going to fit into a Jewish family, but eventually she received her answer – that at least she isn't as awful as Chrissie. Faint praise, but she was happy to take it, and the lovely ring Sacha gave her.

And we learned much about Jac's attitude to balloons. She puts up with them for Emma's sake, but hates them because they bring back memories of bleak parties in children's homes, she told Oliver Valentine – who was a little deflated to hear this. And almost my favourite line of the night among many was Oliver Valentine referring to their balloon modeller of a patient: "I hope you let him down gently." Ollie is cracking jokes again and Hanssen has seen off a coup by Selfie. All's right with the world.

A spark or an agreement

(*Series 18, ep. 16 'Kiss and Tell' by Jeff Povey 26.1.16*)

Mr T has bought a babygro with Winnie the Pooh on it! Not for himself (though if anyone could pull that look off it's Mr T) but for the baby that he and Mo plan to have. Not this month, though, because Mo did a test and it was negative.

This upset Mr T. Not so much that she's not pregnant yet, because who knows better than him that it doesn't always happen straight away. But because he wasn't there when she did the test. He wants to be fully involved – he's even thinking of baby names and school places.

Mo and Mr T have been circling around each other for so long they even have their own hashtag, so Mr T decided it was time to test out whether they had a spark or just an agreement by kissing her. He said if they did that they'd know. So they did that, and claimed they knew that there was no spark. But we saw their faces – there so *was* a spark.

Digby was back on Keller. "The little fella's back on Keller," quipped Dominic, and of course one of the lovely side effects of this is we get to see Dig and Dom back together again. There was also a pep talk from Hanssen: "Dr Digby! Walk with me." "Walking," said Digby, falling into step beside the world's tallest CEO, who said what he needed to say and dismissed Diggers with "You can stop walking now."

Patient o' the week was none other than Morven's dad Austin (Clinton Blake), who'd succumbed early to the curse of being a Holby relative, and succumbed late to a nasty parasite he picked up in Panama. Austin had a medical theory that was more or less ignore it and it won't happen. This was rather borne out by events, because he only came in for a hernia repair but as soon as they found out about this parasite he seemed to go downhill before our very eyes, and was at death's door and on the transplant list within the hour.

It gave Digby the chance to be strong and magnificent though. When Austin barfed blood and told Digby he was scared, I think I fell in love with Digby a little bit more when he told him, "I'm here."

In AAU, Serena was discovering, via a patient who was a friend of her late mother, that somewhere out there Adrienne had another daughter. Serena has a sister she never knew she had! There seems to be a lot of this sort of thing among the Holby staff. Just please don't tell me Serena's secret sister is Adele.

Do what makes you happy
(Series 18, ep. 17 'Serenity' by Michelle Lipton 2.2.16)

Major Bernie Wolfe is eventually going to be a new doctor on Keller, but this week she was a new patient on Darwin and, as such, spent the entire episode lying down. She still managed to make her mark, though, because she's Jemma Redgrave and she radiates charisma even when horizontal. We've already learned that she has a husband called Marcus who works at The Mythical St James's. He wants her to choose between her army career and a life in Holby with him. Despite having a close personal colleague in Afghanistan who sends her flowers, she's going to have to plump for Holby eventually. Personality-wise she's brave, tough and no nonsense in the manner of Fleur Fanshawe, but I think I need to see her upright before I get a proper idea of what she's like.

Her main function this week was to be a patient with complicated CT and neuro needs, which meant that Selfie and Dr Oliver Valentine had to work together to sort her out. I did wonder why, as the procedure was going to be so delicate and tricky, they didn't get Mo to do it, as she was around (isn't Mo senior to Ollie?), but obviously Mo isn't going out with Selfie's daughter so that scenario would have had far less dramatic potential.

As it was, Ollie proved (yet again) that he's an excellent surgeon, and that he wasn't going to take any nonsense from the charm-free neurosurgeon. And, on Bernie's advice, Zosia followed her heart and decided that her birthday would be better spent watching Ollie attempt to make fresh pasta, rather than going for her father's rival bid of a table at a swanky restaurant. Ollie is "the real deal," she told Selfie. Ollie proved this with his birthday gift of an extremely posh stethoscope engraved with "My heart is in your hands" – in Latin. I bet Digby's jealous when he sees that, because it's a top geek gift.

Keller was all about Dominic, who is a terrible driver. Why Digby let him drive his car to work I have no idea. It could have been so much worse – at any given time there'll be at least five anguished patients and/or staff members roaming the car park just asking to get run over – but it was bad enough when he knocked the wing mirror off another car, because the car happened to belong to Ric Griffin. This put Ric in a bad mood, and he strongly suspected Dominic after he'd had a look at the CCTV footage. Dominic was typically economical with the truth and said, all wide-eyed innocence, that he didn't even have a car.

Dominic's patient was Ted, who'd swallowed a key. Dominic was so sweet with Ted, who was confused and forgetful and had a tendency to wander off. Unfortunately he wandered in the direction of Ric's office and sat in his chair, where the key started to make its reappearance to the outside world while Ted informed Ric about Dominic breaking the wing mirror. You'd imagine Ric wouldn't be very happy and he wasn't, but he was impressed with the way Dominic had dealt with Ted. Hurrah! My favourite line was in Ric's office. Ric asked Dominic to sit down and Dominic's face was a picture when he said, "Is this the chair that..?". I also loved Ric spraying air freshener around his room.

Serena's boyfriend Robbie the Copper was lurking around AAU again. He wanted to use his police contacts and expertise to track down Serena's sister-she-never-knew-she-had, but Serena said no. Her mind was changed by a patient who'd hidden in the landing gear of Major Bernie Wolfe's army plane (shocking lack of security there). It got Serena thinking about relatives etc and she gave Robbie the go-ahead to find her sister. No sooner said than done. Her name is Marjorie. Or wasMarjorie, because she died a couple of years ago. Well, there's the chance to introduce a new character gone out of the window. But wait – Marjorie had a son, Jason, who is very much alive and will be visible to the naked eye as early as next week.

Nothing to lose

(Series 18, ep. 18 'A Partnership, Literally' by Andy Bayliss 9.2.16)

We all thought we'd seen the last of That Lee, the dastardly villain who broke Dominic's heart, and stole his mother's running away money and Digby's granddad's medals. But no – there was another nasty twist to the tale.

When Dominic's patient Alison told Dominic he reminded her of her husband, she couldn't quite put her finger on why. Everybody else could, as soon as her husband was revealed to be none other than Lee. He insisted that he really loved Dominic, but Alison was pregnant and soon Lee and Dominic were fighting in the staff room, where someone had left a handy cake knife. Ric Griffin waded into the fray, and the ensuing fight scene was rather gripping and well done. Someone got stabbed – but who was the stabber and who was the stabbee?

At the end of the episode, Dominic was being taken away by the police. Lee had been stabbed in the fight (he didn't die, though, because he was lucky enough to be stabbed in probably the best hospital in the whole of Wyvernshire), and it had been Dominic holding the knife. Surely all it'll take will be a witness statement from Ric and a character reference from Digby, and Dom will be recognised as a lover and not a fighter?

On AAU, Serena popped an email off to the nephew-she-never-knew-she-had, Jason. And within five minutes Jason himself was popping into AAU in person, initially being mistaken for a member of a visiting inspection team. Oh how we laughed.

Jason has Aspergers, and well done to Holby for casting Jules Robertson, who has autism himself, in the role. Jason takes life super-literally (when Cara told him Serena only really had time for patients I was glad he drew the line at just getting in a hospital bed, rather than making himself an actual patient by some hideous means) apart from when he's likening people to birds. He wanted to know why there was a bald eagle in the Linden Cullen Memorial Shrubbery – correctly identifying Jac as the top of the food-chain, bird-wise.

Every single person thought he was adorable – even Jac, who would normally have taken someone's head off for calling her a bald eagle, treated him to her nicest dimply smile and seemed to get where he was coming from immediately. Cara trotted around wishing he would compare her to a bird and he even had Hanssen acting out his favourite TV show The World's Strongest Man. Serena liked the idea of being "Auntie Campbell," though Fletch did advise her that "it's more usual to use your first name."

Jason's presence was the basis of a lot of fun and comedy, but I hope that's not all there is to him, especially as he's apparently going to be a semi-regular in the cast. His carer, Allan, turned up right at the end to sound a note of caution to Serena about how vulnerable Jason is, so maybe some different aspects of his life will come more into play.

On Darwin Major Bernie Wolfe has made a brilliant recovery from her surgery and was already walking, with help. She'd have walked right out of the hospital if there hadn't been a chance that she might have had TB. This required her to go into quarantine for a while, giving her time to decide not to go to Kabul and to possibly apply for a job on Keller instead. I'm not sure why there's a vacancy on Keller as they already have Sacha and Ric, but there you go – fluid staffing configurations etc.

And in other news, Zosia is already tiring of Ollie's pasta-making efforts. She should get him a bread machine for Valentine's – that'll keep him busy for a while.

I'm worried about Ric

(Series 18, ep. 19 'All That Glitters' by Sue Mooney 16.2.16)

I'm worried that soon there won't be enough livers to go round on Holby. Morven's dad needs one, and Morven wanted to give him a piece of hers but she isn't a match, so now Digby is stepping forward (bless! He really does love Morven doesn't he?). But at the same time we've seen Ric clutching his side rather like the bad old days when he used to go "Nnngh!" when he had cancer which spread to his liver. Hashtag PrayForRic, because we've only just got him back on a fairly regular basis and I don't want to lose him again. I think we need his brand of grizzled gravitas as a contrast to some of the other more excitable elements of the staff team.

I don't know what's going on with Mo and Mr T. She's currently pretending she doesn't care about him at all and is looking elsewhere for sperm. I can't help thinking this is a terrible mistake because he is perfect. Mo busied herself with looking after a patient's son's school project hamster ("Alert and responsive"), which created an implausible yet lovely scene where the hamster wheeled past Hanssen in his little exercise ball (the hamster's, not Hanssen's – that would have to be a vast exercise ball). The scene would have been even lovelier if Hanssen had spotted the hamster, but I suppose he's too far up to be noticing things at ground level.

He also had on his mind the ongoing complaint that Lee had made against Dominic for stabbing him. That Lee, he really is the gift that keeps on giving, stress-wise.

Hero syndrome

(Series 18, ep. 20 'All Fall Down' by Patrick Homes 23.2.16)

No news about Ric and the pain in his side this week. He was briefly glimpsed and he seemed healthy enough – no sign of a "Nnngh!" So maybe he's fine after all.

Or maybe, if his cancer has come back, it's just been parked for a while as the ever-circling poo bird of fate prepares to drop its load on poor Digby.

While having a blood test to see if he could donate a bit of his liver to Morven's dad, Digby took his top off in case he barfed down it. Essie didn't think to hand him a cardboard sick bowl, because she was too busy staring at a mole on his back.

Essie was worried that Digby might have skin cancer, and there was a very odd scene where he was summoned to Hanssen's office and commanded to take his top off, and Hanssen ordered Essie to organise an immediate mole removal – without addressing Digby and asking his opinion about it first. This may have been clinically sensible, but it was a totally bizarre way to deal with a colleague and patient.

Major Bernie Wolfe had her first day as a locum consultant on Keller, but as they already had Sacha and Ric available they were a bit over-resourced. Instead she spent the shift putting her trauma experience to good use on Darwin, where she performed the traditional debut ninja level surgery. For the rest of the time she dealt with the physical and emotional wellbeing of a patient who was ex-army. I wonder how many more ex-army people will turn up at Holby now, or whether Bernie has now had enough post-military brains-speak to enable her to get on with civilian life.

The main thing was how would she get on working with Jac Naylor? I know it's early days, but after a bit of a territorial scuffle they got on very well. Jac likes a plain speaking, no bullshit colleague, and that's certainly what you get with Ms Wolfe.

It's also what you get with Serena's nephew Jason, who is very literal and needed Hanssen's help to discover that "break a leg" can also be a nice thing to say to someone, as long as that person is in showbiz. Apart from this, and his carer telling everyone he's vulnerable, Jason doesn't seem that vulnerable at all – he quite happily wanders round the hospital making friends and charming everyone. All the same, whenever he goes missing, Serena rushes tearfully around the hospital feeling guilty and frantic with worry. Expect more of this, as she's decided to fully integrate him into her family and is introducing him to her daughter.

And finally – am I alone in thinking the ground is being laid for a Hanssen/Bernie Wolfe romance? Jason noticed that Hanssen is rather impressed by his newest staff member, but is it purely admiration for her clinical skills?

We've all been to Normandy with Digby

(Series 18, ep. 21 'One Under' by Kate Verghese 1.3.16)

"Normandy" was Digby's code word for when he was due to find out if he had cancer. He needed a code word because he was hiding it from Morven, and trying his best to hide it from himself. When Holby doctors are worried about their own health, they tend to fill the time by getting heavily involved with a patient (in the medical sense rather than the romantic, because that would be unethical).

Digby's patient was a teenage boy who'd been hit by a train, and frankly his chances weren't good. Despite being in the world's number one medical facility, he still died. Digby was the last one to give up, even when Bernie, Sacha and everybody else was saying it was time to stop.

The good news for Digby is that his mole has been successfully removed and the cancer hasn't spread, so he's fine. Despite a tedious hiccup, in which Morven got the idea that he was going on holiday with Zosia to Normandy, all ended well and Morven gave him a well-deserved hug.

I'm very happy that this was only a blip, because I love Morven and Digby as a couple. He said in this episode that she makes him feel normal, which wouldn't be a huge endorsement coming from anyone else, but from Digby it is.

Some people find Morven irritating, and I can't really see why. I can, however, see exactly why you would find Adele irritating. I don't know where the writers are going with this character – surely they've had time by now to realise that telling us every week how wonderful and special she is just isn't working because we're not believing it? In the days before she was Saint Adele of the Trillion Skills and she was just Mo's little sister, I rather liked her. Now almost every week we have to endure her being Wise and Right and adding yet more skills to her terrifying CV. Having effortlessly made the transition from being a key player in Elliot Hope'a groundbreaking Kibo project, to being a top quality nurse on Keller, via her part time job for NASA and her consultative role at the UN, this week she made the transition to neurosurgery.

Selfie has very high standards for nurses, because one little slip can make the difference between a happy outcome and not being able to breathe unaided. So when Adele dropped a suction tube in theatre and left him up to his knuckles in a bloody brain, that should have been Adele's short-lived neuro career over, surely? But no – he only went and offered her a full time job, because he recognises sheer brilliance when he sees it. Did she accept this with suitable humility and a vow to keep improving and do better? She did not. She decided to give the esteemed and experienced neurological consultant and former CEO some ground rules. "It has to be a partnership of equals," she told him, and he meekly agreed. This was about as plausible as Jac Naylor running a Zumba class in Pulses.

Meanwhile on AAU Raf and Cara were doing that tedious thing of both liking each other but pretending not to, saving their hankering looks for when nobody but the camera was looking at them. Presumably it's going to take one or both of them to be in jeopardy before they admit what they really feel.

A welcome distraction

(Series 18, ep. 22 'On the Ropes' by Julia Gilbert 8.3.16)

I wasn't going to review Holby City this week. I watched half the episode on Tuesday night as usual, but I couldn't concentrate on it because my dad was in hospital. On Wednesday, he died. It wasn't a shock and it wasn't unexpected, but it's always a shock and always unexpected when it's your dad, isn't it?

So I didn't think I'd be reviewing Holby at all. Then I found myself watching the second half of the episode last night, because I wanted the distraction that only a high quality continuing drama can bring, and nothing fits that bill better than Holby. I still wasn't able to concentrate much, though, so this isn't going to be a proper review.

Was it just my befuddled state of mind or was it an odd episode? There was Ric having a bout of existential angst, but being as solid as a rock compared to Dominic, who was having a bout of post-Lee weepiness. A strange new character in the form of the tea making Sir Dennis Hopkins-Clarke had been parachuted in to whip Darwin from under Mo's nose. Is he permanent? And it looks like Serena has got herself a proper keeper in the form of that policeman Robbie, who was thrilled to meet nephew Jason, possibly because he shares his love of lurking on AAU for no good reason. And I love Bernie Wolfe's hair, and her gorgeous Redgrave voice.

The sweetest thing

(Series 18, ep. 24 'Who You Are' by Patrick Homes 22.3.16)

Morven and Digby are such a sweet couple. They're so adorable they knock Ollie and Zosia into second place and could only possibly be beaten if Mo and Mr T got together. Morven's proposal to Digby in that most romantic of settings, the Linden Cullen Memorial Shrubbery, was so touching – and provoked one of Digby's best "nicest smile in the NHS" smiles.

I found myself wishing, as usual, that the writers would give them a few months of happiness at least (not forgetting that they already have her father's illness to cope with). I should really stay away from spoilers.

It was a busy day for the Linden Cullen Memorial Shrubbery. I'm far too innocent to speculate what Sacha and Essie might have been up to in its leafy depths, but I don't think it was anything you'd see on *Gardeners' World*.

Meanwhile, what is going on with Ric Griffin? It seems that he and Jess didn't part on good terms and after missing several calls from her he's now unable to reach her because her phone number is dead. He's all angry about something and he's had Jesse transferred to AAU for no good reason apart from possibly because he has "Jess" in his name.

And poor Mo had her hands full with the new consultant, Sir Dennis Bigoted-Dinosaur, who is not only the holder of some extremely offensive views, but he's also fairly rubbish at surgery and hasn't done any for a long time. Jac seems to be blissfully unconcerned about all this, and Ollie and Zosia turned against Mo because Sir Dennis had been giving them tricky procedures to do on their own (so he wouldn't have to) and now he isn't anymore. Mo is made of feisty stuff though, and she's not going to let a temporary twonk get the better of her.

Please not Digby!

(Series 18, ep. 25 'A Friend In Need' by Rebecca Wojciechowski 29.3.16)

This was the most beautifully written and acted episode. The scenes between Dominic and Digby were heartbreakingly perfect as Dominic was the one to discover that his friend's cancer had spread. The moment when he put Digby's glasses on for him was such a tender expression of his care and Digby's vulnerability – I had to make a very big effort not to cry loud snotty tears, particularly as I was watching it on a train. Beautiful, Hanssen-level acting from David Ames and Rob Ostlere.

Elsewhere, Adele was very committed to neurosurgery. We knew this because she said so every five minutes. It took the death of her old holiday rep friend, Denise Welch, to make her realise that she wasn't that committed to neurosurgery after all. After a glittering career progression in which she's been expert in everything from hearts to brains to radio presenting, she's finally found her true calling in the world of palliative care. Unbelievably, Holby is not the centre of palliative care excellence (well, they can't be brilliant at every specialism), so she's off to The Mythical King/St/ Whatever John's to be trained. Or to train them, because she's bound to know better.

And lovely Nurse Cara Martinez finally plucked up the courage to ask Dr Raf Not Smug on a date (a proper date, not involving Fletch and the Fletchlings) – but then realised that she wasn't over her miserable husband, Jed 'Alias' Martinez, who has been banged up for five years. This has prompted Cara to seek a new post on Darwin.

The one with the Norse gods

(Series 18, ep. 26 'Handle With Care' by Tony Higgins 5.4.16)

If you see the phrase "Norse God" and immediately think "Henrik Hanssen," you'd have agreed with whoever voted for him to win the Sexiest Doctor prize in the annual Holby Awards. He beat stiff competition from Oliver Valentine and Dr Raf Not-Smug for the accolade, and accepted it with the slightly ironic grace the situation demanded.

For other Norse gods we must turn to Digby, and his new hobby of making copper medallions of all our favourites from the Thor movies and giving them to his friends and colleagues to wear (I was quite pleased that Loki was meant for Dominic). Never mind that it turned their skin green, it kept him occupied and that's what he needs at the moment.

What he doesn't really need is people pussy-footing around him, but that's what darling Dominic spent most of the day doing, because he wants to help. Sadly with the best will in the world you're not going to be able to stop a doctor with cancer coming across patients with cancer, and Dominic realised (with Sacha's help) that the best way to help Digby was to be normal around him. Which meant the skin-discolouring Norse god (the medal, not Hanssen) had to go for a start.

AAU won the best ward award and Serena made an excellent speech which managed to insert a supportive word for the junior doctors (striking again today) into the script. Hurrah! But elsewhere Serena was having a very difficult day as her nephew's carer was taken ill suddenly and it became clear that Serena was in no position to give Jason the support he needs full time. It's particularly painful for Serena because this is the position she found herself in with her mother, and she's grown very fond of Jason. It was a lovely touch when Jason became distressed that the person who was able to relate to him and calm him down best was Henrik Hanssen, who took him for a quiet sit on the roof. Jason said he felt he could trust Hanssen. "You don't lie," he told him.

Someone who does lie is Sir Dennis Bigoted-Dinosaur, who was once again doing his best to sideline Mo. Luckily Cara is a very astute person (apart from where Jed 'Alias' Martinez is concerned) and on her first shift on Darwin she soon had him sussed. I wonder what's going to happen with him, plot-wise? He seems an entirely superfluous character at the moment, but maybe his presence is going to spur Mo to a new phase of her career and her development as a character. Meanwhile she was last seen driving off with Jesse in her little pink car. His mother has just died, bless him, and Mo offered to take him to London (a shortish drive if Holby is in Borehamwood but quite the undertaking without sandwiches and a Thermos of coffee if we're still pretending it's Bristol).

Jesse gets his priorities in order

(Series 18, ep. 27 'Dark Night of the Soul' by Michelle Lipton 12.4.16)

Lift doors opening: CEO with nosebleed! But why? The action goes back to ten hours earlier, but luckily for us it's been compressed into one hour of quality drama, so we don't have too long to wait to find out.

It turned out that the cause of Hanssen's nosebleed was the least of the action in what was a very busy and traumatic night shift, not least for Mo and Jesse. The Curse of Holby relatives and friends reached giddy proportions when both Jesse's father Thomas and Mo's mother Ina were both admitted at the same time, straight from Jesse's mother's funeral.

We discovered that Jesse had been actively avoiding visiting his mother since she'd become disabled by a stroke, and he did his best to avoid spending time with his father in hospital. Luckily Morven was on hand with her speciality doctoring, which throws in lots of TLC along with the FBC's, U's and E's and LFT's. She discovered that Thomas was diabetic but was refusing medication – he didn't see any point living on lentils without his wife. "There are worse things than dying," he said, though in my opinion there are worse things than lentils because I'm quite partial. Anyway, Jesse eventually realised that he'd just been drifting since Adele dumped him in the Linden Cullen Temple of Anguish. It was time to get his priorities straight, which meant taking his dad to Trinidad to help him scatter his mum's ashes in her home country. Thus we had to say goodbye to the prettiest anaesthetist since Zubin, while Jesse went off to concentrate on cracking out of prison to terrorise Denise on *EastEnders* (I don't know if he's actually pencilled in to do that, but I'd vote for it).

Meanwhile, Mo was in a dilemma. On the one hand a mother with a heart condition that Mo felt (and Ollie agreed) could benefit from surgery. On the other side, Sir Dennis Bigoted-Dinosaur, whose conservative treatment of the patient involved getting a DNR signed, because at the ripe old age of sixty something she was surely knocking on heaven's door already. The ensuing drama involved Sir Dennis cocking up Ina's drugs and overdosing her, Jesse and Mo preparing to do maverick surgery on her, Jac stepping in, and Sir Dennis snoozing throughout the proceedings. Jesse's career would have been hanging on a knife edge if he hadn't already decided to quit. I did love his parting words in the boardroom – "Mr Hanssen, Mr Griffin, Mo, it's been a pleasure. Jac… yeah."

Sir Dennis, it turns out, was more than Jac's mentor at the start of her career and paid her tuition fees. He suggested to her that she would behave in just the same way as him and would do anything to hold on to power. That might have been true of Early Jac, but we know her better than that and I can't help thinking Sir Dennis's Holby days are numbered.

But what of Keller, I hear you ask. Well indeed. Keller patient o' the week had broken his penis. Who knew that was even a thing? We didn't get even a glimpse of this injury, which possibly left the prosthetics team feeling rather thwarted but avoided the BBC switchboard being jammed by complaints.

Bernie and Ric disagreed about how to treat the problem. Ric proposed a "degloving." I quite often google Holby procedures out of interest or for spelling, but I didn't want to go near that one. Luckily for the patient, Bernie didn't want to go near it either, and did an equally horrific-sounding but less traumatic procedure. Poor Dominic looked quite faint, but was able to get stuck in and do some of the procedure himself.

Ric and the owner of the penis were soon bonding happily over a shared interest in boxing and playing cards, and this is what got Hanssen's nose into trouble. An impromptu card game in the staff room led Bernie to encourage Ric to show off his boxing moves, and Hanssen loomed through the door straight in the path of a right hook. Ouch.

Time to be brave

(Series 18, ep. 28 'Prioritise the Heart' by Julia Gilbert 19.4.16)

I'd forgotten what a brilliant actor Heather Peace is. She appeared in Holby yesterday as Alex, locum anaesthetist. This was the same Alex who'd been in the army with Bernie and sent her flowers when she first arrived at Holby as a patient. The charged atmosphere between them just screamed "unfinished business" – even Dominic noticed.

There was such chemistry between Heather Peace and Jemma Redgrave and their scenes together were intense and emotional. Bernie and Alex were in love and Bernie was struggling with the choice she'd made to try and make a success of her marriage and family life. Bernie had a little heart-to-heart with Dominic in the Linden Cullen Memorial Shrubbery. "How wonderful life could be if only I was brave enough," she told him. Dominic said she shouldn't live a lie. When we last saw her she was heading off home to have a difficult conversation with her husband. Meanwhile, Alex has gone, because she couldn't bear to have her heart broken again. She told Bernie to come and find her when she's sorted her life out. I really hope she does just that, because Holby needs an anaesthetist now Jesse's gone, and Alex would be an excellent addition to the cast.

I wonder whether we're going to be seeing a lot more of Mr T (MR T!!!) in the coming weeks? In an episode where he stood up for himself as Mo's professional equal, he got approval from Hanssen to expand his department – and he wants to go into womb transplants. I'm hoping this means a sharing of skills and facilities with Darwin, because then we wouldn't have to wait for a pregnant heart patient to turn up before getting him up there.

The romance between him and Mo is still brewing nicely. He really is her best cheerleader – he brought her a big bunch of balloons to celebrate her first day as a consultant (now nasty Sir Dennis Bigoted-Dinosaur has been ousted – hurrah!). At the end, they released the balloons (with no regard to the wildlife of Wyvernshire, but still) and made a wish. And we saw Mo's hand almost – almost– reach for his.

Romance was also in the air on AAU, where Serena was contemplating moving into a lovely new house with Robbie the Bobby. Or Robbie the soon-to-be-ex-bobby, because it was his last shift before retiring. TV policemen having their last shift are usually faced with a hideous murder that haunts them until they're forced out of retirement to crack the case. On Robbie's last day there was nothing more heinous going on in Holby than a spot of shoplifting, but the shoplifters were Serena's nephew Jason and his "girlfriend," Lola. Sadly Jason was being exploited by this girl, and when Serena discovered that he was living in a bleak room and people were taking advantage of him, she had no choice but to ask him to live with her. She hoped Robbie wouldn't mind, but he did mind because he's not as nice as Serena hoped he was.

Someone who is nice is Digby, and he was trying to cheer Morven up by booking a weekend away to Verona. She went all stroppy because she can't just swan off while her dad's ill etc, but Fletch told her to cut Digby a bit of slack. He's wise, that Fletch.

Truly brave

(Series 18, ep. 29 'Out of Sight Out of Mind' by Johanne McAndrew and Elliot Hope 26.4.16)

Essie makes a mean shepherd's pie, apparently. I start with Essie because I've been a bit critical of her in the past (when she was being Chrissie 2.0), but in an episode like this, where she's very much embedded in the general goings-on of Keller and doing her transplant coordinator thing, I really like her. She has a warmth, steadiness and dependability which is exactly what you'd want from a nurse.

It's also exactly what Digby needs at the moment, though he's pretending hard that it isn't. Everyone was worried about him in this episode, as his cancer treatment was taking its toll on him and he looked quite pale and fragile at times. Sacha, Essie and Dominic wanted him to go home and rest, but when Morven's dad was brought in following a car accident, he insisted on staying.

Much of the story revolved around Morven's brother AJ (Petrice Jones), who has been sitting on the fact that he's a donor match for his father – because he's going to be a father himself and didn't want to take the risk of surgery. Digby's illness seems to have given him a new depth of understanding and wisdom and he – and Austin – understood AJ's position, whereas all Morven could think was that he'd let their father down.

Luckily, a liver was found for Austin, so AJ (Austin Junior?) gets to keep the whole of his, and hopefully Austin will live to see his new grandchild.

And Digby finally got a bit of sleep, on a heap of cushions thoughtfully provided by Essie in a touching scene where Dominic got to use him as a ventriloquist's dummy (Sacha doesn't let him do that to the patients) and Morven snuggled down for a sleep with him.

Meanwhile, Digby's other bezzie mate, Zosia, wasn't coping very well knowing that her friend was ill. She threw all her energy into one of those cases where there's an adorable patient for whom the outlook is bleak, but there's a risky procedure which just might work. Mia (Sue Vincent), a foster mother with a heart of gold and a nasty tumour (not of gold), didn't have long to live, but Zosia thought she'd be a good candidate for Jac's new balloon stent trials. Mo was against the scheme, thinking that palliative care was a gentler option, and it seemed she'd been proved right when Mia suffered a stroke in theatre and subsequently died. Mo reassured Zosia that it had been worth a try, and that the knowledge gained about the new procedure would save lives in the future, so like the AJ story it wasn't a case of right or wrong. Camilla Arfwedson was brilliant in some of the scenes with Mia – she totally nails that smiling-on-the-verge-of-tears thing that I always think must be so hard to do.

Bernie Wolfe was on AAU this week because Raf was off sick. Get well soon, Raf – but his absence meant we got to see more of Serena and Bernie in action together, and what a superb double act they make. They have a very similar sense of humour ("You don't need a corkscrew if you're drinking straight from the box," Bernie said – but that could easily have been Serena). This made for some excellent dialogue as Bernie was served with divorce papers, and nobody gives better divorce advice than Serena ("Expect the worst – anything less is a bonus").

Bernie struggles to be frank

(Series 18, ep. 30 'The Coward's Way' by Kate Verghese 3.5.16)

I do love Jemma Redgrave. In a very short time she's established Bernie Wolfe as an interesting, multi-dimensional character. Even before we discovered the truth about Alex there was always a below-the-surface vulnerability about her, though she presents herself as feisty and confident.

Her confidence clearly doesn't carry through to her personal life, because despite her decision to stop living a lie and ask her husband for a divorce, when he appeared on Keller as a locum it was clear that she hadn't told him the whole story. Even worse, she was terrified that Dominic would tell him about Alex. So she texted Dominic (who was keeping Digby company in chemo) to say please don't say anything. But who knew there was a Dominic Copeman (as opposed to Copeland) in Anaesthetics? What a coincidence! And it seems that he loves a gossip, and soon everyone and the lady in Pulses knew, and Bernie's secret love was no secret any more.

You can understand her husband being a bit cross about this news, but I was disappointed by Serena's reaction. She was angry that she'd been open with Bernie about her own personal life and but Bernie hadn't been honest about hers, which is sort of fair enough but I didn't think it warranted giving Bernie the cold-shoulder. I hope that when Serena's had a bit of a think she'll realise that Bernie's situation is complicated, and the delicious Campbell/Wolfe double act will be back on again.

Talking of double acts, there's a precious one on AAU in the shape of Raf and Fletch ("Faf"? Better than "Retch," I'd have thought). This lovely friendship was almost disrupted by the arrival of Naomi Palmer (Lorna Brown) from Psych. Fletch took an instant shine to her, which puzzled me because she seemed almost entirely tedious. There was a nice scene, though, where Raf and Fletch bickered like an old married couple while Naomi attempted to mediate.

There was a little Fletchling wandering around. This one was called Mikey (Kai O'Loughlin), and it was yet another brilliant piece of casting as he was like a mini-me of Fletch. He was a proper cheeky chappie type, who very sweetly helped a man with agoraphobia take his first steps back into a happy life, via the Linden Cullen Memorial Shrubbery. As such he was for more useful than Psych Naomi.

Zosia could perhaps have benefited from some of Fletch Jr's wisdom, as she was once again having trouble coming to terms with Digby's cancer enough to support him. Perhaps the most brutal advice would be "it's not about you, it's about him," but I'm going to cut Zosia some slack because she's lovely. It wasn't terribly helpful when the sight of a tumour in theatre gave her the theatre-wobbles, though. Luckily Ollie was on hand to take over.

He's doing his best to understand what Zosia is going through and to help her. Jac was a little less sympathetic. "I don't do the pastoral stuff," she said. "So – purely to cover my own back – would you like some time off or something?"

Incurable romantic

(Series 18, ep. 31 'It Tolls for Thee' by Joe Ainsworth 10.5.16)

Holby City was trending on Twitter last night, as viewers up and down the country blinked away their tears to share their thoughts about what was a brilliant episode.

It wasn't an episode I'd been looking forward to. I avoid serious spoilers (the detailed ones that almost make watching the programme pointless), but it was obvious from all the hints that things were not going to go well for Digby – even if you factor in that he got married to a gorgeous woman who makes him very happy.

I've always loved Digby since he first appeared. One of the most brilliant medical students of his year, he also had to cope with a lack of social skills and general anxiety (as well as a nasty car crash, a mugging and being pounced on by Zosia). At the same time, he has such a beautiful smile and is obviously such a nice person that you're always on his side. He's quirky and funny and he has a backpack with horses on it. He's adorable. His colleagues think so, too, and his relationships with Chantelle, Zosia, Morven, Sacha and especially Dominic have been precious to behold.

So for a character like that to get cancer that spreads and becomes fatal – that's hard to watch. For it to happen when he's just fallen in love is even harder.

Full credit to everyone involved in this episode. Rob Ostlere was heartbreaking – I think everyone watching would have wanted to give Digby a hug, and the scene where Sacha did just that had me in bits. Morven was a beautiful bride and was trying to be strong, as was Dominic, whose facial expression often says more than a thousand words could.

The big drama was nicely balanced with some stress-relieving humour, with writer Joe Ainsworth giving Serena, Bernie and Fletch some comedy gold in the form of a man with a bath tap up his bum (cue lots of "He's feeling hot and cold" type jokes).

Serena seemed to have thawed towards Bernie a little bit after last week, which was good to see, because they make a great double act (and there are already 'Berena' fans out there hoping for more). Sadly Serena has been suspended, after carelessly leaving her laptop in her car. The car was stolen, and thousands of patient records have made their way on to the internet, which is a PR nightmare for Hanssen. It was good to see that, even in the midst of a PR nightmare he can still take the time to sit at a table and eat a hard boiled egg very nicely. It's also exciting to learn that Holby has its own 'IT boffins.' I remember when all the computers in the ED went down because of a corrupted USB stick, and it was left to Max the porter to sort it out. No sign of an IT boffin when one was really needed.

All of this would have been enough for most hours of top quality continuing drama (speaking of which – that BAFTA should have gone to Holby). But there was another, huge, part to the story. The Mo and Mr T 'will they/won't they' relationship that has been rumbling on for literally years moved on in a massive way yesterday. The episode started with Mo waking up in Mr T's bed (I'm guessing it was his bed because of the duvet cover. I can't imagine zoo animals being Mo's thing). It seemed their relationship had finally 'moved to the next level.' A nation threw its collective hat in the air and shouted 'Hurrah!' As did Mr T. Mo, however, seemed less keen. Mr T had been offered a job in

Gothenburg, and he was about to leave. Sleeping with him, it seemed, was Mo's idea of a goodbye present and seemed like a good idea at the (slightly drunken) time.

Normally I'd have been wondering what she was thinking, loving him and leaving him like that. The fool! But I have to admit that, for the first time ever, I found Mr T a bit annoying in this episode. He was just so full-on and more or less had the wedding speech written and the little Effanga-Thompsons registered at good schools. I could understand why Mo would have second thoughts. Though I did laugh out loud when he gave a random man in a wheelchair a high-five. On the other hand, for 99% of the time, Mr T has been a complete darling, so I wasn't that surprised when Mo had third thoughts and realised she'd hurt a very good man very badly.

When Jac appeared briefly in her motorbike gear and suggested a dash to the airport, I thought she was going to offer Mo a lift like she did for Sacha when he dashed to catch up with Chrissie (but look how that turned out). She didn't, and maybe that would have been the difference between getting to Stansted in time and not. We'll never know. Mo missed her chance – though as Jac pointed out, there's always the phone.

So much going on, then, and all top quality, unmissable stuff. Like I said – that BAFTA should have gone to Holby.

I've always got your back

(*Series 18, ep. 32 'Running Out' by Wendy Granditer 17.5.16*)

All three stories in this episode dealt with issues of loyalty, friendship and support. Some relationships were strengthened, but one seems to have broken up altogether.

Maybe I should start with the broken one and then proceed via the strengthened-yet-sad one, and end with the strengthened-and-happy one so we're not too depressed by the end.

Remember last week when Serena's car was stolen and lots of confidential information from her laptop made its way to the press and the interweb? This week the impact of Serenaleaks (as she wouldn't thank me for calling it) was most strongly felt on Darwin, when "news" emerged of a doctor with bipolar. Then Zosia's name was published online, possibly by her patient.

Zosia, considering dreadful things were being said about her in the press, and one of her best friends is terminally ill, was remarkably calm and focused on trying to work out what the patient was not telling her about his condition. Somewhat disgustingly (why am I surprised?) Selfie used it as an excuse to manipulate Ollie. He told him to remember that he was Zosia's superior as well as her boyfriend, and left Ollie's lack of backbone to do the rest. A stronger character would have nodded and smiled and inwardly told Selfie to shove off, but Ollie nodded and smiled and then told Mo he didn't think Zosia was up to assisting in theatre. Mo, bless her, tried to cover this up, but when Zosia found out she was not happy, and Ollie found himself dumped. Is "Zollie" over? Or will he win her back with his newly-honed pasta making skills and beautiful blue eyes?

Meanwhile, Digby and Dominic are breaking my heart. There are some people you meet in life who change you and make you a better person, and that's what Digby has done for Dominic. I'm not saying there won't be any situation in the future when Dominic doesn't lie to get his own way, or threaten a patient with the pointy end of a syringe – he wouldn't be Dominic if he wasn't a tiny bit strange and very sassy. But he's mellowed and become a kinder, more caring person.

Digby went to visit his parents in this episode, to tell them that he was married, and that he has cancer. We didn't get to see Felicity Digby and her husband, but we didn't really need to. I can picture them from Digby's description – cold, proper, emotionally absent. I bet they never had pets and they probably have a dining room that's only ever used on Sundays. Digby needed to rehearse what he was going to say. Dominic played the part of his mum: "Have you changed your hair? It looks different." "Dom, my mum's not going to ask me about my hair," Digby said. Dominic realised that Felicity was obviously nothing like his own mum. "It's tangent, tangent, tangent in the Copeland household."

I've probably said before (more than once, sorry) that David Ames has the most expressive face, but he really does. He can switch from saying something funny to looking desperately sad in a second, but it's not just a facial expression. You understand what he's thinking and feeling. And Rob Ostlere's Digby is so funny and sweet, vulnerable but touchingly brave. Honestly, I know he's fictional and everything but I really am thinking of doing a fun run to raise money for a miracle cure. Who's with me?

I bet that Bernie Wolfe would be game for a fun run, and the good news is that Serena Campbell would probably join her (as long as she was back to do Jason's dinner on time). Serena returned to

AAU from her brief suspension following Serenaleaks to discover Bernie installed in her office – and what a messy pup she turns out to be. Even worse than Elliot Hope, and he was living in his car for half the time so he had an excuse.

Serena wasn't happy to learn that Bernie was there to keep an eye on her, in case she mislaid any more laptops or let any more random police officers wander round the department for no good reason. It was all too much, and Serena resigned. Then she un-resigned again, realising that she and Bernie work well together, and she needs someone to keep an eye on Fletch and Raf while she's getting Jason's dinner ready. This is excellent news, because Jemma Redgrave and Catherine Russell are a dream team.

Like Digby and Dominic. But not, apparently, like Zosia and Ollie.

Breaking hearts, one week at a time

(Series 18, ep. 33 'When I Grow Up' by Martin Jameson 24.5.16)

For those of us hoping for Hanssen to pull a miracle cure out of the bag for Digby, like he did for Ric Griffin, he is leaving it a little late. And I rather fear that if he was going to do it, he'd have done it in this episode.

There was a lot of Hanssen this week, as he'd decided to station himself on Keller for the day. The first thing we discovered about him is that his middle name is Love. It's pronounced 'Loovay,' apparently, but his stethoscope is engraved with 'Henrik Love Hanssen.' It's too delicious.

The stethoscope as a symbol of the practice and vocation of medicine, and Love as a symbol of, well, love, featured prominently in this episode, as Digby came to the realisation that the future he'd imagined for himself might be disappearing.

Hanssen was a supportive presence to Digby throughout. "Your career is not over yet," he told him, as he encouraged him in dealing with a 15 year old girl who had terminal cancer.

Sadly, by the end of the episode Digby knew otherwise, and resigned. "So what am I meant to do without you?" Dom wanted to know. Sacha and Essie thought about laying on some drinks and cakes, but Digby didn't want a fuss.

As he was leaving, he found a present in his locker from Hanssen. A stethoscope engraved with his name. Trying it out by listening to his own heart beating, Digby smiled and cried and I think the entire Holbyverse (is that a thing? It is now) smiled and cried along with him.

Light relief was to be found on AAU in the Fletch/Raf double act. Still squabbling like an old married couple, they were both entertained and exasperated in equal measure by their patient, who thought he was "the sole manifestation of the fabric of god on earth." Surely that's Jac Naylor? Anyhoo, with great power comes great responsibility, which means he couldn't be anaesthetised because who knew what might happen to the world while he was asleep? The only way he would agree to the surgery he needed was for his power to be temporarily delegated to Fletch. If only Fletch had been able to effect a miracle cure on Digby while he was in possession of these powers. Sadly he wasn't, and nor did he manage to sort out the refugee crisis or prevent a bus crash on the bypass.

He did, however, get a date with Psych Naomi. This was a bit of a disappointment for Raf, who likes her himself, but he didn't want to get in Fletch's way. Worse was to come when he overheard Zosia yelling at Ollie for kissing Nurse Cara Martinez.

Yup, in a moment of tequila fuelled madness, Ollie pounced at Cara just as Zosia walked in the door to try and sort out their differences. Ouch. At this rate, Mo had better watch herself. She's the only female speaking cast member on Darwin who has managed to avoid being "romanced" by Dr Valentine so far.

Broken boy soldier

(Series 18, ep. 34 'The Sky Is Falling' by Andy Bayliss 31.5.16)

Still determined to break our hearts one week at a time, this week Holby gave us the sad sight of lovely Arthur Digby arriving at the hospital by ambulance, with breathing difficulties, and the even sadder sight of him in a hospital bed. Symbolically, Dominic had been fiddling with one of Digby's military figures and snapped it in half accidentally. Was it curtains for Digby?

All wasn't lost, however. There was always Jac's prototype removable stent, which would make a huge difference to Digby's quality of life and send him on his way – if not with a spring in his step, at least being able to breathe unaided.

The aforementioned stent was destined for another patient. By manipulative means, Zosia (who in her turn was being manipulated by Selfie, who has been at her shoulder like a bad angel quite a lot recently) made sure Arthur got the treatment he needed. I think we have to park quietly to one side that Zosia's actions were unethical. Just the look of relief on Morven's face when she heard the surgery had gone well was enough for me.

And Dominic glued the little Napoleon figure back together.

The episode had started with Digby giving first aid to a patient, Ruth, who'd collapsed outside, in a lovely scene which was a reminder of everything we love about Digby – his kindness, his skill, his nerdy awkwardness.

Ruth ended up in AAU, where there was a power struggle going on between Serena and Bernie. Serena was even competitive about who should look after Morven. Auntie Serena's nephew Jason didn't help this process with his own brand of brutal honesty (Jules Robertson has excellent comic timing and I especially loved his scenes with Jemma Redgrave). Jason also provided something else for Serena and Bernie to compete over – Bernie thought Serena was being over protective of him, and Serena thought Bernie didn't understand how hard it was to try and manage Jason's expectations.

It seems possible that Bernie and Serena are being lined up for a romantic relationship, and given the abilities of the two actors involved and the chemistry between them, I think that's an interesting prospect.

It was a huge week for Dominic. If his best friend being ill and undergoing surgery wasn't stressful enough, he also had to look after Alison – the partner of Dominic's nasty ex, Lee. Dominic didn't want anything to do with her at first, but he was forced to get involved and by helping her he also helped himself to face his feelings about Lee.

All the feels

(Series 18, ep. 35 'I'll Walk You Home' by Andy Bayliss 7.6.16)

If you had dry eyes at the end of that episode, you're a stronger person than I am. Was that a brilliant hour of television, or what?

Arthur Digby's last episode was always going to be emotional, no matter which way it went (miracle cure, or slow decline with last few months spent travelling and off-screen demise, or… not). He's a very well-loved character, not just loved by fans but by so many other characters in the hospital. He's worked on several wards and come into contact with so many people who love and respect him for his sweet, gentle nature and earnest commitment to his job. So young, just at the start of what promised to be a glittering career. And just married to his soulmate. Whatever happened to him was going to impact on everybody.

The episode, beautifully written by Andy Bayliss, balanced carefully along the line between hope and despair for much of the time. That the half way mark included one of the most joyous and funny moments ever in Holby – the dance routine with even Ric Griffin and (hilariously) Hanssen joining in – and ended with the sadness of Digby quietly dying, surrounded by his friends, was extraordinary.

I loved the way Malick, Chantelle and Ethan were involved in the episode, to remind us that Digby has an importance that extends outside of the present story confines. I especially loved the hallucinatory sequences, which were strange, beautiful and tender. Most of all, I loved Morven's parting speech to Digby. Ellie Fanyinka was incredible, delivering so much emotion and conveying all of Morven's love for Arthur. Her line that he gave so much to so many people but kept a little bit back just for her was beautiful.

I'd expected Dominic to be the one to make me cry the most, but his reaction at the bedside was restrained, shrugging off Ric's comforting hand and leaving the room. For once, Dominic didn't want to do his emoting in public (though he had some lovely scenes with Digby and Sacha earlier in the episode, and nobody can be in any doubt that losing his best friend will have hit him hard). Zosia breaking down and Jac running to hug her was an intense moment of pure grief that will have finished off anyone who wasn't crying already. The detail that had me in a messy heap was the close-up on Arthur squeezing Morven's hand and her saying, "I know."

Rob Ostlere didn't physically have much to do in the final moments except lie still, but in the earlier scene where he collapsed in Hanssen's office he was heartbreaking. One moment he was filled with optimism and a sense of freedom, but you could see him deteriorate second by second. When Hanssen promised him everything would be alright, you knew that he knew which way things were going to go. Hanssen almost lost his trademark composure during this scene. His lip actually wobbled at one point.

So it's farewell to Arthur Digby, who's given us plenty to smile about and plenty to worry about during his Holby career. I'm going to miss him and his rucksack with the horses on it, his love of a good pen, the banter with Dominic, the way he finds courage when he needs it most. Above all, I'm going to miss the most beautiful smile in the NHS.

Those left behind

(Series 18, ep. 36 'Missing You Already' by Joe Ainsworth 16.6.16)

This episode didn't turn out how I expected it to. I'd expected the huge emotions of last week's epic episode to carry on, with profound and beautiful words at the funeral to match Morven's beautiful words as Digby lay dying. Instead we had a church full of beepers going off, and our regular cast members speeding back to the hospital, which was rapidly filling up with wounded people following a train crash. "It's what Arthur would have done," somebody said, and it is exactly what he'd have done, and why it was right to return the action quickly to the hospital. It wasn't just the place where Arthur died, it was where he'd lived his life doing the doctor thing and saving lives. It's what binds all the characters together.

So instead of a weep-fest we had a more subtle look at how people have to carry on after a death. Though there were tears, of course – Serena breaking down in the Linden Cullen Memorial Shrubbery and being comforted by Bernie was a particularly poignant moment.

Dominic had a patient, Marisa (Alice O'Connell), who was supposed to bear a striking resemblance to Digby, though she didn't really. Maybe that was the point – that when you miss somebody you see reminders of them everywhere. I liked her, anyway – she was so excited to be in the middle of a scene that was just like in a medical drama: "This place is awesome!" She was only disappointed that they didn't order the FBC's and LFT's "Stat!" It is Holby and not Chicago, after all. Dominic wasn't coping well with the loss of Digby, trying to hide behind work – which is never a good plan. Having his mother Carol around didn't help ("Mothers. Can't live with them, can't poison them slowly in their sleep" he said, and I loved that little echo of Psycho-Dom), although her memories of Digby were sweet and funny and it's always good having Carol around "checking on my Dazzle" because she's ace. Dominic eventually had a meltdown, witnessed by Hanssen, who has told him to take a week off – but not before getting him to deliver a eulogy at Albie's.

There was some excellent comedy provided by Jac, of all people, giving romantic advice to Oliver Valentine, telling him he needed to take his chance with Zosia. "It's got grief shag written all over it," she told him. He tried to put that plan into action, but it didn't go too well – Zosia's emotional defences are well and truly up.

Being in the middle of trauma mayhem is very much Dr Bernie Wolfe's area of expertise, although she was also struggling with domestic issues because her husband is being a twonk about the divorce. Bernie and Serena were largely cooperative, and Serena put in a good word with Hanssen, who is going to get Bernie to head up a complete overhaul of trauma care.

But what of Dr Morven Digby, the grieving widow? We didn't see all that much of her (though more than we saw of Digby's parents who had non-speaking roles and were left sobbing quietly), but in the scene in Albie's at the end she almost had me in tears again, because she looked quite lost and separate from everyone, even among her friends. She's usually such a sparkling, sparky person and she looks like her light has gone out for now.

So we didn't see much of Digby's funeral, but we saw a lot of what he left behind.

Luck is for lesser surgeons

(Series 18, ep. 37 'The Lone Ranger' by Atiha Sen Gupta and Katie Douglas 23.6.16)

The Digby Stent. It sounds like a particularly subdued type of dance for someone who prefers their dancing to contain as little movement as possible. Actually it's a game-changer of a fictional device, and the credit for it must go to Jac Naylor and her crack team on Darwin.

Or must it? At the press conference to launch it, Jac was informed that apparently those dastardly Germans had already launched something very much like it. Instantly, Jac was on the warpath, and it led her to be even more horrible to her team than usual, and to forge ahead putting the aforementioned stent into an adorable opera singer (Ronny Jhutti), risking the wrath of the patent holders in Berlin and, more importantly, Hanssen. I very much enjoy Jac/Hanssen showdowns, because she isn't scared of him and he always seems to want to save her from herself.

It took the whole episode before the quivering finger of suspicion finally settled on Selfie. He told Zosia it wasn't him, though frankly I'd trust him as far as I could drop-kick him, and with my knees that's not far.

Meanwhile, Dominic went back to work after a bit of leave and discovered that the new registrar on Keller was none other than Syed from EastEnders, only he's had a haircut, is now Dr Isaac Mayfield, and was the person Dominic had woken up next to that very morning. Oops. That's got to make for an awkward day at the office. Isaac seems to be in the cocky/confident category of new doctors and didn't waste any time getting stuck into a radical approach to a knackered spleen. It didn't go quite according to plan, but that didn't dismay him. And he and Dominic went home together at the end of the shift.

Dominic is worrying his friends by apparently holding on to his grief about Arthur and not letting it out. Even a trip to the Linden Cullen Memorial Shrubbery, which worked a treat for Serena getting in touch with her grief last week, didn't do it for him. Zosia shed a little tear and said she missed Arthur, though. Essie thinks Dominic needs a bereavement counsellor, but he's not keen.

He could use the services of Psych Naomi, but she's too busy pootling around on AAU being lusted after by both Fletch and Raf. She seems more drawn to Raf – he's got more money, doesn't have kids and he's more organised re marking birthdays etc. However – it was Cara's last shift, and when she said goodbye to Raf it was sad, because after their kiss and her move to Darwin, their storyline just fizzled out. It was a very low-key exit for Cara – though she did get a lovely scene where she stood up to Jac about the way she was treating her team, and a sad hug from Morven, who was being stored in a locker room for that specific purpose.

A proper friend

(Series 18, ep. 38 'Another Day in Paradise – Part 1' by Nick Fisher 28.6.16)

It was the hottest day since Holby records began, but before you cancel your scheduled holiday to Tenerife and book a static caravan in Holby instead, it actually didn't look like fun. Everyone was irritable and fed up, and that was even before you throw in the added pressures of grief, heartbreak, jealousy and Jac Naylor.

For everyone who'd expected Dominic's reaction to Arthur's death to be totally heartbreaking, this was the episode that finally delivered that. He's been holding everything in for a few weeks, talking to Arthur's photo but not allowing himself to cry. That all changed when he seemed to get a message from "the other side," via a patient who was in touch with the dead via the medium of flatulence. The message he received was to sail Arthur's ship, a beautiful model of a sailing ship that Arthur had left incomplete.

Dominic left it incomplete, too, as an attempt to fix it in the staff room was ended abruptly by Hanssen. "At what point did our patients become Spanish galleons?" he said – a sentence I'm sure he never expected to utter when he got out of bed that morning. Adorably, Hanssen then finished the model himself, and he and Dominic went off to sail it. They first looked at an exciting new fish pond in the Linden Cullen Memorial Shrubbery, which I'm going to call the Arthur Digby Reminiscence Pool. It was a lovely thing, but they needed something a bit bigger in scale. Off they went to a park with a pond, and the ship sailed – for about a minute, and then sank.

It was this that finally allowed Dominic to let go, and he sobbed all over Hanssen's lovely suit. It was an incredibly touching scene, with Hanssen's wise, fatherly, comforting presence giving Dominic the safety to let his grief out. Dominic worried that he'd been a terrible friend to Arthur, but Hanssen knew that Dominic had been exactly what Arthur needed (and vice versa). "Unquestionably you loved him," Hanssen said. "I did," said Dominic, "And I still do." "Well, what more could any friend want?" Hanssen said, producing a clean white handkerchief to wipe the snot off his suit.

Passions of a different sort were seething on AAU. Fletch had been dumped by Psych Naomi, who wasted no time in flexing her flirt muscles at Raf. Is he going to let her get in the way of his bromance with Fletch? Oh, Raf, think of the Fletchlings! They already have nits – don't add to their distress by breaking up the happy home.

Meanwhile the AAU patient o' the week had got himself mixed up with some criminal activity, which culminated in a gang of thugs turning up in the Car Park of Doom. Someone was set on fire, Jac had something nasty sprayed at her and it all got quite tense for a minute or two.

Jac was in the car park because she'd just arrived at the hospital having wasted her morning waiting for a dentist appointment. She'd left Oliver Valentine with the responsibility for a famous tennis player who was about to have ground-breaking surgery. Ollie was feeling the pressure, particularly as Selfie kept trying to hijack his patient to get him to fund his Self Centre. Ollie did good work, but no moment was finer than when he was pursuing Selfie and his patient along a corridor and crashed into some shelves. Ollie is very good at collisions.

It's the heat

(Series 18, ep. 39 'Another Day in Paradise – Part 2' by Nick Fisher 5.7.16)

This was my favourite kind of Holby episode – there was a lightness of touch about the whole thing, with lots of funny dialogue. There were some lovely character combinations – Sacha in particular was beautifully used to bring out the sweeter and more human side of Jac, while appearing in his own story line that involved a hilarious scene with Ric.

Jac was suffering from the effects of being sprayed with nasty gas last week (this was the second of a two-parter), which was unfortunate timing because she had to do ground-breaking surgery on that hot-shot tennis player. No worries – Mr Oliver Valentine had been training for this moment and working his precious socks off for her, so he was ready.

Sadly, he was also being a bit lippy, and Jac – eyes all red and watery – was in no mood to take any of that kind of nonsense, so she dumped him from the case and drafted in Mo.

Last week Mo was resisting bacon and being emotional. This week she almost vomited in a patient's open chest cavity. For the avoidance of doubt, she confirmed to Jac that she's pregnant – with, it must be assumed, a Baby T. Sweet! But entirely useless when there's groundbreaking surgery to be done. So Ollie was back on the op, and he was wearing his finest "sulky-yet-smug" face as he scrubbed in.

The surgery didn't go exactly to plan and Ollie had to revert to a more conventional procedure. This annoyed Jac, but what annoyed her most was when Ollie laid into her on a variety of issues, one of which was her parenting of Wee Emma. Jac had told Sacha earlier that she'd missed the signs that Emma has whooping cough, so we knew she was already feeling guilty. There was a kind of thrilling dread in seeing Ollie call her out on her mothering skills, and it was inevitable he'd get a smack in the face for his trouble.

All was well that ended well as far as the tennis player was concerned, though. Bigger surgery meant a longer recovery time – which he welcomed so he could have a nice break from tennis. He was also a massive flirt and seeing him flirt with Jac (wanting to work on all of her strokes) was rather delicious. Jac, however, decided she needed some time off to be with Emma. Before anyone panics, Holby series producer Simon Harper confirmed on Twitter that she will be back.

Parenthood was very much on Essie's mind. She was ovulating, which meant Sacha had to Perform. That would be pressure enough, but it was still the hottest day in Holby since records began, and it seemed that everyone knew what was afoot. "You have big sex night, yes?" the Keller patient o' the week (who was adorable) said when he spotted the bottle of Pulses Own Brand Sparkling Wine Sacha was carrying. There was already someone in the on-call room, as Sacha discovered a little too late, so Essie suggested the romantic confines of the car.

We didn't see what happened (thank goodness), but we gathered from the post-mortem that the whole experience had been a bit... limp. "Oh my goodness," said Dom when he overheard what they were talking about. "Oh my goodness. You two are disgusting."

Then there was a wonderful scene in which Sacha asked Ric Griffin for advice about Viagra. It was the timing and the reactions of the pair of them that was so funny. Eventually Sacha and Essie had a heart to heart, and she ripped up her ovulation spreadsheets.

On AAU it was all about the Raf/Fletch bromance. Fletch was thinking of moving himself and the Fletchlings out of Di Lucca Towers. "I feel like we're cramping his style," he said. "Raf has style?" said Serena. What was upsetting Fletch was Raf getting together with Psych Naomi, but when Serena advised him to prioritise his children rather than a romance with a not terribly suitable woman, he saw sense. While Raf was setting out for a date with Psych Naomi, Fletch was ringing Evie to organise a (paddling) pool-side barbecue. I know which sounds more fun to me.

You have the bridge, Ms Effanga

(Series 18, ep. 40 'Children of Men' by Ed Sellek 12.7.16)

At the beginning of the episode Mo was telling a non-speaking and barely glimpsed medical person that she wanted to have a termination. For the rest of the episode she struggled with her decision, via the medium of dealing with a stroppy daughter-of-patient who'd previously been a patient of hers and Mr T's. It should perhaps be a lesson to me to pay more attention to the patients, but I can honestly say I didn't really remember this one. It probably didn't matter anyway, because the point was that she reminded us (and Mo) what a lovely man Mr T is, so Mo rang him and left a voice message. In return she received a text telling her not to contact him again. Ouch! That's so not-standard Mr T behaviour – Mo has hurt him good and proper.

With one tall, calm and lovely Holby man far away in Sweden, Mo sought the advice of a tall, calm and lovely Swedish man close at hand in Holby. Hanssen always steps up to the mark when needed, and he always has a nice clean hanky about his person if you need to have a cry. By the end of the episode Mo had decided to cancel her termination and Hanssen was supplying her with ginger beer for her morning sickness. I'd have him pencilled in as godfather, too – he'd be fabulous.

On Keller, Ric was concerned about Isaac. He's the cockier type of junior doctor, the sort who is annoying yet (usually) ultimately rewarding to mentor, but Ric has seen enough of those in his time. What he was more concerned about was whether Isaac could be trusted not to hurt Dominic. Ric was annoyed when he caught them kissing (more than once), but only because he's aware that Dominic is very vulnerable at the moment (remember how central Ric was to the Lee storyline, and then there's obviously the loss of Digby). He sees a "superficial attitude" and a lack of respect in Isaac that he doesn't much care for.

AAU was busy with a shortage of staff, a scaffolding collapse in the high street, and one of the Fletchlings wandering about. I do love it that Serena calls them Fletchlings, too.

It was Mikey, the one who is a mini-me of Fletch and who looks like he's about to launch into a song from Oliver! at any given moment. I love the Fletch/Mikey double act almost as much as I love the Fletch/Evie double act. Mikey also had a lot of scenes with AAU patient o' the week Ivor (Ryan Sampson), a junkie with a nasty abscess (even nastier after Mikey had whacked him with his school bag).

As we saw Ivor leave the hospital, I had a sneaky feeling that he'd be back . It looks like we won't have long to wait for that to happen, and the abscess will be the least of our worries. Also next week – new doctor Jasmine Burrows. You may have heard the name Burrows on Holby before.

Welcome to the madhouse

(Series 18, ep. 41 'A Perfect Life' by Julia Gilbert 19.7.16)

I can imagine that when Sacha was at school he was one of those kids who gets "Tries very hard" on every school report. A for effort, and so on. Because he does try, and in his professional life he succeeds. In his romantic relationships with women, though, it's the actual trying that seems to put them off. He jumped through hoops trying to persuade Chrissie that he was up to her exacting standards, and it's been much the same story with Essie. I had thought, after their little talk about how her desire to have a baby was getting in the way of their desire for each other, that things might go smoothly for a while. Then the useless lump only went and tried to save her life. Good grief, what can you do with a man like that?

Ivor (Ryan Sampson), last week's patient with the nasty abscess and the even nastier drug habit, was back this week and his leg had gone even yuckier. Sacha prescribed methadone. A new pharmacist, Mel (Jocelyn Jee Esien), thought he would be better off with morphine, but Sacha didn't want to start giving a junkie morphine. Ignoring the pharmacist's advice was probably a mistake, and it led to Mel and Essie in a hostage situation with Ivor in the pharmacy.

This was all quite tense, with Mel having an asthma attack and then getting a nasty crack on the head. All the same, Essie thought she was dealing with it because she could relate to Ivor, having been no stranger to chemical enhancement herself when she was younger. Still, I can't blame Sacha for hurtling in when he thought she was in danger. It certainly didn't look to the casual glance like she had things under control, particularly as Mel was on the floor and in need of brain surgery. But Sacha is in the doghouse again.

On AAU, they have a new Trauma Unit. It's a bed behind a plastic curtain, and it has its own red Trauma Phone and everything. Exciting! Hanssen was excited, anyway. I wondered whether it made him remember the heady days when Sahira Shah the Registrah had her own Trauma Phone. We shall never know.

With Bernie temporarily away dealing with her divorce, Serena was about to get stuck in to the very first Trauma when the familiar cry went up, "Auntie Serena! Where are you?" It's been a while since we saw Jason, but he wasn't just randomly wandering about this time. He was the actual cause of the injuries to the AAU patient o' the week – who was his girlfriend Celia (Zara Jayne). She was easy to recognise because she was the one with a park railing through her.

Had Celia received her injuries trying to escape an attempted sexual assault by Jason? Serena worried that might be the case, but the truth was much more innocent. All he needed was a bit of relationship advice from those two romance experts, Fletch and Raf. Girls like "good manners and kindness" according to Raf, and "nice presents" according to Fletch.

Talking of romance, Serena and Bernie were definitely holding eye gaze a little longer than usual in the scene in Albie's at the end. They were there to celebrate Serena's decision to step down as Deputy CEO so she can concentrate on her family and her patients rather than piles of paperwork.

There was a new girl on AAU, for about two minutes. Then she was sent to Darwin, where she was supposed to be meeting her mentor, Mr Oliver Valentine. She imagined he'd be pompous and stuffy with a wife named Pandora, she told Oliver Valentine, without checking who she was speaking to.

Oliver Valentine spent his formative years at Holby being mentored by Jac Naylor, and now the circle of Holby life sees him mentoring this new girl, who is almost certainly Jac's sister. She has the same name as Jac's sister (Jasmine Burrows) anyway, but you can't take anything for granted in Holby land. I can't wait to see her and Jac together. She looks like she won't be scared of Jac at all, and that has to be a first for a newbie. She's bright, perky, beautiful and brave enough to stick a chest drain in when there's nobody else around to do it. In other words, she is Prime Holby Material.

I got you, babe

(*Series 18, ep. 42 'From Bournemouth With Love' by Ailsa Macaulay 26.7.16*)

At one point in this episode, Morven told recurring character Hugh (Keith Barron), that she thought Arthur's favourite place had been right there in that very hospital. It's hardly surprising, really. Is there any other workplace in the world where the staff are so supportive, kind and protective, while at the same time being at least 100% more attractive than the general population? Ok, there's Selfie, but you have to mix it up with the occasional bad guy and even he has his moments.

The episode dealt a lot with grief and moving on – variants of the old "life's too short" axiom kept cropping up at regular intervals. It was Morven's first day back at work after losing Arthur (apart from that time she popped up in the locker room to say goodbye to Cara). "I'm Dr Digby now," she said, and that little phrase captured a whole world of love, bravery, pain and pride. [Side note: When I was a kid our GP's were a husband and wife combo, and to differentiate between them everyone called them "Dr Corrigan and Dr Mrs Corrigan." Now I'm all grown up, again I have a husband and wife GP combo, only now everyone – patients, receptionists – calls the female GP "the lady doctor." Which (a) makes her sound like she has the same area of specialism as Mr T and (b) makes it sound like I live in Victorian England].

Grief is making Morven wear her hair flatter, and it's (understandably) made her personality flatter, too. It was a very realistic portrait of grief, as she struggled to bring her focus back to her work and to real life. It was made more challenging by having to deal with the new wife of Hugh. Again understandably Morven felt he'd moved on too quickly after losing his beloved wife, but she was seeing everything through the lens of her own pain and Hugh helped her to realise that future happiness is possible and not a betrayal of the person who's gone. She was also helped by Bernie, who is marvellous at just being with someone who's hurting and being a calm, reassuring presence. A little chat with Dominic also helped, and last but not least Arthur had left a little gift in the form of a memory stick with a video of him and Morven doing karaoke Sonny and Cher. It was lovely to see Digby again, and also his rucksack with the horses on it, which Morven took home.

Elsewhere, Oliver Valentine had a job offer. Prof Elliot Hope wanted to lure him to Pakistan to help run a hospital there. Ollie was very tempted, especially when he came up against Selfie in one of his best "I hate you, Valentine" moods and Mo failed to support him in the way he felt Jac would have done (not because she likes him but because she always goes in to bat for Team Cardiothoracics). In the end he did his usual fabulous work in theatre, Mo admitted she was wrong, and I can't remember if he withdrew his resignation or not, but there are at least three women who hope he did – me, Zosia and Jasmine. I'm enjoying how Jasmine and Zosia are both hankering after him. With Jasmine you can see that it's mainly lust – he's available, he's pretty, so why wouldn't you? Whereas with Zosia she's trying so hard not to care, but you can see that she cares really deeply about him.

Dominic is beginning to care about Isaac, too, though it's taking quite a bit to overcome the barriers he's put up around his already quite barrier-strewn personality following Lee's betrayal and Arthur's death. Essie and Keller patient o' the week Vince (Syrus Lowe) both helped him to realise that "life goes on" and Isaac is quite a catch. I imagine he could get irritating, because he's a bit fond of a "prank." Covering Ric's car in Post-It notes was quite creative, though.

In other news, Serena, Ric, Sacha and Hanssen all had to participate in a Mindfulness Leadership Course, which hilariously involved yoga in the Linden Cullen Memorial Shrubbery. Mindfulness? The only thing on Serena's mind was apparently how much she needed a nice glass of Shiraz to get over it.

The beep wobbles

(Series 18, ep. 43 'Back in the Ring' by Jeff Povey 2.8.16)

I'm not sure who commissioned the Digby memorial plaque that was unveiled by Ric in the Linden Cullen Memorial Shrubbery, but I'd be asking for a refund (it was rubbish) and also having serious words with the handy-person who made such a hash of nailing it up above the Pondering Pond.

It raised the question – what would be a fitting memorial for the late and much-loved doctor? I assume that those pesky Germans have rebadged the Digby Stent now, so that's out.

It fell to Ric to solve this puzzle, and eventually he came up with the idea of an academy called the Arthur Digby Foundation, to seek out new medical talent wherever it might manifest itself (starting with Ric's former boxing sparring partner, who was back again with a leaking aneurysm and a new interest in medicine). I don't know who's going to pay for all this, but let's not worry our pretty heads about that because it's a lovely idea.

It was a difficult day for Ric. He's perhaps been worried that he didn't do everything humanly possible for Digby (though of course he did), and this was made worse when Morven asked him about that very thing. Morven's sadness breaks my heart, btw. This all led to Ric having a fit of what I shall call the "beep wobbles" – when you're in the middle of some delicate surgery, the machines are going beep, there's blood everywhere and you go a bit funny and someone has to take over. I really hope it doesn't happen in real life as often as it happens in Holby.

Ric asked Hanssen whether he'd ever suffered from the beep wobbles himself. "Sometimes even magnificence doesn't bring you much joy," said Henrik, enigmatically.

Talking of joy, though, every scene between Hugh Quarshie and Guy Henry was a thing of pure bliss. My favourite piece of dialogue:

Hanssen: "The team will benefit from your imperious gravitas."
Ric: "Are you chatting me up?"
Hanssen: "Possibly."

Glorious.

That wasn't the only beautiful Keller double act this week. Sacha and Dominic were busy providing comic relief, when an over-tired and over-caffeinated Sacha ("I can taste Colombia. It's on my lips") sent Ric a bit of a sweary first draft email by mistake, and then had to try to get into Ric's computer to delete it before it was seen. The best bit was when Sacha shoved Dominic aside to get to the computer, and Dominic went gliding gracefully backwards on his chair. If you haven't seen it I know that doesn't exactly sound like a highlight, but the look on Dom's face made me laugh out loud.

On Darwin, meanwhile, recurring patient Lexy (the vicar who married Digby and Morven) was back, because her Herzig was malfunctioning. Not many people can say that, because not many people have got one. Jasmine was very excited to get that experience under her belt. She's also been looking quite interested in adding Oliver Valentine to her CV, but was he ready to move on from Zosia? Lexy has a habit of turning up when Ollie needs advice, and her advice this time was that he needed to move on. I felt it was quite ambiguous advice, and he could have taken it to mean that he needed to make things right with Zosia. He didn't, though. They passed each other in the corridor, and it was too sad – she loves him to bits but she's holding it all in. He loves her, too, but when we last saw him he was literally giving the green light to Jasmine.

Slightly too early to have come via the Arthur Digby Academy for Medical Wannabees, Jason has started work on AAU in an administrative capacity. His first job was to detect that Auntie Serena is not as productive as she could be, mainly because she's always watching Jason. I think he should really work on a different ward, because his presence does seem to totally distract her. She was rather brusque with a patient who thought he had "a brain tumour camouflaged to look like a brain." I know doctors have to spend a lot of time dealing with hypochondriac, googling time wasters, but when he said his father had had a brain tumour I thought she could have been a tad more sympathetic. Luckily Bernie was on hand with this week's Tricky Diagnosis – electromagnetic hypersensitivity. And Jason was on hand to disable the wi fi in a side room so Bernie could test her theory out. Value for money already.

The cake eating man and the tell-tale kidney
(Series 18, ep. 44 'Indefensible' by Kate Verghese and Nick Fisher 4.8.16)

Another triumph for the casting department, this time in the form of Bernie's son Cameron (Nic Jackman). He really did look like he could be related to Bernie, not just in looks but something about his manner – that quality that Bernie has that I can only describe as "stillness." He had that too, and obviously it's not all about the casting but also the actors working well together.

Cameron succumbed to the Curse of The Holby Relative by becoming a patient, following a car accident for which he was taking the blame. It was a complicated and interesting story which had Bernie covering for Cameron and Serena covering for Bernie when the alleged passenger in the car was found to have a kidney injury that could only be caused to the person driving.

The most important aspect of the story was that Cameron had once met Alex (the woman Bernie was in love with in the army) and he spotted straight away that Bernie looks at Serena the same way she used to look at Alex. Ooh! I'm not sure Bernie had even realised that herself – but she has now. This is getting very interesting.

I know we have rather a lot of people's relatives joining the hospital staff in one capacity or another (Serena's nephew, Mo's dad, Jac's sister, Selfie and Selfie Jr, Raf and Dr Amy Smug etc etc), but I wouldn't mind at all if Cameron decided to join Holby when he's finished with medical school. I think he'd be quite an asset.

Talking of relatives, Sacha and Essie aren't yet legally related, and it's looking less likely that they ever will be. Mel the Pharmacist had made them a mock-up of a proposed wedding cake, and it was fabulous (as is Mel, who is eccentric, random, funny and rather touching). The cake featured "a surgeon doing a bowel resection in fondant icing," which was the best thing ever, but Essie failed to be impressed. Mel seems to have a bit of a crush on Sacha. She complained that she has two cats and she bakes – for anyone. "Whereas you have a bold, brave, cake-eating man," she told Essie. Once again Sacha finds himself being under-appreciated by his official partner, while others are well able to see what a glorious specimen of humanity he really is.

Morven – looking incredibly beautiful but also incredibly sad – was spending her day off on Darwin doing a research project. Bless her, she can't cope with being home alone. Luckily it seems she doesn't have to, as Jasmine needed somewhere to live, so she'll be moving in. They might drive each other mad, but hopefully Jasmine's sunny personality will help to bring some smiles back to Morven's life.

We've got a long wait to find out what happens next, because the BBC have decided that we really want to spend our Tuesday evenings watching pole vaulting or some such nonsense for the next couple of weeks.

Unfinished business

(*Series 18, ep. 45 'Little Acorns' by Johanne McAndrew and Elliot Hope 23.8.16*)

Guy Self. Selfie. Self-centred, selfish, self-absorbed, self-promoting, always the villain of the piece. And yet an episode which started with Selfie in typically arrogant mode with the publication of his memoirs (Head Space – sadly not currently available from Amazon and all good book shops) ended with him in tears – and frankly, I was almost in tears with him.

The cause of this turnaround was the appearance – as a patient – of his mother Valerie, beautifully played by Brigit Forsyth. Zosia didn't know that Granny was still alive, and she seemed so nice, too. But it was clear that Selfie was a haunted man. It wasn't until Valerie made her presence felt at a meeting where Selfie was trying to impress bigwigs that her sweet facade started to crack – and as soon as Zosia wasn't around, we caught a glimpse of something very nasty indeed.

Then, in a scene that was powerfully played by both John Michie and Camilla Arfwedson, Selfie told his daughter that Valerie had been a tyrant, who locked him in a cupboard and beat him if he wasn't perfect. His father had committed suicide because of it, and Selfie still had the physical scars all over his back, and the emotional scars all over his personality.

I now feel bad for (almost) every negative thing I've ever said about Selfie. And I never thought I'd be saying that.

The Curse of the Holby Relative was running high this week. As well as Valerie, Fletch's daughter Evie was admitted to AAU after falling down the stairs at home. Or was she pushed by that wee imp Mikey? Fletch has been struggling with life as the lone parent of four kids. Even with Raf's support, things have been too much but he never likes to admit it and ask for help – just like when he got into a life of crimewith Clifford. With two of his children in trouble he finally had no choice but to talk to a rather lovely social worker (Patrick Regis) who just happened to be languishing on the ward recovering from a nasty cycling accident.

While Selfie was busy going all sympathetic on us, a new villain appeared in the form of the snake-like Tristan Wood (Jonathan McGuinness). He's the husband of Patsy Brassvine and co-holder of the Brassvine-Wood purse strings. Sacha said you can never trust a Tristan, and he was right in this case. Ric had more-or-less been offered the post of Deputy CEO, but then an issue came up about whether a piece of equipment should have been purchased or leased, and he went to Tristan to complain. When Ric walked away from Sacha muttering that the promised (by the Brexit campaign) £350 million quid would have come in handy, it was a hurrah! moment like Serena's speech about the junior doctors a while back. But it was Ric's last hurrah really, because Tristan didn't want that kind of meddling going on, so rather than give Ric the Deputy CEO job he decided there wouldn't be a Deputy CEO after all and they could spend the money on shiny new equipment instead.

If he thought that would be the last he'd hear from Ric, he was wrong. Ric found him in Albie's and made it quite clear that the battle may be lost but the war isn't over. Brilliant.

Happy families

(*Series 18, ep. 46 'Fractured' by Rebecca Wojciechowski 25.8.16*)

Jac has apparently been away on some happy-clappy retreat thing with Emma (can you imagine it? No, me neither). The short-term effect was to make her smile a lot and be all co-operative and amenable with her colleagues, and it didn't last long. There was no long-term effect.

Any thought of peace and good will to all got blown out of the water as soon as she discovered the identity of her new F1. Jasmine, who'd been bouncing about like a medically-trained puppy and impressing Jac with her knowledge and her keenness, didn't wait all that long before telling Jac who she really is – her half sister. Jac's reaction was about what we'd expect, given her relationship with the toxic Paula. "If anyone finds out we're related, you'll never work in medicine again," Jac told her sister.

It's going to be fascinating to watch how the relationship between these two evolves. Jasmine said that she hadn't had an easy time with Paula – including not knowing that she was dying. I can't imagine Jasmine giving up easily, either, even though Jac has gone into her usual state of emotional armour-plating. Meanwhile, Jasmine is consoling herself with Oliver Valentine.

In what was a very well-crafted episode, Selfie was at the same time struggling with his own issues with his mother. Valerie died in the operating theatre, and in the conversation that followed it was clear that Jac and Selfie have more in common than either of them would like to think. It's part of what attracted them to each other (though I didn't really buy that attraction at the time, but that's because I don't think anyone but Joseph is good enough for Jac) and it's part of what makes Jac hate him so much. In fact she hates him so much that even though he offered to leave (having said he would to try and persuade Jac to do a Herzig procedure on Valerie), Jac said she didn't want him to. She wants him gone, but on her terms: "I will get rid of you, and it will be painful."

On AAU, Evie was trying to prolong her stay so she didn't have to go back to her role as Lead Fletchling. It's all a bit much at Di Lucca Towers, what with Fletch being tired all the time, Mikey kicking off, and the core diet being jacket potatoes. She even asked if she could live with Serena, which was understandable given that Serena was being absolutely lovely with her. Obviously Serena said no, but Evie would be a lot more fun than her own daughter, who let her down at the very last minute before they were due to go on a spa break.

Sacha and Essie, meanwhile, had the spark restored to their relationship thanks to Mel the Pharmacist, who organised a picnic for them in one of Holby's many empty rooms. It seems that the strain of trying for a baby hasn't been taking its toll as much as the strain of being on a reproduction-enhancing diet – particularly as it was Fajita Tuesday at Pulses.

A hospital's a dangerous place

(Series 18, ep. 47 'Protect and Serve' by Joe Ainsworth 30.8.16)

For those who watch Holby but not Casualty, the 'Previously' segment brought us up to speed on Connie's accident and Saturday's helicopter crash. Then we saw Fletch, who'd been a part of the helicopter mayhem, giving us a little talk about what a difficult but rewarding job he had. Directly to camera he said, "You just gotta remember, a hospital's a dangerous place." Nobody who's watched Holby for very long would doubt that for a minute, but it added an extra twist of tension.

Fletch had the unenviable task of looking after Stephanie Simms, the woman who'd caused Connie and Grace's car accident. She was under police guard, because there was a chance she'd try to escape. She spent most of the time trying to get inside Fletch's head by asking him about his children. She's a manipulative one, but Fletch was on to her. "If you get a chance, give that bitch a morphine overdose," Connie told him, which in hindsight might have been the best course of action, but he's way too professional for that sort of thing.

To add to the general worries on AAU there was also a patient who'd been sort of stalking Bernie, and he thought that Stephanie Simms was out to get her. Fletch thought he needed a psych consult, but Bernie wasn't convinced until she saw the patient's somewhat disturbing sketch pad. The next thing we knew, we were in the basement. Nothing good ever happens in the basement, and when it also contains the evil Stephanie trying to escape and the disturbed sketch pad man trying to stop her before she can harm Bernie, you've got a perfect storm of basement trouble. Bernie wasn't even there, but Fletch was, just in time to see the man threaten Stephanie with a screwdriver. Then the screwdriver ended up embedded in Fletch.

Not Fletch! He's so absolutely lovely, and he looks like he gives such good hugs (he'd hugged Morven earlier, because the poor love was shattered after a double shift looking after the post-Casualty casualties). Serena and Bernie did their best for him in the operating theatre, but it's not looking all that good for him.

Serena and Bernie sat outside the operating theatre, deflated and emotional. Bernie said it was all her fault because she hadn't taken sketch pad man seriously enough. Serena said that was stuff and nonsense because Bernie was just about the most wonderfulest doctor since Hippocrates (or words to that effect) – and then Bernie kissed her. Serena only looked a tiny bit surprised, and then kissed her back. A nation of #Berena fans threw their hats in the air and shouted "Hurrah!" We've seen those meaningful looks and extended eye gaze moments and knew this was always on the cards – but what I really want to see is how they'll both react now. Will Serena start flirting madly with Ric Griffin in an attempt to prove her heterosexual credentials? Will they both try to pretend nothing happened (like Ollie and Zosia after their first kiss)? Or will they woman up and accept that #Berena is a Thing? We'll have to wait and see.

In the meantime, Morven had been home, cleaned the house from top to bottom and done several days of volunteering at a homeless shelter, where she met Bernie's lovely son Cameron. Jasmine was doing a stint riding in an ambulance with Jez and Iain off of Casualty (the latter fairly well recovered from his helicopter ordeal) and they all went for a night out together. They didn't go to Albie's though, because Casualty staff are not allowed in there.

You don't know what you've got till it's gone

(Series 18, ep. 48 'Brave New World' by Katie Douglas 6.9.16)

I know not everyone is on board with the whole #Berena thing. There are some who are against it for the same reasons that *Coronation Street* has had to fend off complaints recently, and I've got no time for that view. There are others who would have preferred Bernie and Serena to have remained as supportive colleagues, and that does make sense and would have been a nice relationship to explore. But where could that have gone, drama-wise, much beyond "Gosh that was a hard day. Let's kick back with a nice bottle of Shiraz"? It certainly wouldn't have delivered such blissfully toe-curling scenes as we had last night, as Serena 'fessed up to a comatose Fletch that she kissed a girl and she liked it, and the even more blissful scenes she shared with Bernie. I'm all for a storyline that brings out the beautifully subtle and elegant comic talents of Catherine Russell. She and Jemma Redgrave are brilliant together, and I'm looking forward to watching this story develop.

While one relationship teeters on the threshold of beginning, another was on the way out. I haven't been a great fan of the Sacha/Essie relationship, mainly because for most of the time she was frowning disapprovingly at him, giving him what I took to calling "Chrissie face," and he'd had enough of that with the real Chrissie. I have warmed to Essie recently and I have to say the scenes of their break-up were very sad. Bob Barrett and Kaye Wragg acted their socks off. It was Sacha's birthday, too.

The issue of whether to have children or not was what tore them apart, and there was a poignant moment when Essie congratulated Mo on her pregnancy, and Mo responded that it wasn't ideal, but when life gives you lemons you just have to crack on and make lemonade.

The reason that Mo was less than thrilled about her situation was that Mr T (MR T!!!) was back – but he wasn't alone. There was a soon-to-be-Mrs T with him, in the form of new nurse Inga Olsen, and they are hideously couply ("Work kiss!"). Mr T was still obviously angry with Mo about the way she treated him, but all the same, when nobody was looking apart from we the viewers at home, you can tell he still loves her. Not wanting to complicate the situation she's told him that the baby isn't his.

And what about Inga? She confused me a little bit the first time she appeared in her uniform, because I thought Cara was back. Then I thought it was Jasmine. My ageing eyesight can only cope with so much blonde-ness. Inga gives every appearance of being as nice as pie, but possibly a rather indiscreet pie, judging by the way she dropped news of Mo's pregnancy when she knew Mo hadn't told anyone but Hanssen yet.

Finally – how is Fletch doing? For a start, Alex Walkinshaw scores extra points with me by actually looking like someone who's just woken up from a coma after he was woken up from his coma. He looked all sleepy and confused, and like his mouth was dry. He wasn't helped by Serena waffling on about whether he'd actually heard anything that had been said to him while he was asleep – things like, "Serena Campbell – lesbian" (he might have heard that, but he wouldn't have seen the amused smile that accompanied it). So all is well with Fletch and he's on the road to recovery. Unless you hung on to wait for the preview of next week's episode, in which case – Be Very Worried.

I'm looking out for him

(*Series 18, ep. 49 'Say a Little Prayer' by Sian Evans 13.9.16*)

I was absolutely gripped by this week's episode. I don't think there's a Holby fan on the planet who doesn't like Fletch. He's a genuine, kind, caring, funny man who just wants to help people and make a living so he can support his kids. So I was rooting for Fletch, and I love Raf and the bromance between them, so I was rooting for Raf, too. As well as being engaged with the human side of the story, I was intrigued by the puzzle of Fletch's mystery illness that got worse and worse, and even had the best medics in TV-land stumped for a while. It was nail-biting stuff, and thank heavens for Bernie, an oasis of calm among all the angst.

A special mention also for Kai O'Loughlin, who plays Mikey Fletcher. This week he subdued his cheeky chappie persona a bit (usually he seems about to burst into a chorus of 'Consider Yourself At Home' at any moment, which is a lovely thing to watch but wouldn't have been appropriate here) and he was brilliant. He's completely believable as Fletch's son and has masses of charm, personality and talent. His scene with Hanssen was absolutely precious. I was glad it was Mikey who provided the clue that eventually led to a diagnosis. "He's okay now. I'm looking out for him," he said.

Elsewhere, romantic issues were high on the agenda. Oliver Valentine and Jasmine are apparently an item, and Jasmine has quickly gone from being ever-so-casual about relationships to insisting that Ollie told Zosia what was going on. Unfortunately, it seems that Zosia isn't at all over him. All he had to do was speak a bit of Spanish (he was translating for a patient and her rather over-dramatic friend) and Zosia went a little bit breathless. At various points it seemed that Ollie is not over Zosia either, but Jasmine had other ideas and Zosia caught them having a store room moment. I really didn't like the way Jasmine undermined Zosia on the ward later, particularly as she had a very smug look on her face as she did so. That's not very sensitive or very nice, and perhaps Little Miss Sunshine isn't as sunny as she looks. She does have Paula Burrows' genes, after all.

On Keller, Sacha and Essie were doing their best to move on after their breakup last week. Sacha's shirt was loud even by his standards. It literally took Hanssen's breath away, but he declined to comment. "I think Dr Copeland is a better arbiter of the sartorial zeitgeist than am I," he said. Sacha had enrolled on a cookery course and was going to try out for the hospital choir. Essie was trying out a new hairstyle and had signed up for scuba diving. It seems that moving on is quite literally hard work, so they gave up, temporarily, and went for a drink instead. Whether they get back together or not, I hope they stay friends. They had such fun winding Dominic up after he accidentally broke a hideously naff statuette that neither of them liked. I loved Dominic's initial response to it: "What the merry hell is that?" It made me laugh out loud, and considering that Fletch was in the throes of a mystery creeping paralysis at the time, that was quite an achievement.

Another roll of the dice

(Series 18, ep. 50 'Emotionally Yours' by Chris Murray 20.9.16)

Dr Isaac Mayfield has certainly changed his taste in men. His current beau is the wonderful Dr Dominic Copeland, but in this episode we met his ex. Miles Richardson, King of the Revolutionary Spleen Procedure (Jonathan Firth), was one of those creepy/scary/weird people that, if they sidled up to you at a party, you would make every excuse to get away from. I think he was supposed to have charisma, but he was nasty and manipulative and I didn't like him at all. He wasn't very nice to our Dominic, which made Dom go all possessive and defensive with Isaac. Given his history with Lee and the fact that he's only just starting to trust Isaac, I think this was an understandable response.

I can also understand Jac's response to her half sister, Little Miss Sunshine. The interactions between them generally involve Jasmine bouncing up and down like an attention-seeking toddler, and Jac batting her away like an irritating fly. This may change as Jac discovers that Jasmine has excellent medical skills, but for now she's making Jasmine work extra hard for any crumb of recognition. When Jasmine asked her how she was planning to do a tricky procedure Jac said, "That's for me to know and you to witness in awe and wonder," which was a classic and beautiful Jac line, but not really what you want in a teaching hospital.

This week Jac found out that Jasmine and Oliver Valentine are an item, and she correctly (in my opinion) pointed out that "He's a one woman man, and you're not her." But so much for sisterly support.

Talking of sisterly support, the beautiful double act of Bernie and Serena continued on AAU, where for much of the time they had nothing much to do apart from watching Ric Griffin being dazzled by a glamourous French patient (Félicité Du Jeu). But they did it in such a fun way, with plenty of meaningful glances. Serena and Ric went to Albie's for a drink at the end of the shift and got to discussing relationships. Serena admitted that there was someone special in her life, and told him it was Bernie. "That is not what I was expecting," said Ric.

Recognise the symptoms

(Series 18, ep. 51 'Life in the Freezer' by Michelle Lipton 27.9.16)

It seems out of character for someone like Serena – so poised and strong – to be literally running after a romantic interest, begging them not to leave. This is how we know that Bernie Wolfe is more than just "romantic interest." Falling for Bernie must be, to Serena, like being given a glimpse inside a previously locked room, and then having the door shut in your face just as you're on the threshold.

It also makes sense that Bernie would run away. She's been in the place Serena is now, when she fell for Alex, and she's seen the heartbreak it can bring. The scene where Bernie talked to Dominic on the roof shows that she's quite fatalistic about relationships.

We can only hope that Bernie will be back eventually, because the scenes between Catherine Russell and Jemma Redgrave were jaw-droppingly good. The connection between Bernie and Serena is obvious in every scene, whether they're working together to help a patient or having a laugh at Ric Griffin's expense. It's been built up in a very deliberate and detailed way.

The same could be said for Mo and Mr T, and it still can be said for Mo and Mr T, even though he's engaged and she's pretending that the baby she's carrying isn't his.

Did we know prior to this that Mr T is a twin? Conveniently for us (but possibly less convenient for her) his sister Delwen (Elizabeth Bower) had a heart problem, which brought her to Darwin. Mr T tells her everything, apparently, so she was fully clued up on all the details of Mo and Mr T's relationship, and lying in her hospital bed she had plenty of time to work out that "Woody" probably is the father of the baby.

Delwen's speculation – and indeed Delwen herself – was almost cut short thanks to Jasmine biting off a bit more than she could chew, medically-speaking. This has given Jac the excuse she's been looking for to have Jasmine transferred to Keller.

Meanwhile, Mo had been feeling unwell all day, and when she started bleeding she needed Mr T's expertise to reassure her that all was well with the baby. And he let slip that it's a boy. He also asked Mo to be "best man" at his wedding, which is taking being friend-zoned to a whole new level.

It was the end of an era for Zosia and Dominic. Isaac has asked Dominic to move in with him, and after a few misunderstandings and muddles, Zosia realised that this meant he would be moving out. The choice for her was whether to get new flatmates, or move out herself. She's decided a clean break is what's needed, but was I the only one who felt a bit emotional at the thought that they'd be leaving the flat they'd shared with Digby?

Sharp knives and Inga

(Series 18, ep. 52 'Snakes and Ladders' by Michelle Lipton 4.10.16)

The phrase "emotional roller coaster" is over-used, but I'm going to use it anyway, because this series has been one. Also, that's the mental image I had at the end of this episode (which also marked the end of series 18) that we were left poised at the top of the roller coaster, ready to start series 19 with twists and turns already lined up – Mo's baby, Fletch's recovery, Dominic and Isaac, Serena and Bernie, Jasmine and Jac. And, if you've seen the Autumn trailer, big stuff for Zosia, Selfie and Hanssen, a new doctor, and a bizarre new look for Sacha.

I can't wait, to be honest, but in the meantime I need to concentrate on what was going on last night.

Inga seems nice, doesn't she? It's that word "seems" that's the pertinent point, though. Kaisa Hammarlund is doing a lovely job of portraying a woman who is as nice as apple pie – though it might be an apple pie with a few less-appetising ingredients under the crust. Only Mo has noticed that Inga isn't the sweet fluffy cloud she first appears to be. "I think being around sharp knives and Inga at the same time is a recipe for disaster," Mo told Zosia, and this has got to be a worry in a hospital full of scalpels and other sharp stuff. Inga's weapon of choice when she discovered that Mo was the evil woman who broke Mr T's heart wasn't a knife, though – it was a large jug of urine. Possibly still warm.

Jac was amused. "Two women fighting over Derwood Thompson," she said. "Just when I thought the world couldn't get any weirder."

There was a beautiful scene at the end of the episode, in which Mo and Jac got stuck into a bottle of wine (just Jac for the wine) and a large quantity of cheese, and had a bit of a catch-up. We learned that Jac and Jonny are co-parenting Emma in a friendly and civilised way – they even went to a petting zoo together. There was a bit of brains-speak when Jac said what a good father Jonny is and how she regrets trying to shut him out of Emma's life, because after all that's what Mo is doing to Mr T. We also learned that Mo has been avoiding Jonny, and I think that's entirely realistic. He knows her better than anybody, and it would be hard not to tell him who the baby's father is. And Jonny would doubtlessly feel that Mr T has a right to know.

It's not easy being a lone parent – just ask Raf. The poor man is floundering a bit trying to look after the Fletchlings while Fletch recovers. He's going to have to do it for a bit longer, now, as an accident during physio has set Fletch back a few weeks. This storyline did a nice job of pulling in several story strands, as Fletch's frustration with his situation made Morven angry with him because at least he's ended series 18 still alive, unlike Arthur. We also found out that "Berena" is quite the topic of hot gossip around the hospital, and Fletch most probably did hear Serena's little speech about this when he was in a coma. There was a glorious appearance from Mikey Fletcher ("Alright Serena! Raf about?") and assorted other Fletchlings. And I wanted to hug Raf for being such a good friend and caring so much about the Fletchlings.

So much love around the place at the moment. Things were a little trickier on Keller, as Isaac tried to impress Ric so he could win the prized Registrar Scheme and get to go Anywhere In The World on a paid-for placement. Ric is no big fan of Isaac, so Dominic tried to give him a little help by handing him the credit for this week's Tricky Diagnosis. Obviously this backfired spectacularly when Dr Jasmine Burrows, on her first Keller shift, told Hanssen what had really happened. With some skilful diplomacy Dominic made everything all right in the end. He even found he hated Jasmine less than he expected – it seems that Zosia has probably been having a moan to him about how she snatched Ollie from under her very nose.

Favourite dialogue of the week – Jasmine: "I've been shadowing Dr Copeland." Hanssen: "Oh, bad luck."

Also by Sue Haasler:

Holby City: Behind the Screen - the official BBC book.

Novels:
Two's Company
Time After Time
True Colours
Better Than the Real Thing
Half a World Away (to be published in 2018)

suehaasler.com

Printed in Poland
by Amazon Fulfillment
Poland Sp. z o.o., Wrocław